VBA
Developer's Handbook™

Second Edition

Ken Getz

Mike Gilbert

SYBEX®

San Francisco • Paris • Düsseldorf • Soest • London

Associate Publisher: Richard Mills
Contracts and Licensing Manager: Kristine O'Callaghan
Acquisitions & Developmental Editor: Christine McGeever
Editors: Susan Berge, Raquel Baker
Technical Editor: David Shank
Book Designer: Kris Warrenburg
Graphic Illustrator: Tony Jonick
Electronic Publishing Specialist: Nila Nichols
Production Editor: Leslie E. H. Light
Proofreaders: Nancy Riddiough, Patrick J. Peterson, Molly Glover, Nelson Kim, Jennifer Campbell
Indexer: Ted Laux
CD Coordinator: Christine Harris
CD Technician: Keith McNeil
Cover Designer: Design Site
Cover Illustrator: Jack D. Meyers
Library of Congress Card Number: 2001089612

ISBN: 0-7821-2978-1

Manufactured in the United States of America

10 9 8 7 6

*To Peter: Your patience and understanding
(especially that patience thing) have made it
possible to write books like this. Your working very
long hours didn't hurt, either.*

—K.N.G.

*To Revi, Lynn, David, Tree, Michelle, Cynthia,
and Karishma: true friends and good souls all.
Thanks for being there when I needed you.*

—M.T.G.

ACKNOWLEDGMENTS

As with any book, this one wouldn't have been possible without the contributions of many people besides the authors. First of all, we'd like to thank our tireless developmental editor, Melanie Spiller, without whom we wouldn't be writing the kinds of books we write. Melanie continues to be an inspiration, a confidant, and someone whose edits continue to provide new insights into how to get technical writing done right. This is the seventh book we've done with Melanie, and every one has been made better by her patience, understanding, and care.

In addition, we've had the benefit of not one, but two careful, caring editors from Sybex for this edition: Raquel Baker and Susan Berge survived our ever-changing schedule and our procrastination, complaining, and (yes, we can say it) anal-retentiveness, with amazing grace and good nature. It's been a pleasure working with both Raquel and Susan, and we'd do it again in a heartbeat. There are many others at Sybex we'd like to thank, as well, including all the folks in layout, production, and other departments we never get to meet.

We'd also like to pay special tribute (again) to our technical editor, David Shank. His eye for detail is unsurpassed, and in the course of reviewing this book, he provided innumerable comments that measurably improved the content and examples. If the book is complete and accurate, blame Dave. (On the other hand, any errors or omissions are clearly our responsibility and not Dave's.) This is our fourth book with David (he also worked his way through *Access 97 Developer's Handbook*, *Visual Basic Language Developer's Handbook*, and *Access 2000 Developer's Handbook: Desktop Edition*), and given the choice, we'd work with him on any and every future project. David currently works on developer documentation at Microsoft, having cowritten what may be the definitive book on Office development: *Microsoft Office 2000/Visual Basic: Programmer's Guide* from Microsoft Press. We don't know how David does it, but he's made an indelible contribution to each of these books.

Thanks to Dan Haught of FMS, Inc., who originally prepared an outline for a book similar to this one and then decided to go a different route; his company created *Total Access SourceBook* and *Total VB SourceBook*, source code libraries for Microsoft Access and Visual Basic, respectively, which include material that parallels the topics covered in this book. Dan kindly provided us with his detailed outline, from which we began the process of writing the book. For more information on FMS, Inc. and their products, visit their Web site at `http://www.fmsinc.com`. Thanks also to Luke Chung of FMS, Inc., who provided us with documentation and examples involving numeric rounding and calculation errors, which were helpful in the creation of Chapter 2.

We'd also like to thank Mary Chipman and Andy Baron, senior consultants with MCW Technologies. They both dug through the VBA issues surrounding numeric operations and provided much of the material in Chapter 2 of this book. Thanks to Terry Kreft, who added some new material to this chapter for this edition, as well.

Dev Ashish, the keeper of the Web site where you'll find answers to almost any Microsoft Access question (see the Access Web at `http://www.mvps.org/access/`), revised Chapter 9, "Retrieving and Setting System Information," for this edition of the book. Dev loves digging into the Windows API, and this chapter shows that off. He tirelessly dug through new Windows 2000 API calls, helping to add many new properties and methods to the existing classes in this chapter.

Michael Kaplan of Trigeminal Software, Inc. crafted Chapter 11 for us in the previous edition of this book and revised it for this edition. This chapter, covering the issues involved in working with networks programmatically, was greatly enhanced by Michael's contributions, based on his research and experience with networks and network management. We'd also like to thank those experts who provided us with suggestions, ideas for chapter topics, and code review, including Jim Ferguson, Mike Gunderloy, and Brian Randell. Several readers wrote to us with suggestions, complaints, and ideas, including Philip Andrew, Doug Behl, Manuel Lopez, Mindy Martin, Sanjay S. Mundkur, Peter Mundy, Carl Parmenter, and Brian Wells. (We've surely missed a few and apologize in advance.) We truly appreciate the ideas, support, and encouragement. Malcolm Stewart, of Microsoft's Access support group, provided the NEATCODE.MDB sample database from which we began much of our research into some of the various programming topics.

In addition, we'd like to thank Neil Charney. Neil has been working with Office and VBA for the past four years and is currently group product manager for VBA and Microsoft Office Developer at Microsoft. Neil has been instrumental in getting us the information and contacts we needed to write this book. In addition to Neil, we'd also like to thank the members of the entire VBA development team, especially Theresa Venhuis, David Holmes, Tom Quinn, and Russell Spence, who not only are the ones responsible for the technology but were also gracious enough to put up with our nitpicky questions. We'd also like to thank all the companies that provided samples, demos, and information for the book's CD-ROM.

Finally, Greg Reddick and Paul Litwin deserve special thanks. Paul not only provided ideas and spiritual and moral support, he also graciously granted permission for us to use some of the work he did for our sister book, *Access 2000 Developer's Handbook*, also published by Sybex. Greg laboriously updated his naming conventions for Office 2000 and VBA, and we've included this document as Appendix A.

ABOUT THE AUTHORS

Ken Getz

Ken Getz is a senior consultant with MCW Technologies, focusing on the Microsoft suite of products. He has received Microsoft's MVP award (for providing online technical support) every year since 1993 and has written several books on developing applications using Microsoft products. Ken is a technical editor for *Access-Office-VB Advisor* magazine, which is published by Advisor Media, Inc. He is also a contributing editor for *Microsoft Office & Visual Basic for Applications Developer* magazine, published by Informant Communications Group, Inc. Currently, Ken spends a great deal of time traveling around the country for Application Developer's Training Company, presenting training classes for Access and Visual Basic developers. He also speaks at many conferences and trade shows throughout the world, including Microsoft's Tech*Ed, Advisor Publication's DevCon, and Informant's Microsoft Office and VBA Solutions conference. You can reach Ken at kgetz@developershandbook.com.

Mike Gilbert

Mike Gilbert works at Microsoft as a program manager designing object models for business productivity and Web collaboration products. Prior to joining Microsoft, he was a senior consultant with MCW Technologies, specializing in application development using Microsoft Access, Visual Basic, SQL Server, and Microsoft Office. He writes for several periodicals and is a contributing editor to *Microsoft Office &Visual Basic for Applications Developer* magazine. He is also a regular speaker at conferences such as Microsoft Tech*Ed and the Microsoft Office and VBA Solutions conference. You can reach Mike at mgilbert@developershandbook.com.

CONTENTS AT A GLANCE

TABLE OF CONTENTS

INTRODUCTION

Visual Basic for Applications (VBA) started its life as a tool that would allow Excel, and then other Microsoft Office applications, to control their own environment programmatically and would work with other applications using OLE Automation. In 1996, the VBA world exploded when Microsoft allowed other vendors to license the VBA language engine and environment for their own products. At the time of this writing, hundreds of vendors have licensed this exciting technology, making it possible for users of many products to control their applications and any Automation server using VBA.

The best part about all this for the VBA developer is that the skills you learn in one product will carry directly to any other VBA host. The programming environment is the same, the debugging tools are the same, and the language is the same. Finally, Basic programmers (after all, VBA is still a variant on the original BASIC language) are getting some respect. Using tools that end-users can appreciate and work with, you can write applications that they can live with, modify, and extend.

Here's what Microsoft doesn't make clear: VBA is a language, a development environment, and a forms package. This book is only about one part of that triumvirate: the language. We've attempted to dig into details of VBA, the language, that you won't find elsewhere. We've not made any attempt to discuss the forms package that's part of VBA, nor have we spent any time discussing the development environment.

What this means is that this book applies to anyone using VBA 6, and that includes Office 2000, Visual Basic 6, and the myriad of other products that have licensed the VBA 6 technology. In essence, this book is host-agnostic, and all the code runs equally well in VB6 or Access 2000.

About the Book

VBA has become the glue that ties together the various pieces of multi-platform solutions, and many new programmers are being tossed into situations in which they need programming help. In this book, you'll find creative solutions to many programming problems.

Is this book a replacement for the VB or VBA programmer's reference manuals? Not even close! Nor does it intend to provide you with a complete reference. This book is about ideas, about solutions, and about learning. We've taken our combined years of Basic programming; come up with a list of topics that we think are interesting and that provide challenges to many developers; and created a book that, we hope, collates all the information in useful and interesting ways.

First and foremost, this book is *not* product specific. That is, whether you're using Microsoft Office 2000 or any other product that hosts VBA 6 or later, you'll be able to take advantage of the code in this book. Because we've provided the code in three formats (as Microsoft Access 2000 databases, Microsoft Excel 2000 workbooks, and as separate text files with VB6 project files), anyone who has a CD-ROM reader can immediately make use of this code. We'll say it again: Although we used Office 2000 in developing this book, *the code provided here should work in any product that hosts VBA 6.*

For these reasons, we've focused on code, not the user interface, so you'll find very few examples in the book that actually *look* like anything much. For the most part, the examples involve calling code from the Immediate window. Don't expect lots of pretty examples with forms you can dig into—that wasn't our goal at all. We've provided the tools; now *you* provide the spiffy interface!

Our goal in writing this book was both to provide useful code and to explain that code so you can modify and extend it if you need to add more or different functionality. We've covered a broad range of topics but haven't even made an attempt to be the absolute final word on these, or any, topics. Doing so would require a book ten times the size of this one. No, this book is meant as a starting place for explorations into new topics, in addition to providing a ton of useful code.

Is This Book for You?

This book is aimed squarely at the legions of developers, both new to, and experienced with, VB and VBA development, who need help with specific coding situations. But if you're looking for a description of how the If...Then construct works or for someone to hold your hand while you write your first VBA procedure, perhaps this isn't the right book for you. On the other hand, if you want to work through a great deal of code, copy and paste code and complete modules from our samples directly into your applications, and work through the code line by line, you've come to the right place.

This book will appeal to three separate audiences:

VBA beginner to intermediate   You've written a few procedures and are trying to put together an application. You need help writing specific procedures; stopping to figure out the code on your own would be an insurmountable task. You can copy and paste code from the book right into your modules, skip the boring part where we describe how the code works, and get back to work on your application.

VBA advanced   You've written a lot of code and are facing more and greater coding challenges. You need specific procedures written and could do it yourself, but there are other pressing needs (like getting your application finished yesterday). You can take the routines from this book, modify them to exactly meet your needs, and work through the explanations provided here to add to your working knowledge about the use of VBA.

VBA expert Even if you're among the most experienced of VBA programmers, there are some procedures you'll need and just haven't written yourself. You can take the code provided here as a starting point and embellish and fine-tune to your heart's content. Of course, you may find a better way to rewrite the code we've provided; if so, we'd love to hear from you!

If you find yourself in any one of these three categories, have we got some code for you!

What You Need to Know

To make it possible to stuff as much code as possible into this book, we've had to dispense with material specifically geared for beginners. If you're not sure where to put the code, how to create a module, or even what the different variable types are in VBA, perhaps you'd do best to put this book aside for a week or so and study the reference materials provided with the VBA host you're working with. Make sure you have a good grasp of the following topics before jumping into this book:

- Creating modules
- Creating procedures
- Using variables and their data types
- Using VBA syntax (including If…Then, For…Next, and other control structures)

If you take the time to review these concepts before delving into this book, you'll get a great deal more out of the material here.

Conventions Used in the Book

Having worked on a number of projects together, we've found that a consistent style and defined conventions make it much simpler for multiple programmers to work together on a project. To make it easier for you to understand our code (and for us to understand each other's), we've adopted a naming standard, which we've stuck to both throughout this book and in all our professional work.

We've used version 6 of the Reddick VBA (RVBA) naming conventions for the naming of objects, which have been accepted by many VB and VBA developers as the naming standard to follow. Greg Reddick, a noted Access and Visual Basic developer and trainer, developed the standard, which bears his name. Even if you don't subscribe to the RVBA standard, you'll likely appreciate the fact that it has been used consistently throughout this book. These conventions, which were first published in *Smart Access,* are included in their entirety in Appendix A.

In addition to following the RVBA standard, we've prefaced all Public functions, subroutines, and user-defined types that you may wish to use for your own code, with the "dh" prefix (which stands for *Developer's Handbook*). Also, we have aliased all Public Windows API declarations using a "dh_api" prefix, and we have prefixed all Public constants with "dhc". These conventions should avoid naming conflicts with any existing code in your applications. However, if you import multiple modules from various chapters' samples into a single application, you may find naming conflicts as a result of our using consistent naming throughout the chapters. In that case, you'll need to comment out any conflicting API declarations or user-defined types.

A note about error handling: When writing utility procedures, such as those found in this book, it's always a toss-up whether to include extensive error handling. We decided, both for the sake of simplicity and because we both hate using service routines that display error messages, to include very little error handling, except in cases where the procedures need it for their own use. This means that your code, calling our procedures, will need to trap and handle errors that bubble up from the code provided here. Of course, if you'd rather, you can simply add your own error handling to the procedures you import. For more information on using error handling, please see Appendix C, which is included on the CD-ROM that accompanies this book.

Appendices

In addition to the fifteen chapters, we've included four appendices. Appendix A is included in the book. Appendices B, C, and D are included on the CD-ROM that accompanies this book.

- Appendix A contains the complete Reddick VBA naming conventions.

- Appendix B contains a chapter borrowed from our "sister" book (*Access 2000 Developer's Handbook: Desktop Edition*, also from Sybex), which introduces the use of the Windows API in VBA applications. If you've never looked into how VBA apps can use the Windows API, you'll want to at least skim this appendix before working with the code in Chapters 9 through 13.

- Appendix C focuses on writing bulletproof, well-tuned VBA applications, including handling errors, creating event logs, and creating a procedure-tracking stack for your applications. Because many of this book's readers already have the concepts presented in this appendix under their belts, we've moved this from being a full chapter into the appendix territory for this edition of the book.

- Appendix D contains a Folder and File object model—that is, a set of classes you can use for modeling the file system. This code was originally in Chapter 12. However, we noticed that in this edition, Chapter 14's coverage of the FileSystemObject made this home-grown set of classes (perhaps) redundant. On the other hand, there's something to be said for having modifiable source code, so we've included this as an appendix. Feel free to dig in if you're interested.

Using the Chapter Samples

The CD-ROM includes an Installer (Setup.exe) that will install the chapter projects on your hard drive in a folder named vbadh. Within the vbadh folder, there is a folder for each chapter that has code examples. In these folders, you'll find all the example files used in the book. We've provided each chapter's examples in at least three formats. First, each chapter's folder includes a Microsoft Excel 2000 workbook containing all the modules discussed in the chapter, ready for you to experiment with. In addition, we've provided each module as a separate BAS or CLS file (along with a Visual Basic VBP file), so you can import these into your projects in whatever VBA host you're using. Finally, to make it simpler for Microsoft Access 2000 developers, we've created one database file for each of the chapters, with all the modules imported for you.

Tell Us Who You Are

In order to make it easy for us to contact you with information about updates to the book and other useful information about VB and VBA development, we've set up a Web site that you can visit: http://www.developershandbook.com. At this Web site, you can fill out a form with information about yourself so we can let you know about changes, errata, enhanced examples, and other updates. Be the first person on your block to know about updates to *VBA Developer's Handbook*. Visit and sign up now.

How to Use This Book

We can think of two ways in which you might want to use this book. You may just want to start at the beginning and plow straight through until you've reached the other side. That's fine, but keep some sticky notes at hand so you can mark interesting code as it goes by. Otherwise, you'll never remember where all the fun stuff was.

However, it's more likely that you'll peruse this Introduction, browse through a few chapters, and then use the book as a reference when you need it. That's fine, too. Just do us two favors:

- If you're not comfortable with class modules, work your way through Chapter 5, at least, to find out how they work and what they bring to the VBA "party."

- If you've never used Windows API calls, be sure to visit Appendix B on the CD-ROM that accompanies this book. This appendix introduces ways in which the Windows API can contribute to your programming efforts and explains how to use this valuable technique.

Both of these topics are crucial to a complete understanding of much of the rest of the book, and attempting to work through the remaining chapters without an understanding of at least these prerequisites will make for a steep climb.

Focusing on Business Logic

In 1991, Microsoft released Windows 3, the first widely adopted version of Windows, and ushered in the era of the graphical user interface (the efforts of companies like Xerox and Apple notwithstanding). At the time, the only way to create Windows applications was by using the C language and DOS-based tools like Microsoft C 7. To make Windows more accessible to the legions of programmers who grew up on Microsoft's BASIC offerings, the company released Visual Basic 1 in 1992. VB 1 was heralded as revolutionary in terms of Windows development tools because it insulated the programmer from most of the tedious details of Windows programming, like memory allocation and message loops, and let them focus instead on an application's business logic.

The race was on to adapt VB technology to other programming tasks, such as automating applications through a "macro" language. Programmers saw many variations on this theme throughout the early 1990s, including WordBasic, Project Basic, and Access Basic, all with their own idiosyncrasies in syntax and capabilities. It quickly became apparent that a common syntax was needed if BASIC was to maintain its importance in the realm of Windows development. Microsoft responded to this need in 1993 with the introduction of Visual Basic for Applications (VBA) in Excel 5 for Windows. It wasn't long until the entire Microsoft Office product line had adopted VBA as the automation language of choice. By 1995, VBA had become a common component for Access, Word, and Excel, sharing its core technology (and source code) with Microsoft Visual Basic.

At the same time, other companies in the software industry were recognizing the importance of providing an automation language along with a program's core functionality. The mid-1990s saw the introduction of a number of embedded language technologies, most based on BASIC. During this period, Microsoft created a version of the VBA development environment and run-time engine (version 5) that could be factored out of Office and offered to third-party software developers. The first company to license VBA from Microsoft was Visio Corporation. Visio released the first VBA 5–enabled product, Visio 4.5, in late 1996. Ironically, Microsoft acquired Visio in 1999. Today, more than 100 companies have licensed

VBA from Microsoft, making it one of the most widely adopted programming technologies in the world. For the latest information on VBA, you can visit the VBA Web site at `http://msdn.microsoft.com/vba/`.

A Language Is about Data

By looking at the differences between VB 1 and, say, QuickBasic, you can begin to understand what makes up the core language and what belongs to the particular platform and development environment. At the heart of any programming language is the ability to model, store, and manipulate data. After all, that's the goal of most computer programs—accept input, perform calculations, and produce output. All BASIC variants enable you to do this using variables, operators, and keywords.

Of course, unless you or your user can supply a program with data input or view, the program's output is not of much use. That's why each implementation of a language includes functions for obtaining and displaying data. Therefore, the question is whether or not these functions are really part of the language. The approach we've adopted in this book is that, for the most part, the Visual Basic language is not about input or output but strictly about data manipulation. Adopting this approach has enabled us to present examples that work in any recent variant of the language, regardless of development environment.

What this means is that we don't cover functions that deal with capturing user input, monitoring the keyboard or mouse, drawing user interfaces, or printing. We also don't cover the object models of VB or other VBA hosts, like Access or Excel. Instead, we focus on manipulating variables and data structures to accomplish common tasks, like computing dates, writing to disks, controlling other applications through Automation, and reading system information. For the most part, input and output in this book's samples is limited to the Visual Basic equivalent of a command line, the Immediate window.

The Visual Basic Family

Microsoft often refers to the current lineup of BASIC derivatives as the Visual Basic family. There are currently three family members, Visual Basic, VBA, and VBScript, each with their own role to play in enabling software development using the Visual Basic language.

Visual Basic is the senior member of the group and represents the stand-alone programming system that ships as part of Microsoft's Visual Studio development suite, as well as a separate product. The role of Visual Basic (or just VB) is to provide software developers with a tool for creating stand-alone components and applications. Even though VB's initial appeal was the ease with which developers could create graphical interfaces, you can use VB to create pure, code-only components. This has become an attractive way to factor a program's functionality, leading to pieces that can easily be reused.

Visual Basic consists of a graphical development environment that enables you to design your user interface, write program logic, and compile and debug your application using the same tool. While it appears to the user as integrated, there are actually a number of separate components that make up the VB development experience:

Development environment   Provides the user interface components for viewing and editing code and creating forms. It also provides interactive windows for debugging tasks. The development environment is also extensible, enabling third parties to create *add-ins* that assist developers in working with VB projects and *designers* that create components that become an integral part of a compiled application.

Visual Basic forms engine   Provides all the user interface functionality and is an inextricable part of the VB experience. In addition to the native capability to display windows with primitive controls, like labels and text boxes, the forms engine is responsible for supporting the ActiveX control architecture that provides developers with a rich set of interface options. Many developers have wished for the ability to use VB forms in other products, but the truth is that the two are so closely related that this is impossible.

Visual Basic language engine   Is responsible for parsing and compiling source code. It translates variables, keywords, and operators into a proprietary set of operation codes (op-codes) and performs optimizations for constructs like For Next loops. Some people still think Visual Basic is an interpreted language. It isn't. The language engine has almost no knowledge of any of the user interface or other components that make up a typical VB application, although there are a few exceptions, such as keywords for primitive drawing operations held over from earlier versions of the language.

Run-time engine   Acts as a counterpart to the language engine and is charged with executing the op-codes generated by the language engine. The run-time engine also provides debugging capability and implements the hooks necessary to interact with the development environment's user interface.

Automation infrastructure   Opens up the development environment to external components and mediates communication among them. Many of the capabilities you associate with VB, such as database access, are actually provided by separate components. VB uses COM Automation as the glue that ties these components together. This infrastructure also enables you to create your own components and is the foundation for VBA class modules.

Native code compiler   Is the most critical aspect of Visual Basic as a distinct member of the VB family. After the language engine compiles source code into op-codes that the run-time engine can execute, the native code compiler turns these into machine instructions, producing a Windows executable or COM DLL. In fact, VB uses the same compiler and linker as Visual C++. Visual Basic is the only member of the VB family that can create stand-alone executable programs.

The other two family members, VBA and VBScript, inherit their features (and, to some extent, their source code) from Visual Basic. Visual Basic for Applications was designed as a hosted component to provide automation services to any COM-based application. It uses the VB environment, Automation infrastructure, language, and run-time engines to deliver these capabilities. It is important to understand this if you are to overcome skepticism regarding the power of VBA. It has the same core components as VB; the only thing it lacks is the forms engine (although it does have its own) and the ability to create stand-alone components. In every other respect, the language engine is just as powerful. In a sense, VB could be described as VBA plus a forms engine and compiler. That's why we chose to write this book in the first place, and why we still refer to language constructs as belonging to VBA rather than VB.

At the other end of the spectrum from VB, VBScript was designed to offer light-weight automation capabilities and is optimized for Web-based applications. It was subject to a very different set of design constraints than VB and VBA; thus, it lacks many of their features and, it could be argued, some of their power. For instance, VBScript is just one implementation of a script engine using Microsoft's ActiveX Scripting technology framework. ActiveX Scripting is a framework that enables an application like Internet Explorer to host any number of different script languages simply by installing a separate language component. JScript and Perl are two examples of languages that have been implemented using this technology. Furthermore, VBScript was designed to be installed over the Internet, which placed tight constraints on the size of the script engine. For this reason, it has no integrated development environment or debugging tools and is just a subset of the complete VB language; although this is rapidly changing to include more and more core language features.

Because VBA is a "universal" language, all the code examples in this book should operate equally well in Office 2000, Office XP, VB6, and any other host product that includes VBA 6 (including Visio, AutoCad, and myriad other products that have licensed this technology from Microsoft). The file formats for Office 2000 and Office XP remain essentially unchanged (Access 2002 does provide a new file format, but it's able to transparently load and work with

Access 2000 files, and that's the format we've chosen to use here), so all the examples work equally well in both products.

Why This Book Is Useful

We hope it's now clear what the Visual Basic language is and what this book covers. Simply stated, the Visual Basic language is the core syntax, compiler, and run-time engine shared by all members of the Visual Basic family (with small exceptions for VBScript). It does not concern itself with particular user interface implementations or host environments. In focusing on the pure language, this book attempts to be a valuable resource for all developers wishing to get the most out of their development tools, be those VB, VBA in Office, or third-party applications.

We leave it up to you to understand how to create forms or take advantage of the object model provided by your particular VB language host. Although we must delve into these areas occasionally, such as in our discussion of Automation, we make no claim to be even a reasonable resource for this information. This book is meant to complement any other material you discover that is geared directly toward your development tool. If you keep this volume side-by-side with your VB, Access, Excel, or Internet Explorer books and consult it as often, then we've succeeded in our efforts to deliver to you valuable knowledge on what we call the Visual Basic language.

chapter 1

Manipulating Strings

- Understanding how string values are stored and used in VBA

- Using the built-in VBA string-handling functions

- Searching for and replacing text

- Gathering information about strings

- Converting strings

- Working with substrings

Almost any VBA application will need t o handle string (text) data at one point or another. VBA itself provides a useful set of string-handling functions, but the functionality of other functions as a whole is not nearly as full-featured as that provided by other, more text-centric programming languages. This chapter first makes a quick pass through the existing functions and then provides many useful routines to add to your string-handling bag of tricks. Surely, no chapter on this topic could cover every possible combination of useful functions, but the ones we've provided here should give you a good start in writing your own VBA solutions.

The sample files you'll find on the CD-ROM that accompanies this book are listed in Table 1.1:

TABLE 1.1:   String-Handling Functions

Filename	Description
STRINGS.XLS	Excel file with sample functions
STRINGS.BAS	Text file with sample functions
TESTSTR.BAS	Text file with test procedures
PROPER.MDB	Access 2000 database, containing sample for dhProperLookup
PROPER.TXT	Text version of sample for dhProperLookup
PROPER.XML	XML-based recordset for dhProperLookup
STRINGS.VBP	Visual Basic project with sample code
STRINGS.MDB	Access 2000 database, containing sample functions

WARNING   Because the modules for this chapter take advantage of ADO, you'll need to make sure your own project includes a reference to the Microsoft ActiveX Data Object 2.1 Library before you import the StringsBAS module into the project. Use the Tools ➤ References menu (or Project ➤ References menu, in Visual Basic) to add the necessary reference. Otherwise, your code will not compile once you've added the Strings module to your project.

How Does VBA Store Strings?

A VBA string is simply a collection of bytes. To make it easier for VBA to work with strings, each string also maintains its own information about its length. In addition, unlike other programming languages, VBA takes care of creating, destroying, and resizing string buffers. You needn't worry about how VBA finds strings in memory, whether they're contiguous in memory, or how or when VBA reclaims the memory of the string used once you're done with it.

VBA provides two types of strings: *fixed-length* and *dynamic*. Fixed-length strings are those you declare with a fixed size, like this:

```
Dim strFixed As String * 100
```

In this case, strFixed will always contain exactly 100 characters, no matter how many characters you've placed into it. When VBA first creates the variable, at runtime, it fills the variable with 100 spaces. From then on, if you attempt to retrieve the length of the string, the output will always be 100:

```
Debug.Print Len(strFixed)
```

VBA fills the extra positions with spaces. You'll need to use the Trim function in order to use the string in any other expression (see the section "Working with Portions of a String" later in this chapter for more information). Fixed-length strings can be no longer than 65,526 characters.

TIP   Online help for VBA states that a fixed-length string can be up to 2^{16} (or 65,536) characters long. Not so—if you attempt to create one with more than 65,526 characters, VBA won't compile your code.

Dynamic strings, on the other hand, have no fixed size. As you add or remove characters from these objects, VBA takes care of locating memory in which to place the text and allocates and deallocates memory as necessary for your text. To declare a dynamic string, you use a declaration like this:

```
Dim strDynamic As String
```

In this case, if you retrieve the length of the string, the result will accurately reflect the amount of text you've placed into the variable. Dynamic strings can contain up to around two billion characters.

How do you decide which type of string to use? Dynamic strings require a bit more processing effort from VBA and are, accordingly, a bit slower to use. On the other hand, you make up the time by not needing to use the Trim function to remove excess space every time you use the string. As you'll see by working through the examples in this chapter, we use fixed-length strings only when it's necessary. When working with a single character at a time, it makes sense to use a fixed-length string declared to contain a single character. Because you know you'll always have only a single character in the string, you'll never need to trim off excess space. You get the benefits of a fixed-length string without the extra overhead.

Unicode versus ANSI

The 32-bit Windows "universe" supports two character storage mechanisms: ANSI and Unicode. The ANSI storage standard uses a single byte for every character, with only 256 different characters allowed in any ANSI character set. If you want to display characters from a different set of 256, you must load a separate code page. This limitation makes it difficult to create internationalized applications. Windows 95 and Windows 98 use this approach for compatibility with previous versions of Windows. The Unicode standard allows for 65,536 characters, each taking up two bytes. The Unicode character set includes just about all the known written characters and ideograms in a single entity. In this way, an application that embraces the Unicode standard can support (once its text has been translated) just about any written language. Windows NT and Windows 2000 support the Unicode standard.

No matter what operating system you're using, VBA stores strings internally in Unicode format. That is, every character takes up two bytes of space. When VBA needs to communicate with Windows 95 or Windows 98 (when you include Windows API calls in your code, for example), it must first convert strings to ANSI format. This happens automatically when you use the ANSI version of a Windows API call that involves strings. The only other time you'll care about how VBA stores strings is when you want to convert a string into an array of bytes—a useful technique that we'll take advantage of a few times in this chapter. In this case, a string containing five characters becomes an array of bytes containing ten bytes. For example, a string containing the text *Hello* would contain the following ten bytes, once converted to a byte array:

```
72   0   101   0   108   0   108   0   111   0
```

Each pair of bytes (72 and 0 for the *H*, for example) represents the Unicode storage for a single character. However, if you were running Microsoft Excel in Korea, for example, and were entering text in your native language, the second byte wouldn't be 0. Instead, it would be a value that combined with the first byte to represent the character you'd typed.

Using Strings and Byte Arrays

Because it's often faster and simpler to work with arrays of bytes than to work with individual characters in a string (and you'll find some examples in this chapter that use this technique), VBA provides a simple way to convert strings into byte arrays and back. Simply assigning a string to a byte array variable causes VBA to copy the data into the array. When you're done working with the array, you can assign it right back into the string variable. For example, the following code fragment copies data from a string into a byte array, performs processing on the array, and then copies the array back into the string:

```
Sub StringToByteArray()
    Dim strText As String
    Dim aByt() As Byte
    Dim intI As Integer
    strText = "Hello"
    ' VBA allows you to assign a string into
    ' a byte array and then back again.
    aByt() = strText
    For intI = LBound(aByt) To UBound(aByt)
        Debug.Print aByt(intI);
    Next intI
    Debug.Print
    strText = aByt()
    Debug.Print strText
End Sub
```

Although you won't use this technique often, if you need to process each byte of a string, it's the best solution.

WARNING   In previous versions of Basic, many programmers used string variables to contain binary data (that is, non-textual data, such as bitmaps, sound files, and so on). In VBA, this isn't necessary, nor is it advisable. Instead, use arrays of bytes for non-textual data. Because VBA performs ANSI-to-Unicode conversions on the fly, you're almost guaranteed that your non-text data will be ruined once you place it into a string variable.

Using Built-In String Functions

VBA provides a large number of string-handling functions. This section introduces many of those functions, broken down by the area of functionality, and discusses the most useful of the built-in functions. The remainder of the chapter provides techniques that combine the built-in functions to perform tasks for which you would otherwise need to write custom code.

Comparing Strings

VBA provides three ways for you to compare the contents of one string with another: comparison operators (such as =, <, and so on), the Like operator, and the StrComp function. In addition, you can specify the method of comparison for each module using the Option Compare statement in the declarations area.

Option Compare

The Option Compare statement, if it's used at all, must appear in a module before any procedures, and it tells VBA how you want to make string comparisons within the module. The choices are as follows:

Option Compare Binary   Comparisons are made based on the internal sort order of the characters, using their binary representation. In this situation, characters are treated case sensitively (that is, A isn't the same as a).

Option Compare Text   Comparisons are made based on the text sort order of the current locale. Characters are treated, at least in English, case insensitively.

Option Compare Database   Is available only in Microsoft Access. Comparisons are made based on the locale ID of the current database.

TIP　If you don't specify an Option Compare setting, VBA uses Option Compare Binary. In that case, if you attempt to perform a simple comparison between *A* and *a*, you'll get a False return value. If you're working with strings and performing comparisons, make sure you're aware of the Option Compare setting for the module.

Comparison Operators

You can use the simple logical operators to compare two strings, like this:

```
If strText1 < strText2 Then...
```

In this case, VBA performs a character-by-character comparison according to the Option Compare setting in force in the current module. The result of the comparison will most likely change, based on that setting. You can use the set of simple comparison operators shown here.

Operator	Description
<	Less than
<=	Less than or equal to
>=	Greater than or equal to
=	Equal to
<>	Not equal to

In addition, VBA supplies the Like operator for comparing two strings. This operator allows you to specify wildcards, character lists, and character ranges in the comparison string, not just fixed characters. The following is a listing of all the options for the comparison string using the Like operator:

Characters in Pattern	Matches in String
?	Any single character
*	Zero or more characters
#	Any single digit (0–9)
[charlist]	Any single character in *charlist*
[!charlist]	Any single character not in *charlist*

The string containing the wildcard information must be on the right-hand side of the Like operator. That is, unlike many mathematical operators, this one is not commutative: The order of the operands is significant.

For example, the following code fragment would compare a string with a template that checks for valid Canadian Postal codes:

```
strTemp = "W1F 8G7"
If strTemp Like "[A-Z]#[A-Z] #[A-Z]#" Then
    ' You know strTemp is a valid Canadian Postal Code
End If
```

To check whether the single character in strTemp was a vowel, you could use this expression:

```
If strTemp Like "[AEIOUaeiou]*" Then
    ' You know the first character in strTemp is a vowel
End If
```

If you want to see whether the word stored in strTemp doesn't start with a vowel, you could use an expression like this:

```
If strTemp Like "[!AEIOUaeiou]*" Then
    ' You know the word in strTemp doesn't start with a vowel
End If
```

You'll find the Like operator to be invaluable when you need to validate input. Rather than parse the string yourself, you can use wildcards to allow various ranges of characters.

The behavior of the Like operator depends on the Option Compare setting. Unless you specify otherwise, each module uses Option Compare Binary (case-sensitive comparisons).

There are a number of issues you need to be aware of when using the Like operator (sorting, order of the characters within the range, and so on). Be sure to check out the online help for this topic for more information.

Using the StrComp Function

The StrComp function provides a way for you to compare strings, overriding the Option Compare statement within a given module. To use StrComp, you specify the two strings and a comparison method (binary, text, or database), and the function returns a value indicating how the two strings compared. In general, you call StrComp like this:

```
intRetVal = StrComp(strText1, strText2, CompareOption)
```

The two text strings can be any string expressions. The CompareOption value should be one of the items from Table 1.2 or a locale ID integer that specifies a local sort order for comparisons. Depending on the parameters, StrComp returns one of the values from Table 1.3.

TIP   The CompareOption parameter for StrComp is optional. If you omit it, VBA uses the option selected by the Option Compare setting for the module. If you omit the Option Compare, of course, VBA will use binary comparisons (vbBinaryCompare).

WARNING   Online help incorrectly supplies a fourth value, not shown in Table 1.2 (vbUse-CompareOption, −1). This value doesn't appear to work in the current version of VBA. For any function that takes a comparison option as a parameter, you may not use the vbUseCompareOption value. (No matter what the online help tells you.)

TABLE 1.2: Compare Options for StrComp

Constant	Option Compare Equivalent
vbBinaryCompare	Option Compare Binary
vbDatabaseCompare	Option Compare Database (Microsoft Access only)
vbTextCompare	Option Compare Text

TABLE 1.3: Return Values for StrComp

If	StrComp Returns
strText1 is less than strText	−1
strText1 is equal to strText	0
strText1 is greater than strText2	1

Using the StrComp function, even if you normally perform case-sensitive comparisons, you can override that requirement for one comparison:

```
If StrComp(strText1, strText2, vbTextCompare) = 0 Then
    ' You know that strText1 and strText2 are the same, as far
    ' as the text comparison goes.
End If
```

Converting Strings

Rather than provide individual functions to convert strings from one format to another, VBA includes the single StrConv function. This function allows you to specify a string, as well as a conversion parameter indicating the conversion you'd like to make. In general, you call the function like this:

$$strOutput = StrConv(strInput, Conversion, [LocaleID])$$

where *strInput* is the string to be converted; *Conversion* is a value from the following table; and *LocaleID* (optionally) specifies the Windows LocaleID to use for the conversion. (If you don't specify a locale ID, VBA will use the current locale's information in order to perform the conversion.) StrConv returns the converted string as its return value.

Constant	Description
vbUpperCase	Converts the string to uppercase characters.
vbLowerCase	Converts the string to lowercase characters.
vbProperCase	Converts the first letter of every word in the string to uppercase.
vbUnicode	Converts the string to Unicode using the default code page of the system.
vbFromUnicode	Converts the string from Unicode to the default code page of the system.

As you can see, the StrConv function performs two basic tasks: converting the case (upper, lower, proper) of strings and converting strings from ANSI to Unicode and back.

TIP   If you're working in a Japanese or other Far East locale, you'll want to check out the options for StrConv that are available only in those locales. See the VBA online help for more information.

Creating Strings: The Space and String Functions

VBA provides two functions that make it easy for you to create specific strings. The Space function lets you create a string consisting only of spaces; you indicate the number of spaces, and VBA does the rest. The general syntax looks like this:

strOut = Space(*lngSpaces*)

Although this function has many uses, we've used it most often in two particular situations:

- Creating string buffers when calling external DLLs (the Windows API, in particular)

- Padding strings so they're left or right justified within a buffer of a particular size

You can use an expression like this to create a 10-character string of spaces:

```
strTemp = Space(10)
```

If you need more flexibility, you can use the String function to create a string of any number of a specified character. For this function, you specify the number of characters you need and the specific character or ANSI value to repeat:

```
strOut = String(lngChars, strCharToRepeat)
' or

strOut = String(lngChars, intCharToRepeat)
```

For example, either of the following fragments will return a string containing 10 occurrences of the letter *a*. (The ANSI value for *a* is 97.)

```
strOut = String(10, "a")
strOut = String(10, 97)
```

Although you're unlikely to need this particular string, the following code fragment creates a string consisting of one *A*, two *B*s, three *C*s, and so on.

```
Dim intI As Integer
Dim strOut As String
For intI = 1 To 26
    strOut = strOut & String(intI, Asc("A") + intI - 1)
Next intI
```

Calculating the Length of a String

Simple yet crucial, the Len function allows you to determine the length of any string or string expression. To use the function, pass it a string or string expression:

```
lngCharCount = Len(strIn)
```

Certainly, you'll often need to find the length of a string expression. But the Len function also has an extra benefit: It's fast! VBA stores strings with a long integer preceding the string that contains the length of the string. It's very simple for VBA to retrieve that information at runtime. For example, what if you need to know whether a particular string currently contains no characters? Many programmers write code like this to check for an empty string:

```
If strTemp = "" Then
    ' You know strTemp is empty
End If
```

Because VBA can calculate string lengths so quickly, you're better off using code like this to find out if a string is empty:

```
If Len(strTemp) = 0 Then
    ' You know strTemp is empty
End if
```

Performing one non-optimized comparison isn't going to make any difference in the speed of your application, but if you check for empty strings often, consider using the Len function instead.

Formatting Data

VBA allows you to format the output display of a string using placeholders that represent single characters from the input string. In addition, you can use the Format function to convert an input string to upper- or lowercase. The placeholders and conversion characters shown in Table 1.4 allow you to reformat an input string.

For example, if strTemp contains the string "8364928", the following fragment returns "(   )836-4928":

```
strOut = Format("8364928", "(@@@)&&&-&&&&")
```

This fragment returns "()836-4928":

```
strOut = Format("8364928", "(&&&)&&&-&&&&")
```

TABLE 1.4:   Placeholders and Conversion Characters for the Format Function

Character	Description
@	Character placeholder for a character or a space. If the input string has a character in the position where the At symbol (@) appears in the format string, display it; otherwise, display a space in that position.
&	Character placeholder for a character or nothing. If the input string has a character in the position where the ampersand (&) appears, display it; otherwise, display nothing.
<	Displays all characters in lowercase format.
>	Displays all characters in uppercase format.
!	Forces left to right fill of placeholders. The default is to fill placeholders from right to left. The character can be placed anywhere in the format string.

In addition, the Format function allows you to format normal strings one way and empty or null strings another. Every character following the symbol will be converted. For example, you may want to indicate an empty value differently from a value with data. To do this, use two sections in the placeholder string separated with a semicolon (;). The first section will apply to non-empty strings, and the second will apply to empty strings. That is, the following statement places a formatted phone number into strOut if strIn contains a non-empty string, or it places "No phone" into strOut if strIn is an empty string or Null:

```
strOut = Format(strIn, "(@@@)&&&-&&&&;No phone")
```

To convert text to upper- or lowercase as it's formatted, add the > or < character to the format string. (It doesn't matter where you place the > or < character within the string. If it's in there, VBA formats the string correctly.) Every character following the symbol will be converted. For example, the following fragment converts the input text to uppercase and inserts a space between letters:

```
Format("hello there", ">@ @ @ @ @ @ @ @ @ @")
```

TIP   Although it's beyond the scope of this chapter, the Format function can also provide user-defined formatting for dates and numeric values. Check out Chapter 2 for more information on using Format with date values.

VBA also supplies two simple functions, UCase and LCase, that you can use to convert your functions to upper- and lowercase. Pass the function the string you want converted, and its output will be the converted string. The following example places the word "HELLO" into strOut:

```
strOut = UCase("hello")
```

This chapter presents three ways to convert text to upper- or lowercase: the UCase/LCase functions, the > and < characters in the Format function, and the vbUpperCase and vbLowerCase constants with the StrConv function. Use the technique that's most comfortable for you.

Because using the Format function can be overkill in some circumstances, VBA also supplies simpler, special-case functions for situations when you simply need to format a date, a number, or a percent.

FormatCurrency, FormatNumber, FormatPercent

The FormatCurrency, FormatNumber, and FormatPercent functions each accept a numeric expression and optional parameters that specify how you want the output value to be formatted. The obvious differences between the functions are that the FormatCurrency function formats its output as currency, while the other two functions simply format their output as a numeric value. FormatPercent also multiplies its result by 100 and tacks on a percent (%) sign. However, no matter what choices you make, the output value from all of these functions is always a string. Table 1.5 lists the parameters for the FormatCurrency, FormatNumber, and FormatPercent functions. (All display options other than those shown in Table 1.5 are controlled by the Windows regional settings.) These parameters make it simple to format currency, numeric, and percent values.

Several of these functions include parameters that would appear to be Boolean values (True or False) but, in fact, support three values: True, False, or Use Default. That is, you can set these options to be either True or False specifically, or you can use the default value specified in the Windows regional settings. To make it easier for you to specify which of these three values you'd like to use, VBA provides an enumerated type, vbTriState. All functions that can accept one of these three values allow you to choose from the constants vbTrue (–1), vbFalse (0), or vbUseDefault (–2).

TABLE 1.5:   Formatting Function Parameters

Parameter	Required/ Optional	Data Type	Default	Description
Expression	Required	Numeric		Numeric value to be formatted.
NumDigitsAfterDecimal	Optional	Numeric	–1 (Use regional settings.)	Number of places after the decimal to be displayed. Use –1 to force regional settings.
IncludeLeadingDigit	Optional	vbTriState	vbUseDefault	Display leading 0 for fractional values?
UseParensForNegativeNumbers	Optional	vbTriState	vbUseDefault	Display parentheses around negative numbers?
GroupDigits	Optional	vbTriState	vbUseDefault	Group digits. In the United States, this means to group every three digits from the right with a comma separator to indicate groupings of thousands?

None of these functions does much that the more generic Format function can't. But they're a lot simpler to use (no character masks to memorize). Figure 1.1 shows a session in the Immediate window, trying out various parameters for the FormatCurrency and FormatPercent functions. (FormatNumber would return similar results, but without the currency symbol.)

FIGURE 1.1

You can use the Immediate window to test out the FormatCurrency and FormatPercent functions.

```
? FormatCurrency(1234567.89)
$1,234,567.89
? FormatCurrency(1234567.89, NumDigitsAfterDecimal:=3)
$1,234,567.890
? FormatCurrency(.5)
$0.50
? FormatCurrency(.5, IncludeLeadingDigit:=vbFalse)
$.50
? FormatCurrency(1234567.89, GroupDigits:=vbFalse)
$1234567.89
? FormatCurrency(-1234567.89)
($1,234,567.89)
? FormatCurrency(-1234567.89, UseParensForNegativeNumbers:=vbFalse)
-$1,234,567.89
? FormatPercent(33/51)
64.71%
? FormatPercent(33/51, NumDigitsAfterDecimal:=1)
64.7%
```

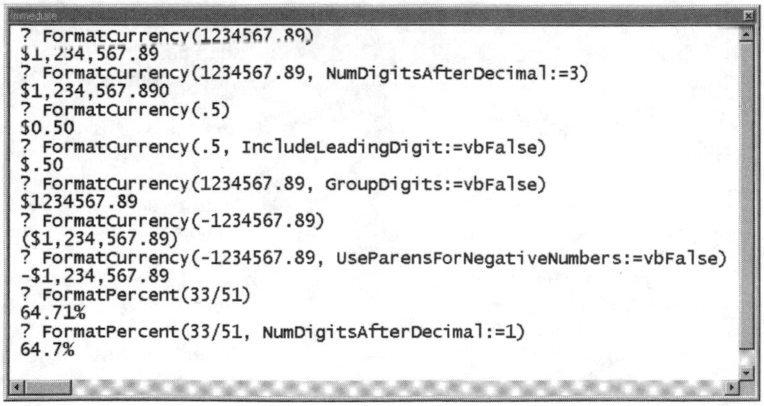

FormatDateTime

The FormatDateTime provides a simple-to-use, but very limited, technique for formatting dates and times. It lacks the flexibility and power of the built-in Format function, but it is quite simple to use. It accepts a date/time value and, optionally, a formatting specifier, and returns a string formatted as a date and/or time. Table 1.6 lists the parameters for the FormatDateTime function. Table 1.7 lists all the possible date formatting constants. Choose from these values when formatting a date.

T A B L E 1 . 6 : Parameters for the FormatDateTime Function

Parameter	Required/ Optional	Data Type	Default	Description
Expression	Required	Numeric		Numeric value to be formatted
NamedFormat	Optional	Numeric	vbGeneralDate (0)	Named format, selected from the values shown in Table 1.7, indicating how you want the date formatted

T A B L E 1 . 7 : Date Formatting Constants

Constant	Value	Description
vbGeneralDate	0	Return date and/or time. If there is a date part, include a short date. If there is a time part, include a long time. Include both date and time parts if both are available.
vbLongDate	1	Return a date using the long date format specified by your computer's regional settings.
vbShortDate	2	Return a date using the short date format specified by your computer's regional settings.
vbLongTime	3	Return a time using the time format specified by your computer's regional settings.
vbShortTime	4	Return a time using the 24-hour format (hh:mm).

Figure 1.2 shows a short debugging session, demonstrating the range of formatting possibilities with the FormatDateTime function.

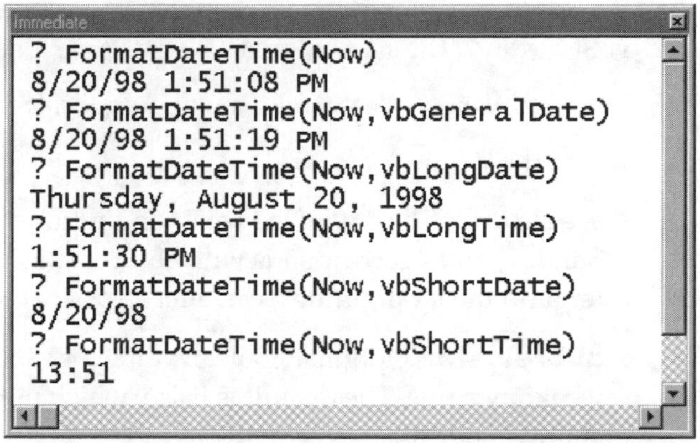

FIGURE 1.2

The FormatDateTime function is simple, but limited, as you can see from this debugging session.

```
Immediate                                                    ☒
? FormatDateTime(Now)
8/20/98 1:51:08 PM
? FormatDateTime(Now,vbGeneralDate)
8/20/98 1:51:19 PM
? FormatDateTime(Now,vbLongDate)
Thursday, August 20, 1998
? FormatDateTime(Now,vbLongTime)
1:51:30 PM
? FormatDateTime(Now,vbShortDate)
8/20/98
? FormatDateTime(Now,vbShortTime)
13:51
```

MonthName and WeekdayName

Although seemingly simple, these two functions don't have counterparts in previous versions of VBA. In VBA 5, if you need to find the name of a month, given its number, you might resort to writing a function like the MonthName shown here. (Actually, this is a complete replacement for the VBA 6 function, in case you need such a function in the previous version of VBA. And yes, you could use a simple Select Case statement, based on the Month value, but how would you get your function to work in other languages if you did that?)

```
Function MonthName(Month As Long, _
  Optional Abbreviate As Boolean = False) As String
    Dim strFormat As String

    If Abbreviate Then
        strFormat = "mmm"
    Else
        strFormat = "mmmm"
    End If
    MonthName = Format(DateSerial(2000, Month, 1), strFormat)
End Function
```

But you needn't write or call this function: VBA 6 includes a built-in MonthName function. Given a month number and a Boolean value indicating whether you want to abbreviate the name, MonthName returns the localized month name.

WeekDayName fills the same need, but instead returns the name of the day of the week corresponding to a numeric value (1 through 7, or vbSunday through vbSaturday). The syntax for WeekDayName looks like this:

strName = WeekdayName(*weekday, [abbreviate], [firstdayofweek]*)

where the various parts are

weekday   The day of the week, as a number. Normally, 1 corresponds with Sunday, and 7 corresponds with Saturday, although the *firstdayofweek* parameter (and the local settings) can alter this behavior.

abbreviate   Optional Boolean value that allows you to abbreviate the output weekday name. The default is False, which means that the weekday name isn't abbreviated.

firstdayofweek   Optional numeric value indicating the first day of the week. You can use vbUseSystem (0) to use the system value, or you can specify a particular day using the constants vbSunday (1) through vbSaturday (7).

Figure 1.3 shows a sample debugging session using these two functions.

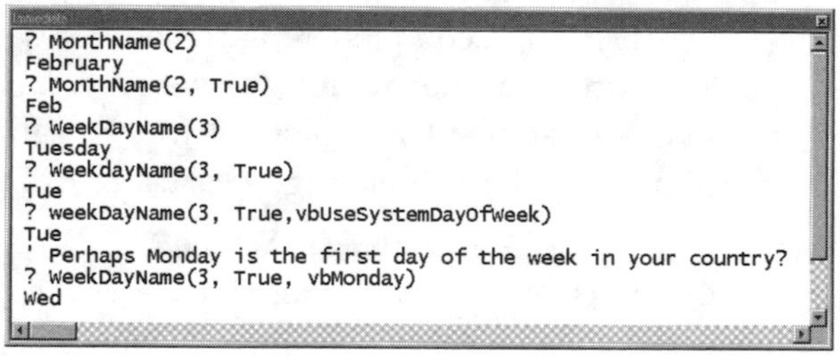

FIGURE 1.3
You can use the Immediate window to test out Month-Name and WeekDayName.

```
? MonthName(2)
February
? MonthName(2, True)
Feb
? WeekDayName(3)
Tuesday
? WeekdayName(3, True)
Tue
? weekDayName(3, True,vbUseSystemDayOfWeek)
Tue
' Perhaps Monday is the first day of the week in your country?
? WeekDayName(3, True, vbMonday)
Wed
```

Reversing a String

StrReverse returns the string you send it, with the order of the characters reversed. We're having a hard time finding a real use for this (except for writing your own InstrRev function, but that's built into VBA now, too). Perhaps this is a good use:

```
Public Function IsPalindrome(strTest As String) As Boolean
    ' Is strTest a palindrome (the same forwards as backwards)?
    IsPalindrome = (StrComp( _
      strTest, StrReverse(strTest), vbTextCompare) = 0)
End Function
```

It's not clear how often you'll need to know if a given string is the same forward and backward (that's what a palindrome is: a string that's the same in both directions), but should you ever need to know, this function does the work. For example, one of the famous palindromes "Madam, I'm Adam" works correctly in IsPalindrome, but only if you supply the value correctly. This function call returns True:

```
? IsPalindrome("madamimadam")
```

StrReverse does exactly what it was intended to do, for those who need this functionality.

Justifying a String

VBA provides two statements, LSet and RSet (note that these aren't functions) that allow you to justify a string within the space taken up by another. These statements are seldom used in this context but may come in handy. In addition, LSet gives you powerful flexibility when working with user-defined data types, as shown later in this section.

LSet and RSet allow you to stuff a new piece of text at either the beginning or the end of an existing string. The leftover positions are filled with spaces, and any text in the new string that won't fit into the old string is truncated.

For example, after running the following fragment, the string strOut1 contains the string "Hello   " ("Hello" and three trailing spaces) and strOut2 contains "   Hello" (three leading spaces and then "Hello").

```
strOut1 = "ABCDEFG"
strOut2 = "ABCDEFG"
LSet strOut1 = "Hello"
RSet strOut2 = "Hello"
```

TIP   Let's face it: Most programmers don't really take much advantage of LSet and RSet with strings. They're somewhat confusing, and you can use other string functions to achieve the same result. However, using LSet with user-defined types is key to moving data between different variable types and is discussed in the following paragraphs.

LSet also supplies a second usage: It allows you to overlay data from one user-defined type with data from another. Although the VBA help file recommends against doing this, it's a powerful technique when you need it. Simply put, LSet allows you to take all the bytes from one data structure and place them on top of another, not taking into account how the various pieces of the data structures are laid out.

Imagine that you're reading fixed-width data from a text file. That is, each of the columns in the text file contains a known number of characters. You need to move the columns into a user-defined data structure, with one field corresponding to each column in the text file. For this simple example, the text file has columns as described in the following list.

Column Name	Width
FirstName	10
LastName	10
ZipCode	5

To work with the data from the text file, you've created a user-defined data structure:

```
Type TextData
    FirstName As String * 10
    LastName As String * 10
    ZipCode As String * 5
End Type
```

You've used the various file-handling functions (see Chapter 5 for class modules to help work with text files) to retrieve a line of text from the file, and a String variable named strTemp now contains the following text:

```
"Peter     Mason     90064"
```

How do you get the various pieces from strTemp into a TextData data structure? You could parse the characters out using other string-handling functions, but you needn't—LSet can do the work for you.

The only limitation of this technique is that you cannot use LSet to move data between a simple data type and a user-defined data type. It works only with two simple data elements (the technique shown earlier in this section) and with two user-defined data types. Attempting to write code like the following will fail:

```
Dim typText As TextData
' This won't work
LSet typText = strTemp
```

To cause LSet to coerce data from one type to another, you'll need to copy your text data into yet another user-defined type. However, all this takes is a data type with a single fixed-length string, like this:

```
Type TextTemp
    strText As String * 25
End Type
```

Given that data type, it takes just one extra step to perform the conversion. You must copy the text into the strText member of the TextTemp data type. With the text there, you can use LSet to copy the bytes from the temporary data structure on top of the real data structure.

```
Dim typTest As TextData
Dim typTemp As TextTemp
' Copy the data into the temporary data structure,
' and from there into the real data structure.
typTemp.strText = strText
LSet typTest = typTemp
' Test the data and see if it arrived OK.
Debug.Print typTest.FirstName
Debug.Print typTest.LastName
Debug.Print typTest.ZipCode
```

As you can see, LSet provides a very specific usage, but it can save you many lines of code if you've got to move a large number of fields from a text string into a data structure.

WARNING　We've just barely scratched the surface of all the interesting, and potentially dangerous, tricks you can play with LSet. Beware that VBA does no checking for you when you use LSet to move data from one data structure to another.

Searching for a String

In many of the solutions presented later in this chapter, procedures will need to search a string for the inclusion of another string. The InStr function can determine whether one string contains another, and it can start looking at a specified location in the string. In addition, you can optionally specify whether the search should be case sensitive.

In general, the syntax for the InStr function looks like this:

lngLocation = InStr(*[lngStart,] strSearched, strSought[, Compare]*)

Table 1.8 explains the parameters and their return values.

T A B L E   1 . 8 :   Parameters for the InStr Function

Part	Description
lngStart	Optional. Sets the starting position for each search. If omitted, the search begins at the first character position. The lngStart argument is required if you specify the Compare argument.
strSearched	Required. String expression being searched.
strSought	Required. String expression sought.
Compare	Optional. Specifies the type of string comparison. The compare argument can be omitted, or it can be one of the values from Table 1.2. If Compare is omitted, the Option Compare setting for the module determines the type of comparison. If specified, you must also specify intStart (normally, use a value of 1 for that parameter).
Return value	0 if strSought is not found in strSearched; character position where the first occurrence of strSought begins (1 through the length of strSearched) if strSought is found; intStart (or 1, if intStart is omitted) if strSought is zero-length

For example, the following example returns 3:

```
lngPos = InStr("This is a test", "is")
```

This example, which starts looking later in the string, returns 6:

```
lngPos = InStr(4, "This is a test", "is")
```

Finding the Last Occurrence of a Substring

At one time or another, you've likely written a function that needs to know the location of the final backslash in a full path. Most likely, you either looped backward through the string, one character at a time, searching for the final backslash. Or, perhaps you used InStr, looking forward until you didn't find any more matches. Both approaches work, and both are inefficient. The InStrRev function works similarly to the InStr function, locating the position of one string within another. Instead of looking from left to right for the sought string, InStrRev looks from right to left. Just as with InStr, you can specify the starting position and the comparison mode. The only difference is the direction of the search. One more difference is that if you don't specify a starting position, the search begins at the final character, not the first character. If you want to explicitly specify a starting position, you can do that. You can also pass –1 for the starting position, to indicate that you want to start at the end of the string. Whether you omit the parameter or specify –1, you don't need to calculate the length of the string before performing a search that starts at the final character of the string.

The syntax for calling InstrRev looks like this:

lngLocation = InstrRev(*stringcheck*, *stringmatch*[, *start*[, *compare*]])

Table 1.9 describes each of the parameters and the return value.

TABLE 1.9: Parameters for the InStRev Function

Part	Description
stringcheck	Required. String expression being searched.
stringmatch	Required. String expression sought.
start	Optional. Sets the starting position for each search. If omitted, the search begins at the final character position. Use –1 (or omit) to indicate you want the search to start at the final character.
compare	Optional. Specifies the type of string comparison. The compare argument can be omitted, or it can be one of the values from Table 1.2. If compare is omitted, the Option Compare setting for the module determines the type of comparison. If specified, you must also specify intStart (normally, use a value of 1 for that parameter).
Return value	0 if stringmatch is not found in stringcheck; character position where the first occurrence of stringmatch begins (1 through the length of stringcheck) if stringmatch is found; start (or the length of stringcheck, if start is omitted, or start is –1) if stringmatch is zero-length.

Figure 1.4 shows two instances of calling InStrRev, searching for "\" within a string containing a file path. Use the numbers on the figure to help verify the return values.

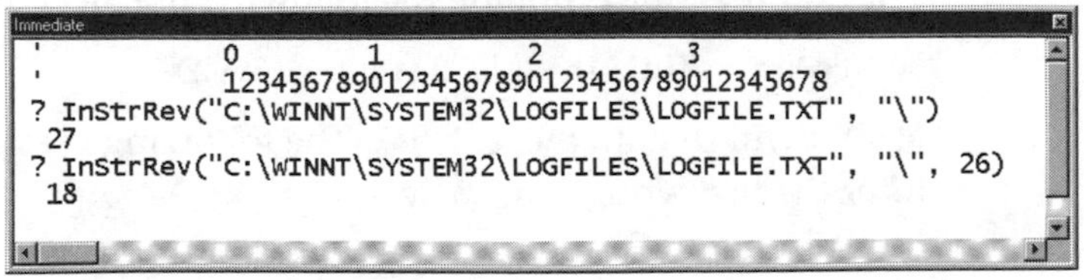

FIGURE 1.4
InStrRev searches within one string for another, starting at the right.

```
Immediate
'            0         1         2         3
'            12345678901234567890123456789012345678
? InStrRev("C:\WINNT\SYSTEM32\LOGFILES\LOGFILE.TXT", "\")
 27
? InStrRev("C:\WINNT\SYSTEM32\LOGFILES\LOGFILE.TXT", "\", 26)
 18
```

Working with Portions of a String

Many string operations involve extracting a chunk of a string, and VBA makes this task simple by providing a series of functions that let you retrieve any portion of a string. Combined with the InStr function (see the previous section), you'll be able to find substrings and then extract them as necessary.

VBA supplies three simple functions for working with substrings: Left, Mid, and Right. The Left function allows you to extract the left portion of a string:

strOut=Left(*strIn*, *lngChars*)

and returns the first *lngChars* characters from *strIn*. For example, this fragment returns the first two letters of the specified string:

```
strLeft2 = Left("This is a test", 2)
```

The following fragment returns the first word from strIn:

```
' This code fails miserably if there's no space in strIn.
' You can't ask Left for the first -1 characters in a string!
strWord = Left(strIn, InStr(strIn, " ") - 1)
```

The Right function performs the same trick, but takes characters from the right side of the string instead. The following fragment appends a backslash (\) to the filename stored in strFileName, if it's not already there:

```
If Right(strFileName, 1) <> "\" Then
    strFileName = strFileName & "\"
End If
```

The Mid function is a bit more complex because it does more. It allows you to retrieve any specified piece of a string. You supply the string, the starting location, and (optionally) the number of characters to retrieve, and VBA does the rest. If you don't specify the number of characters to retrieve, you get the rest of the characters. The formal syntax for Mid looks like this:

strOut = Mid(*strIn*, *lngStart*[, *lngLen*])

For example, after running the following line of code:

```
strOut = Mid("This is a test", 6, 2)
```

strOut will contain the text "is". The following example places all the text of strIn, after the first word, into strRest:

```
strRest = Mid(strIn, InStr(strIn, " ") + 1)
```

TIP Don't ever do what we've done in these examples! That is, never pass an unchecked value to Left, Right, or Mid unless you've included error handling in your procedure. In the examples that retrieved the first word, or all text after the first word, it's quite possible that the variable didn't actually contain a space, and InStr will return 0. In that case, you'll be passing –1 to the Left or Mid, and the functions won't take kindly to that. In cases like this, make sure you've checked the value returned from InStr before you call Left or Mid. For more information on slicing a word from a multi-word string, see the section "Working with Substrings" later in this chapter.

One common use of the Mid function is to loop through a string, one character at a time, working with each character. For example, the following loop prints each character in a string:

```
Dim strTest As String
Dim intI as Integer
strTest = "Look at each character"
For intI = 1 To Len(strTest)
    Debug.Print Mid(strTest, intI, 1)
Next intI
```

In addition to using the Left, Mid, and Right functions to extract portions of a string, you may need to remove leading or trailing white space from an existing string. VBA provides the LTrim, RTrim, and Trim functions to take care of these tasks. Each of these simple functions does one thing: LTrim removes leading spaces, RTrim removes trailing spaces, and Trim removes both leading and trailing spaces. The following fragment demonstrates the usage and results of these functions:

```
Dim strTest As String
strTest = "    This is a test    "
strTest = RTrim(strTest)
' strTest is now "    This is a test"
strTest = LTrim(strTest)
' strTest is now "This is a test"

strTest = "    This is a test    "
strTest = Trim(strTest)
' strTest is now "This is a test"
' You could use LTrim(RTrim(strTest))
' to replace the call to Trim, if you have the urge!
```

TIP   None of the Trim, LTrim, or RTrim functions removes white space from within a string. If you want to remove extraneous spaces (and, optionally, tabs) from within a string, see the dhTrimAll function, described in the section titled "Removing All Extra White Space" later in the chapter.

Replacing Portions of a String

Although you'll find several routines later in this chapter that make it easy to replace various portions of a string with other text, VBA includes a single statement that implements much of the functionality you'll need. The Mid statement (yes, it has the same name and parameters as the Mid function) allows you to replace text within a string with text supplied by another string.

To replace a substring within a string, use the Mid statement *on the left-hand side* of a line of code. The syntax for the Mid statement is as follows:

Mid(*strText*, *lngStart*[, *lngLength*]) = *strReplace*

The *lngStart* value indicates where in *strText* to start replacing. The *lngLength* value indicates how many characters from *strReplace* to place in *strText* at *intStart*.

For example, after calling the following code:

```
Dim strText As String
strText = "That car is fast."
Mid(strText, 6, 3) = "dog"
```

the variable strText will contain the text "That dog is fast." Although the Mid statement has its uses, it's rather limited because you can't control how much of the original string is replaced. You can control only how much of the replacement string is used. That is, if you try the following code:

```
Dim strText As String
strText = "That car is fast."
Mid(strText, 6, 4) = "fish"
```

there's no way to tell VBA to replace the word *car* with the word *fish*. Because the words are of differing lengths, you'll end up with "That fishis fast." The Replace function, discussed in the next section, can perform a search and replace operation within a VBA string for you.

Search and Replace in Strings

New in VBA 6, the VBA Replace function allows you to replace one substring within another string a certain number of times, starting anywhere within the string, case sensitive or not. You just have to wonder how many developers have written their own version of this function over the years. (We've certainly written it a number of times ourselves.) Replace is built into VBA, and it works well. Table 1.10 lists and describes the parameters for the Replace function.

The syntax for the Replace function looks like this:

modifiedString = Replace(*expression, find, replace*[, *start*[, *count*[, *compare*]]])

T A B L E 1 . 1 0 :   Parameters for Replace

Parameter	Required/Optional	Data Type	Description
expression	Required.	String	String to search in.
find	Required.	String	Substring being searched for.
replace	Required.	String	Replacement substring.
start	Optional. Default is 1, indicating that the search should start at the beginning.	Long	Position within expression where substring search is to begin.
count	Optional. Default is –1, indicating that you want all substitutions made.	Long	Number of substring substitutions to perform.
compare	Optional. Default is vbBinaryCompare.	Long	Kind of comparison to use when evaluating substrings. Choose one of vbBinaryCompare, vbDatabaseCompare, or vbTextCompare, or supply a Windows locale ID. See Table 1.2 for more information.

WARNING   Beware! If you specify a value for Start, that's where the output string starts. The output from Replace may not contain the entire input string with replacements made if you specify a value for the Start parameter. This certainly took us by surprise, but it's documented as working this way.

Figure 1.5 shows some examples using the Replace function. Note the effect of each of the parameters on the output string.

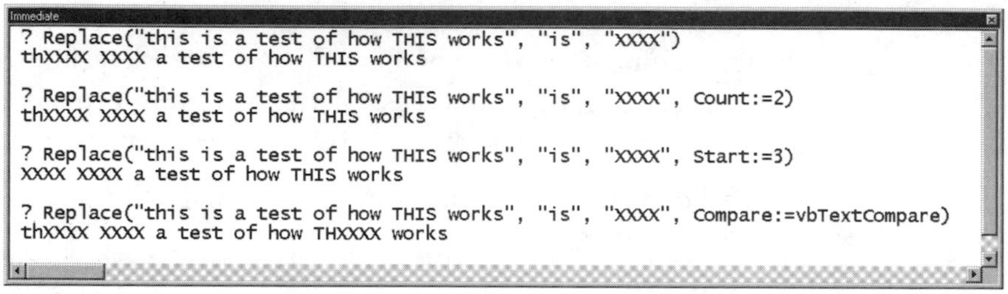

FIGURE 1.5

The Replace function allows you to replace one string within another.

```
Immediate
? Replace("this is a test of how THIS works", "is", "XXXX")
thXXXX XXXX a test of how THIS works

? Replace("this is a test of how THIS works", "is", "XXXX", Count:=2)
thXXXX XXXX a test of how THIS works

? Replace("this is a test of how THIS works", "is", "XXXX", Start:=3)
XXXX XXXX a test of how THIS works

? Replace("this is a test of how THIS works", "is", "XXXX", Compare:=vbTextCompare)
thXXXX XXXX a test of how THXXXX works
```

However, Replace does have its limitations. It can only replace a single substring with another substring. What if you want to replace one character at a time from an input map with the corresponding character in an output map? For example, what if you want to convert from text-based telephone numbers (1-800-CAR-TALK) into the corresponding string of digits (1-800-227-8255). You know how much of a pain that conversion is, manually. (And it turns out that in many countries telephones don't even have the letters printed on the buttons anymore!) What you need is a function that uses Replace for each character in an input string, mapping that character to the corresponding character in another string. The dhTranslate function, shown later in this chapter, provides this capability (without using the Replace function).

You'll find the Replace function to be useful in your development efforts. If you need to replace a single string with a single replacement string, you can't beat it. Many of the examples from the second half of this chapter use it, and others could use it but don't. It turns out that in many cases, you can handcraft code that runs faster. That's exactly what we've done in several cases, including the dhTranslate function.

Working with Arrays of Strings

The three string functions, Split, Join, and Filter, all work with arrays of strings. (And they're all new in VBA 6.) They're all useful and are all somewhat tricky to write on your own. The next few sections outline how to use each of these functions and provide examples of why you might want to use them.

Split a String into an Array

The Split function takes a string and a delimiter, and returns an array full of the pieces of the string. For example, the following function, GetLastWord, splits the input string up into an array of words and returns the final word in the array.

```
Public Function GetLastWord(strText As String) As String
    Dim astrWords() As String

    If Len(strText) = 0 Then
        GetLastWord = strText
    Else
        astrWords = Split(strText, " ")
        GetLastWord = astrWords(UBound(astrWords))
    End If
End Function
```

TIP   The GetLastWord function, shown here, is somewhat limited. We've created a more full-featured version, dhLastWord, discussed later in the chapter.

The syntax for the Split function is as follows:

outputArray = Split(*expression*[, *delimiter*[, *limit*[, *compare*]]])

Table 1.11 describes the parameters for the function.

TABLE 1.11:   Parameters for the Split Function

Parameter	Required/Optional	Data Type	Description
expression	Required.	String	String expression containing substrings and delimiters.
delimiter	Optional. Default is " ".	String	String character used to identify substring limits.
count	Optional. Default is –1, indicating you want all the substrings.	Long	Number of substrings to be returned.
compare	Optional. Default is vbBinaryCompare.	vbCompare Method	Numeric value indicating the kind of comparison to use when evaluating substrings. See Table 1.2 for a list of values.

Some things to note about the Split function:

- If the input string is an empty string, the output value will be a simple variant, not an array. Therefore, you must always check the input value (as does the GetLastWord function, shown previously) and handle that special case individually.

- If your input string contains multiple delimiters next to each other, or ends with a delimiter, the output array will contain empty elements corresponding to those delimited items. Be aware that Split isn't terribly smart—it takes what it gets and splits the input string based on the parameter you specify. If your input string contains extra delimiters, you'll get extra elements in the output array.

- If the Delimiter parameter is an empty string, the function returns an array with one element: the entire input string. (We do wish that there were some way to get the output array to contain an array of all the characters in the input string, one character per array element. But, there's no such way. As a matter of fact, there's no easy way to do that at all in VBA. You must loop through each character in turn. You could copy the string into a byte array, but that's even uglier.)

- The documentation specifies that you could use –1 (vbUseCompareOption) for this and other functions to specify the compare mode. This value is not allowed by any of the functions at runtime. You might check your version of Office 2000 or Visual Basic to see if this parameter value works as it's documented, or if they removed it from the documentation altogether. (You may have a later version than we did when writing this text.)

Perhaps you've had a need to extract a particular token from within a string (for example, to find the fourth token in a string like "Name | Address | City | State | Zip", with the delimiter " | "). The Extract function, shown in Listing 1.1, does this work for you. It allows you to specify an input string, the particular item you need, and a string containing a delimiter character. It returns the particular substring you requested. If you specify a substring that's out of range (that is, asking for the sixtieth substring from a string with only four words), it returns an empty string. For example, the following expression returns the value "Los Angeles":

```
Debug.Print _
  Extract("Joe Clark|123 Smith Street|Los Angeles|CA|90065", 3, "|")
```

Feel free to analyze how Extract does its work, but that's not the point here—it counts on Split to do its work and would be more complex without the availability of that useful VBA function.

TIP

Although Extract is useful, it's still more limited than you might like. We've provided the dhExtractString function, discussed later in the chapter, which is more powerful.

Listing 1.1: A Simple Function to Extract a Single Substring Using Split

```
Function Extract( _
 ByVal strIn As String, _
 ByVal intPiece As Integer, _
 Optional ByVal strDelimiter As String = " ") As String

    Dim astrItems() As String

    On Error GoTo HandleErrors

    If Len(strDelimiter) = 0 Then
        ' No delimiter supplied. Return
        ' the entire input string.
        Extract = strIn
    Else
        ' Split the string into
        ' an array, and return the requested piece.
        ' Don't forget that the array returned by Split
        ' is always 0-based.
        astrItems = Split( _
         Expression:=strIn, _
         Delimiter:=strDelimiter, _
         Compare:=vbTextCompare)
        Extract = astrItems(intPiece - 1)
    End If

ExitHere:
    Exit Function
```

```
HandleErrors:
    Select Case Err.Number
        Case 9      ' Subscript out of range.
            ' The caller asked for a token that doesn't
            ' exist. Simply return an empty string.
            Resume ExitHere
        Case Else
            Err.Raise Err.Number, Err.Source, _
             Err.Description, Err.HelpFile, Err.HelpContext
    End Select
End Function
```

Join Array Elements Back into a String

The Join function does just the opposite of the Split function, and it's a lot simpler. It takes an array containing string values, along with a delimiter value, and creates an output string with the values concatenated. For example, the combination of the Split and Join functions allows you to take a string, split it apart into tokens (normally, into words), do something to each word in turn, and then put it back together. Perhaps you'd like to convert text to pig latin. Of course, that requires working with each word individually. That's exactly what the pair of Split and Join was meant for. The ToPigLatin function shown in Listing 1.2 uses both to accomplish its high-minded goals.

Listing 1.2: Convert Text to Pig Latin Using the Split and Join Functions

```
Public Function ToPigLatin(strText As String) As String
  Dim astrWords() As String
  Dim i As Integer
  If Len(strText) > 0 Then
    ' Break the string up into words.
    astrWords = Split(strText)
    For i = LBound(astrWords) To UBound(astrWords)
      ' Convert each word to pig latin.
      ' Warning: you may not agree with these conversion
      ' rules. We didn't make them up! (And the
      ' exact conversion isn't our point here.)
```

```
' 1. If a word begins with a consonant,
' the first letter is moved to the end
' of the word, and 'ay' is added.
' Example: The word 'bridge' would become 'ridgebay'.

' 2. If a word begins with an vowel, the
' first letter is moved to the end,
' and 'ey' is added.
' Example: The word 'anchor' would become 'nchoraey'.

' 3. Exception to rule #2: if the vowel is
' an 'e', use 'ay' instead of 'ey'.
' Example: The word 'elevator' would become 'levatoreay'.


        Select Case LCase(Left$(astrWords(i), 1))
          Case "a", "i", "o", "u"
            astrWords(i) = Mid$(astrWords(i), 2) & _
              Left(astrWords(i), 1) & "ey"
          Case "a" To "z"
            ' Most vowels have been caught already, do it doesn't
            ' hurt to have cases for them again. Don't
            ' change the order of the cases, however!
            astrWords(i) = Mid$(astrWords(i), 2) & _
              Left(astrWords(i), 1) & "ay"
        End Select
      Next i
      ToPigLatin = Join(astrWords)
    End If
End Function
```

WARNING   In case you were planning on taking this translator to the big time, note that it doesn't work on hyphenated words ("next-door" should be converted to "extnay-oorday", but it won't be—Split is only looking for spaces as its delimiters. To get this right, you'd want to modify ToPigLatin so that it accepts an optional delimiter (defaulting to a space, of course) as one of its parameters. Then, you'd have to look at each word for hyphens, and call Split once again, splitting each word into sub-words. Then, you could call ToPigLatin recursively, passing in the hyphen delimiter. We'll leave this as an exercise for the reader, although it's not difficult at all.

Filter an Array, Looking for Specific Values

The Filter function allows you to filter an array of strings, returning a subset array of strings, that either contains or doesn't contain the text you're searching for. If you've used Split to create an array of strings, you can then use Filter to return an array containing just the strings that contain a specified substring. You might need to look hard to find a pressing need for this function, but it seems like it could be useful, in the right circumstances. That is, should you ever need to create a new string from all the words containing a particular substring within a larger string, Split, Join, and Filter make a great team.

Table 1.12 contains the parameters you pass into the Filter function. The syntax for the Filter function looks like this:

$result$ = Filter($sourcearray$, $match$[, $include$[, $compare$]])

TABLE 1.12:   Parameters for the Filter Function

Parameter	Required/Optional	Data Type	Description
sourcearray	Required	Array of strings	One-dimensional array of strings to be searched.
match	Required	String	String to find within each element of the InputStrings value.
include	Optional	Boolean	Should Filter return an array of strings that contain Value, or those that don't? If True, returns those that do. If False, returns those that don't.
compare	Optional	Long	Numeric value indicating the kind of string comparison to use. See Table 1.2 for a list of values.

For example, the WordsContaining function, shown in Listing 1.3, uses the Split, Join, and Filter functions to return a new string consisting of all the words from the input string that contain the requested substring. Figure 1.6 shows a small debugging session testing out the WordsContaining function.

FIGURE 1.6

The WordsContaining function does its job, returning subsets of words.

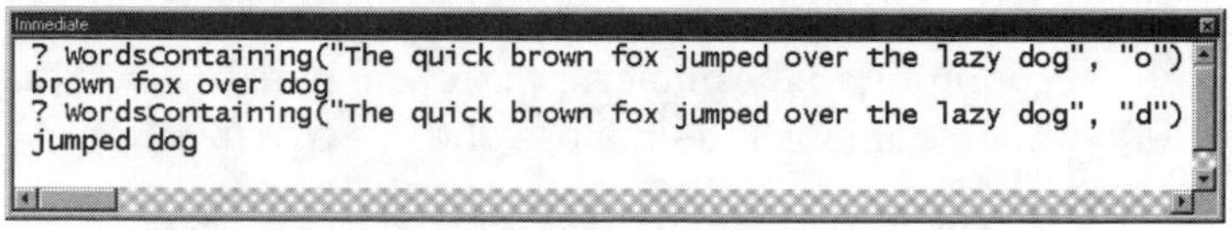

```
Immediate
? WordsContaining("The quick brown fox jumped over the lazy dog", "o")
brown fox over dog
? WordsContaining("The quick brown fox jumped over the lazy dog", "d")
jumped dog
```

Listing 1.3: Find Words Containing a Substring Using the Split, Join, and Filter Functions

```
Public Function WordsContaining( _
 strIn As String, strFind As String) As String
   ' Return a string containing all the words
   ' in the input string containing a supplied substring.
   Dim astrItems() As String
   Dim astrFound() As String

   If Len(strIn) > 0 And Len(strFind) > 0 Then
     astrItems = Split(strIn)
     astrFound = Filter(astrItems, strFind, True, vbTextCompare)
     WordsContaining = Join(astrFound)
   Else
     WordsContaining = strIn
   End If
End Function
```

ANSI Values

It's the job of the operating system's character set to map numbers representing text characters to those characters. When using the ANSI character set, Windows maps the values 0 through 255 to the 256 different characters that are available in each Windows code page. (When using Unicode, Windows NT does the same sort of mapping, with values from 0 to 65535.) Each individual character represents a value between 0 and 255, and VBA provides two functions, Asc and Chr, to convert back and forth between the values and the characters themselves. These functions are inverses of each other—that is, using both functions on a value returns the original value.

The Asc function returns the character code corresponding to the first character of the string expression you pass it. The Chr function returns a character corresponding to the numeric value you pass it. For example, the following code fragment demonstrates the use of these two functions:

```
Dim intCh as Integer
Dim strCh as String * 1
intCh = Asc("This is a test")
' intCh now contains 84, the value corresponding to
' the "T" character.
strCh = Chr(intCh)
' strCh now contains "T", the letter corresponding to
' the value 84.
```

Speed Considerations with the Asc and Chr Functions

The following two logical expressions are equivalent:

```
If Asc(strChar) = intANSIValue Then
' and
If strChar = Chr(intANSIValue) Then
```

However, you'll want to use the first construct because it's actually quite a bit more efficient to compare two numeric values than it is to compare two strings. If you're comparing a large number of characters to specific ANSI values, make sure you convert the character to ANSI rather than convert the ANSI value into a character. This optimization can save you considerable processor time if you use it often.

Working with Bytes

In addition to all the functions VBA provides for working with standard strings, you'll find a set of functions for working with bytes within the strings and a set for working directly with the characters in Unicode strings.

If you want to work with the bytes that make up a string, you can use the LeftB, RightB, MidB, LenB, AscB, InStrB, and ChrB functions. Each of these functions does what its normal relative does, but each works on bytes instead of characters, as shown in Figure 1.7. For example, for a 10-character string, Len returns 10, but LenB returns 20 (each character takes two bytes). The first fragment in Listing 1.4

loops through all the characters in a string, printing each to the Debug window. The second loop in the fragment works through all the *bytes* in the string and lists each one. In this case, the output will include a 0 between bytes because the alternate bytes are 0 for English characters.

Listing 1.4: Loop through Characters and Bytes

```
Sub DumpBytes()
    ' Dump the characters, and then bytes, of
    ' the text "Hello" to the Debug window.
    Dim intI As Integer
    Dim strTest As String
    strTest = "Hello"
    For intI = 1 To Len(strTest)
        Debug.Print Asc(Mid(strTest, intI, 1));
    Next intI
    Debug.Print
    For intI = 1 To LenB(strTest)
        Debug.Print AscB(MidB(strTest, intI, 1));
    Next intI
    Debug.Print
End Sub
```

TIP   Generally, you won't write code using MidB, like that shown in Listing 1.4. Instead, you'll convert the string into a byte array and work with each element of the byte array. However, the other byte functions are necessary in order to extract just the bytes you need from the string.

FIGURE 1.7
Looping through bytes as opposed to characters

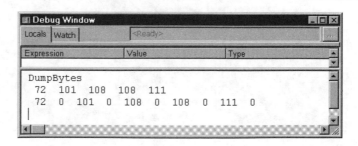

About the Functions Ending in $

VBA supplies all the functions that return strings in two formats—one with a dollar sign ($) at the end and one without. Why did they bother? The versions without $s return variants, and the ones with $s return strings. The variant versions are able to propagate a null value through an expression; the string functions cannot. That is, if the input value is a variant containing Null, the variant functions return Null, and the string functions trigger a run-time error. The string functions, on the other hand, are faster; because they don't need to perform any data type conversions, they can do their work faster.

How do you decide which version to use? If you're concerned about wringing the best performance out of your application and you can ensure that you won't be sending null values to these functions, by all means, use the string-specific version of any function you can.

Putting the Functions Together

Now that you've seen all the basic string-handling functions, you can start to put them together in various combinations to tackle more complex situations. The remainder of this chapter, which provides a number of techniques for use in real-world situations built up from our personal function libraries, is broken into four sections:

- Searching for and Replacing Text
- Gathering Information about Strings
- Converting Strings
- Working with Substrings

Using Optional Parameters

Many of the procedures in the following sections accept one or more optional parameters. In each case, if you don't specify the parameter in your function call, the receiving function assigns that parameter a value.

When you use optional parameters, you have two basic choices:

- Use a Variant parameter and check for the parameter using the IsMissing function.

- Use a strongly typed parameter and assign a default value in the formal declaration.

We've opted for the second alternative because this allows for type-checking when calling the procedure. On the other hand, it also removes the possibility of using the IsMissing function to check for the omission of the parameter.

Searching for and Replacing Text

In this section, you'll find techniques for finding and replacing text within strings. Although these procedures require more code than almost any other procedures in the chapter, they're used by many of the later solutions, so it makes sense to present them first.

In particular, this section includes solutions to performing the following tasks:

- Replace any character in a specified list with a single other character.

- Remove all white space, leaving one space between words.

- Remove trailing Null and padding from string.

- Replace tokens within a string (by position in an array passed in).

Replacing Any Character in a List with Another Character

Editing text often involves replacing any one of a list of characters with another single character. For example, if you want to count the number of words in a sentence, you may need to take the input sentence, replace all the punctuation characters with spaces, and then count the spaces. Or you may want to just remove all extraneous characters. For example, you might want to convert a phone number in the format (213) 555-1212 into the format 2135551212. The function provided in this section, dhTranslate, makes both these tasks simple. (See Listing 1.5 for the entire function.)

Using dhTranslate, you could replace all punctuation characters with spaces, like this:

```
strText = dhTranslate(strText, " ,.!:;<>?", " ")
```

To remove extraneous characters, you could call dhTranslate like this:

```
strText = dhTranslate("(213)555-1212", "()-", "")
```

But dhTranslate does more than that: If you specify a mapping between the set of search characters and the set of match characters, it will replace characters in a one-to-one correspondence. That is, imagine you want to replace letters in a phone number with the corresponding digit. You know, someone says to call l-800-CALLKEN, but you really want to store just the digits to be dialed. You can use dhTranslate to map specific characters to digits, like this:

```
strPhone = dhTranslate("1-800-CALLKEN", _
  "ABCDEFGHIJKLMNOPRSTUVWXY", _
  "22233344455566677788899")
```

That function call will replace each letter with its appropriate digit.

If the replacement string is shorter than the search string, dhTranslate pads it to make it the same width as the search string. That is, when you call dhTranslate with a short replacement string:

```
strText = dhTranslate(strText, " ,.!:;<>?", " ")
```

the function converts the third parameter into a string with the same number of characters as the second parameter, internally, so it's as though you'd called the function like this:

```
strText = dhTranslate(strText, " ,.!:;<>?", "          ")
```

That way, each character in the second string has been mapped to a space for its replacement character.

To call dhTranslate yourself, pass three required parameters and one optional parameter, like this:

```
strText = dhTranslate(strIn, strMapIn, strMapOut[, lngCompare])
```

The parameters for dhTranslate are as follows:

- *strIn* is the string to be modified.

- *strMapIn* is the string containing characters to find.

- *strMapOut* is the string containing 0 or more characters to replace the corresponding characters from strMapIn. If this string is shorter than strMapIn, the function pads the string with its final character to match the length of strMapIn.

- *lngCompare* is optional. Select a comparison value from Table 1.2 (as you have with many other functions in this chapter) to determine how the function compares strings. If you don't specify a value, the function assumes you want to use binary comparisons (vbBinaryCompare).

The function's return value is a copy of the original string (strIn) with the requested modifications.

Listing 1.5: Translate One Set of Characters to Another Set

```
Public Function dhTranslate( _
 ByVal strIn As String, _
 ByVal strMapIn As String, _
 ByVal strMapOut As String, _
 Optional lngCompare As VbCompareMethod = vbBinaryCompare) As String

    Dim lngI As Long
    Dim lngPos As Long
    Dim strChar As String * 1
    Dim strOut As String

    ' If there's no list of characters
    ' to replace, there's no point going on
    ' with the work in this function.
    If Len(strMapIn) > 0 Then
        ' Right-fill the strMapOut set.
        If Len(strMapOut) > 0 Then
            strMapOut = Left$(strMapOut & String(Len(strMapIn), _
                Right$(strMapOut, 1)), Len(strMapIn))
        End If

        For lngI = 1 To Len(strIn)
            strChar = Mid$(strIn, lngI, 1)
            lngPos = InStr(1, strMapIn, strChar, lngCompare)
            If lngPos > 0 Then
                ' If strMapOut is empty, this doesn't fail,
                ' because Mid handles empty strings gracefully.
                strOut = strOut & Mid$(strMapOut, lngPos, 1)
            Else
                strOut = strOut & strChar
            End If
        Next lngI
    End If
    dhTranslate = strOut
End Function
```

Before it does any other work, dhTranslate checks to make sure strMapIn actually contains some text. If not, there's no work to do, and the function quickly exits.

Next, dhTranslate ensures that the strMapOut parameter contains as many characters as strMapIn. To do that, it takes the right-most character of strMapOut, creates a string of that character as wide as strMapIn, appends it to strMapOut, and then truncates the string to the same width as strMapIn:

```
' Right-fill the strMapOut set.
If Len(strMapOut) > 0 Then
    strMapOut = Left$(strMapOut & String(Len(strMapIn), _
      Right$(strMapOut, 1)), Len(strMapIn))
End If
```

For example, if strMapIn is "1234567890" and strMapOut is "ABCDE", the code creates a string of *E*s that is 10 characters long (the same length as strMapIn), appends it to the end of strMapOut (so it becomes "ABCDEEEEEEEEEE"), and then truncates the entire string to the length of strMapIn (10 characters, or "ABCDEEEEEE"). This mechanism makes it possible to replace a series of characters, supplied in strMapIn, with a single character, supplied in strMapOut.

Finally, dhTranslate performs the replacements, using brute force. For each character in the input string, dhTranslate attempts to find that character in strMapIn:

```
strOut = strIn
For lngI = 1 To Len(strOut)
    strChar = Mid$(strIn, lngI, 1)
    lngPos = InStr(1, strMapIn, strChar, lngCompare)
    ' The code continues...
Next lngI
```

If the InStr search found a match, lngPos will be greater than 0. dhTranslate finds the appropriate matching character in strMapOut and replaces that character in the output string.

```
If intPos > 0 Then
    ' If strMapOut is empty, this doesn't fail,
    ' because Mid handles empty strings gracefully.
    strOut = strOut & Mid$(strMapOut, intPos, 1)
Else
    strOut = strOut & strChar
End If
```

In this way, one character at a time, dhTranslate uses either the character from the input string or its replacement from strMapOut. Either way, it returns strOut as its return value.

Many other functions within this chapter count on dhTranslate to do their work for them. You'll surely find many uses for it in your own applications, as well.

Removing All Extra White Space

If you need to remove all extraneous white space from a string (and certainly, the dhCountWords function later in this chapter that counts the number of words in a string has reason to need this functionality), the dhTrimAll function will help. This function traverses a string and makes a new output string, copying over only a single space every time it finds one or more spaces inside the string. You can optionally request dhTrimAll to remove tabs, as well.

For example, the following function call:

```
strOut = dhTrimAll("    This is     a test" & _
   "       of how   this works")
```

places "This is a test of how this works" into strOut. By default, the function removes tabs as well as spaces. If you want the function to disregard tabs and remove only spaces, send a False value for the second parameter. Listing 1.6 shows the entire dhTrimAll function.

Listing 1.6: Remove All White Space from a String

```
Function dhTrimAll( _
 ByVal strInput As String, _
 Optional blnRemoveTabs As Boolean = True) As String

    Const conTwoSpaces = "  "
    Const conSpace = " "

    strInput = Trim$(strInput)
    If blnRemoveTabs Then
        strInput = Replace(strInput, vbTab, conSpace)
    End If
```

```
       Do Until InStr(strInput, conTwoSpaces) = 0
           strInput = Replace(strInput, conTwoSpaces, conSpace)
       Loop
       dhTrimAll = strInput
    End Function
```

How does dhTrimAll do its work? It starts by calling the Trim function to remove any leading or trailing spaces. Then, it continues by replacing all the tabs with spaces, if necessary, using the built-in Replace function:

```
If blnRemoveTabs Then
    strInput = Replace(strInput, vbTab, conSpace)
End If
```

The rest of the procedure is a simple loop: the code checks to see if the input string contains two contiguous spaces, and if so, replaces the pair with a single space. It continues this same action until the input string contains no pairs of spaces, side by side. Once that condition is true, the function has done its job and can return the output string.

```
Do Until InStr(strInput, conTwoSpaces) = 0
    strInput = Replace(strInput, conTwoSpaces, conSpace)
Loop
```

Removing Trailing Null and Padding from a String

Although you'll probably need the dhTrimNull function only if you're working with the Windows API, it's invaluable when you do. API functions don't know what the source of the string is, and they tend to place null-terminated strings into the buffers you send them. Unfortunately, VBA needs to have the length of the string set explicitly, so you need to find the first null character (Chr$(0), or vbNull-Char) in the string and truncate the string there using the Left function. Examples in later chapters will use this function, and it's important to have it ready to go when you need it.

The dhTrimNull function, in Listing 1.7, accepts a single string and returns the same string, truncated at the first null character.

Listing 1.7: Trim Strings at the First Null Character

```vb
Public Function dhTrimNull(ByVal strValue As String) As String
    Dim lngPos As Long

    lngPos = InStr(strValue, vbNullChar)
    Select Case lngPos
        Case 0
            ' Not found at all, so just
            ' return the original value.
            dhTrimNull = strValue
        Case 1
            ' Found at the first position, so return
            ' an empty string.
            dhTrimNull = vbNullString
        Case Is > 1
            ' Found in the string, so return the portion
            ' up to the null character.
            dhTrimNull = Left$(strValue, lngPos - 1)
    End Select
End Function
```

To do its work, dhTrimNull calls the InStr function, passing it the original string to search in and the constant vbNullChar to search for. Depending on the return value of InStr (stored in lngPos), the function does one of three things:

- If lngPos is 0, the function returns the original string. There weren't any null characters in the string to begin with.

- If lngPos is 1, the first character was null, so the function returns an empty string.

- If lngPos is greater than 1, the function uses the Left function to pull out the part up to, but not including, the null character.

Using all three cases removes any possibility that you'll attempt to pass an illegal starting position to the Left function.

Replacing Numbered Tokens within a String

If you're creating text resources that need to be translated to local languages, or if you just need to replace a series of tokens in a string with a series of text strings, the function shown in Listing 1.8 will help you out. This function allows you to pass in a list of text strings to replace numbered tokens (%1, %2, and so on) in a larger text string.

If you separate the text for your application from the application's user interface, it's far easier to prepare the application for international use. However, it's inevitable that some of your strings will need to contain replaceable parameters. Using dhTokenReplace makes it simple to perform those replacements at runtime. For example, running the following fragment:

```
strText = dhTokenReplace("Unable to add file %1 to %2", _
   "C:\AUTOEXEC.BAT", "C:\FOO.ZIP")
```

would place the text "Unable to add file C:\AUTOEXEC.BAT to C:\FOO.ZIP" into strText. (The assumption here is that the resource string "Unable to add…" is coming from a table, a resource file, or some other source external to your application and is translated for use in countries besides your own.) But what if, in a particular language, the correct phrasing would be (translated back into English) "C:\FOO.ZIP is unable to contain C:\AUTOEXEC.BAT"? In that case, the translator could modify the resource to be "%2 is unable to contain %1", and your code would still function correctly.

Even if you're not producing internationalized applications, dhTokenReplace will make your work simpler. Being able to replace multiple substrings in one pass can make your applications run faster and certainly will make them code faster.

Using ParamArray to Pass an Array of Parameters

Although the ParamArray construct has been available in the past few versions of VBA, few programmers have run across it. It's not used often, but when you need it, it's indispensable. In this case, being able to pass a virtually unlimited number of parameters to a function makes it possible to write one function that can handle unlimited situations.

To use this feature, you declare your function to accept a ParamArray parameter, like this:

```
Public Function dhTokenReplace(ByVal strIn As String, _
   ParamArray varItems() As Variant) As String
```

Then, when you call the function, you can pass as many items as you like after the required parameter(s), and VBA will convert them into an array and pass them to the procedure. Your procedure receives the array in the parameter you declared as ParamArray, and you can use any array-handling technique to work with the parameters.

The rules? The ParamArray parameter must be

- The final parameter

- Not mixed with the Optional, ByVal, or ByRef keyword

- Declared as an array of variants

Listing 1.8: Replace Numbered Tokens in a String

```
Public Function dhTokenReplace(ByVal strIn As String, _
  ParamArray varItems() As Variant) As String
    On Error GoTo HandleErr

    Dim lngPos As Long
    Dim strReplace As String
    Dim intI As Integer

    For intI = UBound(varItems) To LBound(varItems) Step -1
        strReplace = "%" & (intI + 1)
        lngPos = InStr(1, strIn, strReplace)
        If lngPos > 0 Then
            strIn = Left$(strIn, lngPos - 1) & _
                varItems(intI) & Mid$(strIn, lngPos + Len(strReplace))
        End If
    Next intI

ExitHere:
    dhTokenReplace = strIn
    Exit Function

HandleErr:
    ' If any error occurs, just return the
    ' string as it currently exists.
```

```
        Select Case Err.Number
            Case Else
                ' MsgBox "Error: " & Err.Description & _
                '   " (" & Err.Number & ")"
        End Select
        Resume ExitHere
    End Function
```

To do its work, dhTokenReplace loops through all the elements of the input array, from the upper bound back down to the lower bound:

```
For intI = UBound(varItems) To LBound(varItems) Step -1
    ' (Code removed)
Next intI
```

NOTE   If dhTokenReplace didn't work its way backward through its tokens, it would have trouble if you specified more than 10 parameters. It would replace "%1" with some replacement text, and that would also replace the "%1" in "%10", rendering each of the two-digit replacement values inoperative. By working backward, this problem won't occur.

For each item in the array, the code builds a new item number (such as "%1", "%2", and so on) and then searches for the string within the text:

```
strReplace = "%" & (intI + 1)
lngPos = InStr(1, strIn, strReplace)
```

If InStr found a match (that is, lngPos is greater than 0), dhTokenReplace modifies the input string to contain all the text before the match, then the replacement text, and then all the text after the match:

```
If lngPos > 0 Then
    strIn = Left$(strIn, lngPos - 1) & _
      varItems(intI) & Mid$(strIn, lngPos + Len(strReplace))
End If
```

That's it! Repeating the steps for each item in the input array ends up with all the tokens replaced with text.

WARNING Make sure you call the dhTokenReplace function correctly. That is, supply a single text string, containing text and "%x", with values to be replaced. Follow that string with individual text parameters, containing the strings to be placed into each of the replacement tokens. If you're an advanced developer, it may be tempting to supply a string and an array of replacements, but that technique won't work with this function. If you like, you could modify the function to work that way, but we like the simplicity provided by the ParamArray modifier.

Gathering Information about Strings

In this section, you'll find techniques for retrieving information about an existing string, including:

- Determining whether a character is alphanumeric
- Determining whether a character is alphabetic
- Determining whether a character is numeric
- Counting the number of times a substring appears in a string
- Counting the number of tokens in a delimited string
- Counting the number of words in a string

Determining the Characteristics of a Character

When validating text, you may want to check the contents of each individual character in a string. You may want to know whether any specific character is alphabetic (A–Z, in English), alphanumeric (A–Z, 0–9 in English), or just numeric (0–9). The first two tests are most quickly accomplished using API calls, and the final one can be accomplished a few different ways.

NOTE Although the examples in this section focus only on the ANSI character set, the examples on the CD-ROM also take into account the Unicode character set. See the sidebar "Working with Wide Character Sets" later in this chapter for more information.

Is This Character Alphabetic?

Should you need to verify that a given character is alphabetic (and not numeric, punctuation, a symbol, and so on), you might be tempted to just check the character and see whether it's in the range of A–Z or a–z. This would be a mistake for two reasons:

- If you want your application to be able to be localized for countries besides your own, this code is almost guaranteed to break in any other language.

- Using VBA to handle this task is almost certainly the slowest way possible.

A better bet is to let Windows handle this task for you. Using the IsCharAlpha API function, you can allow Windows to decide whether the selected character is alphabetic. That way, the test runs faster, and you needn't worry about internationalization issues—Windows will know, for the local environment, whether a given character is alphabetic.

To use the API function, you must first declare the function. (This declaration is included in the sample code for this chapter.)

```
Private Declare Function IsCharAlphaA Lib "USER32" _
 (ByVal bytChar As Byte) As Long
```

To use the IsCharAlphaA API function, you can call the dhIsCharAlpha function:

```
Function dhIsCharAlpha(strText As String) As Boolean
    ' Is the first character of strText an alphabetic character?
    dhIsCharAlpha = CBool(IsCharAlphaA(Asc(strText)))
End Function
```

This simple wrapper function converts the first letter of the text you pass to a numeric value (using the Asc function), calls IsCharAlphaA, and converts the result to a Boolean value.

TIP   The function you'll find in the sample project is a bit more complex than this representation because it attempts to handle both ANSI and Unicode character sets. See the "Working with Wide Character Sets" for more information. This applies to the next few functions, as well.

To verify that the first letter of a value a user supplies is alphabetic, you might use dhIsCharAlpha like this:

```
If dhIsCharAlpha(strText) Then
    ' You know the first letter of strText is alphabetic.
End If
```

Is This Character Alphanumeric?

Expanding on the previous function, if you need to know whether a character is either alphabetic or numeric, Windows provides a simple function for this test, as well. You can use the IsCharAlphaNumericA API function, declared like this:

```
Private Declare Function IsCharAlphaNumericA Lib "USER32" _
  (ByVal byChar As Byte) As Long
```

Just as before, we've provided a simple wrapper function for the API function, making it easier to call:

```
Function dhIsCharAlphaNumeric(strText As String) As Boolean
    ' Is the first character of strText an alphanumeric character?
    dhIsCharAlphaNumeric = CBool(IsCharAlphaNumericA(Asc(strText)))
End Function
```

This function will return True if the first character of the value you pass it is either a letter or a digit.

Is This Character Numeric?

Although the task of determining whether a character is numeric could be quite simple, finding the best approach took a few iterations. We ended up with two techniques that are almost identical in their performance, and you'll need to choose one based on your own preferences.

The first technique uses the two previous solutions—that is, a character is numeric if it's alphanumeric but not alphabetic. Therefore, dhIsCharNumeric performs the first determination.

```
Function dhIsCharNumeric(strText As String) As Boolean
    ' Is the first character of strText a numeric character?
    dhIsCharNumeric = dhIsCharAlphaNumeric(strText) _
     And Not dhIsCharAlpha(strText)
End Function
```

An alternative technique is to use the Like operator, discussed in the section "Comparison Operators" earlier in this chapter. If you're checking only to see whether a character is numeric, this is the best solution; it involves no API calls and no declarations. If you're already using the other two API-reliant functions, you might as well use them here. This alternative checks the first character of the string you send it, comparing it to "[0–9]*":

```
Function dhIsCharNumeric1(strText As String) As Boolean
    ' Is the first character numeric?
    ' Almost identical in speed to calling the two API functions.
    dhIsCharNumeric1 = (strText Like "[0-9]*")
End Function
```

Working with Wide Character Sets

Unfortunately, the two techniques shown here that call the Windows API will fail if your version of Windows uses wide (two-byte) characters or if you want your solutions to run on machines that use wide characters. In these cases, you'll need to take extra steps.

The simplest solution is to determine the maximum character width in the selected character set and choose the correct API function to call based on that determination. (The code examples on the CD-ROM do take these extra steps.) The 32-bit Windows API specification includes two versions of most functions that involve strings: one for the ANSI environment and one for DBCS and Unicode environments. In the examples shown here, we've used the ANSI solution because that solution works for English text.

To determine whether you need to use the alternate API calls, you can use the dhIs-CharsetWide function. Once you've got the return value from that function, you can decide whether to call the ANSI or the Unicode version of the API functions, like this:

```
Function dhIsCharAlphaNumeric(strText As String) As Boolean
    If dhIsCharsetWide() Then
        dhIsCharAlphaNumeric = _
        CBool(IsCharAlphaNumericW(AscW(strText)))
```

```
        Else

            dhIsCharAlphaNumeric = _
            CBool(IsCharAlphaNumericA(Asc(strText)))
        End If
    End Function
```

Note that you must also call the AscW function when working with the "wide" versions of the API functions.

Counting the Number of Times a Substring Appears

The InStr built-in VBA function can tell you whether a particular string appears within another string (InStr returns a position within the string if the substring is there and 0 if it's not), but it can't tell you how many times the substring appears. If you want to count occurrences (and several of the other functions in this chapter will need to do this), you can use the dhCountIn function, shown in Listing 1.9.

Listing 1.9: Find the Number of Occurrences of a Substring

```
Public Function dhCountIn(strText As String, strFind As String, _
    Optional lngCompare As VbCompareMethod = vbBinaryCompare) As Long

    Dim lngCount As Long
    Dim lngPos As Long

    ' If there's nothing to find, there surely can't be any
    ' found, so return 0.
    If Len(strFind) > 0 Then
        lngPos = 1
        Do
            lngPos = InStr(lngPos, strText, strFind, lngCompare)
            If lngPos > 0 Then
                lngCount = lngCount + 1
                lngPos = lngPos + Len(strFind)
            End If
        Loop While lngPos > 0
    Else
        lngCount = 0
```

```
        End If
        dhCountIn = lngCount
    End Function
```

Of course, if there's nothing to find, the function just returns 0:

```
If Len(strFind) > 0 Then
    ' the real code goes here
Else
    intCount = 0
End If
```

To perform the search, the code loops through the input text, looking for the search string, until it no longer finds any matches (that is, until the return value from InStr is 0). Along the way, if it finds a match, it increments the value of intCount and moves the start position to the character after the end of the sought string in the input text. This not only speeds up the search (why look for the text at the very next character after you just found it if the text you're looking for is, say, four characters long?), it also avoids finding overlapping matches. Here's the code fragment that does the major portion of the work:

```
lngPos = 1
Do
    lngPos = InStr(lngPos, strText, strFind, lngCompare)
    If lngPos > 0 Then
        lngCount = lngCount + 1
        lngPos = lngPos + Len(strFind)
    End If
Loop While lngPos > 0
```

To find the number of vowels in a string, you might write code like this:

```
intVowels = dhCountIn(strText, "A") + dhCountIn(strText, "E") + _
  dhCountIn(strText, "I") + dhCountIn(strText, "O") + _
  dhCountIn(strText, "U")
```

TIP

The dhCountIn function, like all the functions in this chapter that perform searching, is case sensitive by default. If you want to perform case-insensitive searches, either modify the source code or pass in the appropriate optional parameter value (vbTextCompare).

Counting Vowels Revisited

You could use the dhCountIn function to count vowels, as shown in the previous example. You might also take advantage of the dhTranslate and Split functions to do the same job. That is, you can have dhTranslate replace all vowels with a single vowel, and then use the Split function to split the text, based on that single vowel. The size of the array returned from Split tells you how many vowels you have. For example, you might write the code this way (see the next section for more information on using dhTranslate in this manner):

```
Public Function CountVowels(ByVal strIn As String) As Long
    ' An alternative way to calculate vowels in a piece of text.
    Dim astrItems() As String

    strIn = dhTranslate(strIn, "AEIOU", "A", vbTextCompare)
    astrItems = Split(strIn, "A")
    CountVowels = UBound(astrItems) - LBound(astrItems)
End Function
```

Counting the Number of Tokens in a Delimited String

The dhCountTokens function, shown in Listing 1.10, is a general-purpose function that allows you to find out how many "chunks" of text there are in a string, given text delimiters that you supply. The function interprets any one of the characters in your list of delimiters as a token separator, so

```
Debug.Print dhCountTokens("This is a test", " ")
```

returns 4, as does

```
Debug.Print dhCountTokens("This:is!a test", ": !")
```

Because every delimiter character must delimit a token, the following example returns 10:

```
Debug.Print dhCountTokens("This:!:is:!:a:!:test", ": !")
```

You'll have to look carefully to see them, but the individual tokens are

```
This, "", "", is, "", "", a, "", "", test
```

Listing 1.10: Count the Number of Tokens in a String

```
Public Function dhCountTokens(ByVal strText As String, _
 ByVal strDelimiter As String, _
 Optional lngCompare As VbCompareMethod = vbBinaryCompare) As Long

    Dim strChar As String * 1

    ' If there's no search text, there can't be any tokens.
    If Len(strText) = 0 Then
        dhCountTokens = 0
    ElseIf Len(strDelimiter) = 0 Then
        ' If there's no delimiters, the output
        ' is the entire input.
        dhCountTokens = 1
    Else
        strChar = Left$(strDelimiter, 1)

        ' Flatten all the delimiters to just the first one in
        ' the list.
        If Len(strDelimiter) > 1 Then
            strText = dhTranslate(strText, strDelimiter, _
              strChar, lngCompare)
        End If
        ' Count the tokens. Actually, count
        ' delimiters, and add one.
        dhCountTokens = dhCountIn(strText, strChar) + 1
    End If
End Function
```

The dhCountTokens function is somewhat tricky—it uses the dhCountIn function, which can count the occurrence of only a single item. Rather than call dhCountIn multiple times, once for each different delimiter, dhCountTokens "flattens" the delimiters in the input text. That is, it first calls the dhTranslate function to map all the different delimiters to the first character in your list of delimiters:

```
strChar = Left$(strDelimiter, 1)

' Flatten all the delimiters to just the first one in
' the list.
If Len(strDelimiter) > 1 Then
    strText = dhTranslate(strText, strDelimiter, strChar)
End If
```

That is, if you called dhCountTokens as

```
Debug.Print dhCountTokens("This:!:is:!:a:!:test", ": !")
```

after the code fragment listed previously, strText would contain

```
"This:::is:::a:::test"
```

Now it's just a matter of counting the number of times the first delimiter appears in the string and adding 1. (If there are four delimiters, there must be five tokens.)

```
dhCountTokens = dhCountIn(strText, strChar) + 1
```

That's all there is to it. The next section shows a typical reason to call dhCountTokens.

Counting Vowels Re-Revisited

Now that you've got the dhCountTokens function ready to use, you could rewrite the CountVowels function discussed in the previous section, like this:

```
Public Function CountVowels2(ByVal strIn As String) As Long
    ' An alternative way to calculate vowels in a piece of text.
    CountVowels2 = _
        dhCountTokens(strIn, "aeiou", vbTextCompare) - 1
End Function
```

For example, if a string breaks down into 16 tokens, it must contain 15 vowels. This simple function shows the power of the parsing functions included in this chapter.

Counting the Number of Words in a String

Although the dhCountTokens function provides you with total flexibility, you're more often going to want to count specific types of delimited objects. Counting words is a typical task, and dhCountWords uses techniques similar to those used in dhCountTokens to make the task simple. The code, shown in Listing 1.11, takes the following steps:

1. Checks the length of the input text. If it's 0, there's not much point in continuing.

2. Calls dhTranslate to convert all the delimiters to spaces. The function uses a standard set of delimiters, declared as follows:

```
Const dhcDelimiters As String = " ,.!:;<>?"
```

3. Calls dhTrimAll to remove leading and trailing spaces and converts all groups of spaces to a single space within the text.

4. Calls dhCountIn to count the spaces in the string and adds 1 to the result.

For example, calling dhCountWords like this:

```
dhCountWords("Hi there, my name is Cleo, what's yours?")
```

returns 8, the number of words in the string.

Listing 1.11: Count the Number of Words in a String

```
Public Function dhCountWords(ByVal strText As String) As Long
    If Len(strText) = 0 Then
        dhCountWords = 0
    Else
        ' Get rid of any extraneous stuff, including delimiters and
        ' spaces. First convert delimiters to spaces, and then
        ' remove all extraneous spaces.
        strText = dhTrimAll(dhTranslate(strText, dhcDelimiters, " "))
        ' If there are three spaces, there are
        ' four words, right?
        dhCountWords = dhCountIn(strText, " ") + 1
    End If
End Function
```

Converting Strings

This section presents a series of techniques for performing common tasks involving the conversion of a string from one form to another. The section includes the following topics:

- Converting a number into a string with the correct ordinal suffix
- Converting a number to roman numerals
- Performing a "smart" proper case conversion
- Encrypting/decrypting text using XOR password encryption
- Returning a string left-padded or right-padded to a specified width
- Using Soundex to compare strings

TIP Another common string conversion trick is the conversion from a numeric value into written text (as you might when writing a check, for example). You'll find a procedure that does this work for you in Chapter 2.

Converting a Number into a String with the Correct Ordinal Suffix

If you want to be able to represent a numeric value as its ordinal position in a set, you'll need to write a function that, when provided with an integer, returns a string containing the value and its suffix as a string. The simple dhOrdinal function, shown in Listing 1.12, does what you need; it takes in a numeric value and returns a string containing the ordinal representation of that value. For example:

```
dhOrdinal(34)
```

returns "34th", and

```
dhOrdinal(1)
```

returns "1st".

The dhOrdinal function counts on standard rules to calculate the suffix (once it's removed all but the final two digits, using the Mod operator:

- All values between 11 and 19, inclusive, use "th".

Otherwise:

- Numbers that end in 1 use "st".
- Numbers that end in 2 use "nd".
- Numbers that end in 3 use "rd".
- All numbers that haven't yet been claimed use "th".

Listing 1.12: Convert a Value to Its Ordinal Suffix

```
Public Function dhOrdinal(lngItem As Long) As String
    Dim intDigit As Integer
    Dim strOut As String * 2
    Dim intTemp As Integer
```

```
' All teens use "th"
intTemp = lngItem Mod 100
If intTemp >= 11 And intTemp <= 19 Then
    strOut = "th"
Else
    ' Get that final digit
    intDigit = lngItem Mod 10
    Select Case intDigit
        Case 1
            strOut = "st"
        Case 2
            strOut = "nd"
        Case 3
            strOut = "rd"
        Case Else
            strOut = "th"
    End Select
End If
dhOrdinal = lngItem & strOut
End Function
```

The code first uses the Mod operator to retrieve the final two digits and checks for values between 11 and 19—these should all use the "th" suffix. For other values, the code looks at the "ones" digit because that's all it takes to determine which suffix to use. To find the digit that ends each number, the code uses the Mod operator, which returns the remainder when you divide by the second operand. For example:

```
41 Mod 10
```

returns 1, the remainder you get when you divide 41 by 10.

TIP   The dhOrdinal function would need to be completely overhauled for any language besides English; it's not clear that the ordinal suffixes would even group the same way in any other language. If you intend to distribute applications globally, be sure to allot time for rewriting this function for each localized language.

Converting a Number into Roman Numerals

If you're creating legal documents programmatically, or if your job involves copyright notifications (well, it is somewhat difficult coming up with compelling scenarios for this one), you're likely to require the capability to convert integers into roman numerals. Although this need may not come up often, when it does, it's tricky enough that you'll want to avoid having to write the code yourself.

The dhRoman function, in Listing 1.13, can accept an integer between 1 and 3999 (the Romans didn't have a concept of 0), and it returns the value converted into roman numerals. For example:

```
Debug.Print dhRoman(1997)
```

displays "MCMXCVII", and

```
Debug.Print dhRoman(3999)
```

displays "MMMCMXCIX".

WARNING   Attempting to convert a number greater than 3999 or less than 1 will raise a run-time error in dhRoman.

Listing 1.13: Convert Numbers to Roman Numerals

```
Public Function dhRoman(ByVal intValue As Integer) As String

    Dim varDigits As Variant
    Dim lngPos As Integer
    Dim intDigit As Integer
    Dim strTemp As String

    ' Build up the array of roman digits
    varDigits = Array("I", "V", "X", "L", "C", "D", "M")
    lngPos = LBound(varDigits)
    strTemp = ""
    Do While intValue > 0
        intDigit = intValue Mod 10
        intValue = intValue \ 10
        Select Case intDigit
            Case 1
                strTemp = varDigits(lngPos) & strTemp
            Case 2
                strTemp = varDigits(lngPos) & _
                 varDigits(lngPos) & strTemp
```

```
        Case 3
            strTemp = varDigits(lngPos) & _
             varDigits(lngPos) & varDigits(lngPos) & strTemp
        Case 4
            strTemp = varDigits(lngPos) & _
             varDigits(lngPos + 1) & strTemp
        Case 5
            strTemp = varDigits(lngPos + 1) & strTemp
        Case 6
            strTemp = varDigits(lngPos + 1) & _
             varDigits(lngPos) & strTemp
        Case 7
            strTemp = varDigits(lngPos + 1) & _
             varDigits(lngPos) & varDigits(lngPos) & strTemp
        Case 8
            strTemp = varDigits(lngPos + 1) & _
             varDigits(lngPos) & varDigits(lngPos) & _
             varDigits(lngPos) & strTemp
        Case 9
            strTemp = varDigits(lngPos) & _
             varDigits(lngPos + 2) & strTemp
      End Select
      lngPos = lngPos + 2
    Loop
    dhRoman = strTemp
  End Function
```

How does dhRoman do its work? As you probably know, all numbers built in roman numerals between 1 and 3999 consist of the seven digits I, V, X, L, C, D, and M. The I, X, C, and M digits represent 1, 10, 100, and 1000; V, L, and D represent 5, 50, and 500, respectively. The code loops through all the digits of your input value from right to left, using the Mod operator to strip them off one by one:

```
Do While intValue > 0
    intDigit = intValue Mod 10
    intValue = intValue \ 10
    ' (Code removed)
    intPos = intPos + 2
Loop
```

At each point in the loop, intDigit contains the right-most digit of the value, and intValue keeps getting smaller, one digit at a time. For example, the following table shows the values of the two variables while dhRoman tackles the value 1234:

intValue	intDigit	intPos	Character
123	4	0	I
12	3	2	X
1	2	4	C
0	1	6	M

In addition, intPos indicates which array element to use in building the string as the code moves through the ones, tens, hundreds, and thousands places in the value.

Based on the value in intDigit, the code uses a Select Case construct to choose the characters to prepend to the output string. (That's right—prepend. dhRoman constructs the output string from right to left, adding items to the left of the string as it works.) For example, for the value 1234, dhRoman finds the digit 4 when int-Pos is 0. The code says to use

```
strTemp = varDigits(intPos) & _
  varDigits(intPos + 1) & strTemp
```

in this case. Because intPos is 0, the output is IV (varDigits(0) & varDigits(1)). If the 4 had been in the hundreds place (imagine you're converting 421 to roman numerals), then intPos would be 2, the expression would say to use varDigits(4) & varDigits(5), and the output would be "CD" for this digit.

You won't use this function every day. However, when you do need to convert a value to roman numerals, it will be waiting.

Performing a "Smart" Proper Case Conversion

Although VBA provides the built-in StrConv function to convert words to proper case, it does just what a brute-force hand-coded solution would do: It converts the first letter of every word to uppercase and forces the rest of each word to lower-case. This doesn't help much for articles (*a*, *the*, and so on) or prepositions (*of*, *for*, and so on) or for handling proper names like *MacDonald* or *Port of Oakland*. Writing code to handle all the special cases would be prohibitively difficult, but if a "smart" proper-casing routine were to look up the exceptions to the rules in a table, the routine might work a bit better than through code alone.

One possible solution, dhProperLookup (in Listing 1.14), walks through the text you pass it, building up "words" of alphabetic characters. As soon as it finds a non-alphabetic character, it checks out the most current word it's collected and looks it up in a table. If it's there, it uses the text it finds in the table. If not, it performs a direct conversion of the word to proper case. The code then continues the process with the rest of the text. Once it hits the end of the string, it handles the final word and returns the result.

Listing 1.14: A "Smart" Proper Case Function

```
Public Function dhProperLookup( _
 ByVal strIn As String, _
 Optional blnForceToLower As Boolean = True, _
 Optional rst As ADODB.Recordset = Nothing, _
 Optional strField As String = "") As Variant


    Dim strOut As String
    Dim strWord As String
    Dim lngI As Long
    Dim strC As String * 1

    On Error GoTo HandleErr

    strOut = vbNullString
    strWord = vbNullString

    If blnForceToLower Then
        strIn = LCase$(strIn)
    End If

    For lngI = 1 To Len(strIn)
        strC = Mid$(strIn, lngI, 1)
        If dhIsCharAlphaNumeric(strC) Or strC = "'" Then
            strWord = strWord & strC
```

```
        Else
            strOut = strOut & dhFixWord(strWord, rst, strField) & strC
            ' Reset strWord for the next word.
            strWord = vbNullString
        End If
NextChar:
    Next lngI

    ' Process the final word.
    strOut = strOut & dhFixWord(strWord, rst, strField)

ExitHere:
    dhProperLookup = strOut
    Exit Function

HandleErr:
    ' If there's an error, just go on to the next character.
    ' This may mean the output word is missing characters,
    ' of course. If this bothers you, just change the Resume
    ' statement to resume at "ExitHere."
    Select Case Err
        Case Else
            ' MsgBox "Error: " & Err.Description & _
            '    " (" & Err.Number & ")"
    End Select
    Resume NextChar

End Function
```

To call dhProperLookup, you can pass the following set of parameters:

- *strIn* (required) is the text to be converted.

- *blnForceToLower* (optional; default = True) causes the function to convert all the text to lowercase before performing the proper case conversion. If you set the parameter to False, dhProperLookup won't affect any characters except the first character of each word.

- *rst* (optional; default = Nothing) is an open ADO recordset, containing the list of special cases. This recordset can come from a database, from an XML file, or from any other source of an ADO recordset. The recordset must have been opened using some cursor type besides the default, which doesn't allow for random access within the recordset.

- *strField* (optional; default = "") is a string expression containing the name of the field to be used for lookups in the recordset referred to by rst. If you specify the recordset, you must also specify this field name.

WARNING Because of an anomaly in the current version of ADO, the dhFixWord function (the function that retrieves special cases from the recordset) will fail if your special case text includes more than one apostrophe.

For example, suppose you have a database named PROPER.MDB containing a table named tblSpecialCase. In that table, a field named Lookup contains special cases for spelling. The sample code shown in Listing 1.15 opens the database, creates a recordset, and calls the dhProperLookup function.

Listing 1.15: Test the dhProperLookup Function

```
Sub TestProperMDB()
    ' Test procedure for dhProperLookup

    Dim rst As ADODB.Recordset

    Set rst = New ADODB.Recordset
    rst.Open "tblSpecialCase", _
      "Provider=Microsoft.Jet.OLEDB.4.0;" & _
      "Data Source = " & ActiveWorkbook.Path & "\Proper.MDB", _
      adOpenKeyset

    Debug.Print dhProperLookup( _
      "headline: cruella de ville and old macdonald eat dog's food", _
      True, rst, "Lookup")
End Sub
```

TIP The examples in this chapter assume that you're running them from within the sample Excel workbook. As you can see, this particular example uses Active-Workbook.Path, a property of the current Excel workbook that's only valid for a saved workbook. If you use this sample code in another application, or in a new Excel workbook, you'll need to take this into account. This issue is already handled in the Access and VB versions of the samples on the CD-ROM.

If tblSpecialCase contains at least the words *a*, *and*, *de*, and *MacDonald*, the output from the call to dhProperLookup would be

```
Headline: Cruella de Ville and Old MacDonald Eat a Dog's Food
```

If you don't supply recordset and field name parameters for dhProperLookup, it performs the same task as would a call to StrConv, although it does its work somewhat less efficiently than the built-in function. (In other words, unless you intend to supply the recordset, you're probably better off calling the built-in function.) To do its work, dhProperLookup starts by checking the blnForceToLower parameter and converting the entire input string to lowercase if the parameter's value is True:

```
If blnForceToLower Then
    strIn = LCase$(strIn)
End If
```

To work its way through the input string, dhProperLookup performs a loop, visiting each character in turn:

```
For lngI = 1 To Len(strIn)
    strC = Mid$(strIn, lngI, 1)
    ' (Code removed)
Next lngI
```

The code examines each character. If the character is alphanumeric or an apostrophe, it's appended to strWord. If not, the loop has reached the end of a word, so the code calls the dhFixWord procedure to perform the conversion and then tacks the word and the current (non-word) character onto the end of the output string.

```
If dhIsCharAlphaNumeric(strC) Or strC = "'" Then
    strWord = strWord & strC
Else
    strOut = strOut & dhFixWord(strWord, rst, strField) & strC
    ' Reset strWord for the next word.
    strWord = vbNullString
End If
```

TIP
Rather than setting strWord to be "", the code uses vbNullString instead. This optimization allows your code to run a tiny bit faster. Because this code executes for each character you're converting, you need all the help you can get! VBA provides the vbNullString constant, and although this constant's value is not really "" (it contains a reference to a known, "null" string pointer), when you assign it to a string variable, VBA converts it into its value, "". You can use vbNullString in any situation where you might otherwise use "" in your code.

Once the loop has concluded, one final step is necessary: Unless the text ends with a character that's not part of a word, the code will never process the final word. To make sure that last word ends up in the output string, dhProperLookup calls dhFixWord one last time, with the final word:

```
' Process the final word.
strOut = strOut & dhFixWord(strWord, rst, strField)
```

The dhFixWord function, shown in Listing 1.16, does its work using a recordset containing the special cases for specific words' spellings passed in from dhProperLookup. Supplying that information is up to you, and the function presented here counts on your having created an ADO recordset object filled with the rows of special names. If you have not supplied the recordset and field name, dhFixWord simply capitalizes the first letter of the word you've sent it and then returns.

Listing 1.16: dhFixWord Converts a Single Word to Proper Case

```
Private Function dhFixWord( _
 ByVal strWord As String, _
 Optional rst As ADODB.Recordset = Nothing, _
 Optional strField As String = "") As String

    ' "Properize" a single word
    Dim strOut As String

    On Error GoTo HandleErr

    If Len(strWord) > 0 Then
        ' Many things can go wrong. Just assume you want the
        ' standard properized version unless you hear otherwise.
        strOut = UCase(Left$(strWord, 1)) & Mid$(strWord, 2)
        ' Did you pass in a recordset? If so, lookup
        ' the value now.
        If Not rst Is Nothing Then
            If Len(strField) > 0 Then
                rst.MoveFirst
                rst.Find strField & " = " & _
                  "'" & Replace(strWord, "'", "''") & "'"
                If Not rst.EOF Then
                    strOut = rst(strField)
                End If
```

```
            End If
        End If
    End If

ExitHere:
    dhFixWord = strOut
    Exit Function

HandleErr:
    ' If anything goes wrong, anything, just get out.
    Select Case Err.Number
        Case Else
            ' MsgBox "Error: " & Err.Description & _
            ' " (" & Err.Number & ")"
    End Select
    Resume ExitHere
End Function
```

The dhFixWord function does the bulk of its work in a few simple lines of code:

```
rst.MoveFirst
rst.Find strField & " = " & _
  "'" & Replace(strWord, "'", "''") & "'"
If Not rst.EOF Then
    strOut = rst(strField)
End If
```

It uses the recordset's FindFirst method to look up a string in the format

```
Lookup = 'macdonald'
```

If it finds a match in the table, it replaces the output string with the word it found. In this case, it would replace the value of strOut with the text "MacDonald". (The rest of the code in dhFixWord simply validates input and prepares the lookup string.)

What's missing from this solution? First of all, it's not terribly smart. It can work only with the specific words you've added to the list. If you've added *McGregor* but not *MacGregor*, there's no way for the code to know how to handle the word that's not there. It's not possible to work with proper names that contain spaces (such as *de Long,* for example), although you could add many of the proper name prefixes to the lookup table to avoid their being capitalized incorrectly. The code checks only for alphabetic characters and apostrophes as legal characters in words. You may find you need to add to the list of acceptable characters. In that case, you may want to create a list of acceptable characters as a constant and use the InStr function to see whether strC is in the list. For example, to treat apostrophes and hyphens as valid word characters, you could declare a constant:

```
Const conWordChars = "'-"
```

and modify the check for characters like this:

```
If dhIsCharAlphaNumeric(strC) Or _
  (InStr(conWordChars, strC) > 0) Then
```

Where Does the Recordset Come From?

In this example (and others throughout this book), you may need to supply an ADO record-set as a parameter value. In the traditional sense, a recordset normally comes from a table in some database. However, using ADO, a recordset can come from many different places. You can read data from a standard database, or from a text file, or from an XML file; or you can even create the recordset on-the-fly, with no connection to stored data. If you're distributing an application, you may find it easiest to distribute your lookups for the dhProperLookup as a text file rather than as a full MDB file. We actually tried this out, creating a recordset from tblSpecialCase and then calling the Save method to create an XML file, like this:

```
Sub CreateProperXML()
    ' Create XML file for recordset.

    Dim rst As ADODB.Recordset
    Dim strPath As String
    Dim strFile As String

    strPath = ActiveWorkbook.Path
    Set rst = New ADODB.Recordset
    rst.Open "tblSpecialCase", _
      "Provider=Microsoft.Jet.OLEDB.4.0;" & _
      "Data Source = " & strPath & "\Proper.MDB", _
      adOpenKeyset

    On Error Resume Next
    strFile = strPath & "\Proper.xml"
    Kill strFile
```

```
                rst.Save strFile, adPersistXML

                rst.Close
                Set rst = Nothing
        End Sub
```

Then, to test this out, you can try code like this:

```
        Public Sub TestProperXML()
            ' Test procedure for dhProperLookup

            Dim rst As ADODB.Recordset
            Dim strText As String

            ' You don't even need a database. You can use a
            ' saved XML file.
            Set rst = New ADODB.Recordset
            rst.Open ActiveWorkbook.Path & "\Proper.xml", , _
            adOpenKeyset, adLockReadOnly, Options:=adCmdFile

            strText = _
              "headline: cruella de ville and old macdonald " & _
              "eat dog's food"
            Debug.Print dhProperLookup(strText, True, rst, "Lookup")

            rst.Close
            Set rst = Nothing
        End Sub
```

As you can see, this technique requires that you supply only a single text file (Proper.xml) in order to open a recordset—no need to bring along a big database, just to use dhProper-Lookup. You may find it interesting to open Proper.xml in a text editor—it's simply a text file, containing all your data.

Encrypting/Decrypting Text Using XOR Encryption

If you need a simple way to encrypt text in an application, the function provided in this section may do just what you need. The dhXORText function, in Listing 1.17, includes code that performs both the encryption and decryption of text strings. That's right—it takes just one routine to perform both tasks.

To encrypt text, pass dhXORText the text to encrypt and a password that supplies the encryption code. To decrypt the text, pass dhXORText the exact same parameters again. For example:

```
dhXORText(dhXORText("This is a test", "Password"), "Password")
```

returns "This is a test", the same text encrypted and then decrypted.

Listing 1.17: Use the XOR Operator to Encrypt Text

```
Public Function dhXORText(strText As String, strPWD As String)  _
  As String
    ' Encrypt or decrypt a string using the XOR operator.
    Dim abytText() As Byte
    Dim abytPWD() As Byte
    Dim intPWDPos As Integer
    Dim intPWDLen As Integer
    Dim intChar As Integer

    abytText = strText
    abytPWD = strPWD
    intPWDLen = LenB(strPWD)
    For intChar = 0 To LenB(strText) - 1
        ' Get the next number between 0 and intPWDLen - 1
        intPWDPos = (intChar Mod intPWDLen)
        abytText(intChar) = abytText(intChar) Xor _
          abytPWD(intPWDPos)
    Next intChar
    dhXORText = abytText
End Function
```

The dhXORText function counts on the XOR operator to do its work. This built-in operator compares each bit in the two expressions and uses the following rules to calculate the result for each bit:

If Bit1 is	And Bit2 is	The result is
1	1	0
1	0	1
0	1	1
0	0	0

Why XOR? Using this operator has a very important side effect: If you XOR two values and then XOR the result with either of the original values, you get back the other original value. That's what makes it possible for dhXORText to do its work. To try this, imagine that the first byte of your text is 74 and the first byte of the password is 110.

```
74 XOR 110
```

returns 36, which becomes the encrypted byte. Now, to get back the original text,

```
36 XOR 110
```

returns 74 back. Repeat that for all the bytes in the text, and you've encrypted and decrypted your text.

To perform its work, dhXORText copies both the input string and the password text into byte arrays. Once there, it's just a matter of looping through all the bytes in the input string's array, repeating the password over and over until you run out of input text. For each byte, XOR the byte from the input string and the byte from the password to form the byte for the output string.

Figure 1.8 shows a tiny example, using "Hello Tom" as the input text and "ab" as the password. Each byte in the input string will be XOR'd with a byte from the password, with the password repeating until it has run out of characters from the input string.

FIGURE 1.8
XOR each byte from the input string and the password, repeated.

Original text:

H	0	e	0	l	0	l	0	o	0		0	T	0	o	0	m	0
72	0	101	0	108	0	108	0	111	0	32	0	84	0	111	0	109	0

Password (repeated):

a	0	b	0	a	0	b	0	a	0	b	0	a	0	b	0	a	0
97	0	98	0	97	0	98	0	97	0	98	0	97	0	98	0	97	0

Output:

41	0	7	0	13	0	14	0	14	0	66	0	53	0	13	0	12	0

The code loops through each character of the input string—that's easy!

```
For intChar = 0 To LenB(strText) - 1
    ' (Code removed)
Next intChar
```

The hard part is to find the correct byte from the password to XOR with the selected byte in the input string: The code uses the Mod operator to find the correct character. The Mod operator returns the remainder, when you divide the first operand by the second, which is guaranteed to be a number between 0 and one less than the second operand. In short, that corresponds to rotating through the bytes of the password, as shown in Table 1.13 (disregarding the null bytes). If the password were five bytes long, the "Position Mod 2" ("Position Mod 5", in that case) column would contain the values 0 through 4, repeated as many times as necessary.

```
' Get the next number between 0 and intPWDLen - 1
intPWDPos = (intChar Mod intPWDLen)
abytText(intChar) = abytText(intChar) Xor abytPWD(intPWDPos)
```

TABLE 1.13: Steps in the Encryption of the Sample Text

Char from Input	Position	Position Mod 2	Char from Password	XOR
H (72)	0	0	a (97)	41
e (101)	1	1	b (98)	7
l (108)	2	0	a (97)	13
l (108)	3	1	b (98)	14
o (111)	4	0	a (97)	14
(32)	5	1	b (98)	66
T (84)	6	0	a (97)	53
o (111)	7	1	b (98)	13
m (109)	8	0	a (97)	12

TIP   As you can probably imagine, passwords used with dhXORText are case sensitive, and you can't change that fact. Warn users that passwords in your application will need to be entered exactly, taking upper- and lowercase letters into account.

WARNING   Although no XOR-based algorithm for encryption is totally safe, the longer your password, the better chance you have that a decryption expert won't be able to crack the code. The previous example, using "ab" as the password, was only for demonstration purposes. Make sure your passwords are at least four or five characters long—the longer, the better.

Returning a String Left-Padded or Right-Padded to a Specified Width

If you're creating a phone-book listing, you may need to left-pad a phone number with dots so it looks like this:

```
............(310) 123-4567
.................555-1212
```

Or you may want to left-pad a part number field with 0s (zeros), so "1234" becomes "001234", and all part numbers take up exactly six digits. You may want to create a fixed-width data stream, with spaces padding the fields. In all of these cases, you need a function that can pad a string, to the left or to the right, with the character of your choosing. The two simple functions dhPadLeft and dhPadRight, in Listing 1.18, perform the work for you.

To call either function, pass a string containing the input text, an integer indicating the width for the output string, and, optionally, a pad character. (The functions will use a space character if you don't provide one.)

For example:

```
dhPadLeft("Name", 10, ".")
```

returns "......Name" (the word *Name* preceded by six periods).

```
dhPadRight("Hello", 10)
```

returns "Hello   " (*Hello* followed by five spaces).

NOTE   Neither dhPadLeft nor dhPadRight will truncate your input string. If the original string is longer than you indicate you want the output string, the code will just return the input string with no changes.

Listing 1.18: Pad with Characters to the Left or to the Right

```
Public Function dhPadLeft(strText As String, intWidth As Integer, _
 Optional strPad As String = " ") As String

    If Len(strText) > intWidth Then
        dhPadLeft = strText
    Else
        dhPadLeft = Right$(String(intWidth, strPad) & _
          strText, intWidth)
    End If
End Function


Public Function dhPadRight(strText As String, intWidth As Integer, _
 Optional strPad As String = " ") As String

    If Len(strText) > intWidth Then
        dhPadRight = strText
    Else
        dhPadRight = Left$(strText & _
          String(intWidth, strPad), intWidth)
    End If

End Function
```

Both functions use the same technique to pad their input strings: They create a string consisting of as many of the pad characters as needed to fill the entire output string, append or prepend that string to the original string, and then use the Left$ or Right$ function to truncate the output string to the correct width. For example, if you call dhPadLeft like this:

```
dhPadLeft("123.45", 10, "$")
```

the code creates a string of 10 dollar signs and prepends that to the input string. Then it uses the Right$ function to truncate:

```
Right$("$$$$$$$$$$123.45", 10)
' returns "$$$$123.45"
```

Using Soundex to Compare Strings

Long before the advent of computers, people working with names knew it was very difficult to spell surnames correctly and that they needed some way to group names by their phonetic spelling rather than by grammatical spelling. The algorithm demonstrated in this section is based on the Russell Soundex algorithm, a standard technique used in many database applications.

WARNING   The Soundex algorithm was designed for, and works reliably with, surnames only. You can use it with any type of string, but its effectiveness diminishes as the text grows longer. It was intended to make it possible to match various spellings of last names, and its discriminating power is greatest in short words with three or more consonants.

The Soundex algorithm is based on these assumptions:

- Many English consonants sound alike.

- Vowels don't affect the overall sound of the name as much as the consonants do.

- The first letter of the name is most significant.

- A four-character representation is optimal for comparing two names.

For example, all three of the following examples return "P252", the Soundex representation of all of these names:

```
dhSoundex("Paszinslo")
dhSoundex("Pacinslo")
dhSoundex("Pejinslo")
```

All three provide very distinct spellings of the difficult name, yet all three return the same Soundex string. As long as the first letters match, you have a good chance of finding a match using the Soundex conversion.

The concept, then, is that when attempting to locate a name, you'd ask the user for the name, convert it to its Soundex representation, and compare it to the Soundex representations of the names in your database. You'd present a list of the possible matches to the user, who could then choose the correct one.

The Soundex algorithm follows these steps:

1. Use the first letter of the string, as is.

2. Code the remaining characters, using the information in Table 1.14.

3. Skip repeated values (that is, characters that map to the same value) unless they're separated by one or more separator characters (characters with a value of 0).

4. Once the Soundex string contains four characters, stop looking.

The full code for dhSoundex, in Listing 1.19, follows these steps in creating the Soundex representation of the input string.

TABLE 1.14: Values for Characters in a Soundex String

Letter	Value	Comment
W,H		Ignored
A,E,I,O,U,Y	0	Although removed from the output string, these letters act as separators between significant consonants
B,P,F,V	1	
C,G,J,K,Q,S,X,Z	2	
D,T	3	
L	4	
M,N	5	
R	6	

Listing 1.19: Convert Strings to Their Soundex Equivalent

```
Const dhcLen = 4

Public Function dhSoundex(ByVal strIn As String) As String

    Dim strOut As String
    Dim intI As Integer
    Dim intPrev As Integer
    Dim strChar As String * 1
    Dim intChar As Integer
```

```
        Dim blnPrevSeparator As Boolean
        Dim intPos As Integer

        strOut = String(dhcLen, "0")
        strIn = UCase(strIn)
        blnPrevSeparator = False

        strChar = Left$(strIn, 1)
        intPrev = CharCode(strChar)
        Mid$(strOut, 1, 1) = strChar

        intPos = 1
        For intI = 2 To Len(strIn)
            ' If the output string is full, quit now.
            If intPos >= dhcLen Then
                Exit For
            End If
            ' Get each character, in turn. If the
            ' character's a letter, handle it.
            strChar = Mid$(strIn, intI, 1)
            If dhIsCharAlpha(strChar) Then
                ' Convert the character to its code.
                intChar = CharCode(strChar)

                ' If the character's not empty, and if it's not
                ' the same as the previous character, tack it
                ' onto the end of the string.
                If (intChar > 0) Then
                    If blnPrevSeparator Or (intChar <> intPrev) Then
                        intPos = intPos + 1
                        Mid$(strOut, intPos, 1) = intChar
                        intPrev = intChar
                    End If
                End If
                blnPrevSeparator = (intChar = 0)
            End If
        Next intI
        dhSoundex = strOut
    End Function
```

Now that you've found the Soundex string corresponding to a given surname, what can you do with it? You may want to provide a graduated scale of matches.

That is, perhaps you don't require an exact match but would like to know how well one name matches another. A common method for calculating this level of matching is to use a function such as dhSoundsLike, shown in Listing 1.20. To use this function, you supply two strings, not yet converted to their Soundex equivalents, and dhSoundsLike returns a number between 0 and 4 (4 being the best match) indicating how alike the two strings are. (If you'd rather, you can pass in two Soundex strings, and dhSoundsLike won't perform the conversion to Soundex strings for you. In that case, set the optional blnIsSoundex parameter to True.)

Listing 1.20: Use dhSoundsLike to Compare Two Soundex Strings

```
Public Function dhSoundsLike(ByVal strItem1 As String, _
  ByVal strItem2 As String, _
  Optional blnIsSoundex As Boolean = False) As Integer

    Dim intI As Integer

    If Not blnIsSoundex Then
        strItem1 = dhSoundex(strItem1)
        strItem2 = dhSoundex(strItem2)
    End If
    For intI = 1 To dhcLen
        If Mid$(strItem1, intI, 1) <> Mid$(strItem2, intI, 1) Then
            Exit For
        End If
    Next intI
    dhSoundsLike = (intI - 1)
End Function
```

It's hard to imagine a lower-tech technique for performing this task. dhSounds-Like simply loops through all four characters in each Soundex string. As long as it finds a match, it keeps going. Like a tiny game of musical chairs, as soon as it finds two characters that don't match, it jumps out of the loop and returns the number of characters it found that matched; the more characters that match, the better the rating.

To test out dhSoundsLike, you could try

```
Debug.Print dhSoundsLike("Smith", "Smitch")
```

which returns 3, or

```
Debug.Print dhSoundsLike("S125", "S123", True)
```

which returns 3, as well. Of course, you're not likely to call dhSoundsLike with string literals. More likely, you'd call it passing in two string variables and compare their contents.

NOTE   There are variants of this algorithm floating around that aren't as effective as the one used here. Those (admittedly simpler) algorithms don't notice repeated consonants that are separated by a vowel and therefore oversimplify the creation of the Soundex string for a given name. The algorithm presented here is more complex but yields more reliable results.

Working with Substrings

To finish off the chapter, this section provides a few techniques for parsing and extracting substrings from a longer string. Specifically, you'll find out how to perform these tasks:

- Return a specific word, by index, from a string.
- Retrieve the first or last word in a string.
- Convert a delimited string into a collection of tokens.

Returning a Specific Word, by Index, from a String

Of all the functions in this chapter, the function in this section, dhExtractString, has received the most use in our own applications. It allows you to retrieve a chunk of a string, given a delimiter (or multiple delimiters), by the position within the string. Rather than write laborious code to parse a string yourself, you can use dhExtractString to pull out just the piece you need. For example, if you need to take the following string:

```
ItemsToBuy=Milk,Bread,Peas
```

and retrieve the item names individually, you could either write the code to parse the string or call dhExtractString in a loop:

```
Public Sub TestExtract(strIniText As String)

    ' Test sub for dhExtractString
    Dim intI As Integer
    Dim strText As String

    intI = 2
    Do While True
        strText = dhExtractString(strIniText, intI, "=,")
        If Len(strText) = 0 Then
            Exit Do
        End If
        Debug.Print strText
        intI = intI + 1
    Loop
End Sub
```

NOTE   You might wonder why you would use dhExtractString rather than the built-in Split function. You can easily retrieve an array of strings from the Split function. Then you can retrieve just the item you need from that array. Our function provides two benefits over Split (whether they're benefits or detriments depends on your exact needs): dhExtractString allows you to specify more than one alternate character as a delimiter (Split allows only a single delimiter), and Split splits up the entire string, even if you need only the first piece of the string. When you need only the second word of a paragraph, there's no point asking Split to do its work, splitting up the entire paragraph into words so you can retrieve the second word. In timing tests, dhExtractString was often significantly faster than Split because dhExtractString stops working as soon as it retrieves the item you need.

You can be creative with dhExtractString: You can call it once with one set of delimiters and then again with a different set. For example, you might have tackled the previous problem by first parsing the text to the right of the equal sign as a single chunk:

```
strVals = dhExtractString(strIniText, 2, "=")
```

Then you could pull the various comma-delimited pieces out of strVals:

```
strItem1 = dhExtractString(strVals, 1, ",")    ' Returns "Milk"
strItem2 = dhExtractString(strVals, 2, ",")    ' Returns "Bread"
strItem3 = dhExtractString(strVals, 3, ",")    ' Returns "Peas"
```

As you can see, you can supply a single delimiter character or a list of them. That is, you could also parse the previous expression using code like this:

```
strItem1 = dhExtractString(strIniText, 2, ",=")       ' Returns "Milk"
strItem2 = dhExtractString(strIniText, 3, ",=")       ' Returns "Bread"
strItem3 = dhExtractString(strIniText, 4, ",=")       ' Returns "Peas"
```

You'll find the full listing for dhExtractString in Listing 1.21.

WARNING   The return value from dhExtractString can be somewhat misleading. If the input string contains two contiguous delimiter characters, dhExtractString sees that as an empty string delimited by those two characters. This means that you cannot loop, calling dhExtractString, until it returns an empty string (unless you're sure the string contains no contiguous delimiters). You'll need to call dhCountIn first, find out how many substrings there are, and then iterate through the string that many times. See the section "Converting a Delimited String into a Collection of Tokens" later in this chapter for an example of using this technique.

TIP   If you don't supply dhExtractString with a delimiter or a list of delimiters, it will default to using the standard text delimiters in the dhcDelimiters constant. Of course, you can change those default values simply by modifying the constant in the code.

⟩ Listing 1.21: Extract a Specified Substring

```
Public Function dhExtractString(ByVal strIn As String, _
 ByVal intPiece As Integer, _
 Optional ByVal strDelimiter As String = dhcDelimiters) As String

    Dim lngPos As Long
    Dim lngPos1 As Long
    Dim lngLastPos As Long
    Dim intLoop As Integer

    lngPos = 0
    lngLastPos = 0
    intLoop = intPiece
```

```
        ' If there's more than one delimiter, map them
        ' all to the first one.
        If Len(strDelimiter) > 1 Then
            strIn = dhTranslate(strIn, strDelimiter, _
             Left$(strDelimiter, 1))
        End If
        strIn = dhTrimAll (strIn)
        Do While intLoop > 0
            lngLastPos = lngPos
            lngPos1 = InStr(lngPos + 1, strIn, Left$(strDelimiter, 1))
            If lngPos1 > 0 Then
                lngPos = lngPos1
                intLoop = intLoop - 1
            Else
                lngPos = Len(strIn) + 1
                Exit Do
            End If
        Loop
        ' If the string wasn't found, and this wasn't
        ' the first pass through (intLoop would equal intPiece
        ' in that case) and intLoop > 1, then you've run
        ' out of chunks before you've found the chunk you
        ' want. That is, the chunk number was too large.
        ' Return "" in that case.
        If (lngPos1 = 0) And (intLoop <> intPiece) And (intLoop > 1) Then
            dhExtractString = vbNullString
        Else
            dhExtractString = Mid$(strIn, lngLastPos + 1, _
             lngPos - lngLastPos - 1)
        End If
    End If
End Function
```

The first thing dhExtractString does is to "flatten" multiple delimiters down to the first item in the list. That is, if you pass a group of delimiters, such as a comma, a space, and a hyphen, the function first replaces all of these with a comma character (,) in the input string:

```
If Len(strDelimiter) > 1 Then
    strIn = dhTranslate(strIn, strDelimiter, Left$(strDelimiter, 1))
End If
```

Next, dhExtractString loops through the string until it's found the delimiter it needs. If you've asked for the fourth token from the input string, it will loop until it finds the third instance of the delimiter. It also keeps track of the last position at which it found a delimiter (lngLastPos) and the position of the delimiter it's just found (lngPos). If the current search for a delimiter using InStr fails (it returns 0), the loop indicates that the current position is one character past the end of the input string and just exits the loop:

```
Do While intLoop > 0
    lngLastPos = lngPos
    lngPos1 = InStr(lngPos + 1, strIn, Left$(strDelimiter, 1))
    If lngPos1 > 0 Then
        lngPos = lngPos1
        intLoop = intLoop - 1
    Else
        lngPos = Len(strIn) + 1
        Exit Do
    End If
Loop
```

The logic for determining whether to return an empty string or a chunk of the input string is complex (perhaps too complex). There are three conditions that must all be met in order for dhExtractString to return an empty string:

lngPos1 = 0   This indicates that the input string ran out of delimiters before it stopped looking for tokens. This could happen, of course, if you requested the final token from a string—there wouldn't be a delimiter after that token, so lngPos1 would be 0.

intLoop <> intPiece   The intLoop variable counts down, starting at the value of intPiece, as it loops through the delimiters in the input string. If intLoop is the same as intPiece, this indicates there was only one token to begin with, and no delimiters at all. In such a case, dhExtractString returns the entire input string, not an empty string.

intLoop > 1   If intLoop is 0, it indicates that the loop progressed through all the delimiters in the string, and you may have selected the final token in the input string. It also may indicate that you asked for a token past the number of tokens in the string. (That is, perhaps you asked for the sixth word in a sentence that contains only four words. In that case, the function should return an empty string, and it will because the other two conditions will also be true.)

Unless all three of these conditions are met, the code extracts the string starting at lngLastPos + 1 and takes lngPos – lngLastPos – 1 characters:

```
If (lngPos1 = 0) And (intLoop <> intPiece) And (intLoop > 1) Then
    dhExtractString = vbNullString
Else
    dhExtractString = Mid$(strIn, lngLastPos + 1, _
     lngPos - lngLastPos - 1)
End If
```

TIP   Remember that dhExtractString treats consecutive delimiters as though there was an empty token between them. Requesting the second token from "This;;is;a;test", using " ;" as the delimiter, you'll receive an empty string as the return value.

You'll see that several of the other functions in this section use dhExtractString to do their work. We're sure you'll find this extremely useful parsing function invaluable in any code you write that extracts portions of text strings.

Retrieving the First or Last Word in a String

Each of the two functions presented in this section, dhFirstWord and dhLast-Word, breaks its input string into two pieces: the selected word and, optionally, the rest of the string. Calling dhFirstWord (see Listing 1.22) returns the first word of the input string and fills an optional parameter with the rest of the string. Calling dhLastWord (see Listing 1.23) returns the final word of the input string and fills an optional parameter with the first portion of the string. For example:

```
Dim strRest As String
Dim strReturn As String
strReturn = dhFirstWord("First words are mighty important", strRest)
```

returns "First" and places " words are mighty important" (note the leading space) into strRest. On the other hand:

```
Dim strRest As String
Dim strReturn As String
strReturn = dhLastWord("First words are mighty important", strRest)
```

returns "important" and places "First words are mighty " (note the trailing space) into strRest.

Listing 1.22: Return the First Word from a String

```
Public Function dhFirstWord( _
 ByVal strText As String, _
 Optional ByRef strRest As String = "") As String

    Dim strTemp As String

    ' This is easy!
    ' Get the first word.
    strTemp = dhExtractString(strText, 1)

    ' Extract everything after the first word,
    ' and put that into strRest.
    strRest = Mid$(strText, Len(strTemp) + 1)

    ' Return the first word.
    dhFirstWord = strTemp
End Function
```

Listing 1.23: Return the Final Word from a String

```
Public Function dhLastWord( _
 ByVal strText As String, _
 Optional ByRef strRest As String = "") As
String

    Dim intCount As Integer
    Dim strTemp As String

    ' Find the number of words, and then
    ' extract the final word.
    intCount = dhCountWords(strText)
    strTemp = dhExtractString(strText, intCount)

    ' Extract everything before the last word,
    ' and put that into strRest.
    strRest = Trim(Left$(strText, Len(strText) - Len(strTemp)))
    dhLastWord = strTemp

End Function
```

The dhFirstWord function is simple because it can use the dhExtractString function discussed earlier in this chapter. It first pulls out the first word:

```
strTemp = dhExtractString(strText, 1)
```

Then it places the rest of the string into strRest:

```
strRest = Mid$(strText, Len(strTemp) + 1)
```

NOTE   The dhFirstWord and dhLastWord functions needn't make any explicit check to see whether you've passed in a variable for the strRest parameter. If you haven't specified the parameter, VBA uses only the local copy of the value and just doesn't pass anything back. No harm done, and it saves adding logic to check the status of that parameter.

The dhLastWord function is bit more complex, because the code must first find the number of words in the string, and then extract the correct one:

```
intCount = dhCountWords(strText)
strTemp = dhExtractString(strText, intCount)
```

Once it has the final word, it can extract the previous portion of the string and place it into strRest:

```
strRest = Left$(strText, Len(strText) - Len(strTemp))
```

Of course, once you have as many string functions under your belt as you do by now, you can probably create several alternatives to either of these tasks. You may find it interesting to pursue other methods, and perhaps your solutions will be even more efficient!

Converting a Delimited String into a Collection of Tokens

VBA provides support for easy-to-use, variable-sized Collection objects, and you may want to parse a string into a collection of words. The function in this section, dhExtractCollection, lets you specify input text and, optionally, the delimiters to use in parsing the text. It returns a collection of strings, filled in from your input text.

For example, the following code parses a text string and then prints each word to the Immediate window:

```
Function TestExtractCollection()
    Dim varText As Variant
    Dim colText As Collection
    Set colText = dhExtractCollection( _
      "This string contains a bunch of words")
    For Each varText In colText
        Debug.Print varText
    Next varText
    TestExtractCollection = colText.Count
End Function
```

The collection returned from dhExtractCollection has all the properties and methods of any other collection in VBA. The example routine uses a simple For...Next loop to visit each item in the returned collection, and the Count property to inspect the number of items in the collection. Listing 1.24 includes the full listing of dhExtractCollection.

Listing 1.24: Return a Collection Filled with Substrings

```
Public Function dhExtractCollection(ByVal strText As String, _
  Optional ByVal strDelimiter As String = dhcDelimiters) As Collection

    Dim colWords As Collection
    Dim lngI As Long
    Dim strTemp As String
    Dim strChar As String * 1
    Dim astrItems() As String

    Set colWords = New Collection

    ' If there's more than one delimiter, map them
    ' all to the first one.
    If Len(strDelimiter) = 0 Then
        colWords.Add strText
    Else
        strChar = Left$(strDelimiter, 1)
        If Len(strDelimiter) > 1 Then
            strText = dhTranslate(strText, strDelimiter, strChar)
        End If
```

```
        astrItems = Split(strText, strChar)

        ' Loop through all the tokens, adding them to the
        ' output collection.
        For lngI = LBound(astrItems) To UBound(astrItems)
            colWords.Add astrItems(lngI)
        Next lngI
    End If

    ' Return the output collection.
    Set dhExtractCollection = colWords
End Function
```

Given the rest of the routines in this chapter, dhExtractCollection is simple. Its first step, after declaring a local collection object to contain all the strings, is to "flatten" the list of delimiters to a single delimiter character so the built-in Split function can return an array filled with tokens from the input string:

```
Dim colWords As Collection
Set colWords = New Collection
' (Code removed)
strChar = Left$(strDelimiter, 1)
If Len(strDelimiter) > 1 Then
    strText = dhTranslate(strText, strDelimiter, strChar)
End If
astrItems = Split(strText, strChar)
```

Next, the function loops through the number of words in the input string, using the LBound and UBound functions to control the loop. For each word it finds, it adds the word to a local collection:

```
For lngI = LBound(astrItems) To UBound(astrItems)
    colWords.Add astrItems(lngI)
Next lngI
```

Finally, the function sets its return value to the local collection, returning that collection to the function's caller:

```
Set dhExtractCollection = colWords
```

Note that there's no reason not to use dhExtractCollection to find a particular word in a string, if that's what you need. For example, either

```
dhExtractCollection("This is a test").Item(2)
```

or

```
dhExtractCollection("This is a test")(2)
```

will return the word "is". You'll get the same result calling

```
dhExtractString("This is a test", 2)
```

and dhExtractString is a bit more efficient. But there's no reason besides speed not to call dhExtractCollection, and you may find its syntax easier to use.

Summary

VBA programs seem unable to avoid working with strings as part of each and every application. This chapter has provided an overview of the built-in VBA functions and a long laundry list of additional procedures that provide additional functionality. Specifically, this chapter covered

- How VBA stores and uses strings
- Many of the built-in string functions and options for:
    - Comparing strings
    - Converting strings
    - Creating strings
    - Calculating the length of a string
    - Formatting a string
    - Justifying a string
    - Searching for a string
    - Working with and replacing portions of a string
    - Using ANSI values and bytes

- Additional functions for:
  - Searching and replacing text
  - Gathering information about strings
  - Converting strings
  - Working with substrings

For similar chapters covering dates and numbers, see Chapters 2 and 3, respectively.

chapter 2

Working with Numbers

- Understanding how numeric values are stored in VBA

- Using the built-in VBA numeric functions

- Generating random numbers

- Using custom numeric functions

At some point in the development process of your application, you're most likely going to need to work with numbers. You'll be faced with choosing how to store the numeric values you're working with, and you'll probably want to use some of the built-in numeric functions. You may find that you need to create your own functions to expand the functionality VBA provides.

This chapter explains how VBA stores and computes numbers and takes a look at the built-in numeric functions. The remainder of the chapter provides and explains several advanced functions using mathematical algorithms.

The sample files you'll find on the CD-ROM that accompanies this book are listed in Table 2.1.

TABLE 2.1: Sample Files

Filename	Description
NUMBERS.XLS	Excel 2000 workbook containing sample code
NUMBERS.MDB	Access 2000 database containing sample code
NUMBERS.VBP	VB6 project containing sample code
NUMBERS.BAS	Numeric functions listed in this chapter
TEST.BAS	Test functions listed in this chapter
QUICKSORT.BAS	Quicksort procedure from Chapter 7

How Does VBA Store Numeric Values?

As human beings, we count things in base 10, mainly because we have 10 fingers. The earliest mathematicians found that fingers made handy counting tools, and it was easier to group larger numbers of items in groups of 10 than in groups of eight, two, or any other arbitrary number. However, your computer, not having 10 fingers, does not group things by 10s; it uses a base 2, or binary, representation of numbers to store and track information. Because a base-2 system requires only two digits, 0 and 1, it's convenient for mapping numbers to electronic circuits, where open and closed switches can represent 1s and 0s.

NOTE A convenient way of indicating the base of any particular number is to place the base as a subscript to the number, so decimal 10 could be shown as 10_{10}, and binary 10 could be shown as 10_2. In the following chapter the subscript will be used in the body text for any number that is not base 10.

Our counting system relies on two factors: The first is the value of the digit used and the second is the placing of the digit. So, for example, the number 111 uses only the digit 1, but that digit has three separate meanings due to the three positions where it is placed within the number.

NOTE The position of a digit within a number is directly related to the concept of powers of the base, and those positions start numbering from 0, moving from right to left within a number. Therefore, the number 123 is another way of saying $(1 * 10^2) + (2 * 10^1) + (3 * 10^0)$. (In case you've forgotten your high-school algebra, 10 to the 0 power is 1, 10 to the 1 power is 10, and 10 to the 2 power is 100.)

Just as each position in a decimal number can contain any digit from 0 to 9, each position in a binary number, called a bit, can contain only a 0 or a 1. Bits are usually grouped in packages of eight, called bytes. One byte can hold 256 combinations of 0s or 1s and can therefore be used to represent only 256 different numbers. To represent larger ranges of numbers, more bytes are required.

NOTE In a similar way to decimal numbers, each position in a binary number represents a power of the base, so 100_2 is the same as 2^2, 10_2 is the same as 2^1, and 1_2 is the same as 2^0.

You need to take two factors into account when considering numbers you want to store in a variable in VBA. First, how big do the numbers need to be? If you're counting stars in the universe, you need to be able to store larger numbers than if you are counting legs on a pig. The second factor is precision. When counting stars in the universe, you may accept being off by a few million, but your leg count needs to be exactly right. The question of precision becomes especially tricky when you're dealing with very large numbers and numbers that include fractions; the fact that you're counting in base 10 and your computer uses base 2 for storage can create pitfalls for the unwary.

VBA supports several data types for storing numeric values in variables. Which one you choose for a particular variable will depend on how large the numbers you're working with can become and on how much precision is needed.

The general rule of thumb when choosing a variable's data type is to choose the smallest possible one that will fit the task and, if possible, avoid the floating-point data types (Single and Double). For example, if you're counting bovine append-ages, which rarely exceed four per animal and never go less than zero, you might use a Byte variable (it can hold values from 0 up to 255). If you need fractions only because you're working with money, use the Currency data type. If you use a Double just to be on the safe side (because it seems to cover the largest possible range and precision), you could run into unanticipated complications when your base-2 computer tries to store or manipulate floating-point numbers. (We'll have more on that later.)

The available data types for storing numeric values are summarized in Table 2.2.

TABLE 2.2: VBA Numeric Data Types

Data Type	Storage Size	Range
Byte	1 byte	0 to 255
Integer	2 bytes	–32,768 to 32,767
Long (long integer)	4 bytes	–2,147,483,648 to 2,147,483,647
Single (single-precision floating-point)	4 bytes	–3.402823E38 to –1.401298E–45 for negative values; 1.401298E–45 to 3.402823E38 for positive values
Double (double-precision floating-point)	8 bytes	–1.79769313486232E308 to –4.94065645841247E–324 for negative values; 4.94065645841247E–324 to 1.79769313486232E308 for positive values
Currency (scaled integer)	8 bytes	–922,337,203,685,477.5808 to 922,337,203,685,477.5807
Decimal (available only as a Variant subtype)	14 bytes	+/–79,228,162,514,264,337,593,543,950,335 with no decimal point; +/–7.9228162514264337593543950335 with 28 places to the right of the decimal; smallest nonzero number is +/–0.0000000000000000000000000001
Variant (with numbers)	16 bytes	Any numeric value up to the range of a Double

The data types summarized in Table 2.2 and the ranges they support are examined in detail in the following sections. They can be divided into three groups: those that can hold only whole numbers, those that can hold fractions using floating-point mathematics, and a hybrid group, called *scaled integers*, that uses whole numbers to store fractions.

NOTE   You can use the Variant data type to store values of any of the other data types. VBA provides a function, TypeName, that returns the data type of any value or variable that is passed to it. If a Variant is passed to TypeName, the subtype of the variant is returned. The use of TypeName is demonstrated in the section "Floating-Point Numbers and the Errors They Can Cause" later in this chapter.

NOTE   No matter what it appears that we're saying here, be wary about using Byte variables to hold small values. If you actually were keeping track of pigs' legs, in code, we'd recommend that you use an Integer, not a Byte. VBA handles Byte values specially, because they're really meant for storing bytes in an array of bytes (see Chapter 1 for more information on byte arrays). You'll pay a price in terms of performance if you use a Byte variable for anything but working with arrays of bytes.

Whole Numbers

The Byte data type is the most straightforward, and the most limited, of the numeric data types. It is simply stored as an 8-bit binary number. For example, the number 10 would be stored as 00001010_2, which represents 1 times 2 to the first power ($2^1 = 2$), plus 1 times 2 to the third power ($2^3 = 8$). No negative numbers can be stored in a Byte, and the largest number that can be stored is 11111111_2, or 255.

To understand the ranges of the other data types, you need to know about another important difference between decimal and binary numbers. In addition to the digits 0 through 9, the decimal system uses two special symbols that are essential for representing certain values: the decimal point and the minus sign. Since binary numbers are so useful precisely because numeric values can be represented using only 0s and 1s, ways have been developed to represent fractions and negative numbers without the use of any special symbols.

For example, the Integer data type, which uses 16 bits of storage, employs one of these bits to indicate the sign, positive or negative. This leaves 15 bits to represent the absolute value of the number. The largest number that can be represented with 15 bits is $2^{15} - 1$, or 32,767. The reason it's $2^{15} - 1$ and not simply 2^{15} is that one number is needed to represent 0. Because there's no need for a negative 0, one extra negative number can be represented, which is why the range starts at –32,768 ($-1 * 2^{15}$).

The Long data type stores only whole numbers, just as the Byte and Integer data types do. With the storage size increased to 4 bytes (32 bits), the largest possible number becomes $2^{31} - 1$ (approximately 2 billion), and the lowest possible negative number is -2^{31}.

TIP   To use computer memory most efficiently, always choose one of the whole number data types, if possible. The only time you should consider one of the floating-point data types to store whole numbers is when the numbers you are working with could exceed 2 billion (the largest Long value), or if you need to work with fractional data. In the section "The 'Hidden' Decimal Data Type" later in this chapter, you'll learn how to use this new data type to store large numbers more safely.

Floating-Point Numbers and the Errors They Can Cause

The two floating-point data types that cause developers headaches are Single and Double. To understand why those headaches come about, you need to know a little about how the floating-point data types use binary digits to store potentially large numbers and fractions.

The Single data type uses the same number of bytes as the Long data type (4 bytes), but it uses these 32 binary digits in a completely different way. The method used for both Single and Double data types is an industry standard that was developed by the Institute of Electrical and Electronics Engineers (IEEE). (Coincidentally, the acronym is also the sound most people make when trying to understand this concept, "Eye-Eeeeeeee!") A full explanation of floating point mathematics is beyond the scope of this book, but the basic strategy behind it is quite simple.

Floating-point numbers are similar to scientific notation in that they express a number as the product of two other numbers. For example, the decimal number 1500 can be expressed in scientific notation as $1.5 * 10^3$, or 1.5E3, and the number .0015 can be expressed as $1.5 * 10^{-3}$, or 1.5E–3. This way of expressing numbers consists of two parts. The first part is a multiplier, called the *mantissa*. The second part is an *exponent*. Positive exponents are used for whole numbers and negative exponents for fractions. The number of digits allowed in the mantissa determines the level of precision, and the maximum size of the exponent determines the range.

In binary floating-point numbers, the bits that are available get divided between those that represent the mantissa and those that represent the exponent. For example, a Double uses 1 bit for the sign (positive or negative), 11 bits for the exponent, and 52 bits for the mantissa for a total of 64 bits, or 8 bytes.

As you can see in Table 2.2, Single and Double data types can hold some huge positive and negative numbers and some tiny fractions. However, unlike the Integer and Long data types, the floating-point data types cannot store every possible number within their ranges. Some of the numbers within that range, including some large whole numbers, cannot be represented exactly, so they get rounded to the nearest available value. Since there is an infinite number of possible fractional values within any given range, there will always be an infinite number of precise fractions that will also have to be rounded.

Another reason floating-point numbers get rounded is that binary (base 2) numbers cannot represent all fractions exactly. Of course, decimal numbers are also unable to exactly represent certain fractions. For example, the fraction $1/3$ cannot be exactly represented by any combination of powers of 10. The decimal representation of $1/3$, .3333333, does not exactly equal $1/3$, and no matter how many more 3s are added on after the decimal point, it never will. Similarly, some fractional numbers that can be exactly represented in decimal notation, like 0.0001, can never be precisely stored as binary values. There is just no exact combination of powers of 2 that can accomplish the task. This rounding that sometimes occurs with floating-point numbers can cause errors, as you can see in the procedure shown in Listing 2.1.

More on Binary Inaccuracy

To understand why a binary representation of a value has problems with numbers such as 0.0001, you need to dig a bit deeper into the concept of positional representation of digits within a value. Earlier we noted that (using binary) $1_2 = 2^0$ and that $10_2 = 2^1$; carrying on the trend we can see that $0.1_2 = 2^{-1}$ and $0.01_2 = 2^{-2}$ and so on.

If $10_2 = 2^2$ (which is equal to 4) and $1_2 = 2^0$ (which is equal to 1), then $0.1_2 = 2^{-1}$ (which is equal to 0.5) and $0.01_2 = 2^{-2}$ (which is equal to 0.25).

If you tried to convert 0.0001_{10} to binary, you would get a number something like $0.0001100110011001100110011001100110011001100110011001100110011001_2$ (note the repeating groups), at which point it would still not be resolved. If you convert this binary value back to decimal, you actually get the value $0.000099999999999999907031652_{10}$. Although it's close to 0.0001_{10}, it's not exactly right.

Listing 2.1: Demonstrating Floating-Point Errors

```
Public Sub TestFloatingPoints()

    Dim intI As Integer
    Dim sngSum As Single
    Dim dblSum As Double

    Debug.Print "Both results should be 1.0"

    For intI = 1 To 10000
        sngSum = sngSum + 0.0001
    Next intI

    'This prints "Single: 1.000054"
    Debug.Print TypeName(sngSum) & ":"; sngSum

    For intI = 1 To 10000
        dblSum = dblSum + 0.0001
    Next intI
    'This prints, "Double: .999999999999906"
    Debug.Print TypeName(dblSum) & ":"; dblSum
End Sub
```

The TestFloatingPoints procedure, in Listing 2.1, sums the value 0.0001 in a loop, repeating 10,000 times. The code attempts this first using a Single variable, and then again using a Double. The result, in a perfect world, would be 1.0 in both cases. As you find, if you run the procedure, the result for the Single variable is a little greater than 1, and the result for the Double variable is a little less than 1. If nothing else, this procedure demonstrates two ways errors can occur. The first problem is that rounding can cause mathematical operations to produce incorrect results. The second problem is that the same operation can produce different results depending on the floating-point data type that is used. Not only did the use of Single and Double data types both produce wrong numbers, but the wrong numbers were not even the same wrong numbers! This means that if you compare a Single number to a Double number and test for equality, the test may fail even if the numbers seem like they should be equal.

To make this situation even more maddening, some floating-point rounding errors can remain completely hidden when the numbers are displayed, and some equality test results can defy the laws of logic. For example, in the code shown in Listing 2.2, dbl1 equals sng1, sng1 equals sng2, sng2 equals dbl2, but dbl1 does not equal dbl2!

Listing 2.2: Rounding Errors Cause Erroneous Inequality

```
Public Sub TestEquality()
    Dim sng1 As Single
    Dim sng2 As Single
    Dim dbl1 As Double
    Dim dbl2 As Double

    sng1 = 69.82
    sng2 = 69.2 + 0.62
    dbl1 = 69.82
    dbl2 = 69.2 + 0.62

    'This prints: "sng1 = 69.82, sng2 = 69.82"
    Debug.Print "sng1 = " & sng1 & ", sng2 = " & sng2

    'This prints: "dbl1 = 69.82, dbl2 = 69.82"
    Debug.Print "dbl1 = " & dbl1 & ", dbl2 = " & dbl2

    'This prints: "dbl1 = sng1: True"
    Debug.Print "dbl1 = sng1: "; (dbl1 = sng1)

    'This prints: "sng1 = sng2: True"
    Debug.Print "sng1 = sng2: "; (sng1 = sng2)

    'This prints: "sng2 = dbl2: True"
```

```
        Debug.Print "sng2 = dbl2: "; (sng2 = dbl2)

        'This prints: "dbl1 = dbl2: False" !!!
        Debug.Print "dbl1 = dbl2: "; (dbl1 = dbl2)

        ' Strip off the whole number portion.
        dbl1 = dbl1 - 69
        dbl2 = dbl2 - 69
        sng1 = sng1 - 69
        sng2 = sng2 - 69

        ' You'll be amazed!
        ' This prints: "sng1:  0.8199997 "
        Debug.Print "sng1: "; sng1

        ' This prints: "sng2:  0.8199997"
        ' No wonder the inequality fails!
        Debug.Print "sng2: "; sng2
        ' This prints: "dbl1:  0.819999999999993"
        Debug.Print "dbl1: "; dbl1

        ' This prints: "dbl2:  0.820000000000007"
        ' No wonder the inequality fails!
        Debug.Print "dbl2: "; dbl2
    End Sub
```

In the section "Rounding Numbers" later in this chapter, you'll find algorithms you can use to round floating-point numbers to the level of precision you need. By using these functions, you can avoid the hidden rounding errors that were discussed in this section. Another way to avoid these errors is to use the scaled integer data types whenever possible, as described in the next section.

Scaled Integers

Rounding errors can occur when you're working with decimal fractions that don't have exact binary equivalents. The Currency and Decimal data types use a method called *integer scaling* to avoid these errors. This method relies on the fact that all decimal *whole* numbers do indeed have exact binary equivalents. Even though the same can't be said for fractions in base 10, any decimal *integer* value can be exactly represented as some combination of powers of 2. Scaled integers convert decimal fractions to whole numbers before storing them in binary form, by multiplying them by a number large enough to eliminate the decimal point.

The Currency Data Type

You can use the Currency data type to store any number that falls within its range and has no more than four decimal places. The number is multiplied internally by 10,000, thereby eliminating the need for the decimal point, and then stored in binary form as an integer. This prevents the rounding errors that can occur when decimal fractions are stored as binary floating-point numbers. The procedure shown in Listing 2.3 demonstrates how using the Currency data type can solve problems with floating-point data types.

Listing 2.3: Solve Rounding Errors with the Currency Data Type

```
Sub TestCurrency()
    Dim intI As Integer
    Dim dblSum As Double
    Dim curSum As Currency

    For intI = 1 To 10000
        dblSum = dblSum + 0.0001
    Next intI
    'This prints "Double: .999999999999906"
    Debug.Print TypeName(dblSum) & ":"; dblSum

    For intI = 1 To 10000
        curSum = curSum + 0.0001
    Next intI
    'This prints "Currency: 1"
    Debug.Print TypeName(curSum) & ":"; curSum
End Sub
```

The "Hidden" Decimal Data Type

Although it's not easy to find, VBA includes one more numeric data type: Decimal. The Decimal data type was introduced in version 5.0 of VBA and still hasn't reached full data type standing. As you'll see, you cannot declare a variable "As Decimal."

Using 12 bytes, the Decimal data type extends the advantages of the Currency data type to numbers that can be much larger and more precise than Currency values. The range of values you can store using the Decimal data type is variable and depends on the number of decimal places of precision you need. As more decimal places are required, the available range gets smaller. At one extreme, you can store a number with 28 decimal places, but the number would have to fall within the very narrow range between approximately −8 and 8. At the other extreme, if you're working with whole numbers that require no decimal places, huge positive and negative values can be stored. At this time, you can use the Decimal data type only with variables that are declared as Variants, which can hold anything you care to stuff into them. It's not now possible to directly declare a variable as Decimal: You must use the CDec function to specifically cast a Variant value into this particular data type. The procedure shown in Listing 2.4 illustrates how you can use the CDec function to create a Decimal Variant and avoid floating-point errors.

Listing 2.4: Use the New Decimal Variant Subtype

```
Public Sub TestDecimal()
    Dim intI As Integer
    Dim dblSum As Double
    Dim varDblSum As Variant
    Dim varDecSum As Variant

    For intI = 1 To 10000
        dblSum = dblSum + 0.0001
    Next intI
    'This prints, "Double: .999999999999906"
    Debug.Print TypeName(dblSum) & ":"; dblSum

    For intI = 1 To 10000
        varDblSum = varDblSum + 0.0001
    Next intI
    'This prints, "Variant Double: 0.999999999999906"
    Debug.Print "Variant " & TypeName(varDblSum) & ":"; varDblSum

    For intI = 1 To 10000
        varDecSum = varDecSum + CDec(0.0001)
    Next intI
    'This prints,"Variant Decimal: 1"
    Debug.Print "Variant " & TypeName(varDecSum) & ":"; varDecSum
End Sub
```

TIP Because of the hidden errors floating-point data types can introduce, you should always use the scaled integer data types when you can. They are slightly less efficient in their use of memory because they need more bytes of storage, but your code will be more efficient if you avoid the need to use special code to handle rounding.

Using Built-In Numeric Functions

VBA provides a large variety of built-in numeric functions. This section presents these functions, broken into several categories. The remainder of the chapter provides techniques and algorithms for performing more complex computations and a few tasks that are not covered by the built-in functions.

NOTE In addition to functions that manipulate numeric values, VBA also includes functions for formatting numeric data (FormatNumber, FormatCurrency, and so on). Chapter 1 covers these in detail.

Mathematical and Trigonometric Functions

Table 2.3 lists the built-in VBA mathematical and trigonometric functions. Each of these takes an argument, called *number* in the table, which can be any valid numeric expression.

TABLE 2.3:   Mathematical and Trigonometric Functions in VBA

Function	Description	Syntax
Atn	Returns a Double specifying the angle that is the arctangent of a number in radians	Atn(*number*), where *number* is the ratio between two sides of a right triangle
Cos	Returns a Double specifying the ratio that is the cosine of an angle	Cos(*number*), where *number* is an angle in radians
Sin	Returns a Double specifying the ratio that is the sine of an angle	Sin(*number*), where *number* is an angle in radians

TABLE 2.3: Mathematical and Trigonometric Functions in VBA *(continued)*

Function	Description	Syntax
Tan	Returns a Double specifying the ratio that is the tangent of an angle	Tan(*number*), where *number* is an angle in radians
Exp	Returns a Double specifying *e* (the base of natural logarithms) raised to a power	Exp(*number*). If the value of *number* exceeds 709.782712893, an error sometimes referred to as the antilogarithm occurs.
Log	Returns a Double specifying the natural logarithm of a number	Log(*number*), where *number* is any valid expression greater than 0
Sqr	Returns a Double specifying the square root of a number	Sqr(*number*), where *number* is any valid expression greater than or equal to 0
Sgn	Returns a Variant (integer) indicating the sign of a number	Sgn(*number*), where *number* is any valid numeric expression

Trigonometry is the mathematics of right triangles. It allows you to calculate angles by knowing the ratio between the lengths of two sides of a right triangle or to calculate the ratios by knowing the angles. VBA uses radians as the unit of measure for angles. Because 180 degrees equal π (pi) radians (π being roughly 3.14159265358979), you can convert degrees to radians by multiplying degrees by $\pi/180$, and you can convert radians to degrees by multiplying radians by $180/\pi$. The functions we created to handle these conversions are shown in Listing 2.5 and use a reasonably precise approximation of π. Note the explicit conversion of the argument to the Decimal Variant subtype. This increases the accuracy of the calculation.

Listing 2.5: Radian-to-Degree Conversion Functions

```
Public Function dhDegToRad(varDegrees As Variant) As Variant
    ' Converts degrees to radians
    Const PI = 3.14159265358979
    dhDegToRad = (CDec(varDegrees) / 180) * PI
End Function

Public Function dhRadToDeg(varRadians As Variant) As Variant
    ' Converts radians to degrees
    Const PI = 3.14159265358979
    dhRadToDeg = (CDec(varRadians) / PI) * 180
End Function
```

Logarithmic Functions

VBA's logarithmic functions use natural logarithms. The natural logarithm is the logarithm to the base e, where the constant e is approximately 2.718282. You can calculate base–n logarithms for any number x by dividing the natural logarithm of x by the natural logarithm of n as follows:

```
Log_n(x) = Log(x) / Log(n)
```

The following function, dhLogN, converts any decimal number to a logarithm with any base. Of course, because base 10 is the most common logarithmic scale, the base is optional and defaults to 10:

```
Public Function dhLogN(varDecimal As Variant, _
 Optional varLogBase As Variant = 10) As Variant
    dhLogN = CDec(Log(varDecimal) / Log(varLogBase))
End Function
```

> **TIP**
>
> In case the theory of logarithms has escaped you temporarily, $Log_{10}(x)$ returns the power you'd have to raise 10 to, in order to end up with x. For example, $Log_{10}(100)$ is 2, and $Log_{10}(1000)$ is 3. In the same vein, $Log_8(64)$ is 2, and $Log_{64}(8)$ is 0.5. The dhLogN function performs these types of calculations for you.

Just as VBA's Log function returns the natural log of a number (that is, the power you'd need to raise the value **e** to, in order to end up with the argument), it also provides the inverse function, Exp. The Exp function returns the value **e** to the specified power. For example, Exp(2) returns e * e, or 7.38905609893065. When working with advanced trigonometric formulas, or working with chemistry or physics, these functions can be important.

Determining Sign

The Sgn function returns an integer indicating whether its argument is positive, negative, or 0. It returns +1 if its argument was positive, –1 if its argument was negative, or 0 (if its argument was 0). For example, Sgn(3) returns 1, Sgn(–3) returns –1, and Sgn(3 – 3) returns 0.

> **WARNING**
>
> As with any of the mathematical functions that take numeric expressions as arguments, if you pass Sgn a null value, you'll get back a runtime error (error 94, "Invalid use of Null").

Derived Trigonometric Functions

VBA doesn't supply every possible useful trigonometric function, but you can combine the built-in trigonometric functions to create more complex functions. Table 2.4 shows the formulas you can use to derive these more complex functions from the ones VBA provides.

T A B L E   2 . 4 :   Derived Trigonometric Functions

Function	Derived Equivalents
Secant	Sec(X) = 1 / Cos(X)
Cosecant	Cosec(X) = 1 / Sin(X)
Cotangent	Cotan(X) = 1 / Tan(X)
Inverse Sine	Arcsin(X) = Atn(X / Sqr(–X * X + 1))
Inverse Cosine	Arccos(X) = Atn(–X / Sqr(–X * X + 1)) + 2 * Atn(1)
Inverse Secant	Arcsec(X) = Atn(X / Sqr(X * X – 1)) + Sgn((X) – 1) * (2 * Atn(1))
Inverse Cosecant	Arccosec(X) = Atn(X / Sqr(X * X – 1)) + (Sgn(X) – 1) * (2 * Atn(1))
Inverse Cotangent	Arccotan(X) = Atn(X) + 2 * Atn(1)
Hyperbolic Sine	HSin(X) = (Exp(X) – Exp(–X)) / 2
Hyperbolic Cosine	HCos(X) = (Exp(X) + Exp(–X)) / 2
Hyperbolic Tangent	HTan(X) = (Exp(X) – Exp(–X)) / (Exp(X) + Exp(–X))
Hyperbolic Secant	HSec(X) = 2 / (Exp(X) + Exp(–X))
Hyperbolic Cosecant	HCosec(X) = 2 / (Exp(X) – Exp(–X))
Hyperbolic Cotangent	HCotan(X) = (Exp(X) + Exp(–X)) / (Exp(X) – Exp(–X))
Inverse Hyperbolic Sine	HArcsin(X) = Log(X + Sqr(X * X + 1))
Inverse Hyperbolic Cosine	HArccos(X) = Log(X + Sqr(X * X – 1))
Inverse Hyperbolic Tangent	HArctan(X) = Log((1 + X) / (1 – X)) / 2
Inverse Hyperbolic Secant	HArcsec(X) = Log((Sqr(–X * X + 1) + 1) / X)
Inverse Hyperbolic Cosecant	HArccosec(X) = Log((Sgn(X) * Sqr(X * X + 1) + 1) / X)
Inverse Hyperbolic Cotangent	HArccotan(X) = Log((X + 1) / (X – 1)) / 2

Here's an example of how you can use the formulas in Table 2.4 to create your own custom trigonometric functions:

```
Public Function dhHyperbolicSine(ByVal dblNumber As Double) As Variant
    ' Calculates hyperbolic sine using the Exp function
    dhHyperbolicSine = (CDec(Exp(dblNumber)) - CDec(Exp(-dblNumber))) _
    / 2
End Function
```

Numeric Conversions and Rounding

As mentioned earlier in this chapter, the various numeric data types differ in the levels of precision they support. Therefore, rounding often occurs automatically when you convert a number from one data type to another. Sometimes that's the reason you want to convert to a different data type—to round the number. However, there are other ways of rounding, and sometimes you'll want to use them without having to resort to converting the number to a different data type. This section describes the built-in numeric conversion functions VBA provides, how you can use them for rounding, and how you'll sometimes need other rounding algorithms to get the results you want.

Conversion Functions

Table 2.5 lists the VBA functions that perform numeric conversions from one data type to another. Decimal to hexadecimal and decimal to octal conversions are discussed in the section "Base Conversions" later in this chapter.

TABLE 2.5: Numeric Conversion Functions

Function	Returns	Rounding
CByte(*expression*)	Byte (range 0–255)	To whole number; 0.5 rounded to nearest even number
CInt(*expression*)	Integer	To whole number; 0.5 rounded to nearest even number
CLng(*expression*)	Long Integer	To whole number; 0.5 rounded to nearest even number
CCur(*expression*)	Currency	To four decimal places; rounding to five decimal places is undocumented (See the "Rounding Numbers" section for more information.)

TABLE 2.5: Numeric Conversion Functions *(continued)*

Function	Returns	Rounding
CDec(*expression*)	Decimal Variant	To a variable number of decimal places depending on the size of the number
CSng(*expression*)	Single	To the nearest floating-point number in the range
CDbl(*expression*)	Double	To the nearest floating-point number in the range
CVar(*expression*)	Variant Double if numeric; Variant Date/Time if delimited by #; Variant String otherwise	Same as Double for numeric values

The *expression* argument that's passed to any of the numeric conversion functions can be any valid numeric or string expression. String expressions must be interpretable as numbers using the conventions of the installed locale. For example, CLng("–34,734.687") would return –34735 in locales that use commas as thousand separators. If *expression* doesn't fall within the acceptable range for that data type, a runtime error occurs (error 13, "Type mismatch," or error 6, "Overflow").

WARNING You can also use another VBA function, Val, to convert expressions to numbers. However, there's an important disadvantage to using Val for this purpose. Unlike the conversion functions in Table 2.5, Val does not provide internationally aware conversions. Different decimal separators, thousands separators, and currency options will be correctly recognized by the conversion functions according to the *locale* setting of your computer. However, Val doesn't have the ability to use the computer's locale setting and therefore may not recognize numbers that were typed using standards other than those used in the United States.

Rounding Numbers

The CInt and CLng functions, used to convert to the Integer and Long Integer data types, round fractions to whole numbers. They'll sometimes round up and sometimes round down when passed numbers ending in .5. The rounding in these cases will always result in an even number. For example, CInt(1.5) evaluates to 2, and CInt(2.5) also evaluates to 2.

The CCur function, which converts a number to the Currency data type, rounds numbers to four decimal places of precision. Unfortunately, Microsoft hasn't documented the rule used in rounding Currency values that have five digits to the right of the decimal place, where the fifth digit is a 5. Sometimes these numbers are rounded up, and sometimes they're rounded down. The examples in Table 2.6 demonstrate that there is no clear pattern to this undocumented rounding behavior.

TABLE 2.6:   Unpredictable Currency Rounding

Type in Immediate Window	Result
?CCur(.00005)	0.0001
?CCur(.00015)	0.0001
?CCur(.00025)	0.0003
?CCur(.00035)	0.0003
?CCur(.00045)	0.0004
?CCur(.00095)	0.0009
?CCur(.00995)	0.01
?CCur(.00895)	0.0089
?CCur(.01895)	0.019

Because such seemingly random rounding behavior might not be reliable enough for your computations, you may want to round numbers yourself to a specified number of decimal places instead of letting VBA do it with the CCur function. A little later in this section, you'll see the dhRound custom function, which you can use to round values predictably to a specified number of decimal places.

Two VBA functions, Int(*number*) and Fix(*number*), remove the fractional part of a number. They don't round the number; they just chop off the part to the right of the decimal place. Both functions return an Integer if the result falls within the Integer range (−32,768 to 32,767) and a Long if the result is outside the Integer range but within the Long range (−2,147,483,648 to 2,147,483,647). It doesn't matter which of these functions you use for positive numbers, but for negative numbers, you have to remember that Int returns the first negative Integer less than or equal to *number*, whereas Fix returns the first negative Integer greater than or equal to *number*. Table 2.7 shows the output of Int and Fix in the Immediate window.

TABLE 2.7: Using Int and Fix

Type in Immediate Window	Result
?Int(–9.4)	–10
?Fix(–9.4)	–9
?Int(9.6)	9
?Fix(9.6)	9

NOTE   Fix(*number*) is equivalent to Sgn(*number*) * Int(Abs(*number*)).

Beware of using Int with expressions. Doing so will sometimes yield unanticipated results. For example, Int((1.55 * 10) + 0.5) evaluates to 16, as you would expect. However, Int((2.55 * 10) + 0.5) evaluates to 25, even though you would expect it to evaluate to 26. (Why? It turns out that 2.55 * 10 is actually slightly less than 25.5, because of binary round-off issues. Then, when you add 0.5, the result is slightly less than 26. The Int function truncates the result, which ends up being 25.) For this reason, it's best to set your expression equal to a variable first and then pass the variable to Int, as the procedure shown in Listing 2.6 illustrates.

Listing 2.6: Use a Variable to Control the Int Function

```
Sub TestInt()
    Dim dblNumber As Double

    ' Prints: "25"
    Debug.Print Int((2.55 * 10) + 0.5)

    dblNumber = (2.55 * 10) + 0.5
    ' Prints: "26"
    Debug.Print Int(dblNumber)
End Sub
```

As discussed earlier in this chapter, rounding often presents problems with floating-point numbers because some decimal numbers are rounded unpredictably when converted to floating-point binary numbers. VBA has finally added a

Round function, in the most current incarnation of the language, but it still has a few flaws:

- Numbers supposedly round to the nearest even value. That is, Round(9.585, 2) is supposed to return 9.58, and Round(9.595, 2) is supposed to return 9.60. Contrary to what everyone thinks a Round function should do, this one uses the IEEE standard, which dictates that the function should round to the nearest even value.

- Unless you supply the number to be rounded using the Decimal data type, you can't be guaranteed that the function will work correctly (such as that is, given the previous bullet point). To demonstrate this, see Figure 2.1. In that debugging session, the request to round 9.575 to two decimal places returned (incorrectly) 9.57. Rounding 9.585 to two decimal places also fails, but testing with 9.595 works fine. On the other hand, if you always convert the number to be rounded into a Decimal data type first, VBA's Round function always rounds correctly. (Again, taking into account that "correctly" means "to the nearest even value.")

- The VBA Round function does not correctly handle rounding to tens, or hundreds, and so on. The way we learned how to round numbers, if you ask to round to –2 places, your number is rounded to the 100s. That is, rounding 1234 to –1 decimals returns 1230, and rounding 1234 to –2 decimals returns 1200. The built-in Round function simply doesn't allow you to specify negative values for the number of decimals.

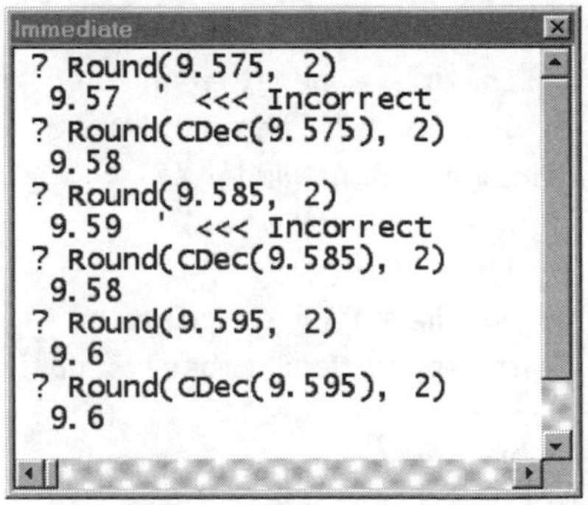

FIGURE 2.1
The built-in Round function performs somewhat erratically.

```
Immediate
? Round(9.575, 2)
 9.57  ' <<< Incorrect
? Round(CDec(9.575), 2)
 9.58
? Round(9.585, 2)
 9.59  ' <<< Incorrect
? Round(CDec(9.585), 2)
 9.58
? Round(9.595, 2)
 9.6
? Round(CDec(9.595), 2)
 9.6
```

What's going on here? Why isn't Round working as it should? It turns out that unless you specify otherwise, Round assumes that you're passing it a Double. In its use of that Double, Round must convert the value to binary and back, and in doing so, causes some inaccuracies in the least-significant decimal places. If you've ever studied computer science, you've most likely seen the standard algorithm for rounding a value to a specific number of decimal places. Listing 2.7 shows a working Round function that uses the algorithm we learned in school. (This version also allows you to pass in a True value as a third parameter indicating that you want it to use IEEE-style rounding. This way, you get the round-to-the-nearest-even-value behavior, and the function takes care of the conversion to Decimal type for you.)

Listing 2.7: A Generic Rounding Function

```
Public Function dhRound( _
  ByVal Number As Variant, NumDigits As Long, _
  Optional UseIEEERounding As Boolean = False) As Double
    ' Rounds a number to a specified number of decimal
    ' places. 0.5 is rounded up

    Dim dblPower As Double
    Dim varTemp As Variant
    Dim intSgn As Integer

    If Not IsNumeric(Number) Then
        ' Raise an error indicating that
        ' you've supplied an invalid parameter.
        Err.Raise 5
    End If
    dblPower = 10 ^ NumDigits
    ' Is this a negative number, or not?
    ' intSgn will contain -1, 0, or 1.
    intSgn = Sgn(Number)
    Number = Abs(Number)

    ' Do the major calculation.
    varTemp = CDec(Number) * dblPower + 0.5

    ' Now round to nearest even, if necessary.
    If UseIEEERounding Then
        If Int(varTemp) = varTemp Then
            ' You could also use:
            ' varTemp = varTemp + (varTemp Mod 2 = 1)
            ' instead of the next If ...Then statement,
```

```
            ' but we hate counting on True == -1 in code.
            If varTemp Mod 2 = 1 Then
                varTemp = varTemp - 1
            End If
        End If
    End If
    ' Finish the calculation.
    dhRound = intSgn * Int(varTemp) / dblPower
End Function
```

TIP

You can round numbers to whole digit places (for example, round 1234 to 1200) by specifying a negative value for the number of places. That is, specifying 0 for NumDigits rounds to the ones place, −1 rounds to tens, −2 rounds to hundreds, and −3 rounds to thousands.

NOTE

If you don't care about IEEE rounding, we've also included a simplified version of dhRound in the basNumbers module (dhRoundSimple). You can use this version, if you'd rather.

Subtracting Floating-Point Numbers While Maintaining Precision

You might assume that VBA wouldn't have problems with simple subtraction, because the result of subtraction can't have more decimal places than either of the two numbers involved, but you would be wrong. Table 2.8 shows some of the surprising results in the Immediate window for subtracting various decimal values, all of which look like they ought to result in 0.1. To avoid errors in subtraction, you need to first prepare your values, either by rounding to the correct number of digits, or by using the CDec function to convert to the special Decimal data type.

TABLE 2.8: Errors in Floating-Point Subtraction

Type in Immediate Window	Result
?100.8−100.7	9.99999999999943E−02
?10.8−10.7	0.100000000000001
?1.8−1.7	0.1

You can safely subtract one floating-point value from another by using the Decimal data type. We created a subtraction function, shown in Listing 2.8, that overcomes the rounding error.

Listing 2.8: Use Decimal Variants for Subtraction

```
Public Function dhSubtract(varVal1 As Variant, _
    varVal2 As Variant) As Double
      dhSubtract = CDec(varVal1) - CDec(varVal2)
End Function
```

Random Numbers

The subject of generating random numbers often causes confusion. First, there's the Randomize statement:

> Randomize [*number*]

Then there's the Rnd function:

> Rnd[(*number*)]

Why two functions? Which one do you use?

VBA generates random numbers by starting with a seed value and then running that seed through a proprietary algorithm that creates a number greater than or equal to 0 and less than 1. Starting with a particular seed will always result in exactly the same "random" number. The VBA Randomize statement initializes the Rnd function by creating a new seed value. If you don't use the optional argument for Randomize, the new seed value is based on the system timer.

If you elect not to use Randomize at all and just call the Rnd function with no arguments, Rnd always uses the same number as a seed the first time it's called. Each subsequent time Rnd is called during that session, it uses the number that was generated by the last call as its new seed. So, unless you use Randomize or supply an argument to Rnd, you'll always get the same sequence of numbers. The *number* argument passed to Rnd affects the value that's returned, as summarized in Table 2.9.

TABLE 2.9: Pass an Argument to Rnd

Rnd Argument	Number Generated by Rnd
< 0	The same number every time, depending on the negative argument used
> 0	Next random number in the sequence, regardless of the positive argument used
= 0	Repeats the most recently generated number
Not supplied	Next random number in the sequence (same as with a positive argument)

The number returned by Rnd is a Single value that's greater than or equal to 0 and less than 1. If you want to create random integers within a certain range of values, you can use the following formula:

$$i = Int((\textit{<high number>} - \textit{<low number>} + 1) * Rnd) + \textit{<low number>}$$

For example, if you want to create a random number between 1 and 10, the expression would look like this:

```
i = Int((10 - 1 + 1) * Rnd) + 1
```

Using 10 as the upper bound won't give you a very wide range of numbers, and after running this procedure a few times, you'll run into duplicates. There's a misconception that using the Randomize function in front of Rnd will eliminate duplicates, but this is not true. Randomize will only reset the random number generator so that it starts at a different place in the set of numbers it generates; nothing keeps it from returning duplicates in a given sequence. The following procedure generates a set of random numbers:

```
Dim i As Integer
Randomize
For i = 1 To 10
    Debug.Print Int(Rnd * 10) + 1;
Next i
```

The output from the Immediate window when run five times might return results like these:

```
2  7  1  2  10 4  1  10 5  7
6  2  8  1  8  5  2  2  8  7
6  9  7  2  3  10 6  10 4  2
5  9  6  8  5  4  4  10 1  6
9  5  9  3  3  7  2  9  5  6
```

What this means is that if you want to avoid duplicates in a list of integers, you have to keep track of them yourself. We've provided the procedure shown in Listing 2.9 to shuffle numbers from 1 to 10, producing a random list of the 10 integers with no duplicates.

Listing 2.9: Generate Random Numbers with No Duplicates

```
Public Function dhRandomShuffle(Optional lngItems As Long = 10) _
As Long()
    Dim alngValues() As Long
    Dim i As Long
    Dim lngPos As Long
    Dim lngTemp As Long

    ReDim alngValues(1 To lngItems)

    ' Fill in the original values.
    For i = 1 To lngItems
        alngValues(i) = i
    Next i

    ' Loop through all the items except the last one.
    ' Once you get to the last item, there's no point
    ' using Rnd, just get it.
    For i = lngItems To 2 Step -1
        ' Get a random number between 1 and i
        lngPos = Int(Rnd * i) + 1
        lngTemp = alngValues(lngPos)
        alngValues(lngPos) = alngValues(i)
        alngValues(i) = lngTemp
    Next i
    dhRandomShuffle = alngValues()
End Function
```

The dhRandomShuffle procedure creates an array large enough for the number of items you've requested and fills the array with the numbers from 1 up to your requested value. The procedure works its way from the end of the array back to the beginning, picking a random number between 1 and the current location in the array, and swaps the value at the selected location with the value at the current location. By the time the function has reached the beginning of the array, the numbers are in random order, and the function returns the array as its return value. Table 2.10 simulates shuffling a 10-item array.

TABLE 2.10: Simulation of Shuffling an Array (Items Swapped in the Current Step Marked in Bold)

Selected Item	1	2	3	4	5	6	7	8	9	10
4	1	2	3	**10**	5	6	7	8	9	**4**
4	1	2	3	**9**	5	6	7	8	**10**	4
1	**8**	2	3	9	5	6	7	**1**	10	4
3	8	2	**7**	9	5	6	**3**	1	10	4
2	8	**6**	7	9	5	**2**	3	1	10	4
3	8	6	**5**	9	**7**	2	3	1	10	4
2	8	**9**	5	**6**	7	2	3	1	10	4
2	8	**5**	**9**	6	7	2	3	1	10	4

To test the dhRandomShuffle procedure, we've provided the TestShuffle procedure, shown below. This procedure calls dhRandomShuffle, requesting 10 items. It takes the return value from dhRandomShuffle and iterates through all its items, printing them to the Immediate window.

```
Sub TestShuffle()
    Dim alngItems() As Long
    Dim i As Long

    alngItems = dhRandomShuffle(10)

    For i = LBound(alngItems) To UBound(alngItems)
        Debug.Print Right$(Space(4) & alngItems(i), 4);
    Next i
    Debug.Print
End Sub
```

Financial Functions

VBA provides a number of built-in functions you can use for performing financial calculations. These are divided into three basic groups: depreciation functions, annuity functions, and cash-flow functions, as described in the following sections.

Depreciation Functions

The depreciation functions are used in accounting to calculate the amount of monetary value a fixed asset loses over a period of time. For example, a business that owns a truck needs to calculate the amount the truck depreciates each year to determine the current value of the truck at any point in time. Because depreciation affects taxes, governments often mandate the depreciation formulas that can be used. For example, the double-declining method of depreciation uses the following formula:

Depreciation over period = ((cost – salvage) * 2) / life

Table 2.11 summarizes the VBA depreciation functions and their arguments, and Table 2.12 describes the arguments used in depreciation functions.

T A B L E 2 . 1 1 : Depreciation Functions

Function	Description
DDB(*cost*, *salvage*, *life*, *period*[, *factor*])	Returns a Double specifying the depreciation of an asset for a specific time period using the declining balance method
SLN(*cost*, *salvage*, *life*)	Returns a Double specifying the straight-line depreciation of an asset for a single period
SYD(*cost*, *salvage*, *life*, *period*)	Returns a Double specifying the sum-of-years' digits depreciation of an asset for a specified period

T A B L E 2 . 1 2 : Arguments Used in Depreciation Functions

Argument	Description
Cost	Initial cost of the asset
Salvage	Value of the asset at the end of its useful life
Life	Length of the useful life of the asset; must be in the same unit of measure as *Period*
Period	Period for which asset depreciation is calculated
[*Factor*]	Optional rate at which the balance declines; if omitted, 2 (double-declining method) is assumed

Annuity Functions

An annuity is a series of payments that represents either the return on an investment or the amortization of a loan. Negative numbers represent monies paid out, like contributions to savings or loan payments. Positive numbers represent monies received, like dividends. Tables 2.13 and 2.14 summarize the VBA annuity functions and their arguments.

TABLE 2.13: Annuity Functions

Function	Description
FV(*rate, nper, pmt*[, *pv*[, *type*]])	Returns a Double specifying the future value of an annuity based on periodic fixed payments and a fixed interest rate
Rate(*nper, pmt, pv*[, *fv*[, *type*[, *guess*]]])	Returns a Double specifying the interest rate per period for an annuity
NPer(*rate, pmt, pv*[, *fv*[, *type*]])	Returns a Double specifying the number of periods for an annuity
IPmt(*rate, per, nper, pv*[, *fv*[, *type*]])	Returns a Double specifying the interest payment for a given period of an annuity
Pmt(*rate, nper, pv*[, *fv*[, *type*]])	Returns a Double specifying the payment for an annuity
PPmt(*rate, per, nper, pv*[, *fv*[, *type*]])	Returns a Double specifying the principal payment for a given period of an annuity
PV(*rate, nper, pmt*[, *fv*[, *type*]])	Returns a Double specifying the present value of an annuity based on periodic fixed payments to be paid in the future at a fixed interest rate

TABLE 2.14: Arguments Used in Annuity Functions

Argument	Description
Rate	Interest rate per period; must use the same unit for *Period* as used for Nper
Nper	Total number of payment periods in the annuity
Pmt	Payment to be made each period
Pv	Present value (or lump sum) that a series of payments to be paid in the future is worth now
[Fv]	Optional value of the annuity after the final payment has been made (if omitted, 0 is assumed, which is the usual future value of a loan)
[Type]	Optional number indicating when payments are due: 0 if payments are due at the end of the payment period and 1 if payments are due at the beginning of the period; if omitted, 0 is assumed

We created a procedure, shown in Listing 2.10, that uses the Pmt function to calculate the monthly payment on a loan.

Listing 2.10: Calculate the Payment on a Loan

```
Public Function dhCalcPayment(ByVal dblRate As Double, _
ByVal intNoPmts As Integer, _
ByVal curPresentValue As Currency, _
Optional varFutureVal As Variant = 0, _
Optional varWhenDue As Variant = 0) As Double
    ' Calculates payments using Pmt function
    If varWhenDue <> 0 Then
        ' set to only other possible value
        ' of 1 indicating payment to occur
        ' at beginning of period
        varWhenDue = 1
    End If
    dhCalcPayment = Pmt((dblRate / 12), intNoPmts, _
      -CDbl(curPresentValue), varFutureVal, varWhenDue)
End Function
```

Cash-Flow Functions

The cash-flow functions perform financial calculations based on a series of periodic payments and receipts. As with the annuity functions, negative numbers represent payments and positive numbers represent receipts. However, unlike the annuity functions, the cash-flow functions allow you to list varying amounts for the payments or receipts over the course of the loan or investment. Payments and receipts can even be mixed up within the cash-flow series.

Tables 2.15 and 2.16 summarize the VBA cash-flow functions and their arguments.

TABLE 2.15: Cash-Flow Functions

Function	Description
IRR(*values*()[, *guess*])	Returns a Double specifying the internal rate of return for a series of periodic cash flows
MIRR(*values*(), *finance_rate*, *reinvest_rate*)	Returns a Double specifying the modified internal rate of return for a series of periodic cash flows
NPV(*rate*, *values*())	Returns a Double specifying the net present value of an investment based on a series of periodic cash flows and a discount rate

TABLE 2.16: Arguments Used in Cash-Flow Functions

Argument	Description
Values()	Array of cash-flow values; the array must contain at least one negative value (a payment) and one positive value (a receipt)
Rate	Discount rate over the length of the period, expressed as a decimal
Finance_rate	Interest rate paid as the cost of financing
Reinvest_rate	Interest rate received on gains from cash reinvestment
[Guess]	Optional value you estimate will be returned; if omitted, *Guess* is 0.1 (10 percent)

In order to look at how Net Present Value (NPV) and Internal Rate of Return (IRR) work, you must understand how Discount Rate works. Take an example where the rate of interest for a particular investment is 20 percent. The discount rate is $1/(1 + 20/100)$ or 0.8333 in the first year; in the second year it would be $(1/(1 + 20/100)) \wedge 2$ or 0.6944.

The NPV function, in effect, gives an evaluation of the profitability of an investment. Imagine that a company was looking at buying a machine for $17,000, they predicted the machine would make money for them at the rate of $6,000 per year, and they expect a yield of 20 percent from their investment. This would produce results as shown in Table 2.17.

TABLE 2.17: Cash Flows for an NPV Exercise

Year	Cash Flow	Discount Rate (20% Interest)	NPV of Cash Flows
1	6000	0.833333333333333	5000
2	6000	0.694444444444444	4166.66666666666
3	6000	0.578703703703703	3472.22222222222
4	6000	0.482253086419752	2893.51851851851
5	6000	0.40187757201646	2411.26543209876
Totals	30000		17943.672839506

This tells them that purchasing the machine would be a profitable exercise (because 17943 − 17000 is greater than 0). If, on the other hand, the machine had cost $18,000, the company would have lost money in the future (because 17943 − 18000 is less than 0). The function provided in Listing 2.11 illustrates how you can use the NPV function to calculate the net present value of a business investment.

Listing 2.11: Calculate the Net Present Value of an Investment

```
Public Function dhNetPresentValue(ByVal dblRate As Double, _
  ParamArray varCashFlows()) As Double
    ' Calculates net present value
    Dim varElement As Variant
    Dim i As Integer
    Dim lngUBound As Long
    Static dblValues() As Double

    ' get upper bound of ParamArray
    lngUBound = UBound(varCashFlows)
    ' size array to ParamArray
    ReDim dblValues(lngUBound)
    i = 0
    ' place elements of ParamArray into Array
    For Each varElement In varCashFlows
        dblValues(i) = varElement
        i = i + 1
    Next
    dhNetPresentValue = NPV(dblRate, dblValues())
End Function
```

The IRR cash-flow function uses multiple iterations to arrive at its final return value. It starts with the value, *Guess,* and continues running calculations until it achieves a result that's accurate to within 0.00001 percent. If a satisfactory result hasn't been reached after 20 attempts, the function fails.

The IRR function takes the cash-flow information provided in the Values array and attempts to find the discount rate where cash-flow-in matches cash-flow-out. The higher the discount rate returned by IRR, the more profitable the investment.

As an example of this, imagine that a firm was considering the purchase of two different machines (Machine D and Machine E): Machine D costs $80,000 to purchase, and Machine E costs $90,000 to purchase.

Table 2.18 shows the predicted cash flows for the two machines and the discount rate returned by the IRR function, based on the predicted cash flows.

TABLE 2.18:   Cash Flows for an IRR Exercise

	Machine D	Machine E
Purchase	−80000	−90000
Year 1	40000	40000
Year 2	30000	40000
Year 3	30000	35000
Year 4	25000	30000
Year 5	5000	8000
IRR	*0.2384 (23.84%)*	*0.2527 (25.27%)*

This indicates that although Machine E costs more, its profitability outweighs that of Machine D and would therefore be the better purchase.

Base Conversions

To convert numbers between base 16 (hexadecimal), base 8 (octal), and base 10 (decimal), your best bet is to use the built-in VBA functions Hex, Oct, and CLng, which are summarized in Table 2.19.

TABLE 2.19:   Base Conversion Functions

Function	Description
Hex(*number*)	Returns a String representing the hexadecimal value of a number
Oct(*number*)	Returns a Variant representing the octal value of a number, up to 11 octal characters. Returns Null if the number is Null, 0 if the number is Empty (Only a Variant that has not been initialized is Empty.)
CLng(*string*)	Returns Double numeric values that are contained in a string, including Hexadecimal and Octal values that use the radix prefixes, &H and &O

Hexadecimal and Octal Conversion

The Hex and Oct functions return a string with the hexadecimal or octal value in it. However, the radix prefixes, &H and &O, are not added to the string. For example, Hex(255) returns "FF," not "&HFF," which is how you would represent the number in code. If you ever want to convert to hexadecimal or octal and then back to decimal, be sure to add the prefix that a VBA conversion function like CLng will need to recognize the number, as illustrated in Table 2.20.

TABLE 2.20: Converting to Hex and Back to Decimal

Type in Immediate Window	Result
?Hex(255)	FF
?CLng(Hex(255))	Error 13 (type mismatch)
?CLng("&H" & Hex(255))	255

NOTE   The Hex function rounds fractions to the nearest whole number before performing the conversion. For example, Hex(256) returns 100, and Hex(256.4) also returns 100. Although it's possible to represent fractional data in hexadecimal format (see the dhDecToHex function in the sample), there's no practical reason to do so. VBA conversion functions like CLng recognize only whole hexadecimal numbers.

Binary Conversions

VBA doesn't include any built-in binary conversion functions. The custom functions shown in Listing 2.12 can be used to convert hexadecimal numbers to binary (base 2) numbers, to convert binary to hexadecimal, and to convert decimal numbers to binary.

Each of these functions does its work in a slightly different manner:

- The dhHexToBinary function works its way through each "digit" of the Hex value and uses a Select Case statement to convert each digit (0 through F) into its corresponding four binary bits.

- The dhBinaryToHex function does the opposite. Once it's padded the original binary string with enough leading zeros so that the number of digits is divisible by four, it takes each four-digit chunk and uses Select Case to convert the chunk back to the corresponding hex digit.

- The dhBinaryToDec function takes advantage of the dhBinaryToHex function. Once the input value's converted to Hex, the procedure uses the CLng function to convert from hex to decimal.

- The dhDecToBinary function first uses the built-in Hex function to convert the decimal value to Hex. Then, it calls the dhHexToBinary procedure to convert to binary and removes any leading zeros.

Listing 2.12: Binary Conversion Functions

```
Public Function dhHexToBinary(strNumber As String) As String
    Dim strTemp As String
    Dim strOut As String
    Dim i As Integer
    For i = 1 To Len(strNumber)
        Select Case Mid(strNumber, i, 1)
            Case "0"
                strTemp = "0000"
            Case "1"
                strTemp = "0001"
            Case "2"
                strTemp = "0010"
            Case "3"
                strTemp = "0011"
            Case "4"
                strTemp = "0100"
            Case "5"
                strTemp = "0101"
            Case "6"
                strTemp = "0110"
            Case "7"
                strTemp = "0111"
            Case "8"
                strTemp = "1000"
            Case "9"
                strTemp = "1001"
            Case "A"
                strTemp = "1010"
            Case "B"
                strTemp = "1011"
            Case "C"
                strTemp = "1100"
            Case "D"
                strTemp = "1101"
            Case "E"
                strTemp = "1110"
            Case "F"
                strTemp = "1111"
            Case Else
```

```
                        ' This can't happen, right?
                        strTemp = ""
            End Select
            strOut = strOut & strTemp
        Next i
        dhHexToBinary = strOut
End Function

Public Function dhBinarytoHex(ByVal strNumber As String) As String
    Dim strTemp As String
    Dim intI As Integer
    Dim intLen As Integer
    Dim strOut As String
    ' First, pad the value to the left, with "0".
    ' To do this, find the length of the string
    ' rounded to the next highest multiple of 4.
    intLen = Len(strNumber)
    ' Find the next higher multiple of 4:
    intLen = Int((intLen - 1) / 4 + 1) * 4
    strNumber = Right$(String(intLen, "0") & strNumber, intLen)
    ' Now walk through each group of 4 digits, converting each
    ' to hex.
    For intI = 1 To intLen Step 4
        Select Case Mid(strNumber, intI, 4)
            Case "0000"
                strTemp = "0"
            Case "0001"
                strTemp = "1"
            Case "0010"
                strTemp = "2"
            Case "0011"
                strTemp = "3"
            Case "0100"
                strTemp = "4"
            Case "0101"
                strTemp = "5"
            Case "0110"
                strTemp = "6"
            Case "0111"
                strTemp = "7"
            Case "1000"
                strTemp = "8"
            Case "1001"
                strTemp = "9"
```

```
                    Case "1010"
                        strTemp = "A"
                    Case "1011"
                        strTemp = "B"
                    Case "1100"
                        strTemp = "C"
                    Case "1101"
                        strTemp = "D"
                    Case "1110"
                        strTemp = "E"
                    Case "1111"
                        strTemp = "F"
                End Select
                strOut = strOut & strTemp
        Next intI
        dhBinarytoHex = strOut
    End Function

    Public Function dhBinaryToDec(ByVal strNumber As String) As Long
        dhBinaryToDec = CLng("&H" & dhBinarytoHex(strNumber))
    End Function

    Public Function dhDecToBinary(ByVal lngNumber As Long) As String
        Dim strTemp As String
        Dim intI As Integer
        strTemp = Hex(lngNumber)
        strTemp = dhHexToBinary(strTemp)
        ' Rip off leading 0s.
        Do While Left(strTemp, 1) = "0"
            strTemp = Mid(strTemp, 2)
        Loop
        dhDecToBinary = strTemp
    End Function
```

Custom Math and Numeric Functions

In this section we've provided several handy custom functions that perform basic mathematical and statistical calculations. You'll also find a function that converts numbers to text. These functions will save you time if you ever need the calculations they perform, but the programming techniques employed are pretty straightforward, so the functions are presented with little additional comment.

Mathematical Functions

Several mathematical functions have already been presented in this chapter. These were mostly built-in VBA functions and combinations thereof. Here are a few more that you can use in specialized situations.

Finding the Greatest Common Factor (GCF) of Two Integers

The *greatest common factor* (GCF) of two numbers is the largest number that will evenly divide into each. The function shown in Listing 2.13 accepts two arguments and computes their GCF.

Listing 2.13: Compute the Greatest Common Factor of Two Numbers

```
Public Function dhGreatestCommonFactor( _
 ByVal lngX As Long, ByVal lngY As Long) As Long

    Dim lngTemp As Long
    lngX = Abs(lngX)
    lngY = Abs(lngY)
    lngTemp = lngX Mod lngY
    Do While lngTemp > 0
        lngX = lngY
        lngY = lngTemp
        lngTemp = lngX Mod lngY
    Loop
    dhGreatestCommonFactor = lngY
End Function
```

Finding the Lowest Common Multiple (LCM) of Two Integers

A similar numeric relationship between two numbers is the *lowest common multiple* (LCM). The LCM of two numbers is the smallest number of which the two numbers are factors. Listing 2.14 shows a function that computes this.

Listing 2.14: Compute Two Numbers' Lowest Common Multiple

```
Public Function dhLowestCommonMultiple( _
 ByVal intX As Integer, ByVal intY As Integer) As Long
    ' Returns the smallest number of which both
    ' intX and intY are factors
    intX = Abs(intX)
    intY = Abs(intY)
    dhLowestCommonMultiple = _
     intY * (intX \ dhGreatestCommonFactor(intX, intY))
End Function
```

Is This Number Prime?

Prime numbers can be divided evenly only by themselves and by 1. There are many algorithms for figuring out whether a number is prime. Listing 2.15 illustrates a function that employs one of the more commonly used methods. It uses several If statements to eliminate common cases like 0, 1, 2, and other even numbers. It then uses a For...Next loop to determine the "primeness" of other numbers. Be aware that for large numbers, this function can take a bit of time to run.

Listing 2.15: Determine Whether a Number Is Prime

```
Public Function dhIsPrime(ByVal lngX As Long) As Boolean
    ' Find out whether a given number is Prime.
    ' Treats negative numbers and positive numbers
    ' the same.

    Dim intI As Integer
    Dim dblTemp As Double
    dhIsPrime = True
    lngX = Abs(lngX)

    If lngX = 0 Or lngX = 1 Then
        dhIsPrime = False
    ElseIf lngX = 2 Then
        ' dhIsPrime is already set to True.
    ElseIf (lngX Mod 2) = 0 Then
        dhIsPrime = False
```

```
        Else
            For intI = 3 To Int(Sqr(lngX)) Step 2
                dblTemp = lngX / intI
                If dblTemp = lngX \ intI Then
                    dhIsPrime = False
                    Exit Function
                End If
            Next intI
        End If
End Function
```

Geometric Calculations

There's a whole host of problems involving geometry that you can solve using VBA (computing the surface area of a sphere, for instance). If you paid attention during junior high geometry class, you probably already know how to write the required VBA code. If, on the other hand, that's just a distant memory, we've provided you with some code that will do the trick. Listing 2.16 shows these functions.

⟳ Listing 2.16: Miscellaneous Geometry Functions

```
Const PI = 3.14159265358979

Public Function dhAreaofCircle(ByVal dblRadius As Double) As Double
    ' Return the area of a circle
    dhAreaofCircle = PI * dblRadius ^ 2
End Function

Public Function dhAreaOfSphere(ByVal dblRadius As Double) As Double
    ' Return the area of a sphere
    dhAreaOfSphere = 4 * PI * dblRadius ^ 2
End Function

Public Function dhAreaOfRectangle(ByVal dblLength As Double, _
 ByVal dblWidth As Double) As Double
    ' Return the area of a rectangle
    dhAreaOfRectangle = dblLength * dblWidth
End Function

Public Function dhAreaOfTrapezoid(ByVal dblHeight As Double,
```

```
    ByVal dblSide1 As Double, _
    ByVal dblSide2 As Double) As Double
        ' Return the area of a trapezoid
        dhAreaOfTrapezoid = dblHeight * (dblSide1 + dblSide2) / 2
End Function

Public Function dhVolOfPyramid(ByVal dblHeight As Double, _
    ByVal dblBaseArea As Double) As Double
        ' Return the volume of a pyramid
        dhVolOfPyramid = dblHeight * dblBaseArea / 3
End Function

Public Function dhVolOfSphere(ByVal dblRadius As Double) As Double
        ' Return the volume of a sphere
        dhVolOfSphere = PI * (dblRadius ^ 3) * 4 / 3
End Function
```

Converting Currency Numbers to Text

If you're programming an application that writes checks, you may need to translate numbers to a textual description. For example, the value $149.56 would be translated as "one hundred forty-nine and fifty-six hundredths." The dhNumToStr function shown in Listing 2.17 demonstrates how to do this by using some of the built-in numeric functions, as well as some string functions, which were discussed in Chapter 1. Listing 2.17 also shows the dhHandleGroup function, which dhNumToStr calls.

WARNING　The dhNumToStr function uses zero-based arrays. For it to work properly, make sure you don't use the Option Base 1 statement in any module where you place this function.

Listing 2.17: Convert a Number to Descriptive Text

```
Public Function dhNumToStr(ByVal varValue As Variant) As String
        On Error GoTo HandleErrors

        Dim intTemp As Integer
        Dim varNames As Variant
```

```
Dim lngDollars As Long
Dim intCents As Integer
Dim strOut As String
Dim strTemp As String
Dim intI As Integer

If Not IsNumeric(varValue) Then Exit Function

' 999,999,999.99 is the largest possible value.
If varValue > 999999999.99 Then Exit Function
varNames = Array("", "Thousand", "Million")

varValue = Abs(varValue)
lngDollars = Int(varValue)
intCents = (varValue - lngDollars) * 100

If lngDollars > 0 Then
    ' Loop through each set of three digits,
    ' first the hundreds, then thousands, and then
    ' millions.
    Do
        intTemp = lngDollars Mod 1000
        lngDollars = Int(lngDollars / 1000)
        ' Prepend spelling of new triplet of digits to the
        ' existing output.
        If intTemp <> 0 Then
            strOut = dhHandleGroup(intTemp) & " " & _
             varNames(intI) & " " & strOut
        End If
        intI = intI + 1
    Loop While lngDollars > 0
    ' Handle the cents.
    strOut = RTrim(strOut) & " and " & _
     Format$(intCents, "00") & "/100"
End If

ExitHere:
    dhNumToStr = strOut
    Exit Function
```

```
HandleErrors:
    ' Handle all errors by returning an empty string
    strOut = ""
    Resume ExitHere
End Function

Private Function dhHandleGroup(ByVal intValue As Integer) As String
    ' Called by dhNumToStr
    Static varOnes As Variant
    Static varTens As Variant
    Dim strOut As String
    Dim intDigit As Integer

    If IsEmpty(varOnes) Then
        varOnes = Array("", "One", "Two", "Three", "Four", "Five", _
            "Six", "Seven", "Eight", "Nine", "Ten", _
            "Eleven", "Twelve", "Thirteen", "Fourteen", "Fifteen", _
            "Sixteen", "Seventeen", "Eighteen", "Nineteen", "Twenty")
    End If
    If IsEmpty(varTens) Then
        ' Elements 0 and 1 in this array aren't used.
        varTens = Array("", "", "Twenty", "Thirty", "Forty", _
            "Fifty", "Sixty", "Seventy", "Eighty", "Ninety")
    End If

    ' Get the hundreds digit, and then the rest.
    intDigit = intValue \ 100
    intValue = intValue Mod 100

    ' If there's a hundreds digit, add that now.
    If intDigit > 0 Then strOut = varOnes(intDigit) & " Hundred"

    ' Handle the tens and ones digits.
    Select Case intValue
        Case 1 To 20
            strOut = strOut & varOnes(intValue)
        Case 21 To 99
            intDigit = intValue \ 10
            intValue = intValue Mod 10
            If intDigit > 0 Then
                strOut = strOut & " " & varTens(intDigit)
            End If
```

```
        If intValue > 0 Then
            strOut = strOut & "-" & varOnes(intValue)
        End If
    End Select

    dhHandleGroup = strOut
End Function
```

Statistics

This section presents several useful statistical functions, including functions to calculate factorials, to compute various types of averages and standard deviation, and to find minimum and maximum values.

Factorials

Statistical functions often make use of factorial calculations. You can use the two functions shown in Listing 2.18 to calculate recursive and nonrecursive factorials. You may have a preference for one over the other (some people find recursion confusing or upsetting), but they both return the same values.

Listing 2.18: Compute Recursive and Nonrecursive Factorial Expressions

```
Public Function dhFactorialRecursive(intX As Integer) As Double
    If intX < 0 Or intX > 170 Then
        dhFactorialRecursive = 0
    ElseIf intX = 0 Then
        dhFactorialRecursive = 1
    Else
        dhFactorialRecursive = intX * _
          dhFactorialRecursive(intX - 1)
    End If
End Function

Public Function dhFactorial(intX As Integer) As Double
    Dim i As Integer
    Dim dblX As Double

    If intX < 0 Or intX > 170 Then
        dhFactorial = 0
```

```
        Else
            dblX = 1
            For i = 2 To intX
                dblX = dblX * i
            Next i
            dhFactorial = dblX
        End If
End Function
```

Mean, Median, Mode, and Standard Deviation of an Array

The most common statistical functions are those that determine the mean, median, mode, and standard deviation of a series of numbers. The mean is nothing more than the arithmetic average of the series. The median, on the other hand, is the number that occurs in the "middle" of the series. The mode is the number that occurs most frequently. It's usually close to the mean, but since it's one of the numbers in the series, it might not be exact. Finally, the standard deviation is a measurement of how closely numbers in the series are gathered around the mean. Listing 2.19 shows four functions that compute these values based on an array passed as an argument.

NOTE The dhArrayMedian and dhModeOfArray functions use the dhQuickSort function from Chapter 7 to sort the array prior to determining the mode. For a complete discussion of sorting, see Chapter 7.

Listing 2.19: Mean, Median, Mode, and Standard Deviation Functions

```
Public Function dhArrayAverage(varArray As Variant) As Variant
    Dim varItem As Variant
    Dim varSum As Variant
    Dim lngCount As Long

    If IsArray(varArray) Then
        For Each varItem In varArray
            varSum = varItem + varSum
            lngCount = lngCount + 1
```

```
            Next
                dhArrayAverage = varSum / lngCount
        Else
                dhArrayAverage = Null
        End If
End Function

Public Function dhArrayMedian(varArray As Variant) As Variant
        Dim varItem As Variant
        Dim varTemp As Variant
        Dim varMedian As Variant
        Dim intI As Integer
        Dim lngTemp As Long
        Dim lngLBound As Long
        Dim lngElements As Long

        If IsArray(varArray) Then
            ' Sort the array
            Call dhQuickSort(varArray)
            ' Compute the number of array elements
            ' and the index of the "middle" one

            lngLBound = LBound(varArray)
            lngElements = (UBound(varArray) - lngLBound + 1)
            ' Find the midpoint in the array. For an odd
            ' number of elements, this is easy (it's the
            ' middle one)...
            If (lngElements Mod 2) = 1 Then
                dhArrayMedian = varArray(lngLBound + _
                  (lngElements \ 2))
            Else
                ' For an even number of elements, it's the
                ' midpoint between the two middle values...
                lngTemp = ((lngElements - 1) \ 2) + lngLBound
                dhArrayMedian = ((varArray(lngTemp + 1) - _
                  varArray(lngTemp)) / 2) + varArray(lngTemp)
            End If
        Else
                dhArrayMedian = Null
        End If
End Function
```

```
Public Function dhArrayStandardDeviation(varArray As Variant) As Double
    Dim lngN As Long
    Dim dblSumX As Double
    Dim dblSumX2 As Double
    Dim dblVar As Double
    Dim intCounter As Integer

    lngN = 0
    dblSumX = 0
    dblSumX2 = 0
    For intCounter = LBound(varArray) To UBound(varArray)
        If Not IsNull(varArray(intCounter)) Then
            lngN = lngN + 1
            dblSumX = dblSumX + varArray(intCounter)
            dblSumX2 = dblSumX2 + varArray(intCounter) ^ 2
        End If
    Next intCounter

    dblVar = 0
    If lngN > 0 Then
        dblVar = (lngN * dblSumX2 - dblSumX ^ 2) / (lngN * (lngN - 1))
        If dblVar > 0 Then
            dhArrayStandardDeviation = Sqr(dblVar)
        End If
    End If
End Function

Public Function dhArrayMode(varArray As Variant) As Variant
    Dim varItem As Variant
    Dim varLast As Variant
    Dim lngCount As Long
    Dim lngOccur As Long
    Dim lngLastOccur As Long
    Dim lngTotalOccur As Long

    If IsArray(varArray) Then
        ' Sort the array so elements are in order
        Call dhQuickSort(varArray)

        ' Capture the first item
        varItem = varArray(LBound(varArray))

        ' Loop through all the elements
```

```vba
        For lngCount = LBound(varArray) To UBound(varArray)
            ' Increment the occurrence counter
            lngOccur = lngOccur + 1

            ' If the value is not the same as the last one,
            ' see if the occurrences of the last value
            ' exceed the current maximum
            If varArray(lngCount) <> varLast Then
                If lngLastOccur >= lngTotalOccur Then
                    ' If so, make it the new maximum and
                    ' capture the prior value
                    lngTotalOccur = lngLastOccur
                    varItem = varArray(lngCount - 1)
                End If

                ' Record this element as the last one visited
                varLast = varArray(lngCount)

                ' Reset the counter
                lngOccur = 0
            End If

            lngLastOccur = lngOccur
        Next

        ' Return the value with the most occurrences
        ' (make sure to check the final value)
        If lngOccur > lngTotalOccur Then
            dhArrayMode = varArray(lngCount - 1)
        Else
            dhArrayMode = varItem
        End If
    Else
        dhArrayMode = Null
    End If
End Function
```

Finding Minimum and Maximum Values

Surprisingly, VBA does not include functions for determining the minimum or maximum values in a series of numbers. It's relatively easy, however, to construct a function to do this using an array. Listing 2.20 shows two functions we've created that compute the minimum or maximum values, given an array.

Listing 2.20: Custom Maximum and Minimum Functions

```
Function dhArrayMax(varArray As Variant) As Variant
    ' Return the maximum value from an array

    Dim varItem As Variant
    Dim varMax As Variant
    Dim i As Long

    If IsArray(varArray) Then
        If UBound(varArray) = -1 Then
            dhArrayMax = Null
        Else
            varMax = varArray(UBound(varArray))
            For i = LBound(varArray) To UBound(varArray)
                varItem = varArray(i)
                If varItem > varMax Then
                    varMax = varItem
                End If
            Next i
            dhArrayMax = varMax
        End If
    Else
        dhArrayMax = Null
    End If
End Function

Function dhArrayMin(varArray As Variant) As Variant
    ' Return the minimum value from an array

    Dim varItem As Variant
    Dim varMin As Variant
    Dim i As Long

    If IsArray(varArray) Then
        If UBound(varArray) = -1 Then
            dhArrayMin = Null
        Else
            varMin = varArray(LBound(varArray))
            For i = LBound(varArray) To UBound(varArray)
                varItem = varArray(i)
```

```
            If varItem < varMin Then
                varMin = varItem
            End If
        Next i
        dhArrayMin = varMin
    End If
Else
    dhArrayMin = varArray
End If
End Function
```

Summary

VBA has many useful functions for handling numbers, but there are problems in using these functions that are not apparent on the surface. This chapter has provided an overview of the built-in functions, as well as some of the problems inherent in floating-point data types and rounding. Several handy custom functions for performing numeric calculations were also presented. Specifically, this chapter covered

- How VBA stores and computes numbers:
  - Understanding the different data types in VBA
  - Problems with floating-point numbers and how to solve them
- Built-in numeric functions:
  - Mathematical
  - Type conversion and rounding
  - Generating random numbers
  - Financial
  - Base conversions
- Custom functions:
  - Mathematical
  - Geometric
  - Converting numbers to text
  - Statistics

For similar chapters covering strings and dates, see Chapters 1 and 3, respectively.

chapter 3

Working with Dates and Times

- Understanding how date/time values are stored in VBA

- Using the built-in VBA date/time functions

- Extending the built-in functions with new generalized procedures

- Using the Windows API to manage system time and time zone issues

This chapter is devoted to providing solutions to common problems involving date and time values, including manipulating date values, finding a particular date, and working with elapsed times. Although VBA supplies a rich set of functions that help you work with date/time values, their use can be confusing, and there are many programmatic questions that require functions other than those supplied by the built-in VBA date-handling functions.

Table 3.1 lists the sample files you'll find on the accompanying CD-ROM.

TABLE 3.1: Sample Files

Filename	Description
DATETIME.XLS	Excel 2000 workbook with sample functions (contains all the modules)
DATETIME.MDB	Access 2000 database with sample functions (contains all the modules)
DATETIME.BAS	Text file with sample functions
DATETIMEADO.BAS	Sample functions, using ADO recordsets
HOLIDAYS.MDB	Access 97 database containing tblHolidays
HOLIDAYS.TXT	Exported text version of tblHolidays
HOLIDAYS.XML	XML file containing sample holiday recordset
SYSTEMTIMEINFO.CLS	Class module containing system time and time zone information properties
TESTDATETIME.BAS	Module containing test procedures
DATETIME.VBP	Visual Basic 6 project containing demo code

What Is a Date, and How Did It Get There?

All other definitions aside, to VBA, a date is an 8-byte floating-point value that can contain information indicating a specific point in time. In particular, the integer portion of the value contains a number of days since December 30, 1899. The fractional portion of the date value represents the portion of the day stored in the value. For example, if the current date is 5/22/97 at 3:00 P.M., VBA stores the value internally as 35572.625. That is, the current date is 35572 days after 12/30/1899, and 3:00 P.M. is 625/1000th of a full day. In general, you don't have to care about the storage mechanism; VBA handles the conversions gracefully to and from the internal floating-point format and the external date display.

TIP
> Note that a date/time value to VBA represents only a point in time, not an elapsed time. If you want to work with elapsed times, you'll need to write some code. We've provided procedures, discussed later in this chapter, that allow you to calculate and format elapsed times. You should never treat VBA date/time values as anything but what they are, however: simply, a point in time.

NOTE
> Perhaps it seems odd that the 0 date, to VBA, is 12/30/1899. This means that day 1 is 12/31/1899, and day 2 is 1/1/1900. Why the odd numbering? The story we heard (and this may be totally apocryphal, so don't hold us to this) is that some other company—to remain unnamed—released an extremely popular spreadsheet product before Microsoft's first spreadsheet. This other spreadsheet stored dates in the same fashion as described here, and Microsoft wanted to provide a compatible date format. The other company had designated 12/31/1899 as day 0, and 1/1/1900 as day 1. Unfortunately, the other company had neglected to notice that 1900 wasn't a leap year. (See the section titled "Is This a Leap Year?" later in the chapter for more information on why 1900 wasn't a leap year.) Microsoft developers, working on their first spreadsheet, worked to find a way so that their dates, correctly taking into account the fact that 1900 wasn't a leap year, could coincide with the dates used by their competitor. Their solution? Back up the 0 date one day, so that only the days before March 1, 1900 would be different from the competitors'. Maybe it's true; maybe it's not. It makes a good story.

An Added Benefit

Because VBA stores dates internally as serial values, you get the added benefit of being able to treat dates as numeric values in expressions if you want. Although VBA supplies the DateAdd function, covered in more detail in the section "Performing Simple Calculations" later in this chapter, you needn't use it if you're adding a number of days to a given date value. For example, to get tomorrow's date, you could just add 1 to today's date, like this:

```
dtmTomorrow = Date + 1
```

Date is a built-in VBA function that returns the date portion (the integer part) of the current date and time retrieved from Windows. Adding 1 to that value returns a date that represents the next day.

The same mechanism works for subtracting two dates. Although VBA supplies the DateDiff function for finding the interval spanned by two date/time values, if you just need to know the number of days between the two dates, you can simply subtract one from the other. For example, to find the number of days between 5/22/97 and 1/10/97, you could use an expression like this:

```
intDays = #5/22/2000# - #1/10/2000#
```

Afterward, intDays will contain the value 133, the number of days between May 22 and January 10 in a leap year.

Supplying Date Values

Like some weird date-munching omnivore, VBA's expression engine can "eat" dates in any of several formats. As long as you enclose date literals within number signs (#) and format the literal in some reasonable, unambiguous way, VBA should be able to understand what you mean.

VBA understands any of the following formats (if you're running a VBA host in the United States, that is):

```
#January 1, 1998#
#Jan 1 1998#
#1-Jan-98#
#1 Jan 1998#
#1 1 98#
```

TIP   VBA uses your Windows international settings to determine how to parse the value you've entered. This does, of course, cause trouble with dates entered with nothing differentiating days and months. (How is VBA supposed to know, unless you tell it otherwise, that #5/1/98# represents May 1 and not January 5?) To be completely unambiguous, especially in cases in which your application must run in various localized VBA hosts, you might consider abandoning date literals in code altogether and using the DateSerial function instead. This function, discussed in the section "Putting the Pieces Together" later in this chapter, takes three distinct values representing the year, month, and day portions of a date and returns a date value representing the selected date. Using this mechanism, you'll never have any issues with localized versions of your code parsing date literals differently than you'd expected.

When converting from other data types into dates, VBA stores the portion to the left of the decimal point (the whole number part) as the date and the portion to the right of the decimal point as the time. For example, if you were to write code like this:

```
Dim dbl As Double
Dim dtm As Date
dbl = 3005 / 12.6
dtm = dbl

Debug.Print dbl
Debug.Print dtm
```

the output would be

```
238.492063492063
8/25/1900 11:48:34 AM
```

Judging from the results, it looks like 8/25/1900 is 238 days after 12/30/1899, and .4920634... is about 11:48:34 A.M.

The Built-In VBA Date Functions

Although VBA provides a large number of built-in functions, there aren't many logical groups as tightly entwined as the VBA functions handling date and time manipulations. The next few sections provide details and examples of using the intrinsic functions to solve simple problems. The remainder of the chapter provides more complex solutions that, in each case, use these basic building blocks.

Exactly When Is It?

VBA provides three functions enabling you to determine the current date and time set in your computer's hardware. These functions—Now, Date, and Time—check your system clock and return all or part of the current setting. None of these functions requires any parameters, and the functions can be summarized simply:

Function	Return Value
Now	Returns the current date and time
Date	Returns the date portion of the current date and time
Time	Returns the time portion of the current date and time

Although these functions seem somewhat redundant, they do each have their purpose. For example, if you want to display only the current time without the date portion, it's simpler to call the Time function than to call the Now function and remove the date portion.

TIP You can use the Date and Time *statements* to set the current date and time as well. Placing either keyword on the left-hand side of an equal sign allows you to assign a new value to the system date and time.

For example, the following fragment checks the current time, and if it's past 1:00 P.M., executes some code.

```
If Time > #1:00 PM# Then
    ' Only execute this code if it's after 1 PM.
End if
```

On the other hand, the following comparison wouldn't make any sense in this context because the value in Now (a value like 34565.2345) is guaranteed to be greater than #1:00 PM# (the value 0.5416666667):

```
If Now > #1:00 PM# Then
    ' Only execute this code if it's after 1 PM.
End if
```

NOTE Unlike most other functions, Now, Date, and Time don't require trailing parentheses. In fact, if you enter the parentheses, VBA often politely removes them for you.

TIP You may run across the Date$ and Time$ functions if you're reading other people's code. These functions represent special cases of the Date and Time functions. In each case, the string version (Date$ and Time$) returns a string representing the date or time. Date$ always returns a string in the format mm-dd-yyyy; Time$ always returns a string in the format hh:mm:ss.

What If You Just Want One Portion of a Date/Time Value?

To retrieve just the *date* portion of a date/time value, use the built-in DateValue function. This function, discussed in the section "Converting Text to Date/Time Format" later in this chapter, takes in either a string or a date value and returns only the date portion. Using DateValue, you can compare the date portion of a Date variable to a specific date value, like this:

```
If DateValue(dtmSomeDate) = #5/14/70# Then
    ' You know the date portion of dtmSomeDate is 5/14/70
End If
```

On the other hand, if you need just the *time* portion of a date variable, you can use the TimeValue function. Using this function, you could write code that checks the time portion of a date variable against a particular time, like this:

```
If TimeValue(dtmSomeDate) > #1:00 PM# Then
    ' You know the date variable contained a time portion
    ' with a time after 1:00 PM.
End If
```

Pulling the Pieces Apart

Of course, if you're working with dates, you're also working with years, months, days, hours, minutes, and seconds. You might also like to work with a date in terms of its placement within the year, or which quarter it's in, or which day of the week it is. VBA provides simple and useful functions for retrieving all this information, and more.

Retrieving Just the Part You Need

To start with, you'll find the functions listed in Table 3.2 to be helpful in extracting simple information from a date value. Each of these functions accepts a date parameter and returns an integer containing the requested piece of information. (You can also use the DatePart function, described in the section "One Function Does It All" later in this chapter, to retrieve any of these values. It's simpler to call the functions in Table 3.2 if you just need one of the values listed.)

TABLE 3.2:   Simple Date/Time Functions

Function	Return Value
Year	Year portion of the date
Month	Month portion of the date
Day	Day portion of the date
Hour	Hour portion of the date
Minute	Minutes portion of the date
Second	Seconds portion of the date

You can use any of these functions to retrieve a portion of a date value. For example, the following fragment displays the current year value:

```
MsgBox "The current year is " & Year(Now)
```

and the following fragment displays the month and day of a date variable:

```
Dim dtmDate As Date
dtmDate = #1/15/1947#
MsgBox "Month: " & Month(dtmDate) & " Day: " & Day(dtmDate)
```

The following fragment checks the current time and allows you to take an action at 1:12 P.M.:

```
If Hour(Time) = 13 And Minute(Time) = 12 Then
    ' You know it's 1:12 PM
End If
```

WARNING   Don't try sending the Date function to functions that return time portions of a date/time value. Because the return value from the Date function doesn't include any time information (its fractional portion is 0), the Hour, Minute, and Second functions will all return 0. The same warning applies to the Day, Month, and Year functions: Don't send them the Time function, because the return value from that function doesn't include any date information.

What Day of the Week Is This?

In addition to working with months and days, you may need to know the day of the week represented by a date value. Of course, you could calculate this yourself (there are published algorithms for calculating the day of a week, given a date), but why bother? VBA knows the answer and can give it to you easily, using the built-in WeekDay function. (You can also use the DatePart function, discussed in the next section, to retrieve the same information.)

To determine the day of the week represented by any date value, use the Week-Day function. Supply it with a date value, and it will return the day of the week on which that date falls. For example,

```
Debug.Print WeekDay(#5/16/1956#)
```

returns 4, indicating that May 16 fell on a Wednesday in 1956.

Sunday Isn't Always the First Day of the Week

Online help indicates that you can pass a second parameter to WeekDay, indicating the first day of the week. In some countries, Monday is considered the first day of the week, so most of the VBA date functions allow you to specify what you consider to be the first day of the week. If you don't specify a value, VBA uses the Windows setting for your local country. If you specify a constant (vbSunday through vbSaturday) for this parameter, VBA treats that day as the first day of the week and offsets the return value accordingly. If you supply the constant value vbUseSystemDayOfWeek, the function uses its default, the value supplied by Windows.

For example, the following lines represent a sample session in the Immediate window (run in the United States, where Sunday is the first day of the week):

```
? WeekDay(#5/1/98#)
6
? WeekDay(#5/1/98#, vbUseSystemDayOfWeek)
6
? WeekDay(#5/1/98#, vbMonday)
5
```

Note that as you change the value of the FirstDayOfWeek parameter, the return value changes as well. You need to be aware that WeekDay (and the corresponding functionality in the DatePart function) doesn't return a fixed value but, rather, a value relative to the local first day of the week.

Of course, if you want a fixed value, no matter where your code runs, simply specify the first day of the week. The following example returns 6 no matter where you run it:

```
? WeekDay(#5/1/98#, vbSunday)
```

One Function Does It All

In addition to the functions described in the previous sections, VBA supplies the DatePart function. This function allows you to retrieve any portion of a date/time value and also performs some simple calculations for you. (It can retrieve the quarter of the year containing your date value, as well as all the other, simpler information.)

To call DatePart, pass to it a string indicating which information you want returned and a date value. The function returns the requested piece of information from the date value you send it. Table 3.3 lists the possible values for the DatePart function's Interval argument.

TABLE 3.3: Values for the Interval Argument of the DatePart Function

Setting	Description
yyyy	Year
q	Quarter
m	Month
y	Day of year
d	Day
w	Weekday
ww	Week
h	Hour
n	Minute
s	Second

For example, the following two lines of code are equivalent:

```
Debug.Print Day(Date)
Debug.Print DatePart("d", Date)
```

But these two lines have no simple alternatives:

```
' Return the ordinal position of the current day within the year.
Debug.Print DatePart("y", Date)
' Return the quarter (1, 2, 3, or 4) containing today's date.
Debug.Print DatePart("q", Date)
```

DatePart allows you to optionally specify the first day of the week (just as you can do with the WeekDay function) in its third parameter. It also allows you to optionally specify the first week of the year in its fourth parameter. (Some countries treat the week in which January 1st falls as the first week of the year, as does the United States. Other countries treat the first four-day week as the first week, and still others wait for the first full week in the year and call that the first week.)

Performing Simple Calculations

VBA supplies two functions, DateAdd and DateDiff, which allow you to add and subtract date and time intervals. Of course, as mentioned above, if you're just working with days, you don't need these functions—you can just add and subtract the date values themselves. The following sections describe each of these important functions in detail.

Adding Intervals to a Date

The DateAdd function allows you to add any number of intervals of any size to a date/time value. For example, you can calculate the date 100 days from now or the time 35 minutes ago. The function accepts three required parameters, as shown in Table 3.4. Table 3.5 lists the possible values for the Interval parameter.

TABLE 3.4: Parameters for the DateAdd Function

Parameter	Description
Interval	A string expression indicating the interval of time to add
Number	Number of intervals to add. It can be positive (to get dates in the future) or negative (to get dates in the past)
Date	Date to which the interval is added

TABLE 3.5: Possible Interval Settings for DateAdd

Setting	Description
yyyy	Year
q	Quarter
m	Month

TABLE 3.5:   Possible Interval Settings for DateAdd *(continued)*

Setting	Description
y	Day of year
d	Day
w	Weekday
ww	Week
h	Hour
n	Minute
s	Second

For example, to find the date one year from the current date, you could use an expression like this:

```
DateAdd("yyyy", 1, Date)
```

rather than add 365 days to the current date (a common, although incorrect, solution). What about calculating the time two hours from now? That's easy, too:

```
DateAdd("h", 2, Now)
```

DateAdd will never return an invalid date, but if you try to add a value that would cause the return date to be before 1/1/100 or after 12/31/9999, VBA triggers a runtime error.

WARNING   Watch out! The abbreviation for adding minutes to a date/time value is "n," not "m," as you might guess. (VBA uses "m" for months.) Many VBA developers have used "m" inadvertently and not noticed the error until the program was in use.

Subtracting Dates

If you need to find the number of intervals between two dates (where the interval can be any item from Table 3.5), use the DateDiff function. Table 3.6 lists the parameters for this function.

TABLE 3.6: Parameters for the DateDiff Function

Parameter	Required?	Data Type	Description
Interval	Yes	String	Interval of time used to calculate the difference between Date1 and Date2
Date1, Date2	Yes	Date	The two dates used in the calculation
FirstDayOfWeek	No	Integer constant	The first day of the week. If not specified, Sunday is assumed.
FirstWeekOfYear	No	Integer constant	The first week of the year. If not specified, the first week is assumed to be the week in which January 1 occurs.

For example, to calculate the number of hours that occurred between two date variables, dtmValue1 and dtmValue2, you could write an expression like this:

```
DateDiff("h", dtmValue1, dtmValue2)
```

DateDiff's return value can be confusing. In general, it performs no rounding at all, but the meaning of the difference varies for different interval types. For example,

```
DateDiff("h", #10:00#, #12:59:59#)
```

returns 2 because only two full hours have elapsed between the two times.

When working with months or years, DateDiff returns the number of month or year borders that have been crossed between the dates. For example, you might expect the following expression to return 0 (no full months have been traversed), yet the function returns 1 because a single month border has been crossed:

```
DateDiff("m", #11/15/2000#, #12/1/2000#)
```

The same goes for the following expression, which returns 1 even though only a single day has transpired:

```
DateDiff("yyyy", #12/31/2000#, #1/1/2001#)
```

When working with weeks, DateDiff becomes, well, strange. VBA treats the "w" (weekday) and "ww" (week) intervals differently, but both return (in some sense) the number of weeks between the two dates. If you use "w" for the interval, VBA counts the number of the day on which Date1 falls until it hits Date2. It counts Date2 but not Date1. (This explanation requires visual aids, so consult Figure 3.1 for an example to work with.) For example,

```
DateDiff("w", #12/5/2000#, #12/18/2000#)
```

returns 1 because there's only one Wednesday following 12/5/2000 before stopping at 12/18. On the other hand,

```
DateDiff("w", #12/5/2000#, #12/19/2000#)
```

returns 2 because there are two Wednesdays (12/6 and 12/13) in the range.

Using "ww" for the range, DateDiff counts calendar weeks. (That is, every time it hits the first day of the week, it bumps the count.) Therefore, the previous two examples both return 2, using the "ww" interval; in both cases, there are two Sundays between the two dates. Just as with the "w" interval, VBA counts the end date if it falls on a Sunday, but it never includes the starting date, even if it is a Sunday. Given that caveat, DateDiff should return the same answer for either the "w" or "ww" interval if Date1 is a Sunday.

FIGURE 3.1
A visual aid for DateDiff calculations

December 2000	December ▾		2000 ▾			
Sun	Mon	Tue	Wed	Thu	Fri	Sat
26	27	28	29	30	1	2
3	4	5	6	7	8	9
10	11	12	13	14	15	16
17	18	19	20	21	22	23
24	25	26	27	28	29	30
31	1	2	3	4	5	6

TIP If you use date literal values (like #5/1/2001#), VBA uses the exact date you specify in its calculations. If, on the other hand, you use a string that contains only the month and date (like "5/1"), VBA inserts the current year when it runs the code. This allows you to write code that works no matter what the year is when you run it. Of course, this makes it difficult to compare dates from two different years because there's no way to indicate any year except the current one. But if you need to perform a calculation comparing dates within the current year, this technique can save you time.

Converting Text to Date/Time Format

Sometimes your code needs to work with date values that are stored as strings. Perhaps you've received data from some outside source and need to convert it to date format, or perhaps the user has entered a value into a text box somewhere and you now need to work with it as a date. VBA provides four functions to help you make the necessary conversions: IsDate, DateValue, TimeValue, and CDate. Each of these functions accomplishes a slightly different task, and their differences aren't apparent from the online help.

The IsDate function takes in a single value (a string or a date value) and determines if VBA can correctly interpret the value as a date. If so, the function returns True; otherwise, False. For example, each of the following expressions returns True when run in the Immediate window (in the United States):

```
? IsDate(#12/30/2000#)
? IsDate("12/30/2000")
? IsDate("30/12/2000")
? IsDate(#12-30-2000#)
? IsDate("December 30 2000")
```

Obviously, VBA is quite lenient in terms of what it accepts as a date, and it will attempt to convert the value to a date using the CDate function shown below. You should note, however, that VBA may return True when you'd expect it to return False. In the preceding examples, the date value "30/12/2000" returned True, even though the string represents an invalid date in the current locale. Under the covers, VBA determined that if it swapped the month and day, this would be a legal date, and it attempts to do this for you. You may not like this behavior, but that's how it works.

WARNING   The IsDate function does not validate a date/time value. All it does is determine if, by some means, no matter how much effort it takes, VBA can manage to interpret the data you send it as a date. It may not be a valid date or a reasonable one, but VBA will be able to convert it into some type of date value. For example, try passing "3a1-2-3" to IsDate—it returns True. Then try passing the same value to the DateValue and TimeValue functions—you may be surprised at the results.

DateValue and TimeValue each accept a single argument (usually a string expression) and convert that value into either a date or a time. (As mentioned earlier in this chapter, you can also use these functions to extract just the time or date portion of a combined date/time value.) DateValue can convert any string that matches the internal date formats and any recognizable text month names as well. If the value you send it includes a time portion, DateValue just removes that information from the output value.

For example, all of the following expressions return the same value (assuming the variable intDate contains the value 30):

```
DateValue("12 30 2001")
DateValue("December 30 2001")
DateValue("December " & intDate & " 2001")
DateValue("12/30/01 5:00 PM")
DateValue("30/12/2001")
```

The final example returns December 30 no matter where you are, of course, only because the date is unambiguous. Try that with a date like "12/1/2001," and you'll get the date as defined in your international settings (December 1 in the United States, January 12 in most of the rest of the world).

The TimeValue function works similarly to the DateValue function. You can send it a string containing any valid expression, and it returns a time value. If you send TimeValue a string containing date information, it disregards that information as it creates the output value.

For example, all of the following return the same time value:

```
TimeValue("5:15 PM")
TimeValue("17:15")
TimeValue("12/30/2001 5:15 PM")
```

The CDate function coerces any value it can get its hands on into a date/time value, if it can. Unlike the TimeValue and DateValue functions, it returns a full date/time value, with all the information it was sent intact. In addition, it can convert numeric values into dates. For example, all of the following examples return the same value. (The last example is redundant, of course, but it works.)

```
CDate("12/30/2001 5:15 PM")
CDate(37255.71875)
CDate(#12/30/97 5:15 PM#)
```

Most often, you'll use CDate to convert text into a full date/time value, and you'll use DateValue and TimeValue to convert text into a date or a time value only.

Putting the Pieces Together

What if, rather than text, you've got the pieces of a date or a time as individual numeric values? In that case, although you could use any of the functions in the previous section to perform the conversion (building up a complex string expression and then calling the function), you're better off using the DateSerial and TimeSerial functions in this case. Each of these functions accepts three values—

DateSerial takes year, month, and day, in that order; TimeSerial takes hour, minutes, and seconds, in that order—and returns a date or a time value, much like the DateValue and TimeValue functions did with a single expression as input. Many of the functions presented in the remainder of this chapter use the DateSerial or TimeSerial function to create a date from the three required pieces.

For example, what if you need to know the first day of the current month? The simplest solution is to write a function that uses an expression like this:

```
FirstDayInCurrentMonth = DateSerial(Year(Date), Month(Date), 1)
```

As you'll see, this is exactly the technique the dhFirstDayInMonth function, discussed later in this chapter, uses. By creating a new date that takes the year portion of the current date, the month portion of the current date, and a day value of 1, the function returns a new date that corresponds to the first day in the current month.

The TimeSerial function works just the same way. You pass it hour, minutes, and seconds values, and it creates the appropriate time value for you. You'll use both functions together to build a full date/time value if you've got six values containing the year, month, day, hour, minutes, and seconds. That is, you might find yourself with an expression like this:

```
DateSerial(intYear, intMonth, intDay) + _
  TimeSerial(intHour, intMinutes, intSeconds)
```

Because a date/time value is simply the sum of a whole number representing days and a fraction representing time, you can use both functions together to create a full date/time value.

One useful feature of VBA's built-in date functions is that they never return an invalid date. For example, asking for DateSerial(2000, 2, 35), which certainly describes a date that doesn't exist, politely returns 3/6/2000. If you use an expression such as DateSerial(1999, 12, 0), DateSerial happily returns the 0th day of December. From a computer's point of view, that date is 11/30/1999. We'll actually use these features to our benefit, as you'll see in the section "Is This a Leap Year?" later in this chapter.

Odd Behaviors

DateSerial and TimeSerial both have some behaviors that you might consider odd, unless you really stop and think about them. First, consider what this expression should return:

```
DateSerial(0, 0, 0)
```

On first trying this, we expected this function call to return the zero date (12/30/ 1899). But it doesn't; it returns 11/30/1999. After some discussion, the result became clearer. DateSerial saw the year 0 and attempted to interpret that as a valid year. If you supply the value 75 for the year, DateSerial assumes you mean 1975, and if you supply 23 for the year, DateSerial assumes you mean 2023. (The choices made here are based on the built-in cutoff for interpreting two-digit years, as discussed in the sidebar, "The Turn of the Century Approacheth and Passeth" later in the chapter.) If you've entered 0 for the year, DateSerial assumes you mean the year 2000. Then, you've asked for the 0th month in 2000. Because January is month number 1, month 0 is December 1999. Then, you've asked for day 0 within the selected month. Because day 1 would be 12/1/1999, day 0 is 11/30/1999. And so it goes.

As another interesting example, try this expression:

```
TimeSerial(0, -60, 0)
```

You might expect this to return a value corresponding to 11:00 P.M. on 12/29/1899. That is, because you've not specified a date, the expression uses the zero date, 12/30/1899, and because you've requested a value of –60 minutes, you might assume you'd get a value 60 minutes before midnight. That's not the way Time-Serial works, however. Remember that a time is a fractional portion of a date/time value, and the date is the whole number portion of the value. When you enter TimeSerial(0, -60, 0), VBA converts the expression into its corresponding date value: –0.0417 (that is, 1/24th of a day). But, because VBA interprets that value as a date/ time pair, the date part, –0, might as well be 0. The time part is 0.0417 (positive) either way. That is, the result would be the same, using either of these expressions:

```
TimeSerial(0, -60, 0)
TimeSerial(0, 60, 0)
```

This may not be what you expect, but it is the way it works. (It's interesting to note that the DateAdd function does handle negative time intervals the way you might expect. See the section "Adding Intervals to a Date" earlier in the chapter for more information.)

Displaying Values the Way You Want

In your applications, you most likely will want to display dates in a variety of formats. VBA supplies the Format function, which you can use to format date values just the way you need. (You can also use the Format function to format numeric values, and string values as well. See the VBA online help for more information on the specifics of using Format with other data types.)

When you use the Format function, you supply an expression to be formatted (a date/time value, in this case) and a string expression containing a format specifier. Optionally, you can also supply both a constant representing the first day of the week you want to use and a constant representing the manner in which you want to calculate the first week of the year. (For more information on these two parameters, see Table 3.6 earlier in this chapter.)

The format specifier can be either a built-in, supplied string or one you make up yourself. Table 3.7 lists the built-in date/time formats.

TABLE 3.7:   Named Date/Time Formats for the Format Function

Format Name	Description	Use Local Settings
General Date	Displays a date and/or time, depending on the value in the first parameter, using your system's Short Date style and the system's Long Time style	Yes
Long Date	Displays a date (no time portion) according to your system's Long Date format	Yes
Medium Date	Displays a date (no time portion) using the Medium Date format appropriate for the language version of the host application	No
Short Date	Displays a date (no time portion) using your system's Short Date format	Yes
Long Time	Displays a time (no date portion) using your system's Long Time format; includes hours, minutes, seconds	Yes
Medium Time	Displays time (no date portion) in 12-hour format using hours and minutes and the AM/PM designator	Yes
Short Time	Displays a time (no date portion) using the 24-hour format; for example, 17:45	Yes

To test out these formats, we took a field trip to a fictional country. The region's time settings for Windows are displayed in Figure 3.2, and their date settings are shown in Figure 3.3. The screen in Figure 3.4 shows some tests, using the Format function, with the various date and time formats.

FIGURE 3.2
Regional settings for times
in a fictitious environment.
(Screen shot taken in
Windows 2000.)

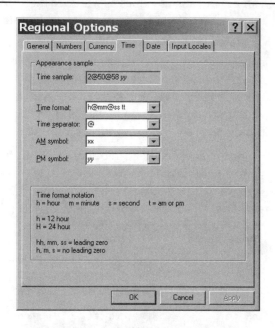

FIGURE 3.3
Regional settings for
dates in the same fictitious
environment. (Screen shot
taken in Windows 2000.)

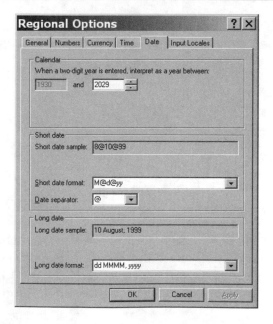

FIGURE 3.4
Test of regional date formats in the Microsoft Excel Immediate window

```
Immediate                                              ×
? Format(#12/15/2001 1:15 PM#, "General Date")
12@15@01 1@15@00 yy
? Format(#12/15/2001 1:15 PM#, "Long Date")
15 December, 2001
? Format(#12/15/2001 1:15 PM#, "Medium Date")
15-Dec-01
? Format(#12/15/2001 1:15 PM#, "Short Date")
12@15@01
? Format(#12/15/2001 1:15 PM#, "Long Time")
1@15@00 yy
? Format(#12/15/2001 1:15 PM#, "Medium Time")
01@15 yy
? Format(#12/15/2001 1:15 PM#, "Short Time")
13@15
```

Back from your field trip, if you're feeling creative, or hampered by the limitations of the named time and date formats, you can create your own formats using the options shown in Table 3.8. If you build a string containing combinations of these characters, you can format a date/time value any way you like. Figure 3.5 demonstrates a few of the formats you can create yourself, using the characters listed in Table 3.8.

FIGURE 3.5
Use the Format function with user-defined formats for complete control.

```
Immediate                                              ×
? Format(#12/15/2000 1:15 PM#, "hh:mm:ss mmm dd, yyyy")
13:15:00 Dec 15, 2000

? Format(#12/15/2000 1:15 PM#, "ddd, dd mmmm, yyyy")
Fri, 15 December, 2000
```

TABLE 3.8: User-Defined Time/Date Formats for the Format Function

Character	Description	Use Regional Settings?	Comments
(:)	Time separator. Separates hours, minutes, and seconds when time values are formatted	Yes	In some locales, this character may have been translated and may not be a colon (:). Output value is determined by local settings.
(/)	Date separator. Separates the day, month, and year when date values are formatted	Yes	In some locales, this character may have been translated and may not be a slash (/). Output value is determined by local settings.

T A B L E 3 . 8 : User-Defined Time/Date Formats for the Format Function *(continued)*

Character	Description	Use Regional Settings?	Comments
c	Displays the date as ddddd and displays the time as ttttt, in that order	Yes	Same as the named General Date format
d	Displays the day as a number without a leading 0 (1–31)	No	
dd	Displays the day as a number with a leading 0 (01–31)	No	
ddd	Displays the day as an abbreviation (Sun–Sat)	Yes	
dddd	Displays the day as a full name (Sunday–Saturday)	Yes	
ddddd	Displays the date as a complete date (including day, month, and year)	Yes	Same as the named Short Date format
dddddd	Displays a date as a complete date (including day, month, and year)	Yes	Same as the named Long Date format
w	Displays the day of the week as a number (1 for Sunday through 7 for Saturday)	No	Output depends on the setting of the FirstDayOfWeek parameter.
ww	Displays the week of the year as a number (1–54)	No	Output depends on the FirstWeekOfYear parameter.
m	Displays the month as a number without a leading 0 (1–12)	No	If "m" follows "h" or "hh," displays minutes instead
mm	Displays the month as a number with a leading 0 (01–12)	No	If "mm" follows "h" or "hh," displays minutes instead
mmm	Displays the month as an abbreviation (Jan–Dec)	Yes	
mmmm	Displays the month as a full month name (January–December)	Yes	

TABLE 3.8:   User-Defined Time/Date Formats for the Format Function *(continued)*

Character	Description	Use Regional Settings?	Comments
q	Displays the quarter of the year as a number (1–4)	No	
y	Displays the day of the year as a number (1–366)	No	
yy	Displays the year as a two-digit number (00–99)	No	
yyyy	Displays the full year (100–9999)	No	
h	Displays the hour as a number without leading zeros (0–23)	No	
hh	Displays the hour as a number with leading zeros (00–23)	No	
n	Displays the minute as a number without leading zeros (0–59)	No	
nn	Displays the minute as a number with leading zeros (00–59)	No	
s	Displays the second as a number without leading zeros (0–59)	No	
ss	Displays the second as a number with leading zeros (00–59)	No	
ttttt	Displays a time as a complete time (including hour, minute, and second)	Yes	Same as the named Long Time format
AM/PM	Uses the 12-hour clock	No	Use "AM" for times before noon and "PM" for times between noon and 11:59 P.M.
am/pm	Uses the 12-hour clock	No	Use "am" for times before noon and "pm" for times between noon and 11:59 P.M.

TABLE 3.8: User-Defined Time/Date Formats for the Format Function *(continued)*

Character	Description	Use Regional Settings?	Comments
A/P	Uses the 12-hour clock	No	Use "a" for times before noon and "p" for times between noon and 11:59 P.M.
a/p	Uses the 12-hour clock	No	Use "A" for times before noon and "P" for times between noon and 11:59 P.M.
AMPM	Uses the 12-hour clock and displays the AM/PM string literal as defined by your system	Yes	The case of the AM/PM string is determined by system settings

If you want to include literal text in your format string, you have two choices. You can do either of the following:

- Precede each character with a backslash (\).

- Enclose the block of text within quotes inside the string.

The first method becomes quite tedious and difficult to read if you have more than a few characters. The second method requires you to embed a quote inside a quoted string, and that takes some doing on its own.

For example, if you want to display a date/time value like this:

```
May 22, 2002 at 12:01 AM
```

you have two choices. With the first method, you could use a format string including \ characters:

```
Format(#5/22/2002 12:01 AM#, "mmm dd, yyyy \a\t h:mm AM/PM")
```

Using the second method, you must embed quotes enclosing the word "at" into the format string. To do that, you must use two quotes where you want one in the output. VBA sees the two embedded quotes as a single literal quote character and does the right thing:

```
Format(#5/22/2002 12:01 AM#, "mmm dd, yyyy ""at"" h:mm AM/PM")
```

Either way, the output is identical.

The Turn of the Century Approacheth and Passeth

How does VBA handle the year 2000 issue? Actually, quite gracefully. Normally, users are accustomed to entering two-digit year values, and this, of course, is what has caused the great, late 20th-century computer controversy. VBA interprets two-digit years in a somewhat rational manner: If you enter a date value with a two-digit year between 1/1/00 and 12/31/29, VBA interprets that as a date that begins with "20." If you enter a date with a two-digit year between 1/1/30 and 12/31/99, VBA interprets that as being a date that begins with "19." If you're using Windows 98 or Windows 2000, you can modify this "window" in the Regional settings Control Panel applet. The following list summarizes how VBA treats date values entered with a two-digit year value, by default:

- Date range 1/1/00 through 12/31/29: treated as 1/1/2000 through 12/31/2029

- Date range 1/1/30 through 12/31/99: treated as 1/1/1930 through 12/31/1999

TIP   If you want to make things simpler, you can also use the FormatDateTime function, discussed in Chapter 1, to format your date and time values. Because the function outputs strings, its description fell into that chapter. It could just as easily have ended up here.

Beyond the Basics

Once you get the built-in date-handling functions under your belt, you'll find innumerable other tasks you need to solve involving dates and times. The remainder of this chapter presents a series of solutions to common problems that require stand-alone procedures, grouped by their functionality. The three sections deal with three types of date/time issues:

- Finding a specific date

- Manipulating dates and times

- Working with elapsed time

Finding a Specific Date

In this section, you'll find solutions to many simple problems that involve locating a date. Specifically, the routines include

- Returning the first or last day of a specified month

- Returning the first or last day of the week, given a date

- Returning the first or last day of the year, given a date

- Returning the first or last day of the quarter, given a date

- Returning the next or previous specific weekday, given a date

- Finding the next anniversary date

- Returning the date of the nth particular weekday (Monday, Tuesday, and so on) of a month

- Returning the next or previous working day, given a date

- Returning the first or last working day of a specified month

Using Optional Parameters

Many of the procedures in the following sections accept one or more optional parameters. In each case, if you don't specify the parameter in your function call, the receiving function assigns that parameter a value. In most cases, this allows you to omit the date parameter, and the function assumes the current date when it runs.

When you use optional parameters, you have two basic choices:

- Use a Variant parameter, and check for the parameter using the IsMissing function.

- Use a strongly typed parameter, and assign a default value in the formal declaration.

We've opted for the second alternative because this allows for type checking when calling the procedure. On the other hand, this technique also removes the possibility of using the IsMissing function to check for the omission of the parameter. Because the value you assign to the parameter in the formal declaration can only be a constant, not a function value, our solution when working with dates was to use the value 0 to indicate that you'd omitted the date parameter. For example, you'll see declarations like this:

```
Function dhFirstDayInMonth(Optional dtmDate As Date = 0) As Date
```

This requires the procedure to check for the 0 value and replace it with the current date:

```
' Did the caller pass in a date? If not, use
' the current date.
If dtmDate = 0 Then
    dtmDate = Date
End If
```

We assumed you would be very unlikely to ever actually use the date 0 (12/30/1899) as a parameter to one of these procedures. If you do attempt to send 12/30/1899 to any of the procedures that accept an optional date parameter, the procedure will treat your input as though you'd entered the current date. If you must allow that date as input, you'll need to either remove the optional parameter or find some other workaround.

TIP   Unless specified otherwise, all the procedures that follow are saved in the sample module named DateTime.

Finding the Beginning or End of a Month

Finding the first day in a specific month is easy: Use the DateSerial function, breaking out the year and month portions of the specified date, asking for the day value 1. The dhFirstDayInMonth function, in Listing 3.1, performs this function call after first checking the incoming parameter and converting it to the current date if necessary. Calling the function as

```
dhFirstDayInMonth(#5/7/70#)
```

returns 5/1/70, of course.

Determining the last day in the month requires using an obscure, but documented, detail of the DateSerial function. It turns out that any (or all) of the three parameters to the DateSerial function can be numeric expressions. Because VBA will never return an invalid date, you can request the day before the first day of a month by incrementing the month value by 1 and decrementing the day by 1. The dhLastDayInMonth function in Listing 3.1 does just that. Using this expression:

```
DateSerial(Year(dtmDate), Month(dtmDate) + 1, 0)
```

it finds the 0th day of the following month, which is, of course, the final day of the requested month.

Listing 3.1: Find the First or Last Day in a Month

```
Public Function dhFirstDayInMonth(Optional dtmDate As Date = 0) As Date
    ' Return the first day in the specified month.

    ' Did the caller pass in a date? If not, use
    ' the current date.
    If dtmDate = 0 Then
        dtmDate = Date
    End If

    dhFirstDayInMonth = DateSerial( _
     Year(dtmDate), Month(dtmDate), 1)
End Function

Public Function dhLastDayInMonth(Optional dtmDate As Date = 0) As Date
    ' Return the last day in the specified month.

    ' Did the caller pass in a date? If not, use
    ' the current date.
    If dtmDate = 0 Then
        dtmDate = Date
    End If

    dhLastDayInMonth = DateSerial( _
     Year(dtmDate), Month(dtmDate) + 1, 0)
End Function
```

Finding the Beginning or End of a Week

Finding the first or last day in a week counts on the fact that you can subtract integers from a date value and end up with another date value. If the specified date was a Sunday, to find the first day of the week (assuming Sunday was the first day of the week), you'd subtract 0 from the date. If the date was a Monday, you'd subtract 1; if Tuesday, you'd subtract 2, and so on. Because the WeekDay function returns a number between 1 and 7, all you need to do is subtract the WeekDay return value from the date and then add 1. The dhFirstDayInWeek function, in Listing 3.2, does this work for you.

NOTE To be completely correct, the dhFirstDayInWeek and dhLastDayInWeek functions specify the first day of the week for the WeekDay function, using the vbUseSystemDayOfWeek constant. This way, the first and last days in the week correspond to the local settings.

The dhLastDayInWeek function in Listing 3.2 uses the same concepts. This time, however, you want to add 6 to the first day of the week. That is (assuming you're in the United States), if the date in question is a Wednesday, you subtract the Weekday return value (4), which takes you to Saturday. Adding 1 takes you to the first day of the week, and adding 6 more takes you to the last day of the week.

Listing 3.2: Find the First or Last Day in a Week

```
Public Function dhFirstDayInWeek(Optional dtmDate As Date = 0) As Date
    ' Returns the first day in the week specified by the
    ' date in dtmDate. Uses localized settings for the first
    ' day of the week.

    ' Did the caller pass in a date? If not, use
    ' the current date.
    If dtmDate = 0 Then
        dtmDate = Date
    End If

    dhFirstDayInWeek = dtmDate - _
     Weekday(dtmDate, vbUseSystemDayOfWeek) + 1
End Function

Public Function dhLastDayInWeek(Optional dtmDate As Date = 0) As Date
    ' Returns the last day in the week specified by the
    ' date in dtmDate.
    ' Uses localized settings for the first day of the week.

    ' Did the caller pass in a date? If not, use
    ' the current date.
    If dtmDate = 0 Then
        dtmDate = Date
    End If
```

```
    dhLastDayInWeek = dtmDate - _
     Weekday(dtmDate, vbUseSystemDayOfWeek) + 7
End Function
```

To call dhFirstDayInWeek and dhLastDayInWeek, pass a date value to specify a date, or pass no parameter to use the current date. For example, the following code calculates the first and last day in two different weeks:

```
Debug.Print "First day in the current week: " _
 & dhFirstDayInWeek()
Debug.Print "Last day in the current week: " & dhLastDayInWeek()
Debug.Print _
 "First day in the week of 1/1/98: " & dhFirstDayInWeek(#1/1/98#)
Debug.Print _
 "Last day in the week of 1/1/98: " & dhLastDayInWeek(#1/1/98#)
```

Finding the Beginning or End of a Year

Finding the first or last day in a year is simple, compared to the other functions in this section. Once you understand the DateSerial function, it's just a matter of building up a date value that's January 1 or December 31 in the specified year. Because those dates are fixed as the first and last days in the year, no more calculation is necessary. The dhFirstDayInYear and dhLastDayInYear functions, in Listing 3.3, show all that's necessary.

⤳ Listing 3.3: Find the First or Last Day in a Year

```
Public Function dhFirstDayInYear(Optional dtmDate As Date = 0) As Date
    ' Return the first day in the specified year.

    ' Did the caller pass in a date? If not, use
    ' the current date.
    If dtmDate = 0 Then
        dtmDate = Date
    End If

    dhFirstDayInYear = DateSerial(Year(dtmDate), 1, 1)
End Function

Public Function dhLastDayInYear(Optional dtmDate As Date = 0) As Date
    ' Return the last day in the specified year.
```

```
' Did the caller pass in a date? If not, use
' the current date.
If dtmDate = 0 Then
    dtmDate = Date
End If

dhLastDayInYear = DateSerial(Year(dtmDate), 12, 31)
End Function
```

To call either of these functions, either pass no value (to work with the current year) or pass a date value indicating the year. The functions will each return the requested date. For example, the following code fragment calculates the first and last days in two ways:

```
Debug.Print "First day in the current year: " & _
  dhFirstDayInYear()
Debug.Print "Last day in the current year: " & dhLastDayInYear()
Debug.Print _
  "First day in the next year: " & _
  dhFirstDayInYear(DateAdd("yyyy", 1, Date))
Debug.Print _
  "Last day in the previous year: " & _
  dhLastDayInYear(DateAdd("yyyy", -1, Date))
```

Finding the Beginning or End of a Quarter

Finding the beginning or end of a quarter takes a bit more effort than do the other functions in this section because there's little support for working with quarters (January though March, April through June, July through September, October through December) in the VBA function library. Listing 3.4 shows the functions that solve this problem, dhFirstDayInQuarter and dhLastDayInQuarter.

Listing 3.4: Find the First and Last Day in a Quarter

```
Public Function dhFirstDayInQuarter(Optional dtmDate As Date = 0) _
As Date
    ' Returns the first day in the quarter specified by the
    ' date in dtmDate.
```

```
        Const dhcMonthsInQuarter As Integer = 3
        Dim intMonth As Integer

        ' Did the caller pass in a date? If not, use
        ' the current date.
        If dtmDate = 0 Then
            dtmDate = Date
        End If

        ' Calculate the first month in the quarter.
        intMonth = Int((Month(dtmDate) - 1) / dhcMonthsInQuarter) * _
         dhcMonthsInQuarter + 1

        dhFirstDayInQuarter = DateSerial(Year(dtmDate), intMonth, 1)
End Function

Public Function dhLastDayInQuarter(Optional dtmDate As Date = 0) _
 As Date
        ' Returns the last day in the quarter specified by the
        ' date in dtmDate.

        Const dhcMonthsInQuarter As Integer = 3
        Dim intMonth As Integer

        ' Did the caller pass in a date? If not, use
        ' the current date.
        If dtmDate = 0 Then
            dtmDate = Date
        End If

        ' Calculate the last month in the quarter.
        intMonth = Int((Month(dtmDate) - 1) / dhcMonthsInQuarter) * _
         dhcMonthsInQuarter + (dhcMonthsInQuarter + 1)

        dhLastDayInQuarter = DateSerial(Year(dtmDate), intMonth, 0)
    End Function
```

Certainly, once you know how to find the first day in the quarter, you know how to find the last; that's just a matter of adding three months and subtracting one day. But how do you find the first day in the quarter containing a specified date? You know the year portion of the date (it's the same as the date you've specified) and the day portion (which has to be 1), but what month do you use? You could, of course, use the brute-force technique, with a Select Case statement like this:

```
Select Case Month(dtmDate)
    Case 1, 2, 3
        intMonth = 1
    Case 4, 5, 6
        intMonth = 4
    ' etc.
End Select
```

But you just *know* there has to be a better way! This is one situation in which it's worth pulling out some paper and thinking through what's really going on. You may find it useful to create a table listing the input and output of a proposed calculation, in this case, to convert from any month to the first month in that quarter:

Month	First Month of Quarter
1	1
2	1
3	1
4	4
5	4
6	4
7	7
8	7
9	7
10	10
11	10
12	10

Remember, you're looking for a mathematical relationship between the two columns. (Reminds you of high school algebra, right?) It looks as though each output "step" is a multiple of 3, plus 1. After much scribbling, you might come up with the following algebraic relation between the two columns, which turns out to be the exact solution dhFirstDayInQuarter uses:

```
First Month of Quarter = Int((Month - 1) / 3) * 3 + 1
```

This expression finds, for each month value, the largest multiple of 3 less than or equal to the number, multiplies the result by 3, and then adds 1. This calculation, based on the value in the first column, returns the value in the second column in every case. Therefore, rather than asking VBA to perform a lookup and a jump for each call to the function, it performs a moderately simple calculation.

Once dhFirstDayInQuarter has found the first month in the quarter, finding the first day is simple: The function calls DateSerial, building a date from the supplied year, the calculated month, and the day value 1. To find the last day in the quarter, dhLastDayInQuarter repeats the calculation from dhFirstDayInQuarter, adds 1 to the month it calculated to move to the next month, and then uses 0 for the day value. As discussed in the section "Finding the Beginning or End of a Month" earlier in this chapter, supplying 0 for the Day parameter to DateSerial returns the final day of the previous month, which is exactly what you want in this context.

Finding the Next or Previous Weekday

In many financial calculations, you'll need to know the next specific weekday after a given date. For example, you might need to know the date of the Friday immediately following April 30, 2002, or the Monday immediately preceding the same date. As when finding the first or last day in a week, calculating these dates counts on the fact that you can subtract an integer from a date value and end up with another date value.

In this case, it seems simplest to just calculate the beginning of the week containing the specified date and then add on enough days to get to the requested date. That code, from the procedures in Listing 3.5, looks like this:

```
dtmTemp = dtmDate - Weekday(dtmDate) + lngDOW
```

Say you're looking for the Thursday before 10/7/97 (a Tuesday). In this case, Weekday(dtmDate) will be 3 (Tuesday's day of the week) and lngDOW will contain 5 (Thursday's day of the week). The expression

```
dtmDate - Weekday(dtmDate) + intDOW
' the same as:
' #10/7/97# - 3 + 5
```

will return the date 10/9/1997. This, clearly, is not the Thursday before 10/7/97, but the Thursday after. The final step of the calculation, then, is to subtract one week, if necessary. The entire set of statements looks like this:

```
dtmTemp = dtmDate - Weekday(dtmDate) + lngDOW
If dtmTemp >= dtmDate Then
    dtmTemp = dtmTemp - 7
End If
```

When would you not need to subtract 7 to move to the previous week? Reverse the dates in the example. If you're looking for the Tuesday before 10/9/97, the expression would be

```
dtmDate - Weekday(dtmDate) + lngDOW
' the same as:
' #10/9/97# - 5 + 3
```

which returns #10/7/1997#, the correct answer. There's no need to subtract 7 to move to the previous week. The same logic applies to calculating the following weekday, but reversed. In this case, you may need to add 7 to move to the next week if the day you were looking for has already occurred in the current week.

Listing 3.5: Find the Previous or Next Specific Weekday

```
Public Function dhPreviousDOW(lngDOW As VbDayOfWeek, _
  Optional dtmDate As Date = 0) As Date
    ' Find the previous specified day of week before
    ' the specified date.

    Dim dtmTemp As Date

    ' Did the caller pass in a date? If not, use
    ' the current date.
    If dtmDate = 0 Then
        dtmDate = Date
    End If

    dtmTemp = dtmDate - Weekday(dtmDate) + lngDOW
    If dtmTemp >= dtmDate Then
        dtmTemp = dtmTemp - 7
    End If
    dhPreviousDOW = dtmTemp
End Function
```

```
Public Function dhNextDOW(lngDOW As VbDayOfWeek, _
 Optional dtmDate As Date = 0) As Date
    ' Find the next specified day of week after the specified date.

    Dim dtmTemp As Date

    ' Did the caller pass in a date? If not, use
    ' the current date.
    If dtmDate = 0 Then
        dtmDate = Date
    End If

    dtmTemp = dtmDate - Weekday(dtmDate) + lngDOW
    If dtmTemp <= dtmDate  Then
        dtmTemp = dtmTemp + 7
    End If
    dhNextDOW = dtmTemp
End Function
```

The following examples demonstrate calling the two functions:

```
Debug.Print "The Monday before 12/25/2000 is " & _
 dhPreviousDOW(vbMonday, #12/25/2000#)
Debug.Print "The Friday after 12/25/2000 is " & _
 dhNextDOW(vbFriday, #12/25/2000#)
Debug.Print "It's " & Date & _
 ". The next Monday is " & dhNextDOW(vbMonday)
```

Finding the Next Anniversary

Often, when working with dates, you have stored away a birthday or a wedding date and need to find out the next occurrence of the anniversary of that date. The function in this section, dhNextAnniversary (Listing 3.6), will do that chore for you. Given a date, it finds the next anniversary of that date, taking into account the current date.

◯ Listing 3.6: Find the Next Anniversary of a Date

```
Public Function dhNextAnniversary(dtmDate As Date) As Date
    ' Given a date, find the next anniversary of that date.

    Dim dtmThisYear As Date

    ' What's the corresponding date in the current year?
    dtmThisYear = DateSerial(Year(Now), Month(dtmDate), Day(dtmDate))

    ' If the anniversary has already occurred, then add 1 to the year.
    If dtmThisYear < Date Then
        dtmThisYear = DateAdd("yyyy", 1, dtmThisYear)
    End If
    dhNextAnniversary = dtmThisYear
End Function
```

This one's actually quite easy. The code follows these steps:

1. Finds the date corresponding to the anniversary in the current year

2. If the date has already passed in the current year, adds one year to the date

To find the anniversary date in the current year, the code uses this expression:

```
dtmThisYear = DateSerial(Year(Now), Month(dtmDate), Day(dtmDate))
```

To correct the result if the date has already passed in the current year, the function uses this fragment:

```
If dtmThisYear < Date Then
    dtmThisYear = DateAdd("yyyy", 1, dtmThisYear)
End If
```

Either way, dtmThisYear contains the next occurrence of the anniversary.

To try out the procedure, you might use code like the following fragment. Given that the current date is 12/15/2001,

```
dhNextAnniversary(#5/16/56#)
```

returns 5/16/2002 because that date has already passed in 2001.

Finding the *n*th Particular Weekday in a Month

Perhaps your application needs to find the third Tuesday in November, 1997. The function presented here, dhNthWeekday, in Listing 3.7, solves this puzzle for you. The function accepts three parameters:

- A date specifying the month and year to start in

- An integer greater than 1 that specifies the offset into the month

- A long integer specifying the day of week to retrieve (Use the vbSunday... vbSaturday constants, defined as part of the VbDayOfWeek enumeration.)

The function returns a date representing the *n*th specific weekday in the month. If you pass an invalid day of week value or an invalid offset, the function returns the date you passed it.

Listing 3.7: Find the *n*th Specific Weekday in a Month

```
Public Function dhNthWeekday(dtmDate As Date, intN As Integer, _
 lngDOW As VbDayOfWeek) As Date

    ' Find the date of the specified day within the month. For
    ' example, retrieve the 3rd Tuesday's date.

    Dim dtmTemp As Date

    If (lngDOW < vbSunday Or lngDOW > vbSaturday) _
     Or (intN < 1) Then
        ' Invalid parameter values. Just
        ' return the passed-in date.
        dhNthWeekday = dtmDate
        Exit Function
    End If

    ' Get the first of the month.
    dtmTemp = DateSerial(Year(dtmDate), Month(dtmDate), 1)

    ' Get to the first lngDOW including or after the first
    ' day of the month.
    dtmTemp = dtmTemp + ((lngDOW - Weekday(dtmTemp) + 7) Mod 7)
```

```
    ' Now you've found the first lngDOW in the month.
    ' Just add 7 for each intN after that.
    dhNthWeekday = dtmTemp + ((intN - 1) * 7)
End Function
```

The function is moderately simple. To do its work, it must:

1. Verify the parameters

2. Find the first day of the specified month

3. Move to the first specified weekday in the month

4. Add enough weeks to find the *n*th occurrence of the specified weekday

If either the day of the week value or the number of weeks to skip is invalid, the function returns the passed-in starting date. The code that handles the verification looks like this:

```
If (lngDOW < vbSunday Or lngDOW > vbSaturday) _
  Or (intN < 1) Then
      ' Invalid parameter values. Just
      ' return the passed-in date.
    dhNthWeekday = dtmDate
    Exit Function
End If
```

Finding the first day of the specified month is, as you know by now, simple. It takes one line of code:

```
dtmTemp = DateSerial(Year(dtmDate), Month(dtmDate), 1)
```

Moving to the first specified weekday requires a bit more work. This procedure uses logic similar to that shown in the section "Finding the Next or Previous Weekday" earlier in this chapter. In this case, the procedure uses the Mod operator to verify that the code never adds more than 6 to the current day. Mod returns the remainder when you divide a value by Mod's second operand, and in this case, using Mod 7 returns a value between 0 and 6, which is exactly what you need:

```
dtmTemp = dtmTemp + ((lngDOW - Weekday(dtmTemp) + 7) Mod 7)
```

Finally, to move to the *n*th occurrence of the weekday, you just need to add the correct multiple of 7 to the date:

```
dhNthWeekday = dtmTemp + ((intN - 1) * 7)
```

For example, to find the date of the third Tuesday in March, 1998, you could call the function like this:

```
dtm = dhNthWeekday(#3/98#, 3, vbTuesday)
```

The return value will be the date #3/17/1998#, the third Tuesday in March, 1998.

Working with Workdays

Many calculations involve the five typical workdays (Monday through Friday), but VBA doesn't provide any support for this subset of dates. The functions in this section provide information about the next and previous workday and finding the first and last workday in a month. Skipping weekend days is simple and not worthy of much explanation. The hard part is dealing with the other factor affecting these calculations: holidays. VBA is blissfully unaware of the real world and knows nothing of national and religious holidays. Supplying that information is up to you, and the functions presented here count on your having created an ADO recordset object filled with the rows of information about holidays. You needn't supply a recordset if you don't need this functionality; the recordset parameter to the functions shown here is optional. If you do supply a reference to an open recordset, you must also pass in the name of the field containing holiday date information so the code knows the field in which to search.

TIP   We've stored all the procedures in this section in the module named DateTimeADO. Because these procedures require a reference to ADO 2.1 (or higher) in your projects, it's important that we kept them separate from the procedures that don't require a special reference. If you want to use these procedures in your own applications, import DateTimeADO into your project, and use the Tools ➤ References menu to locate and select Microsoft ActiveX Data Objects 2.1 (or higher, if you've installed a product that supplies a later version—2.1 was current at the time of this book's writing).

Because all the functions in this section count on the same support routines, it makes sense to explain these underlying procedures first. The first routine, IsWeekend, shown in Listing 3.8, accepts a date parameter and returns True if the date falls on a weekend and False otherwise.

Listing 3.8: Indicate Whether a Date Falls on a Weekend

```
Private Function IsWeekend(dtmTemp As Date) As Boolean
    ' If your weekends aren't Saturday (day 7)
    ' and Sunday (day 1), change this routine
    ' to return True for whatever days
    ' you DO treat as weekend days.
    Select Case WeekDay(dtmTemp)
        Case vbSaturday, vbSunday
            IsWeekend = True
        Case Else
            IsWeekend = False
    End Select
End Function
```

The second support function, SkipHolidays (shown in Listing 3.9), takes a reference to a recordset, a field to search in, a date value, and the number of days to skip (normally +1 or –1). It skips over weekend days and holidays until it finds a date that is neither a weekend nor a holiday. It skips past increments of the parameter passed in, so the same code can be used to skip forward or backward.

Listing 3.9: Move a Date Value over Holidays and Weekends

```
Private Function SkipHolidays( _
 rst As ADODB.Recordset, strField As String, _
 dtmTemp As Date, intIncrement As Integer) As Date
    ' Skip weekend days, and holidays in the recordset
    ' referred to by rst.
    ' Return dtmTemp + as many days as it takes to get to
    ' a day that's not
    ' a holiday or weekend.

    Dim strCriteria As String
    Dim strFieldName As String
    On Error GoTo HandleErr

    ' Move up to the first Monday/last Friday, if the first/last
    ' of the month was a weekend date. Then skip holidays.
    ' Repeat this entire process until you get to a weekday.
    ' Unless rst contains a row for every day in the year (!)
    ' this should finally converge on a weekday.
```

```
        Do
            Do While IsWeekend(dtmTemp)
                dtmTemp = dtmTemp + intIncrement
            Loop
            If Not rst Is Nothing Then
                If Len(strField) > 0 Then
                    strFieldName = strField
                    If Left$(strField, 1) <> "[" Then
                        strFieldName = "[" & strFieldName & "]"
                    End If
                    rst.MoveFirst
                    Do
                        strCriteria = strFieldName & " = " & _
                         "#" & Format(dtmTemp, "mm/dd/yyyy") & "#"
                        rst.Find strCriteria, , adSearchForward
                        If Not rst.EOF Then
                            dtmTemp = dtmTemp + intIncrement
                        End If
                    Loop Until rst.EOF
                End If
            End If
        Loop Until Not IsWeekend(dtmTemp)

ExitHere:
        SkipHolidays = dtmTemp
        Exit Function

HandleErr:
        ' No matter what the error, just
        ' return without complaining.
        ' The worst that could happen is that we
        ' include a holiday as a real day, even if
        ' it's in the table.
        Resume ExitHere
End Function
```

The code starts out by skipping over any weekend days. If you send it a date that falls on a weekend, this first bit of code will loop until it lands on a non-weekend date:

```
Do While IsWeekend(dtmTemp)
    dtmTemp = dtmTemp + intIncrement
Loop
```

Its next task is to ensure that the recordset variable is instantiated, that it points to something, and that the field name has been supplied. Once that happens, if the field name doesn't include a leading [character, the code adds leading and trailing brackets. This guards against problems that can occur if the field name includes spaces.

```
If Not rst Is Nothing Then
    If Len(strField) > 0 Then
        strFieldName = strField
        If Left$(strField, 1) <> "[" Then
            strFieldName = "[" & strFieldName & "]"
        End If
```

Finally, the code enters the loop shown below, checking for a match in the recordset against the current value of dtmTemp. If the code finds a match in the table, it moves to the next day and tries again. It continues in this way until it no longer finds a match in the table. Most of the time, however, this code will execute only once. (There are few, if any, occurrences of consecutive holidays.) Normally, there won't be any match, and the code will drop right out. If the code finds a match in the table, there's rarely more than one. Unless you add a row to the table for each day of the year, this code should be quite fast.

```
Do
    strCriteria = strFieldName & " = " & _
      "#" & Format(dtmTemp, "mm/dd/yyyy") & "#"
    rst.Find strCriteria, , adSearchForward
    If Not rst.EOF Then
        dtmTemp = dtmTemp + intIncrement
    End If
Loop Until rst.EOF
```

Because this step could drop you off on a weekend date, the entire process repeats until you run out of holidays and don't end up on a weekend date. Of course, the outer loop most likely is never going to be used, but it takes care of an important problem.

NOTE There are many ways to create an ADO recordset, and the examples later in the chapter show two different ways to do it. You might want to peruse the example procedures in the TestDateTime module to see how you can create the necessary recordsets. For more information on using ADO, we recommend both our "sister" book, *Access 2000 Developer's Handbook* (Sybex, 1999), and *Visual Basic Developer's Guide to ADO* by Mike Gunderloy (Sybex, 1999).

Finding the Next, Previous, First, or Last Workday in the Month

Once you've got the routines to skip holidays, the rest is simple. If you need to find the previous or next workday, it's just a matter of skipping weekends and holidays until you find another workday. For example, the procedures in Listing 3.10 find the next or previous workday simply by calling the SkipHolidays function. In each case, the function accepts three optional parameters:

- A date, indicating the month in which to search. If this parameter is omitted, the code uses the current date.

- An open recordset, containing holiday information. If this parameter is omitted, the code skips just weekends, not holidays. If it is supplied, you must supply the field name in the next parameter.

- A string containing the name of a field to be searched in the open recordset. This parameter is used only if the recordset parameter isn't omitted, and it is required if you supply the recordset.

As you can see from the code in Listing 3.10, there's not much to these routines, given the workhorse procedure, SkipHolidays.

Listing 3.10: Find the Next or Previous Workday

```
Public Function dhNextWorkday(Optional dtmDate As Date = 0, _
  Optional rst As ADODB.Recordset = Nothing, _
  Optional strField As String = "") As Date

    ' Return the next working day after the specified date.
    ' If you want to look up holidays in a table, pass in
    ' an ADO recordset object containing the rows.

    ' Did the caller pass in a date? If not, use
    ' the current date.
    If dtmDate = 0 Then
        dtmDate = Date
    End If

    dhNextWorkday = SkipHolidays(rst, strField, dtmDate + 1, 1)
End Function
```

```
Public Function dhPreviousWorkday(Optional dtmDate As Date = 0, _
 Optional rst As ADODB.Recordset = Nothing, _
 Optional strField As String = "") As Date

    ' Return the previous working day before the specified date.
    ' If you want to look up holidays in a table, pass in
    ' an ADO recordset object containing the rows.

    ' Did the caller pass in a date? If not, use
    ' the current date.
    If dtmDate = 0 Then
        dtmDate = Date
    End If

    dhPreviousWorkday = SkipHolidays(rst, strField, dtmDate - 1, -1)
End Function
```

If you want to find the first or last workday in a given month, all you need to do is maneuver to the first or last day in the month and then skip holidays forward or backward. For example, the dhFirstWorkdayInMonth function, shown in Listing 3.11, handles this for you. The function accepts the same three optional parameters as the previous examples.

The dhFirstWorkdayInMonth function first finds the first day in the month, using the same code as in other procedures in this chapter. Once it gets to the first day, it calls SkipHolidays, passing the recordset, the field name, the starting date, and the increment (1, in this case). The date returned from SkipHolidays will be the first working day in the month.

Listing 3.11: Find the First Workday in a Given Month

```
Public Function dhFirstWorkdayInMonth(Optional dtmDate As Date = 0, _
 Optional rst As ADODB.Recordset = Nothing, _
 Optional strField As String = "") As Date

    ' Return the first working day in the month specified.
    ' If you want to look up holidays in a table, pass in
    ' an ADO recordset object containing the rows.

    Dim dtmTemp As Date
```

```
' Did the caller pass in a date? If not, use
' the current date.
If dtmDate = 0 Then
    dtmDate = Date
End If

dtmTemp = DateSerial(Year(dtmDate), Month(dtmDate), 1)
dhFirstWorkdayInMonth = SkipHolidays(rst, strField, dtmTemp, 1)
End Function
```

Finding the last workday in the month is very similar. In dhLastWorkdayInMonth, shown in Listing 3.12, the code first finds the final day of the month, using code discussed earlier in this chapter, and then calls the SkipHolidays function to move backward through the month until it finds a day that is neither a weekend nor a holiday.

Listing 3.12: Find the Last Workday in a Given Month

```
Public Function dhLastWorkdayInMonth(Optional dtmDate As Date = 0, _
  Optional rst As ADODB.Recordset = Nothing, _
  Optional strField As String = "") As Date

    ' Return the last working day in the month specified.
    ' If you want to look up holidays in a table, pass in
    ' an ADO recordset object containing the rows.

    Dim dtmTemp As Date

    ' Did the caller pass in a date? If not, use
    ' the current date.
    If dtmDate = 0 Then
        dtmDate = Date
    End If

    dtmTemp = DateSerial(Year(dtmDate), Month(dtmDate) + 1, 0)
    dhLastWorkdayInMonth = SkipHolidays(rst, strField, dtmTemp, -1)
End Function
```

To work with these procedures, you might write a test routine like the one shown in Listing 3.13 (from the module TestDateTime). This procedure assumes the following:

- You have OLEDB and ADO installed on your machine.

- You have a reference set to the ADO 2.1 or higher type library in your project.

- You have an XML file named HOLIDAYS.XML available (and you've modified the code to point to the actual location of HOLIDAYS.XML). You can use the CreateHolidaysXML procedure to create this XML file, based on tblHolidays in the supplied Jet 4 MDB file, Holidays.MDB. (In order for this to work, you must have the Jet 4 OLEDB provider installed on your machine. If you've installed ADO 2.1 or higher, you have this. If not, you'll need to download the most current ADO providers from Microsoft's Web site at http://www.microsoft.com/data.)

- tblHolidays, in Holidays.MDB, includes a date/time field named Date, containing one row for each holiday you want tracked.

TIP   Make sure to run the CreateHolidaysXML procedure after you modify the data in tblHolidays, or this test procedure won't "see" the changes you've made.

NOTE   You needn't use an XML file for transporting your recordset around. You could place your table containing holiday information into any database that OLEDB can open and read from, including MDB files and SQL Server databases. But it's a lot simpler to include a simple text file (that is, the XML file) instead of carting around a big MDB file or installing data into a client's SQL Server installation.

Listing 3.13: Test Routine for the SkipHolidays Function

```
Sub TestSkipHolidays()
    Dim rst As ADODB.Recordset

    Set rst = New ADODB.Recordset
    ' You'll need to modify the path in the next line, to point
    ' to your sample XML file. Use the CreateHolidaysXML
    ' procedure to create the necessary XML file.
    rst.Open ActiveWorkbook.Path & "\Holidays.xml", , _
    adOpenKeyset, adLockReadOnly, Options:=adCmdFile

    Debug.Print dhFirstWorkdayInMonth(#8/1/1999#, rst, "Date")
    Debug.Print dhLastWorkdayInMonth(#12/31/1999#, rst, "Date")
    Debug.Print dhNextWorkday(#12/30/1999#, rst, "Date")
    Debug.Print dhNextWorkday(#5/27/1999#, rst, "Date")
    Debug.Print dhPreviousWorkday(#1/1/2000#, rst, "Date")
    Debug.Print dhPreviousWorkday(#5/23/1999#, rst, "Date")
End Sub
```

If you don't have ADO installed, or you just don't care about holidays, you could also call these routines like this:

```
Debug.Print dhFirstWorkdayInMonth(#1/1/97#)
' or
Debug.Print dhLastWorkdayInMonth(#12/31/97#)
```

In this case, the procedure calls would just skip weekend days, if necessary, to return the first and last workday, respectively.

TIP

The sample CD with this book includes HOLIDAYS.MDB (which contains tblHolidays) that you can use as a start for preparing your list of holidays. If you have any product that can work with Access databases, you're ready to start filling in your own list of holidays for use with these routines. If not, we've included HOLIDAYS.TXT, a text file you can import into your own database program for use with these samples. If you want to use Holidays.MDB and export a recordset to XML, see the CreateHolidaysXML procedure in the TestDateTime module. This procedure opens the Holidays.MDB database, creates a recordset based on tblHolidays, and saves the recordset as an XML file. From then on, all you need is the XML file (a small text file) in order to reopen the recordset on a client's machine.

Manipulating Dates and Times

This section provides solutions to five common date manipulation issues:

- Finding the number of days in a specified month
- Counting the number of iterations of a specific weekday in a month
- Determining whether a specified year is a leap year
- Rounding time to a specified increment
- Converting numbers or strings to dates, given an input format specification

In each case, we've provided a VBA function or two, as well as some examples showing the usage of the function, to help get you started.

How Many Days in That Month?

Although there's no built-in function to determine the number of days in a specified month, it's not a difficult task. There are many ways to accomplish this. You could create a Select Case statement and, knowing the month and year, look up the length of the month. This requires, of course, knowing the year, because leap years affect February's length.

An alternative is to let VBA do as much of any calculation as possible. Because you can subtract one date value from another to determine the number of days between the dates, you can use the DateSerial function to find the first day in the specified month and the first day in the next month and then subtract the first value from the second.

The dhDaysInMonth function, in Listing 3.14, performs the necessary calculations. You send it a date, and it calculates the number of days in the month represented by that date. In this function, as in many others, if you don't pass a date at all, the function assumes you want to use the current date and finds the number of days in the current month.

Listing 3.14: Calculate the Days in a Given Month

```
Public Function dhDaysInMonth(Optional dtmDate As Date = 0) As Integer
    ' Return the number of days in the specified month.

    ' Did the caller pass in a date? If not, use
    ' the current date.
    If dtmDate = 0 Then
        dtmDate = Date
    End If

    dhDaysInMonth = _
     DateSerial(Year(dtmDate), Month(dtmDate) + 1, 1) - _
     DateSerial(Year(dtmDate), Month(dtmDate), 1)
End Function
```

TIP   Although this tip applies to many functions in this chapter, it is key to this particular function. VBA accepts dates in many formats, as you've seen. One that we haven't mentioned is the #mm/yy# format. That is, you can pass just a month and year as a date, and VBA will assume you mean the first of that month. With the dhDaysInMonth function, it's useful to be able to just send in the month and year portion if you don't care to handle the day portion as well. That is, you could pass either #12/31/2001# or #12/2001# as a parameter to this function, and it would return the same value either way.

How Many Mondays in June?

If your application needs to know how many occurrences there are of a particular weekday in a given month, the dhCountDOWInMonth function is for you. This function, shown in Listing 3.15, allows you to specify a date and, optionally, a specific day of the week. It returns the number of times the specified day of the week occurs in the month containing the date. If you don't pass a day of the week value, the function counts the number of times the day indicated by the date parameter occurs within its own month.

Listing 3.15: Count the Number of Specific Weekdays in a Month

```
Public Function dhCountDOWInMonth(ByVal dtmDate As Date, _
  Optional lngDOW As VbDayOfWeek = 0) As Integer

    Dim dtmFirst As Date
    Dim intCount As Integer
    Dim intMonth As Integer

    If (lngDOW < vbSunday Or lngDOW > vbSaturday) Then
        ' Caller must not have specified DOW, or it
        ' was an invalid number.
        lngDOW = Weekday(dtmDate)
    End If
    intMonth = Month(dtmDate)

    ' Find the first day of the month
    dtmFirst = DateSerial(Year(dtmDate), intMonth, 1)

    ' Get to the first lngDOW including or after the first
    ' day of the month.
    dtmFirst = dtmFirst + ((lngDOW - Weekday(dtmFirst) + 7) Mod 7)

    ' Now, dtmFirst is sitting on the first day
    ' of the requested number in the month.

    ' There are either 4 or 5 of each weekday in each month.
    ' Assume there are 5. If that gives you a date outside
    '  the month, there are only 4. If there are 5 of a
    ' given day within a month, the 5th one will be
    ' 28 days after the first.
```

```
        intCount = 5
        If (Month(dtmFirst + 28) <> Month(dtmFirst)) Then
            intCount = 4
        End If
        dhCountDOWInMonth = intCount
End Function
```

The dhCountDOWInMonth function takes four simple steps to do its work. It must do the following:

1. Verify the parameters.

2. Find the first day of the specified month.

3. Move forward within the month to the first day matching the day of week you're interested in.

4. Calculate the number of matching days in the month. The month must contain either four or five instances of a given weekday. Assume there are five. Add 28 days to the starting date, and if the date you get is in a different month than the starting date, set the result to be four.

To verify the parameters, the code checks the lngDOW parameter, making sure the value is between vbSunday and vbSaturday. If not, it overrides the value and uses the day of the week represented by the dtmDate parameter:

```
If (lngDOW < vbSunday Or lngDOW > vbSaturday) Then
    ' Caller must not have specified DOW, or it
    ' was an invalid number.
    lngDOW - WeekDay(dtmDate)
End If
```

Finding the first day of the month requires yet another call to the DateSerial function:

```
' Find the first day of the month
dtmFirst = DateSerial(Year(dtmDate), intMonth, 1)
```

Finding the day matching the required day of the week takes just a single line, using the same logic shown in several earlier procedures:

```
' Get to the first lngDOW including or after the first
' day of the month.
dtmFirst = dtmFirst + ((lngDOW - Weekday(dtmFirst) + 7) Mod 7)
```

Finally, assume the result is five, check the date four weeks later, and see if the months match. If not, set the result to be four:

```
intCount = 5
If (Month(dtmFirst + 28) <> Month(dtmFirst)) Then
    intCount = 4
End If
dhCountDOWInMonth = intCount
```

To test this function, you might write code like this:

```
If dhCountDOWInMonth(#12/1999#, vbFriday) > 4 Then
    MsgBox "There are more than four Fridays in December 1999!"
End If
```

Is This a Leap Year?

Although VBA provides very rich date and time support, it includes no built-in function that will tell you whether a given year is a leap year. Calculating this answer is actually more complex than checking to see whether the year is evenly divisible by four. If that's all it took, you could just check like this:

```
' (Assuming that intYear holds the year in question)
' MOD returns the remainder when you divide, so
' the following expression will return True if
' intYear is evenly divisible by 4.
If intYear MOD 4 = 0 Then
```

But that's not all there is. The year is defined as the length of time it takes to pass from one vernal equinox to another. If the calendar gains or loses days, the date for the equinox shifts. Because the physical year isn't exactly 365.25 days in length (as the calendar says it should be), the current calendar supplies three too many leap years every 385 years. To make up for that, years divisible by 100 aren't leap years unless they're a multiple of 400. Got all that? (In case you're concerned, this schedule will result in an error of only three days in 10,000 years. Not to worry...) This means that 1700, 1800, and 1900 weren't leap years, but 2000 is.

Yes, you could write the code to handle this yourself, and it's not all that difficult. But why do it? VBA is already handling the algorithm internally. It knows that the day after February 28 (in all but a leap year) is March 1 but in a leap year it's February 29. To take advantage of this fact, dhIsLeapYear (shown in Listing 3.16) calculates the answer for you.

Listing 3.16: Is the Specified Year a Leap Year?

```
Public Function dhIsLeapYear(Optional varDate As Variant) As Boolean
    ' Is the supplied year a leap year?
    ' Check the day number of the day
    ' after Feb 28 to find out.

    ' Missing? Use the current year.
    If IsMissing(varDate) Then
        varDate = Year(Date)

    ' Is it a date? Then use that year.
    ElseIf VarType(varDate) = vbDate Then
        varDate = Year(varDate)

    ' Is it an integer? Use that value, if it's value.
    ' Otherwise, use the current year.
    ElseIf VarType(varDate) = vbInteger Then
        ' Only years 100 through 9999 are allowed.
        If varDate < 100 Or varDate > 9999 Then
            varDate = Year(Date)
        End If

    ' If it's not a date or an integer, just use the
    ' current year.
    Else
        varDate = Year(Date)
    End If
    dhIsLeapYear = (Day(DateSerial(varDate, 2, 28) + 1) = 29)
End Function
```

Almost all the code in dhIsLeapYear handles the "optional" parameter; because you can pass either a date or an integer representing a year, you need a larger amount of error-checking code than normal. If you pass nothing at all, the code uses the current year:

```
If IsMissing(varDate) Then
    varDate = Year(Date)
```

If you pass a date, the function uses the year portion of the date:

```
' Is it a date? Then use that year.
ElseIf VarType(varDate) = vbDate Then
    varDate = Year(varDate)
```

If you pass an integer, the code treats that integer as the year to check. Because VBA can only process years between 100 and 9999, it verifies that your integer falls in that range. If you pass a value that's neither a date nor an integer, it uses the current year:

```
ElseIf VarType(varDate) = vbInteger Then
    ' Only years 100 through 9999 are allowed.
    If varDate < 100 Or varDate > 9999 Then
        varDate = Year(Date)
    End If
' If it's not a date or an integer, just use the
' current year.
Else
    varDate = Year(Date)
End If
```

After performing all that parameter checking, the code that calculates the return value is simple: It checks the Day function's return value for the day after the 28th of February in the specified year. If the value is 29, you've got a leap year. If it's something else (hopefully 1, otherwise VBA is in bad shape), it's not a leap year:

```
dhIsLeapYear = (Day(DateSerial(varDate, 2, 28) + 1) = 29)
```

You might try calling the procedure in any of these three ways:

```
If dhIsLeapYear() Then
    ' You know the current year is a leap year.
If dhIsLeapYear(1956) Then
    ' You know 1956 was a leap year.
If dhIsLeapYear(#12/1/92#) Then
    ' You know 1992 was a leap year.
```

The moral of this story (if there is one) is to let VBA do as much work as possible for you. Although you could have written the dhIsLeapYear function to take into account the algorithm used by the Gregorian calendar, what's the point? The VBA developers have done that work already. You'll get better performance (and fewer bugs) by taking advantage of the work that's already been done.

Rounding Times to the Nearest Increment

If you're writing a scheduling application, you may need to round a time to a specified number of minutes. For example, given a time, you may need to find the nearest 5-, 10-, 15-, 20-, or 30-minute interval. The solution isn't trivial, and the code shown in Listing 3.17 takes care of this problem.

To call dhRoundTime(), pass it a date/time value and an interval to round to. (You must use any divisor of 60, but you'll most likely use 5, 10, 15, 20, 30, or 60.) For example,

```
? dhRoundTime(#12:32:15#, 5)
```

returns

```
12:30:00 PM
```

and

```
? dhRoundTime(#12:32:35#, 5)
```

returns

```
12:35:00 PM
```

If you pass dhRoundTime a full date and time value, it will preserve the date portion and just modify the time part.

Listing 3.17: Round Time Values to the Nearest Interval

```
Public Function dhRoundTime( _
 dtmTime As Date, intInterval As Integer) As Date

    ' Round the time value in varTime to the nearest minute
    ' interval in intInterval

    Dim decTime As Variant
    Dim intHour As Integer
    Dim intMinute As Integer
    Dim lngdate As Long

    ' Get the date portion of the date/time value
    lngdate = DateValue(dtmTime)

    ' Get the time portion as a number like 11.5 for 11:30.
    decTime = CDec(TimeValue(dtmTime) * 24)

    ' Get the hour and store it away. Int truncates,
    ' CInt rounds, so use Int.
    intHour = Int(decTime)
```

```
' Get the number of minutes, and then round to the nearest
' occurrence of the interval specified.
intMinute = CInt((decTime - intHour) * 60)
intMinute = CInt(intMinute / intInterval) * intInterval

' Build back up the original date/time value,
' rounded to the nearest interval.
dhRoundTime = CDate(lngdate + _
   ((intHour + intMinute / 60) / 24))
End Function
```

This procedure is probably the most complex in this chapter, at least in terms of the calculations it performs. Its first step is to store away the date portion of the original date/time value so it can preserve the value, which will never be altered by the function:

```
' Get the date portion of the date/time value
lngdate = DateValue(dtmTime)
```

Next, the procedure retrieves the time portion of the parameter and converts it into a decimal number, multiplying the value by 24:

```
' Get the time portion as a number like 11.5 for 11:30.
decTime = CDec(TimeValue(dtmTime) * 24)
```

Because the time portion of a date/time value is the fraction of a full day represented by the time, taking a value representing 12:32:15 P.M. (0.522395833333333) and multiplying it by 24 will result in the value 12.5375. Once you have the time in a format like that, you can round it as needed.

TIP Note the use of the CDec function in this example. Because you do want to preserve the accuracy of the calculation, you want to reduce rounding errors. The Decimal data type (discussed in more detail in Chapter 2) doesn't cause any rounding errors, and although it's not likely that multiplication will cause any rounding problems, it can't hurt to preserve accuracy when possible.

Once the function knows the time, it can tuck away the hour portion, because that value will also never change.

```
' Get the hour and store it away. Int truncates,
' CInt rounds, so use Int.
intHour = Int(decTime)
```

The next step is to pull off just the fractional portion (representing the minutes) and multiply by 60 to find the number of minutes involved. Using the example of 12.5375, multiplying the fractional part by 60 and converting to an integer would return 32, which is the number of minutes involved:

```
' Get the number of minutes, and then round to the nearest
' occurrence of the interval specified.
intMinute = CInt((decTime - intHour) * 60)
```

The crucial step involves rounding the number of minutes to the correct interval:

```
intMinute = CInt(intMinute / intInterval) * intInterval
```

Once you've rounded the value, the final step is to reconstruct the full date/time value. The following line of code adds the hour portion to the minute portion divided by 60, divides the entire time portion by 24 to convert to the appropriate fraction, adds the result to the preserved date value, and returns the entire value:

```
dhRoundTime = CDate(lngdate + _
  ((intHour + intMinute / 60) / 24))
```

You may find it useful to single-step through this procedure, checking the value of various variables as it runs. Try calling dhRoundTime from the Immediate window, passing in various times and divisors of 60 as intervals. Once you get the hang of what dhRoundTime is doing, you'll find it useful in many applications that involve time and scheduling.

Converting Strings or Numbers to Real Dates

The world of data isn't perfect, that's for sure, and data can come to your application in many formats. Dates are particularly troublesome because there are so many ways to display and format them. If you routinely need to gather information from outside sources, you'll appreciate the two functions in this section. The first, dhCNumDate (Listing 3.18), attempts to convert dates stored in numeric values into true Date format. The second function, dhCStrDate (Listing 3.19), performs the same sort of task, but with formatted strings as input.

Some computer systems, for example, store dates as integers such as 19971231 (representing #12/31/1997#) or 52259 (representing #5/22/1959#). The code in dhCNumDate can convert those values into real VBA date/time format, as long as you tell it the layout of the number coming in. For example, to perform the first conversion, you might use

```
dtmBirthday = dhCNumDate(19971231, "YYYYMMDD")
```

The function, knowing how the date number was laid out, could pull out the various pieces.

The dhCStrDate function does similar work but with string values as its input. For example, if all the dates coming in from your mainframe computer were in the format "MMDDYYYY," you could use

```
' strOldDate contains "05221959"
dtmNewDate = dhCStrDate(strOldDate, "MMDDYYYY")
```

to convert the string into a real date.

Listing 3.18: Convert Formatted Numbers to Real Dates

```
Public Function dhCNumDate(ByVal lngdate As Long, _
ByVal strFormat As String) As Variant
    ' Convert numbers to dates, depending on the specified format
    ' and the incoming number. In this case, the number and the
    ' format must match, or the output will be useless.

    Dim intYear As Integer
    Dim intMonth As Integer
    Dim intDay As Integer

    Select Case strFormat
        Case "MMDDYY"
            intYear = lngdate Mod 100
            intMonth = lngdate \ 10000
            intDay = (lngdate \ 100) Mod 100

        Case "MMDDYYYY"
            intYear = lngdate Mod 10000
            intMonth = lngdate \ 1000000
            intDay = (lngdate \ 10000) Mod 100

        Case "DDMMYY"
            intYear = lngdate Mod 100
            intMonth = (lngdate \ 100) Mod 100
            intDay = lngdate \ 10000

        Case "DDMMYYYY"
            intYear = lngdate Mod 10000
            intMonth = (lngdate \ 10000) Mod 100
            intDay = lngdate \ 1000000
```

```
            Case "YYMMDD", "YYYYMMDD"
                intYear = lngdate \ 10000
                intMonth = (lngdate \ 100) Mod 100
                intDay = lngdate Mod 100

            Case Else
                ' Raise an error and get out.
                ' Error 5 normally indicates an invalid parameter.
                Err.Raise 5, "dhCNumDate", "Invalid parameter"
        End Select
        dhCNumDate = DateSerial(intYear, intMonth, intDay)
    End Function
```

TIP   You'll find an interesting code technique in dhCNumDate. Given a number like 220459 (#4/22/59# in date format), retrieving the month portion requires some effort. The code accomplishes this by first using integer division (the \ operator), resulting in 2204. Then, to retrieve just the month portion, the code uses the Mod operator to find the remainder you get when you divide 2204 by 100. You'll find the integer division and the Mod operator useful if you want to retrieve specific digits from a number, as we did in dhCNumDate.

Listing 3.19: Convert Formatted Strings to Real Dates

```
Public Function dhCStrDate( _
 strDate As String, Optional strFormat As String = "") As Date

    ' Given a string containing a date value, and a format
    ' string describing the information in the date string,
    ' convert the string into a real date value.
    '

    Dim strYear As String
    Dim strMonth As String
    Dim strDay As String

    Select Case strFormat
        Case "MMDDYY", "MMDDYYYY"
            strYear = Mid$(strDate, 5)
            strMonth = Left$(strDate, 2)
            strDay = Mid$(strDate, 3, 2)
```

```
            Case "DDMMYY", "DDMMYYYY"
                strYear = Mid$(strDate, 5)
                strMonth = Mid$(strDate, 3, 2)
                strDay = Left$(strDate, 2)

            Case "YYMMDD"
                strYear = Left$(strDate, 2)
                strMonth = Mid$(strDate, 3, 2)
                strDay = Right$(strDate, 2)

            Case "YYYYMMDD"
                strYear = Left$(strDate, 4)
                strMonth = Mid$(strDate, 5, 2)
                strDay = Right$(strDate, 2)

            Case "DD/MM/YY", "DD/MM/YYYY"
                strYear = Mid$(strDate, 7)
                strMonth = Mid$(strDate, 4, 2)
                strDay = Left$(strDate, 2)

            Case "YY/MM/DD"
                strYear = Left$(strDate, 2)
                strMonth = Mid$(strDate, 4, 2)
                strDay = Right$(strDate, 2)

            Case "YYYY/MM/DD"
                strYear = Left$(strDate, 4)
                strMonth = Mid$(strDate, 6, 2)
                strDay = Right$(strDate, 2)

            Case Else
                ' If none of the other formats were matched, raise
                ' an error and get out.
                Err.Raise 5, "dhCStrDate", "Invalid parameter"
        End Select
        dhCStrDate = DateSerial(Val(strYear), Val(strMonth), Val(strDay))
    End Function
```

There's no doubt about it—the code in both these functions relies on brute force. Given the examples already in the functions, you should find it easy to add your own new formats, should the need arise. In each case, it's just a matter of using the correct mathematical or string functions to perform the necessary conversions.

Working with Elapsed Time

No matter how much you'd like VBA date/time values to be able to track elapsed time, they're not built that way. As designed, VBA date/time values store a particular point in time, not a span of time, and there's no way to store more than 24 hours in a given date/time variable. If you want to work with elapsed times, you'll generally have to do some conversion work, storing the elapsed times in a numeric data type and converting them back to a formatted output for display. Other elapsed time issues simply return an integer value indicating the number of elapsed units (year, days, months) between two dates.

This section covers several standard issues when dealing with elapsed times, including these topics:

- Finding the number of workdays between two dates

- Returning a person's age, in years, given the birth date

- Formatting elapsed time using a format specification string

- Formatting cumulative times

Finding Workdays between Two Dates

Many applications require you to calculate the number of days between two dates (and you can simply use DateDiff or subtract the first date value from the second, if that's all you need). In addition, many business applications need to know the number of workdays between two dates, and that's a bit more complex. The function in this section, dhCountWorkdays, uses the SkipHolidays and IsWeekend procedures presented previously (see the section "Working with Workdays") to skip holidays and weekends. Listing 3.20 shows the entire function. (You can find the dhCountWorkdays function in the module named DateTimeADO. It's grouped in this module because it relies on ADO to find holidays, as discussed previously in the chapter.)

Listing 3.20: Count the Number of Workdays between Two Dates

```
Public Function dhCountWorkdays( _
  ByVal dtmStart As Date, ByVal dtmEnd As Date, _
  Optional rst As ADODB.Recordset = Nothing, _
  Optional strField As String = "") _
```

```
    As Integer

        ' Count the business days (not counting weekends/holidays) in
        ' a given date range.

        Dim intDays As Integer
        Dim dtmTemp As Date
        Dim intSubtract As Integer

        ' Swap the dates if necessary.
        If dtmEnd < dtmStart Then
            dtmTemp = dtmStart
            dtmStart = dtmEnd
            dtmEnd = dtmTemp
        End If

        ' Get the start and end dates to be weekdays.
        dtmStart = SkipHolidays(rst, strField, dtmStart, 1)
        dtmEnd = SkipHolidays(rst, strField, dtmEnd, -1)
        If dtmStart > dtmEnd Then
            ' Sorry, no Workdays to be had. Just return 0.
            dhCountWorkdays = 0
        Else
            intDays = dtmEnd - dtmStart + 1

            ' Subtract off weekend days.  Do this by figuring out how
            ' many calendar weeks there are between the dates, and
            ' multiplying the difference by two (because there are two
            ' weekend days for each week). That is, if the difference
            ' is 0, the two days are in the same week. If the
            ' difference is 1, then we have two weekend days.
            intSubtract = (DateDiff("ww", dtmStart, dtmEnd) * 2)

            ' The answer to our quest is all the weekdays, minus any
            ' holidays found in the table.
            ' If rst is Nothing, this call won't subtract any dates.
            intSubtract = intSubtract + _
             CountHolidays(rst, strField, dtmStart, dtmEnd)

            dhCountWorkdays = intDays - intSubtract
        End If
    End Function
```

To call dhCountWorkdays, pass it two dates (the starting and ending dates). In addition, if you want to take holidays into account, pass it a reference to an open ADO recordset and the name of the field within the recordset containing the holiday date information. For more information on working with this type of function, see the section "Working with Workdays" earlier in this chapter. Unlike the functions presented there, however, this one requires a bit of effort to find the right answer.

There are, of course, many ways to solve this problem. The solution we came up with takes these steps:

1. Move the starting date forward, skipping weekend and holiday dates, until it finds a workday:

   ```
   dtmStart = SkipHolidays(rst, strField, dtmStart, 1)
   ```

2. Take the same step with the ending date, moving backward.

   ```
   dtmEnd = SkipHolidays(rst, strField, dtmEnd, -1)
   ```

3. If the starting date is now past the ending date, there are no workdays in the interval, so just return 0:

   ```
   If dtmStart > dtmEnd Then
       ' Sorry, no workdays to be had. Just return 0.
       dhCountWorkdays = 0
   ```

4. Calculate the difference between the dates so far:

   ```
   intDays = dtmEnd - dtmStart + 1
   ```

   Now for the tricky part, the final three steps:

5. Subtract the number of weekend days. DateDiff, using the "ww" interval specifier, gives you the number of weeks, and there are two weekend days per weekend:

   ```
   intSubtract = (DateDiff("ww", dtmStart, dtmEnd) * 2)
   ```

6. Subtract the number of holiday days. If you've not supplied a recordset variable, the CountHolidays function returns without doing any work, reporting no holidays in the interval:

   ```
   intSubtract = intSubtract + _
   CountHolidays(rst, strField, dtmStart, dtmEnd)
   ```

7. Finally, return the total number of workdays in the interval:

```
dhCountWorkdays = intDays - intSubtract
```

To work with these procedures, you might write a test routine like the one shown in Listing 3.21 (from the TestDateTime module). This procedure makes these assumptions:

- You have OLEDB and ADO installed on your machine.

- You have a reference set to the ADO 2.1 or higher type library in your project.

- You have an XML file named HOLIDAYS.XML available (and you've modi-fied the code to point to the actual location of HOLIDAYS.XML). You can use the CreateHolidaysXML procedure to create this XML file, based on tbl-Holidays in the supplied Jet 4 MDB file, Holidays.MDB. (In order for this to work, you must have the Jet 4 OLEDB provider installed on your machine. If you've installed ADO 2.1 or higher, you have this. If not, you'll need to download the most current ADO providers from Microsoft's Web site at `http://www.microsoft.com/data`.)

- tblHolidays, in Holidays.MDB, includes a date/time field named Date, con-taining one row for each holiday you want tracked.

Listing 3.21: Test Procedure for dhCountWorkdays

```
Sub TestCountWorkdays()
    Dim rst As ADODB.Recordset

    ' You'll need to modify the path in the next line, to point
    ' to your sample database.
    Set rst = New ADODB.Recordset
    rst.Open ActiveWorkbook.Path & "\Holidays.xml", , _
    adOpenKeyset, adLockReadOnly, Options:=adCmdFile

    Debug.Print dhCountWorkdays(#7/2/2000#, #7/5/2000#, rst, "Date")
    Debug.Print dhCountWorkdays(#7/2/2000#, #7/5/2000#)

    Debug.Print dhCountWorkdays(#12/27/1999#, #1/2/2000#, rst, "Date")
    Debug.Print dhCountWorkdays(#12/27/1999#, #1/2/2000#)
End Sub
```

Calculating Age

Calculating someone's age, given that person's birth date, is a commonplace need in data manipulation. Unfortunately, VBA doesn't give a complete and correct method for calculating a person's age.

You might be tempted to use this formula:

```
Age = DateDiff("yyyy", Birthdate, Date)
```

to calculate age, but this doesn't quite work. If the birth date hasn't yet occurred this year, the Age value will be off by 1. For example, imagine your birthday is December 31, and you were born in 1950. If today is October 1, 2000, subtracting the year portions of the two dates (2000 – 1950) would indicate that you were 50 years old. In reality, by the standard way of figuring such things, you're still only 49. (And you'd better take advantage of it while you can!)

To handle this discrepancy, the dhAge function in Listing 3.22 not only subtracts one Year portion of the dates from the other, it checks whether the birth date has already occurred this year. If it hasn't, the function subtracts 1 from the calculation, returning the correct age.

In addition, dhAge allows you to pass an optional second date: the date on which to calculate the age. If you pass nothing for the second parameter, the code assumes you want to use the current date as the ending date. That is, if you use a call like this:

```
intAge = dhAge(#5/22/59#)
```

you'll find the current age of someone born on May 22, 1959. If you call the function like this:

```
intAge = dhAge(#5/22/59#, #1/1/2010#)
```

you'll find out how old the same person will be on the first day of 2010.

Listing 3.22: One Solution for Calculating Age

```
Public Function dhAge(dtmBD As Date, _
 Optional dtmDate As Date = 0) As Integer

    Dim intAge As Integer

    If dtmDate = 0 Then
        ' Did the caller pass in a date? If not, use
        ' the current date.
        dtmDate = Date
    End If
```

```
        intAge = DateDiff("yyyy", dtmBD, dtmDate)
        If dtmDate < DateAdd("yyyy", intAge, dtmBD) Then
            intAge = intAge - 1
        End If
        dhAge = intAge
    End Function
```

TIP   You might also be tempted to solve this problem by dividing the difference between the two dates, in days, by 365.25. This works for some combinations of dates, but not for all. It's just not worth the margin of error. The functions presented here are simple enough that they're a reasonable replacement for the simple division that seems otherwise intuitive.

If you're looking for the smallest possible solution, perhaps at the expense of readability, you could use the version in Listing 3.23 instead. It relies on the fact that a true expression is equal to the value –1 and a false expression is equal to 0. The function adds –1 or 0 to the year difference, depending on whether the specified birth date has passed.

⟳ Listing 3.23: A Second Solution for Calculating Age

```
    Public Function dhAge1(dtmBD As Date, _
     Optional dtmDate As Date = 0) As Integer

        Dim intAge As Integer

        If dtmDate = 0 Then
            ' Did the caller pass in a date? If not, use
            ' the current date.
            dtmDate = Date
        End If
        intAge = DateDiff("yyyy", dtmBD, dtmDate)
        dhAge1 = intAge + _
         (dtmDate < DateAdd("yyyy", intAge, dtmBD))
    End Function
```

Formatting Elapsed Time

VBA provides no support for elapsed times or for displaying formatted elapsed times. You'll have to take steps on your own if you want to take two dates, find the difference between them, and display the difference formatted the way you want it. The function in this section, dhFormatInterval, in Listing 3.24 (certainly the longest procedure in this chapter), allows you to specify two dates and an optional format specifier and returns a string representing the difference. As the function is currently written, you can use any of the format specifiers listed in Table 3.9. You are invited, of course, to add your own specifiers to the list by modifying the source code. (For information on retrieving the time delimiter programmatically, see the section "Formatting Cumulative Times" later in this chapter.)

TABLE 3.9:   Available Format Specifications for dhFormatInterval

Format	Example
D H	3 Days 3 Hours
D H M	3 Days 2 Hours 46 Minutes
D H M S	3 Days 2 Hours 45 Minutes 45 Seconds
D H:MM	3 Days 2:46
D HH:MM	3 Days 02:46
D HH:MM:SS	3 Days 02:45:45
H M	74 Hours 46 Minutes
H:MM	74:46 (leading 0 on minutes, if necessary)
H:MM:SS	74:45:45
M S	4485 Minutes 45 Seconds
M:SS	4485:45 (leading 0 on seconds, if necessary)

Listing 3.24: Format the Interval between Two Dates

```
Public Function dhFormatInterval(dtmStart As Date, datend As Date, _
  Optional strFormat As String = "H:MM:SS") As String
    ' Return the difference between two times,
    ' formatted as specified in strFormat.
```

```
Dim lngSeconds As Long
Dim decMinutes As Variant
Dim decHours As Variant
Dim decDays As Variant

Dim intSeconds As Integer
Dim intMinutes As Integer
Dim intHours As Integer

Dim intRoundedHours As Integer
Dim intRoundedMinutes As Integer

Dim strDay As String
Dim strHour As String
Dim strMinute As String
Dim strSecond As String
Dim strOut As String

Dim lngFullDays As Long
Dim lngFullHours As Long
Dim lngFullMinutes As Long

Dim strDelim As String

Const dhcDays As String = "Days"
Const dhcHours As String = "Hours"
Const dhcMinutes As String = "Minutes"
Const dhcSeconds As String = "Seconds"

Const dhcDay As String = "Day"
Const dhcHour As String = "Hour"
Const dhcMinute As String = "Minute"
Const dhcSecond As String = "Second"


' If you don't want to use the local delimiter,
' but a specific one, replace the next line with
' this:
' strDelim = ":"
strDelim = GetTimeDelimiter()
```

```
' Calculate the full number of seconds in the interval.
' This limits the calculation to 2 billion seconds (68 years
' or so), but that's not too bad. Then calculate the
' difference in minutes, hours, and days, as well.
lngSeconds = DateDiff("s", dtmStart, datend)
decMinutes = CDec(lngSeconds / 60)
decHours = CDec(decMinutes / 60)
decDays = CDec(decHours / 24)

' Get the full hours and minutes, for later display.
lngFullDays = Int(decDays)
lngFullHours = Int(decHours)
lngFullMinutes = Int(decMinutes)

' Get the incremental amount of each unit.
intHours = Int((decDays - lngFullDays) * 24)
intMinutes = Int((decHours - lngFullHours) * 60)
intSeconds = CInt((decMinutes - lngFullMinutes) * 60)

' In some instances, time values must be rounded.
' The next two lines depend on the fact that a true statement
' has a value of -1, and a false statement has a value of 0.
' The code needs to add 1 to the value if the following expression
' is true, and 0 if not.
intRoundedHours = intHours - (intMinutes > 30)
intRoundedMinutes = intMinutes - (intSeconds > 30)

' Assume all units are plural, until you find otherwise.
strDay = dhcDays
strHour = dhcHours
strMinute = dhcMinutes
strSecond = dhcSeconds

If lngFullDays = 1 Then strDay = dhcDay
Select Case strFormat
    Case "D H"
        If intRoundedHours = 1 Then strHour = dhcHour
        strOut = _
         lngFullDays & " " & strDay & " " & _
         intRoundedHours & " " & strHour
```

```
Case "D H M"
    If intHours = 1 Then strHour = dhcHour
    If intRoundedMinutes = 1 Then strMinute = dhcMinute
    strOut = _
     lngFullDays & " " & strDay & " " & _
     intHours & " " & strHour & " " & _
     intRoundedMinutes & " " & strMinute

Case "D H M S"
    If intHours = 1 Then strHour = dhcHour
    If intMinutes = 1 Then strMinute = dhcMinute
    If intSeconds = 1 Then strSecond = dhcSecond
    strOut = _
     lngFullDays & " " & strDay & " " & _
     intHours & " " & strHour & " " & _
     intMinutes & " " & strMinute & " " & _
     intSeconds & " " & strSecond

Case "D H:MM"        ' 3 Days 2:46"
    strOut = lngFullDays & " " & strDay & " " & _
     intHours & strDelim & Format(intRoundedMinutes, "00")

Case "D HH:MM"       ' 3 Days 02:46"
    strOut = lngFullDays & " " & strDay & " " & _
     Format(intHours, "00") & strDelim & _
     Format(intRoundedMinutes, "00")

Case "D HH:MM:SS"   ' 3 Days 02:45:45"
    strOut = lngFullDays & " " & strDay & " " & _
     Format(intHours, "00") & strDelim & _
     Format(intMinutes, "00") & strDelim & _
     Format(intSeconds, "00")

Case "H M"           ' 74 Hours 46 Minutes"
    If lngFullHours = 1 Then strHour = dhcHour
    If intRoundedMinutes = 1 Then strMinute = dhcMinute
    strOut = lngFullHours & " " & strHour & " " & _
     intRoundedMinutes & " " & strMinute

Case "H:MM"          ' 74:46 (leading 0 on minutes, if necessary)
    strOut = lngFullHours & strDelim & _
     Format(intRoundedMinutes, "00")
```

```
        Case "H:MM:SS"      ' 74:45:45"
            strOut = lngFullHours & strDelim & _
             Format(intMinutes, "00") & strDelim & _
             Format(intSeconds, "00")

        Case "M S"          ' 4485 Minutes 45 Seconds
            If lngFullMinutes = 1 Then strMinute = dhcMinute
            If intSeconds = 1 Then strSecond = dhcSecond
            strOut = lngFullMinutes & " " & strMinute & " " & _
             intSeconds & " " & strSecond
        Case "M:SS"         ' 4485:45 (leading 0 on seconds)"
            strOut = lngFullMinutes & strDelim & _
             Format(intSeconds, "00")

        Case Else
            strOut = vbNullString
    End Select
    dhFormatInterval = strOut
End Function
```

For example, to test out the function, you might write a test routine like the sample shown in Listing 3.25 (from the module named TestDateTime). This sample exercises all the predefined format specifiers.

Listing 3.25: Test Routine for dhFormatInterval

```
Sub TestInterval()
    Dim dtmStart As Date
    Dim dtmEnd As Date

    dtmStart = #1/1/97 12:00:00 PM#
    dtmEnd = #1/4/97 2:45:45 PM#

    Debug.Print dhFormatInterval(dtmStart, dtmEnd, "D H")
    Debug.Print dhFormatInterval(dtmStart, dtmEnd, "D H M")
    Debug.Print dhFormatInterval(dtmStart, dtmEnd, "D H M S")
    Debug.Print dhFormatInterval(dtmStart, dtmEnd, "D H:MM")
    Debug.Print dhFormatInterval(dtmStart, dtmEnd, "D HH:MM")
    Debug.Print dhFormatInterval(dtmStart, dtmEnd, "D HH:MM:SS")
    Debug.Print dhFormatInterval(dtmStart, dtmEnd, "H M")
    Debug.Print dhFormatInterval(dtmStart, dtmEnd, "H:MM")
```

```
        Debug.Print dhFormatInterval(dtmStart, dtmEnd, "H:MM:SS")
        Debug.Print dhFormatInterval(dtmStart, dtmEnd, "M S")
        Debug.Print dhFormatInterval(dtmStart, dtmEnd, "M:SS")
    End Sub
```

Let's face it: The dhFormatInterval function defines the term *brute force*. Although we attempted to make this routine as simple as possible, it requires several steps to provide all this flexibility.

How does it work? The function first calculates the difference between the two dates in seconds and then calculates the total number of days, hours, minutes, and seconds. In addition, it calculates the number of leftover hours, minutes, and seconds so it can display those, too. Finally, it also calculates rounded values for hours and minutes. That way, if you choose not to display seconds, the minutes value will be rounded accordingly. The same goes for hours: If you decide not to display minutes, the hours value must be rounded to the nearest full hour. Once the routine has those values, it uses a large Select Case statement to determine which type of output string to create and takes the steps to create the correct result.

WARNING   Because dhFormatInterval calculates the difference between the two dates in seconds and places that value in a long integer, you're limited to around 68 years between the two dates. Most likely that won't be a terrible limitation, but you should be aware of it before using this function in a production application.

Formatting Cumulative Times

As we've already stated, VBA has no way of storing, or measuring, elapsed times in its date/time fields. When you assign 8:30 to a Date variable, you may *think* you're entering the number of hours someone worked, but you're actually entering a specific time: 8:30 A.M. on December 30, 1899. VBA has no qualms about performing aggregate calculations on date/time fields—they're stored internally as floating-point values, so there's no problem performing the calculation—but the result will not be what you had in mind.

The task, then, is to allow you to enter time values as you've become accustomed. You'll need to convert them to some simple value for calculations and then format the output as a standard time value for display. To make all this happen, you'll need the two functions included here, dhCMinutes and dhCTimeStr. The dhCMinutes function accepts a date/time value as a parameter and returns the time portion, converted to the corresponding number of minutes. Given that value, you can easily sum up a series of time values. Then, when you're ready to display your sum, you'll need the dhCTimeStr function. This one, given a number of minutes, returns a string representing the total, in hh:mm format.

For example, imagine you need to find the sum of 8:30, 12:30, and 13:25 (in each case, a span of time). To sum the three time values and convert that sum back into a time format, you could use an expression like this:

```
dhCTimeStr(dhCMinutes(#8:30#) + dhCMinutes(#12:30#) + _
  dhCMinutes(#13:25#))
```

The result of that expression would be the string "34:25."

Each of the functions consists of just a few lines of code. The dhCMinutes function, shown in Listing 3.26, uses the TimeValue function to extract the time portion of the date and multiplies the resulting fraction by 24*60, resulting in the number of minutes represented by the fractional portion.

Listing 3.26: Convert a Date/Time Value into Elapsed Minutes

```
Public Function dhCMinutes(dtmTime As Date) As Long
    ' Convert a date/time value to the number of
    ' minutes since midnight (that is, remove the date
    ' portion, and just work with the time part.) The
    ' return value can be used to calculate sums of
    ' elapsed time.

    ' Subtract off the whole portion of the date/time value
    ' and then convert from a fraction of a day to minutes.
    dhCMinutes = TimeValue(dtmTime) * 24 * 60
End Function
```

The function that converts the number of minutes back to a string formatted as a time value, dhCTimeStr (Listing 3.27), is just as simple. It takes the number of minutes and performs an integer division (using the \ operator) to get the number of hours. Then it uses the Mod operator to find the number of minutes (the remainder when you divide by 60). The function formats each of those values and concatenates them as a string return value.

Listing 3.27: Convert Elapsed Minutes into a Formatted String

```
Public Function dhCTimeStr(lngMinutes As Long) As String
    ' Convert from a number of minutes to a string
    ' that looks like a time value.
    ' This function is not aware of international settings.
    '
    dhCTimeStr = Format(lngMinutes \ 60, "0") & _
      GetTimeDelimiter() & Format(lngMinutes Mod 60, "00")
End Function
```

There's just one small wrinkle here: Not everyone uses the same time delimiter character. The built-in VBA formatting specifiers take that into account, but in this case, you're supplying your own formatting. The solution is to ask Windows for the local time delimiter, of course. Although you can retrieve the information directly from the Registry, that requires much more work and isn't the recommended method. The answer is to use the Windows API, calling the GetLocale-Info function. This function requires you to specify a LocaleID value (a number representing the current "locale" that's being used on your computer) and a constant indicating which locale-specific information you want to retrieve. It digs into the registry for you, finds the information you need, and returns it. (In order to determine your current LocaleID value, the function first calls the GetSystemDefault-LCID function.)

The function GetTimeDelimiter (Listing 3.28) does the work for you, so any function needing to format time values can use the native delimiter.

TIP You'll find the GetLocaleInfo function invaluable if you want to do any work requiring localized settings. Visit `http://msdn.microsoft.com` for more information on this and all the other Windows API functions.

Listing 3.28: Retrieve the Local Time Delimiter

```
Private Function GetTimeDelimiter() As String
    ' Retrieve the time delimiter. Use the GetLocaleInfo
    ' API function to return information about the current
    ' user's settings.
```

```
        Dim lngLCID As Long
        Dim lngLen As Long
        Dim strBuffer As String
        Const MAX_CHARS = 4

        lngLCID = GetSystemDefaultLCID()
        strBuffer = Space(MAX_CHARS + 1)
        lngLen = GetLocaleInfo(lngLCID, LOCALE_STIME, _
          strBuffer, Len(strBuffer))
        ' lngLen includes the trailing Null character.
        GetTimeDelimiter = Left$(strBuffer, lngLen - 1)
    End Function
```

WARNING   If you use the GetTimeDelimiter function in your own applications, you'll also need to copy the associated API declarations into your application as well. Be careful when copying functions that use API calls out of their sample modules. You may find that you must copy the API information as well.

Handling Time Zone Differences

Perhaps you've noticed, but it's not the same time all over the world. When it's midnight in Los Angeles, it's eight in the morning in London. In some applications, you may need to have some way to compare exact times, taking into account the time zone differences between the locations where events occurred. Perhaps you want to know whether a sales order from California came in before an order for the same item in London, but all you have are local times when the orders were placed.

In order to make it possible to retrieve information about absolute times, Windows stores times internally as an absolute value, based on the time in Greenwich, England, home of the prime meridian. (Think back, hard, to third grade. It will all come back to you.) This *coordinated universal time* (oddly abbreviated as UTC within Windows documentation) allows code to be able to compare times and dates based on some absolute, as opposed to local times. For every earthly location Windows is aware of, you can determine the bias (the number of minutes the current locale is removed from Greenwich, England), the state of daylight saving time, and the dates daylight saving time starts and stops.

Working with these values requires a bit of Windows API manipulation, and to keep things simple, we wrapped up all the workings in a simple class module. Yes, class modules won't be covered until Chapter 5, so we won't dwell here on how this class works—instead, we'll focus on how you can use it in your own code.

Using the SystemTimeInfo Class

You can think of the SystemTimeInfo class, provided with the chapter samples, just as you might think of any other object you work with in VBA. That is, just as you might program a form, a control, or an ADO recordset, you can program an instance of the SystemTimeInfo class. It has several properties, some read/write, some read-only. (It doesn't have any methods, or events, but it could.) In order to use the SystemTimeInfo class, it must exist as part of your project, and you must write code to get it into memory so you can use it (much like an ADO recordset object):

```
Dim sti As SystemTimeInfo
Set sti = New SystemTimeInfo
```

Once you've created the object, you can work with its various properties, like this:

```
Debug.Print "The current time zone name is " & sti.CurrentTimeZoneName
Debug.Print "The current time zone bias is " & sti.Bias
```

In this chapter, we won't delve into how the SystemTimeInfo class works—for information on creating and using class modules, see Chapter 5. We've skipped ahead a little because it just makes sense, given the particular API calls, to create a class module here. (For more info on using the Windows API in general, see Appendix B, located on the CD-ROM.)

In general, a class module contains public property procedures (procedures that run when you attempt to set or retrieve the value of a property of the object) and public procedures (treated as methods of the object). In this case, the System-TimeInfo class contains the properties listed in Table 3.10. Once you've created an instance of a SystemTimeInfo object, you can use any of these properties to determine (or, in some cases, change) the time zone behavior of the machine running your code. Although you won't need this function in every application, if you ever do need to be able to compare times and dates in different locales, you may find this class useful.

TABLE 3.10: Properties Provided by the SystemTimeInfo Class

Property	Data Type	Description
Bias	Long	Read-only long representing the number of minutes between the UTC and the current time. Takes into account daylight saving time. For example, Pacific daylight time has a bias of 420 minutes, meaning that UTC time is local time + 420 minutes. The standard bias for this region is 480 minutes, but when daylight saving time is active, you must subtract 60 minutes. The class module handles all these issues for you. For a particular bias (standard or daylight), see the appropriate property, StandardBias or DaylightBias.
CurrentTimeZoneName	String * 32	Read-only string containing the name of the current time zone. The name may be different in different times of the year. For example, the name may be Pacific standard time, or Pacific daylight time, depending on whether daylight saving time is active. For a particular time zone name, see the appropriate property, StandardTimeZoneName or DaylightTimeZoneName.
DaylightBias	Long	Read/write long containing the number of minutes between UTC time and local time, if daylight saving time is currently active. Normally, this value is either –60 or 0. That is, when daylight saving time is active, the local clock has normally been set ahead one hour (making the offset between UTC and local time 60 minutes less). Some states (Arizona, for example) don't use daylight saving time, so this value is 0 in that state. If you want to retrieve the current bias, taking into account daylight saving time, see the Bias property.
DaylightTimeZoneName	String * 32	Read/write string containing the name of the time zone, if daylight saving time is currently active. To retrieve the current name, whether daylight saving time is active or not, see the CurrentTimeZoneName property.
StandardBias	Long	Read/write long containing the number of minutes between UTC time and local time, if daylight saving time is not currently active. When daylight saving time is not active, you can use a formula such as UTC = local time + StandardBias to calculate times. (Daylight saving time normally adds 60 minutes from the local time, subtracting 60 minutes from the bias.) If you want to retrieve the current bias, taking into account daylight saving time, see the Bias property.

TABLE 3.10: Properties Provided by the SystemTimeInfo Class *(continued)*

Property	Data Type	Description
StandardTimeZoneName	String * 32	Read/write string containing the name of the current time zone, if daylight saving time is not currently active. To retrieve the current name, whether daylight saving time is active or not, see the CurrentTimeZoneName property.
SystemDateTime	Date	Read/write date value, allowing you to set or retrieve the system date/time value, which corresponds to UTC time. (That is, the SystemDateTime property minus the Bias property will give you the current date/time. You can use an expression like this, should you need to perform this calculation: DateAdd("n", -sti.Bias, sti.SystemDateTime).) If you need to know the local date/time, use the Now function instead.

The following procedure demonstrates all the properties of the SystemTimeInfo class:

```
Sub TestSystemTimeInfo()
    Dim sti As SystemTimeInfo
    Set sti = New SystemTimeInfo

    Debug.Print "Current time zone name is : " & _
      sti.CurrentTimeZoneName
    Debug.Print "Current time zone bias is : " & _
      sti.Bias

    Debug.Print "Daylight time zone name is: " & _
      sti.DaylightTimeZoneName
    Debug.Print "Daylight time zone bias is: " & _
      sti.DaylightBias

    Debug.Print "Standard time zone name is: " & _
      sti.StandardTimeZoneName
    Debug.Print "Standard time zone bias is: " & _
      sti.StandardBias

    Debug.Print "System date/time (UTC) is : " & _
      sti.SystemDateTime
    Set sti = Nothing
End Sub
```

NOTE   Windows provides many more time and date handling functions, most of which work with file dates and times. Chapter 12 covers many of these in its coverage of working with disk files. See that chapter if you're interested in working with file dates and times. For more information on working with classes and class modules, see Chapter 5.

Summary

Almost any VBA application will sooner or later need to work with date values, and this chapter has provided solid coverage of the built-in date functions, as well as many procedures that use those functions to provide more general functionality. Specifically, we covered these topics:

- How dates are represented in VBA
- All the built-in date functions:
    - Date, Time, Now
    - DatePart, WeekDay, Year, Month, Day, Hour, Minute, Second
    - DateAdd, DateDiff
    - DateValue, TimeValue, CDate
    - DateSerial, TimeSerial
    - Format
- Additional extended functions, for:
    - Finding a specific date
    - Manipulating dates and times
    - Working with elapsed time
    - Working with Windows system date and time, and time zone information

Given the functions presented in this chapter and the information about writing your own additional functions, you should be ready to handle any date/time challenge facing you in your own applications. For similar chapters covering text and numbers, see Chapters 1 and 2, respectively.

chapter 4

Using VBA to Automate Other Applications

- Understanding how Automation works

- Writing simple Automation code

- Creating integrated solutions with Microsoft Office 2000

- Creating event sinks to monitor other applications

The term *Automation* refers to a technology that allows two separate application components to communicate with each other. Communication can take the form of data exchanges or commands issued by one component for another to carry out. The driving force behind the creation and exploitation of this technology is the desire to combine numerous independent software components into a single integrated solution. Almost since its beginning, the Visual Basic language has supported the programming interfaces that make Automation possible. In this chapter, we explain the basics of Automation and explore ways to use it to create integrated solutions using applications like those found in Microsoft Office. After reading this chapter, you should have an understanding of how the pieces of the Automation puzzle fit together and how you can use them to your advantage.

Table 4.1 lists the sample files included on the CD-ROM for this chapter.

TABLE 4.1: Sample Files

Filename	Description
AUTOMATE.XLS	Excel file with sample functions
AUTOMATE.MDB	Access 2000 database with sample functions
AUTOMATE.BAS	General Automation functions
AUTOMATE.VBP	Visual Basic project file with sample functions
EXCEL.BAS	Excel Automation functions
GLOBALS.BAS	Global constants
WORD.BAS	Word Automation functions
WORDEVNT.CLS	Word WithEvents class module
INVOICE.DOT	Sample Word document template
MAIN.FRM	Start-up form for the Visual Basic project
STATREQ.XLS	Sample Excel workbook

Automation Basics

Under the covers, Automation is a very complex technology that involves numerous programming interfaces. Fortunately, VBA has encapsulated those interfaces and made Automation relatively simple to implement. Its greatest strength is that it lets you work with objects from other applications using the same techniques you use now with objects built into VBA or those you create using class modules. Before beginning to write integrated solutions using Automation, you should be familiar with the basics. In this section, we explain the terminology we'll be using, where Automation information is stored, and how to examine an Automation component's objects, properties, and methods.

Terminology

There have been some changes in Automation terminology since we began writing about it in earlier books and magazine articles. In addition, some of the terms used in this book have meanings that differ when taken outside the context of Automation. In both cases, it's important that you understand the specific meanings of these terms.

Changes in Terminology

In the beginning, Microsoft created Object Linking and Embedding and it saw that it was good. But the masses cried, "That's too much to remember! Give us a three-letter acronym!" So Microsoft decried that Object Linking and Embedding would be henceforth known as OLE and it saw that that was also good. And OLE grew and prospered and before long it encompassed much and so Microsoft created ActiveX, which it said was OLE but with much greatness. And the customers rejoiced, yea, the programmers were confused. And then there came the Internet with much promise and mystery. So Microsoft created COM and proclaimed that COM was supreme and forever and that Object Linking and Embedding, and OLE, and ActiveX had never been. And Microsoft rejoiced, yea, the customers and programmers were confused.

Well, if there's one thing Microsoft can't be accused of, it's letting its names for technology get stale. Over the past decade, we've seen a number of technologies designed to enable software to work better together. As this book was being written, the *nom du jour* was COM, short for Component Object Model. (And COM+ is right around the corner!) COM is the all-encompassing term for everything we once knew as Object Linking and Embedding, OLE, and ActiveX. (Despite this, the term ActiveX is still used for some subset technologies.) The following list provides both the old and new terms for some of the technologies involved.

- OLE Automation is now COM Automation or simply Automation.
- OLE Automation components are now COM components.
- OLE custom controls or OLE controls are now ActiveX controls.
- OLE document objects are now ActiveX documents.

Terminology Used in This Chapter

Now, let's clarify some common terms used in this chapter.

Automation requires a client (sometimes called a *controller*) and a server. The *server* is the application or component that provides services to the client. It may exhibit behaviors independently of the client, but, for the most part, it depends on the client's giving it commands to do things. The *client*, on the other hand, is the application that uses the services of an Automation server. In a narrow context, a client application is one that implements a development language that allows you to write code that controls a server. (Of course, you could create your own client from scratch using C++ as the development tool.) Automation clients include Microsoft Visual Basic, Excel, Word, PowerPoint, and Outlook. In fact, any application that supports VBA has Automation client capabilities. An Automation client need not be a development tool, but development tools such as Access and Visual Basic are the ones of most interest here.

In addition to understanding clients and servers, you should be familiar with the difference between object classes and objects. *Object classes* are the types of objects that an Automation server makes available for you to control. Object classes have a defined set of properties, methods and, in some cases, events that dictate how instances of that object class look and act. When you write Automation code, you manipulate *objects*—particular instances of object classes. The same holds true for VBA class modules and the instances you create and manipulate. (For more information on class modules, see Chapter 5.) You can think of objects and object classes as being similar to variables and data types. VBA supports a fixed set of data types, but you can declare and use as many variables of a single type as you wish. In this chapter, when we discuss a server application's *object model,* we are talking about its set of object classes. When you write VBA code, you're using instances of those classes, which are called objects.

What's the Value of Automation?

Automation's biggest benefit is its capacity to let you use pre-built, robust, and debugged software components in your applications. Just imagine having to build your own spreadsheet module instead of using Microsoft Excel. Obviously, for simple tasks, you may decide to "roll your own," but as the complexity of a component increases, the benefits of using off-the-shelf software increase, as well. Automation takes component reuse one step further by allowing you to control objects using your own code, extending whatever built-in intelligence the objects may have. Finally, the architecture of Automation lets you do this unobtrusively. That is, you control objects using Automation the same way you control them in VBA, by using sets of properties, methods, and events. With a few extensions to your current understanding of VBA and its objects, you can start controlling other applications' objects, such as those found in Microsoft Office (Access, Excel, Word, PowerPoint, FrontPage, and Outlook) and ActiveX controls.

Object Classes

Before you can start controlling objects, you need to understand which objects are available to you. As you install applications and ActiveX controls, these components will make entries in the Windows Registry that mark them as controllable to Windows. (Technically speaking, Automation servers are those applications that support the IDispatch programming interface.) Because each application may make more than one object class available to Automation clients, you need to know not only the application name, but the object type, as well. This information is encapsulated in the program identifier, or ProgID, for the particular object class. ProgIDs are expressed as follows:

ApplicationName.ObjectClass

For example, Microsoft Excel exports a controllable Chart class that has an associated ProgID of Excel.Chart. Furthermore, this convention lets you append a version number to the ProgID to restrict manipulation of the object to a particular version of the software. Excel.Chart.5 refers to a Chart object that is manipulated by Excel version 5. Most applications register a pointer to the latest version installed on your computer, so leaving off the version number will force VBA to use the latest version.

WARNING   As software versions are released at an ever-increasing pace, it occasionally becomes necessary to have multiple versions of a particular program installed on your computer. Furthermore, sometimes you will install an older version of a program on a computer that already has a newer version installed. When this happens with an Automation component, the older version sometimes overwrites the Registry information so that an unqualified ProgID (one with no version number appended) will point to the older version. Automation clients that use this ProgID and depend on features that exist only in the newer version will no longer work. When this happens, you should reinstall the newer version. This should restore the Registry settings. However, as a precaution, you can use qualified ProgIDs if you depend on certain features that aren't available in all versions.

While it is not always the case, most applications that feature a user interface (as opposed to "UI-less" servers, which operate transparently behind the scenes) register an Application class. Normally, this object represents the highest-level object in the application's object model, and from it you can derive most other object types. As we discuss the examples in this chapter, the use of ProgIDs should become clear.

Type Libraries: The Key to Classes

These days, almost all COM components implement *type libraries*. Type libraries are databases that list the objects, methods, properties, and events offered by a server application. Automation clients, such as VBA, can use the information stored in a library to "learn" about another application. Type libraries offer a number of benefits:

- VBA does not actually have to run the server application to interrogate its object model.

- The VBA editor and interpreter can use type libraries to perform syntax checking on your Automation code.

- You can obtain context-sensitive help for another application's keywords.

Type libraries can exist as separate files or be implemented as part of an application EXE or DLL. Most components' type libraries that exist as separate files have a TLB or OLB (for object library) file extension, and you use them in your VBA project by adding them to the list of references in the References dialog. Most well-behaved components make the proper Registry entries to make this happen automatically. However, occasionally you must add it to the references list yourself. To do this, follow these steps:

1. Open the Visual Basic development environment.

2. Select the References command from either the Project menu (VB) or the Tools menu (VBA). You should see a list of references similar to the ones shown in Figure 4.1.

3. Check the box next to the reference you want to add.

4. If the reference is not listed, click the Browse button and locate the type library or executable file of the component you want to use.

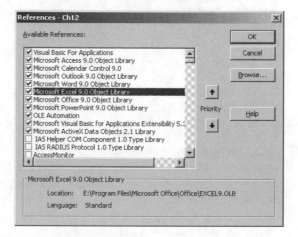

FIGURE 4.1
References dialog showing loaded and available references

Once you've loaded a type library, you can use the objects, properties, and methods in your VBA code. VBA will be able to correctly verify syntax, as well as provide context-sensitive help for the server component's keywords. One important issue is that the complete path to the type library is stored with your VBA project. If you move the type library or install your application on another computer, you will need to reestablish the link to the type library.

NOTE   Type libraries are also essential to *early binding*, the preferred approach to Automation, described in the following sections.

Type Libraries, References, and Broken Apps

In the many years we've been writing, teaching, and speaking on Automation, a few issues regarding server applications and references have been raised again and again. A common one is, "If I use Automation to control Application X, do my users need Application X in order to run my solution?" The answer, of course, is yes. Automation does not magically compile a server application's functionality into your program; it merely controls the application at runtime. The server application must be installed in order for your program to work.

Another common question is, "What happens if the application isn't installed and a user tries to run my program?" The answer depends on whether you've used a type library reference or not. If not, and your code is running in a VBA host like Access, the first time you try to start an Automation session, VBA will raise a run-time error that you can trap and handle as you see fit. However, if you have used a type library, it's a bit trickier since VBA tries to resolve type library references prior to executing code. However, in this case, you can be proactive and run code to validate references. Fortunately the VBA project information is available through the object model at runtime, and you can fix up any broken links.

To do this, you must completely separate the code that uses Automation servers from the code that checks for valid references in different code modules. This is necessary because of VBA's demand load behavior. VBA loads and compiles modules only as needed but will preload modules when they contain procedures referenced by a loaded module. (Of course, this is necessary to compile the requested module completely.) By having a completely separate module that runs a start-up procedure to check references, you have the opportunity to find missing type library references before getting a compile error.

However, if you're running your code in a compiled VB application, you're out of luck. You cannot change the project information (and thus references) at runtime. You should make sure you have very robust error handling to account for code that won't be able to run due to the missing Automation server.

Browsing Objects with Object Browser

Once you've added references to an Automation component's type library, you can use the VBA Object Browser to view a list of the component's classes, properties, methods, and events. To make Object Browser available, open the Visual Basic environment and press the F2 key, click the Object Browser toolbar button or select the View ➢ Object Browser menu command. Figure 4.2 shows Object Browser open to the Application class of Microsoft Excel's type library.

When Object Browser first opens, it displays a list of all the classes exposed by every referenced Automation component, including the current VBA project. You can use the Project/Library drop-down list at the top left of the screen to select a single component, thus making the list of classes a bit more manageable. Object Browser changes the contents of the Classes and Members lists to reflect the change. The Classes list shows all the object classes available from the Automation component. Selecting any one of them causes Object Browser to display the methods and properties for that class in the right-hand list. Icons denote various elements of the type library, such as constants, classes, properties, and methods.

Note that collections are also shown in the left-hand (object) list. When you select a collection, usually denoted as the plural form of the object class name, Object Browser displays the methods and properties for the collection, not the object.

FIGURE 4.2
Object Browser showing details on Excel's Application object

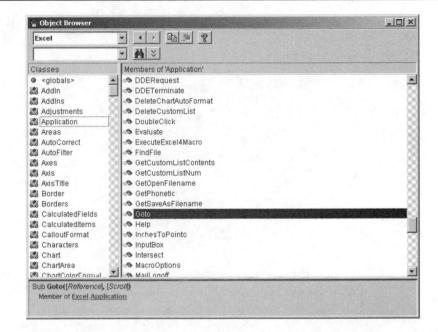

If you're not sure of the exact name of a property or method, you can use Object Browser's search engine. Enter a text string in the text box just below the list of libraries and click the Find button (the one with binoculars on it). After searching the selected type libraries, Object Browser opens the Search Results pane, as shown in Figure 4.3. You can collapse the pane by clicking the button with the up arrows.

Figures 4.2 and 4.3 also show the Application object's Goto method highlighted in the right-hand list. Note the syntax example at the bottom of the dialog. Object Browser shows you the calling syntax of the property or method, including any arguments. You can highlight any portion of the syntax and use the Copy button to copy the highlighted portion to the clipboard for subsequent pasting into a module. If you don't highlight any of the syntax, the Copy button simply copies the method or property name to the clipboard. If the type library being viewed supports a help file, pressing the Help button (the one with a question mark) or pressing F1 opens that file to the proper page for the displayed property or method.

FIGURE 4.3

Object Browser displaying
search results

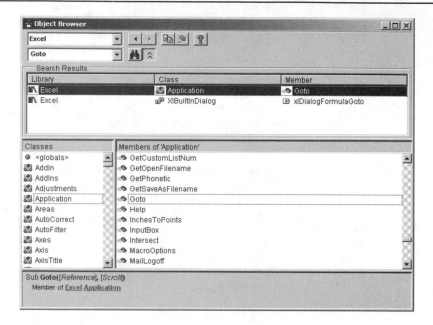

Object Browser can be especially helpful when you're using an Automation component for the first time. It gives you a class-by-class overview of the object model, allowing you to browse the individual classes and their properties and methods. As you become more familiar with a component, you'll be able to write Automation code from memory, but until then, Object Browser is a good place to start learning about what's available and how to use it.

Creating Object Instances

All Automation sessions begin with the client application creating an instance of a server object. By *creating* an object instance, we mean establishing a conversation with the server application and telling it which of its objects you wish to control. The result of this creation process is a pointer to an instance of the server's object stored in an object variable. Using this object variable, you can control the server application's object using the same techniques you use to control VBA objects—by manipulating their methods and properties.

Early Binding and Late Binding

There are two approaches to creating instances of Automation component objects: early binding and late binding. Each approach has its own pros and cons.

With *early binding,* you add a reference to a component's type library at design time to inform VBA about the Automation server and its objects. This technique is called early binding because VBA knows which object classes the component supports (along with all their properties and methods) before you execute your code.

On the other hand, late binding does not require a reference to a type library. Instead, you instantiate objects at runtime. This approach is known as late binding because VBA has no way of knowing what type of object will be created until runtime.

Most Automation components support early binding, and you should use early binding whenever possible. Early binding offers several benefits:

Speed   Because you tell VBA about a component in advance, it does not need to worry that a particular property or method might not be supported. With late binding, extra communication takes place to determine whether the server supports a given property or method *with each line of code!* This decreases performance.

VBA editor support   When you use early binding, VBA can perform syntax checking on your source code and provide developer IntelliSense features like statement completion.

Online help   Early binding gives you context-sensitive help for components that have help files. Just highlight any member name and press F1.

However, early binding has a drawback. Since you must use a reference to a type library, if the type library or application is not installed on a user's workstation, your solution will not compile or run. Late binding, at least, lets your code compile and run because it does not require a reference in the first place. (However, statements that reference the Automation server's objects, properties, and methods will still fail.) In general, you should use late binding only when an Automation component does not support early binding.

A Simple Early Binding Example

Controlling Automation components using early binding is extremely simple and very similar to the way you work with built-in VBA components and custom classes constructed using VBA class modules. To demonstrate early binding, we've created a simple example that uses Microsoft Excel as an Automation server. If you already know everything there is to know about early binding, you can skip to the next section. Otherwise follow these steps:

1. Create a new project in your favorite VBA development tool. (You can even use Excel if you like.)

2. Open the Visual Basic environment.

3. Add a new module to the project.

4. Open the References dialog by selecting the References menu command.

5. Locate "Microsoft Excel 9.0 Object Library" in the list and mark the check box. Click OK to close the dialog.

6. Enter the VBA code shown in Listing 4.1 in the new module. (If you're using VB, it's probably easier to put the code in the Form_Load procedure of the project's start-up form.)

7. Highlight any line of code in the TestXL procedure and press F8 to step through the code.

Listing 4.1: A Simple Procedure Demonstrating Automation Basics

```
Sub TestXL
    Dim objXL As Excel.Application

    ' Create a new instance of Excel
    Set objXL  = New Excel.Application

    ' Reference a few properties
    MsgBox objXL.Name & " " & objXL.Version
    objXL.Visible= True
    objXL.Quit
    Set objXL = Nothing
End Sub
```

> **NOTE** Notice that we prefaced the object class (Application) with the name of the server (Excel). It's good practice to qualify the object class with the server name whenever the object class might be ambiguous. (Other Automation servers also have an Application object.) If you're unsure of the server name to use, look at the list of libraries in Object Browser. Object Browser uses the name of each component, which is what you should use to qualify objects exported by that component.

As you step through the code, you'll notice several things happen. First, you'll observe a slight delay and some disk activity as you execute the New statement. This is because a new instance of Excel is being launched. After the new instance loads, VBA continues executing code and displays the dialog announcing Excel's name and version.

At this point, a new copy of Excel will be running, but you won't be able see it. That's because when Excel is launched in response to a request from an Automation client, it makes its main window invisible. This behavior is application-specific. For more information on how the other Microsoft Office applications react, see the section "Differences in Application Behavior" later in this chapter.

To make Excel's main window visible, execute the next statement. Excel's Application object has a Visible property that controls this behavior. Changing the property to True displays Excel's main window.

Executing the next statement (objXL.Quit) terminates Excel. You'll notice another slight delay as Excel shuts down. The final statement, which sets the object variable to the intrinsic constant Nothing, is a housekeeping task that frees any memory VBA was using to manage the Automation session.

What Happens When You Say "New" Anyway?

Another question might be, "Why do my Automation solutions seem so fragile?" The answers to both questions can be found by looking at how Windows manages Automation servers—through the system registry.

The registry entries required to support Automation were actually designed to make using Automation easier by abstracting attributes like the physical location of an Automation server. However, sometimes these entries get altered or corrupted and nothing seems to work, so it makes sense to understand a bit how this abstraction happens.

In this chapter, we've discussed using an Automation server's ProgID to initiate an Automation session. In fact, this is a convenience designed for us humans. In reality, COM Automation is based on each server having its own Globally Unique Identifier (GUID), which is a 64-bit integer, normally expressed in hexadecimal notation. For example, Excel 2000's GUID is 00024500-0000-0000-C000-000000000046. Easy to remember, right?

The registry lists all Automation components by GUID under the HKEY_LOCAL_MACHINE\
Software\Classes\CLSID key. For instance, if you look up Excel's GUID, you'll find a key
with the GUID's name containing a number of subkeys, such as LocalServer32, ProgID,
and VersionIndependentProgID. LocalServer32 contains a value that is the path to
EXCEL.EXE on your machine. (The path also includes the \automation command line
switch.) If this doesn't point to the location where Excel is really installed, you're in trouble! The other two subkeys, ProgID and VersionIndependentProgID, contain the strings
Excel.Application.9 and Excel.Application, respectively, and exist so that given a GUID, you
can determine the ProgID.

But VBA works in the reverse fashion, taking the ProgID and looking up the GUID. How
does this work? Well, if you look at the HKEY_LOCAL_MACHINE\Software\Classes key,
you'll see there are probably hundreds of ProgID keys, Excel.Application being one of
them. Digging into this key reveals, you guessed it, a CLSID subkey containing the matching GUID. So, you can see how a tool like VBA can easily find the right GUID and pass it to
the COM Automation functions in Windows to provide you with a pointer to a running
Automation server. You should also be able to see how chaos can result if any of these
many registry keys and values are corrupted. So, if you ever get Automation errors where
Windows can't find or start Automation servers, you should first check to make sure your
registry isn't messed up.

When to Instantiate

In the previous example, you saw how a new instance of Excel was created when
you executed a New statement. This forced VBA to create a new instance of Excel
explicitly. As an alternative (and just like VBA class modules), if you *declare* an
object variable using the New keyword, the object is instantiated the first time you
reference one of its properties or methods. For instance, you could modify the
prior example shown in Listing 4.1 to make it look like the one shown in Listing 4.2.

Listing 4.2: Using Implicit Instantiation to Launch Excel

```
Sub TestXLDelayed()
    Dim objXL As New Excel.Application

    ' Excel is started on the next line automatically
    MsgBox objXL.Name & " " & objXL.Version
    objXL.Visible= True
    objXL.Quit
    Set objXL = Nothing
End Sub
```

In this case, Excel will be launched automatically the first time VBA references a property or method, in this case, by the Name property in the MsgBox statement. However, in general, we don't recommend this technique, even though it saves you typing one line of code. The reason is that in a complex application, it may not be obvious (as it is here) when the object becomes instantiated. This can make debugging Automation problems more difficult. Therefore, you should always use explicit instantiation.

NOTE　　You cannot use a specific Automation server version (such as Excel.Application.9) with the New keyword. If you need access to version-specific objects, you must use the CreateObject or GetObject functions described in the next section.

CreateObject and GetObject

CreateObject and GetObject are VBA functions (as opposed to a keyword, like New) used to instantiate Automation component objects. Both return pointers to an instantiated object that you must store in an object variable. You can declare a variable using the generic Object data type, or you can use a server-specific data type if you have added a reference to the server's type library to your VBA project. For example:

```
' If you don't want to use the type library, do this:
Dim objExcel As Object

' If you are using the type library you can do this:
Dim objExcel As Excel.Application
```

Both CreateObject and GetObject are essential to working with late-bound Automation servers (those that don't use a type library) but can also be used with early binding.

Using CreateObject

CreateObject accepts two arguments: a string containing a component object's ProgID, as described in the section "Object Classes" earlier in this chapter, and an optional machine name for use with remote servers (see the sidebar "Using Distributed COM with Automation Servers"). When you call CreateObject, VBA attempts to create an object of the type specified using the application specified. If it cannot create the object, perhaps because the application is not installed or does not support the object type, it fails with a run-time error.

If you want to try a simple example of late-bound Automation using CreateObject, create the procedure shown in Listing 4.3 and walk through it.

Listing 4.3: Instantiating Excel without Using a Type Library

```
Sub TestXLLateBound()
    Dim objXL As Object

    ' This creates a new instance
    Set objXL = CreateObject("Excel.Application.9")

    ' The rest is pretty much the same as before
    MsgBox objXL.Name & " " & objXL.Version
    objXL.Visible = True
    objXL.Quit
    Set objXL = Nothing
End Sub
```

You'll notice that this is almost the same code as in the prior examples, except that we've used a generic Object variable to store the pointer to Excel's Application object. If you don't include a reference to a component's type library, you must use the Object data type. We've also used CreateObject to instantiate the object variable rather than the New keyword. Note that the ProgID (Excel.Application.9) is passed as text. We could have stored this in a variable that VBA could evaluate at runtime. This is something that is not possible if you use the New keyword because the ProgID must be hard coded as part of the New statement.

Using Distributed COM with Automation Servers

Distributed COM (or DCOM for short) is an extension to standard COM that enables you to control applications and components installed on other workstations than the one your code runs on. It is an extremely powerful technology that supports application features like fault tolerance and load balancing. Prior to VBA 6, support for DCOM was available only through the operating system, and VBA had no knowledge of it. When DCOM was enabled (through a complex set of steps involving machine name/automation server mapping and security administration), calls from VBA to Automation servers were intercepted and routed over the network via remote procedure calls (RPCs). While complex to set up, when DCOM worked, it worked well.

VBA 6 makes using DCOM even easier by letting you simply select the machine name where an Automation server is located in the CreateObject function call. For example, suppose you wanted to launch a copy of Excel on a remote workstation called myserver. You would write code like this:

```
Set objXL = CreateObject("Excel.Application", "myserver")
```

Of course, you still need to enable DCOM on the remote workstation and set up security attributes. (After all, you wouldn't want someone launching applications on your machine, would you?) But, if you have need for advanced application features, the effort may be worth it.

Using GetObject

GetObject is similar to CreateObject, but instead of accepting a single argument for ProgID, it allows for two optional arguments: a document name and/or a ProgID. The general form of a GetObject statement is

Set *objectvariable* = GetObject([*docname*], [*ProgID*])

Note that both arguments are optional, but you must supply at least one of them. GetObject is a more flexible function that you can use to create an object from an application's document (an Excel workbook file, for example) or from an existing instance of an application. The flexibility of GetObject is revealed by the combination of arguments used. Table 4.2 explains the results of these combinations.

T A B L E   4 . 2 :   Various Uses of the GetObject Function

Combination	Example	Results
Document name only	Set objAny = GetObject("C:\BOOK1.XLS")	The application associated with the document type is launched and used to open the specified document. If the application supports it, an existing instance will be used. If the document is already open, the object pointer will refer to that instance.
Object class only	Set objAny = GetObject (, "Excel.Application")	If the server application is running, an object pointer is created for the running instance. Otherwise, GetObject returns a run-time error.

TABLE 4.2: Various Uses of the GetObject Function *(continued)*

Combination	Example	Results
Object class and empty document name	Set objAny = GetObject ("", "Excel.Application")	Same behavior as CreateObject. Opens a new instance of the application.
Both document name and object class	Set objAny = GetObject("C:\BOOK1.XLS","Excel.Application")	Same behavior as passing only the document name, except you can pass document names that aren't normally associated with the server (as determined by the file extension).

As you can see, GetObject is more complex than CreateObject, although it does offer the benefit of using running instances of applications rather than launching new copies each time your Automation code runs. This is especially critical on low-memory computers.

Understanding Class Instancing

In the preceding examples using the Application class, a new copy of Microsoft Excel is launched each time VBA requests a new instance of the class. This is because the Application class is, by default, a single-use class. Automation server classes fall into two broad categories: single-use and multiple-use.

Single-Use Classes

Single-use classes cause a new instance of the application to launch when a client application instantiates them. We've illustrated this in Figure 4.4. Each instance of the Application class created by client applications references an Application object created by a separate copy of Excel.

FIGURE 4.4
Single-use classes are each hosted by a different copy of the application.

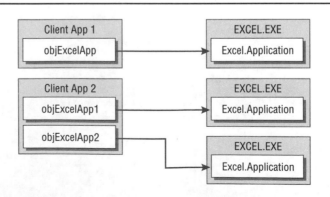

Multiple-Use Classes

On the other hand, *multiple-use classes* allow multiple Automation client applications to share the *same instance* of the class. An example of a multiple-use class is Microsoft Outlook's Application class. Only one instance of the class can exist at any given time. Figure 4.5 illustrates this type of class. Even though client applications might instantiate the class using the New keyword or CreateObject, all references point to the same instance in the server application. Applications that expose multiple-use classes are typically those that allow you to launch only one instance from the Windows shell.

FIGURE 4.5
Multiple-use classes are all hosted by a single copy of the application.

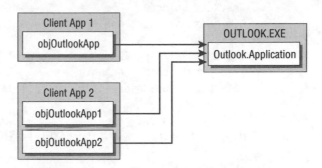

What's more, classes that are single-use by default can sometimes be used like a multiple-use class, as illustrated in Figure 4.6. For example, you can use Excel's Application class as though it were a multiple-use class, even though it is single-use by default. To accomplish this, you must first ensure that a copy of the application is already running. Then, instead of using the New keyword or CreateObject function to instantiate an object, use a normal Set statement or the GetObject function. The code in Listing 4.4 demonstrates this.

FIGURE 4.6
Using a single-use class as though it were multiple-use

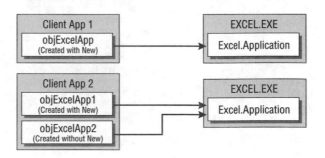

While you can use most single-use classes in the multiple-use role, the converse is not true. Each time you request a new instance of a multiple-use class, you receive a new reference to a pre-existing instance if one exists. Only the first request results in a copy of the application being launched. Therefore, you should be careful about programmatically terminating a multi-use server because other clients (or users) might be using it.

Listing 4.4: Using GetObject to Attach to a Running Instance of Excel

```
Sub TestXLExisting()
    Dim objXL As Excel.Application

    ' Use an existing instance (this will fail
    ' if Excel isn't running!)
    Set objXL = GetObject( ,"Excel.Application.9")

    ' The rest is the same
    MsgBox objXL.Name & " " & objXL.Version
    objXL.Visible = True
    objXL.Quit
    Set objXL = Nothing
End Sub
```

Table 4.3 lists the programs in Microsoft Office 2000 and indicates whether they are single-use or multiple-use by default.

TABLE 4.3: Single-Use and Multiple-Use Office 2000 Applications

Application	Default Behavior	Multiple-Use?
Access	Single-use	Yes
Excel	Single-use	Yes
FrontPage	Multiple-use	N/A
Outlook	Multiple-use	N/A
Publisher	N/A	N/A
PowerPoint	Multiple-use	N/A
Word	Single-use	Yes

Reference Counting and Server Termination

When working with multiple references to object instances, you need to be aware of *reference counting* by the server application. Every time you ask a server application for an object instance using New, CreateObject, or GetObject, the server application increments an internal counter. Conversely, when you destroy an object reference by setting it equal to Nothing (or when the object variable goes out of scope), the server decrements the counter. With multiple-use classes, this can lead to problems if you're not careful.

Most Automation servers terminate automatically when the internal reference count reaches zero. Furthermore, some will not terminate unless the count is zero. For this reason, you should take care when creating multiple references to a single Automation class in your program. If you must do this for whatever reason, be sure to destroy all references to the server when your application terminates. There is no way to determine a server's internal reference count using VBA code.

Some applications will not terminate automatically when the reference count reaches zero if you've done something that enabled the user to interact with the application. For example, displaying Excel's main window will prevent Excel from terminating if the user creates a new workbook.

Controlling Other Applications

Now that you understand the basics of Automation, you're ready to start writing code to control Automation components. The rest of this chapter explains how you can write code like this, using several applications in Microsoft Office to illustrate.

Learning an Application's Object Model

The techniques involved in using another component's objects through Automation are the same as those for manipulating VBA objects; the only difference is the set of objects themselves. Before beginning to write Automation client code, you must familiarize yourself with the server component's object model. Unfortunately, the availability and quality of documentation vary enormously, even among Microsoft products. As a general rule, those applications that have their own development language (such as VBA in Microsoft Excel, Outlook, Word, FrontPage, and PowerPoint) have better documentation than those that don't (for example,

MapPoint). Resources are available that you can use to learn another application's object model. Two of them are listed here:

- The *Microsoft Office 2000/Visual Basic Programmer's Guide* is included with Microsoft Office 2000 Developer, as well as separately from Microsoft Press, and contains information on creating integrated solutions with Microsoft Office, including object model descriptions.

- The *Microsoft Developer Network Library* is an online and CD-ROM resource for those developing solutions with any type of Microsoft technology. You can access a portion of the library (as well as sign up for a paid membership that includes quarterly CD mailings) at `http://msdn.microsoft.com/`.

As mentioned earlier, you can also use Object Browser to interrogate a component's object model. Even with online help, this tends to be a trial-and-error method that does not offer the supplementary information that other documentation sources do.

Perhaps one of the most productive ways to get an overview of an object model is by inspecting a graphical view of the relationships between objects. Office 2000 includes help files for each application that include a diagram like the one shown in Figure 4.7. However, finding the diagram can be tricky.

FIGURE 4.7

Office 2000 includes help files with object model diagrams.

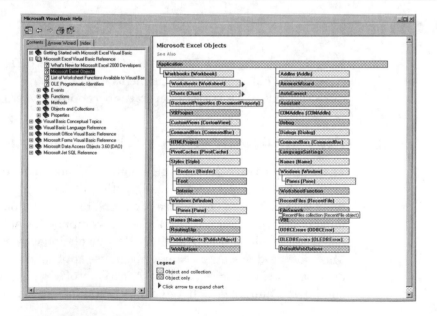

First, you need to make sure you've installed the VBA help files. (They're an optional component of the standard install.) Then, the easiest way to locate the diagrams is to do the following:

1. Launch the Visual Basic development environment.

2. Set a reference to an application's type library.

3. Open the Object Browser and select the application's type library from the drop-down list.

4. Click the Help button.

The application's object model diagram should appear as the default help topic. If you don't see it, you should be able to select it from the help browser's topic list. It would be nice if it were easier than this but, alas, the perky Office Assistant seems woefully unaware of object models.

Differences in Application Behavior

When creating Automation objects, be aware that component applications exhibit unique behavior when used as Automation servers. Differences in an application's behavior will dictate how you use it in your Automation client code. Table 4.4 lists differences in behavior of the Application object among the programs that make up Microsoft Office 2000. The table explains four facets of Office application behavior:

- Does the application open as a hidden window when launched through Automation?

- Does the application include a Visible property for toggling the visible state of the main window?

- Does the application terminate automatically when its internal reference count equals zero?

- Does the application have a UserControl property to indicate that the user has interacted with the application?

As you use other Automation components, you may want to note how they behave in respect to the list provided.

TABLE 4.4:   Differences in Behavior among Microsoft Office 2000 Applications

Application	Opens Hidden?	Visible Property?	Terminates When Ref Count = 0?[1]	UserControl Property?
Access	Yes	Yes[2]	Yes	Yes
Excel	Yes	Yes	Yes	Yes
PowerPoint	Yes	Yes	No	No
Outlook	Yes	No[3]	No	No
Word	Yes	Yes	No	Yes

1. Assumes user has not interacted with the application.
2. Does not always work correctly. You may want to use the Windows API ShowWindow function instead.
3. You must use the Windows API ShowWindow function to change the visible state.

Memory and Resource Issues

One very important piece of information to keep in mind when creating integrated solutions using Automation is how controlling multiple applications at the same time will affect the overall performance of a user's system. Large server applications, such as Excel and Word, consume a lot of memory. While it is now more difficult to produce the dreaded "Out of System Resources" error, thanks to better memory management in Windows 9.x and NT, RAM is still an issue. Due to disk swapping, computers with fewer than 32 megabytes of RAM may perform poorly when many large applications are running. If low memory is a problem, you may want to consider closing each server after using it.

The other side of the coin is the time it takes to start and stop large applications. If you frequently use large applications as Automation servers, you may want to leave them open despite the effect this will have on memory consumption. In other words, you will likely have to experiment to get the right mix of performance and memory utilization.

Creating Automation Solutions with Microsoft Office

Statistically speaking, if you are reading this book, you probably already own a copy of Microsoft Office or have access to one. This gives you an opportunity to leverage the vast functionality in those applications by creating integrated solutions based on Automation. To get you started, we'll spend a good portion of this chapter demonstrating several sample applications that use Office components. You'll be able to see examples of how each can be controlled from VBA. We'll also point out some of the minor differences and idiosyncrasies that still exist in this supposedly integrated suite of products.

Specifically, we'll illustrate Automation using two moderately simple examples:

- Creating and manipulating documents and tables using Microsoft Word
- Charting database data using Microsoft Excel

Each of the two examples will highlight a slightly different aspect of using Automation. First, the Word application demonstrates the basics of controlling an Automation component and shows how to work with a document-oriented server. The Excel example shows how to use existing documents as the target of Automation commands.

TIP   You can find more examples of using other Automation servers in Microsoft Office in *Access 2000 Developer's Handbook: Volume I, Desktop Edition*, from Sybex.

The Office Object Models

While we don't have nearly enough room in this chapter to fully explain the object models of Office applications, we can describe some of their more significant aspects. This will provide a good basis for explaining the sample applications in the rest of the chapter. We've included diagrams from the Office help files that illustrate abridged versions of the object models. They include just a few of the applications' classes. Table 4.5 lists the classes that are exposed to Automation clients. All the other classes implemented by the applications are available through collections, methods, and properties of the exposed classes.

TABLE 4.5:   Object Classes Exposed by Microsoft Office 97 Applications

Server Name	Class Name	Description
Access	Application	Pointer to an instance of Microsoft Access.
Excel	Application	Pointer to an instance of Microsoft Excel.
	Chart	Pointer to a new Chart object. Launches Excel and opens a new workbook if necessary.

TABLE 4.5:   Object Classes Exposed by Microsoft Office 97 Applications *(continued)*

Server Name	Class Name	Description
	Sheet	Pointer to a new Worksheet object. Launches Excel and opens a new workbook if necessary.
FrontPage	Application	Pointer to an instance of Microsoft FrontPage.
Outlook	Application	Pointer to an instance of Microsoft Outlook.
PowerPoint	Application	Pointer to an instance of Microsoft PowerPoint.
Word	Application	Pointer to an instance of Microsoft Word.
	Document	Pointer to a new Document object. Launches Word if necessary.

Excel

Excel has what might be described as the granddaddy of Office object models. It was the first application to integrate VBA (with version 5 in 1993), and with that came a very rich object model that allowed developers complete control over Excel worksheet-based applications. Figure 4.8 illustrates a small portion of the object model.

FIGURE 4.8

A very small portion of the Excel object model

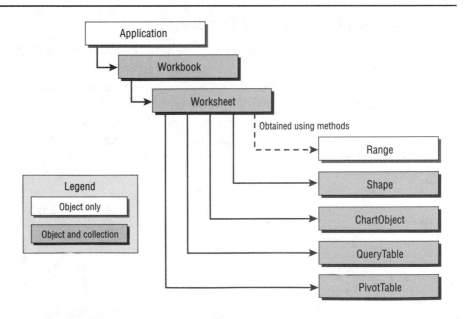

As you can see in Figure 4.8, Excel's object model follows its user interface design very closely. Its top-level class, Application, represents the main Excel application. Descending from that is a Workbooks collection representing all open workbooks (XLS files). And contained within each workbook is a collection of Worksheets.

Within each worksheet are collections of objects representing embedded charts, lines, pictures, and so on. What you won't see is any collection symbolizing data in individual cells. This is because implementing a Cells collection, for example, would require managing 16,777,216 objects (because an Excel worksheet is 256 columns wide by 65,536 rows deep)! Instead, you use methods to return references to data. These references are stored using a generic Range object. A range can be a single cell, a block of cells, a discontinuous group of cells, or an entire row or column. You'll find numerous methods designed to return Range objects—for example, Cells, Range, Column, Row, Union, and Intersect. Once you have a valid Range object, you can use some of its more than 160 properties and methods to manipulate data, change formats, and evaluate results.

Word

Word 97 was the first version of Microsoft's flagship word processor to have an exposed object model. While it has been an Automation component since version 2, prior versions have exposed only a single class, Word.Basic, representing Word's macro interpreter. You used this class to execute WordBasic commands against the current instance of Word. Without a rich object model, writing Automation code was cumbersome. WordBasic macros operate only on the currently selected text or object, so it took a great deal of code to ensure that the proper element was selected before you could execute a command that modified it.

Fortunately, this limitation became history with Word 97, and Microsoft has extended the object model in Word 2000. Figure 4.9 illustrates a small portion of Word's object model.

Word's object model shares a number of similarities with that of Excel. At its root is the Application object, which contains a collection of Document objects, one for each open document. Each Document object has several properties that allow you to manipulate text, including Sections, Paragraphs, Sentences, and Words. Each property returns a pointer to a Range object. Word Range objects are similar in concept to those in Excel in that they give you access to the contents and formatting of blocks of text.

FIGURE 4.9
Highlights of Word's object
model

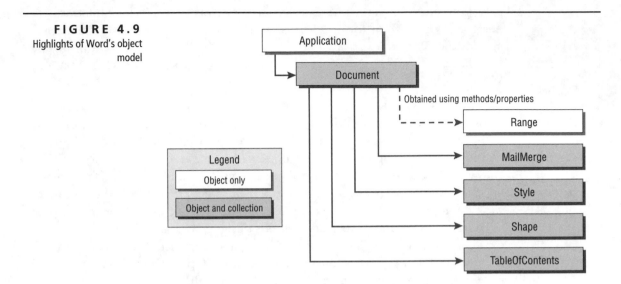

FIGURE 4.9
Highlights of Word's object
model

PowerPoint

While PowerPoint has had an object model since PowerPoint 95, it wasn't until Microsoft integrated the VBA development environment in PowerPoint 97 that developers really began taking advantage of its functionality. PowerPoint has a rich object model that, like Excel and Word, is aimed at managing the contents of documents. (In Excel, workbooks are the "documents.") However, PowerPoint's document paradigm deals with presentations and slides. Figure 4.10 shows a portion of the PowerPoint object model, which should look familiar to you by now. It features the requisite Application object and Presentations and Slides collections.

Manipulating textual information in PowerPoint is a bit more convoluted than in Word or Excel because of the unstructured, free-form nature of PowerPoint slides. Each Slide object has a collection of Shapes representing the various graphical components placed on the slide. For those shapes that can contain text, there is a TextFrame object, which controls how contained text is displayed (margins, orientation, and so on). Finally, the TextFrame object contains a TextRange object with text and formatting properties and methods.

FIGURE 4.10

PowerPoint's object model deals with Presentation and Slide objects.

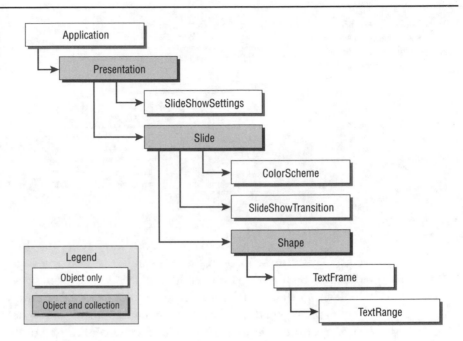

FIGURE 4.10
PowerPoint's object model deals with Presentation and Slide objects.

Outlook

Microsoft added an object model to Outlook in its first release, Outlook 97, and made minor enhancements in Outlook 98, an interim release. With Outlook 2000, Microsoft has added new members to the object model, as well as greatly expanding Outlook's support of events. However, Outlook's object model is unlike any of the other Office products primarily because it does not follow the same document-centric metaphor. The data it manipulates is far less structured and, like its predecessor Schedule+, the object model can be difficult to learn and use. Furthermore, Outlook is designed to be an integral part of your electronic messaging system and, as such, must cope with various service providers, addressing schemes, storage mechanisms, and electronic mail functions.

Figure 4.11 illustrates the Outlook object model, which may at first appear less complex than that of the other applications. It has an Application class at its root, but that's where similarities end.

FIGURE 4.11

Outlook's object model is quite different from other Office applications.

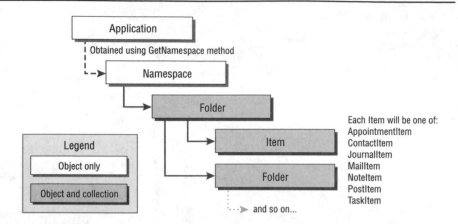

First, Outlook requires that you create a reference to what it calls a Namespace class. This represents one of the messaging service provider layers that Outlook depends on for data storage (although MAPI is the only type of namespace Outlook supports). MAPI (Messaging Application Programming Interface) implements persistent data storage using a hierarchical folder metaphor similar to disk subdirectories. Outlook's Namespace class contains a Folders collection representing the top-level folder of each installed storage system. Each of these, in turn, contains a Folders collection with members for each subfolder (Inbox, Outbox, and so on). Every folder object has a Folders collection, allowing for infinite nesting of data storage.

Data in folders is represented by an Items collection. Each element of this collection can be one of a variety of object classes that represent such things as mail messages, appointments, journal entries, contacts, and tasks. It is this uncertainty about what a folder contains that makes programming with Outlook challenging.

Office Objects

Finally, Microsoft Office implements a set of objects that individual programs share. These include the Office Binder, Office Assistant, command bars, a file search tool, PhotoDraw, and Microsoft Graph. You'll find information about these objects in online help.

Example: Word as a Report Writer

It might seem odd to suggest using Word as a report writer given the other options available to developers these days. Word documents are often more flexible and certainly more powerful than many reports created using specialized tools, since a user can take the output and modify it further. They are also more portable and produce richer HTML output for Web applications. For this reason (and because it's a great demonstration of basic Word Automation techniques), we've chosen to create a sample that accomplishes the following tasks:

- Launches Microsoft Word if it is not already running.

- Creates a new Invoice document based on a Word template with several bookmarks defined.

- Copies customer and order data from an Access database to the invoice header in Word.

- Copies line item data from an ADO recordset to a Word table.

- Previews the document using Word's print preview mode.

NOTE   To run this sample, you'll need to have Word installed on your computer and have the sample template INVOICE.DOT in the same directory as the sample database, AUTOMATE.MDB. You will also need to modify the conPath constant in basAutomation to reflect the directory where you copied the sample files from this chapter.

Creating the Word Template

The sample application code relies on the existence of a Microsoft Word template file with predefined bookmarks. Figure 4.12 shows the template open in Microsoft Word. The vertical gray bars on the left side of the document are Word bookmarks. The sample uses the bookmarks to denote where to insert text. Consider creating Word templates containing static elements and bookmarks for your applications rather than creating entire documents from scratch.

You define a bookmark by setting the insertion point at the spot in the document where you want to create the bookmark and then choosing the Insert ➤ Bookmark command. Figure 4.13 shows the dialog that appears. It lists any existing bookmarks, and you can click the Go To button to go to the point in the document marked by the bookmark. To create a new bookmark or redefine an existing one, enter the name of the bookmark in the text box and click the Add button.

FIGURE 4.12
The sample invoice template uses bookmarks to define data insertion points.

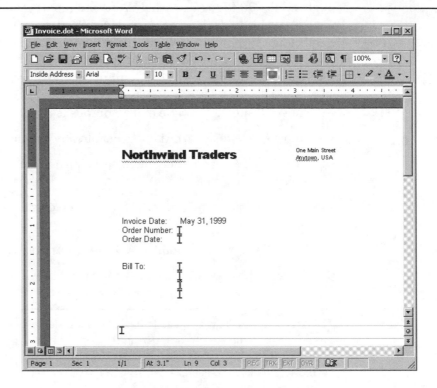

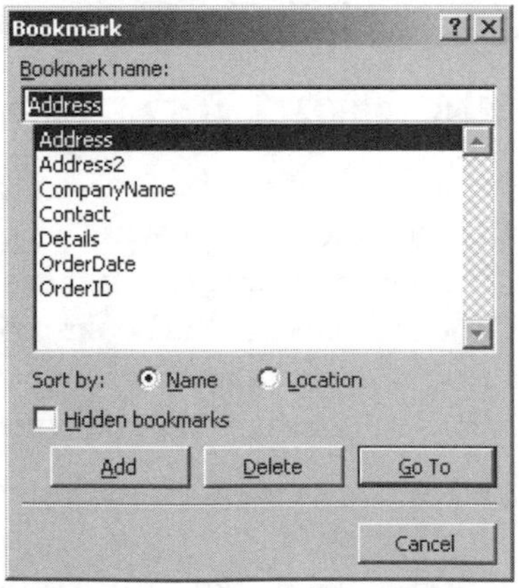

FIGURE 4.13
Word's Bookmark dialog, showing bookmarks defined in the sample template

You can see in Figure 4.13 that our sample template has a number of bookmarks already defined. We'll use these bookmarks to drive the data transfer process.

Building the Invoice

Once you've copied the invoice template to your hard disk, you can test our application by running the PrintInvoiceWithWord procedure. (Remember: Make sure INVOICE.DOT is in the same directory as AUTOMATE.MDB). The procedure is contained in basWord, and it creates the invoice in three steps:

- Loads the template in Word.

- Adds header information.

- Builds the details table.

NOTE   We've included the code for PrintInvoiceWithWord in several chunks in the next few sections. For a complete listing, open the procedure yourself in the Visual Basic Editor.

NOTE   To try this example you'll need to call the PrintInvoiceWithWord function and pass an order number that exists in the sample database. You can choose any order contained in the Orders table in AUTOMATE.MDB. Order number 10250 is a safe choice. For your convenience we've also provided a test routine, TestInvoice, in basWord.

Loading the Template in Word

The first step is to launch Microsoft Word and load a new document based on the invoice template. Word implements a Documents collection representing all open documents, and you create new ones by calling the collection's Add method. Here's the code that does it (objWord is declared as a Word Application object):

```
' Launch Word and load the invoice template
Set objWord = New Word.Application
objWord.Documents.Add _
  conPath & "\Invoice.dot"
objWord.Visible = True
```

The Add method accepts as its first argument the name of a document template to base the new document on. You can see we've provided a complete path to INVOICE.DOT contained in the same folder as the sample database. If you omit the path, Word looks in the standard Office template folders. You can also omit the template entirely, in which case, Word will base the new document on the default template, NORMAL.DOT.

Adding Header Information

Once Word creates the new document, you can begin adding text to it. Our sample procedure uses bookmarks to control the location of inserted text. While you can insert text at any point in a document using objects and collections like Paragraphs, Sentences, Words, and Characters, you'll find it much easier to use predefined bookmarks. Bookmarks retain the same relative location in a document as additional content is added or removed. The aforementioned collections change, and this often makes it hard to position text at a precise location. Listing 4.5 shows the Automation code that copies the invoice header from an ADO Recordset object to the Word document.

TIP A complete coverage of ADO is beyond the scope of this book. For a more in-depth discussion of database access and query processing using ADO, we encourage you to check out *Visual Basic Developer's Guide to ADO* or *Access 2000 Developer's Handbook, Volume 1: Desktop Edition*, both from Sybex.

Listing 4.5: Copying the Invoice Header from an ADO Recordset

```
' Add header information using predefined bookmarks
With objWord.ActiveDocument.Bookmarks
    .Item("OrderID").Range.Text = rst!OrderID
    .Item("OrderDate").Range.Text = rst!OrderDate
    .Item("CompanyName").Range.Text = rst!CompanyName
    .Item("Address").Range.Text = rst!Address
    .Item("Address2").Range.Text = rst!City & ", " & _
        rst!Region & " " & rst!Country & " " & _
        rst!PostalCode
End With
```

The code in Listing 4.5 shows how to reference individual bookmarks using the Document's Bookmarks collection. Bookmark objects implement a Range method that returns a reference to a text range enclosed by the bookmark. In our example, this is a simple insertion point, although, bookmarks can span blocks of text and other objects.

Once the procedure has a reference to a bookmark's Range object, it's a simple matter to set the Text property to a value from the Recordset object.

Building the Details Table

The final stage in the process is to add invoice details based on the currently selected order. This involves querying the database for the required information, transferring the data to Word, and building and formatting a Word table. Listing 4.6 shows the code that accomplishes these tasks.

Listing 4.6: Constructing a Word Table from Recordset Data

```
' Build SQL string for details
strSQL = "SELECT [Product Name], [Unit Price], Quantity, " & _
  "Disc, Extended FROM [Order Details Formatted] " & _
  "WHERE OrderID = " & lngOrderID

' Get details from database and create a table
' in the document
Set rst = New Recordset
rst.Open strSQL, cnn
With CreateTableFromRecordset( _
  objWord.ActiveDocument.Bookmarks("Details").Range, rst, True)

    ' Apply formatting
    .AutoFormat wdTableFormatProfessional
    .AutoFitBehavior wdAutoFitContent

    ' Fix up paragraph alignment
    .Range.ParagraphFormat.Alignment = wdAlignParagraphRight
    .Columns(1).Select
    objWord.Selection.ParagraphFormat.Alignment = wdAlignParagraphLeft
    objWord.Selection.MoveDown
End With
```

Getting the data is pretty straightforward—we simply use a predefined query, Order Details Formatted, to create an ADO Recordset object.

After creating the Recordset, our procedure calls a custom function called CreateTableFromRecordset (see Listing 4.7). CreateTableFromRecordset is a very useful generic function that builds a table in a Word document given an ADO Recordset. PrintInvoiceWithWord takes the table returned by CreateTableFromRecordset, applies some formatting, and then fixes up paragraph alignment of the columns containing numeric data—it's a pretty simple task.

⟳ Listing 4.7: A Generic Table-Building Function

```
Function CreateTableFromRecordset( _
  rngAny As Word.Range, _
  rstAny As ADODB.Recordset, _
  Optional fIncludeFieldNames As Boolean = False) _
  As Word.Table

    Dim objTable As Word.Table
    Dim fldAny As ADODB.Field
    Dim varData As Variant
    Dim strBookmark As String
    Dim cField As Long

    ' Get the data from the Recordset
    varData = rstAny.GetString()

    ' Create the table
    With rngAny

        ' Creating the basic table is easy,
        ' just insert the tab-delimted text
        ' add convert it to a table
        .InsertAfter varData
        Set objTable = .ConvertToTable()

        ' Field names are more work since
        ' you must do them one at a time
        If fIncludeFieldNames Then
            With objTable

                ' Add a new row on top and make it a heading
                .Rows.Add(.Rows(1)).HeadingFormat = True

                ' Iterate through the fields and add their
                ' names to the heading row
                For Each fldAny In rstAny.Fields
                    cField = cField + 1
                    .Cell(1, cField).Range.Text = _
                    fldAny.Name
                Next
            End With
        End If
    End With
    Set CreateTableFromRecordset = objTable
End Function
```

CreateTableFromRecordset works like this: First it calls the recordset's Get-String method, which returns the recordset's data as a tab and carriage return delimited string. Once we have the data, we copy it to the Word document using the InsertAfter method of the Word Range object passed to the procedure. The Range object indicates where in the document you want to create the table. Next, the procedure calls the Range object's ConvertToTable method to morph the newly inserted text into a table. This technique of creating a table from delimited text is the fastest way to create tables in Word using Automation—far faster than copying data one row and column at a time.

From here, it's relatively simple to add field names to the table by inserting a new row in the table and iterating through recordset fields, copying their names to each newly added cell. Once the process is complete, the function returns a pointer to the newly created table.

Figure 4.14 shows the completed document. Even though this was a relatively simple example, it illustrated two techniques for automating Word and manipulating bookmarks and tables, which you will find useful in your applications.

FIGURE 4.14
A completed invoice created using Automation to control Microsoft Word

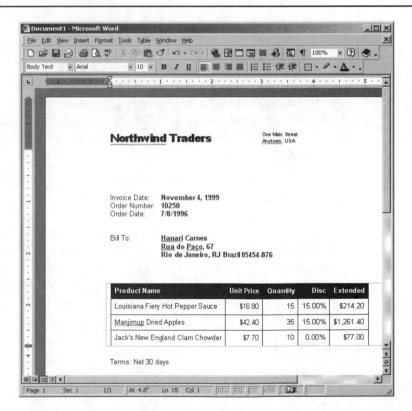

Example: Populating an Excel Worksheet

Microsoft Excel is probably one of the most satisfying Automation servers you can work with. It has a rich, well-documented object model that lets you control just about every element of an Excel worksheet, right down to individual character formatting within a cell. In this section, we show you how to update a simple worksheet and chart with data in an Access database. We've already discussed most of what you need to know about using Automation servers, so we'll keep this section brief.

TIP　　　To run this sample, you'll need to modify the conPath constant in basAutomation to reflect the directory where you copied the sample files from this chapter.

Using an Existing File

What we haven't discussed is using an Automation server to manipulate an existing document. Manipulating existing documents is a technique that becomes critical when you need to retrieve data from a file that was edited by another process or even a (gasp!) human being. Because you don't have complete control over it, you must be careful when altering and saving it to make sure you don't inadvertently overwrite another person's changes. Using existing files is also a good compromise between completely manual and completely automated creation of documents. For example, the VBA code required to create a complex Excel chart can be quite long. It is often better to use an existing chart and modify only a few properties.

From a programming standpoint, you can approach this problem in one of two ways. You can either create an instance of Excel's Application object and use it to open an existing file, or you can use the GetObject function, which will return a reference directly to the workbook. In this example, we've used GetObject to demonstrate how to use it with existing documents. GetObject lets you specify a document name and path instead of a ProgID. As long as the file type is correctly registered, Windows will start the appropriate Automation component application (if it's not already running) and load the specified file.

Our Scenario

The scenario for our sample Excel application involves a fictitious airline. AUTOMATE.MDB contains a table of airport codes (tblAirports) and a table filled with randomly generated lost-luggage rates (tblLostCount) for each North American airport for the months of January 1999, January 2000, January 2001, and January 2002. (The sample code is written to use a date in January of the current year so if you're still using the sample code in 2003 you'll either need to add more data or change the code).

In our example, we've also created an Excel workbook called STATREQ.XLS that allows users to request data on any given airport. You might think of it as a query form a user could fill out and send to someone else for processing. The workbook contains two worksheets. The Query worksheet, shown in Figure 4.15, lets the user fill in an airport code (the standard, three-character code assigned by the International Air Transport Association) in a cell. Our example procedure will query the database and, based on the current date, return information on month-to-date lost-luggage rates. The second worksheet in STATREQ.XLS, Results, provides a table of data and a chart. In our example, we show you how to perform the following steps using Automation to control Excel:

1. Open the workbook.

2. Retrieve the airport code from the Query worksheet.

3. Query the Access database.

4. Return the results to the worksheet.

5. Redefine the data range the chart uses to reflect new data.

FIGURE 4.15
Query worksheet in
STATREQ.XLS

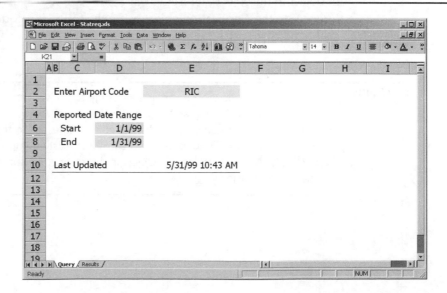

Creating an Object from an Existing Document

There is no user interface for our simple example function. Rather, we've created one procedure, called UpdateAirportStats, in basExcel, which handles all the processing. BasExcel, in AUTOMATE.MDB on the companion CD-ROM, shows the entire subroutine. We've saved space by printing only the relevant portions here. If you view the module in Design view, you can see from the variable declarations that we use quite a few Excel object variables in the procedure.

The first thing the procedure does is call GetObject, passing it the path to the STATREQ.XLS file:

```
Set objXLBook = GetObject( _
    conPath & "STATREQ.XLS")
```

As long as Excel is installed correctly and the path is valid, GetObject should return a reference to an Excel workbook. This differs from the other examples we've discussed so far, which used the Application object of each Automation server. Keep this in mind as you create object references to documents. The object you create will be somewhere in the middle of the object hierarchy, not at the top, as is the case with Application objects.

Because we will want to manipulate Excel's Application object in addition to a Workbook object, we need a way to create a reference to it. Fortunately, rather than using another call to GetObject or CreateObject, we can use the Parent property of Excel objects to return a reference to the object immediately above the current object in the object hierarchy. Using the Parent property, we can create references to the Application object using the following code:

```
Set objXLApp = objXLBook.Parent
```

WARNING With Excel 97, Microsoft has made a change to the way an XLS file is referenced using GetObject. Passing an XLS file now returns a Workbook object. In prior versions, GetObject returned a Worksheet object representing the first worksheet in the XLS file. This will undoubtedly break some existing applications. If you have existing VBA code that uses GetObject in this fashion, be sure to take note of this change in behavior.

Updating the Worksheets and Chart

The bulk of the processing in UpdateAirportStats involves running a query against the tblLostCount table and poking the results into the Results worksheet in STATREQ.XLS. We do this by first querying the data and placing the results in a Variant array using the GetRows method of an ADO Recordset object:

```
' Run our query (note that it has
' parameters we need to set)
strSQL = "SELECT tblLostCount.DateLost," _
& " tblLostCount.LostCount" _
& " FROM tblLostCount" _
& " WHERE (((tblLostCount.DateLost)" _
& " Between [pStart] And [pEnd]) AND ((" _
& " tblLostCount.IATACode)=[pIATACode]))"

Set cnnLost = New ADODB.Connection
cnnLost.Open "Provider=Microsoft.Jet.OLEDB.4.0;" & _
  "Data Source=" & conPath & "AUTOMATE.MDB"
Set cmdLost = New Command
With cmdLost
    .ActiveConnection = cnnLost

    .CommandText = strSQL
    .Prepared = True

    .Parameters("[pIATACode]") = varIATACode
    .Parameters("[pStart]") = varStart
    .Parameters("[pEnd]") = varEnd

    Set rstLost = .Execute()
End With

' Snag all the results into an array using GetRows
' and a large (2 ^ 15) row count to get all rows
varResults = rstLost.GetRows(2 ^ 15)
rstLost.Close
```

We then clear any existing data using the Clear method of a Range object corresponding to the data shown in Figure 4.16. This figure also shows the Chart object, which we will update once all the data has been copied.

FIGURE 4.16

Results worksheet showing a data table and chart

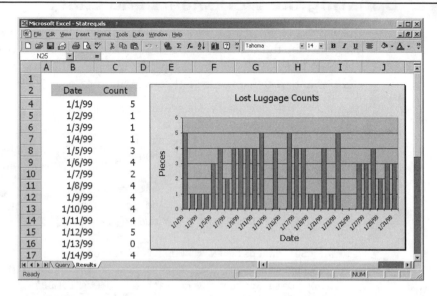

The code that clears the existing data is shown here. Notice that we use the worksheet's Range method with a named cell range.

```
objResultsSheet.Range("rngDataAll").Clear
```

We can now copy the results of our query into the Excel worksheet. The simplest and fastest way to do this is to construct a Range object that refers to the block of cells where the data belongs and set its FormulaArray property equal to the query results stored in our Variant array. The other alternative, iterating through each cell in the range, is extremely slow because Excel is running as an out-of-process server. (If you want to know more, see the sidebar "In-Process versus Out-of-Process Servers" later in the chapter.) The following code demonstrates how to use the FormulaArray property. Note that we need to use Excel's Transpose function because the array returned by GetRows is not oriented correctly.

```
Set objXLRange = objResultsSheet. _
  Range("B4:C" & 4 + UBound(varResults, 2))

objXLRange.FormulaArray = _
  objXLApp.Transpose(varResults)
```

The last task remaining once the data is on the worksheet is to redefine the source for the chart to reflect the current amount of data. We use Excel's Union method (a method of the Application object) to combine the data range computed in the prior step with cells B2 and C2, which contain the headings for the data and chart. We use this with the ChartWizard method of the Chart object on the Results worksheet to set the new data source equal to the existing data set:

```
objResultsSheet.ChartObjects(1). _
  Chart.ChartWizard Source:=objXLApp. _
  Union(objResultsSheet.Range("B2:C2"), _
  objXLRange)
```

NOTE   If you run the UpdateAirportStats from the example Excel project, Excel will load STATREQ.XLS in the same application instance as AUTOMATE.XLS. This just proves that an application can be run interactively and as an Automation server simultaneously.

In-Process versus Out-of-Process Servers

Automation components can be grouped into two categories that describe how the operating system treats their program code. *In-process* servers are loaded into the same memory address space (or *process space*) as the client application. ADO is an example of an in-process server, as are ActiveX controls. For example, when you reference an ADO object, you're communicating with an instance of ADO loaded into Access's process space using Automation. You can also create your own in-process servers using Visual Basic, where they are called COM DLLs.

On the other hand, *out-of-process* servers are loaded into their own address space. All the Microsoft Office applications, as well as normal Automation servers you create in Visual Basic, are out-of-process servers.

From a practical standpoint, the biggest difference between the two types of servers is the rate at which communication takes place between them and your client application. As a rule, in-process servers are much faster than out-of-process servers. This is because Windows does not need to manage data and communications between two separate processes and address spaces.

While you can't control what type of server an Automation server is, you can modify your code when using out-of-process servers. Try to avoid repeated references to objects, properties, and methods. In our example, we've taken advantage of the fact that you can insert several cells' worth of data into an Excel worksheet with a single statement. We avoided referencing individual cells one at a time.

Tapping into Events Using WithEvents

You've just seen how you can control other applications using Automation. This is a powerful capability but very one-sided. That is, your code tells the Automation server to do something and that's it. What if the server could tell your code things without your code having to ask? Wouldn't that be handy sometimes? Well, servers can by exposing events that you can "listen to" using a feature called WithEvents.

> **NOTE**   WithEvents is also explained in Chapter 6 in regard to custom VBA class modules.

What Is WithEvents?

WithEvents is a VBA keyword used in conjunction with an object variable declaration. It signals to VBA that, in addition to exposing the object's properties and methods, you want VBA to notify you of any events that that object exposes. WithEvents is most useful when using Automation components like those in Microsoft Office or with your own custom class modules (see Chapter 6 for more information on the latter). But, in theory, you can use WithEvents with any Automation component that exposes events.

> **NOTE**   WithEvents uses the same mechanism that AcitveX controls use to send events to forms.

How do you know if an Automation component exposes events? The easiest way to find out is by looking at the component's entries in Object Browser. When you select a class that exposes events, Object Browser lists them along with properties and methods, marking them with a lightning bolt icon. Figure 4.17 shows Object Browser displaying information on Microsoft Word's Application class. Near the bottom of the Members list, you can see the events exposed by the class.

FIGURE 4.17
Object Browser displaying
events exposed by Word's
Application class

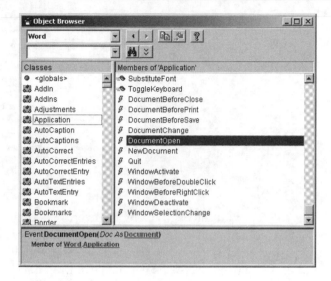

Using WithEvents

You use WithEvents in a variable declaration. However, there are a couple of
catches. You can use it only in a class module (including form modules), and it
must appear in the declarations section. You can't declare a variable using With-
Events in the body of a procedure. We've included a class module called
clsWordEvents in the sample database, which contains the following declaration:

```
Private WithEvents mobjWordApp As Word.Application
```

Note that the WithEvents keyword is listed before the object variable name.
When you add a declaration using WithEvents to the declarations section of a
class module, VBA adds an entry to the Object drop-down list that corresponds to
the variable name. Selecting that entry from the list displays the object's events
in the Procedure list. Figure 4.18 shows clsWordEvents open in Design view with
the DocumentChange event procedure selected. You can see that we've responded
to the event by opening a dialog that displays the name of the current active
document.

FIGURE 4.18

Editing mobjWordApp's
DocumentChange event
procedure

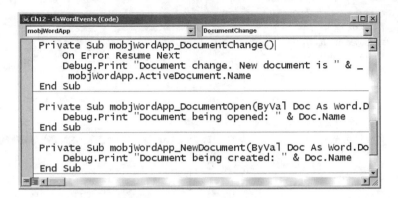

```
Ch12 - clsWordEvents (Code)                                    _□X
mobjWordApp                          ▼   DocumentChange          ▼
Private Sub mobjWordApp_DocumentChange()
    On Error Resume Next
    Debug.Print "Document change. New document is " & _
        mobjWordApp.ActiveDocument.Name
End Sub

Private Sub mobjWordApp_DocumentOpen(ByVal Doc As Word.D
    Debug.Print "Document being opened: " & Doc.Name
End Sub

Private Sub mobjWordApp_NewDocument(ByVal Doc As Word.Do
    Debug.Print "Document being created: " & Doc.Name
End Sub
```

Before you can begin using the event functionality exposed by an Automation component, you must do two things that are normally taken care of for you when using ActiveX controls. You need to instantiate the Automation component class, and you need to create an instance of the VBA class where the component class variable is declared.

We satisfied the first requirement in the Initialize event of our class using the following code:

```
Private Sub Class_Initialize()
    Set mobjWordApp = New Word.Application
    mobjWordApp.Visible = True
End Sub
```

To satisfy the second requirement, you need to create a new instance of the clsWordEvents class. We have included an example in basAutomation:

```
Global gobjWordEvents As clsWordEvents

Sub InitWordEvents()
    Set gobjWordEvents = New clsWordEvents
End Sub
```

That's all you need to create a custom event sink for Microsoft Word. Note that we've declared the object variable as Global. If we had declared it in the body of the InitWordEvents procedure, it would have been destroyed, along with our event sink, when the procedure terminated.

NOTE   If you declare a variable using WithEvents in a module belonging to a user interface object, like a VBA form, the event sink will be created as soon as you open the object.

Figure 4.19 illustrates how event sinking with VBA works. Our object variable, gobjWordEvents, points to an instance of our VBA class, clsWordEvents. The class instance, in turn, contains another pointer (mobjWordApp) that references an instance of Word's Application class. As the Application class generates events, Word calls our VBA event procedures defined in clsWordEvents. The gobjWordEvents variable is required only to give our event sink "life."

FIGURE 4.19
How VBA event sinking works

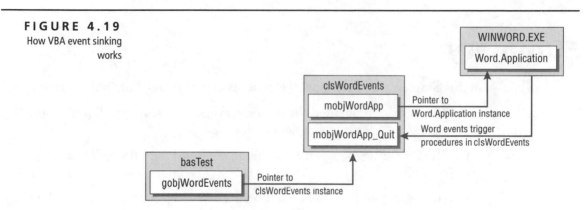

To see WithEvents in action, run InitWordEvents and open the Immediate window. Then open, close, activate, and save several documents in the Microsoft Word instance that appears. You'll see messages printed to the Immediate window as each event fires, as shown in Figure 4.20.

FIGURE 4.20
Monitoring events in Microsoft Word

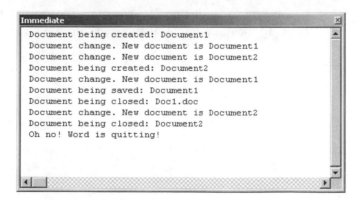

WARNING Event procedures created using WithEvents are nothing more than functions that an Automation component calls when an event occurs. Just as with normal functions, the Automation component cannot continue processing until an event procedure finishes. Beware of anything that could prevent or delay the completion of an event procedure.

Summary

In this chapter, we've explored the basic concepts behind Automation, including:

- The role of Automation clients and servers, the use of type libraries, and the creation of objects in another application

- The similarities between Automation code and the VBA code you write every day

- How to manipulate other applications using objects, properties, and methods, just as you do VBA objects

We used several sample applications that demonstrated how to use the other programs in the Microsoft Office suite in integrated solutions. In each example, we stressed the similarities between Automation code and plain VBA code.

You can use VBA to control other applications. Automation can also help you become more productive by giving you the tools to integrate other robust, feature-filled applications into a customized solution.

chapter 5

Creating Your Own Objects with VB Class Modules

- ■ Exploring class modules and how they work

- ■ Creating your own object classes

- ■ Implementing custom properties and methods

With the introduction of Visual Basic 4 in 1993, Microsoft endowed Basic developers with a new tool: class modules. While other Basic dialects (prior versions of Visual Basic and Access Basic, as examples) had already introduced object-oriented constructs, class modules gave you the ability to create and manipulate your own classes of objects. If you have programmed in other object-oriented languages, such as SmallTalk or C++, you are familiar with the benefits this ability provides. If you haven't, we hope to surprise you with the power they give you as a programmer. We make heavy use of class modules in this book to do everything from implementing data structures such as linked lists to abstracting Windows API functions. This chapter explains what class modules are and how they work and provides some examples of how you can use them in your applications.

TIP	If you purchased the first edition of this book or are familiar with the basics of class module usage, you might find it expeditious to skip ahead to Chapter 6, where we discuss more advanced class module topics.

Since this chapter deals with creating your own objects, it assumes you are familiar with using objects provided by VBA or a host application. That is, you should be comfortable with concepts such as properties and methods, as well as how to declare and use object variables.

Table 5.1 lists the sample files included on the CD-ROM. You'll find all the sample code discussed in the chapter in these files.

TABLE 5.1:   Sample Files

Filename	Description
CLASSES.XLS	Excel workbook containing sample code
CLASSES.MDB	Access 2000 database containing sample code
CLASSES.VBP	Visual Basic project containing sample code
TEXT1.CLS	TextFile class module
CLIP.CLS	Clipboard class module
TEST.BAS	Test procedures for class modules

TIP Trying to understand object-oriented programming (OOP) techniques for the first time can be a daunting task. Many people find the line that distinguishes OOP from procedural programming very fine. If you fit this description, you may find it helpful to work through the examples as we present them in this chapter.

Why Use Class Modules?

If you've been developing applications or routines using Basic for any length of time, you might be asking yourself, "Why use class modules anyway? I've been getting along without them for some time." Well, like any product feature, class modules have their benefits and costs. The primary cost is the learning curve required to understand them so you can use them effectively. While many VBA programmers take working with built-in objects (such as the Debug and Err objects) for granted, they find the idea of creating their own object types difficult to comprehend. We hope that after reading this chapter you won't feel that way.

Once you've mastered the basics of class modules, the benefits become clear. They make your code more manageable, self-documenting, and easier to maintain, especially if you deal with complex sets of related data. The sections that follow examine some reasons for using class modules.

Encapsulate Data and Behavior

One of the primary benefits of object-oriented programming in general, and VBA class modules in particular, is the ability to *encapsulate* data and behavior in high-level programming constructs. What does this really mean? It means you associate all the variables and procedures that are conceptually linked to some "thing" and make it part of a programmable entity. This entity is easily manipulated using VBA code and remains a discreet part of your application, never mingling its data or behavior with other entities. In essence, class modules allow you to create and use your own object types in your application. Why would you want to do this? Well, imagine you want to write an application that tracks information on employees in your company. Using traditional Basic, you might create separate variables to store each employee's name, manager, and salary, among other things. If you're really clever, you might create an array of user-defined data types, and you might also write procedures to handle such tasks as hiring or transferring an employee or giving an employee a raise. The problem with this approach is that there is nothing inherent in the program or the language that ties together all these bits of information and processes. Figure 5.1 illustrates this situation. All the data and all the processes are free floating. It's up to you, the programmer, to ensure that each element is used correctly, and the task increases in difficulty if there are many developers working on the source code.

FIGURE 5.1
Managing data using traditional Basic constructs

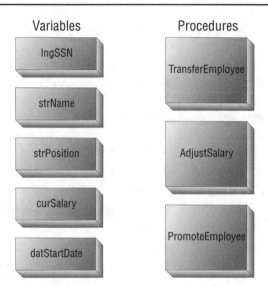

With nothing enforcing relationships among the items in Figure 5.1, chaos can result. For example, suppose two or more separate procedures modify the salary data using a particular set of rules. Changes to the rules necessitate changes to the program logic in several places.

Encapsulating these data and program components in an object makes the management task much easier. First of all, any references to data (properties) must be associated with a particular object, so you always know what "thing" it is you're operating on. Second, processes that operate on an object are defined as part of that object. In other words, the processes are defined as methods of the object. The consumers of the object (other procedures in your program) are insulated from the inner workings of each method and cannot modify properties directly unless you allow them to. This "shield" enforces a degree of control over data that the object represents. Finally, since each property and method is defined in one place (the object type's definition), any code modifications need be implemented only once. An object's consumers will benefit automatically from the change. Figure 5.2

represents this type of object-oriented development. All data and processes are defined as part of the object, and the application program interacts with them through a central point, a reference to an *instance* of the object.

FIGURE 5.2
Managing data using object-oriented techniques

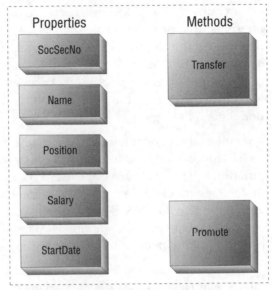

Employee Object

Is VBA Really Object Oriented?

At this point many of you who have experience in other object-oriented languages are probably thinking, "What are they talking about? VBA isn't really object oriented!" While we concede that VBA does not exhibit some of the characteristics of a "true" object-oriented language, such as polymorphism and implementation inheritance, we believe that it just doesn't matter. So what if VBA isn't as feature rich as C++ or SmallTalk? For most people, it's much easier to understand than those languages, and what's really important is that VBA offers a way for developers to think about applications in terms of a group of related objects, not as masses of disparate data structures.

Hide Complex Processes from Other Developers

If you find the idea of encapsulating data and processes within an object compelling, you'll be even more excited about another benefit of using class modules: the ability to abstract complex processes, hiding their detail from other developers (or even yourself). Suppose you are trying to create an application that manages internal purchases within an organization. Determining the amount to charge one department for goods or services received from another (called the transfer price) can be a complicated task. With traditional programming techniques, the logic for computing the transfer price might be an integral component of the application. Not only does it make the program code harder to maintain, it means you must understand the logic.

By using object-oriented techniques, on the other hand, you could create object classes for each good or service being transferred, making the transfer-price computation logic part of each object class. This makes the application code easier to understand and write. You need only know that there is an object being transferred and that the object knows how to compute the transfer price. The logic for computing that price is maintained separately, perhaps by another programmer more familiar with the intricacies of transfer pricing theory.

When you create an object, you define an *interface* to that object. This isn't a user interface but a list of the object's properties, methods, and collections. This is all that users of the object (other programmers) need to know to use the object. It's then up to you to implement each feature in the object's source code using VBA class modules.

Making Development Easier

In the preceding example, another programmer was charged with the task of maintaining the transfer pricing logic encapsulated in the object being transferred. This brings up a continual challenge facing development managers: how to coordinate large, complex programming projects. Object-oriented techniques (which include using VBA class modules) can make managing projects easier. Because objects are autonomous entities that encapsulate their own data and methods, you can develop and test them independent of the overall application. Programmers can create custom objects using VBA class modules and then test them using only a small amount of generic Basic code. Once a programmer has determined that a custom object behaves as desired, you can merge it into the overall project by including the appropriate class modules.

How Class Modules Work

Have we convinced you that object-oriented techniques in general, and VBA class modules in particular, are worth learning about? If so, you're ready for this section of the chapter, which explains how VBA class modules work by discussing the difference between object classes and object instances. (If we haven't yet, just bear with us. It'll be worth it.)

Class Modules Are Like Document Templates

VBA class modules define the properties and methods of an object but cannot, by themselves, be used to manipulate those properties. In other words, when you create a new class module and declare, let's say, a procedure within it, you cannot just call that procedure from elsewhere in your code. This differs from standard modules. An object's definition is called an *object class.* You can think of VBA class modules, and thus object classes, as being similar to document templates in applications like Microsoft Word, Excel, PowerPoint, and FrontPage. A document template defines what a new document will look like when you create one from it. It may include a set of defined styles or boilerplate text. It may even contain some macros, thus implementing its own behavior.

In the case of VBA class modules, you don't create boilerplate text or styles but instead define a set of properties, including their data types and whether they are read-only or read/write, and methods, including the data type returned (if any) plus any parameters they might require. You'll see how to add a class module to your VBA project and use it to define properties and methods in the next section.

Class Instances Are the Documents

To make use of an object class, you must create a new *instance* of that class. In our analogy, object instances are the documents you create from a template. Each has the set of properties and methods defined by the class, but you can also manipulate class instances individually as real programming entities just as you can edit, save, and print individual documents separately from the template. When you create a new instance of a class, you can change its properties independent of any other instance of the same class.

A Simple Example: A Text File Class

To demonstrate the basic techniques required to create and use class modules, this section shows you how to create a class that represents a text file. It will include properties that let you manipulate the filename and contents, as well as methods for reading and writing the contents from and to disk. Not only will this relatively simple example illustrate class module concepts, but you'll find it a useful class to add to your VBA projects that must work with text files as an alternative to the Scripting Runtime component described in Chapter 14.

NOTE   You'll find the sample code for this section in CLASSES.XLS and CLASSES.MDB. If you don't have a copy of Microsoft Access or Excel, look in the individual files TEXT1.CLS and TEST.BAS.

Creating an Object Class

Before you can start working with your own custom objects, you must create the object class from which they will be fabricated. You do this by adding a new class module to your project.

Inserting a New Class Module

To add a new class module to your VBA project, select Class Module from the Insert menu (or select Add Class Module from the Project menu, if you're using VB). VBA opens a new module window and adds a reference to the new class to the Project Explorer window. You edit class modules pretty much the same way you do normal code modules. The only difference is that class modules have two events, Initialize and Terminate, associated with the creation and destruction of a class instance. (See the section "The Initialize and Terminate Events" later in this chapter.)

Naming Your Class

All class modules have a Name property that is integral to the definition of an object class: It determines the class name. The class name is what appears when you look in the Object Browser. VB, VBA, and countless applications and components define classes you can use in your applications. Figure 5.3 shows the Object Browser open in the sample project. The Classes list on the left-hand side lists all the classes available to you (or you can filter them by library using the drop-down list), with the ones you've implemented using class modules shown in bold.

FIGURE 5.3
Browsing classes available
in the sample project

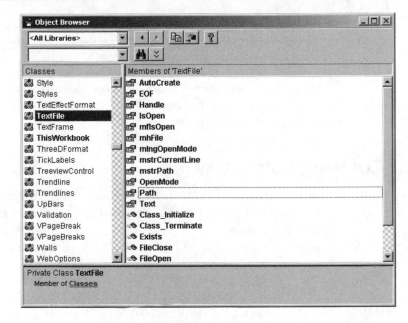

To name a class module, select the class module's code window or its reference in the Project Explorer window and open the Properties window. Set the Name property, being sure to assign the name you want to use in any VBA programs that use the class. Figure 5.4 shows the Properties window for one of the classes introduced in this chapter.

FIGURE 5.4
Setting the Name property
of a class module

NOTE   The other class property shown in Figure 5.4, Instancing, is used in Visual Basic programs that act as COM Automation servers—a topic not discussed in this book—and to share classes with other VBA projects, a topic we discuss in Chapter 6.

Normally you'll want to choose a name that is both unique and emblematic of the class module's purpose (e.g., TextFile). A more extensive discussion of class naming can be found in Chapter 6.

Creating a Property

Now you know how to create a new class in your project. Yippee. Most classes are not very useful unless they have properties you can set and retrieve. Properties store values representing characteristics of the object. While we have seen classes that implement methods for setting and returning values, we don't recommend this approach; methods are normally used to symbolize actions an object takes.

NOTE   For a more in-depth discussion of when to use properties and methods, see "Specifying Class Members" in Chapter 6.

There are two ways to create a property. The simplest approach is to create a Public variable in the declarations section of the class module. (For the second approach, see the section "Using Property Procedures" later in this chapter.) Consumers of your class will then be able to set and retrieve a value stored in that variable. (In other words, the property is read/write.) The variable's name determines the name of the property used by other parts of your program, so, as with class names, choose something with symbolic or literal meaning. Our sample class defines a property called AutoCreate using the following statement in the declarations section:

```
Public AutoCreate As Boolean
```

The AutoCreate property controls whether a new file is automatically created if it doesn't already exist.

While using Public variables to define properties is the simplest approach, it does have several drawbacks:

- Your class has no way of knowing when an outside process has changed the value of the property. This may be critical to your object for, say, restricting values to a given range or taking other actions in response to a change in value.

- You can't restrict property values or perform other data validation. For example, you might want to restrict a property representing a person's age to positive real numbers.

- You can't create read-only properties. Often it's important for your program to retrieve property values but not to set them, especially if they are calculated based on other data.

To overcome these drawbacks, you'll have to use Property procedures, a topic discussed in the section "Using Property Procedures" later in this chapter.

TIP　　You can declare Private variables in your class modules. Just as with standard modules, these become available only to procedures within the module.

Creating a Method

Just as declaring a Public variable creates a property, declaring a Public procedure creates a method. You can create Public functions and Public subs, the only difference being that a Public function can return a value to the calling process. Our class implements, among other things, a FileOpen method that carries out the task of opening the file specified by the Path property of the class. Listing 5.1 shows the VBA code that makes up the FileOpen method. Pay close attention to the Select Case statement that calls the VBA Open statement.

NOTE　　We would have liked simply to call our method Open, but this conflicted with a reserved word of our host application, Visual Basic. You may find that VBA reports a syntax error when declaring methods or properties. In these cases, make sure you haven't inadvertently used a reserved word, and change the method or property name if necessary.

↻ **Listing 5.1: FileOpen Method of the TextFile Class**

```
Public Function FileOpen() As Boolean
    On Error GoTo HandleError

    ' If a file is already open, close it
    If Me.IsOpen Then
      Me.FileClose
    End If
```

```
    ' Get next available file handle
    mhFile = FreeFile

    ' Open file based on file open mode property
    Select Case Me.OpenMode
      Case tfOpenReadOnly
        If Me.AutoCreate Then
          Open Me.Path For Binary Access Read As mhFile
        Else
          Open Me.Path For Input Access Read As mhFile
        End If
      Case tfOpenReadWrite
        Open Me.Path For Binary Access Read Write As mhFile
      Case tfOpenAppend
        Open Me.Path For Append Access Read Write As mhFile
      Case Else
        ' Bad value of OpenMode, throw an error
        Err.Raise conErrInvalidProcCall
    End Select

  ' Set IsOpen property variable and return value
    mfIsOpen = True
    FileOpen = True

    ' Read first line into buffer
    Me.ReadNext
ExitProc:
    Exit Function
HandleError:
    FileOpen = False
    Resume ExitProc
End Function
```

While the code shown in Listing 5.1 is not earth shattering by any standard (it uses low-level file I/O functions that have been around for years), you should be able to see the benefits of encapsulating the code in a class. You no longer have to remember all the various forms of the Open statement. All you need to do is set the object's Path and OpenMode properties and call its FileOpen method. The code encapsulated in the class does the rest, including error handling!

One item of note in Listing 5.1 is the use of the reserved word *Me* (for example, "Select Case Me.OpenMode"). You use Me in class modules to refer to the current instance of that class. You may already be used to using Me in Visual Basic and Access form modules. In fact, the module behind a VB or Access form, Access report, or Office document *is* a class module! While you could refer to variables or procedures directly, using Me lets you use the same object-oriented coding style that external consumers of your object use.

TIP   Using the Me object has another benefit. If you've implemented a property using a property procedure (described later in the chapter), VBA will call the procedure. If you simply refer to the variable directly, you won't be referencing the property value the same way external processes do.

Table 5.2 lists all the properties and methods of the TextFile class. You may find it useful to look through the class module and see how all the methods and properties have been declared.

TABLE 5.2:   Methods and Properties of the Simple TextFile Class

Member	Description
AutoCreate property	If True, then a new file is created during the Open method if one does not already exist
EOF property	Returns True if you've reached the end of the text file (read-only)
Exists method	Determines whether the file exists, based on a directory search. Returns True or False
FileClose method	Closes the text file
FileOpen method	Opens the requested file, once you've supplied the Path (and optionally, the OpenMode) property. If you don't supply an OpenMode value, the code assumes you want read-only access.
Handle property	Contains the operating system file handle for the opened file (read-only)
IsOpen property	Contains True if the file is currently open, False if not (read-only)
OpenMode property	Contains the file open mode: 0 for read-only 1 for read/write 2 for append 3 for read-only (fails if file does not exist) (Read/write until the file is open, read-only after that)

TABLE 5.2:   Methods and Properties of the Simple TextFile Class *(continued)*

Member	Description
Path property	Contains the path of the text file (read/write until the file has been opened, read-only after that)
ReadNext method	Reads the next line of text into the internal buffer. Use the Text property to retrieve the value.
Text property	Contains the text of the current line from the text file (read-only)

Using the Object Class

Once you've defined a class and given it a few properties and methods, you can use it in other VBA procedures. The first step in using a class is creating a new instance of the class. As we mentioned earlier, you can't simply refer to variables or call procedures the way you would with a standard module. If you don't believe us, try running the following code from the Immediate window with the sample project active:

```
Call FileOpen
```

VBA reports a compile error, "Sub or function not defined," because it can't locate the procedure name in its global namespace. It remains "hidden" until you create a new instance of the TextFile class, and then you may call it only as a method of the class instance you create.

Creating New Class Instances

To create a new class instance, declare an object variable based on the class. You'll use it to store a reference to a new class instance. Variables referencing custom classes adhere to the same rules as those referencing VBA or host application objects. You can declare them using the Dim, Private, Public, or Global reserved word. For example, the following code fragment declares a variable called objFile that will hold an instance of the TextFile class:

```
Dim objFile As TextFile
```

NOTE   Note that the data type in this example is the class name we defined earlier.

The next step is to create a new instance of the object and store a reference to it in the variable. To do this, you use the Set statement in conjunction with the *New* keyword, as in:

```
Set objFile = New TextFile
```

Although the syntax might seem redundant, you must use the New keyword in the Set statement to create a new instance of the object. If you don't, VBA will generate an "Object variable or With block variable not set" runtime error if you try to use any of the properties or methods of the class. Simply declaring an object variable with a Dim statement is not enough to create a new object instance.

Save a Line of Code, but at What Cost?

It is possible to create a new instance along with the variable declaration by adding the New keyword to the variable declaration. For example,

```
Dim objFile As New TextFile
```

Immediately after declaring an object variable in this manner, you can start using the object's properties and methods without first using Set. The first time VBA encounters the object variable it will automatically instantiate the object. We don't recommend this approach, however. Why not?

This method of implicit instantiation saves one line of code, but it does have a drawback—in a complex application it may not be clear where and when VBA instantiates the object. Knowing when an object is instantiated could be crucial while debugging an application. For this reason we recommend you use explicit instantiation—that is, use a separate Set New statement—in your applications.

Using Properties and Methods

Once you've got a variable storing a reference to a new class instance, you can use the properties and methods defined by the class module. Listing 5.2 shows some sample code that uses the TextFile class to open a file (we've used AUTOEXEC.BAT in this case because it's on most people's PCs) and print each line using the properties (Path, EOF, Text) and methods (FileOpen, ReadNext, FileClose) of the class.

NOTE   Although we have not included full listings of class modules in this chapter, you can find them in the VBA projects on the accompanying CD-ROM.

Listing 5.2: Print a File's Contents Using the TextFile Class

```
' Create new instance of TextFile class
Set objFile = New TextFile

' Set the Path property
objFile.Path = "C:\AUTOEXEC.BAT"

' Try to open the file--if successful,
' read until the end of the file,
' printing each line
If objFile.FileOpen() Then
  Do Until objFile.EOF
    Debug.Print objFile.Text
    objFile.ReadNext
  Loop
  objFile.FileClose
End If

' Destroy class instance
Set objFile = Nothing
```

Now, isn't this code better than including the low-level I/O routines themselves in your code? In fact, if you've used DAO or ADO in VB, Access, or VBA, the code should look very familiar. It's similar to the way you manipulate database data using Recordset objects.

So What Have We Done?

The few lines of code in Listing 5.2 have accomplished a number of things. First, the code created a new instance of the object and stored a reference to it in the object variable objFile. Then it used the reference to call the object's properties and methods.

NOTE

The reference stored would be called a *pointer* in other languages such as Pascal and C++. A pointer is an integer that holds the memory address of another piece of data. In other words, it *points to* the other piece of data. VBA doesn't expose the actual value of the pointer, as other languages do, but you don't really need it. All you need to know is that it points to some object you've defined and you can use it to access that object's properties and methods. We use the terms *pointer* and *reference* interchangeably in this chapter to refer to the contents of an object variable. The only time you need to think pointers is in terms of *reference counting* and *termination*, which we describe in detail in Chapter 6.

One important point to remember is that you can have more than one pointer to the same object. As long as an object has at least one pointer to it, VBA will keep it in memory. For example, the code in Listing 5.3 demonstrates how you can create two pointers to the same object by setting a second pointer variable equal to the first. You can tell whether two pointers refer to the same object by using the Is operator in a conditional statement.

Listing 5.3: Create Multiple Pointers to the Same Class Instance

```
Dim objFirst As TextFile
Dim objSecond As TextFile

' Create new instance of TextFile class
Set objFirst = New TextFile

' Create a second pointer to the new instance
Set objSecond = objFirst

' Compare the two pointers
If objFirst Is objSecond Then
   ' Both pointers refer to same object
End If
```

In a sense, VBA keeps the object alive until nothing points to it—until it is no longer needed. When does this happen? It can happen when the object variable pointing to the object goes out of scope. You can also explicitly break the connection between a pointer and the object it points to by setting the pointer variable to the intrinsic constant Nothing. That's what we did in Listing 5.2. While this was unnecessary because our pointer was local in scope, it is good programming style to explicitly release objects you no longer need rather than relying on the rules of variable scope to do it for you.

WARNING   There are cases when even setting the variable to Nothing does not destroy the pointer. This normally happens only if you have circular references. We describe what these are and how to correct them in the section "Circular Reference Issues" in Chapter 6.

The Initialize and Terminate Events

It is important to consider when an object instance is created and destroyed, because you have the opportunity to run VBA code in response to each event. Unlike regular VBA modules that have no events, class modules have Initialize and Terminate events that are triggered, respectively, when an instance of the class is first created and when the last pointer to it is released or destroyed. You can use the Initialize event to do such things as setting default property values and creating references to other objects. Use the Terminate event to perform cleanup tasks.

Listing 5.4 shows the Initialize and Terminate event code for the TextFile class. During processing of the Initialize event, the code sets the default open mode property. In the Terminate event, the code checks to see whether a file is still open (if you have not explicitly called the FileClose method) and then closes it. If you want a more obvious example of when these events are triggered, try inserting a MsgBox statement in each and watching what happens as you use instances of the class.

Listing 5.4: TextFile's Initialize and Terminate Events

```
Private Sub Class_Initialize()
  ' Set default file open mode property
  Me.OpenMode = tfOpenReadOnly
End Sub

Private Sub Class_Terminate()
  ' If a file is still open then close it
  ' before terminating
  If Me.IsOpen Then
    Me.FileClose
  End If
End Sub
```

Using Property Procedures

You now know the basic techniques for creating and using class modules in VBA. If you've looked at the complete source code for the sample TextFile class, however, you will have noticed some things that we've not yet discussed. The remainder of this chapter is devoted to some of these, beginning with the second way to implement custom properties, Property procedures. Chapter 6 builds on what we've described here with a discussion of more advanced techniques.

What Are Property Procedures, and Why Use Them?

You've already seen how to implement properties simply by declaring a Public variable in the declarations section of a class module. Consumers of your class can then reference that property using the syntax *object.property.* We also mentioned that the one major drawback to this approach is that your class has no way of knowing when the value of the property has changed. Property procedures solve this problem. *Property procedures* are VBA procedures that are executed when a property is set or retrieved. During the processing of a property procedure, you can take action regarding the property.

Property procedures come in three varieties: Property Get, Property Let, and Property Set. Property Get procedures retrieve (or get) the values of class instance properties. Property Let and Property Set procedures, on the other hand, set the values of properties. The distinction between the two is that Property Let is used for scalar values (Integer, String, and so on), while Property Set is used for object data types. The sections that follow explain each of these in detail.

Retrieving Values with Property Get

The Property Get procedure is probably the easiest of the three types of property procedures to understand. In its basic form, it consists of a declaration, which includes the property name and data type, and a body, just like a normal function. It's up to you to return a property value by setting the procedure name equal to the return value. For example, the following code is the Property Get procedure for the Path property of the sample class:

```
Property Get Path() As String
    ' Return the path of the file from the
    ' Private class variable
    Path = mstrPath
End Property
```

The name of the Property procedure, Path, defines the property name, and the return type (String, in this case) defines the property's data type. When another procedure references the property using code like this:

```
Debug.Print objFile.Path
```

VBA calls the procedure, and the value of a Private class module variable (mstr-Path) is returned. Of course, you can do anything within a Property procedure that you can within any VBA procedure (such as perform a calculation or query a database), so how you arrive at the value to be returned is completely up to you.

Going beyond the simple example shown above, you can create Property Get procedures that accept arguments, although it is rather unconventional (normally only methods accept arguments). Property procedure arguments are declared just like arguments of normal VBA procedures. You could use parameters to implement multivalued properties. For example, suppose your application required you to compute weekly payroll dates. You might create a class with a PayDay property that accepts a week number and returns the associated payroll date. The declaration of that property might look like this:

```
Property Get PayDay(ByVal intWeek As Integer) As Date
  ' Compute the appropriate payroll date
  PayDay = datSomeDate
End Property
```

Your program could then access the property by passing the arguments inside parentheses, after the property name:

```
datPayDay = objPayRoll.PayDay(12)
```

NOTE In practice there are very few properties that accept parameters, even though it is possible to create them. Normally developers use methods instead, adding a verb to the member name, as in GetPayDay(*number*) and SetPayDay(*number*).

Setting Values with Property Let

The counterpart to Property Get is Property Let. You create Property Let procedures to allow consumers of an object to change the value of a property. Listing 5.5 shows the Property Let procedure for the Path property of the sample class.

Listing 5.5: Property Let Procedure for the Path Property

```
Property Let Path(ByVal strPath As String)
  ' Set the path property of the file--
  ' If a file is already open, close it
  If Me.IsOpen Then
    Me.FileClose
  End If
  mstrPath = strPath
End Property
```

Notice that the code in Listing 5.5 uses the same name (Path) as the Property Get procedure. Property procedures are the only VBA procedures that can have the same name within a single module. Notice also the argument to the procedure, strPath. VBA passes the value set by the object's consumer in this argument. For example, if another VBA procedure used a statement like this:

```
objFile.Path = "C:\AUTOEXEC.BAT"
```

VBA would pass the string "C:\AUTOEXEC.BAT" to the Property procedure in the strPath argument.

NOTE   This syntax takes a little getting used to. Normally parameter values are not passed to a procedure using an assignment statement, but Property Let (and Property Set) procedures are the exception.

Like Property Get procedures, Property Let procedures can accept additional parameters. In this case, the last argument in the list is the property value set by the calling procedure. Continuing the above example, suppose your VBA program allowed procedures to set the payday of a given week. Your Property Let procedure might look like this:

```
Property Let PayDay(ByVal intWeek As Integer, _
  ByVal datPayDay As Date)
  ' Change the appropriate payroll date
End Property
```

You could then set the property value using code like this:

```
objPayRoll.PayDay(12) = #3/22/2000#
```

The date value (in this case, March 22, 2000) is passed to the Property procedure in the last argument, datPayDay. The week number is passed to the procedure in intWeek.

The two primary benefits of using a Property Let procedure rather than a Public variable are (1) taking action in response to a property value change and (2) performing data validation. The Path Property Let demonstrates the first benefit, closing an existing file before allowing the property value to be changed. For an example of data validation, see the OpenMode Property Let statement described in the section "Creating Enumerated Types" later in this chapter.

Read-Only and Write-Only Properties

You need not have Property Get and Property Let procedures for each property you wish to implement. By defining only a Property Get procedure, you create, in effect, a read-only property—one that can be retrieved but not set. Likewise, defining only a Property Let procedure produces a write-only property (although these are rare in practice).

We make heavy use of read-only properties in our sample TextFile class for properties like Handle, which makes no sense to set directly as it's derived from the operating system. While consumers of the class can't set the value of read-only properties, procedures inside the class can by writing directly to the Private variables that store the property values.

Creating Object Properties

The Property Set procedure, designed to let you create object properties, is a variation of the Property Let procedure. *Object properties* are properties that are themselves pointers to objects, rather than scalar values. For example, suppose you wanted to create a property of one class that was itself a pointer to an instance of another class. You would need to define a Property Set procedure to allow consumers of the first class to set the property value.

The code in Listing 5.6 defines a Property Set procedure called SaveFile that might be part of a class representing text documents. The class stores a pointer to the TextFile object used for persistent storage of the document's contents.

Listing 5.6: Property Set Procedure for an Object Property, SaveFile

```
' Private variable used to store a reference
' to the TextFile object associated with this class
Private mobjSaveFile As TextFile

Property Set SaveFile(objFile As TextFile)
  ' Make the private class variable point
  ' to the TextFile object passed to the procedure
  Set mobjSaveFile = objFile
End Property
```

VBA procedures could then set the pointer defined by the SaveFile property to point to another instance of the TextFile class. (Important: note the use of the Set reserved word.)

```
Set objDoc.SaveFile = New TextFile
```

Once the reference has been established, the procedure could then manipulate properties and call methods of the TextFile object pointed to by the document object's SaveFile property:

```
objDoc.SaveFile.Path = "C:\AUTOEXEC.BAT"
objDoc.SaveFile.FileOpen
```

At this point you might be wondering, "If I use Property Set to set the value of an object property, how do I retrieve its value?" As it turns out, you can use Property Get procedures for both scalar values and object pointers. You just need to declare the return value as an object data type. For instance, if you wanted to write the corresponding Property Get procedure for the SaveFile property, it might look like this:

```
Property Get SaveFile() As TextFile
  ' Return the pointer contained in the
  ' private class variable
  Set SaveFile = mobjSaveFile
End Property
```

Again, notice the use of the Set reserved word in all assignment statements involving object pointers.

Creating Enumerated Types

Often when developing custom classes you'll find yourself needing to define a series of constants for a given property or method. The OpenMode property of our TextFile class is a good example. There are only three discrete values that OpenMode can have and these are represented by constant values. While normal VBA constants are useful, you can provide even more usability by defining an *enumerated type* for a set of constants. Enumerated types provide you with enhanced developer IntelliSense features when using your class. We've created an enumerated type for OpenMode constants that provides the pop-up list of possible values while coding, shown in Figure 5.5.

FIGURE 5.5
An enumerated type defines the list of constants displayed while writing code.

Defining an Enumerated Type

You create an enumerated type just like a user-defined type—using a multiline structure. Here's the definition for the enumerated type used by the OpenMode property:

```
' Enumeration for file open mode
Public Enum TextFileOpenMode
    tfOpenReadOnly
    tfOpenReadWrite
    tfOpenAppend
End Enum
```

As you can see, the code block begins with the *Enum* keyword (optionally modified by Public or Private keywords) and a unique name for the type. Unless you declare the type as Private, the type name must be unique with respect to the scope of the entire project. *End Enum* terminates the code block. The lines in between represent each enumerated constant value. You'll notice in our example that we've included only constant names and no values. This is perfectly valid, and VBA will assign each constant a long integer value starting at zero and incrementing by one. Therefore tfOpenReadOnly evaluates to 0, tfOpenReadWrite is 1, and tfOpenAppend is 3. We've omitted values since we only need to distinguish between different constants—the actual numeric values have no intrinsic meaning. If you want or need to, however, you can assign specific values, as in this example:

```
' This uses some specific values
Public Enum TextFileOpenMode
    tfOpenReadOnly = -1
    tfOpenReadWrite = 1
    tfOpenAppend
End Enum
```

In this case the first two constants have explicitly assigned values. The other constant is assigned an incrementing value starting at the last explicit value (i.e., the number 2).

NOTE   Enumerated type constants are limited to long integers. You cannot create enumerated types using other data types.

Using Enumerated Types with Methods and Properties

Once you've defined an enumerated type, you use it just as you would any other data type, for example, in variable, argument, and return type definitions. It's this usage that provides the IntelliSense features in the editor. The OpenMode property of our TextFile class uses the TextFileOpenMode type as its return and argument data types:

```
Property Get OpenMode() As TextFileOpenMode
    ' Retrieve the open mode of the file
    OpenMode = mlngOpenMode
End Property
Property Let OpenMode(ByVal lngMode As TextFileOpenMode)
```

```
If Not Me.IsOpen Then
    Select Case lngMode
        Case tfOpenReadOnly, tfOpenReadWrite, tfOpenAppend
            mlngOpenMode = lngMode
        Case Else
            Err.Raise conErrInvalidProcCall
    End Select
End If
End Property
```

Whenever you use an enumerated type in place of a normal data type, VBA displays the list of constant values when it detects that you're editing an assignment or comparison statement. This makes it very easy to remember which choices apply and is extremely helpful for other developers using your classes.

WARNING   Simply defining an argument or variable using an enumerated type does not limit the values to those defined as part of the enumerated type. VBA treats the variable or argument internally as a long integer, and thus you can substitute any long integer value in place of one of the constants. That's why our code uses a Select Case statement to ensure that the parameter is one of the allowable values. If it's not, the procedure raises runtime error 5, "Invalid procedure call or argument."

Applying Class Module Techniques to the Windows API

The Windows API (Application Programming Interface) is an extremely powerful library of functions from which all Windows applications are created. Numbering in the thousands, API functions let Windows programmers do everything from creating new application windows to managing memory to obtaining critical operating information, such as free disk space. Through VBA's ability to call external library functions, including those in the Windows API (WinAPI for short), you can tap into this power. Traditionally, however, calling WinAPI functions has been a complex undertaking, requiring knowledge of internal Windows architecture and the C programming language, the *lingua franca* of Windows developers. By taking advantage of VBA class modules, though, you (or someone else) can encapsulate Windows API functionality in easy-to-use object classes. In this section we suggest one example, creating a class module containing Windows clipboard functions, as a way of proving the usefulness of class modules. Other chapters of this book explore the Windows API in more depth, and you'll find we use class modules extensively.

Working with the Clipboard

The Windows clipboard is an ideal candidate for our example class for two reasons. First, working with the clipboard is complex, requiring no fewer than 12 API functions to move text to and from it. Second, with the exception of Visual Basic, there is no way to interact with it using VBA alone. In this example we show you how to create a VBA class with methods to copy text to the clipboard and back.

Before discussing the required functions, let's look at what needs to be done to put a text string onto the clipboard:

1. Allocate a block of global memory to hold the text.

2. Lock the memory so Windows doesn't move it while you're working with it.

3. Move the text from VBA's memory into the global memory block.

4. Unlock the global memory block. (You can't send the clipboard locked memory.)

5. Empty the current contents of the clipboard.

6. Open the clipboard. This gives you access to it.

7. Point the clipboard at your global memory block. This is, in effect, what "copies" the data to the clipboard.

8. Close the clipboard.

9. Free the global memory.

And that's just getting the text there! Getting it back involves a similar number of steps.

Designing the Clipboard Class

To make things simpler, we've created a Clipboard class that implements three methods and one property, as described in Table 5.3.

TABLE 5.3: Methods and Properties of the Clipboard Class

Member	Description
Text property	Sets or retrieves text from the clipboard
GetText method	Retrieves text from the clipboard
SetText method	Places text on the clipboard
GetErrorText	Returns the textual description of a clipboard error given an error code

NOTE   You might be asking yourself why we implemented seemingly redundant methods, GetText and SetText, when the class has a Text property. The reason is that even though using a property like Text is more intuitive, the Clipboard object implemented by Visual Basic uses methods. By implementing both we make it easy to copy code from a VB project that uses the built-in clipboard object to a VBA project that uses our custom class. For new VBA projects you can simply use the Text property (which itself calls the methods).

Listing 5.7 shows the code that makes up the property and methods. Note the relative complexity of GetText and SetText.

Listing 5.7: Contents of the Clipboard Class Module

```
Function SetText(Text As String) As Variant
    Dim varRet As Variant
    Dim fSetClipboardData As Boolean
    Dim hMemory As Long
    Dim lpMemory As Long
    Dim lngSize As Long

    varRet = False
    fSetClipboardData = False

    ' Get the length, including one extra for a CHR$(0)
    ' at the end.
    lngSize = Len(Text) + 1
    hMemory = GlobalAlloc(GMEM_MOVABLE Or _
        GMEM_DDESHARE, lngSize)
```

```
      If Not CBool(hMemory) Then
          varRet = CVErr(ccCannotGlobalAlloc)
          GoTo SetTextDone
      End If

      ' Lock the object into memory
      lpMemory = GlobalLock(hMemory)
      If Not CBool(lpMemory) Then
          varRet = CVErr(ccCannotGlobalLock)
          GoTo SetTextGlobalFree
      End If

      ' Move the string into the memory we locked
      Call MoveMemory(lpMemory, Text, lngSize)

      ' Don't send clipboard locked memory.
      Call GlobalUnlock(hMemory)

      ' Open the clipboard
      If Not CBool(OpenClipboard(0&)) Then
          varRet = CVErr(ccCannotOpenClipboard)
          GoTo SetTextGlobalFree
      End If

      ' Remove the current contents of the clipboard
      If Not CBool(EmptyClipboard()) Then
          varRet = CVErr(ccCannotEmptyClipboard)
          GoTo SetTextCloseClipboard
      End If

      ' Add our string to the clipboard as text
      If Not CBool(SetClipboardData(CF_TEXT, _
          hMemory)) Then
          varRet = CVErr(ccCannotSetClipboardData)
          GoTo SetTextCloseClipboard
      Else
          fSetClipboardData = True
      End If

SetTextCloseClipboard:
      ' Close the clipboard
```

```vb
        If Not CBool(CloseClipboard()) Then
            varRet = CVErr(ccCannotCloseClipboard)
        End If

SetTextGlobalFree:
    If Not fSetClipboardData Then
        'If we have set the clipboard data, we no longer own
        ' the object--Windows does, so don't free it.
        If CBool(GlobalFree(hMemory)) Then
            varRet = CVErr(ccCannotGlobalFree)
        End If
    End If

SetTextDone:
    SetText = varRet
End Function

Public Function GetText() As Variant
    Dim hMemory As Long
    Dim lpMemory As Long
    Dim strText As String
    Dim lngSize As Long
    Dim varRet As Variant

    varRet = ""

    ' Is there text on the clipboard? If not, error out.
    If Not CBool(IsClipboardFormatAvailable _
        (CF_TEXT)) Then
        varRet = CVErr(ccClipboardFormatNotAvailable)
        GoTo GetTextDone
    End If

    ' Open the clipboard
    If Not CBool(OpenClipboard(0&)) Then
        varRet = CVErr(ccCannotOpenClipboard)
        GoTo GetTextDone
    End If

    ' Get the handle to the clipboard data
    hMemory = GetClipboardData(CF_TEXT)
```

```
    If Not CBool(hMemory) Then
        varRet = CVErr(ccCannotGetClipboardData)
        GoTo GetTextCloseClipboard
    End If

    ' Find out how big it is and allocate enough space
    ' in a string
    lngSize = GlobalSize(hMemory)
    strText = Space$(lngSize)

    ' Lock the handle so we can use it
    lpMemory = GlobalLock(hMemory)
    If Not CBool(lpMemory) Then
        varRet = CVErr(ccCannotGlobalLock)
        GoTo GetTextCloseClipboard
    End If

    ' Move the information from the clipboard memory
    ' into our string
    Call MoveMemory(strText, lpMemory, lngSize)

    ' Truncate it at the first Null character because
    ' the value reported by lngSize is erroneously large
    strText = Left$(strText, InStr(1, strText, Chr$(0)) - 1)

    ' Free the lock
    Call GlobalUnlock(hMemory)

GetTextCloseClipboard:
    ' Close the clipboard
    If Not CBool(CloseClipboard()) Then
        varRet = CVErr(ccCannotCloseClipboard)
    End If

GetTextDone:
    If Not IsError(varRet) Then
        GetText = strText
    Else
        GetText = varRet
    End If
End Function
```

```
Property Get Text() As String
' Wrapper for GetText method

    Dim varRet As Variant

    varRet = Me.GetText
    If IsError(varRet) Then
        Err.Raise vbObjectError + varRet, , GetErrorText(CLng(varRet))
    Else
        Text = CStr(varRet)
    End If
End Property

Property Let Text(strText As String)
' Warpper for SetText method

    Dim varRet As Variant

    varRet = Me.SetText(strText)
    If IsError(varRet) Then
        Err.Raise vbObjectError + varRet, , GetErrorText(CLng(varRet))
    End If
End Property
```

You can see from the comments in the code that it follows the steps listed in the previous section.

NOTE   Note the use of Err.Raise in the Text property procedures to raise a custom runtime error. Handling errors inside class modules is discussed in the section "Error Handling in Classes" in Chapter 6.

Testing the Clipboard Class

Using our Clipboard class is about as easy as understanding the code in Listing 5.7 is difficult! To place text on the clipboard, all you have to do is declare a new instance of the class and call its Text property. Similarly, to retrieve text from the clipboard, retrieve the Text property value. The following code illustrates these steps:

```
Sub TestClip()
    Dim objClip As Clipboard

    ' Instantiate the object
    Set objClip = New Clipboard

    ' Put some text on the clipboard
    objClip.Text = "Test String"

    ' Take it off
    Debug.Print objClip.Text
End Sub
```

If this example doesn't convince you of the value of class modules, we doubt anything will. We've encapsulated several pages of complex API source code into a single, simple property. As you use VBA and the Windows API together, you'll likely see other functions that would benefit from encapsulation in this manner—in fact, you'll find a great deal more in other chapters of the book!

Summary

This chapter has provided you with the basic information necessary to begin using VBA class modules, one of the most powerful features of VBA. By encapsulating complex functionality and code in class modules, you can develop applications that are easier to program and maintain. Of course, it all starts with thinking about the problem you're trying to solve in terms of object classes. Once you've identified the components, it is relatively easy to model them using class modules. Simply create one class for each "thing" you want to model.

This chapter also explored class module coding techniques. We showed you how to create a class, its properties, and methods and how to create and use an instance of that class. Finally, we presented a useful class example for manipulating the Windows clipboard.

When deciding how to take advantage of VBA class modules, you are limited only by your imagination. Just keep the following tips in mind:

- Create one class for each "thing" you want to model.

- Use Property procedures when you need to control how property values are set and retrieved.

- Use enumerated types to help yourself (and others) use your classes.

Chapter 6 continues our discussion of class modules by looking at more advanced techniques like collections, object models, and error handling.

Advanced Class Module Techniques

- Establishing a hierarchy of object classes

- Creating and managing collections of objects

- Developing interface classes

- Enabling classes with custom events

Once you've mastered the basics of using VBA class modules, there's still a lot more to learn about these powerful tools. As your classes get more complex and as their numbers increase, it becomes more important to know how to use them most effectively. This chapter continues what Chapter 5 started by discussing a number of advanced topics. By reading this chapter, you'll learn about creating object model hierarchies, a required skill for developing complex, class-based applications. Creating collections of objects is another required skill, and you'll see how to use VBA class modules to create collections far more useful than VBA's built-in collection object. We also discuss a number of other topics that will round out your knowledge of class modules, including error handling, interface classes and the Implements keyword, and custom events. Before diving into source code, we begin the chapter by taking a look at the design principle around object models and class hierarchies.

Table 6.1 lists the sample files included on the CD-ROM. You'll find all the sample code discussed in the chapter in these files.

TABLE 6.1: Sample Files

Filename	Description
ADVCLASS.XLS	Excel workbook containing sample code
ADVCLASS.MDB	Access 2000 database containing sample code
ADVCLASS.VBP	Visual Basic project containing sample code
TEXT2.CLS	TextFile2 class module
TEXT3.CLS	TextFile3 class module
TEXT4.CLS	TextFile4 class module
LINE.CLS	Line class module
LINES.CLS	Lines collection class module
TEST.BAS	Test functions
CUST.CLS	Sample Customer class
INVOICE.CLS	Sample Invoice class
EVENTS.CLS	Custom events test class
ICALLBACK.CLS	Callback interface class
IWCALL.CLS	Immediate window callback class

TABLE 6.1: Sample Files *(continued)*

Filename	Description
LBCALL.CLS	List box callback class
REF1.CLS	Circular reference test class
REF2.CLS	Circular reference test class
MAIN.FRM	Start-up form for the Visual Basic project
EVENTS.FRM/EVENTS.FRX	Custom events test form
IMPL.FRM/IMPL.FRX	Callback test form
REF.XLS	Project reference test project

Object Model Design Principles

In this chapter, we show you how to take multiple classes and link them together in what's known as an *object model*. An object model expresses the relationships between classes. Usually, a natural hierarchy is formed by object relationships. Consider the diagram in Figure 6.1, which graphically depicts the object model for a fictitious accounting application.

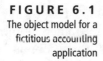

FIGURE 6.1
The object model for a fictitious accounting application

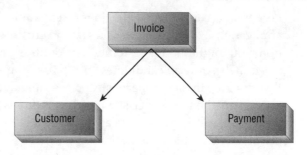

You can see from Figure 6.1 that a relationship exists between invoice and customer and between invoice and payment. It is generally a good idea to create a sketch like the one in Figure 6.1 before beginning to program an application. It makes it very clear what object classes exist and how they relate to one another.

The exact way in which the classes are arranged, plus the way each class itself is designed, determines how useful the object model is and how easy it is for other developers to understand. Therefore, it makes sense to spend some time thinking about the overall design before you begin writing code. There are several factors you should consider when designing an object model for an application:

- What classes are you going to need?

- What members (properties, methods, events, etc.) will each class require?

- How should you name your classes and members?

- Are there relationships between classes, and how will you represent them?

- Are any relationships one-to-many?

In this and the next sections, we'll provide guidelines and coding examples that should help you address these factors in your applications.

Determining Class Requirements

Not surprisingly, the first question you need to ask yourself revolves around the classes you require to effectively model your application. There is no fixed rule that adequately serves every situation, but there are guidelines that you can follow that should help you. As you become more experienced in creating objects, you'll take these guidelines into account implicitly.

Conceptual Data Objects

Perhaps the easiest way to begin is by examining the different data entities in your application. For example, if you were to create a customer management application, you might model customers, accounts, salespeople, and promotions as data objects. These are all candidates for representing as classes since they all have things that describe them (properties), and they all have things that they do or have done to them (methods). Data classes are also pretty easy to define since they map closely to any database schema you create, usually having a one-to-one relationship with the main data tables you define.

User Interface Constructs

Another area of your application to look at is the user interface (UI). Often it makes sense to model your user interface using classes, even if you're using a tool like Visual Basic that provides object-based UI tools. The reason is that classes let you extend the interfaces of built-in UI objects to add additional business logic. The same holds true for Office documents programmatically exposed through VBA. For example, suppose you are developing an expense-reporting application using Microsoft Excel and using Excel worksheets as your main user interface element. Your code could manipulate instances of the Worksheet class directly but it's likely that expense reports, being a particular type of worksheet, have additional business logic associated with them. The solution is to either extend the Worksheet class by adding additional properties and methods, or to create a new class that "wraps" the Worksheet class and exposes its own interface.

Application Processes

A third area of your application to examine for the potential to apply class module techniques are processes that operate on data or services that your application provides. These are processes not necessarily linked to a particular data object, like a customer, but more generic services like disk storage or memory allocation. For instance, take the example of an application that writes disparate types of data to a single data store like Microsoft Exchange. An alternative to encoding the logic for reading and writing data in each data object class would be to create a single class to manage storage that could operate on any data object passed to it. The advantage to this approach is that if you decide to add or change the data storage mechanism, you need to add or change a single class containing the specific code. Your data classes remain unchanged.

Remember: Draw Strict Boundaries

Above all, when developing your list of classes, remember to draw very clear boundaries between classes. The key to proper encapsulation and the long-term capacity for reuse is making sure each class implements very discrete areas of functionality. For example, avoid defining a class that represents both customers and invoices unless you're sure that's the best way to model your application. It will be unlikely that you could use the class for other applications later on that need only one or the other data object. And, never mix user interface logic with data logic. This ties the class to a particular user interface implementation and makes it difficult or impossible to reuse it in other applications that use different technology.

Specifying Class Members

Once you've decided what classes your application will need, you can specify the exact properties, methods, and events each one will have. While this might seem like an obvious step, it's important to approach it with just as much care as any other part of the design process. The members you decide to implement (and, just as important, those you don't) determine the usefulness of your class. Once again, there is no set rule for defining members, except a set of guidelines that you can follow.

Keep It Simple

The first, and most important, rule for deciding what properties, methods, and events a class needs is to start simple and try to keep it that way. You don't necessarily have to implement everything someone would want to do with a class in the class itself. After all, you and other developers need to write some code that uses the class; otherwise, programming an application would be very boring! Furthermore, once you implement and start using a class, it becomes nearly impossible to change it because developers and applications depend on the initial interface you define. In other words, it's very easy to add new members over time in response to experience and feedback, but it's very difficult to remove or change existing ones.

Choose Properties for Values and Methods for Actions

When designing a custom class, it's entirely up to you to decide which members should be represented as properties and which as methods. Under the covers, in the COM world, there is no difference—everything's a function call—but properties and methods are closer conceptually to object-oriented principles. Traditionally, properties are used to represent simple values implemented using single variables or calculations based on in-memory data. On the other hand, methods usually denote an implementation requiring non-trivial amounts of code and indicate some appreciable measure of "work" required to achieve the desired result.

Sometimes it is necessary to implement as a method what would normally be considered a property. You might do this because retrieving or setting the value requires more work than referencing a variable, and you want to imply this in the object model. (For example, a property that determines if a printer is functioning properly might require several, possibly time-consuming, steps. So, you might choose to implement this as a method instead.) This approach also applies when changing a property setting requires more than one value. In this case, a method with multiple arguments is more appropriate.

TIP   Whenever you choose to implement a method when a property might also make sense, a good way to call this out in the object model is to prefix *Get* and/or *Set* to the name, as in SetThreeDFormat and GetSetting.

Don't Reinvent the Wheel

One common urge felt by application designers when designing classes is to come up with a better way to implement existing functionality. You can even see this "not invented here" attitude reflected in software from large commercial companies like Microsoft. For example, for years the accepted way to determine the number of items in a collection was to inspect the *Count* property. However, recently, Microsoft's Internet technologies (IE, MSHTML, MSXML) implemented object models in which collection items were inventoried using a property called *length*. Developers making the transition from applications like VB and Office to Web technologies have had to deal with this difference. While we're sure someone thought there was a good reason for this, we use it as an example of how changing the way common tasks are performed usually serves no purpose but to annoy and confuse developers. If you're implementing commonly recognized functionality, do your customers a favor and just design it the way everybody's used to.

Avoid Overusing Computed Properties

Another common urge, and one that violates the first rule of simplicity, is to add a large number of computed properties to a class. A computed property is one that's derived from other property values. A good example would be the Total property of an invoice line item. Chances are it's a read-only property based on the Price and Quantity properties and, therefore, is something the consumer of your class could derive herself. The question you should ask yourself is, "How often will someone need to compute this property?" In our example, the Total property is probably used often, and, therefore, it makes sense to include it as an intrinsic class property. On the other hand, something like IsQuantityGreater-ThanTwelve is probably not worth implementing in the class because it won't be used that often. Okay, we're being a little extreme in this case, but only to make a point. Remember that the developers using your class can always compute whatever value they need. You don't have to do it all for them.

Help the Developer

That's not to say you shouldn't add members that help the developer perform tasks that would be inconvenient, difficult, or impossible otherwise. The Total property, mentioned in the last section, is one example because it's used often. Therefore, not implementing it would only make needless work for the developer. Another example commonly found in object hierarchies is the Parent property of an object. Parent provides a pointer to the object immediately above the current one in the hierarchy and makes it easy for a developer to write code that navigates the entire tree. Microsoft Office object models feature this property extensively.

Other examples include *active object* properties. These properties, such as Active-Window, ActiveForm, or ActiveControl, are found in user interface object models and return pointers to objects that have the input focus, or appear at the top of the three-dimensional on-screen Z-order. If your application maintains state information internally, it often makes sense to expose things like the active window as properties of a class. And it's not limited to user interface objects, either. Data properties, like ActiveConnection and CurrentUser, are other examples.

Extend Your Classes Using Events

One tool that aids in keeping your classes simple is the ability to create custom events, a subject we cover in detail later in this chapter. Events are your way to let other developers take action in response to things you do inside the class's code. They relieve you of the burden of trying to figure out in advance everything a developer might want your class to do. Consider the example of a data class that implements a method for deleting a record from a database. In developing the class, you might ask yourself, "I wonder if the developer would want to write to a log file that the record was deleted. Should I add this to the class's code?" By implementing the right events, such as BeforeDelete and AfterDelete, you let the developer decide what additional action needs to be taken. Again, you don't need to think of everything yourself, and your class is kept simple.

Object Model Naming

Believe it or not, what you name your classes and their members can be a very controversial issue. That's because, like everything else involved in the design process, the decisions you make affect the general usability of the object model. Here's what you should think about when deciding on a name.

NOTE   Many of the example names in this section come from Microsoft Excel's object model.

Say What It Does

The most important consideration is to choose names that represent the functionality of the class and its members. Typically, this means brief, English word descriptions like Form, Workbook, Visible, Caption, etc.

> **NOTE**   Even if you localize your application class, member names should remain in English to accommodate scripting languages that rely on names to access properties and methods.

When necessary, you can use short phrases to describe members. But be careful not to make them too long because this quickly becomes inconvenient for other developers. Also, use abbreviations when necessary—for example, PromptFor-SummaryInfo, ActivateMicrosoftApp, WorkbookBeforeSave.

Prefixing

It's common practice when writing code to prefix names with letters that indicate the data type and other information. You can apply the same rules to classes, but you should keep in mind how the classes will be used. Classes exposed to VB and VBA applications normally don't include prefixes on class, member, or argument names because this makes it easier to read the declarations in the Object Browser and editor IntelliSense prompts.

One suggested exception is an *interface class*. An interface class defines the interface for an object but not for its implementation. You normally use interface classes with one or more *implementation classes* by adding the Implements keyword to an implementation class's declarations section. Interface class names are often prefixed with a capital *I* to indicate that they define the interface only and have no intrinsic functionality. We explain interface classes and the Implements keyword later in this chapter.

> **NOTE**   Occasionally, you will see object models where every non-interface class is prefixed with a capital *C*. While this does distinguish an implementation class from the interface class it's based on, unless you have a large number of interface classes, the *C* is redundant, and you're better off omitting it.

Capitalization

Traditionally, object models have featured class, member, and argument names that begin with capital letters and include other capital letters at word breaks when the name is made up of more than one word (for example, Workbook, ActiveWindow). Recently, Microsoft's Web technologies have adopted a naming convention that changed the initial letter to lowercase, referred to as "camel case" (for example, length, parentWindow). Now that there are two precedents, the convention you choose depends on what realm your application belongs in and who your developers are. If you are developing a traditional Windows application and the developers using your object model are VB or VBA programmers, you should stick to the traditional initial-caps convention. On the other hand, if you're developing components for Web applications, follow those guidelines. In either case, be consistent across your object model.

Verbs, Nouns, and Adjectives

Another choice you need to make is whether to use verbs, nouns, or adjectives in your member names. Normally, nouns and adjectives are used to denote properties, and verbs are used to denote methods. While this is a subtle difference, verbs imply more substantial action than simply to "set or retrieve this value." Examples of noun and adjective properties include Worksheets, Visible, Height, and Name. Common verbs include Calculate, Undo, and CopyPicture.

For Boolean properties, consider prefixing property names with the word *Is* to imply a True or False value (for example, IsOpen, IsCalculated). Unfortunately, the Microsoft object models are not consistent in this regard, but it is a useful suggestion nonetheless.

Event naming is also inconsistent in Microsoft object models. Traditional object models, like those in Microsoft Office, simply use the name of the event as a verb, as in Activate, Close, and Calculate. When the state context is important, it's added to the beginning of the name (for example, BeforeDelete, AfterDelConfirm). Web-based object models use a slightly different approach, beginning each event with the word *on*, as in onload, onfocus, and onclick. (Note, too, that these are all lowercase words.) This makes it easy to distinguish events from methods, something that can be unclear otherwise. (For instance, Excel's Workbooks have both an Activate method and an Activate event.) Again, which convention you choose should be driven by consistency with your focus and developer base, although a hybrid approach is also possible—for instance, combining the *on* prefix with mixed case.

Modeling Class Relationships

Almost without exception, whenever you have an object model with more than a few classes, there will be natural relationships between classes. (If there aren't, perhaps you haven't factored each class correctly.) One of the final steps in object model design is identifying and properly modeling these relationships.

Containment

The most common type of relationship is containment, where one class can be viewed as being contained within, or subordinate to, another. An obvious example, because of its user interface implications, is the relationship between Excel Worksheet and Workbook classes. Just by looking at the user interface, it's easy to see that a Worksheet is contained within a Workbook. Therefore, it should appear subordinate to the Workbook class in the object model.

NOTE   This also implies a parent-child relationship, meaning that the Worksheet class should implement a Parent property that holds a pointer to the Workbook that it's contained within.

Another, non-UI example is the relationship between an Excel add-in and the Application class. An add-in is a feature of the application and, therefore, is subordinate to it in the object model, even though there is no user interface to provide this guideline.

One-to-Many Relationships

Both of the previous examples, worksheets and add-ins, are one-to-many relationships. That is, one workbook can contain one or more worksheets, and there may be one or more add-ins loaded in the application. In these cases, you'll need to implement a collection of objects, and it is the collection class, not the individual object class, that becomes the subordinate object. For example, Excel's Workbook class actually implements a property that returns a pointer to a Worksheets collection. The individual object class then becomes subordinate to the collection class. We show you how to create collections and collection classes later in this chapter.

Developing Object Hierarchies

Now that we've covered the theory behind designing object models, its time to show you the techniques you use in VBA to implement them. Since Chapter 5 covered the basics of individual class design, we pick up where it left off and discuss implementing object model hierarchies. For the first few examples, refer back to Figure 6.1, which depicted a fictitious accounting object model involving customers, invoices, and payments.

TIP　Visual Basic includes a wizard (the Class Builder Wizard) that can assist you in creating classes and object models. It's available from the VB Add-in Manager. It features a menu-driven and tree-view interface but gives you no control over the code it produces. If you aren't particular about coding style or naming conventions, you might find this tool useful.

Once you have an object model that represents your application, you can begin constructing class modules—one for each object in the diagram. To represent relationships between objects, declare pointers to child objects in the declarations section of the parent class module. For example, to model the relationship between invoice and customer (assuming classes named Invoice and Customer, respectively), you would create a Customer property of the Invoice class that returned a pointer to a Customer class instance:

```
Private mobjCustomer As Customer

Property Get Customer() As Customer
    ' Return pointer to Customer instance
    Set Customer = mobjCustomer
End Property
```

TIP　Note that you can, in fact, declare object variables and properties with the same name as the class they are based on.

As with any class, you need to create a new instance of the Customer class. Normally, the correct place to do this is in the Invoice class's Initialize event:

```
Private Sub Class_Initialize()
    ' Create a new Customer instance
    Set mobjCustomer = New Customer
End Sub
```

By placing the code here, a Customer class instance is automatically created when you create a new instance of the Invoice class. You can then use the invoice object to set properties of the customer instance, as the following code fragment demonstrates:

```
Dim objInvoice As Invoice

Set objInvoice = New Invoice
Set objInvoice.Customer.FirstName = "Jane"
Set objInvoice.Customer.LastName = "Smith"
' and so on...
```

The ability to create object hierarchies using class-level pointer variables is an extremely powerful feature of VBA. It lets you develop and test objects, like the Customer object in this example, separately and then assemble them into a robust, object-oriented representation of your application.

NOTE   The technique just described works great for one-to-one relationships, but what about one-to-many relationships? For example, what if an invoice could have a number of customers associated with it? In this situation, you need to use a collection, as discussed in the section "Creating Your Own Collections" later in this chapter.

Creating a Parent Property

In many object models, classes within the hierarchy implement a property that contains a pointer to the instance of the class immediately above it in the hierarchy. This makes it convenient to traverse the hierarchy using VBA code. Traditionally, this property is named Parent, representative of the parent-child relationship between classes. For example, the Excel Worksheet class implements a Parent property that points to the Workbook instance in which the worksheet is contained.

You can implement a Parent property in your own classes by creating Property Set and Property Get procedures in the child class. For example, suppose you want to be able to reference the Invoice object from the Customer object it contains. Listing 6.1 shows you how to do this.

Listing 6.1: Implement a Parent Property

```
' Private variable to store pointer to parent
Private mobjParent As Invoice

Property Set Parent(objParent As Invoice)
  ' If property hasn't been set yet, do so
  If mobjParent Is Nothing Then
    Set mobjParent = objParent
  End If
End Property

Property Get Parent() As Invoice
  ' Return the pointer stored in mobjParent
  Set Parent = mobjParent
End Property
```

In this case, Parent is a *write-once* property. That is, after you set the value of the property, it cannot be set again. This prevents you from changing an object's parent after establishing the initial value. (Imagine how you would've felt as a child if someone had changed your parents after you were initialized!) You set the value after creating a new object instance by using the Me object to refer to the instance of the parent class. The best place to do this is in the parent class's Initialize event because it sets up the parent-child relationship right away. Here's the updated code from the Invoice class's Initialize event:

```
Private Sub Class_Initialize()
    ' Create a new Customer instance
    Set mobjCustomer = New Customer

    ' Establish the parent-child relationship
    Set mobjCustomer.Parent = Me
End Sub
```

It would be nice if there were a way to declaratively define the relationship so that you didn't have to write the code yourself. This would ensure that it always got populated with a value, but there is currently no mechanism in VBA for one class to know which instance of another class created it.

NOTE   In this example, we've declared the Property procedures to accept and return a specific object type: Invoice. If you are creating a class that might be used by a number of other classes (and thus have different types of parents), you can use the generic Object data type or the Implements keyword (described later), if all parents are derived from the same base type.

Self-Referencing

One type of relationship you can model using VBA class modules is the relationship between one instance of a class module and another instance of the same class. Consider the case of a class representing a person. You could use the class to model a variety of interpersonal relationships (parent-child, employee-manager, and so on).

Self-referencing is simply a specialized type of hierarchy. In the declarations section of a class module, just create a pointer to an instance of the same class. When an instance of the class is created by a VBA procedure, you can instantiate the pointer or leave it with its default value, Nothing.

NOTE   In Chapter 8, we'll use VBA's ability to create self-referencing classes to model data structures, such as linked lists and queues.

Collections of Objects

Often, when creating an object model for an application, you will find that the relationship between two objects is one-to-many. That is, one instance of a class relates to many instances of another class. The set of related objects is called a *collection*, and, like a single child object, the parent object contains the set. Fortunately, VBA includes a Collection class that you can use to create and manipulate your own custom collections.

Collection Basics

This section begins by discussing collections in general and then shows you how to use VBA's Collection object to create your own. If you're already familiar with the way collections work, you might want to skip ahead to the section "Creating Your Own Collections."

Using Collections

It's likely that you are already familiar with collections from your experience using VBA or other Microsoft Basic dialects. For example, Microsoft Excel implements a Workbook object representing the data stored in an XLS file. This object, in turn, contains a collection of unique Worksheet objects. Each Worksheet object represents an individual worksheet tab within the workbook file.

If you're familiar with how collections of objects work, you already know that you refer to objects in a collection using the collection name along with the name of one of the objects it contains. You can also use the relative position of the object in the collection by specifying a numeric index. For example, to print the Visible property of a particular worksheet in the active workbook, you could use either of these statements:

```
Debug.Print ActiveWorkbook.Worksheets("Sheet1").Visible
Debug.Print ActiveWorkbook.Worksheets(1).Visible
```

> **NOTE** In some aspects, collections are similar to arrays in that both contain a set of similar objects, and each can be referenced using a numeric index. Collections are much more robust when dealing with sets of objects because a collection implements built-in methods for adding, removing, and referencing objects. You must write your own procedures for manipulating arrays.

Collection Properties and Methods

As an object, a collection implements a number of methods and properties designed to help you put other objects into the collection, take them out, and reference particular ones. Unfortunately, not all products and components implement these properties and methods the same way. For example, to add a new worksheet to an Excel workbook, you call the Add method of the Worksheets collection. On the other hand, to add a new table to a database using ADOX, you first create a new instance of the Table class. After setting properties of the new Table object, you call the Append method of the Catalog class's Tables collection.

Sound confusing? Don't worry. If you're interested only in creating your own collections of objects using VBA, you'll need to know about only three methods and one property:

The Add method   Adds objects to a collection. You pass a pointer to the object and an optional unique identifier as parameters.

The Remove method   Removes objects from a collection. You pass an object's unique identifier (or position in the collection) as a parameter.

The Item method   References a particular object in a collection and returns a pointer to it. You pass an object's unique identifier (or position in the collection) as a parameter.

The Count property   Returns the number of objects in the collection.

We'll revisit these in the section "Creating Your Own Collections" later in this chapter.

Manipulating Objects in a Collection

Once an object is in a collection, you manipulate its properties and methods directly by referring to its place in the collection using either a unique identifier (or *key*) or its numeric position. An earlier example in this chapter demonstrated this technique using the Visible property of an Excel worksheet. You can also capture a pointer to the object in a variable. For example:

```
Dim wks As Worksheet
Set wks = ActiveWorkbook.WorkSheets(1)
```

Both techniques have been available in Microsoft Basic since the introduction of its object-oriented features. VBA added two new ways to work with objects and collections. The first, the With statement, is not limited to collections, but it can make working with complex object models much easier. The With statement lets you specify an object and then work with that object's properties or methods simply by starting each line with the dot separator character. Consider the following example from Microsoft Excel:

```
With Workbooks("BOOK1.XLS"). _
  Worksheets("Sheet1").ChartObjects("Chart1").Chart
    .Rotation = 180
    .Elevation = 30
    .HasLegend = True
End With
```

This method of referring to the Chart object embedded on Sheet1 of BOOK1.XLS is certainly easier, not to mention faster, than repeating the collection syntax over and over!

Another VBA feature specific to collections is the For Each loop. Like a regular For loop, a For Each loop uses a "counter" variable to iterate through a series of values. However, each value in the series is a pointer to an object in a collection. To use a For Each loop, you first declare a variable of the appropriate object type. You then use it in the For Each statement, along with a reference to the collection you want to loop through. During each iteration of the loop, the variable is reset to point to successive objects in the collection. For example, to display all the worksheets in an Excel workbook, you could use code like this:

```
Dim wksEach As Worksheet
For Each wksEach In ActiveWorkbook.Worksheets
  wksEach.Visible = True
Next
```

You can use both of these constructs with collections you create using VBA's Collection class.

Creating Your Own Collections

VBA allows you to create your own collections using a special Collection class. An instance of the VBA Collection class contains pointers to other objects.

Instantiating a Collection and Adding Objects

To use the VBA Collection class, you must create a new instance of it in your VBA code. For example:

```
Dim SomeObjects As Collection

Set SomeObjects = New Collection
```

You can then add objects to the collection using the object's Add method. Assuming the variable objSomething contained a pointer to an object, you could use a statement like this:

```
SomeObjects.Add objSomething
```

However, when you add an object to a collection in this manner, the only way to refer back to it is by its position in the collection. Typically, you don't want to rely on an object's position; it might change as other objects are added or removed. Instead, specify an alphanumeric key as the second parameter to the Add method:

```
SomeObjects.Add objSomething, "Object1"
```

Once you've done this, you can refer to the object later by either its position or the unique key:

```
Set objSomething = SomeObjects(1)
' or
Set objSomething = SomeObjects("Object1")
```

Selecting unique key values for objects can be tricky. For more information, see the section "Setting Unique Object Keys" later in this chapter.

NOTE   Collections created using VBA's Collection object are one based, and there is no way to change this. The first object added is object 1, the second is object 2, and so on. As objects are removed from the middle of the collection, higher numbers are adjusted downward to maintain continuity. You can also add objects to a collection at a specific point by specifying either the optional *before* or *after* parameters of the Add method. (See online help for more information.) It is for these reasons that you should not depend on an object's position in a collection.

You can represent one-to-many relationships in your object model by creating a collection as a property of an object class. For example, suppose the SomeObjects collection in the previous example was declared as a Public variable of a class called Application. To add an object to the collection, you would use a statement like this (assuming objApp contained a pointer to an instance of Application):

```
objApp.SomeObjects.Add objSomething, "Object1"
```

Likewise, referring back to the object would require you to include a reference to the parent class:

```
Set objSomething = objApp.SomeObjects("Object1")
```

While simple to implement, this approach does have its drawbacks. To find out what these are, as well as how to overcome them, see the section "Creating a Collection Class" a little later in this chapter.

Collections and Pointer Lifetime

It's important to note that adding an object to a collection creates a new pointer to the object. The new pointer is stored as part of the collection. Consider the following code fragment:

```
Dim objSomething As SomeObject
Dim colObjects As Collection

' Instantiate the collection
Set colObjects = New Collection

' Create a new object and add it to the collection
Set objSomething = New SomeObject
colObjects.Add objSomething

' Destroy the object pointer
Set objSomething = Nothing
```

What happens to the new instance of SomeObject after the objSomething pointer is set to Nothing? The answer is nothing. Even though the code explicitly destroyed the pointer contained in objSomething, an implicit pointer exists as part of the colObjects collection. Therefore, the new object instance is not terminated until it is removed from the collection.

Also, pay attention to where you declare the Collection object variable. As a variable, it obeys VBA's rules concerning scope and lifetime. For instance, if you declare a Collection object variable in the body of a procedure, it will disappear when the procedure terminates, destroying all the object pointers it contains! Typically, collections are declared as module or global variables if they're needed elsewhere in a program.

TIP   You can use this behavior to your advantage. Suppose you wanted to clear out a collection by destroying all the object pointers it contained. You could loop through each object and remove it individually from the collection, but an easier approach would be to set the Collection variable to Nothing.

Creating a Collection Class

VBA makes it simple to create your own collections using the Collection object. The Collection object does have one serious drawback, however: There is no way to limit the type of objects placed into a VBA collection. Traditionally, collections contain similar objects, but you can place pointers to any object type in a VBA collection. Unless you are extremely careful, this could lead to problems, especially in large development projects where you might have many people working on the same source code.

To demonstrate the potential for problems, consider this example, which refers to an object's properties or methods using collection syntax:

```
SomeObjects(1).Amount = 10
```

But what happens if the object represented by SomeObjects(1) doesn't have an Amount property? VBA generates a run-time error. To control the type of objects placed into a collection, you must create a *collection class*.

A collection class is a VBA class that defines a Private Collection object and implements methods to add, remove, retrieve, and count objects in the collection. Since the Collection object is Private, you don't have to worry about external procedures cluttering it up with invalid object pointers. Using a class also gives you the ability to create custom replacements for the standard Add, Remove, and Item methods.

Normally, you create two classes to represent a collection of objects in this manner. One defines the object that will be contained in the collection, and the other defines the collection itself.

To demonstrate this, we've created a new version of the TextFile class introduced in Chapter 5, called TextFile2. Rather than reading one line of text at a time, the TextFile2 class implements a collection containing all the lines in a file and reads them all in at one time. Listing 6.2 shows the module that defines the Line class, which represents a single line of text.

Listing 6.2: The Line Class Module

```
Option Explicit

' Private variables for line of text
Private mstrText As String

' Private ID variable
Private mstrID As String
```

```
' Public variable for changed flag
Public Changed As Boolean

Property Get Text() As String
  ' Return value of private variable
  Text = mstrText
End Property

Property Let Text(ByVal strText As String)
  ' Change private variable and set changed flag
  mstrText = strText
  Me.Changed = True
End Property

Property Get Length() As Long
  ' Use Len function to return string length
  Length = Len(mstrText)
End Property

Property Get ID() As String
  ' Return value of private variable
  ID = mstrID
End Property

Private Sub Class_Initialize()
  ' Set the object's ID property to a random string
  mstrID = TypeName(Me) & CLng(Rnd * (2 ^ 31))
End Sub
```

Listing 6.3 shows the module code for the Lines collection class. Note the Private Collection object in the module's declarations section. Note also the Add, Remove, and Item methods implemented as Public procedures, and the Count Property Get procedure.

TIP   The code in Listing 6.3 also implements a Changed property that indicates whether any of the lines in the collection have been modified. This illustrates another reason for using collection classes: You can create custom properties and methods of your collection, something not possible with standard VBA Collection objects.

Listing 6.3: The Lines Collection Class Module

```
Option Explicit

' Private collection to store Lines
Private mcolLines As Collection

Private Sub Class_Initialize()
    ' Initialize the collection
  Set mcolLines = New Collection
End Sub

Public Sub Add(ByVal strText As String, _
 Optional ByVal varBefore As Variant)

  ' Declare new Line object
  Dim objLine As New Line

  ' Set Text property to passed string
  objLine.Text = strText
  ' Add to private collection, using object's
  ' ID property as unique index
  mcolLines.Add objLine, objLine.ID, varBefore
End Sub

Public Sub Remove(ByVal varID As Variant)
  ' Call Remove method of private collection object
  mcolLines.Remove varID
End Sub

Public Function Item(ByVal varID As Variant) As Line
    ' Set return value of property to item within
    ' the private collection object specified by
    ' the passed index value (Note the return type!)
  Set Item = mcolLines.Item(varID)
End Function

Property Get Count() As Long
    ' Return Count property of private collection
  Count = mcolLines.Count
End Property
```

```
Property Let Changed(ByVal fChanged As Boolean)
  Dim objLine As Line

  ' Set Changed property of each Line to value
  For Each objLine In mcolLines
    objLine.Changed = fChanged
  Next
End Property

Property Get Changed() As Boolean
  Dim objLine As Line
  ' Loop through all Line objects in collection--
  ' if any Changed property is True then the
  ' Changed property of the collection is True
  For Each objLine In mcolLines
    If objLine.Changed Then
      Changed = True
      Exit For
    End If
  Next
End Property
```

NOTE   For simplicity, we've omitted error-handling code from our examples. You should add error handling to your own procedures to catch possible errors, such as calling the Item method with a key value that doesn't exist.

Implementing the Remove method and the Count property in our custom collection class is straightforward. They are simple wrappers around the Collection class's method and property. However, our Add method is a bit more complex. Rather than being a simple wrapper, it has been declared to accept a string parameter representing a line of text and, optionally, an index of an existing Line object before which to insert the new line. After creating a new instance of the Line class, the code sets the Line's Text property to the string passed to the Add method and then adds the object to the Private Collection object, using the new Line's ID property as the unique index.

This is where the magic protection of the collection class comes into play. Since the Add method has strong type parameters, only specific data can be used to create the Line object. When accessing the collection, you can now be sure it contains nothing but valid Lines.

Lastly, the Item method returns a particular object from the collection using an index passed to it.

The arguments to the Item and Add methods that represent an object's index are declared as variants. This is necessary because the index could be either an object's unique alphanumeric identifier or its ordinal position in the collection.

Using a Collection Class

Using a collection class is similar to using any object class. You create a new instance of it and then manipulate its properties and methods. In the case of our Lines class, we've declared a new instance of it in the declarations section of the TextFile2 class module. We made this a Private declaration and added a Property Get method to return a reference to it:

```
Private mobjLines As Lines

Property Get Lines() As Lines
   Set Lines = mobjLines
End Property
```

We can then use the properties and methods of the class to add new instances of Line objects to the collection as the code reads each line of text from the file. Listing 6.4 shows a portion of the FileOpen method of the class. After reading a line of text into the local variable strLine, the code adds a new object to the Lines collection.

Listing 6.4: Add Lines of Text from a File to a Collection

```
Dim strLine As String

' ... other statements to open file

' Read all lines into the Lines collection
Set mobjLines = New Lines
If LOF(mhFile) > 0 Then
  Do Until EOF(mhFile)
    Line Input #mhFile, strLine
    Me.Lines.Add strLine
  Loop
End If
```

Once the collection of lines has been established, printing each one becomes trivial. You simply loop through each element in the collection. Listing 6.5 demonstrates this.

NOTE
You can find the sample code in the TestTF2 procedure in basTest. The procedure reads in a text file (AUTOEXEC.BAT), strips out all blank lines, and saves the file.

Listing 6.5: Use the Collection to Print Each Line

```
Dim cLines As Long

' Assume objFile is an open TextFile2 object

For cLines = 1 To objFile.Lines.Count
  Debug.Print objFile.Lines.Item(cLines).Text
Next
```

WARNING
While our example shows a loop that simply accesses each element of the collection using the Item method, be careful when using the Remove method inside a loop. If you use a For loop, as we do in our examples, you will encounter a run-time error as the loop reaches its halfway point. That's because, as you remove items from the collection, the initial Count property value is no longer valid. To remedy this problem, loop backward from the initial Count to 1.

The Downside to Collection Classes

While collection classes give you an added level of safety and flexibility, there is a downside to using them. This is because, by default, VBA treats your class as a normal object, not a collection, resulting in the loss of two very handy collection operators.

First, with true collections, you normally don't need to specify the Item method when referring to objects within the collection. That's because Item is a collection's *default member*. For example, using VBA with Microsoft Excel, the following two statements are equivalent:

```
Debug.Print Workbooks.Item(1).Name
Debug.Print Workbooks(1).Name
```

However, when using a collection class, you must always specify the Item method because, by default, no property or method is marked as the default member.

NOTE   In the C++ world of COM, a class's default member is the one listed first in the vtable or with its dispid set to 0.

The second feature that will not work with collection classes is the For Each loop because VBA can't find a special *enumeration method* that a collection class must implement. If you wish to enumerate all the objects in your collection, you must use a standard For loop with a numeric variable. Use the Count property to determine the number of objects in the collection, and loop from 1 to this number.

If you want to support these features with your collections, you need to do a little more work. How much work depends on whether you're using Visual Basic or the VBA IDE. Later in the chapter, we explain what you need to do in the section "Collection Class Tricks."

Setting Unique Object Keys

Having said earlier that you should set a unique key for objects added to collections, we should point out that it is not always intuitive or easy to do this. First, an object's key cannot be numeric, making the generation of arbitrary, incrementing keys cumbersome. Second, once you set the key value, you cannot change it. Doing so requires destruction of the object.

Ideally, you would want to use a property of the object being added. For example, the unique key for Excel Worksheet objects is the name of the worksheet. Intuitive, is it not? Unfortunately, you cannot mimic this feature in VBA without writing some code because the name of the object might change. If your object has a property that will not change, great—use that. Otherwise, you have two options. The first and easiest option is to create an arbitrary property of objects added to collections (for example, one called ID) to hold the unique key. Set the value of this property to a random value during the Initialize event of the class. For example, this code fragment sets the value of a Private variable to a random alphanumeric value:

```
Private Sub Class_Initialize()
  ' Set the object's ID property to a random string
  mstrID = TypeName(Me) & CLng(Rnd * (2 ^ 31))
End Sub
```

TIP We use the TypeName function, passing in an instance of the class, to return the class name. Therefore, in this example taken from the sample Line class, the ID property would be set to something like "Line521448990". Using TypeName instead of hard-coding the class name makes the code very portable to other classes.

By setting this value in the Initialize event, you ensure that it will always have a value, since Initialize is always triggered when an instance of the class is created. You can then use the value as the object's unique index in a collection. Consider the code shown in Listing 6.6. A new instance of the Line class is created and then added to a collection named mcolLines. The new ID property of the Line property is used as the unique key.

Listing 6.6: Use an Object's Unique ID Property as a Collection Key

```
Public Sub Add(ByVal strText As String, _
Optional ByVal varBefore As Variant)

    ' Declare new Line object
    Dim objLine As New Line

    ' Set Text property to passed string
    objLine.Text = strText

    ' Add to private collection, using object's
    ' ID property as unique index
    mcolLines.Add objLine, objLine.ID, varBefore
End Sub
```

The second and more complicated approach is to build on the first method by allowing referencing by name by doing a search inside the Item method. Consider the code shown in Listing 6.7. It iterates through the Lines collection looking for one where the Name property matches the text that is passed in. If the procedure finds a match, it returns the object to the calling function. (Of course, this is a contrived example because our Line class doesn't have a Name property, but you should be able to apply the concept to other collection classes that you create.)

Listing 6.7: Allowing Item Referencing by Name

```
Public Function Item(ByVal varNameOrID As Variant) As Line
    Dim objLine As Line
    Dim cLine as Long

    ' If text was passed in try to find the object by it's name
    If Not IsNumeric(varNameOrID) Then
      For cLine = 1 To mcolLines.Count
        If mcolLines.Item(cLine).Name = varNameOrID Then
          Set Item = mcolLines.Item(cLine)
          Goto ExitHere
        End If
      Next
    End If

    ' If we reached this point we haven't found it so
    ' try by index or ID
    Set Item = mcolLines.Item(varNameOrID)
ExitHere:

End Function
```

If no match is found, the method simply reverts to its normal behavior, using the numeric position in the collection or unique ID property to return an object. While this approach requires more code and may be a bit less efficient with large collections, it does give you the flexibility of referencing objects in collections by an updateable property like Name.

Collection Class Tricks

If you're going to go to the trouble of creating a collection class, you'll probably want it to work like other collections. Making it do so requires a little extra work to define a default Item function and enumeration method. This section explains how to do that.

TIP   Default methods or properties are not only useful for collection classes but for other classes, as well. Typically, the most commonly used property or method (such as Name, Value, and so on) is a good candidate for the default. Follow the steps in the next section to create them in your classes.

Specifying Default Members

Specifying a class's default member requires you to set a procedure attribute that has special meaning to VBA. If you use VB, you can do this simply by opening a dialog box and making a few selections. In the VBA IDE, it takes a little more effort. We'll discuss VB first and then show you the workaround for VBA.

The Visual Basic IDE features a Procedure Attributes dialog that contains all the settings you need to create a default member or enumeration method. To access the dialog box, select Procedure Attributes from the Tools menu, making sure the module containing the procedure you want to modify is active. You should see a dialog box like the one in Figure 6.2.

FIGURE 6.2

The Visual Basic Procedure Attributes dialog box

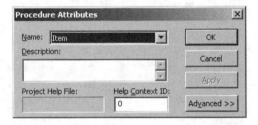

You need to change the Procedure ID property. This field that is located in the Advanced section of the dialog box. Click the Advanced button and you should see the dialog box expand, as in Figure 6.3.

FIGURE 6.3

Advanced Procedure Attributes

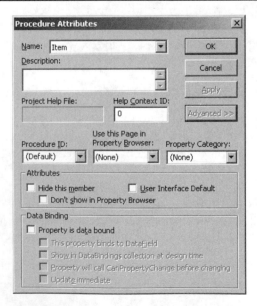

To create a default property or method, first make sure the name of the member is selected in the Name drop-down list. Then select (Default) from the Procedure ID combo box. When you click OK to commit your change and look at the class module in the Object Browser, you should see a little blue marble next to the member name, indicating that it's the default one. Figure 6.4 shows the Lines class. Note that the Item method is listed as the default member both in the Members list and in the description at the bottom of the dialog box.

FIGURE 6.4
Viewing the default
member using the
Object Browser

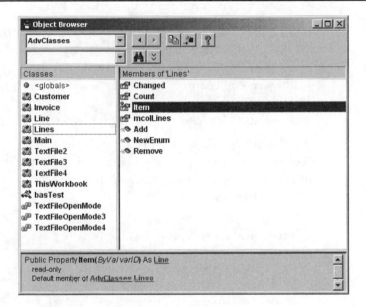

Setting Procedure Attributes in VBA

For some reason, Microsoft chose not to include the Procedure Attributes dialog in the latest version of the VBA IDE, even though VBA will recognize these attributes if they exist. How do you get VBA to recognize them? The only way we've found is to import a module containing the attribute information along with the source code. There are two options for doing this, either by importing the module into Visual Basic and using its Procedure Attributes dialog or by making the changes manually.

In either case, you must start by exporting and removing the module from your VBA project. The simplest way to do this is by selecting the module in the Project Explorer window and choosing the File ➢ Remove menu command. When asked whether you want to save the file before removing it, choose Yes (if you choose No, you'll lose all your code) and then provide a filename using the subsequent dialog.

NOTE   If you export the file and don't remove it from the project, you'll get a duplicate module when you re-import it. So be sure to remove the module as, or after, you export it.

Once you've exported the module from the VBA project, if you have a copy of VB, just open the module in the VB IDE by double-clicking the .CLS file in Windows Explorer. (Or you can add it to an open project by choosing the Project ≻ Add File menu command.) You can now use the Procedure Attributes dialog discussed in the last section. Once you've set the Procedure ID property, save the file and re-import it back into your VBA project. It's not pretty, but it works.

If you don't have a copy of VB, you'll have to make the changes to the exported file manually. Open it in a text editor, like Notepad, and find the method you're interested in (Item in our example). Just after the procedure declaration, add a line of text like the one highlighted here:

```
Public Function Item()
Attribute Item.VB_UserMemId = 0

    ' Other code here...

End Function
```

Make sure that the name of the procedure appears in the Attribute statement and that the attribute value is set to zero. Now, just re-import as before, and VBA will accept the procedure as the default. Perhaps in a future version of the VBA IDE, Microsoft will include the Procedure Attributes dialog, and you'll no longer have to jump through these hoops.

WARNING   If you're using VBA in Access 2000, make sure you import the module using the VBA IDE, not Access's Import dialog. Otherwise, the attribute won't be recognized.

Creating Enumeration Methods

You create an enumeration method in much the same manner, but you must first start by writing code for the method itself. The method must conform to a specific interface that forwards the method call on to the underlying VBA Collection class instance.

An enumeration method is a special function implemented by VBA's Collection class, called _NewEnum (note the underscore). The function is marked with a Procedure ID of –4. You need to create a wrapper function for _NewEnum. Listing 6.8 shows the function we've created for the Lines class. When creating enumeration methods for your own class, you should copy this function exactly as it's shown here; the only change you must make is the name of the Collection variable (mcol-Lines in our case).

Listing 6.8: Enumeration Method for the Lines Class

```
Public Function NewEnum() As IUnknown
    ' Pass call to Collection's enumeration function
    Set NewEnum = mcolLines.[_NewEnum]
End Function
```

You'll notice two unique aspects of the function. First, the return type is declared using the COM data type IUnknown. This is the class from which all other COM classes are derived, and it enables the function to return any type of object. Second, the method call to _NewEnum is enclosed in square brackets. This is necessary because an underscore is not a valid initial character for names in VBA. The editor adds the brackets automatically when you use the IntelliSense features. Figure 6.5 shows an example of selecting _NewEnum from a pop-up list of methods.

FIGURE 6.5

Selecting the hidden
_NewEnum method

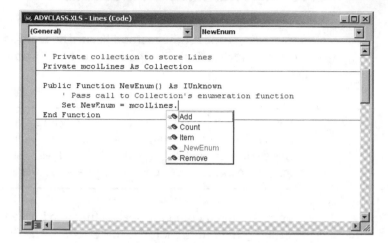

The last step is to mark this as an enumeration method by setting its Procedure ID to
–4. It's this attribute, not the name of the procedure, that enables VBA to use it with
For Each loops. In fact, the name of the VBA procedure is completely irrelevant.

Follow the steps outlined in the previous section to set the Procedure ID attribute.
That is, for VBA, export the module, add the attribute, and re-import the module
back into your VBA project. Note that if you use the VB IDE and Procedure
Attributes dialog, there is no entry in the drop-down list for enumeration. You'll
have to type –4 in the combo box yourself. Alternatively, if you make manual
changes to the .CLS file, you should add an Attribute line to the procedure with a
value of –4, as in this example:

```
Public Function NewEnum() As IUnknown
Attribute NewEnum.VB_UserMemId = -4
    ' Pass call to Collection's enumeration function
    Set NewEnum = mcolLines.[_NewEnum]
End Function
```

You should now be able to use your custom collection class just like you would
use VBA's built-in Collection class. If you examine the sample Lines class in the
Object Browser, you'll see that we've already done this.

WARNING   Procedure attributes may be discarded by VBA if you move, edit, or rename procedures. For this reason, we recommend setting these attributes as the final step in
designing the procedures.

NOTE While we've set the attributes on the Lines collection class, we have not used the default Item method or For Each loops in our sample testing code (for the reason described previously). If you'd like to test these functions, try editing the TestTF2 procedure in basTest to use For Each loops instead of For Next loops.

Creating and Using Custom Events

We've spent the bulk of this chapter (as well as Chapter 5) discussing how to create properties and methods for your custom classes. It's now time to discuss another very powerful feature of VBA—custom events. Events are so powerful because they provide a way for you to extend your classes, opening them to other developers. For example, before writing a line of text to a file using our TextFile2 class, we could raise an event that said, conceptually, "I'm about to write this line of test to the file. Do you want to do anything with it first?" Furthermore, events provide a way for you to separate the data and user interface components of an application. Data components raise events that user interface components respond to. In this way, it's easy to replace one user interface implementation with another because no UI logic is contained in the data class. This section explains how to declare, raise, and respond to custom events using three relatively new VBA keywords: Event, RaiseEvent, and WithEvents.

Defining Custom Events

The first thing you'll need to do is decide on what events your class will support and declare them in the class module's declarations section using the Event keyword. You declare events in a manner similar to procedures, providing a name and parameters, if any. For the purposes of demonstration, we've created another version of the TextFile class, TextFile3, which declares a number of events. Here's the applicable code from TextFile3's declarations section:

```
' Event declarations
Public Event ReadLine(ByVal Text As String)
Public Event WriteLine(Text As String, Skip As Boolean)
Public Event AfterOpen()
Public Event BeforeClose(Cancel As Boolean)
```

Note that all events are declared as Public. Even though this is the only level of scope for class modules, we've included the Public keyword for clarity. You cannot create Private events. Table 6.2 describes the purpose of each event.

TABLE 6.2:   Events Supported by the TextFile3 Class

Event	Description
ReadLine	Raised when a line of text is read and before adding it to the Lines collection. The Text argument contains the text and can be changed by the event listener.
WriteLine	Raised before a line of text is written to a file. The Text argument contains the text and can be changed by the event listener. If the Skip argument is set to True, the line is skipped and not written to the file.
AfterOpen	Raised after a file has been opened and all the lines have been read into the Lines collection.
BeforeClose	Raised before a file is closed. If the Cancel argument is set to True, the file is not closed.

Declaring events using the Event keyword is only the first step in creating events. It only defines what events a class has, not when each is raised. For that, you need to use the RaiseEvent keyword described in the next section.

Raising an Event

To raise an event, you use the RaiseEvent keyword at the point in your code where you want the event to happen. While you declare an event once using the Event keyword in a class module's declaration section, you can use RaiseEvent as many times as you need to in the class's functions and subroutines. As an example, Listing 6.9 shows a portion of TextFile3's FileOpen method. Note that the ReadLine event is raised as each line of text is read, and the AfterOpen event is raised after all lines have been read.

Listing 6.9: Raising Events when a File Is Opened

```
' Read all lines into the Lines collection
Set Lines = New Lines
If LOF(mhFile) > 0 Then
    Do Until EOF(mhFile)
        Line Input #mhFile, strLine
```

```
          ' Raise ReadLine event
          RaiseEvent ReadLine(strLine)

          Me.Lines.Add strLine
     Loop
End If

' Reset the changed property of all lines
Me.Lines.Changed = False

' Fire event
RaiseEvent AfterOpen
```

Using RaiseEvent to trigger custom events is similar to using the Call keyword to execute a procedure. You include the event name and any event parameters in parentheses.

Furthermore, just like VBA procedures, unless you declare an argument using the ByVal keyword, VBA passes the argument to the event listener by reference. This means the listener can change its value, and your code will see the change. That's why it's important to pass a variable, rather than a literal value. For instance, the ReadLine event passed a string variable, strLine, that contains the line of text just read. The event listener is given the opportunity to change the value before it's added to the Lines collection. Another example is the WriteLine event raised in the FileSave method, a portion of which is shown in Listing 6.10.

Listing 6.10: Raising an Event before Saving a Line of Text

```
' Write Lines collection to new file
hFile = FreeFile
Open strPath For Output Access Write As hFile
For cLine = 1 To Me.Lines.Count
    strText = Me.Lines.Item(cLine).Text

    ' Raise WriteLine event
    fSkip = False
    RaiseEvent WriteLine(strText, fSkip)

    If Not fSkip Then
        Print #hFile, strText
    End If
Next
Close hFile
```

In the case of WriteLine, we declared a Boolean variable, fSkip, which we reset to False each time through the For Next loop. After raising the event, we check the variable's value, and only if it's still False do we write the line of text to the file.

So how do you create something that "listens" to your events and responds to them? For that, you need one more keyword, WithEvents, which is described in the next section.

Responding to Events

The final piece of the event puzzle is creating an event procedure that can listen to events generated by an object. Doing this is simple. All you need to do is modify a normal object variable declaration by adding the WithEvents keyword. There is a catch, though. You can only use WithEvents with variables declared at the module level and only within class modules. The reason for this is that VBA uses COM to supply your project with events, and COM requires that both event generators and event listeners be objects, thus the need for class modules.

We've included a class module in the sample project called TestEvents that establishes an event hook for the TextFile3 class. Here's the declaration that tells VBA to hook into TextFile3's events:

```
' WithEvents declaration to establish event hook
Private WithEvents mobjFile As TextFile3
```

It looks just like a regular variable declaration except for the addition of the With-Events keyword. Once you add this keyword to a declaration, the object (mobj-File, in this case) exposes its events through the standard VBA mechanism: event procedures. Figure 6.6 shows the Module window for TestEvents. Notice that mobjFile is displayed in the object list, and all of its events are listed in the procedure drop-down list.

FIGURE 6.6

Selecting event procedures for a custom class

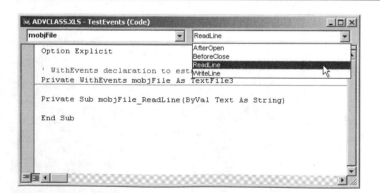

To respond to an event, simply select it from the list and write some code in the event procedure that VBA generates. For example, TestEvents responds to the ReadLine event by writing the line of text to the Immediate window. This is shown in Listing 6.11, along with the rest of the code in the module.

> **NOTE** Notice that, as with any other object that exposes events, the event procedure is named using the object name, an underscore, and the event name (i.e., mobjFile_ReadLine).

Listing 6.11: Code from the TestEvents Class

```
Private Sub Class_Initialize()
    ' Create a new instance of TextFile3 and open a file
    Set mobjFile = New TextFile3
    mobjFile.Path = "C:\AUTOEXEC.BAT"
    mobjFile.FileOpen
End Sub

Private Sub Class_Terminate()
    ' Close the file
    If mobjFile.IsOpen Then
        mobjFile.FileClose
    End If

    ' Destroy the object pointer
    Set mobjFile = Nothing
End Sub

Private Sub mobjFile_ReadLine(ByVal Text As String)
    ' Write the text to the immediate window
    Debug.Print Text
End Sub
```

Of course, nothing is going to happen until a new instance of the TextFile3 class is created. That's what the code in TestEvents' Initialize event does. You can see this in Listing 6.11.

Finally, there's one last thing to do—instantiate the TestEvents class. We accomplish this using a procedure in basTest, as shown in Listing 6.12.

Listing 6.12: Instantiating the TestEvents Class

```
Sub TestFileEvents()
    Dim objEvents As TestEvents

    ' Create new instance--this will open a file
    Set objEvents = New TestEvents

    ' We're all done so just destroy the pointer
    Set objEvents = Nothing
End Sub
```

When you run the procedure, you should see the contents of AUTOEXEC.BAT printed in the Immediate window. Why is there seemingly so little code in the TestFileEvents procedure? Because most of the work is done in TestEvents and TextFile3. If you step through the code, you can see this happen. Code execution follows this path:

1. Code in TestFileEvents creates a new instance of TestEvents (objEvents).

2. Code in TestEvents Initialize event creates a new instance of TextFile3 (mobjFile), sets its Path property, and calls its FileOpen method.

3. Code in the FileOpen method reads a line of text and fires the ReadLine event.

4. TestEvents is "listening" to this event and calls the event procedure mobjFile_ReadLine.

5. Code in the event procedure writes the line of text (stored in the Text parameter) to the Immediate window.

6. Steps 3 through 5 repeat until every line of text is read, at which point control returns to TestEvents Initialize event.

7. There's nothing left to do in the Initialize event, so control returns to TestFileEvents.

8. Code in TestFileEvents destroys the pointer to objEvents by setting it equal to Nothing.

9. This triggers the Terminate event, which closes the file and destroys the mobjFile object pointer.

10. Finally, control returns to TestFileEvents, and the procedure terminates.

If this seems like a complex process, it is, but one that's easily understood after you study it for a while. We can represent the process graphically using the illustration in Figure 6.7.

FIGURE 6.7
A graphical look at how WithEvents works

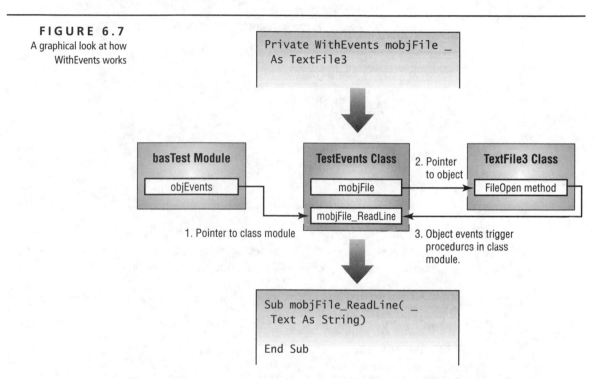

Once you've declared a variable using WithEvents and written code to respond to event procedures, you must "give life" to the class by instantiating it. Our sample code does this using a variable called objEvents, which, in turn, creates and holds a pointer to the TextFile3 class in mobjFile. The entire structure is now "live," and any events generated by the FileOpen method will be captured by code in TestEvents.

Using Forms with WithEvents

If you plan on hooking up events to your user interface using forms in Visual Basic, VBA, or Access, the process is a little simpler. That's because form modules are class modules and are instantiated automatically when you open the form. In this case, you don't need to create and instantiate an additional class in order to respond to events. We've demonstrated this by creating a simple form that displays the contents of a text file (see Figure 6.8).

FIGURE 6.8

A form that uses
WithEvents to display
file contents

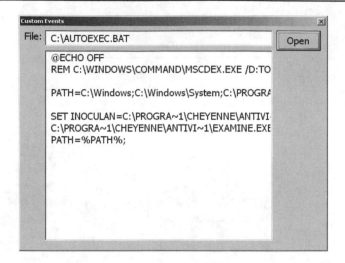

The form's class module takes the place of the TestEvents class in the previous example. That means the WithEvents declaration and event procedures appear in the form's module. Listing 6.13 shows the code in frmEvents.

Listing 6.13: Event-Handling Code in frmEvents

```
Option Explicit

' WithEvents declaration to establish event hook
Private WithEvents mobjFile As TextFile3

Private Sub cmdOpen_Click()
    ' Reinitialize the class instance
    Set mobjFile = New TextFile3

    ' Clear the list box
    Me.lstLines.Clear

    ' Open the file
    mobjFile.Path = Me.txtFile.Text
    mobjFile.FileOpen

    ' Destroy the pointer
    Set mobjFile = Nothing
End Sub
```

```
Private Sub mobjFile_ReadLine(ByVal Text As String)
    ' Add the line to the list
    Me.lstLines.AddItem Text
End Sub
```

This code should look very familiar because it's nearly identical to the code in TestEvents. If you set a breakpoint in the cmdOpen_Click procedure and run the form, you can step through the code and see how it works.

Custom Events Caveats

The capability to create custom events is a powerful one, but it does have its drawbacks. The most significant (although it's not often a problem in practice) is that a class raising event is at the mercy of those objects responding to events, in the sense that it must wait until those objects finish before continuing code execution. If one of the responding objects causes execution to halt, say, by raising a dialog or experiencing a run-time error, there is no way for the initial class to regain control. Furthermore, there is no way for the class-generating events to know what other objects are listening, a somctimes useful piece of information to have. Overcoming these drawbacks requires using custom callback methods instead of events. We explain callbacks in the next section as one use of interface inheritance and the Implements keyword.

Interface Classes and the Implements Keyword

In our discussion of using class modules throughout this chapter (and Chapter 5), we've combined two concepts that are normally treated separately: interfaces and implementations. An *interface* is simply a list of properties, methods, and events supported by a given class. On the other hand, an *implementation* is the code that makes up each of these and determines how a class actually works. VBA insulates you from having to know the difference. When you create a class module, you create its interface implicitly by writing code in Public procedures and by declaring Public variables and events. In other words, you create its interface at the same time as its implementation. C++ programmers treat these separately, creating at least two separate source files for each class: an interface definition file (using something called Interface Definition Language or IDL) and an implementation in the form of C++ source code and header files. Why is it important to know this? Because VBA offers you a way to do the same thing, enabling some interesting and powerful capabilities. But instead of creating IDL and source files, you must create two different classes.

Interface Inheritance

An *interface class* takes the place of an IDL file and enables *interface inheritance*—the ability for one class to inherit the interface defined by another. The interface class contains only property, method, and event declarations. It does not contain any source code. On the other hand, an *implementation class* contains all the code for a given interface. So how does the implementation class know what interface to inherit? You tell it which interface to inherit from by using the Implements keyword in the class module's declaration's section.

After inheriting an interface, you must provide an implementation for each of the interface's properties and methods. These appear as Private procedures in the implementation class in a way similar to WithEvents declarations. In addition to providing implementations for the inherited interface, you can also add your own methods and properties to the class, thus extending the implementation. You can also have multiple levels of inheritance, for example, with class C inheriting from class B, which inherits from class A.

What VBA does not provide in this version is *implementation inheritance*. As you can probably guess, implementation inheritance enables you to use the implementation of an inherited class as the default implementation for any class that inherits from it. Only if you want to define a new implementation do you need to override the default. This powerful feature of C++ and other object-oriented languages reduces the amount of extra implementation code you need to write when inheriting from multiple classes. Perhaps in a future version, VBA will also support this functionality.

As we explore the examples in this section, the use and usefulness of interface inheritance should become clear.

When to Inherit

At this point, you might be asking when interface inheritance is useful, especially if you have to go to extra trouble to implement it. To understand the answer, you need to keep in mind that an interface is like a contract. It defines the exact properties and methods a class must support (although it might define more) and thus how a class can be communicated with and used. Therefore, anywhere you need to enforce a communications contract between classes and you don't control the implementation, you can define an interface class to define the properties and methods you expect. For example:

- You need to develop a procedure to operate on different types of tabular data (for example, Word tables and Excel spreadsheets). You might define an interface class to represent a common view of tabular data and different implementation classes that map different data types to the common interface.

- You need to develop a data manipulation component that updates an unknown user interface with status information. You might define an interface class that defines a set of status properties. Then, any user interface that wants to be informed of status updates need only implement that interface.

We've chosen an example that illustrates the second scenario here, and we describe it in the next section.

Interface Inheritance Example: Callbacks

To illustrate one use of interface inheritance, we've created another version of our friend the TextFile class, this time replacing events with callback methods. You'll recall from the last section that custom events have the drawback of halting the event generator while the event listener deals with an event. An alternative is custom callback methods, where one class, TextFile4 in our case, calls methods in another class rather than simply and blindly broadcasting events.

Defining the Interface

Because we're turning the event model described earlier on its head, we need to define a custom interface that maps procedures to the events we created earlier in the TextFile3 class. We've done this in a VBA class module named ITextFileCallback, shown in Listing 6.14. Notice that it contains no code, only declarations.

NOTE   Traditionally, interface class names begin with a capital *I*.

Listing 6.14: The ITextFileCallback Interface Class

```
' Called when a line of text is read
Public Function ReadLine(Text As String) As Boolean

End Function

' Called before a line of text is written
Public Function WriteLine(Text As String) As Boolean

End Function

' Called after a file is opened
Public Sub AfterOpen()

End Sub

' Called before a file is closed
Public Function BeforeClose() As Boolean

End Function
```

The interface is roughly equivalent to the event structure defined in TextFile3, except the "events" are modeled as functions and subroutines. Methods in TextFile4 will call these procedures using an object passed into the class instance by another class module. Where appropriate, we've declared functions using Boolean return values to hold a success indicator. We can now create any number of implementation classes that inherit from this interface to handle different kinds of display tasks.

Creating Implementation Classes

Remember that an interface is like a contract. Similar to contracts, you can use interface classes with any number of "clients" to provide different implementations of the interface. We've created two classes: one that handles output to the Immediate window (ImmWndCallback) and one that handles output to a list box (ListBoxCallback). The first step in each case was to establish the correct inheritance using the Implements keyword.

If you examine each class module, you'll see they both have the following line of code in their declarations sections:

```
Implements ITextFileCallback
```

This tells VBA that the class will provide an implementation for all the properties and methods defined by the ITextFileCallback interface. Furthermore, as with the WithEvents keyword, using Implements in a class module adds an entry to the Object drop-down list that matches the specified interface. Selecting this entry causes the IDE to list all the interface's properties and methods in the Procedure drop-down list. Figure 6.9 illustrates this.

FIGURE 6.9
Selecting an interface's properties and methods

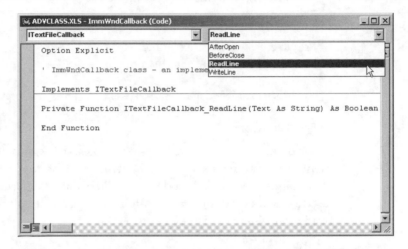

Listing 6.15 shows the code in the ImmWndCallback class module. Notice that every method defined by ITextFileCallback is represented. If you don't provide at least a procedure stub for each interface member, VBA will generate an error. The only method that really does anything useful is ITextFileCallback_ReadLine, which writes a line of text to the Immediate window.

Listing 6.15: Code in the ImmWndCallback Class Module

```
Implements ITextFileCallback

Private Sub ITextFileCallback_AfterOpen()
    ' This method has no implementation
End Sub

Private Function ITextFileCallback_BeforeClose() As Boolean
    ' This method has no implementation--just return True
    ITextFileCallback_BeforeClose = True
End Function
```

```
Private Function ITextFileCallback_ReadLine( _
 Text As String) As Boolean

    ' Write a line to the Immediate Window
    Debug.Print Text

    ' Return success
    ITextFileCallback_ReadLine = True
End Function

Private Function ITextFileCallback_WriteLine( _
 Text As String) As Boolean

    ' This method has no implementation--just return True
    ITextFileCallback_WriteLine = True
End Function
```

The other implementation class, ListBoxCallback, provides an alternative implementation for the interface, adding items to a list box instead of writing text to the Immediate window. The code for ListBoxCallback is shown in Listing 6.16. You'll also notice that it defines an additional property, a pointer to the list box control used by the class to display items.

Listing 6.16: Code in the ListBoxCallback Class Module

```
Implements ITextFileCallback

' Property that determines what list box to write to
Public TargetList As MSForms.ListBox

Private Function ITextFileCallback_ReadLine( _
 Text As String) As Boolean

    ' Add a line of text to the list
    If Not TargetList Is Nothing Then
        TargetList.AddItem Text

        ' Return success
        ITextFileCallback_ReadLine = True
    End If
End Function
```

```
Private Sub ITextFileCallback_AfterOpen()
    ' This method has no implementation
End Sub

Private Function ITextFileCallback_BeforeClose() As Boolean
    ' This method has no implementation--just return True
    ITextFileCallback_BeforeClose = True
End Function

Private Function ITextFileCallback_WriteLine( _
 Text As String) As Boolean

    ' This method has no implementation--just return True
    ITextFileCallback_WriteLine = True
End Function
```

Using the Implementation Class

So far, we've shown you how to create an interface class and two implementation classes that inherit from it. The next step is to modify the TextFile class to use the implementation classes. In our scenario, we will replace the event code with calls to methods of the callback classes. But, how do we tell VBA which class to use since it could be either one? That's where the magic of interface inheritance comes in. Wherever you want to pass an instance of an implementation class, use a reference to the interface class instead.

In our example, the TextFile4 class implements a property called Callback, which accepts a pointer to one of our callback classes, ImmWndCallback or ListBoxCallback. However, the property is defined using the interface class, ITextFile-Callback. Here's the property declaration, defined as a Public variable:

```
' Callback pointer
Public Callback As ITextFileCallback
```

In essence, this says that the Callback property can be set to an instance of the ITextFileCallback or *any class that inherits from it*. That's the power of interface inheritance. Now, wherever we use the TextFile4 class, we need to instantiate one of the callback classes and set it into the Callback property. For example, Listing 6.17 shows the code from frmImplements. In addition to declaring and using an instance of TextFile4, the code also declares and uses an instance of ListBoxCallback.

Listing 6.17. Code from frmImplements That Uses a Callback Class

```
Private Sub cmdOpen_Click()
    Dim objFile As TextFile4
    Dim objLBCallback As ListBoxCallback

    ' Initialize the text file class
    Set objFile = New TextFile4

    ' Initialze and set up the callback class
    Set objLBCallback = New ListBoxCallback
    Set objLBCallback.TargetList = Me.lstLines

    ' Set TextFile4's callback object
    Set objFile.Callback = objLBCallback

    ' Clear the list box
    Me.lstLines.Clear

    ' Open the file
    objFile.Path = Me.txtFile.Text
    objFile.FileOpen

    ' Destroy the pointer
    Set objFile = Nothing
End Sub
```

Figure 6.10 illustrates how this mechanism works.

1. Code in the form's module creates a new instance of the TextFile4 class and stores it in objFile.

2. Code in the form's module then creates a new instance of the ListBoxCallback class (that inherits from ITextFileCallback) and stores it in objLBCallback.

3. Code in the form's module sets objFile's Callback property to the instance of the callback class it just created, objLBCallback.

4. Code in the form's module calls objFile's FileOpen method, and FileOpen calls the ReadLine method in the callback object.

5. Finally, code in the callback object's ReadLine method adds a new item to the form's list box.

FIGURE 6.10
Illustrating how our callback mechanism works

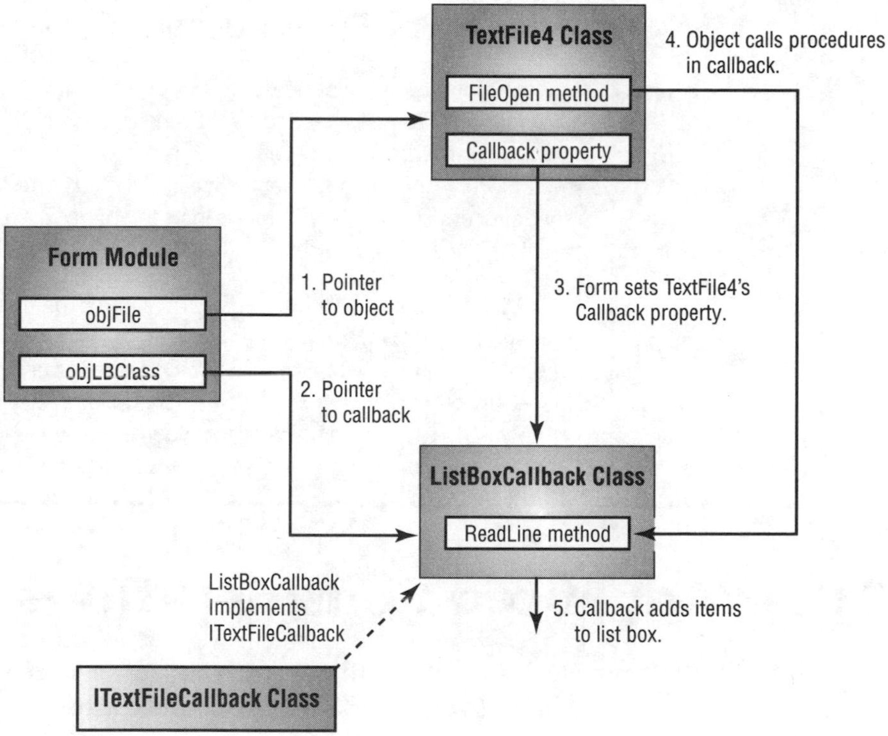

You'll probably find it helpful to step through the code to see the call chain as it happens.

NOTE   Don't confuse our specific callback example with general interface inheritance techniques. Creating multiple callback classes from a single interface class is just one use of interface inheritance.

In summary, interface inheritance depends on creating an interface class that defines a set of properties and methods. You then create one or more implementation classes that provide code to go along with the definitions. You can even have multiple levels of inheritance to represent increasing levels of class complexity, although you'll need to provide implementations at each level since VBA does not yet support implementation inheritance.

So How Is This Better Than Custom Events?

In this section, we presented the callback example as an alternative to using custom events implemented using Event, RaiseEvent, and WithEvents. So how is this better? As you'll recall, the main problem with custom events is that the object generating event has no control over the objects responding to events. Specifically, it has to wait until every event listener is finished processing the event before code can continue executing. Furthermore, it has no control over the order in which event listeners are processed.

With callback classes, the object calling back to all the other objects is in control. In can choose if, when, and in what order to call back to the objects waiting for its "events." In truth, our example is very simple in that the TextFile4 class only makes a provision for a single callback object. In practice, you'll likely want to implement a collection of callback objects and call them each in turn for each event. You can even decide not to call back to certain objects if they take too long to process or if you're just feeling feisty.

Other Advanced Considerations

We complete this chapter with a look at some additional considerations you should be aware of when working with custom classes in VBA. While not critical to custom class design, all of the following issues are worth knowing about as more of your development shifts from traditional, procedural programming to object-oriented implementation.

Error Handling in Classes

We have not discussed error handling in class modules in this chapter or Chapter 5 primarily to keep the examples simple and because, by now, most developers understand the basics of the On Error statement. Class modules add just a bit of extra complexity, and so it makes sense to mention them now.

The main thing to keep in mind is that classes cannot exist on their own; they need other code to instantiate and use them. Therefore, they should never display error information on their own. They should always delegate this task to the code that calls them. Trying to handle errors inside a class module and displaying a dialog box directly also has the effect of irrevocably binding the class to a given user interface implementation, something you should normally avoid. Of course, if run-time errors occur, you can't simply let them go unhandled or ignore them. So, how do you deal with run-time errors in class modules?

Calling Err.Raise

The answer is to use the Raise method of VBA's Err object to propagate errors to the calling procedure. This holds true for errors generated by VBA or custom errors you create to denote certain failure conditions. In the first case, consider the FileOpen method in the same text file classes. It includes an error handler that traps run-time Error 62, which indicates that VBA has reached the end of the file, and ignores it. For all other errors, it uses the Raise method to trigger any error handler in the calling procedure. Here's the relevant snippet of code:

```
ExitProc:
    Exit Function
HandleError:
    Select Case Err.Number
        Case 62 ' Input passed EOF
                ' Just ignore this
        Case Else
            FileOpen = False
            Err.Raise Err.Number, Err.Source, Err.Description
    End Select
    Resume ExitProc
```

Notice how the procedure uses information about the current error (number, source, and description) as arguments to the Raise method. This simply propagates the error to the next level in the call chain. The Raise method accepts up to five arguments for the error number, source (procedure name), description, Help file, and help context ID. We've chosen not to include the help information in our example.

TIP   If you want to test this, modify the TestTF2 procedure in basTest to pass an invalid filename to the class's Path property.

Raising Custom Errors

Custom errors are subtly different in that they are not generated by the VBA runtime but are triggered by your procedure. As such, there is no information contained in the Err object—you need to make it up by supplying the number, description, and so on. As an example, consider the following code snippet that represents a possible error condition for the text file class's Path Property Let statement:

```
Property Let Path(ByVal strPath As String)
    If Len(strPath) = 0 Then
        Err.Raise vbObjectError + 12345, "TextFile2::Path (Let)", _
        "Path cannot be blank."
    End If
    If Me.IsOpen Then
        Me.FileClose
    End If
    mstrPath = strPath
End Property
```

In this case, the procedure passes the Raise method three pieces of data that represent a logic error: a blank path. Let's look at each piece in turn.

The first (and only required) piece of information is the error number. It's defined by an expression, vbObjectError + 12345. Because other error handlers will be using this number to decide on a course of action, it's critical to use a number that will be unique among all other errors the code might encounter. VBA helps you somewhat by supplying a constant, vbObjectError, which represents a very large number (–2,147,221,504 or hexidecimal 80040000)—one beyond the range of all built-in VBA run-time errors. To this, you add a number that uniquely identifies your custom error. You should also choose a large number to avoid conflicts with other classes or components the application might use.

TIP   If you need to compute your custom error number in an error handler, just subtract vbObjectError from the value returned by Err.Number.

The second argument to Raise is the source of the error. The example uses a string that encodes the module name and procedure. Logic in an error handler can use this to determine where the error occurred and possibly display this to the user.

Lastly, the example passes a description of the error as a text string. VBA returns this information in the Description property of its Err object.

TIP	While we've included the literal string inside the procedure, it's a better practice to use constants or other mechanisms for text strings. This makes it easier to modify or localize them.

Breaking on Errors in VBA

One last issue involving error handling in class modules concerns a debugging setting in the Options dialog. Figure 6.11 shows the IDE's Options dialog and the various options for handling run-time errors.

FIGURE 6.11
Error-handling options displayed in the Options dialog box

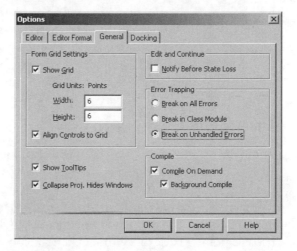

Figure 6.11 shows the option set to its default, Break on Unhandled Errors. This causes VBA to display its standard run-time error dialog box (see Figure 6.12) only when there is no other error handler in the call chain. Normally, this is the behavior you want because it respects your error handlers (and lets you easily spot where you might have forgotten to add one).

FIGURE 6.12
VBA's standard run-time error dialog box

On the other hand, either of the other two settings overrides your error handlers. Break on All Errors, as the text implies, causes VBA to always override your error handlers. Likewise, Break in Class Module overrides your error handlers only in class modules but not in regular modules. Obviously, circumventing your error handlers in not something you'll likely want in production applications.

Fortunately, you can check, if not readily change, these settings using the Windows Registry. These settings map to two values in the HKEY_CURRENT_USER\Software\Microsoft\VBA\6.0\Common key. Visual Basic maintains separate settings for these values in the HKEY_CURRENT_USER\Software\Microsoft\VBA\Microsoft Visual Basic key. The two values are named BreakOnAllErrors and BreakOnServerErrors. When BreakOnAllErrors is set to 1, VBA halts on all runtime errors. Similarly, when BreakOnServerErrors is set to 1, VBA breaks on errors in class modules. When both values are set to 0, only unhandled errors cause VBA to enter break mode. You can inspect these settings using the Registry functions described in Chapter 10. And while you can also change the settings via the Registry, the changes don't take effect until you restart the IDE.

Circular Reference Issues

In the earlier section on constructing a class hierarchy, we showed you how to reference an instance of one class from another. While this is a powerful capability of the language, you must also implement it carefully to avoid potentially difficult-to-diagnose errors. Trouble arises when class instances maintain circular references; that is, when an instance of one class holds a pointer to another, which holds a pointer back to the first instance. Since the rules of COM dictate that class instances cannot be destroyed until all pointers to them are released, this sometimes leads to instances that never terminate. This can lead to cleanup code never being called and memory leakage.

This is much easier to visualize with an example. We've created two classes, Ref1 and Ref2, which have a simple purpose: to maintain pointers to each other. Using these classes, we can easily illustrate circular references. For illustrative purposes, each of these classes also contains code to generate a unique instance identifier and print debugging information to the Immediate window. Three procedures, TestRef1, TestRef2 and TestRef3, demonstrate three different reference scenarios. You will likely find it helpful to step through these examples as we discuss each of the three scenarios.

Delayed Termination

The first test case involves class instances that terminate in a delayed fashion. This occurs when you maintain a pointer to a class instance in your code and that class instance, in turn, maintains a pointer to another class instance. Listing 6.18 shows the code from TestRef1, which illustrates this case.

Listing 6.18: Delayed Termination Due to Internal Pointers

```
Sub TestRef1()
    ' Both objects terminate at same time

    Dim objRef1 As Ref1
    Dim objRef2 As Ref2

    ' Instantiate variables
    Set objRef1 = New Ref1
    Set objRef2 = New Ref2

    ' Set a reference to one from the other
    Set objRef2.Link = objRef1

    ' Destroy the local references
    Set objRef1 = Nothing
    Set objRef2 = Nothing
End Sub
```

If you step through the code, you'll see that it begins by creating an instance of each of the two test classes, Ref1 and Ref2. Code in each class's Initialize events prints a message to the Immediate window. The procedure then sets up an internal pointer from the objRef2 to objRef1 by setting its Link property. This writes another message to the Immediate window. You should now see something like what's illustrated in Figure 6.13.

Internally, the pointer structure looks like Figure 6.14. Code in TestRef1 maintains two pointers, one to each class instance, and the instance of Ref2 maintains a pointer to the instance of Ref1.

FIGURE 6.13

Ref2 is now maintaining a pointer to Ref1.

FIGURE 6.14

Maintaining a unidirectional chain of pointers

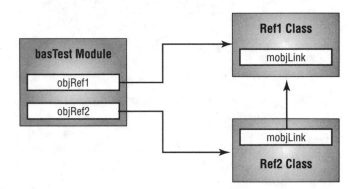

If you now continue to step through code, executing the line of code that sets objRef1 equal to Nothing, you'll see that nothing is written to the Immediate window. In reality, the procedure has destroyed its pointer to Ref1, but since a pointer is also maintained in objRef2, Ref1 cannot terminate. Only after executing the final line of code does Ref1 terminate, at the same time as Ref2. While the behavior does not appear to correspond to the code, at least both objects are destroyed.

Orphaned Objects

The second case is much more insidious because it establishes a circular reference, preventing either object from terminating. This is extremely damaging behavior because it leaves objects in memory with no programmatic way to terminate them. It's also a very difficult case to debug. Listing 6.19 shows the code in a procedure that tests this second case, TestRef2.

Listing 6.19: Code That Creates a Circular Reference

```
Sub TestRef2()
    ' No objects terminate!!

    Dim objRef1 As Ref1
    Dim objRef2 As Ref2

    ' Instantiate variables
    Set objRef1 = New Ref1
    Set objRef2 = New Ref2

    ' Set a reference to one from the other
    Set objRef1.Link = objRef2
    Set objRef2.Link = objRef1

    ' Destroy the local references
    Set objRef1 = Nothing
    Set objRef2 = Nothing
End Sub
```

The only difference between this procedure and the previous one is a single line of code that creates a pointer from the instance of Ref1 to the instance of Ref2. If you could see the pointers in memory, they would look something like the illustration in Figure 6.15. Note the circular reference between the class instances.

FIGURE 6.15
A circular reference is maintained between the class instances.

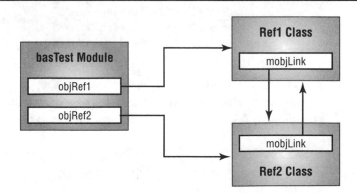

If you step all the way through the code in TestRef2, you'll notice that neither of the two objects terminate, even when you set both objRef1 and objRef2 to Nothing! How can this be? It happens because of the internal pointers maintained by the instances themselves. Hopefully, you can see the problem here. Both objects remain in memory, and, because the procedure has destroyed the pointers in objRef1 and objRef2, there is no longer any way to manipulate them. They will remain in memory until the application is terminated.

WARNING   In the case of in-process COM servers, this case can lead to objects that don't terminate until the machine is rebooted!

Proper Termination

Correcting this problem requires that you pay special attention to any possible circular references created by your class hierarchy. As long as class instances don't point *to each other*, you won't experience this problem. If you do allow circular references (parent-child relationships are the most common case) you should take the extra step of explicitly destroying internal pointers *before* destroying any external ones.

In our example, we could accomplish this by setting the Link property to Nothing before destroying the object pointer. Another potentially safer approach is to create a method of each class that destroys any pointers it maintains and then calls this method prior to termination. For example, both Ref1 and Ref2 implement the Cleanup method shown here:

```
Public Sub Cleanup()
    ' Destroy all object references
    If Not mobjLink Is Nothing Then
        Set mobjLink = Nothing
    End If
End Sub
```

Our final demonstrative procedure, TestRef3, calls this method before setting the object variables to Nothing. This is shown in Listing 6.20. If you step through the code, you'll see that both objects terminate as expected.

Listing 6.20: Calling a Method to Destroy Internal Pointers

```
Sub TestRef3()
    ' Objects terminate normally

    Dim objRef1 As Ref1
    Dim objRef2 As Ref2
```

```
            ' Instantiate variables
            Set objRef1 = New Ref1
            Set objRef2 = New Ref2

            ' Set a reference to one from the other
            Set objRef1.Link = objRef2
            Set objRef2.Link = objRef1

            ' Clean up internal reference
            objRef1.Cleanup
            objRef2.Cleanup

            ' Destroy the local references
            Set objRef1 = Nothing
            Set objRef2 = Nothing
        End Sub
```

Despite the additional effort required, taking these extra steps to ensure proper termination will make your life easier in the long run by eliminating potential debugging headaches and performance problems.

Shared Classes

The final topic in this section involves a new capability of VBA 6—the ability to share class modules between VBA projects. If you've been creating class modules for VBA projects, as we have, you may have been dismayed at having to duplicate common classes among multiple VBA projects. Changes in one project necessitate changes to all the others because there was no way to share the code. (Visual Basic has this capability inherently because projects are made up of files on disk.)

VBA now gives you the ability to share classes between VBA projects using project references. You can reference VBA projects the same way you reference any other COM components. Simply open the References dialog (select the Tools ≻ References menu command), click the Browse button, and locate the project file you're interested in.

NOTE   Project references are limited to the same host application. That is, you can reference one .XLS file from another, but you can't reference a Word VBA project in a .DOC file from an Excel VBA project.

Once you've established a project reference, you can call any Public procedure declared in normal code modules within the referenced project. In fact, you've been able to do this since VBA 5. To share class modules, you must perform two additional tasks.

First, you need to mark the class modules themselves as Public using the Properties window in the VBA IDE. By default, class modules are Private and, thus, cannot be shared. You must change this setting to PublicNotCreatable so other projects can see them. The second thing you must do is to provide a mechanism in the referenced project to create instances of the classes.

Because VBA class modules cannot be created by procedures outside of the project where they are defined, you must create a Public procedure in a normal code module that does this. We've created the following procedure named Get-TextFileObject in basTest:

```
Public Function GetTextFileObject() As TextFile2
    ' Return a new class instance
    Set GetTextFileObject = New TextFile2
End Function
```

All this procedure does is create a new instance of the TextFile2 class and return it to the calling procedure.

To demonstrate how this is used, we've created a second VBA project in REF.XLS that includes a reference to ADVCLASS.XLS. This second project includes it's own version of the test procedure TestTF2, but instead of using the New keyword to create a new instance of the TextFile2 class, it calls GetTextFile-Object:

```
Dim objFile As AdvClasses.TextFile2

' Create new instance of TextFile class
Set objFile = AdvClasses.GetTextFileObject()
```

NOTE   Note that we've prefixed the class and function names with the referenced project name. This serves to disambiguate the names should there be a naming conflict.

If you run the code in REF.XLS, you'll see that it behaves the same way as the code in ADVCLASS.XLS. With the ability to share classes between VBA projects, it's now much easier to make code modifications to common code.

Summary

This chapter picked up where Chapter 5 left off, discussing a number of advanced class module concepts and techniques. As you use more and more classes in your applications, you should find the information in this chapter very useful.

Specifically, this chapter covered the following techniques:

- Class hierarchy design using object properties
- Using the VBA Collection class
- Creating your own collection classes
- Defining and raising custom events
- Developing interfaces classes and using the Implements keyword
- Handling error conditions in class modules
- Dealing with circular references between class instances
- Sharing class modules among VBA projects

chapter 7

Searching and Sorting in VBA

- Creating a StopWatch class to measure elapsed time

- Introducing arrays

- Using the standard Quicksort algorithm

- Sorting collections

- Sorting other types of objects

- Understanding the Binary Search algorithm

If you're working with data in your application, sooner or later you'll need to sort the data, or you'll need to find a particular item within a group of data items. This chapter, which is devoted to searching and sorting data, presents some techniques from which you can choose.

Certainly, the topics of searching and sorting have been covered in much more academic terms, in much greater detail, in other books. We're not attempting to provide a complete discussion of various sorting algorithms here. In fact, we present only one: the common Quicksort algorithm. We do, however, show you how to use the sorting routine and present detailed coverage of exactly how it works. For searching, we present the Binary Search algorithm and demonstrate how you can use it and exactly how it works. Because many readers will be using VBA in conjunction with the Microsoft Jet database engine or some other SQL data source, we provide tips along the way for using the database engine to do the work.

Table 7.1 lists the sample files you'll find on the accompanying CD-ROM.

TABLE 7.1:   Sample Files

Filename	Description
SrchSort.xls	Excel file with all sample functions
SrchSort.mdb	Access 2000 file with all sample functions
BinarySearch.bas	Binary Search module
BubbleSort.bas	Bubblesort module
LinearSearch.bas	Linear search module
QuickSort.bas	Quicksort module
QuickSortable.bas	Quicksort using ISortable class
QuickSortObjects.bas	Quicksort using Object type
TestISortable.bas	Test dhQuickSortable
TestProcs.bas	Test procedures
VQuickSort.bas	Visual Quicksort module
ExistingArray.cls	Sample class for dhQuickSortable
FileData.cls	Sample class for dhQuickSortable

TABLE 7.1: Sample Files *(continued)*

Filename	Description
FileDataObject.cls	Sample class for dhQuickSortObjects
ISortable.cls	Interface class for dhQuickSortable
SimpleArray.cls	Sample class for dhQuickSortable
SortedCollection.cls	Sorted Collection class
StopWatch.cls	StopWatch class module
SrchSort.VBP	VB6 project including all sample modules

Timing Is Everything

Most likely, if you're sorting data, you care about how long it takes to perform the sort. When deciding on the best technique to use for sorting your data, you'll need some help. The StopWatch class discussed in this section can help you determine which is the best technique to use, based on the time it takes to execute. We use this simple StopWatch class all the time and in any situation in which we need to compare the timings of two or more activities.

Introducing the StopWatch Class

It doesn't take much effort to measure elapsed time. VBA itself includes the Timer function, which returns a Single value containing the number of seconds that have elapsed since midnight. This function has three inherent problems if you intend to use it to measure elapsed time in your applications:

- It "turns over" at midnight, so if you happen to be running a test over the bewitching hour, your test results will be meaningless.

- It turns over every 24 hours, so if you want to run a test that lasts longer than that, you're out of luck.

- It isn't terribly accurate. It can measure time only to 1/18-second accuracy because of the particular internal timer it's using.

For these reasons (and there's one even more crucial reason not to use Timer, coming up in a moment), it's probably best that you avoid the Timer function when attempting to measure elapsed times in small increments. What's your alternative? The Windows API provides several ways to measure elapsed time, the simplest of which is the GetTickCount function. This function measures the number of milliseconds (in a long integer) that have elapsed since you started Windows. The GetTickCount function compares favorably to the Timer function:

- It "turns over" only every 49 days or so. If you're interested in millisecond accuracy, you're probably not running tasks that take that long, but it's nice to know it can keep on ticking and ticking!

- It has no concept of days, so there's no issue with running tasks that last longer than a single day.

- It's more accurate than the Timer function. Rather than measuring in 1/18-second increments, it measures in 1/1000-second increments. In addition, because it doesn't involve floating-point math to return its results (as does the Timer function), it's more accurate as well.

Obviously, the StopWatch class will take advantage of this API function. The code for the class, shown in Listing 7.1, is amazingly simple. As you can see in the listing, the class exposes two public methods: StartTimer and EndTimer. The StartTimer method initializes the internal mlngStart variable, storing the time value when the stopwatch was "started." The EndTimer method returns the difference between the current tick value and the time at which the clock was started—effectively, the amount of elapsed time, in milliseconds.

Listing 7.1: The StopWatch Class (Stopwatch.cls)

```
Private mlngStart As Long
Private Declare Function GetTickCount Lib "kernel32" () As Long

Public Sub StartTimer()
    mlngStart = GetTickCount
End Sub

Public Function EndTimer() As Long
    EndTimer = (GetTickCount - mlngStart)
End Function
```

Using the StopWatch Class

To use the StopWatch class, you'll generally write code like this:

```
Dim sw As StopWatch
Set sw = New StopWatch
sw.StartTimer
' Do stuff in here that you want to time
Debug.Print "That took: " sw.EndTimer & "milliseconds."
```

As an example, the final (and most compelling) reason to use GetTickCount as opposed to the built-in Timer function is that the act of calling the Timer function itself takes, in general, several times as long as calling GetTickCount. Don't believe it? Try the code shown in Listing 7.2, from TestProcs.bas. If you run CompareTimers from the Immediate window, you'll see that calling Timer takes substantially longer (five to eight times longer, in our tests) than calling GetTickCount.

Listing 7.2: Compare Timer to GetTickCount (TestProcs.bas)

```
Private Declare Function GetTickCount Lib "kernel32" () As Long

Public Sub CompareTimers()
    Dim lngMax As Long
    Dim sw As New StopWatch
    Dim lngI As Long
    Dim lngResult As Long

    lngMax = 100000
    sw.StartTimer
    For lngI = 1 To lngMax
        lngResult = Timer
    Next lngI
    Debug.Print "Timer: " & sw.EndTimer

    sw.StartTimer
    For lngI = 1 To lngMax
        lngResult = GetTickCount
    Next lngI
    Debug.Print "GetTickCount: " & sw.EndTimer
End Sub
```

To use the StopWatch class in any application, simply import Stopwatch.cls into your project, and call it as shown in the examples. Whenever we make a comment in this book about one technique being faster than another, you can bet we've tried it out both ways with the stopwatch running.

Using Arrays

There are many ways to store data in VBA, but if you're interested in sorting data, it will often be in an array. Although many subtleties are involved in using arrays in VBA, the next few sections outline the concepts you'll need to understand in order to use the techniques supplied in this chapter. If you need more detailed information on creating and using arrays, see the VBA online help. This is a rich topic, and we can't discuss all the subtleties here; we've attempted to explain only what you'll need to know to follow the code examples in this chapter.

What Is an Array, Anyway?

An array is an indexed group of data treated as a single variable. You would consider using an array when you need to work with a group of data items that are related in such a way that you can use an integer to relate the items.

For example, imagine you needed to work with all your salary levels for a six-year range, from 1992 to 1997. Because the year value is an integer, you can use that as an index for the data. You might create an array named SalaryInfo, as shown in Figure 7.1, declared like this:

```
Dim SalaryInfo(1992 To 1997) As Currency
```

Of course, you're not limited to arrays containing information about salaries, or even to arrays of any specific data type. When you declare an array, you can specify any range of values (most arrays start at either 0 or 1, but they don't have to), containing almost any data type. In addition, arrays can contain multiple dimensions of data. To access a particular array element, you might use statements like these:

```
SalaryInfo(1997) = 26500
' or
If SalaryInfo(1997) > SalaryInfo(1996) * 1.10 Then
    MsgBox "The raise from 1996 to 1997 was too great. " & _
    "Make this year's raise smaller!"
End If
```

FIGURE 7.1
An array can use any
integer value range as
its index.

Imagine that rather than storing six years of salary information, you'd like to store salary information by quarter. That is, for each of the four quarters in the year, you'd like information in each of the six years. You might, then, create an array that looks like the one shown in Figure 7.2. To declare an array like this one, you might use a statement like this:

```
Dim SalaryInfo(1992 To 1997, 1 To 4) As Currency
```

where the years range from 1992 to 1997, and for each year, the quarters range from 1 to 4.

FIGURE 7.2
Arrays can contain two or
more dimensions of
information.

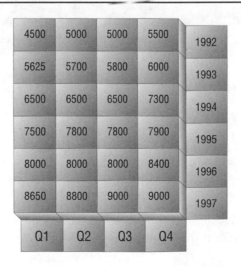

To retrieve or set any item from the array, now you'd use an expression like this:

```
' Give a 15% raise in the fourth quarter, based on the third
' quarter's salary.
SalaryInfo(1997, 4) = SalaryInfo(1997, 3) * 1.15
```

Take it one step further: what if you want to work with information about quarterly salaries of multiple employees? In that case, you might create a three-dimensional array, as shown in Figure 7.3. To declare this array, you might use a statement like this:

```
Dim SalaryInfo(1992 To 1997, 1 To 4, 1 To 3) As Currency
```

(that is, years from 1992 to 1997, quarters from 1 to 4, and employees from 1 to 3). The following code will deduct 10 percent from Employee 3's pay in the final quarter of 1997:

```
SalaryInfo(1997, 4, 3) = SalaryInfo(1997, 4, 3) * .90
```

FIGURE 7.3

Although it's not a common practice, you can use three or more dimensions in your arrays.

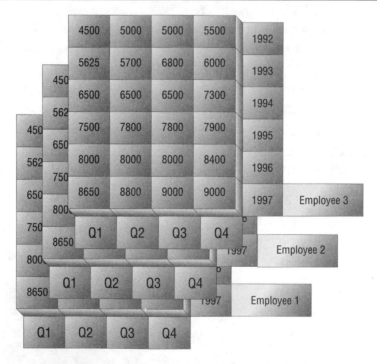

The following sections discuss some of the details of using arrays, and many of the examples in this chapter also use arrays as part of doing their work.

TIP
Although using multidimensional arrays is a useful technique for modeling real-world scenarios, be careful of the complexity you introduce into your applications by using these sometimes difficult-to-envision data structures. In addition, arrays in VBA aren't sparse—that is, empty elements take up just as much memory as elements that are filled with data. Large arrays can be real memory hogs, and you should carefully consider how much of your array is being utilized and whether some other data structure might be more appropriate.

Creating an Array

VBA treats an array much as it would any other variable. The same naming, scoping, and lifetime rules apply. The only difference is that, with an array, you must either specify the lower and upper bounds for the array or at least indicate that you'll *later* indicate those values.

To create an array, dimension array variables like this:

```
' 100 integers
Dim aintItems(1 To 100) As Integer
' 10 rows of data with 2 strings each
Dim astrNames(1 To 10, 1 To 2) As String
' Tell VBA that you'll specify the size later:
Dim astrNames() As String
```

See the section "Sizing an Array" coming up in a moment for more information on resizing an array once you've created it.

TIP
To indicate that a variable contains an array, we've used the "a" prefix on variable names. For example, given a name like "astrNames," you can see that it's an array ("a") containing strings ("str") called "Names." You can pick your own naming convention—this just happens to be how we do it.

Using Data in an Array

Once you've created an array, you can work with any item in the array, referring to the item by its position within the array. For example, if the array astrItems contains

100 strings, you could use code like the following to inspect each of the 100 elements of the array:

```
Dim intI As Integer
For intI = 1 To 100
    Debug.Print astrItems(intI)
Next intI
```

If you wanted to place the current index value into each location in aintItems (an array of 50 integers), you might write code like this:

```
Dim aintItems(1 To 50) As Integer
Dim intI As Integer
For intI = 1 To 50
    aintItems(intI) = intI
Next intI
```

You needn't use a loop of any sort to work with elements of an array. For example, the following procedure, used in the sorting code presented in the section "Sorting Arrays" later in this chapter, swaps two array items. In this case, the array is named varItems, and lngItem1 and lngItem2 contain the indexes of the two items to be swapped:

```
Dim varTemp As Variant
varTemp = varItems(lngItem2)
varItems(lngItem2) = varItems(lngItem1)
varItems(lngItem1) = varTemp
```

> **NOTE** You can also use the For Each...Next construct to loop through the elements of an array, but this isn't recommended. It's slower than using the For...Next construct, and you can't use this construct for setting values in an array—you can use it only to retrieve values. On the other hand, using For Each...Next means you needn't worry about the bounds of the array—the looping construct takes care of those details. If you decide to use For Each...Next to loop through an array, use a variant as the looping variable.

Sizing an Array

An array is generally a static data structure. As such, once you've told VBA the size of the data structure, you won't be able to automatically resize the array without explicitly requesting the change in size.

VBA provides a number of ways to size an array:

- When you declare the array, you can specify its dimensions. (This is normally called a *fixed-size* array.)

  ```
  Dim astrItems(1 To 100) As String
  ```

- When you declare the array, you can leave off the dimensions. Later, when you want to use the array, you can use the ReDim keyword to set its size. (This is normally called a *dynamic* array because you needn't know the size of the array when you create it.)

  ```
  Dim astrItems() As String
  ' Later in the code (intItems contains, perhaps, 100)
  ReDim astrItems(1 To intItems)
  ```

- You can create a dynamic array, along with its dimensions, when you first declare it, using the ReDim keyword:

  ```
  ReDim astrItems(1 To 100) As String
  ```

- You can resize a dynamic array at any time, using the ReDim keyword. Unless you also specify the Preserve keyword, VBA clears the items contained in the array. If you use the Preserve keyword, VBA preserves all the existing items in the array:

  ```
  Dim astrItems() As String
  ' Later in the code:
  ReDim astrItems(1 To 100)
  ' Fill in the items...
  ' Now you find out that you need an additional 100 items:
  ReDim Preserve astrItems(1 To 200)
  ```

TIP Although you needn't specify the lower bound of an array—rather than specifying (1 to 100), for example, you could just use (100) as the array bound—we strongly advise that you always do so. If you don't specify the lower bound, you're counting on using the value specified (or implied) by the module's Option Base setting. By default, a module's Option Base setting is 0, but you can override this by adding an Option Base 1 statement to any module. Either way, if you don't specify the lower bound of an array when you set its size, VBA will use the value selected by the Option Base statement. When you explicitly specify the lower bound, your code is more readable, and you're less likely to be affected by "off by one" errors.

TIP	It's worth noting that you can only use ReDim Preserve and modify the dimensions of an array; you'll need to be especially careful with multidimensional arrays. In that case, you can only redimension the last array dimension, and you can't change the number of dimensions at all. See the ReDim statement in online help for more info, because using ReDim Preserve with multidimensioned arrays may cause you some stress.

Alternatives to ReDim Preserve

Using ReDim Preserve does preserve the contents of your array as it's being resized, but it's not a fast operation. To redimension the array, VBA must grab a chunk of memory for the new array and then, if you've specified the Preserve keyword, copy over all the items in your original array. Finally, it releases the memory used by the original array. You'd do best to avoid ReDim Preserve if at all possible. What are the alternatives? One possibility is to use a collection (see the section "Working with Collections" later in this chapter for more information) to contain your data. Another is to use a dynamic data structure like a linked list, as described in Chapter 8. Finally, you can consider redimensioning your array by adding chunks of items at a time. That is, rather than redimension it every time it requires more items, add a large number of items at a time and redimension only when you run out of items. When you're done adding items, you can make one final call to ReDim Preserve to resize the array correctly.

Using a Variant to Point to an Array

A simple way to work with an array is to "point" a variant variable at the array and use the variant to refer to the array from then on. That is, if astrItems is an array containing 100 strings, you can use code like the following to cause varItems to refer to astrItems:

```
Dim varItems As Variant
Dim astrItems(1 To 100) As String
' Fill in the strings here.
varItems = astrItems
```

Once you take that step, you can use varItems as a single variable, without worrying about the trailing parentheses, but you can also refer to items in the array, using code like this:

```
varItems(1) = "A new string"
```

This assignment happens automatically when you pass an array to a function that expects a variant parameter. For example, the dhQuickSort procedure (in Quicksort.bas) is declared like this:

```
Sub dhQuickSort(varArray As Variant, _
  Optional lngLeft As Integer = dhcMissing, _
  Optional lngRight As Integer = dhcMissing)
```

To call dhQuickSort, pass it either an array or a variant that "contains" an array. For example, any of the following methods is acceptable:

```
Dim varItems As Variant
varItems = Array(1, 2, 3, 4, 5)
Call dhQuickSort(varItems)
' or: ==========
Dim aintItems(1 To 5) As Integer
aintItems(1) = 1
aintItems(2) = 2
aintItems(3) = 3
aintItems(4) = 4
aintItems(5) = 5
Call dhQuickSort(aintItems)
' or: ==========
Dim aintItems(1 To 5) As Integer
Dim varItems As Variant
aintItems(1) = 1
aintItems(2) = 2
aintTtems(3) = 3
aintItems(4) = 4
aintItems(5) = 5
varItems = aintItems
Call dhQuickSort(varItems)
```

If you call dhQuickSort, passing it an array of strings (or any other specific data type), VBA will assign the array to the variant as it calls the procedure. Then, inside the called procedure, you can refer to varItems as though it were the array itself.

To ensure that a variant does, in fact, contain an array, you have three choices:

Use the TypeName function   Call the TypeName function. If your Variant item contains an array, the TypeName function returns the string that ends with "()", like "Integer()" or "String()", depending on the type of data in the array.

Use the IsArray function   Call the IsArray function, passing the variant variable. It will return True if the variant points to an array and False otherwise. You might write code like this at the beginning of a routine that's expecting an array:

```
If Not IsArray(varItems) Then Exit Sub
```

Use the VarType function   Call the VarType function, passing the variant variable. VarType will return vbArray (8192) plus a value corresponding to the type of data in the array—vbInteger (2) through vbByte (17). For example, if you're allowing only an array of strings to be passed into a particular function, you might write code like the following:

```
If VarType(varItems) <> vbArray + vbString Then Exit Sub
```

Using the Array Function

Some examples in this chapter use the Array function to place data into an array. This useful function allows you to list specific values to be placed into an array, and it returns an array containing the values you send it. For example, the following statement places an array containing three integers into a variant:

```
Dim varItems As Variant
varItems = Array(100, 202, 315)
' Almost equivalent to:
Dim varItems(0 To 2) As Integer
varItems(0) = 100
varItems(1) = 202
varItems(2) = 315
```

Note the "almost" in the code comment. In the first example, the indexes used by the items in varItems will use the Option Base statement in the module to determine the start of the range of index values. If there's no Option Base statement or if it's set to 0, the items will be numbered 0, 1, and 2. If you've set the Option Base statement for the module to 1, the elements will be numbered 1, 2, and 3. The array items in the second example will always be numbered 0, 1, and 2, no matter how you modify the Option Base statement for the module. You must be aware of the Option Base setting if you use the Array function. If you want the Array function to always start numbering at 0, you must use a trick: you must call the Array function directly from the VBA type library, using the syntax VBA.Array. Therefore, this code always gives you an array whose first index is 0, no matter how Option Base has been set:

```
varItems = VBA.Array(100, 202, 315)
```

New Array Features

VBA 6 (used in Visual Basic 6 and Office 2000) adds some interesting new features for array users. First of all, although you couldn't do this in previous versions of VBA, you can now return a typed array as the return value of a function. In previous versions, you could return an array stored in a Variant, but you couldn't write a function like this:

```
Function ReturnArray() As String()
    Dim astrValues() As String
    ReDim astrValues(1 To 100)
    ' Put some data into the array.
    astrValues(1) = "Hello"
    astrValues(2) = "There"
    ReturnArray = astrValues()
End Function

Sub TestReturnArray()
    Dim astrValues() As String
    astrValues = ReturnArray()
    Debug.Print astrValues(1)
End Sub
```

Now, there's no problem returning a typed array from a function call. This takes care of a large class of issues you'd otherwise have to deal with when returning an array in a Variant. Most important, this handles the "is there actually an array in there?" problem on return from calling this type of function in VBA 5.

In addition, VBA 6 makes it possible to assign an array from one location to another with a single statement. In previous versions of VBA, you were required to copy each element, one at a time (or to use Windows API calls to copy the whole memory block at once, a frightening concept for most developers). As a matter of fact, the TestReturnArray procedure in the previous code fragment took advantage of this capability when it performed this line of code:

```
Dim astrValues() As String
astrValues = ReturnArray()
```

Whether you can copy an array from one variable to another depends on a number of issues, including the following:

- The type of array (fixed or dynamic) on the left-hand side of the assignment. (You can never assign directly into a fixed-size array.)

- Whether the number of dimensions for the two arrays match.

- Whether the number of elements on both arrays match.

- The data types for the two arrays are compatible. (For example, you'll never be able to copy data from a string array into a numeric array.)

The following table describes the outcome of trying to make an assignment based on the various issues.

Left-Hand Side	Number of Dimensions Match?	Number of Elements Match?	Result
Dynamic	No	Doesn't matter	Succeeds. Left-hand array may ReDim to match right-hand if necessary.
Dynamic	Yes	No	Succeeds. Left-hand array may ReDim to match right-hand if necessary.
Dynamic	No	Yes	Succeeds
Fixed	Doesn't matter	Doesn't matter	Fails at compile time

We take advantage of the ability to assign typed arrays to other arrays in many places throughout the book, and we (to be honest) simply take this ability for granted. Yes, it's new in this version, but it's how you probably expected VBA to work all along, so its use comes naturally in code.

Sorting Arrays

Once you're comfortable with arrays, you'll want to be able to sort the data they contain. This section introduces a common sorting method, the Quicksort algorithm. This algorithm, an accepted advanced sorting technique, is somewhat complex, but it performs well. Once you've written the code, of course, you won't have to revisit it unless you need to modify it. If you're not interested in how the sort does its work, skip ahead to the "Watching Quicksort Run" section.

NOTE   Why this particular sorting algorithm? In choosing a sort method, you want to minimize the number of comparisons and swaps the sort uses to complete its goal. There are simpler sort algorithms (a statement with which you'll undoubtedly agree if you work through the Quicksort example step by step), but the simpler sorts almost always require more comparisons between items and more data movement (swapping items) in order to sort the array. More comparisons and more swaps turn into longer execution time, so Quicksort provides a good compromise: it's complex but understandable, and it's more efficient than simpler sorts.

WARNING   Quicksort isn't optimized for data that's already sorted. That is, if your data comes to the Quicksort algorithm in sorted order, it will take almost as long to sort as if it weren't. Other (perhaps simpler) algorithms will take into account the fact that data is already sorted and drop out sooner. If you're often going to be sorting data that may be in sorted order, you may want to investigate other sorting techniques. (See the discussion in the section "Speed Considerations" later in this chapter for more information.)

How Does Quicksort Work?

The Quicksort algorithm, generally accepted as one of the fastest sort algorithms, uses the "divide and conquer" technique of sorting. Basically, Quicksort divides an array into smaller and smaller partitions, two partitions at a time, such that each left-hand partition contains values smaller than each right-hand partition. When it runs out of partitions, it's done.

Quicksort lends itself to recursion (the concept of a procedure calling itself, passing new parameters), and the recursive implementation of the sort is relatively simple. Given an array to sort, the algorithm boils down to these few steps:

1. Call the sort function, passing the lower and upper bounds of the segment to be sorted.

2. If the lower bound is less than the upper bound, then:

    a. Break the current array into two smaller segments, such that all items in the left segment are less than or equal to each item in the right segment. This will involve swapping some items from one segment to the other.

b. Follow the same algorithm on the smaller of the left and right segments (and this will, most likely, break down the segment into multiple call levels as well). Once that's sorted, follow the same algorithm with the larger, remaining segment.

The sort appears to break down into two major chunks: partitioning the elements and then calling the sort again recursively. You might be grumbling, at this point, about recursive routines and how they use lots of memory. Normally, that's true; this version of the sorting algorithm, however, tries to be conservative about how it uses memory. At each level, it sorts the smaller of the two chunks first. This means it will have fewer recursive levels: the small chunk will end up containing a single element much more quickly than the large chunk. By always working with the smallest chunk first, this method avoids calling itself more often than it has to. The entire dhQuickSort procedure, implementing the Quicksort algorithm, is shown in Listing 7.3.

Listing 7.3: The dhQuickSort Procedure, Implementing the Quicksort Algorithm (Quicksort.bas)

```vba
Private Const dhcMissing = -2

Public Sub dhQuickSort(varArray As Variant, _
 Optional lngLeft As Long = dhcMissing, _
 Optional lngRight As Long = dhcMissing)

    Dim i As Long
    Dim j As Long
    Dim varTestVal As Variant
    Dim lngMid As Long

    If lngLeft = dhcMissing Then lngLeft = LBound(varArray)
    If lngRight = dhcMissing Then lngRight = UBound(varArray)

    If lngLeft < lngRight Then
        lngMid = (lngLeft + lngRight) \ 2
        varTestVal = varArray(lngMid)
        i = lngLeft
        j = lngRight
        Do
            Do While varArray(i) < varTestVal
                i = i + 1
```

```
            Loop
            Do While varArray(j) > varTestVal
                j = j - 1
            Loop
            If i <= j Then
                SwapElements varArray, i, j
                i = i + 1
                j = j - 1
            End If
        Loop Until i > j
        ' To optimize the sort, always sort the
        ' smallest segment first.
        If j <= lngMid Then
            Call dhQuickSort(varArray, lngLeft, j)
            Call dhQuickSort(varArray, i, lngRight)
        Else
            Call dhQuickSort(varArray, i, lngRight)
            Call dhQuickSort(varArray, lngLeft, j)
        End If
    End If
End Sub

Private Sub SwapElements(varItems As Variant, _
  lngItem1 As Long, lngItem2 As Long)
    Dim varTemp As Variant

    varTemp = varItems(lngItem2)
    varItems(lngItem2) = varItems(lngItem1)
    varItems(lngItem1) = varTemp
End Sub
```

When you have a procedure that calls itself recursively, it's imperative that you provide some way to terminate the process. In this case, the code can repeat only as long as the lower bound value is less than the upper bound value. As the dhQuickSort routine calls itself, the lower bound gets higher and higher and the upper bound gets lower and lower. Once these values cross, the sort is done. Therefore, the dhQuickSort procedure starts by checking for this condition:

```
If lngLeft < lngRight Then
    ' Sort this segment (code removed)
End If
```

If, at any call to dhQuickSort, the lower bound isn't less than the upper bound, the sorting stops and the procedure can return to the caller. Once the code has made the determination that it can perform the sort, it takes the following steps:

1. The sort takes the value in the middle of the subset of the array that's being sorted as the "comparison" value. Its value is going to be the dividing factor for the two chunks. There are different schools of thought on how to choose the dividing item. This version of the sort uses the item that's physically in the middle of the chosen list of items:

```
lngMid = (lngLeft + lngRight) \ 2
varTestVal = varArray(lngMid)
```

2. The code first starts from the left, walking along the array until it finds an item that isn't less than the dividing value. This search is guaranteed to stop at the dividing value, which certainly isn't less than itself:

```
i = lngLeft
j = lngRight
' Loop removed here.
Do While varArray(i) < varTestVal
    i = i + 1
Loop
```

3. Next, the code starts from the right, walking backward through the array until it finds an item that isn't more than the dividing value. This search is guaranteed to stop at the dividing value, which certainly isn't more than itself:

```
Do While varArray(j) > varTestVal
    j = j - 1
Loop
```

4. If the position from step 2 is less than or equal to the position found in step 3, the sort swaps the elements at the two positions and then increments the pointer for step 2 and decrements the pointer for step 3:

```
If i <= j Then
    Call SwapElements(varArray, i, j)
    i = i + 1
    j = j - 1
End If
```

5. The sort repeats steps 2 through 4 until the pointer from step 2 is greater than the pointer from step 3 (i > j). At this point, every item to the left of the dividing element is less than or equal to it, and everything to the right is greater than or equal to it.

6. Choosing the smaller partition first, the sort repeats all these steps on each of the subsets to either side of the dividing value until step 1 indicates that it's done:

```
If j <= lngMid Then
    Call dhQuickSort(varArray, lngLeft, j)
    Call dhQuickSort(varArray, i, lngRight)
Else
    Call dhQuickSort(varArray, i, lngRight)
    Call dhQuickSort(varArray, lngLeft, j)
End If
```

To make this technique completely clear, imagine you want to sort an array of 10 integers, positions numbered 1 through 10, as shown in Figure 7.4. The following numbered list corresponds to the steps shown in Figures 7.5, 7.6, 7.7, and 7.8. In the first few steps, the pertinent code will be displayed. Because there isn't much code but there are a lot of steps, once you've seen the appropriate chunk of code, it won't be displayed again.

NOTE   Along the way, the discussion will keep track of the levels of recursion. That is, as you call dhQuickSort from dhQuickSort, it's important to keep track of how many times the procedure has called itself, to make sure you understand the concept of a recursion. In this example, level 1 is your call to dhQuickSort, and subsequent levels represent calls dhQuickSort makes to itself, passing in different limits on the array to be sorted.

NOTE   To make the following steps easier to read, we've used the symbol "j^" to refer to "the item pointed to by j." That is, when the variable j contains the value 1, the item it's pointing to (in the original array) is 79, and the shortcut in the text for that will be j^. (If you require some verbal representation for this notation, you can say—silently, please—"j hat" where you see "j^" in the text. This verbalization stems from a Pascal class one of us took many years ago.)

FIGURE 7.4

The sample array, ready to be sorted

1. Calculate the middle location (5). Then, point i at the first element in the array and j at the final element. While i^ (the item pointed to by i) is less than 26, move i to the right. (It doesn't move at all, because 79 isn't less than 26.) While j^ is greater than 26, move j to the left:

```
lngMid = (lngLeft + lngRight) \ 2
varTestVal = varArray(lngMid)
i = lngLeft
j = lngRight
Do
    Do While varArray(i) < varTestVal
        i = i + 1
    Loop
    Do While varArray(j) > varTestVal
        j = j - 1
    Loop
```

2. Because i is less than or equal to j, swap the elements pointed to by i and j. Then move i one position to the right and j one position to the left.

```
If i <= j Then
    SwapElements varArray, i, j
    i = i + 1
    j = j - 1
End If
Loop Until i > j
```

3. Because i isn't greater than j, the loop goes back to the top. While i^ is less than 26, move i to the right. (It's not, so it doesn't move.) While j^ is greater than 26, move j to the left.

4. Because i is less than or equal to j, swap the elements pointed to by i and j. Then move i one position to the right and j one position to the left.

5. Because i isn't greater than j, the loop goes back to the top. While i^ is less than 26, move i to the right. While j^ is greater than 26, move j to the left.

6. Because i is less than or equal to j, swap the elements pointed to by i and j. Then move i one position to the right and j one position to the left.

7. Because i is now greater than j (i is 5 and j is 4), drop out of the Do...Loop. Now j is less than lngMid (the middle position), so call the entire procedure again, working with elements 1 through j. (You're now leaving level 1 in the recursion and going to level 2.) Once you've sorted the items in positions 1 through 4, you'll call dhQuickSort again to sort the items in positions 5 through 10 (starting in step 13).

```
If j <= lngMid Then
    Call dhQuickSort(varArray, lngLeft, j)
    Call dhQuickSort(varArray, i, lngRight)
```

FIGURE 7.5
Steps 1 through 7

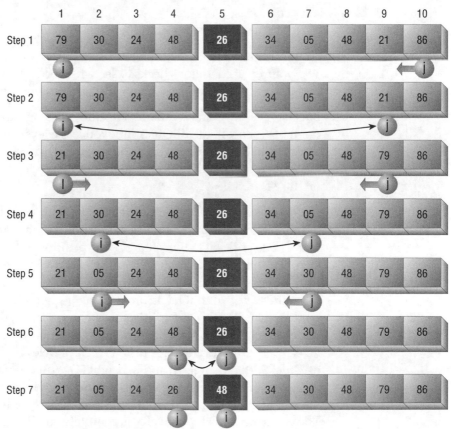

8. Starting over again: the leftmost element is 1 and the rightmost element is 4, so set i and j to point to those items. Calculate the middle location (2). While i^ is less than 5, move it to the right. (It doesn't move at all, because 21 isn't less than 5.) While j^ is greater than 5, move j to the left.

9. Because i is less than or equal to j, swap the elements pointed to by i and j. Then move i one position to the right and j one position to the left.

10. Because i is now greater than j (i is 2 and j is 1), drop out of the Do…Loop. Now j is less than the middle position, so call the entire procedure again, working with elements 1 through j. (You're now leaving level 2 in the recursion and going to level 3.) Of course, once you've sorted items 1 through 1 (not much to sort in that interval, is there?), you'll come back to level 2 and sort items 2 through 4 (starting in step 11).

    ```
    If j <= lngMid Then
        Call dhQuickSort(varArray, lngLeft, j)
    ```

    At this point, you've called dhQuickSort, passing 1 and 1 as the end points. The outermost condition checks to see whether lngLeft is less than lngRight, and if it isn't, it just returns. That's the case now, and you return to level 2.

11. Back at level 2, you now call dhQuickSort, passing i and lngRight as the endpoints. (When you call dhQuickSort, you leave level 2 and move on to level 3 again.) While i^ is less than the middle item (24), move to the right. This places i smack on the 24. While j^ is greater than 24, move it to the left. This places j on the 24 as well.

12. Now, because i is, in fact, less than or equal to j, swap the items i and j point to (not much work here, because i and j point to the same value), and then move j one position to the left and i one position to the right. (This is what step 12 in Figure 7.6 displays.) Because i is now greater than j, it's time to drop out of the loop. At this point, j is less than lngMid (j is 2 and lngMid is 3), so the code calls dhQuickSort, passing lngLeft (2) and j (2). This enters recursion level 4. Of course, as soon as you get there, dhQuickSort determines that lngLeft is not less than lngRight (it's been passed 2 and 2 from level 3), so it drops right back to level 3. Back in level 3, the next step is to call dhQuickSort, passing i (4) and lngRight (4). You can probably guess that the visit to level 4 is going to be short: because dhQuickSort receives lngLeft and lngRight values that are the same, it's going to immediately return to level 3. The call to dhQuickSort, level 3, is complete, and it returns back to level 2.

But level 2 is complete as well—you've sorted both the left and right halves of the first partition (1 to 4)—so it's time to return to the right partition in level 1. Finally, you get to the picture displayed in step 13 of Figure 7.7.

FIGURE 7.6
Steps 8 through 12

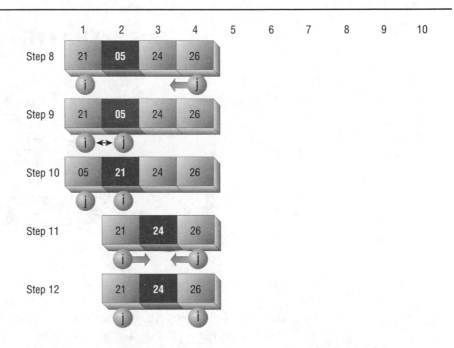

13. You're probably getting the hang of this by now! As long as i^ is less than the middle item (30), move it to the right. It's already pointing to a value greater than 30 (48, in position 5), so it doesn't move. As long as j^ is greater than the middle item (30), move it to the left. All the items to the right of position 7 are greater than 30, so j ends up pointing to the middle item.

14. Because i is less than or equal to j, swap the two items.

15. Move i one position to the right and j one position to the left. (They're both at position 6 now.)

16. As long as i^ is less than the middle item (30), move it to the right. Of course, it's pointing to 34, so it doesn't move at all. As long as j^ is greater than 30, move it to the left; this causes j to move to position 5, where it's pointing to the value 30. Now, because i is greater than j, it's time to drop out of the loop. At this point, the code calls dhQuickSort, passing lngLeft (5) and j (5)

(leaving level 1 and calling level 2). Of course, this visit to level 2 is swift because dhQuickSort finds its new lngLeft and lngRight to be the same.

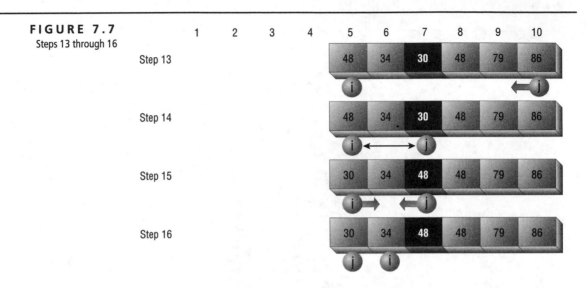

FIGURE 7.7
Steps 13 through 16

17. Now you've returned to level 1, where the code calls dhQuickSort in level 2 again, passing i (6) and lngRight (10) as the parameters. Now, in level 2, with reasonable end points, it's time to continue. As long as i^ is less than the middle item (48), move it to the right. As long as j^ is greater than 48, move it to the left.

18. With i at position 7 and j at position 8, swap the items they point to.

19. Move j one more position to the left and i one more to the right. Now, because i is greater than j, it's time to drop out of the loop. Because j (7) is less than the middle position (8), call dhQuickSort in level 3, passing lngLeft (6) and j (7) as the end points.

20. It's getting tight here: there are only two items to sort, so the middle position is 6 (that's (6 + 7) \ 2). While i^ is less than 34, move it to the right. (It doesn't move.) While j^ is greater than 34, move it to the left. At this point, both i and j are at position 6, pointing at the 34. Because i is less than or equal to j, swap the items to which i and j point. (Yes, it is a fruitless exercise, but that's

what you have to do!) Then move j one position to the left and i one position to the right.

21. Because i is now greater than j (i is 7 and j is 5), drop out of the loop. Call dhQuickSort in level 4, passing lngLeft (6) and j (5). Of course, as soon as you get to level 4, dhQuickSort will return, because its new lngLeft is greater than its lngRight. Back in level 3, call dhQuickSort again, passing i (7) and lngRight (7). Again, the visit to level 4 is awfully short because dhQuickSort returns immediately. At this point, you're done at level 3, so return to level 2.

22. Back in level 2, you've sorted the left portion (steps 20 and 21), and now it's time to call dhQuickSort in level 3 with the right portion. Given the end points 8 and 10, the middle element will be 9, with the value 79. While i^ is less than 79, move i to the right. While j^ is greater than 79, move j to the left. These loops terminate with a situation you've seen before: both i and j point to 79, in position 9. The code swaps 79 with itself and then moves i one more position to the right and j one more to the left.

23. Because i is greater than j, it's time to drop out of the loop. The code calls dhQuickSort in level 4, passing lngLeft (8) and j (8). Of course, this drops right out, back to level 3. Then it calls dhQuickSort in level 4, passing i (10) and lngRight (10). Again, the code returns immediately. Level 3 is done, so it returns back to level 2. Level 2 has sorted both halves, so it returns to level 1. Level 1 has sorted both halves, so it's done. Finally, the entire array has been sorted! Figure 7.8 shows the final steps in this seemingly endless process.

The beauty of computers is that you don't have to follow all these steps every time you execute the sort. Once you've convinced yourself that the algorithm will work in every case, you can use it without thought (and you've probably determined by now that you don't ever want to dig through the Quicksort algorithm at this level of detail again). The "Using Quicksort" section coming up in a moment shows how you can call Quicksort from your own applications.

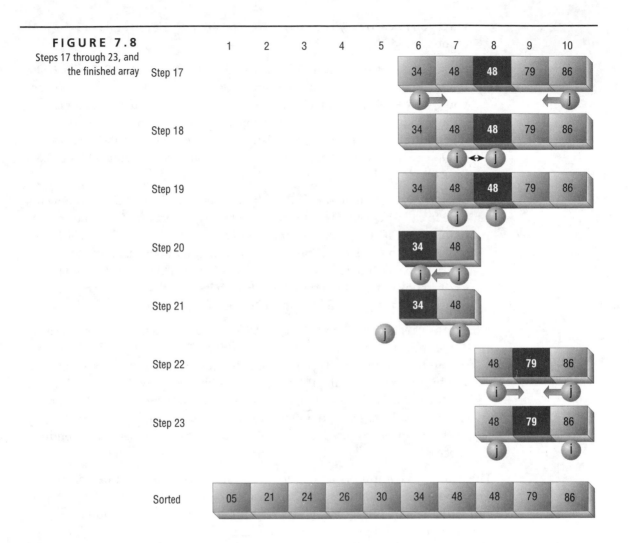

FIGURE 7.8
Steps 17 through 23, and the finished array

Watching Quicksort Run

To make it possible to watch the Quicksort algorithm at work, we've supplied a visual version of the dhQuickSort routine. The VQuickSort.bas module contains an expanded version of the dhQuickSort procedure that prints, to the Immediate window, what it's doing at each step. Although the mechanism of displaying the steps isn't pertinent to the discussion here, you'll find running the TestSortDemo routine instructive. Pass it no parameters to use the sample data discussed in the previous section, or pass it the number of items you'd like sorted. For example, calling

    TestSortDemo

will return a printout demonstrating the same sort as discussed in the 23 steps in the previous section. Calling

    TestSortDemo 6

will choose six random numbers between 1 and 99 and demonstrate the Quicksort algorithm with those numbers. Figure 7.9 shows sample output from calling TestSortDemo.

FIGURE 7.9
Call TestSortDemo to watch Quicksort at work

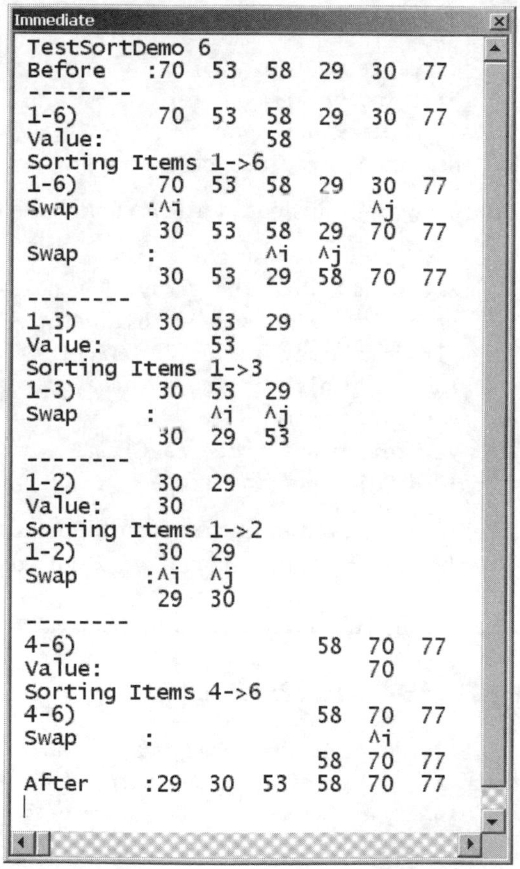

```
Immediate                                            ×
TestSortDemo 6
Before   :70   53   58   29   30   77
--------
1-6)       70   53   58   29   30   77
Value:               58
Sorting Items 1->6
1-6)       70   53   58   29   30   77
Swap     :^i                    ^j
           30   53   58   29   70   77
Swap     :          ^i   ^j
           30   53   29   58   70   77
--------
1-3)       30   53   29
Value:          53
Sorting Items 1->3
1-3)       30   53   29
Swap     :      ^i   ^j
           30   29   53
--------
1-2)       30   29
Value:     30
Sorting Items 1->2
1-2)       30   29
Swap     :^i   ^j
           29   30
--------
4-6)                      58   70   77
Value:                         70
Sorting Items 4->6
4-6)                      58   70   77
Swap     :                     ^i
                          58   70   77
After    :29   30   53   58   70   77
```

Using Quicksort

The dhQuickSort procedure, because it calls itself recursively with smaller and smaller segments of your array, must accept parameters containing the array, as well as the starting and ending points. When you start the sort, however, you'll always want to send the entire array for sorting. To work around this, the boundary parameters are optional. When it starts up, dhQuickSort checks the value of the optional lngLeft and lngRight parameters. If either is dhcMissing (the arbitrary constant value, −2), the procedure knows it must use the LBound and UBound functions to determine the array boundaries.

When passing the array to dhQuickSort, you have two options. You can either pass an actual array or pass a variant that "contains" an array. To pass an actual array, use code like the following:

```
Dim avarItems(1 To 10) As Integer
' Fill in the array here
Call dhQuickSort(avarItems())
' Now, the array has been sorted.
```

To use a variant instead, write code like the following:

```
Dim varItems as Variant
' Get values into the array. For now, just use the Array
'   function, with some sample data:
varItems = Array(1, 10, 29, 37, 45)
' You could also assign an array directly to the
' variant, as in:
' varItems = avarSomeArray()
Call dhQuickSort(varItems)
```

In either case, on the return from dhQuickSort, the array you've passed in will have been sorted, and you can work with the newly arranged data.

Using a Database Engine

There's no doubt about it: if your data is already in a database table, you'll want to use the database engine to retrieve your sorted data! Rather than take on any array-handling technique, simply use a query or a SQL statement to retrieve the data in the order you need. Assuming you have a column named LastName in a table named tblCustomers, no technique for retrieving the data in a sorted fashion will be faster than using a SQL expression:

```
SELECT [LastName] FROM tblCustomers ORDER BY [LastName];
```

The same words of wisdom can be applied to any environment that supplies its own internal sorting. If you've got data in a range in Excel, it makes no sense to copy the data into an array and then sort it. Because Excel makes sorting ranges so simple and fast, you'll want to take advantage of that technique before moving data into a VBA array. Make sure you've investigated internal tools before using VBA to sort your data—you'll almost always do better with the built-in tools.

Speed Considerations

Why choose such a complex sorting algorithm? Yes, it is somewhat daunting, and it would appear, based solely on complexity, that almost any algorithm would be better. That's not true, however. Listing 7.4 includes a simple sort, using a standard Bubblesort algorithm. This technique is easy to understand but can be quite slow in execution. The Bubblesort algorithm works its way through your array, comparing one element to the next. If the items are out of order, it swaps them. After a pass through the entire array, the largest element will have "bubbled" to the top (hence the name). After another pass, the top two elements will have bubbled up. After each pass, you can sort one less item on the next pass. The sort continues until it makes no swaps on a pass or it runs out of items to bubble up.

Listing 7.4: Simple Bubblesort Algorithm (Bubblesort.bas)

```
Sub dhBubbleSort(varItems As Variant)
    ' Standard bubblesort.

    Dim blnSorted As Boolean
    Dim lngI As Long
    Dim lngJ As Long
    Dim lngItems As Long
    Dim varTemp As Variant
    Dim lngLBound As Long

    lngItems = UBound(varItems)
    lngLBound = LBound(varItems)

    ' Set lngI one lower than the lower bound.
    lngI = lngLBound - 1
    Do While (lngI < lngItems) And Not blnSorted
        blnSorted = True
```

```
        lngI = lngI + 1
        For lngJ = lngLBound To lngItems - lngI
            If varItems(lngJ) > varItems(lngJ + 1) Then
                varTemp = varItems(lngJ)
                varItems(lngJ) = varItems(lngJ + 1)
                varItems(lngJ + 1) = varTemp
                blnSorted = False
            End If
        Next lngJ
    Loop
End Sub
```

Yes, the code is much simpler than that used by the Quicksort algorithm. How do they compare? The TestSortTimes procedure, in TestProcs.bas, calls both routines, comparing the results. The test routine creates an array of random numbers and calls each sort procedure. Then it creates an array of ordered numbers (that is, an array that's sorted already) and calls both sorting procedures. The following table shows sample results for 2,000 items. (All times are in milliseconds, for a single iteration of the sort, and all measurements were taken on a Pentium II 400 mHz processor, with 256 meg of memory.)

Array Order	Quicksort	Bubblesort
Random	130	12037
Ordered	30	10

As you can see from the tests, Quicksort does much better than Bubblesort for random numbers. On the other hand, Bubblesort takes great advantage of preordered arrays and outperforms Quicksort on the sorted array.

How does array size affect the length of time it takes to sort the array? Comparing results for random sets of non-sorted numbers, the following table shows the outcome (rounded a bit to make the results clearer):

Items	Quicksort	Bubblesort
500	30	800
1000	50	3200
2000	130	12000
5000	330	76000

Impressive, isn't it? That Bubblesort algorithm simply falls apart, given more than a few hundred items to sort. The time it takes to sort grows exponentially as you increase the number of items to sort. The time Quicksort takes, on the other hand, grows more or less linearly with the number of items in the array it's sorting.

Which one should you choose? It depends, of course, on your data. If you're sorting ten values, it doesn't matter which one you choose. If you're sorting items that are likely in sorted order before you get them, then Bubblesort makes sense. Otherwise, you'll probably do better using the more complex but more efficient Quicksort. Of course, they both require the same amount of effort to call, once they're written, so you can choose based solely on the type of data you're going to be sorting.

Sorting Collections

User-defined collections add tremendous flexibility to VBA solutions. Because collections are dynamic data structures, you can add and remove items at will without worrying about redimensioning and preserving data. On the other hand, they don't lend themselves to sorting. That's too bad, because collections provide a simple way to store and work with large numbers of items in memory. It would be great if you could sort them as well.

What's wrong with collections? Unfortunately, there are a few crucial issues to consider. The following section reviews the basics of using collections and the problems involved in sorting them.

Working with Collections

As you add items to a collection, you must provide a value, and you often use a unique string value (known as the *key*) to identify the collection item. For example, when you open a form in Microsoft Access, under the covers Access adds the form object to the Forms collection and uses the form's name as its unique identifier. Therefore, you can use either of the following techniques:

```
Forms(1)
' or
Forms("frmTest")
```

to retrieve the collection object (a reference to the form).

For Access forms, you can always retrieve the unique identifier; simply examine the Name property of the form. For user-defined collections, however, this isn't possible. For reasons unknown, you cannot retrieve the key for a given item in a user-created collection. This one missing piece of functionality makes it difficult, if not impossible, to perform any sort of manipulation with collection elements. Weird, isn't it? You can use the key to help you find the item, but if you have an item, you can't find the key. Wouldn't it be great if you could add items and their unique keys to a collection and then iterate through the collection in sorted key order? It would be great, but you can't—VBA provides no way to sort the collection by key, and you can't even retrieve the key to do it yourself.

> **TIP**
>
> If you really want the flexibility of a collection, combined with the random access of an array (that is, you want the ability to find an item's key, given its value), you'll want to take a look at the Dictionary object supplied by the Windows Scripting library. Chapter 14 covers the objects provided by the Windows Scripting library in detail.

Why does this prevent you from sorting a collection yourself? Sorting requires moving an element from one place to another. That means copying an item into a temporary location, removing it from the collection, and then copying it into the new location. But you can't do this with collection items; because you can't retrieve the key, any attempt to move an item will cause you to lose its unique identifier!

This means that ordinary sorting techniques, which require you to swap elements, won't work. We've provided an alternative here, and with enough creativity, you'll probably be able to think of a few more on your own. The simplest way to sort a collection is to sort the items as you add them to the collection (that is, keep the collection sorted at all times). The next few sections discuss this method in detail.

Sorting as You Insert

One possible solution to sorting a collection is simple: just maintain it sorted. That is, as you add each item to the collection, make sure you insert it at the correct location. Performing the insertion is simple because VBA allows you to provide a location (or a unique string key value) before which you want to insert the item.

To make this possible, we've created a collection class, named SortedCollection, that provides all the standard functionality of a collection and adds a new feature: as you add items to the collection, code inside the class keeps an internal collection sorted. If you use this class, instead of the built-in Collection class, the data in your collection will always be sorted.

The code in the SortedCollection class, in Listing 7.5, provides all the standard methods and properties of a collection besides the Add method (Count, Item, Remove). Listing 7.6 shows the Add method, which allows you to add items to a collection, maintaining the sorted order of the collection as you add the items. The next few paragraphs explain how this class does its work.

Listing 7.5: Use the SortedCollection Class, Rather Than the Internal Collection Class, to Maintain a Sorted Collection. (SortedCollection.cls)

```
Private mcol As Collection

Private Sub Class_Initialize()
    Set mcol = New Collection
End Sub

Private Sub Class_Terminate()
    Set mcol = Nothing
End Sub

Public Function Count() As Long
    Count = mcol.Count
End Function

Public Sub Remove(Key As Variant)
    On Error GoTo HandleErrors

    mcol.Remove Key
    Exit Sub

HandleErrors:
    Err.Raise Err.Number, _
      "SortedCollection.Remove", Err.Description
End Sub

Public Function Item(Key As Variant)
    On Error GoTo HandleErrors

    Item = mcol.Item(Key)
    Exit Function
```

```
HandleErrors:
    Err.Raise Err.Number, _
      "SortedCollection.Item", Err.Description
End Function

Public Function Enumerate() As IUnknown
    Set Enumerate = mcol.[_NewEnum]
End Function
```

TIP   For more information on Collection classes, see Chapter 6. In addition to what we've covered here, that chapter discusses how you can set the default member of the class, and the enumerator function (so you can use For Each...Next with the class's collection).

The SortedCollection class maintains its own internal collection, mcol, which contains the data that you add to the collection. In the Class_Initialize event procedure, the class instantiates the internal collection, and in the Terminate event, it destroys the collection. The Count, Remove, and Item methods provide "pass-throughs" to the private collection, just like most every collection. The Enumerate function makes it possible to use a For Each...Next loop with this collection but requires special handling. (See Chapter 6 for more details on creating collection classes that allow enumeration.)

⟲ **Listing 7.6: The Add Method Adds Items to the Internal Collection and Keeps the Collection Sorted.**

```
Public Sub Add(varNewItem As Variant, Optional strKey As String = "")

    On Error GoTo HandleErrors

    Dim lngI As Long
    Dim blnAdded As Boolean
    Dim blnUseKey As Boolean

    blnUseKey = (Len(strKey) > 0)

    ' On the first time through here, this loop
    ' will just do nothing at all.
```

```
        For lngI = 1 To mcol.Count
            If varNewItem < mcol.Item(lngI) Then
                If blnUseKey Then
                    mcol.Add varNewItem, strKey, lngI
                Else
                    mcol.Add varNewItem, , lngI
                End If
                blnAdded = True
                Exit For
            End If
        Next lngI
        ' If the item hasn't been added, either because
        ' it goes past the end of the current list of items,
        ' or because there aren't currently any items to loop
        ' through, just add the item at the end of the
        ' collection.
        If Not blnAdded Then
            If blnUseKey Then
                mcol.Add varNewItem, strKey
            Else
                mcol.Add varNewItem
            End If
        End If
        Exit Sub

    HandleErrors:
        Err.Raise Err.Number, "SortedCollection.Add", Err.Description
    End Sub
```

The Add method, shown in Listing 7.6, takes care of adding items to the sorted collection. The first step in the procedure is to determine whether the caller has provided a unique key value:

```
    blnUseKey = (Len(strKey) > 0)
```

If so, the code later in the procedure will know to supply the key to the Add method of the collection object.

The next chunk of the procedure attempts to find the correct location in which to insert the new item. The code looks at each of the values in the collection, and if the value to be added is less than the current collection item, you've found the right place to insert the new item. If you supplied a unique key value, the code calls the Add method of the collection, passing in the new item, the key, and the location before which to insert. If not, it passes only the new item and the location. Once it's inserted the value, it sets a flag so later code can tell that the insertion has been performed and then exits the loop.

```
For lngI = 1 To col.Count
    If varNewItem < col.Item(lngI) Then
        If blnUseKey Then
            col.Add varNewItem, strKey, lngI
        Else
            col.Add varNewItem, , lngI
        End If
        blnAdded = True
        Exit For
    End If
Next lngI
```

Once you're past the end of the loop, there are two reasons why the loop may have ended: either the item was inserted and the code jumped out of the loop or the item wasn't inserted and the loop terminated on its own. In the latter case, the blnAdded flag will be False, and the following chunk of code can then just add the item to the collection. You should get into this situation only if you need to add the new item to the end of the collection—that is, if the value was greater than any existing item or if there was nothing in the collection to start with.

```
If Not blnAdded Then
    If blnUseKey Then
        col.Add varNewItem, strKey
    Else
        col.Add varNewItem
    End If
End If
```

Why the error handler? That is, what can go wrong? The most likely error is one that would occur if you tried to add two elements with the same unique key. If you attempted this, the function would raise error 457, "This key is already associated with an element of this collection." The calling code would have to deal with the error.

What's wrong with this technique? First of all, it's quite slow. It *has* to be, of course, because it's comparing the new item against, on average, half of the existing items in the collection. This means that to insert 20 items into a collection, you'll perform several hundred comparisons. Each of those comparisons is expensive.

Second, because the code is performing simple comparisons between values, you can use only simple data types (strings, numbers, and so on) in the collection. If you want to use this technique with more complex collections, you'll need to modify the code to support more complex comparisons. Because you're most likely to use this technique with simple collections, we've left that alteration for your own exploration.

If you want to use the SortedCollection class in your own applications, import the class, and you should be ready to go. You'll need to write code to instantiate the class and to add items to it. You might write code like that used in the test procedure, TestSortedCollection, shown here:

```
Sub TestSortedCollection()
    ' From the TestProcs module.

    Dim sc As SortedCollection
    Dim lngI As Integer
    Dim intCount As Integer
    Dim varItem As Variant

    Set sc = New SortedCollection

    intCount = 1000
    For lngI = 1 To intCount
        sc.Add Format(Int(99 * Rnd + 1), "00")
    Next lngI

    For Each varItem In sc
        Debug.Print varItem & " ";
    Next varItem

    Set sc = Nothing
End Sub
```

WARNING   The SortedCollection object's ability to be iterated with a For Each loop is fragile at best, unless you're working in Visual Basic 6. In other VBA hosts, there's no built-in way to identify the function to be called when you use For Each loops. There's a tricky work-around, described in Chapter 6, but it's slippery. If you find that the For Each loop doesn't work as advertised in the previous example, check out the steps discussed in Chapter 6 to make this possible in VBA hosts besides VB.

Sorting Other Types of Data

Every example covered so far uses simple data (text or numbers). What if you want to sort an array of user-defined types? Or sort an array of objects? How about this common scenario: you have a user-defined type, like this:

```
Public Type FileInfo
    FullName As String
    Name As String
    Extension As String
End Type
```

and you have an array of these structures containing data about all the files in a particular folder. You'd like to present a list of the files to your users, sorted first by Extension, and within files with the same extension, sorted by Name. Sure, you could take the effort to modify the dhQuickSort procedure to handle this data structure, but then you'd have two copies of dhQuickSort—one for simple data, and one for your array of FileInfo structures. Even if you do accomplish this task, what happens when you want to sort an array of some type of object you've created, or an array of some other user-defined type? You'll need to modify dhQuickSort again, of course.

> **WARNING**   The rest of this section delves into relatively esoteric material. If you've not worked with class modules, this may be difficult going. It's certainly worth working through, as an intellectual exercise, but the rest of this section does count on your understanding how to use class modules in your applications. For more information on working with class modules, see Chapters 5 and 6.

There's a commonly accepted solution to this problem: That is, modify the QuickSort procedure so it doesn't know or care what kind of data it's being sent—remove all data type dependencies from the procedure. Instead, create class modules, one for each type of data you need to sort, and provide a standard interface for sorting. In this case, you could look at the dhQuickSort procedure and notice that there are several operations that are dependent on the particular data being sorted:

- Swapping two elements

- Comparing two elements

- Finding the upper and lower bounds of the array to be sorted

- Finding a specific element you'll compare other elements of the array to

The answer, then, is to not pass dhQuickSort an array of variants to be sorted (because then dhQuickSort needs to know how to compare, swap, and work with the data in the array). Instead, you want to pass in an object reference, where the object you pass in knows how to swap two of its own elements, how to compare two elements, and so on. That is, you need to hide the data-specific functionality in a class and provide methods and properties that the new QuickSort procedure can call.

We actually did this work for the predecessor to this book (*VBA Developer's Handbook*, based on VBA 5). Take a look at how we attempted to solve this issue in that version, why the attempt failed, and how new features in VBA 6 make this all work better now.

> **NOTE**
>
> The solution you'll see here relies on the Implements keyword, new in VBA 6. Actually, this keyword (and the associated functionality) was added to Visual Basic 5, long before VBA and Office developers had use of the keyword. So, it's not actually new in VBA 6—it's just available in all VBA 6 hosts, where previously it was only available in the Visual Basic product line. If you're interested, all the code in this section works fine in Visual Basic 5 but not Office 97 or any other VBA 5 host product.

We first determined the list of methods and properties that the sortable class needs to provide. The following table lists those elements:

Element	Parameters	Return Value	Description
SetCompareValue	lngItem as Long		Stores away a private value, so that later comparisons (for the looping phase of the sort) can compare to the stored value
Compare	lngItem As Long	0 if equal, –1 if less than, 1 if greater than	Compares the item specified by the incoming parameter to the item stored away by a call to the SetCompareValue method

Element	Parameters	Return Value	Description
Swap	lngItem1 As Long, lngItem2 As Long		Swaps the items in the locations specified in the two incoming parameters
UpperBound		Long	Returns the upper bound of the internal storage for the class (normally an array, but it doesn't have to be)
LowerBound		Long	Returns the lower bound of the internal storage for the class (normally an array, but it doesn't have to be)

If a class provides those elements, you should be able to sort the data contained within the class. Of course, you need some way to get data into the class and some way to retrieve the sorted data back out of the class. In addition, it's useful for demonstration purposes to have a way to display the data stored in the class, too. Therefore, the example class has an Add method (so you can add data to the internal data structure), an Item method (so you can retrieve an individual item), and a DumpItems method (to display the entire list of data at once). These aren't required for sorting, but they're necessary if you actually want to use the class.

Once you're committed to sorting this way, you could rewrite dhQuickSort so that it looks like the code in Listing 7.7. This procedure, dhQuickSortObjects, works just like the dhQuickSort procedure, except that this one makes the class passed to it perform all the data manipulations.

Listing 7.7: dhQuickSortObjects Extracts All the Data Manipulation and Places It into the Object Passed In. (QuickSortObjects.bas)

```
' Indicate that a parameter is missing.
Private Const dhcMissing = -2

Public Sub dhQuickSortObjects(oData As Object, _
 Optional lngLeft As Long = dhcMissing, _
 Optional lngRight As Long = dhcMissing)
```

```vb
    Dim i As Long
    Dim j As Long
    Dim lngMid As Long

    If lngLeft = dhcMissing Then
        lngLeft = oData.LowerBound
    End If
    If lngRight = dhcMissing Then
        lngRight = oData.UpperBound
    End If

    If lngLeft < lngRight Then
        lngMid = (lngLeft + lngRight) \ 2
        i = lngLeft
        j = lngRight

        ' Store away the value to be compared
        ' against, in the sortable object's code.
        Call oData.SetCompareValue(lngMid)
        Do
            Do While oData.Compare(i) < 0
                i = i + 1
            Loop
            Do While oData.Compare(j) > 0
                j = j - 1
            Loop
            If i <= j Then
                Call oData.Swap(i, j)
                i = i + 1
                j = j - 1
            End If
        Loop Until i > j
        ' To optimize the sort, always sort the
        ' smallest segment first.
        If j <= lngMid Then
            Call dhQuickSortObjects(oData, lngLeft, j)
            Call dhQuickSortObjects(oData, i, lngRight)
        Else
            Call dhQuickSortObjects(oData, i, lngRight)
            Call dhQuickSortObjects(oData, lngLeft, j)
        End If
    End If
End Sub
```

As you can see in Listing 7.7, the dhQuickSortObjects procedure knows nothing about the data it's sorting, and the oData object must handle all the data manipulation. Now, you need to create a class that knows how to swap, compare, and do everything a sortable class needs to do. Listing 7.8 shows a class (FileDataObject) that you could pass to dhQuickSortObjects. It supplies all the necessary procedures, working with an array of the FileInfo structures shown earlier.

The SetCompareValue method stores away a particular item in the array (mafiItems) for later comparisons. The Compare method compares the extensions of the requested item and stored item, and if they're different, returns the appropriate value. If they're the same, the code then looks at the filenames and compares them. The Swap method swaps two items in the array, and the UpperBound and LowerBound properties return the corresponding UBound and LBound values from the array.

Listing 7.8: The FileDataObject Class Knows How to Manage Its Own Sorting Operations. (FileData.cls)

```vba
Private Type FileInfo
    FullName As String
    Name As String
    Extension As String
End Type

Private mafiItems() As FileInfo
Private mlngCount As Long
Private mfiCompare As FileInfo

Public Sub SetCompareValue(lngItem As Long)
    mfiCompare = mafiItems(lngItem)
End Sub

Public Function Compare(lngItem As Long) As Long

    ' Compare two FileInfo structures, so you can sort
    ' first by extension, and then by name.
    ' First, compare the extensions. If they're not
    ' the same, return the comparison value.
    ' If they're the same, compare the names
    ' and return the comparison value of those.
```

```
        Dim lngResult As Long

        ' Compare extensions.
        lngResult = StrComp( _
         mafiItems(lngItem).Extension, _
         mfiCompare.Extension, vbTextCompare)

        Select Case lngResult
            Case -1, 1
                Compare = lngResult
            Case 0
                ' Extensions are the same, so compare filenames.
                Compare = StrComp( _
                 mafiItems(lngItem).Name, _
                 mfiCompare.Name, vbTextCompare)
        End Select
    End Function

    Public Sub Swap(lngItem1 As Long, lngItem2 As Long)
        Dim fiTemp As FileInfo

        fiTemp = mafiItems(lngItem2)
        mafiItems(lngItem2) = mafiItems(lngItem1)
        mafiItems(lngItem1) = fiTemp
    End Sub

    Public Property Get LowerBound() As Long
        LowerBound = LBound(mafiItems)
    End Property

    Public Property Get UpperBound() As Long
        UpperBound = UBound(mafiItems)
    End Property
```

The FileDataObject class also provides an Add method, so you can add items to its internal array; a Count property, returning the number of items in the array; and an Item method, to return the full name of the file at a specified location within the array. Finally, like all the other classes you'll see in this section, it provides a DumpItems method—by supplying this, it's simple for you, while developing the class, to make sure things are sorting as you'd expect.

To test out the FileDataObject passed into dhQuickSortObjects, try out the
TestQuickSortObjects procedure, in the TestProcs module:

```
Sub TestQuickSortObjects()
    Dim fdo As FileDataObject
    Dim strFile As String

    Set fdo = New FileDataObject

    strFile = Dir("C:\*.*")
    Do While Len(strFile) > 0
        Call fdo.Add(strFile)
        strFile = Dir
    Loop
    Call dhQuickSortObjects(fdo)
    Call fdo.DumpItems("After:")
End Sub
```

This procedure instantiates a new FileDataObject, fills it with filenames from the
C:\ folder (the Add method takes the filename and splits it into the name and
extension parts—see the FileDataObject class for that code), and then calls the
dhQuickSortObjects procedure, passing in the FileDataObject object as a parameter. Before and after all the work is done, the procedure calls the DumpItems
method of the FileDataObject object to display the sorted and unsorted results.

As dhQuickSortObjects does its work, it calls methods of the object passed to it.
That is, when it needs to set a comparison value, it calls the SetCompareValue
method of the FileDataObject object. When it needs to compare two values, it calls
the Compare method. When it needs to swap two values, it calls the Swap method
of the passed-in object. It works great!

And so, you think you've got the problem licked. And so you do, for a little
while. You can merrily create objects, supplying the required methods and properties, and call dhQuickSortObjects with as many different types of objects as you
can devise. Only one (big) problem—it's pretty darned slow. If you compare sorting with dhQuickSort and dhQuickSortObjects, you'll measure a distinct difference in sorting the same types of objects. (One easy way to do this is to create a
class that sorts a simple array and compare its performance with dhQuickSortObjects
to that of an array passed into dhQuickSort directly. There's a big difference in
speed.)

Handling the Speed Problem

You might notice (as we did, when working on the previous version of the book, where we got this far) that you're passing in a variable "As Object" to dhQuickSortObjects. As discussed in more detail in Chapter 4, declaring objects "As Object" forces VBA to bind objects and properties at runtime, rather than at compile time. This late binding (as opposed to early binding, which would occur if you specified the data type at compile time) causes this code to run much slower than it should.

To alleviate the problem, you could modify the code in dhQuickSortObjects to accept oData not "As Object," but "As FileDataObject." That would, we promise, make a difference in the speed at which this procedure can sort your FileDataObject data. And so, feel free to make that change.

Unfortunately, now you're right back where you started—you have a sorting procedure that works only for a particular type of data. If you want to sort data stored a different way, you'd need to cut and paste a new version of dhQuickSortObjects. At least you'll only need to modify one thing—the data type passed in as the first parameter. This, therefore, is not a reasonable alternative. And that's where we got stuck in the previous version of the book: in VBA 5, there wasn't an alternative.

Implements to the Rescue

When we created the DataFileObject class and passed it to the dhQuickSortObjects procedure, we created a sort of "contract" between the class and the procedure. That is, unless the object passed into dhQuickSortObjects provided the required properties and methods, the code would fail at runtime. But it's that "fail at runtime" thing that caused the code to run slowly—because you're passing it in "As Object," VBA can't tell at compile time whether it's going to fail. What you want, in order to gain back the speed you've lost, is for VBA to validate that object passed in and validate it at compile time.

This is a perfect situation for using the Implements keyword. (See Chapter 6 for an introduction to the Implements keyword.) VBA 6 allows you to specify an interface (a contract, as it were), providing a list of all the properties and methods any class that wants to "play along" must provide. This specification doesn't include any code—it's merely a definition of the interface, the properties and methods you need to supply in each class that *implements* the interface. Once you've specified the interface, you can modify your procedure (dhQuickSortObjects) to accept an object that supplies the required properties and methods.

In other words, you specify an object that implements the required interface, and the procedure can do its work, fully confident that the object passed to it supplies all the tools it needs to do its job.

In the sample project, the ISortable class provides the definition of the interface, containing the code shown in Listing 7.9. Note that this class doesn't include any code—it simply defines the properties and methods dhQuickSortObjects requires in order to do its work.

A few things to note:

- Generally, developers name interface classes beginning with an "I". This indicates that the class defines the interface but doesn't implement its functionality.

- The ISortable class contains a public Enum, CompareResults. This enumerated type provides the possible values for the Compare method, and all classes based on this interface will need to use this type when providing their Compare methods.

- Any class that implements this interface will need to supply code for all the methods and properties defined in the interface class. The procedure might just be an empty stub, but VBA is counting on the fact that all classes implementing this interface provide all the necessary procedures. Implementing an interface is like signing a contract that says "I'll provide code for each and every procedure in the contract. If I don't, you can sue me (that is, trigger a compile-time error)."

Listing 7.9: The ISortable Class Provides the Interface Definition. (ISortable.cls)

```
Public Enum CompareResults
    crEqual = 0
    crLess = -1
    crGreater = 1
    crNull = 2
End Enum

Public Sub SetCompareValue(lngItem As Long)

End Sub
```

```
Public Property Get LowerBound() As Long

End Property

Public Property Get UpperBound() As Long

End Property

Public Sub Swap(lngItem1 As Long, lngItem2 As Long)

End Sub

Public Function Compare(lngItem As Long) As CompareResults

End Function
```

Once you've defined an interface class, you can modify dhQuickSortObjects so that, instead of accepting "oData As Object," it accepts "oData As ISortable," like this:

```
Sub dhOQuickSortObjects(oData As ISortable, _
  Optional lngLeft As Long = dhcMissing, _
  Optional lngRight As Long = dhcMissing)
```

Finally, you supply the classes that implement the ISortable interface. To do this, follow these steps:

1. Add the line of code to the FileDataObject class that tells VBA it's going to implement the ISortable interface (adding this effectively signs the contract between you and the ISortable interface):

    ```
    Implements ISortable
    ```

2. Once you've added the Implements statement, VBA adds ISortable to the Object combo box (the left-hand combo box) at the top of the code editor. You select ISortable from the list and provide a procedure for each of its methods and properties. If you choose all the items from the Procedure combo box, one at a time, you'll end up with procedures that look like this:

    ```
    Private Function ISortable_Compare(lngItem As Long) _
      As CompareResults

    End Function

    Private Sub ISortable_SetCompareValue(lngItem As Long)
    ```

```
End Sub

Private Sub ISortable_Swap(lngItem1 As Long, lngItem2 As Long)

End Sub

Private Property Get ISortable_LowerBound() As Long

End Property

Private Property Get ISortable_UpperBound() As Long

End Property
```

3. Your job now is to provide the code for each of these methods and properties. Of course, your FileDataObject class already contains all the code—you can simply move it into the appropriate ISortable procedure and fix up the names of the return values for the functions.

Later, when you pass a FileDataObject object into dhQuickSortObjects, the sorting procedure sees that it's received an object that implements the ISortable interface, and when it calls the Compare method of the object, VBA correctly calls the ISortable_Compare method for you.

We've already set everything up for you in the sample project. The dhQuickSortable procedure (in the QuickSortable module) accepts an object of type ISortable as a parameter. The sample project includes three classes: ExistingArray, FileData, and SimpleArray, demonstrating the use of the dhQuickSortable procedure. If you're interested in sorting various types of objects and their data, you'll want to study each of these simple examples. In addition, the TestISortable module contains three test procedures, one for each sample class, showing how you might sort data in each type of class.

The Drawback

You knew there was a drawback, right? You might have guessed it: Sorting an object's data using the dhQuickSortable procedure will never be as fast as using dhQuickSort. Why not? The dhQuickSort procedure has all its functionality built right into the procedure. No method calls, no overhead, and a lot less effort involved. As a matter of fact, the TestTimes procedure in the TestISortable module compares sorting the same array two different ways. First, it passes the array directly to the dhQuickSort procedure. Then, it uses the ExistingArray class (which effectively sorts exactly the same data in a simple array but does it using the ISortable interface). The procedure, shown in Listing 7.10, demonstrates (at least, on our machines) that calling dhQuickSort seems to take about half as long as calling dhQuickSortable.

Listing 7.10: Compare Calling dhQuickSort and dhQuickSortable. (TestISortable.bas)

```
Sub TestTimes()
    Dim sw As StopWatch

    Dim lngI As Long
    Dim varData() As Variant
    Dim intCount As Integer
    Dim oData As ExistingArray

    ' Change this value to try different
    ' sized sorting sets.
    intCount = 10000

    Set sw = New StopWatch

    ReDim varData(1 To intCount)
    For lngI = 1 To intCount
        varData(lngI) = Format(Int(99 * Rnd + 1), "00")
    Next lngI

    sw.StartTimer
    Call dhQuickSort(varData)
    Debug.Print "QuickSort: " & sw.EndTimer

    For lngI = 1 To intCount
        varData(lngI) = Format(Int(99 * Rnd + 1), "00")
    Next lngI

    sw.StartTimer
    Set oData = New ExistingArray
    oData.Data = varData
    Call dhQuickSortable(oData)
    Debug.Print "OQuickSort: " & sw.EndTimer
End Sub
```

What this proves, we guess, is that if you're only going to sort arrays or a few different data types, it makes sense to use dhQuickSort (and possibly make multiple copies for different data types). If you need to sort lots of different data types and want the ultimate flexibility, you might consider using the ISortable interface and dhQuickSortable. You'll have to try for yourself to determine which is best for you.

Searching

If you've got sorted data, most likely you need to be able to find any particular item in your data set. As with sorting, searching is an entire branch of computer science, and a full discussion is beyond our intent. On the other hand, you won't find as many searching algorithms as you will for sorting. Therefore, we actually come closer here, in the coverage of a single search method, to discussing all the possibilities. (Nothing like narrowing the margins.) In this section, you'll learn about the Binary Search algorithm and how you can apply it to data stored in an array.

Why Use the Binary Search?

Imagine you've picked up a phone book to find the number for the local outlet of the Vegetarian Pizza Kitchen. You could, of course, start at the first name in the phone book, working through the listings one at a time. This might take you a while, considering there are most likely several hundred thousand entries, and you've got to work your way all the way to *V*.

The intelligent phone book user would, of course, look for the *V* entries and go from there. Imagine for a moment that the phone book didn't have letter dividers at all and that you had to scan the entries on a page to know where you were in the book. Now, how could you find the Vegetarian Pizza Kitchen in the fastest way possible? Most likely, you'd put your finger in the middle of the book, see that the *V* entries were later in the book, and discard everything before the location of your finger. Then, taking the second half of the book, you'd check halfway through the pages and decide whether the *V* entries were in the first or second half of the remainder of the book. You might continue in this fashion, breaking the book into smaller and smaller chunks, until you found your entry.

Considering that your phone book might contain 1,000 pages, you threw away 500 possible pages on the first attempt and 250 more on the second. Not bad for two stops! Because the formal Binary Search algorithm works just like this "finger walking," it should be clear to you why Binary Search is very fast for large sets of values: on each lookup, you discard 50 percent of the possible values, until you center in on the location you need. As a matter of fact, the Binary Search algorithm will generally require only $\log_2 n$ lookups if n is the number of items to be searched. This means that for 1,000 items, you shouldn't have to look at more than 10 items before you've either found your item or convinced yourself it's not there. (For logarithm-challenged readers, 2 to the 10th power is 1,024, so $\log_2 1,000$ is just a little less than 10.) The wonderful part of logarithmic growth is that if you double the number of items you have to look through, you will need to, in general, make only one more choice along the way to finding your particular item.

NOTE If you missed this point in the example, don't miss it now: a binary search can work only if the data it's searching through has already been sorted. If you want to use this technique, you'll need to ensure that your data has been sorted, by one means or another, before you use a binary search.

How Does Binary Search Work?

There actually is no single formal Binary Search algorithm; there are many. The code you get depends on whom you ask. In this book, the algorithm you'll find works as follows:

1. Start with a *sorted* array and a value to be found.

2. Set upper and lower limits for the search.

3. While the lower bound is less than the upper bound:

    a. Calculate the middle position of the remaining array.

    b. If the value you're seeking is greater than the middle value, adjust the lower limit; otherwise, adjust the upper limit accordingly.

4. If the item at the lower position is the value you were searching for, return the position index. Otherwise, return a value indicating that the item wasn't found.

The entire dhBinarySearch procedure, implementing the Binary Search algorithm, is shown in Listing 7.11.

Listing 7.11: Use dhBinarySearch to Find a Value in a Sorted Array. (BinarySearch.bas)

```
Function dhBinarySearch( _
 varItems As Variant, varSought As Variant) As Long

    Dim lngLower As Long
    Dim lngMiddle As Long
    Dim lngUpper As Long

    lngLower = LBound(varItems)
    lngUpper = UBound(varItems)
    Do While lngLower < lngUpper
        ' Increase lower and decrease upper boundary,
        ' keeping varSought in range, if it's there at all.
        lngMiddle = (lngLower + lngUpper) \ 2
        If varSought > varItems(lngMiddle) Then
            lngLower = lngMiddle + 1
        Else
            lngUpper = lngMiddle
        End If
    Loop
    If varItems(lngLower) = varSought Then
        dhBinarySearch = lngLower
    Else
        dhBinarySearch = -1
    End If
End Function
```

To fully explain the binary search algorithm, the following series of steps uses the same ten-element array that was used previously in the discussion of the Quicksort algorithm. In this case, the examples attempt to locate a specific number within the array. In the first example, shown in Figure 7.10, the search succeeds. In the second, shown in Figure 7.11, the search fails.

The following set of steps works through the details of the Binary Search algorithm, using the code in dhBinarySearch. In this case, the code is scanning the array shown in step 1 of Figure 7.10, looking for the value 34.

NOTE

In these examples, we'll use the same terminology as in the Quicksort example: to indicate the value in the array at location x, we'll use "x^". If the value of the array varItems at position 5 is 12 (that is, varItems(5) = 12) and the variable x contains the value 5, then x^ is the value 12.

FIGURE 7.10
Use Binary Search to locate a value in the array.

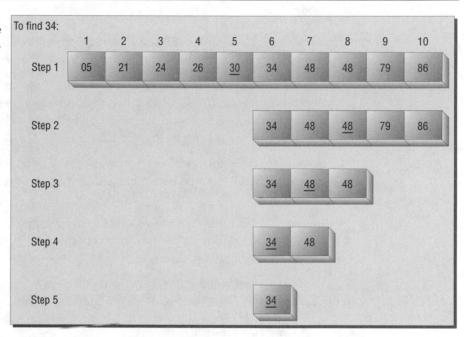

1. Given the array, set the search bounds to be the upper and lower bounds of the array:

    ```
    lngLower = LBound(varItems)
    lngUpper = UBound(varItems)
    ```

    If lngLower is less than lngUpper (and it is), set lngMiddle to be the average of the two:

    ```
    lngMiddle = (lngLower + lngUpper) \ 2
    ```

Because varSought (34) is greater than lngMiddle^ (30), set lngLower to be lngMiddle + 1 (6):

```
If varSought > varItems(lngMiddle) Then
    lngLower = lngMiddle + 1
Else
    lngUpper = lngMiddle
End If
```

2. Because lngLower (6) is still less than lngUpper (10), set lngMiddle to be the average of the two (8). Because varSought is less than lngMiddle^ (48), set lngUpper to be the same as lngMiddle.

3. Because lngLower (6) is still less than lngUpper (8), set lngMiddle to be the average of the two (7). Because varSought is less than lngMiddle^ (48), set lngUpper to be the same as lngMiddle.

4. Because lngLower (6) is still less than lngUpper (7), set lngMiddle to be the average of the two (6). Because varSought (34) isn't greater than lngMiddle^ (34), set lngUpper to be the same as lngMiddle.

5. Because lngLower (6) is no longer less than lngUpper (6), drop out of the loop. Because lngLower^ is the same as varSought, return lngLower as the return value of the function:

```
If varItems(lngLower) = varSought Then
    dhBinarySearch = lngLower
Else
    dhBinarySearch = -1
End If
```

NOTE   It's quite possible that at just this moment, you've determined for yourself that you could have found the 34 in the sample array in the same amount of steps, if not fewer, by simply starting at the beginning and scanning the elements one by one. For small sets of data, you're right—it's almost always faster to just scan the data, looking for the item you need. But this was just an example; you wouldn't normally bother with a binary search for 10 numbers. If you start working with sets of values with 100 or more elements, you'll see a marked speed difference between a linear search and a binary search.

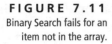

FIGURE 7.11
Binary Search fails for an
item not in the array.

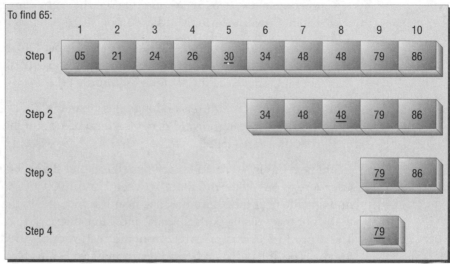

What happens when a binary search fails? The following set of steps, corresponding to the example shown in Figure 7.11, demonstrates what happens as you search for the value 65 in an array that doesn't contain it.

1. Given the array, set the search bounds to be the upper and lower bounds of the array:

```
lngLower = LBound(varItems)
lngUpper = UBound(varItems)
```

If lngLower is less than lngUpper (and it is), set lngMiddle to be the average of the two:

```
lngMiddle = (lngLower + lngUpper) \ 2
```

Because varSought (65) is greater than lngMiddle^ (30), set lngLower to be lngMiddle + 1 (6):

```
If varSought > varItems(lngMiddle) Then
    lngLower = lngMiddle + 1
Else
    lngUpper = lngMiddle
End If
```

2. Because lngLower (6) is still less than lngUpper (10), set lngMiddle to be the average of the two (8). Because varSought is greater than lngMiddle^ (48), set lngLower to be lngMiddle + 1 (9).

3. Because lngLower (9) is still less than lngUpper (10), set lngMiddle to be the average of the two (9). Because varSought is greater than lngMiddle^ (48), set lngUpper to be the same as lngMiddle (9).

4. Because lngLower (9) is no longer less than lngUpper (9), drop out of the loop. Because lngLower^ is not the item being sought, return –1, indicating that the search failed.

Still not convinced that a binary search is better than a linear search? What if you were to put all the numbers between 1 and 1,000 into an array and attempt to find a value near the beginning, one near the end, one in the middle, and a value that's not there, using both a binary and a linear search to compare the timings? The procedure CompareSearch, from the TestProcs.bas module, takes these steps for you. The dhLinearSearch function (from LinearSearch.bas), shown in Listing 7.12, provides a search that starts at the first element of an array, compares each item in turn to the sought value, and exits as soon as it finds a match. If it doesn't find a match, of course, it will end up visiting each element of the array.

Listing 7.12: Linear Search Provides the Slowest Possible W to Find a Value in an Array. (LinearSearch.bas)

```
Function dhLinearSearch(varItems As Variant, _
 varSought As Variant) As Long

    Dim lngPos As Long
    Dim blnFound As Boolean

    blnFound = False
    For lngPos = LBound(varItems) To UBound(varItems)
        If varSought = varItems(lngPos) Then
            blnFound = True
            Exit For
        End If
    Next lngPos
    If blnFound Then
        dhLinearSearch = lngPos
    Else
```

```
        dhLinearSearch = -1
    End If
 End Function
```

To compare a linear search and a binary search, the CompareSearch procedure fills an array with as many items as you request. (It assumes you want 1,000 if you don't specify a size.) It then uses dhBinarySearch to find three items in the array and one that's not. CompareSearch then repeats the process using the LinearSearch function. In each case, the code attempts to find an item that's 10 percent of the way into the array, then one that's 90 percent of the way, then 50 percent, and then one that's not in the array at all. For each test, the sample runs the search 1,000 times. The differences in speed are alarming, as you can see in Figure 7.12. For an array of 1,000 items, to find an item that is in the middle of the array (1,000 times) takes around 20 milliseconds using a binary search and around 670 milliseconds using a linear search—around 30 times longer using a linear search. For 10,000 items, the discrepancy is even greater. Now, a binary search takes 30 milliseconds, but a linear search takes around 6,700! Suddenly, you're looking at an operation taking 300 times as long to perform. (This comparison doesn't even mention the differences in time it takes to find an element near the end of the list. The binary search takes no longer to find a value there than at the middle of the list, but a linear search takes twice as long, of course, on average.)

Remember, for small data sets or if you cannot sort your data, using a linear search is fine. When your array contains 100 or more items, however, you'll want to convert your code to use a binary search, especially if you need to locate items often.

FIGURE 7.12
Compare a linear search to a binary search.

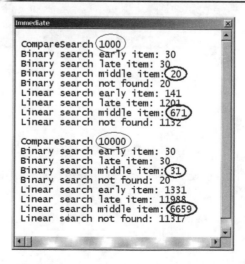

What If Your Data's in a Table?

Just as with sorting, you'll need to think hard about using these array technologies if your data is currently stored in database table or an Excel spreadsheet. That is, you must take into account your local application. No matter how fast your sorting code is, a database engine can sort faster on its own. The same goes for searching: no matter how efficiently you code your search, writing a SQL string that retrieves just the single row you need is going to be faster than loading the data into an array and using a binary search.

Therefore, think twice before using either the searching or sorting techniques presented in this chapter. If your data isn't already in an array, copying it from disk for the sole purpose of searching and sorting it may not be to your advantage. Excel, Access, and Word all supply their own tools for searching and sorting data, and you'll want to exhaust those technologies before copying data into an array and working with it there.

On the other hand, the same warning works in reverse: if you've got data in an array (or any other data structure in memory), you'll generally not want to copy it to a table or an Excel spreadsheet simply to search or sort it. By the time you write all your data to disk in order to have the database engine create a recordset based on the table filled with your data, you could have long since sorted your array and been on your way. It's all a matter of perspective; learn to use the correct tool for the situation.

You can also use an ADO recordset to sort your data. That is, you can create a disconnected recordset, adding the fields yourself and then calling the AddNew method to add each "row" of data. When you're done, you can sort the data using the recordset's Sort method. In our experience, this is by far the slowest way to sort data. You may have a different experience, but unless your data is already in a recordset, we've not found a compelling reason to put it there, just for the purposes of searching or sorting.

Using Binary Search

Calling dhBinarySearch is quite simple; you pass it the array to look in and the item to find:

$$lngPos = dhBinarySearch(varArray, varSought)$$

If the search locates *varSought* in *varArray*, it returns the position at which it found the item. If not, it returns –1.

Don't fall into the same trap we did, over and over, as we worked on this section: before you can use dhBinarySearch, the array to be searched *must be sorted*. Unless you've sorted the array, the Binary Search algorithm will return completely spurious results. If you cannot sort your data, for whatever reason, then you'll need to use dhLinearSearch instead (called in the same fashion as dhBinary-Search).

For example, the following code fragment (in TestProcs.bas) builds an array of random numbers and requests the user to guess as many of the selected numbers as possible. Once the user selects an incorrect value, the procedure displays the number of correct selected values.

```
Sub SillySearch()
    Dim aintItems(1 To 100) As Integer
    Dim intI As Integer
    Dim intPos As Integer
    Dim intCount As Integer
    For intI = 1 To 100
        aintItems(intI) = Int(Rnd * 100) + 1
    Next intI
    Call dhQuickSort(aintItems)
    Do
        intI = _
         Val(InputBox("Choose a number between 1 and 100"))
        intPos = dhBinarySearch(aintItems, intI)
        If intPos > 0 Then
            intCount = intCount + 1
        End If
    Loop Until intPos < 0
    MsgBox "You guessed " & intCount & " correct values!"
End Sub
```

Because dhBinarySearch returns −1 to indicate that it didn't find a match, you won't be able to search in arrays that have negative indexes. That is, if you must search in an array with bounds of −10 to 10, for example, you'll need to modify dhBinarySearch to return a different value that indicates failure.

TIP	Chapter 8 provides another method for searching and sorting: using a binary tree. If you're interested in pursuing other techniques, visit that chapter for more information.

Summary

We're not trying to fool anyone here—this isn't an academic study of various sorting and searching techniques. Instead, we focused on presenting specific solutions to sorting and searching problems, including the following:

- How to determine the relative speed of one solution over another, using the StopWatch class

- How to create and use arrays

- How the Quicksort algorithm works and how to sort an array using the Quicksort algorithm

- How to maintain a sorted collection

- How to use the Implements keyword to create a sort procedure that doesn't know what type of data it's sorting

- How the Binary Search algorithm works and how to find an item in a sorted array using Binary Search

- How Binary Search compares to a linear search and which is best to use in differing circumstances

Armed with the dhQuickSort and dhBinarySearch procedures and an understanding of how they work and how to use them, you should be able to use the procedures to sort and search in simple arrays. You should also be able to modify the procedures to handle different kinds of data as well, should the need arise.

For more information on searching and sorting, see Chapter 8 and its discussion of dynamic data structures. For more information on retrieving system information, as you saw in the StopWatch class, see Chapter 9.

Creating Dynamic Data Structures Using Class Modules

■ Using class modules to implement abstract data structures

■ Emulating a stack

■ Emulating a queue

■ Creating and using ordered linked lists

■ Creating and using binary trees

Almost any application requires that you maintain some data storage in memory. As your application runs, you read and write data in some sort of data structure, and when your application shuts down, it either discards the data structure (and its data) or writes the data to some persistent storage.

VBA provides two built-in data structures: arrays and collections. Each has its good and bad points, and there are compelling reasons to use each of these structures. (For more information on using arrays and collections, see Chapter 7.) On the other hand, if you've previously programmed in other languages or have studied data structures in a college course, you may find the need to use abstract data structures, such as linked lists, binary trees, stacks, and queues, as part of your applications. Although all these structures can be implemented using arrays or collections, neither of those constructs is well suited for linked data structures.

This chapter introduces techniques for using class modules to construct abstract data structures. Amazingly, VBA requires very little code to create these somewhat complex structures. Once you've worked through the examples in this chapter, you'll be able to exploit the power of linked lists, stacks, queues, and binary trees in your own VBA applications. Table 8.1 lists the sample files you'll find on the accompanying CD-ROM.

TABLE 8.1: Sample Files

Filename	Description
DYNAMIC.XLS	Excel file with sample modules and classes
DYNAMIC.MDB	Access 2000 file with sample modules and classes
DYNAMIC.VBP	VB6 project with sample modules and classes
LISTTEST.BAS	Test routines for List class
QUEUETEST.BAS	Test routines for Queue class
STACKTEST.BAS	Test routines for Stack class
TREETEST.BAS	Test routines for Tree class
LIST.CLS	Linked List class
LISTITEM.CLS	ListItem class
QUEUE.CLS	Queue class
QUEUEITEM.CLS	QueueItem class

TABLE 8.1: Sample Files *(continued)*

Filename	Description
STACK.CLS	Stack class
STACKITEM.CLS	StackItem class
TREE.CLS	Tree class
TREEITEM.CLS	TreeItem class
MAIN.FRM	Start-up form for VB project

Dynamic versus Static Data Structures

VBA provides a simple data structure: the array. If you know how many elements you're going to need to store, arrays may suit you fine. On the other hand, arrays present some difficulties:

They are linear only.   You cannot overlay any kinds of relationships between the elements of an array without going through a lot of work.

They're essentially fixed size.   Yes, you can ReDim (Preserve) to resize the array, but all VBA does in that case is create a new data structure large enough for the new array and copy all the elements over, one by one. This isn't a reasonable thing to do often, or for large arrays.

They often use too much space.   No matter how many elements you're going to put into the array, you must pre-declare the size. It's just like the pre-payment rip-off the car rental companies provide—you pay for a full tank, regardless of whether you actually use it. The same goes for arrays: If you dimension the array to hold 50 elements and you store only 5, you're wasting space for the other 45.

Because of these limitations, arrays are normally referred to as *static* data structures.

On the other hand, a *dynamic* data structure is one that can grow or shrink as needed to contain the data you want stored. That is, you can allocate new storage when it's needed and discard that storage when you're done with it.

Dynamic data structures generally consist of at least some simple data storage (in our case, it will be a class module), along with a link to the next element in the structure. These links are often called *pointers* or *references*. You'll see both terms used here.

The study of dynamic data structures could be a full-semester college course on its own, so we can't delve too deeply into it in this limited space. However, we do introduce the basic concepts and show how you can use class modules to create your own dynamic data structures. In addition, we suggest some ways in which you might use these data structures in your own applications.

Simple Dynamic Structures

Linear structures are the simplest class of dynamic data structures. Each element of structures of this type contains some information and a pointer to the next element. The diagram in Figure 8.1 shows a simple data structure in which each element of the structure contains a piece of data and a reference to the next item in the structure. (This structure is normally called a *linked list* because it contains a list of items that are linked together.)

FIGURE 8.1
The simplest type of dynamic data structure

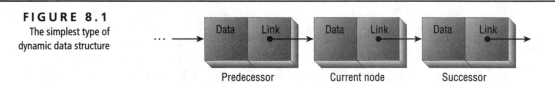

What differentiates one instance of this kind of data structure from another? It's just the arbitrary rules about how you can add or delete nodes. For example, stacks and queues are both types of linear linked data structures, but a stack can accept new items only at its "top," and a queue can accept new items only at its "bottom." With a stack, you can retrieve items only from the same place you added them. But with a queue, you retrieve them from the other end of the structure. This chapter discusses creating both of these simple data structures with VBA class modules.

If you need to be able to traverse your structure in both directions, you can, of course, include links in both directions. Although we won't handle this additional step in this chapter, it takes very little extra work to provide links in both directions. You'll find this extra pointer useful when you must traverse a list in either direction.

Recursive Dynamic Structures

You'll normally use iterative code to loop through the elements of a simple, linear dynamic data structure. On the other hand, many popular dynamic data structures lend themselves to being traversed recursively. For example, programmers often use the *ordered binary tree* structure for data storage and quick retrieval. In this kind of structure, each node has one predecessor and two successors. (Normally, you think of one successor as being the "left child" and the other as the "right child.") Figure 8.2 shows the simplest recursive data structure: a binary tree. The tree data structure is well suited to recursive algorithms for adding items and traversing the nodes.

FIGURE 8.2
Ordered binary trees are an example of a recursive data structure.

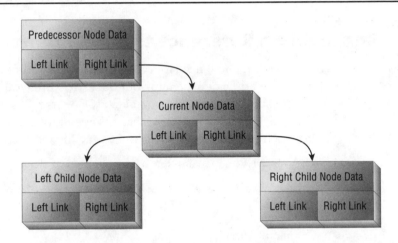

The term *dynamic data structures* always refers to *in-memory* data structures. All the techniques covered in this chapter deal only with data that you work with in the current instance of your application and have nothing to do with storing or retrieving that data from permanent storage. VBA provides its own techniques for reading and writing disk files. You'll use the data structures presented in this chapter once you've retrieved the data you need to work with.

How Does This Apply to VBA?

Because VBA supports class modules and because you can create a new instance of a class (that is, *instantiate* a new member of the class) at any time, you can create class modules that emulate these abstract data structures. Each element of the structure, because it's just like every other element, is just another instance of the class. (For information on getting started with class modules, see Chapter 5.)

You can most easily represent abstract structures in VBA using two class modules: one to represent a data type that does nothing more than point to the real data structure, and another to represent each element of the structure. For example, if you want to create a stack data structure (and you will later in this section), you'll need one class module to act as a pointer to the "top" of the stack. This is where you can add new items to the stack. You'll also need a different class module for the elements in the stack. This class module will contain two pieces of data: the information to be stored in the stack and a reference to the next item on the stack.

Retrieving a Reference to a New Item

At some point, you'll need to retrieve a reference to a new instance of your class. If you want to add a new item to your data structure, you'll need a pointer to that new item so you can get back to it later. Of course, Basic (after all, as many folks will argue, this *is* still just Basic) has never supported real pointers, and dynamic data structures require pointers, right? Luckily, not quite!

VBA allows you to instantiate a new element of a class and retrieve a reference to it:

Dim *objVar* As New *className*

or

Dim *objVar* as *className*

' Possibly some other code in here.

Set *objVar* = New *className*

You choose one of the two methods for instantiating a new item based on your needs. In either case, you end up with a variable that refers to a new instance of the class.

WARNING   Be wary of using the New keyword in the Dim statement. Although this makes your code shorter, it can also cause trouble. This usage allows VBA to instantiate the new object whenever it needs to (normally, the first time you attempt to set or retrieve a property of the object) and, therefore, runs the new object's Initialize event at that time. If you want control over exactly when the new object comes into being (and when its Initialize event procedure runs), use the New keyword with the Set statement. This will instantiate the object when you're ready to, not at some time when you might not be expecting it. In addition, using the New keyword as part of the Dim statement causes VBA to add extra code to your application because it must check at runtime whether it needs to instantiate the object between each line of code where the object is in scope. You don't need this extra overhead.

After either of these statements, *objVar* contains a pointer to the new member of the *className* class. Even though you can't manipulate, view, or otherwise work with pointer values as you can in C/C++, the Set/New combination at least gives VBA programmers almost the same functionality that Pascal programmers have always had, although the mechanism is a bit clumsier: You can create pointers only to classes in VBA, while Pascal allows pointers to almost any data type.

Making an Object Variable Refer to an Existing Item

Just as you can use the Set keyword to retrieve a reference to a new object, you can use it to retrieve a reference to an existing object. If objItem is an object variable that refers to an existing member of a class, you can use code like this to make objNewItem refer to the existing item:

```
Set objNewItem = objItem
```

After this statement, the pointers named `objNewItem` and `objItem` refer to the same object.

What If a Variable Doesn't Refer to Anything?

How can you tell if an object variable doesn't refer to anything? When working with dynamic data structures, you'll find it useful to be able to discern whether a reference has been instantiated. Pascal uses *Nil,* C uses *Null,* and VBA uses *Nothing* to represent the condition in which an object variable doesn't currently refer to a real object.

If you have an object variable and you've not yet assigned it to point to an object, its value is Nothing. You can test for this state using code like this:

```
If objItem Is Nothing Then
    ' You know that objItem isn't currently referring to anything
End If
```

If you want to release the memory used by an object in memory, you must sever all connections to that object. As long as some variable refers to an object, VBA won't be able to release the memory used by that object. (Think of it as a hot-air balloon tied down with a number of ropes; until someone releases the last rope, that balloon isn't going anywhere.) To release the connection, set the object variable to Nothing:

```
Set objItem = Nothing
```

Once you've released all references to an object, VBA can dispose of the object and free up the memory it was using.

Emulating Data Structures with Class Modules

Before you can do any work with dynamic data structures, you need to understand how to use class modules to emulate the elements of these structures. For example, In Figure 8.1, each element of the structure contains a piece of data and a reference to the next element. How can you create a class module that does that?

It's easy: Create a class module named ListItem with two module-level variables:

```
Public Value As Variant
Public NextItem As ListItem
```

The first variable, Value, will contain the data for each element. The second variable, NextItem, will contain a reference to the next item in the data structure. The surprising, and somewhat confusing, issue is that you can create a variable of the same type as the class in the definition of the class itself. It's just this sort of self-referential declaration that makes dynamic data structures possible in VBA.

To add an item to the list, you might write code like this in your class module:

```
Public Function AddItem(varValue As Variant) As ListItem
    Set NextItem = New ListItem
    NextItem.Value = varValue
    ' Set the return value for the function.
    Set AddItem = NextItem
End Sub
```

The first line of the procedure creates a new item in the data structure and makes the NextItem variable in the current element refer to that new element. The second line uses NextItem to refer to the next element and sets its Value variable to the value passed to the current procedure, varValue. The final line sets up the function call to return a reference to the new item that was just added to the list.

In reality, you probably wouldn't write a data structure this way because it provides no way to find a particular item or the beginning or end of the list. In other words, there's something missing that makes these structures possible: a reference to the entire structure. The next section tells you how you should actually create such a data structure.

How about the complicated binary tree structure shown in Figure 8.2? The only difference between this structure and a linear list is that each element in this structure maintains a pointer to two other structures rather than just one. The class module for an element (class name TreeItem) of a binary tree structure might contain these elements:

```
Public Value As Variant
Public LeftChild As TreeItem
Public RightChild As TreeItem
```

Creating a Header Class

Although you can use a class module to emulate the elements of a dynamic data structure, as shown in the previous section, you'll need a different class module to "anchor" the data structure. This class module will generally have only a single instance per data structure and will contain pointers to the beginning, and perhaps the end, of the data structure. In addition, this class often contains the code necessary to add and delete items in the list.

Generally, the header class contains one or more references to objects of the type used in building the data structure, and perhaps other information about the structure itself. For example, a hypothetical class named ListHeader, with the following information, has a reference to the first item in a list and the last item in the list:

```
Private liFirst As ListItem
Private liLast As ListItem
```

Note that the class doesn't contain a self-referential data element. There's generally no reason for a list header to refer to another list header, so this example doesn't contain a reference to anything but the list items. In addition, the header class only needs to contain a reference to the first item in the data structure.

How you work with the items in the data structure—adding, deleting, and manipulating them—depends on the logical properties of the data structure you're creating. Now that you've seen the basics, it's time to dig into some data structures that emulate stacks and queues, each of which has its own ideas about adding and deleting items.

Creating a Stack

A stack is a simple logical data structure, normally implemented using a linked list to contain its data. Of course, you could use an array to implement a stack, and many programmers have done this. However, using an array forces you to worry about the size of the stack, which a linked list structure would not. A stack allows you to control data input and output in a very orderly fashion: New items can be added only to the top of the stack. And, as you remove items, they too are removed from the top. In essence, a stack data structure works like the stack of cafeteria trays at your local eatery or like the pile of problems to solve on your desk (unless you're as compulsive as one of us is—we're not telling which one—and solve your problems in a queue-like fashion). This sort of data storage is often referred to as LIFO (Last In, First Out)—the most recent item added to the stack is the first to be removed.

Why Use a Stack?

Why use a stack in an application? You might want to track forms as a user opens them and then be able to back out of the open forms in the opposite order: That is, you may want to store form references in the stack and then, as the user clicks the OK button on each form, bring the correct form to the top, popping the most recent form from the stack. Or you may want to track the procedure call tree within your application as your user runs it. That way, you could push the name of the procedure as you enter the procedure. On the way out, you could pop the stack. Using this technique, the top of the stack always contains the name of the current procedure. Otherwise, this value is impossible to retrieve. (Perhaps some day VBA will allow you to gather information about the internal call stack programmatically. At this point, you're left handling it yourself.) You could also build your own application profiler. By storing the current time in the stack for each procedure as you push it on the stack and then subtracting that from the current time as you pop the stack, you can find out how long the code was working in each procedure.

Implementing a Stack

Figures 8.3 and 8.4 show a sample stack in memory, before and after a fifth item is added to the stack. At each point, the top of the stack points to the top-most element. After the new element is added, the top of the stack points at the newest element, and that element's link points to the item that used to be at the top of the stack.

It takes very little code to create and maintain a stack. The structure requires two class modules: the Stack and StackItem classes.

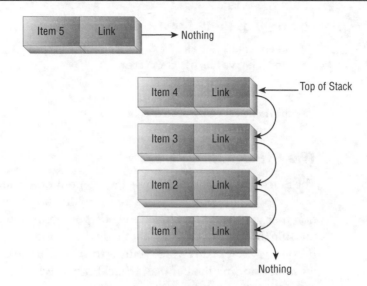

FIGURE 8.3
A sample stack just before adding a fifth item

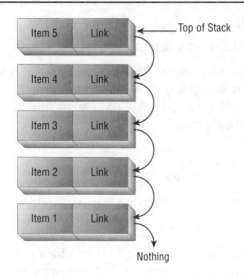

FIGURE 8.4
The same stack after adding the new item

The StackItem Class

It doesn't get much simpler than this. The StackItem class maintains a data item, as well as a pointer to the next item in the structure, as shown in Listing 8.1.

Listing 8.1: Code for the StackItem Class

```
' Keep track of the next stack item,
' and the value of this item.

Public Value As Variant
Public NextItem As StackItem
```

The Stack Class

The Stack class contains a single item: a pointer to the first item in the stack (the stack top). That pointer always points to the top of the stack, and it's at this location that you'll add (push) and delete (pop) items from the stack. The Stack class module implements the two methods (Push and Pop), as well as two read-only properties, StackTop (which returns the value of the element at the top of the stack without popping the item) and StackEmpty (which returns a Boolean value indicating the status of the stack—True if there are no items in the stack and False if there are items).

Pushing Items onto the Stack

To add an item to the stack, you "push" it to the top of the stack. This is similar to pushing a new cafeteria tray to the top of the tray stack. When you push the new tray, each of the other trays moves down one position in the stack. Using linked lists, the code must follow these steps:

1. Create the new node.

2. Place the value to be stored in the new node.

3. Make the new node point to whatever the current stack top pointer refers to.

4. Make the stack top point to this new node.

The code in Listing 8.2 shows the Push method of the Stack class. The four lines of code correspond to the four steps listed previously.

Listing 8.2: Use the Push Method to Add a New Item to the Stack

```
Public Sub Push(ByVal varText As Variant)
    ' Add a new item to the top of the stack.
    Dim siNewTop As StackItem
```

```
      Set siNewTop = New StackItem
      siNewTop.Value = varText
      Set siNewTop.NextItem = siTop
      Set siTop = siNewTop
   End Sub
```

Figures 8.5 and 8.6 demonstrate the steps involved in pushing an item onto a stack. In the example case, you're attempting to push the value 27 onto a stack that already contains three elements.

NOTE   In the figures, to save space, we've collapsed the Dim and As New statements into one line. The examples use separate lines of code for each step, as we've recommended earlier.

FIGURE 8.5
The first three steps in pushing an item onto a stack

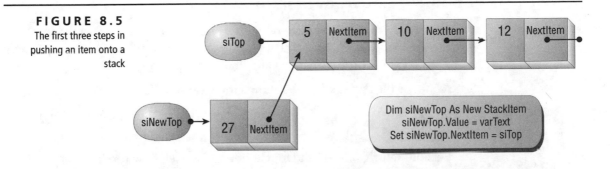

FIGURE 8.6
The final step in pushing an item onto a stack

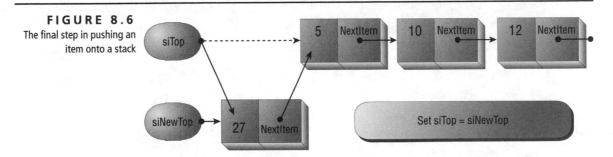

What if the stack is empty when you try to push an item? In that case, siTop will be Nothing when you execute the following code:

```
Set siNewTop.NextItem = siTop
```

The new node's NextItem property will point to Nothing, as it should. Executing the final line of code:

```
Set siTop = siNewTop
```

causes the top of the stack to point to this new node, which then points to Nothing. It works just as it should!

TIP   If you find this final line of code confusing, look at it this way: When you assign siTop to be siNewTop, you're telling VBA to make siTop contain the same address that siNewTop currently contains. In other words, you're telling siTop to point to whatever siNewTop currently points to. Read that a few times while looking at Figure 8.6, and, hopefully, it will all come into focus.

Popping Items from the Stack

Popping an item from the stack removes it from the stack and makes the top pointer refer to the new item on the top of the stack. In addition, in this implementation, the Pop method returns the value that was just popped.

The code for the Pop method, as shown in Listing 8.3, follows these steps:

1. Makes sure there's something in the stack. (If not, Pop doesn't do anything and returns a null value.)

2. Sets the return value of the function to the value of the top item.

3. Makes the stack top point at whatever the first item is currently pointing to. This effectively removes the first item in the stack.

Listing 8.3: Use the Pop Method to Remove an Item from the Stack

```
Public Function Pop() As Variant
    If Not StackEmpty Then
        ' Get the value from the current top stack element.
        ' Then, get a reference to the new stack top.
        Pop = siTop.Value
        Set siTop = siTop.NextItem
    End If
End Function
```

What happens to the node that used to be at the top of the stack? Once there are no more references to an instance of a class module, VBA can remove that instance from memory, effectively "killing" it. If you're not convinced, add a Debug.Print statement to the Terminate event procedure for the StackItem class. You'll see that VBA kills off unneeded objects as soon as there are no more references to the object.

The diagram in Figure 8.7 demonstrates the tricky step: popping an item from the stack. The code causes the stack pointer, siTop, to refer to the item to which siTop previously referred. That is, it links around the current top item in the stack. Once that occurs, there's no reference to the current top item, and VBA can "kill" the item.

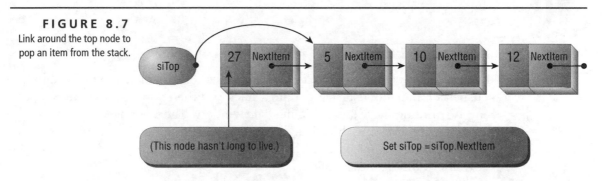

FIGURE 8.7
Link around the top node to pop an item from the stack.

Is the Stack Empty?

You may need to be able to detect whether the stack is currently empty. To make that possible, the example implementation of the Stack data structure provides a read-only StackEmpty property. Providing the information is simple: If siTop is currently Nothing, the stack must be empty.

```
Property Get StackEmpty() As Boolean
    ' Is the stack empty?  It can
    ' only be empty if siTop is Nothing.
    StackEmpty = (siTop Is Nothing)
End Property
```

Given this property, you can write code that pops items until the stack is empty, like this:

```
Do While Not stk.StackEmpty
    Debug.Print stk.Pop()
Loop
```

What's on Top?

You may need to know what's on the top of the stack without removing the item. To make that possible, the example implementation of the Stack data structure includes a read-only StackTop property that returns the value of the item to which siTop points (or Null if siTop is Nothing):

```
Property Get StackTop() As Variant
    If StackEmpty Then
        StackTop = Null
    Else
        StackTop = siTop.Value
    End If
End Property
```

A Simple Example

Listing 8.4 shows a few examples using a stack data structure. The first example pushes a number of text strings onto a stack and then pops the stack until it's empty, printing the text to the Immediate window. The second example calls a series of procedures, each of which pushes its name onto the stack on the way in and pops it off on the way out. The screen in Figure 8.8 shows the Immediate window after running the sample.

Listing 8.4: Using the Stack Data Structure

```
Private stkTest As Stack

Sub TestStacks()

    Set stkTest = New Stack

    ' Push some items, and then pop them.
    stkTest.Push ""Hello"
    stkTest.Push "There"
    stkTest.Push "How"
    stkTest.Push "Are"
    stkTest.Push "You"
    Do Until stkTest.StackEmpty
        Debug.Print stkTest.Pop()
    Loop
```

```
        ' Now, call a bunch of procedures.
        ' For each procedure, push the proc name
        ' at the beginning, and pop it on the way out.
        Debug.Print
        Debug.Print "Testing Procs:"
        stkTest.Push "Main"
        Debug.Print stkTest.StackTop
        Call A
        Debug.Print stkTest.Pop
End Sub

Sub A()
        stkTest.Push "A"
        Debug.Print stkTest.StackTop
        Call B
        Debug.Print stkTest.Pop
End Sub

Sub B()
        stkTest.Push "B"
        Debug.Print stkTest.StackTop
        Call C
        Debug.Print stkTest.Pop
End Sub

Sub C()
        stkTest.Push "C"
        Debug.Print stkTest.StackTop
        ' You'd probably do something in here...
        Debug.Print stkTest.Pop
End Sub
```

TIP

As you can see from the previous example, it's not hard to create a procedure stack, keeping track of the current procedure from within your code. Unfortunately, you must take care of the details yourself. If you do implement something like this, make sure there's no way to exit a procedure without popping the stack, or your stack will get awfully confused about the identity of the current procedure as you work your way back out, popping things from the stack.

FIGURE 8.8
The Immediate window
after the stack example
has run

```
Debug Window                                    ☒
<Ready>                                     [...]
You
Are
How
There
Hello

Testing Procs:
Main
A
B
C
C
B
A
Main
```

Creating a Queue

A queue, like a stack, is a data structure based on the linked list concept. Instead of allowing you to add and remove items at a single point, a queue allows you to add items at one end and remove them at the other. In essence, this forms a First In First Out (FIFO) data flow: The first item into the queue is also the first item out. Of course, this is the way your to-do list ought to work—the oldest item ought to get handled first. Unfortunately, most people handle their workflow based on the stack data model, not based on a queue.

Why Use a Queue?

You'll use a queue data structure in an application when you need to maintain a list of items ordered not by their actual value but by their temporal value. For example, you might want to allow users to select a list of reports throughout the day and, at idle times throughout the day, print those reports. Although there are many ways to store this information internally, a queue makes an ideal mechanism. When you need to find the name of the next report to print, just pull it from the top of the queue. When you add a new report to be printed, it goes to the end of the queue.

You can also think of a queue as a pipeline—a means of transport for information from one place to another. You could create a global variable in your application to refer to the queue and have various parts of the application send messages to each other using the queue mechanism, much as Windows itself does with the various running applications.

> If you're planning on creating an industrial-strength queue in an application to pass information from one user to another, you'll want to study the concepts presented here, but also look into using MSMQ, a server-based product from Microsoft that manages enterprise-wide queuing for you. In one sense, MSMQ works the same way as the queues shown here do. However, in a real sense, comparing MSMQ to the queues shown here is just as accurate as comparing a desktop computer to an abacus. They both perform calculations, but one is far more powerful than the other. If you need disconnected queuing and guaranteed delivery of information in an enterprise-wide environment, you'll want to look into MSMQ.

Implementing a Queue

The diagrams in Figures 8.9, 8.10, and 8.11 show a simple queue before and after adding a new item and before and after removing an item. At each point, you can add a new item only at the rear of the queue and can remove an item only from the front of the queue. (Note that the front of the queue, where you delete items, is at the left of the diagrams. The rear of the queue, where you add items, appears to the right.)

Maintaining a queue takes a bit more code than maintaining a stack, but not much. Although the queue is handled internally as a linked list, it has some limitations as to where you can add and delete items. The underlying code handles these restrictions. The queue structure requires two class modules, one each for the Queue and QueueItem classes.

FIGURE 8.9
A simple queue just before a fourth item is added

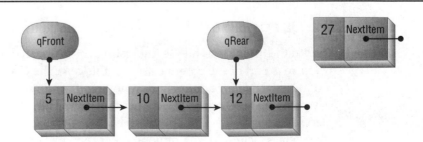

FIGURE 8.10
The simple queue after the
fourth item is added and
before an item is removed

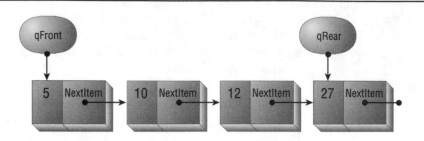

FIGURE 8.11
The simple queue after an
item has been removed

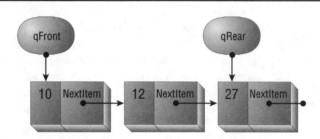

The QueueItem Class

Just like the StackItem class, the QueueItem class stores just a data value and a
pointer to the next data element, as shown in Listing 8.5.

Listing 8.5: Code for the QueueItem Class

```
' Keep track of the next queue item,
' and the text of this item.
Public NextItem As QueueItem
Public Value As Variant
```

The Queue Class

As with the Stack class, all the interesting code required in working with the data
structure is part of the parent class—in this case, the Queue class. It's here you'll
find the methods for adding and removing items in the queue, as well as a read-
only property that indicates whether the queue is currently empty. Because a
queue needs to be able to work with both the front and the rear of the queue, the
Queue class includes two pointers rather than just one, making it possible to add

items at one end and to remove them from the other. These pointers are defined as qFront and qRear, as shown here, and are module-level variables:

```
Private qFront As QueueItem
Private qRear As QueueItem
```

Adding an Item to the Queue

To add an item to a queue, you "enqueue" it. That is, you add it to the rear of the queue. To do this, the Add method follows these steps:

1. Creates the new node.

2. Places the value to be stored in the new node.

3. If the queue is currently empty, makes the front and rear pointers refer to the new node.

4. Otherwise, links the new node into the list of nodes in the queue. To do that, it makes the final node (the node the "rear pointer" currently points to) point to the new item. Then it makes the rear pointer in the queue header object refer to the new node.

The code in Listing 8.6 shows the Add method of the Queue class.

Listing 8.6: Use the Add Method to Add a New Item to a Queue

```
Public Sub Add(varNewItem As Variant)
    Dim qNew As QueueItem
    Set qNew = New QueueItem

    qNew.Value = varNewItem
    ' What if the queue is empty? Better point
    ' both the front and rear pointers at the
    ' new item.
    If IsEmpty Then
        Set qFront = qNew
        Set qRear = qNew
    Else
        Set qRear.NextItem = qNew
        Set qRear = qNew
    End If
End Sub
```

The diagrams in Figures 8.12 and 8.13 demonstrate the steps for adding a new node to an existing queue.

NOTE   As we did earlier, we've collapsed the Dim and New statements in the figures into a single line of code in order to save space. We don't recommend doing this in your own code.

FIGURE 8.12
After you create the new node, the Add method is ready to attach it to the queue.

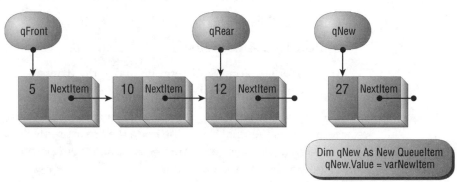

FIGURE 8.13
To finish adding the node, set qRear to point to the new node.

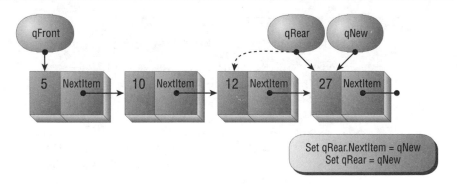

What if the queue was empty when you tried to add an item? In that case, all you need to do is make the head and rear of the queue point to the new node. Afterward, the queue will look like the one in Figure 8.14.

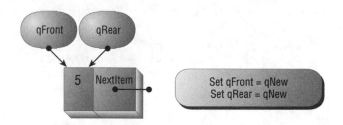

FIGURE 8.14
After a new node is added
to an empty queue, both
the head and rear pointers
refer to the same node.

Removing Items from the Queue

Removing an item from the queue both removes the front node from the data structure and makes the next front-most item the new front of the queue. In addition, this implementation of the queue data structure returns the value of the removed item as the return value from the Remove method.

The code for the Remove method, as shown Listing 8.7, follows these steps:

1. Makes sure there's something in the queue. If not, the Remove method doesn't do anything and returns a null value.

2. Sets the return value of the function to the value of the front queue item.

3. If there's only one item in the queue, sets both the head and rear pointers to Nothing. There's nothing left in the queue.

4. If there was more than one item in the queue, sets the front pointer to refer to the second item in the queue. This effectively kills the old first item.

Listing 8.7: Use the Remove Method to Drop Items from a Queue

```
Public Function Remove() As Variant
    ' Remove an item from the head of the
    ' list, and return its value.
    If IsEmpty Then
        Remove = Null
    Else
        Remove = qFront.Value
        ' If there's only one item
        ' in the queue, qFront and qRear
        ' will be pointing to the same node.
        ' Use the Is operator to test for that.
```

```
            If qFront Is qRear Then
                Set qFront = Nothing
                Set qRear = Nothing
            Else
                Set qFront = qFront.NextItem
            End If
        End If
    End Function
```

The diagram in Figure 8.15 demonstrates the one difficult step in removing an item. The diagram corresponds to this line of code:

```
    Set qFront = qFront.NextItem
```

By moving the front pointer to the item that the first item previously pointed to, you eliminate the reference to the old first item, and VBA removes it from memory. After this step, the queue will contain one less item.

FIGURE 8.15
To remove an item, move the front pointer to the second node in the queue.

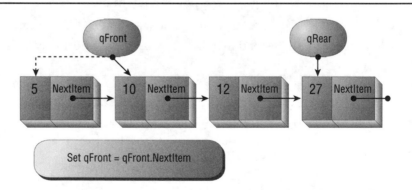

Is the Queue Empty?

You'll often need to be able to detect whether the queue is empty, and the example implementation includes the read-only IsEmpty property for this reason. The queue can be empty only if both the front and rear pointers are Nothing. The code shown here checks for this condition:

```
Public Property Get IsEmpty() As Boolean
    ' Return True if the queue contains
    ' no items.
    IsEmpty = ((qFront Is Nothing) And (qRear Is Nothing))
End Property
```

The IsEmpty property allows you to write code like this:

```
Do Until q.IsEmpty
    Debug.Print q.Remove()
Loop
```

A Simple Queue Example

The code in Listing 8.8 demonstrates the use of the queue data structure. It creates a new queue, adds five words to the queue, and then removes the words, one at a time. The words should come out in the same order in which they were entered. Note that if you'd used a stack for the same exercise, the words would have come out in the opposite order from the order in which they were entered.

Listing 8.8: Using the Queue Data Structure

```
Sub TestQueues()
    Dim qTest As Queue

    Set qTest = New Queue
    With qTest
        .Add "Hello"
        .Add "There"
        .Add "How"
        .Add "Are"
        .Add "You"
        Do Until .IsEmpty
            Debug.Print .Remove()
        Loop
    End With
End Sub
```

Creating Ordered Linked Lists

A linked list is a simple data structure, as shown earlier in Figure 8.1, that allows you to maintain an ordered list of items without having to know ahead of time how many items you'll be adding. To build this data structure, you need two class modules: one for the list head and another for the items in the list. The example presented here is a sorted linked list. As you enter items into the list, the code finds the correct place to insert them and adjusts the links around the new nodes accordingly.

The ListItem Class

The code for the ListItem class, shown here, is simple, as you can see in Listing 8.9. The code should look familiar—it's parallel to the code in Listing 8.1. (Remember, the Stack data structure is just a logical extension of the simple linked list.)

```
Public Value As Variant
Public NextItem As ListItem
```

The class module contains storage for the value to be stored in the node, plus a pointer to the next node. As you instantiate members of this class, you'll set the NextItem property to refer to the next item in the list, which depends on where in the list you insert the new node.

The List Class

The List class includes but a single data element:

```
Dim liHead As ListItem
```

The liHead item provides a reference to the first item in the linked list. (If there's nothing yet in the list, liHead is Nothing.) The List class also includes three Public methods: Add, Delete, and DebugList. The Add method adds a new node to the list, in sorted order. The Delete method deletes a given value from the list if it's currently in the list. The DebugList method walks the list from one end to the other, printing the items in the list to the Immediate window.

Finding an Item in the List

Both the Add and Delete methods count on a Private method, Search, which takes three parameters:

- The value to find (passed by value)
- The current list item (passed by reference)
- The previous list item (passed by reference)

The Search procedure fills in the current and previous list items (so the calling procedure can work with both items). Both parameters are passed using ByRef, so the procedure can modify their values. The function returns a Boolean value indicating whether it actually found the requested value. The function, shown in Listing 8.9, follows these steps:

1. Assumes the return value is False, sets liPrevious to point to Nothing, and sets liCurrent to point to the head of the list:

   ```
   blnFound = False

   Set liPrevious = Nothing
   Set liCurrent = liHead
   ```

2. While not at the end of the list (while the current pointer isn't Nothing), does one of the following:

   - If the search item is greater than the stored value, it sets the previous pointer to refer to the current node and sets the current node to point to the next node.

   - If the search item is less than or equal to the stored value, then you're done, and it exits the loop.

   ```
   Do Until liCurrent Is Nothing
       With liCurrent
           If varItem > .Value Then
               Set liPrevious = liCurrent
               Set liCurrent = .NextItem
           Else
               Exit Do
           End If
       End With
   Loop
   ```

3. Establishes whether the sought value was actually found.

```
If Not liCurrent Is Nothing Then
    blnFound = (liCurrent.Value = varItem)
End If
```

4. Returns the previous and current pointers in ByRef parameters and the found status as the return value.

Listing 8.9: Use the Search Function to Find a Specific Element in the List

```
Function Search(ByVal varItem As Variant, _
 ByRef liCurrent As ListItem, ByRef liPrevious As ListItem) _
 As Boolean
    Dim blnFound As Boolean

    blnFound = False

    Set liPrevious = Nothing
    Set liCurrent = liHead
    Do Until liCurrent Is Nothing
        With liCurrent
            If varItem > .Value Then
                Set liPrevious = liCurrent
                Set liCurrent = .NextItem
            Else
                Exit Do
            End If
        End With
    Loop

    ' You can't compare the value in liCurrent to the sought
    ' value unless liCurrent points to something.
    If Not liCurrent Is Nothing Then
        blnFound = (liCurrent.Value = varItem)
    End If
    Search = blnFound
End Function
```

Taking the most common case (searching for an item in the middle of an existing list), the diagrams in Figures 8.16, 8.17, 8.18, and 8.19 demonstrate the steps in the logic of the Search method. In this example, the imaginary code running is searching for the value 7 in a list that contains the values 3, 5, and 10.

FIGURE 8.16
Check to see if it's time to stop looping, based on the current value and the value to find.

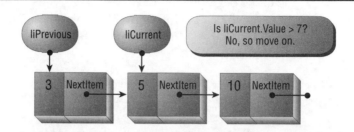

FIGURE 8.17
Set the previous pointer to point to the current node.

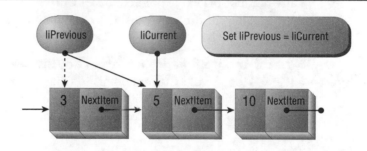

FIGURE 8.18
Set the current pointer to point to the next node.

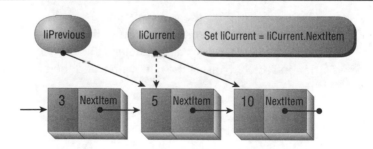

FIGURE 8.19
It's time to stop looping. The item wasn't found, so return False.

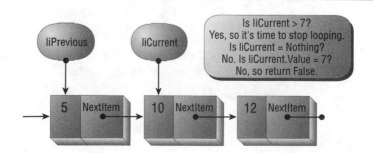

What happens in the borderline cases?

What if the list is currently empty?   In that case, liCurrent will be Nothing at the beginning of the procedure (because you've made it point to the same thing that liHead points to, which is Nothing). The function will do nothing and will return False. After you call the function, liCurrent and liPrevious will both be Nothing.

What if the item to be found is less than anything currently in the list?   In that case, the item should be placed before the item liHead currently points to. As soon as the code enters the loop, it will find that liCurrent.Value is greater than varItem and will jump out of the loop. The function will return False because the value pointed to by liCurrent isn't the same as the value being sought. After the function call, liCurrent will refer to the first item in the list, and liPrevious will be Nothing.

What if the item is greater than anything in the list?   In that case, the code will loop until liCurrent points to what the final node in the list points to (Nothing), and liPrevious will point to the final node in the list. The function will return False because liCurrent is Nothing.

Adding an Item to the List

Once you've found the right position using the Search method of the List class, inserting an item is relatively simple. The Add method, shown in Listing 8.10, takes the new value as a parameter, calls the Search method to find the right position in which to insert the new value, and then inserts it. The procedure follows these steps:

1. Creates a new node for the new item and sets its value to the value passed as a parameter to the procedure:

    ```
    Set liNew = New ListItem
    liNew.Value = varValue
    ```

2. Calls the Search method, which fills in the values of liCurrent and liPrevious. Disregard the return value when adding an item, as you don't care whether the value was already in the list:

    ```
    Call Search(varValue, liCurrent, liPrevious)
    ```

3. If inserting an item anywhere but at the head of the list, adjusts pointers to link in the new item:

```
Set liNew.NextItem = liPrevious.NextItem
Set liPrevious.NextItem = liNew
```

4. If inserting an item at the beginning of the list, sets the head pointer to refer to the new node.

```
Set liNew.NextItem = liHead
Set liHead = liNew
```

Listing 8.10: Use the Add Method to Add a New Item to a List

```
Public Sub Add(varValue As Variant)
    Dim liNew As New ListItem
    Dim liCurrent As ListItem
    Dim liPrevious As ListItem

    Set liNew = New ListItem
    liNew.Value = varValue

    ' Find where to put the new item. This function call
    ' fills in liCurrent and liPrevious.
    Call Search(varValue, liCurrent, liPrevious)

    If Not liPrevious Is Nothing Then
        Set liNew.NextItem = liPrevious.NextItem
        Set liPrevious.NextItem = liNew
    Else
        ' Inserting at the head of the list:
        ' Set the new item to point to what liHead currently
        ' points to (which might just be Nothing). Then
        ' make liHead point to the new item.
        Set liNew.NextItem = liHead
        Set liHead = liNew
    End If
End Sub
```

Inserting an item at the head of the list is easy. All you need to do is make the new node's NextItem pointer refer to the current head of the list and then make the list head pointer refer to the new node. The diagrams in Figures 8.20, 8.21, and 8.22 show how you can insert an item at the head of the list. In this example, you're attempting to insert a node with the value 3 into a list containing 5, 10, and 12. Because 3 is less than any item in the list, the code will insert it at the head of the list.

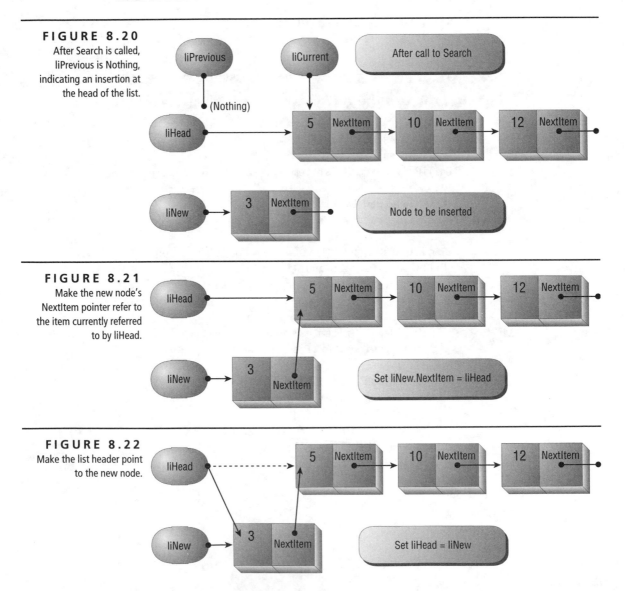

FIGURE 8.20
After Search is called, liPrevious is Nothing, indicating an insertion at the head of the list.

FIGURE 8.21
Make the new node's NextItem pointer refer to the item currently referred to by liHead.

FIGURE 8.22
Make the list header point to the new node.

Inserting an item anywhere in the list besides the head works similarly, but the steps are a bit different. If liPrevious isn't Nothing after the Add method calls Search, you must make the new node's NextItem point to what liPrevious currently points at and then make whatever liPrevious is pointing at point at liNew instead. The diagrams in Figures 8.23, 8.24, and 8.25 illustrate an insertion in the middle (or at the end) of the list. In this series of figures, you're attempting to add an item with value 7 to a list containing 5, 10, and 12.

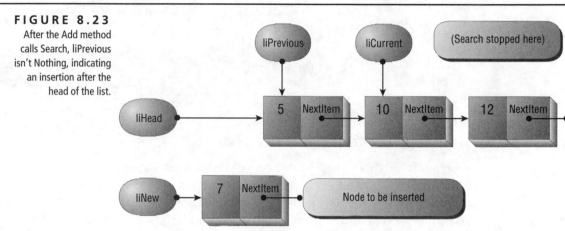

FIGURE 8.23
After the Add method calls Search, liPrevious isn't Nothing, indicating an insertion after the head of the list.

FIGURE 8.24
Make the new item point to the item after the one liPrevious points to.

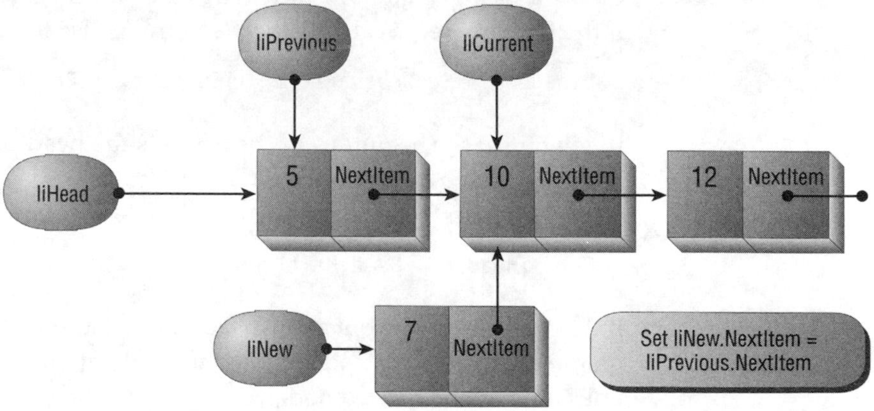

FIGURE 8.25
Make the item that liPrevious points to point to the new item, linking it into the list.

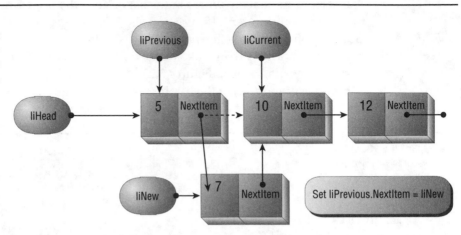

Deleting an Item from the List

Again, just as with adding an item, once you've found the right position using the Search method of the List class, deleting an item doesn't take much code. The Delete method, shown in Listing 8.11, takes the new value as a parameter; calls the Search method to find the item to be deleted; and, if it's there, deletes it. The procedure follows these steps:

1. Calls the Search method, which fills in the values of liCurrent and liPrevious. If the function returns False, there's nothing else to do.

   ```
   blnFound = Search(varItem, liCurrent, liPrevious)
   ```

2. If deleting at the beginning of the list, sets the head pointer to refer to the node pointed to by the selected node. (It links the head pointer to the current second node in the list.)

   ```
   Set liHead = liHead.NextItem
   ```

3. If deleting anywhere but at the head of the list, sets the previous item's pointer to refer to the node pointed to by the item to be deleted. (That is, it links around the deleted node.)

   ```
   Set liPrevious.NextItem = liCurrent.NextItem
   ```

4. When liCurrent goes out of scope, VBA destroys the node to be deleted because no other pointer refers to that instance of the class.

Listing 8.11: Use the Delete Method to Delete an Item from a List

```
Public Function Delete(varItem As Variant) As Boolean
    Dim liCurrent As ListItem
    Dim liPrevious As ListItem
    Dim blnFound As Boolean

    ' Find the item. This function call
    ' fills in liCurrent and liPrevious.
    blnFound = Search(varItem, liCurrent, liPrevious)
    If blnFound Then
        If liPrevious Is Nothing Then
            ' Deleting from the head of the list.
            Set liHead = liHead.NextItem
        Else
            ' Deleting from the middle or end of the list.
            Set liPrevious.NextItem = liCurrent.NextItem
        End If
    End If
    Delete = blnFound
End Function
```

To delete an item from the head of the list, all you need to do is make the header's pointer refer to the second item in the list. The diagrams in Figures 8.26, 8.27, and 8.28 show how you can delete an item at the head of the list.

FIGURE 8.26
If the search ends at the head of the list, liPrevious will be Nothing.

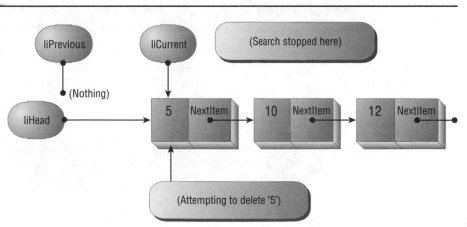

FIGURE 8.27
To delete the first item,
make liHead point to the
second item in the list.

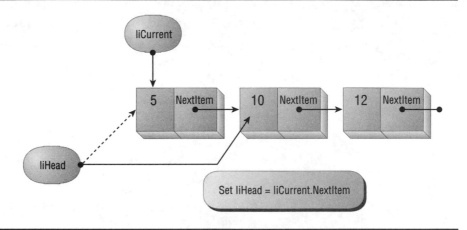

FIGURE 8.28
When liCurrent goes out of
scope, VBA destroys the
deleted item.

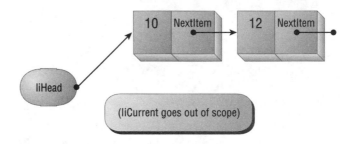

What about deleting an item other than the first? That's easy too: Just link around the item to be deleted. The diagrams in Figures 8.29, 8.30, and 8.31 show how you can delete an item that's not the first item in the list. In this case, you're attempting to delete the node with value 10 from a list that contains 5, 10, and 12.

FIGURE 8.29
The search found the node
to be deleted. (liCurrent
points to it.)

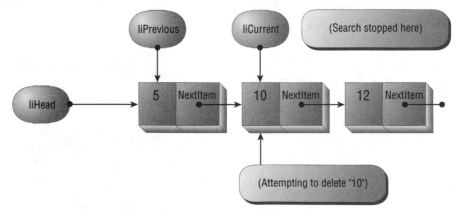

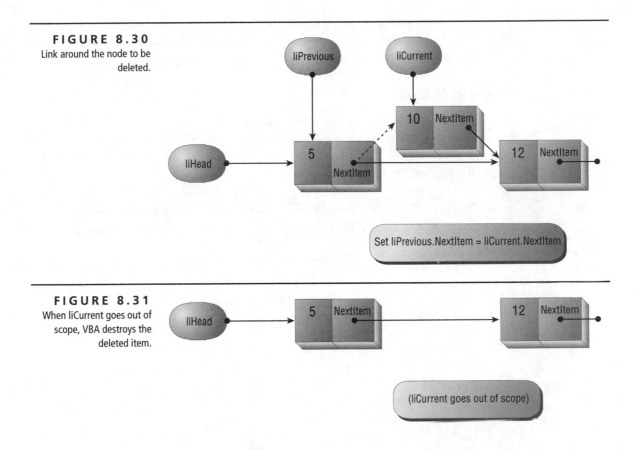

FIGURE 8.30
Link around the node to be deleted.

Set liPrevious.NextItem = liCurrent.NextItem

FIGURE 8.31
When liCurrent goes out of scope, VBA destroys the deleted item.

(liCurrent goes out of scope)

Traversing the List

A list wouldn't do you much good if you couldn't traverse it, visiting each element in turn. The example project includes a DebugList method of the List class. Calling this method walks the list one item at a time, printing each value in turn to the Immediate window:

```
Public Sub DebugList()
    ' Print the list to the Immediate window.
    Dim liCurrent As ListItem
    Set liCurrent = liHead
    Do Until liCurrent Is Nothing
        Debug.Print liCurrent.Value
        Set liCurrent = liCurrent.NextItem
    Loop
End Sub
```

To do its work, the code in DebugList first sets a pointer to the head of the list. Then, as long as that pointer isn't Nothing, the code prints out the current value and sets the current node pointer to refer to the next item in the list.

Testing It Out

The ListTest module includes a simple test procedure that exercises the methods in the List class. When you run this procedure, shown in Listing 8.12, the code will add the 10 items to the list, display the list, delete a few items (including the first and last item), and then print the list again.

Listing 8.12: Sample Code Demonstrating the Ordered Linked List

```
Sub TestLists()
    Dim liTest As List
    Set liTest = New List
    With liTest
        .Add 5
        .Add 1
        .Add 6
        .Add 4
        .Add 9
        .Add 8
        .Add 7
        .Add 10
        .Add 2
        .Add 3
        Call .DebugList
        Debug.Print "====="
        .Delete 1
        .Delete 10
        .Delete 3
        .Delete 4
        Call .DebugList
    End With
End Sub
```

Why Use a Linked List?

That's a good question, because the native VBA Collection object provides much of the same functionality as a linked list, without the effort. Internally, collections are stored as a complex linked list, with links in both directions (instead of only one). The data structure also includes pointers that make it possible to traverse the collection as though it were a binary tree. This way, VBA can traverse the collection forward and backward, and it can find items quickly. (Binary trees provide very quick random access to elements in the data structure.)

It's just this flexibility that makes the overhead involved in using VBA's collections onerous. You may find that you need to create a sorted list, but working with collections is just too slow, and maintaining collections in a sorted order is quite difficult. In these cases, you may find it more worthwhile to use a linked list, as demonstrated in the preceding example, instead.

Creating Binary Trees

A simple binary tree, as shown earlier in Figure 8.2, is the most complex data structure discussed in this chapter. This type of binary tree is made up of nodes that contain a piece of information and pointers to left and right child nodes. In many cases, you'll use binary trees to store data in a sorted manner: As you add a value, you'll look at each existing node. If the new value is smaller than the existing value, look in the left child tree; if it's greater, look in the right child tree. Because the process at this point is the same no matter which node you're currently at, many programmers use recursive algorithms to work with binary trees.

Why use a binary tree? Besides the fact that finding items in a binary tree is faster than performing a linear search through a list or an array, if you insert the items in an ordered fashion, you not only get efficient storage, but you also get sorting for free—it's like finding a prize in the bottom of your cereal box! Who could ask for more?

Traversing Binary Trees

Once you've created a binary tree, you can use one of three standard methods for traversing the tree. All three of the following examples use the tree illustrated in Figure 8.32. In that figure, the nodes contain letters, but their ordering here doesn't mean anything. They're just labeled to make it easy to refer to them.

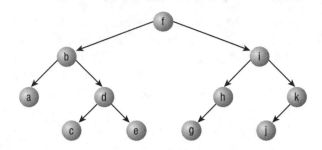

Inorder Traversal

To traverse a tree using inorder traversal, you visit each node; but, as you visit each node, you must first visit the left subtree, then the root node, and then the right subtree, in that order. When visiting the subtrees, you take the same steps. If you listed the value each time you visited a root node in the tree shown in Figure 8.32, you'd list the nodes in the following order:

```
a b c d e f g h i j k
```

Preorder Traversal

Using preorder traversal, you first visit the root node, then the left subtree, and then the right subtree. Using this method, you'll always print out the root value and then the values of the left and right children. Using the example shown in Figure 8.32, you'd print the nodes in this order:

```
f b a d c e i h g k j
```

Postorder Traversal

Using postorder traversal, you visit the left subtree; then the right subtree; and, finally, the root node. Using the example shown in Figure 8.32, you'd visit the nodes in this order:

```
a c e d b g h j k i f
```

What's This Good For?

Binary trees have many analogs in the real world. For example, a binary tree can represent a pedigree tree for a purebred cat. Each node represents a cat, with the left and right links to the cat's two parents. If a parent is unknown, the link will point to Nothing. The diagram in Figure 8.33 shows a parentage tree for a hypothetical purebred cat.

FIGURE 8.33
A binary tree can represent parentage (two parents per node)

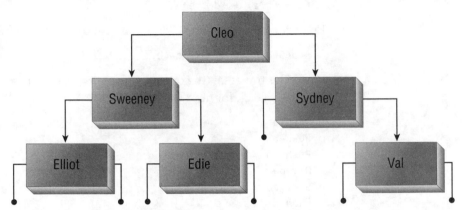

A binary tree can also represent an algebraic expression. If you place algebraic identifiers (constants and variables) in terminal nodes and operators in the interior nodes, you can represent any algebraic expression in a tree. This makes it possible to write expression evaluators: By parsing the expression, placing the various expressions correctly in the tree, and then traversing the tree in the correct order, you can write a simple expression evaluator. The diagram in Figure 8.34 shows how you might represent a simple algebraic expression in a binary tree.

FIGURE 8.34
A binary tree can represent an algebraic expression.

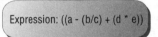

Expression: ((a - (b/c) + (d * e))

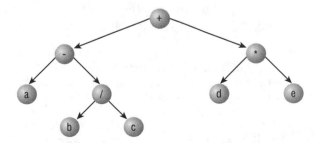

Depending on how you traverse the tree, you could visit the nodes in any of the following manners:

- Inorder traversal:

  (a - (b/c) + (d * e))

- Preorder traversal (the order that might be used by a functional calculator):

  Add(Subtract(a, Divide(b, c)), Multiply(d, e))

- Postorder traversal (the order used by "reverse Polish" notation calculators that use a stack for their calculations):

  ```
  Push a
  Push b
  Push c
  Divide
  Subtract
  Push d
  Push e
  Multiply
  Add
  ```

Implementing a Binary Tree

The following sections discuss in some detail how the code that implements the binary Tree class operates. You'll find the code for this section in Tree.cls, TreeItem.cls, and TreeTest.bas.

The TreeItem Class

As with the structure items in the previous sections, the TreeItem class is simple. It includes just the three necessary data items: the value to be stored at the current node, the pointer to the left child node, and the pointer to the right child node, as shown here:

```
Public Value As Variant
Public LeftChild As TreeItem
Public RightChild As TreeItem
```

Of course, there's nothing stopping you from storing more information in the TreeItem class. For example, you may need to write a program that can parse a text file, create a binary tree containing all the distinct words in the file, and store each word in its own node, along with a list of all the page numbers on which that word occurred. In this case, you might want to store a pointer to a linked list in the TreeItem class, along with the text item. That linked list could store the list of all the page numbers on which the word was found. (See what fun you can have with complex data structures. Just have a few cups of strong coffee first!)

The Tree Class

As with the previous data structures, the base Tree class stores the bulk of the code required to make the data structure work. The class contains but a single data item:

```
Private tiHead As TreeItem
```

As with the other data structures, tiHead is an anchor for the entire data structure. It points to the first item in the binary tree. From there, the items point to other items.

In addition, the Tree class module contains two module-level variables:

```
' These private variables are used when
' adding new nodes.
Private mblnAddDupes As Boolean
Private mvarItemToAdd As Variant
```

The method that adds items to the binary tree uses these module-level variables. If they weren't module-level, the code would have to pass them as parameters to the appropriate methods. What's wrong with that? Because the Add method is recursive, the procedure might call itself many times. Each call takes up memory that isn't released until the entire procedure has completed. If your tree is very deep, you could eat up a large chunk of stack space adding a new item. To avoid that issue, the Tree class doesn't pass these values as parameters; it just makes them available to all the procedures in the Tree class, no matter where they're called.

Adding a New Item

When adding items to a binary tree, you may or may not want to add an item if its value already appears in the data structure. To make it easy to distinguish between those two cases, the Tree class contains two separate methods: Add and AddUnique, shown in Listing 8.13. Each of the methods ends up calling the AddNode procedure, shown in Listing 8.14.

Listing 8.13: The Tree Class Provides Two Ways to Add New Items

```
Public Sub Add(varNewItem As Variant)
    ' Add a new node, allowing duplicates.
    ' Use module variables to place as little as
    ' possible on the stack in recursive procedure calls.
    mblnAddDupes = True
    mvarItemToAdd = varNewItem
    Call AddNode(tiHead)
End Sub

Public Sub AddUnique(varNewItem As Variant)
    ' Add a new node, skipping duplicate values.
    ' Use module variables to place as little as
    ' possible on the stack in recursive procedure calls.
    mblnAddDupes = False
    mvarItemToAdd = varNewItem
    Call AddNode(tiHead)
End Sub
```

The recursive AddNode procedure adds a new node to the binary tree pointed to by the TreeItem pointer it receives as a parameter. Once you get past the recursive nature of the procedure, the code is reasonably easy to understand:

- If the TreeItem pointer, ti, is Nothing, it sets the pointer to a new TreeItem and places the value into that new node:

  ```
  If ti Is Nothing Then
      Set ti = New TreeItem
      ti.Value = mvarItemToAdd
  ```

- If the pointer isn't Nothing, then:

  - If the new value is less than the value in ti, the code calls AddNode with the left child pointer of the current node:

    ```
    If mvarItemToAdd < ti.Value Then
        Set ti.LeftChild = AddNode(ti.LeftChild)
    ```

  - If the new value is greater than the value in ti, the code calls AddNode with the right child pointer of the current node:

    ```
    ElseIf mvarItemToAdd > ti.Value Then
        Set ti.RightChild = AddNode(ti.RightChild)
    ```

- If the new value is equal to the current value, then, if you've instructed the code to add duplicates, the code arbitrarily calls AddNode with the right child pointer. (You could use the left instead, if you wanted.) If you don't want to add duplicates, the procedure just returns.

```
Else
    ' You're adding a node that already exists.
    ' You could add it to the left or to the right,
    ' but this code arbitrarily adds it to the right.
    If mblnAddDupes Then
        Set ti.RightChild = AddNode(ti.RightChild)
    End If
End If
```

- Sooner or later, after calling AddNode for each successive child node, the code will find a pointer that is Nothing, at which point it takes the action in the first step. Because nothing follows the recursive call to AddNode in the procedure, after each successive layer has finished processing, the code just works its way back up the list of calls.

Listing 8.14: The Recursive AddNode Procedure Adds a New Node to the Tree

```
Private Function AddNode(ti As TreeItem) As TreeItem
    ' Add a node to the tree pointed to by ti.
    ' Module variables used:
    '     mvarItemToAdd: the value to add to the tree.
    '     mblnAddDupes: Boolean indicating whether to add items
    '         that already exist or to skip them.
    If ti Is Nothing Then
        Set ti = New TreeItem
        ti.Value = mvarItemToAdd
    Else
        If mvarItemToAdd < ti.Value Then
            Set ti.LeftChild = AddNode(ti.LeftChild)
        ElseIf mvarItemToAdd > ti.Value Then
            Set ti.RightChild = AddNode(ti.RightChild)
        Else
            ' You're adding a node that already exists.
            ' You could add it to the left or to the right,
            ' but this code arbitrarily adds it to the right.
```

```
            If mblnAddDupes Then
                Set ti.RightChild = AddNode(ti.RightChild)
            End If
        End If
    End If
    Set AddNode = ti
End Function
```

Adding a New Node: Walking the Code

Suppose you were to try adding a new node to the tree shown in Figure 8.35 with the value "m". Table 8.2 outlines the process involved in getting the node added. (This discussion assumes that the class module's tiHead member points to the tree shown in Figure 8.35.) For each step, the table includes, in column 1, the recursion level—that is, the number of times the procedure has called itself.

FIGURE 8.35
Revisiting the alphabetic tree, attempting to add a new node

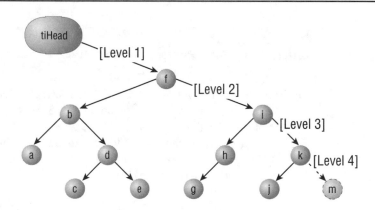

TABLE 8.2: Recursive Steps to Add "m" to the Sample Tree

Level	Action
0	You call the Add method, passing the value "m".
0	The Add method sets mblnAddDupes to True and sets varNewItem to the value "m". It then calls the AddNode method, passing the pointer to the first item in the tree (a node with the value "f", in this case). [Call to Level 1]

TABLE 8.2: Recursive Steps to Add "m" to the Sample Tree *(continued)*

Level	Action
1	AddNode checks to see whether ti is Nothing. It's not. (It points to the node containing "f".)
1	Because "m" is greater then "f", AddNode calls itself, passing the right child pointer of the node ti currently points to. (That is, it passes a pointer to the node containing "i".) [Call to Level 2]
2	AddNode checks to see whether ti is Nothing. It's not. (It points to the node containing "i".)
2	Because "m" is greater then "i", AddNode calls itself, passing the right child pointer of the node ti currently points to. (That is, it passes a pointer to the node containing "k".) [Call to Level 3]
3	AddNode checks to see whether ti is Nothing. It's not. (It points to the node containing "k".)
3	Because "m" is greater then "k", AddNode calls itself, passing the right child pointer of the node ti currently points to (that is, the right child pointer of the node containing "k", which is Nothing). [Call to Level 4]
4	AddNode checks to see whether ti is Nothing. It is, so it creates a new node, sets the pointer passed to it (the right child of the node containing "k") to point to the new node, and returns.
4	There's nothing else to do, so the code returns. [Return to Level 3]
3	There's nothing else to do, so the code returns. [Return to Level 2]
2	There's nothing else to do, so the code returns. [Return to Level 1]
1	The code returns back to the original caller.

Traversing the Tree

As mentioned earlier in this discussion, there are three standard methods for traversing a tree: inorder, preorder, and postorder. Because of the recursive nature of these actions, the code for each is simple; it is shown in Listing 8.15. The class provides three Public methods (WalkInOrder, WalkPreOrder, WalkPostOrder). Each of these calls a Private procedure, passing a pointer to the head of the tree as the only argument. From then on, each of the Private procedures follows the prescribed order in visiting nodes in the tree.

Of course, in your own applications, you'll want to do something with each node besides print its value to the Immediate window. In that case, modify the three Private procedures to do what you need done with each node of your tree.

Listing 8.15: Because of Recursion, the Code to Traverse the Tree Is Simple

```
Public Sub WalkInOrder()
    Call InOrder(tiHead)
End Sub

Public Sub WalkPreOrder()
    Call PreOrder(tiHead)
End Sub

Public Sub WalkPostOrder()
    Call PostOrder(tiHead)
End Sub

Private Sub InOrder(ti As TreeItem)
    If Not ti Is Nothing Then
        Call InOrder(ti.LeftChild)
        Debug.Print ti.Value; " ";
        Call InOrder(ti.RightChild)
    End If
End Sub

Private Sub PreOrder(ti As TreeItem)
    If Not ti Is Nothing Then
        Debug.Print ti.Value; " ";
        Call PreOrder(ti.LeftChild)
        Call PreOrder(ti.RightChild)
    End If
End Sub

Private Sub PostOrder(ti As TreeItem)
    If Not ti Is Nothing Then
        Call PostOrder(ti.LeftChild)
        Call PostOrder(ti.RightChild)
        Debug.Print ti.Value; " ";
    End If
End Sub
```

Traversing a Tree: Walking the Code

In order to understand tree traversal, assume you'd like to perform a postorder traversal of the tree shown in Figure 8.36. Although this example doesn't include many nodes, the steps are the same no matter the size of the tree.

FIGURE 8.36
Use this small example for the tree traversal example

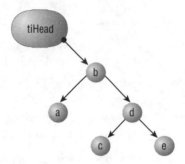

To visit each node in the tree using the postorder traversal, follow the steps listed in Table 8.3. (You'll want to keep a firm finger on the diagram as you work your way through these steps.)

TABLE 8.3: Recursive Steps to Perform a Postorder Traversal

Level	Action
0	Call the WalkPostOrder method of the Tree class.
1	The code in WalkPostOrder calls the PostOrder procedure, passing tiHead as a parameter. [Call to Level 2]
2	PostOrder checks to see whether ti (its parameter) is Nothing. It's not (it's a reference to the node that contains "b"), so it can continue.
2	PostOrder calls itself, passing the left child pointer of the node ti points to. (That is, it passes a pointer to the node containing "a".) [Call to Level 3]
3	PostOrder checks to see whether ti (its parameter) is Nothing. It's not (it's a reference to the node that contains "a"), so it can continue.
3	PostOrder calls itself, passing the left child pointer of the node ti points to. (That is, it passes a pointer that is Nothing.) [Call to Level 4]
4	PostOrder checks to see whether ti (its parameter) is Nothing. It is, so it can't do anything and just returns. [Return to Level 3]
3	PostOrder calls itself, passing the right child pointer of the node ti points to. (That is, it passes a pointer that is Nothing.) [Call to Level 4]

TABLE 8.3: Recursive Steps to Perform a Postorder Traversal *(continued)*

Level	Action
4	PostOrder checks to see whether ti (its parameter) is Nothing. It is, so it can't do anything and just returns. [Return to Level 3]
3	PostOrder prints its value ("a") and then returns. [Return to Level 2]
2	PostOrder calls itself, passing the right child pointer of the node ti points to. (That is, it passes a pointer to the node containing "d".) [Call to Level 3]
3	PostOrder checks to see whether ti (its parameter) is Nothing. It's not (it's a reference to the node that contains "d"), so it can continue.
3	PostOrder calls itself, passing the left child pointer of the node ti points to. (That is, it passes a pointer to the node containing "c".) [Call to Level 4]
4	PostOrder checks to see whether ti (its parameter) is Nothing. It's not (it's a reference to the node that contains "c"), so it can continue.
4	PostOrder calls itself, passing the left child pointer of the node ti points to. (That is, it passes a pointer that's Nothing.) [Call to Level 5]
5	PostOrder checks to see whether ti (its parameter) is Nothing. It is, so it can't do anything and just returns. [Return to Level 4]
4	PostOrder calls itself, passing the right child pointer of the node ti points to. (That is, it passes a pointer that's Nothing.) [Call to Level 5]
5	PostOrder checks to see whether ti (its parameter) is Nothing. It is, so it can't do anything and just returns. [Return to Level 4]
4	PostOrder prints its value ("c") and then returns. [Return to Level 3]
3	PostOrder calls itself, passing the right child pointer of the node ti points to. (That is, it passes a pointer to the node containing "e".) [Call to Level 4]
4	PostOrder checks to see whether ti (its parameter) is Nothing. It's not (it's a reference to the node that contains "e"), so it can continue.
4	PostOrder calls itself, passing the left child pointer of the node ti points to. (That is, it passes a pointer that's Nothing.) [Call to Level 5]
5	PostOrder checks to see whether ti (its parameter) is Nothing. It is, so it can't do anything and just returns. [Return to Level 4]
4	PostOrder calls itself, passing the right child pointer of the node ti points to. (That is, it passes a pointer that's Nothing.) [Call to Level 5]
5	PostOrder checks to see whether ti (its parameter) is Nothing. It is, so it can't do anything and just returns. [Return to Level 4]

TABLE 8.3:   Recursive Steps to Perform a Postorder Traversal *(continued)*

Level	Action
4	PostOrder prints its value ("e") and then returns. [Return to Level 3]
3	PostOrder prints its value ("d") and then returns. [Return to Level 2]
2	PostOrder prints its value ("b") and then returns to WalkPostOrder. [Return to Level 1, and exit]

Optimizing the Traversals

If you worked your way through the many steps it took to traverse the simple tree, you can imagine how much work it takes to perform the operation on a large tree. You could optimize the code a bit by checking to see whether the child node is Nothing before you recursively call the procedure. That is, you could modify InOrder like this:

```
Private Sub InOrder(ti As TreeItem)
    If Not ti Is Nothing Then
        If Not ti.LeftChild Is Nothing Then
            Call InOrder(ti.LeftChild)
        End If
        Debug.Print ti.Value; " ";
        If Not ti.RightChild Is Nothing Then
            Call InOrder(ti.RightChild)
        End If
    End If
End Sub
```

This code would execute a tiny bit faster than the original InOrder tree-traversal procedure (one less procedure call for both children of all the bottom-level nodes), but it's a little harder to read.

The Sample Project

The code in the sample module performs some simple tree manipulations: It adds nodes, walks the tree in all the traversal orders, and deletes some nodes using the TreeDelete method (not covered in this book, but the code is there in the Tree class for you to use). Try the TestTrees procedure in the TreeTest module to see how you might use a binary tree in your applications. The first few tests correspond to the tree shown in Figure 8.32 earlier in this chapter, and you can use the code in the project to test your understanding of the different traversal orders.

What Didn't We Cover?

We actually omitted more about binary trees than we covered here. Binary trees usually fill multiple chapters in textbooks for courses in standard data structures. Consider the following:

- Deleting nodes from binary trees is a science unto itself. The sample project includes code to delete nodes from a tree, but it's just one of many solutions, and possibly not the most efficient one.

- Balancing trees is crucial if you want optimized performance. For example, if you add previously sorted data to a tree, you end up with a degenerate tree—all the nodes are linked as the right child of the parent. In other words, you end up with a linked list. Searching through linked lists isn't particularly efficient, and you lose the benefit of using a binary tree. Courses in data structures normally cover various methods you can use to keep your trees balanced (that is, with the left and right subtrees having approximately the same depth).

- In a course on data structures, you'll normally find a number of variants on binary trees (B-trees, for example) that also take into account data stored on disk.

If you're interested in finding out more about these variants on binary trees, find a good textbook that focuses on data structures. Of course, most such textbooks are written for Pascal programmers (most universities use Pascal as a teaching language), so you'll need to do some conversion. However, it's not hard once you've got the hang of it.

Summary

In this chapter, we've taken a stab at revisiting Computer Science 201: Data Structures or a similar university course you might have taken once. Of course, in this limited space, we can do little more than provide a "proof of concept"—the technique of using self-referential, abstract data structures in VBA works, and it works well. Because of the availability of class modules, you can use the techniques provided here to create hybrid data structures that you just couldn't manage with VBA's arrays and collections. Linked lists of binary trees, collections of linked lists, linked lists of linked lists—all these, and more, are possible, but we suggest drawing pictures on paper first!

Note that all the ideas presented in this chapter rely on data in memory. That is, there's no concept of persistent storage when working with these data structures. If you want to store information contained in one of these abstract structures from one session to the next, you'll need to design some storage mechanism, whether it be in the Registry, an INI file, or a database table. In addition, if you run out of memory, you'll receive a run-time error when you attempt to use the New keyword. Obviously, this shouldn't happen. In production code, you'd want to add error handling to make sure your application didn't die under low-memory conditions.

This chapter presented a number of topics to keep in mind when working with data in memory, including:

- Using class modules to represent elements of linked data structures

- Building stacks, queues, ordered linked lists, and binary trees using class modules

- Using recursion to work with and traverse binary trees

chapter 9

Retrieving and Setting System Information

- Using the API to gather system information

- Controlling Windows accessibility functions

- Setting and retrieving keyboard, mouse, and screen information

- Investigating power management and status information

- Working with system colors

- Retrieving operating system and computer information

If you want to write professional applications, you'll need to be able to maintain some level of control over your users' environments. You may want to temporarily turn off the mouse cursor or modify the Windows accessibility features. You may need to position one window at a particular location within another, requiring you to know the width of the window border. Or, in an attempt to position a window, you may need to know exactly how tall the caption bar is or how wide the vertical scrollbar is. Perhaps you want to control the state of the CapsLock or NumLock key. Perhaps you need to allow users to modify their system colors from within your application.

The goal of this chapter is to provide you with simple, easily callable classes with appropriate properties and methods, which wrap up much of the Windows API functionality dealing with system information. In particular, you'll find classes that supply functionality pertaining to the mouse, keyboard, accessibility functions, system memory, power status, window metrics, border metrics, system colors, and computer and operating system information. Once you've imported the relevant classes into your own applications, you'll be able to determine, and often set, many system parameters that control the way Windows and your applications function. (For more information on writing and using class modules, see Chapter 5.)

Of course, no chapter like this could be considered absolutely complete—no matter how much information you find here, there's always something we had to leave out. You can obtain much more information by digging into the dark corners of the Windows API. There's plenty here to get you started, however, and the techniques we've used to wrap the API functionality should give you ideas for extending the tools provided here, should the need arise.

TIP If you find this information interesting or would like to extend the classes provided here, there's one tool you must have: Microsoft's MSDN CD subscription. This quarterly CD provided almost all the information we used to create the tools in this chapter and is well worth the small expense. This information is also available online at `http://msdn.microsoft.com` under the Platform SDK section. Contact Microsoft for more information about ordering this extremely useful tool, with one caveat: The CD is geared toward C/C++ programmers, and to make the best use of it, you'll need some way to convert the information into a format you can use. Your best bet is to combine the information on the MSDN CD with Daniel Appleman's formidable best-seller, *Visual Basic Programmer's Guide to the Win32 API* (published by SAMS). This book provides VBA-centric coverage of most of the Win32 API. Combined with the MSDN CD, you'll have all the information you need.

Table 9.1 lists the sample files you'll find on the CD-ROM that accompanies this book.

TABLE 9.1: Sample Files

Filename	Description
SYSTEMINFO.XLS	Excel 2000 workbook containing all the sample classes
SYSTEMINFO.MDB	Access 2000 databases containing all the sample classes
SYSTEMINFO.VBP	VB project containing all the sample classes
SYSINFOTEST.BAS	Test procedures
ACCESSIBILITY.CLS	Accessibility class module
FONT.CLS	Font information for the NonClientMetrics class
KEYBOARD.CLS	Keyboard class module
MEMORYSTATUS.CLS	Memory status class module
MOUSE.CLS	Mouse class module
NONCLIENTMETRICS.CLS	Non-client metrics class module
POWERSTATUS.CLS	Power status class module
SCREENINFO.CLS	ScreenInfo class module
SYSTEMCOLORS.CLS	System colors class module
SYSTEMINFO.CLS	Operating system and computer class module

NOTE   The figures in this chapter may look slightly different from what you see on your own screen. Because the various Control Panel applets are different in each of the four operating systems we must cover in this book, we can't print all the various dialog boxes for all the operating systems. What you see here should, however, be easy to equate to what you see on your own computer.

VBA and System Information

VBA provides almost no native support for operations involving system information; because Windows itself provides easy-to-call API functions for determining and controlling the environment, VBA doesn't have to duplicate that functionality.

Of course, some of the API functions are tricky to call, and information you need is scattered throughout the Windows API. In addition, the Windows API provides so many functions for working with system information, and their functionalities overlap so much, that it's difficult to know which one to use in any given circumstance.

To make it simpler to call the selected API functions, we've created a series of class modules that wrap up their functionality. Why class modules? That is, what do you gain by having this functionality wrapped up in a class as opposed to a standard module? Unlike other situations in which you use class modules, in this case you don't care about the multiple instancing. (You'll never need more than one instance of the Keyboard class in your application, for example.) What you do gain is the ability to treat disparate function calls as simple properties. For example, to retrieve information about a particular setting, you'll often use the GetSystem-Metrics API function. To change the same information, you need to use the System-ParametersInfo function. Rather than provide two separate functions for you, one to get and one to change the value, we've provided a single property, with its Let and Get Property procedures. This way, from your application, you can write simple code like this to retrieve a value, change it, and then set it back at a later time:

```
Dim lngBorderColor As Long
Dim sc As SystemColors

Set sc = New SystemColors

' Store away the original color.
lngBorderColor = sc.ActiveBorder
sc.ActiveBorder = 255
' Do work in here...
' Now reset the color and release the object.
sc.ActiveBorder = lngBorderColor
Set sc = Nothing
```

In addition, class modules provide another benefit: Because class modules trigger their Initialize event when you create a new instance of the class, the class can call an API function that initializes a data structure. Several of the system information functions require you to pass a single data structure, with many elements. For these functions, the corresponding class can call the function in its Initialize event, retrieve all the information at once, and return the various pieces of information to you as properties of the class. For more information, see the section "Creating the MemoryStatus Class" later in this chapter.

Windows Versionitis

Each new version of Windows has introduced more version-specific properties that may be valid for only one or more versions of the operating system. Some Windows 2000–specific properties may not be available under Windows 98 or Windows NT. For example, only Windows 2000 allows you to retrieve or set the new menu fade animation by passing SPI_GETMENUFADE or SPI_SETMENUFADE to the SystemParametersInfo API function, whereas support for multiple monitors works in both Windows 98 and Windows 2000.

Typically, if you attempt to set a system property that is invalid for the operating system you are running, the API call will fail with an error code, and generally nothing worse (like a GP fault, for example) will happen. However, it's a good practice to avoid making such calls in the first place.

For this reason, we have added code to the Initialize event of most of the classes in this chapter in which the class determines the operating system version. Later, in various methods and properties in the class, the code uses this information to raise a runtime error if you attempt to set an invalid property for your operating system. Each class that works this way provides a RaiseErrors property that you can set. By default, this property is set to True. If you want the classes to silently fail for calls that are invalid for the operating system, you can set this property to False. Also, because all the classes may raise errors, it is imperative that you include error-handling code in any procedure that contains calls to one of the classes in this chapter.

Each of the classes provided in this chapter is self-contained. If you're interested only in controlling the keyboard, you'll need to import only the single KEYBOARD.CLS module. If you need more information, import the classes you need. The bulk of this chapter, organized to match the class modules themselves, describes in detail each of the properties and methods of the classes. In each case, you can either dig into or skip over the details of how the class works. If you just need the functionality and don't care about the details, skip over the description of the API calls and their usage. If, on the other hand, you want to understand exactly how these classes work or want to expand their functionality, all the information you need is here.

TIP If you find yourself importing multiple classes, you may want to "factor out" the repeated API and constant declarations. Although there aren't a great many repeated declarations from module to module, there's no point adding extra heft to your applications. Once you've imported all the classes you'll need, you can copy the shared declarations to a standard module, remove the "Private" keyword, and use the new shared declarations for your API calls. Don't forget that you'll also need to move the necessary data structures and constants to a shared location.

TIP You may see references to "Windows 9x" in this chapter. Don't worry, it's not a release that you missed: We've used the expression to collectively refer to both Windows 95 and Windows 98.

The API Functions

Although you'll find well over a hundred properties and methods covered in this chapter, we actually used only a few API calls. These API calls generally fall into one of three classes of functions:

- Functions that return a single value. GetComputerName, for example, returns only the name of the current computer, and GetCaretBlinkTime simply returns the number of milliseconds between "blinks" of the text-insert caret.

- Functions that allow you to specify one of any number of parameter values and return different pieces of information depending on the "question" you asked. GetSystemMetrics and SystemParametersInfo fall into this category. These functions allow you to choose an item of interest from a documented list of items, and each returns a single piece of information based on the value you supplied.

- Functions that allow you to pass in a single data structure, which the function fills in with various pieces of information: GlobalMemoryStatus, GetSystemInfo, and GetSystemPowerStatus all fall into this category. Normally, for this type of function, the wrapper class calls the function in response to each Property Get procedure, and the property returns just the element of the structure you require.

The next few sections discuss how you use the second and third types of function (calling the first type is so simple it requires no extra explanation) and demonstrate their usage by presenting examples from this chapter's class modules.

Using the GetSystemMetrics Function

The GetSystemMetrics function can return one of 80 or so values, depending on which you request. In each case, you pass it a single constant value, and it returns the piece of information you need.

TIP

You shouldn't need to worry about specific constants and their values if you're using the classes provided in this chapter. If you're interested, however, your best reference information for GetSystemMetrics (and its partner, SystemParametersInfo) is the MSDN CD.

To find the number of mouse buttons, for example, you might use a call like this:

```
lngMouseButtons = GetSystemMetrics(SM_CMOUSEBUTTONS)
```

and to find out whether there's a mouse with a wheel installed, you could use

```
fWheelMouse = GetSystemMetrics(SM_MOUSEWHEELPRESENT)
```

Of course, you don't have to use either of these. You can retrieve both pieces of information using the Mouse class we've provided:

```
Dim oMouse As Mouse
Set oMouse = New Mouse
lngMouseButtons = oMouse.Buttons
fWheelMouse = oMouse.WheelPresent
```

NOTE

If you see references to "mouse wheels" throughout this chapter, don't go out looking for information on rodent transportation. This term refers to Microsoft's input device with two mouse buttons and a rubberized wheel between the buttons.

You'll find calls to GetSystemMetrics scattered throughout the classes provided with this chapter. When we gathered information for this chapter, it made more sense to group the classes based on the functionality of the information than on its source, so you'll find calls to GetSystemMetrics, and other general-purpose API calls, throughout the various classes.

In addition to API calls, you'll find the declarations for the functions and the constants they use. For example, you'll find this block of code in the declarations area of MOUSE.CLS:

```
Private Const SM_CXCURSOR = 13
Private Const SM_CYCURSOR = 14
Private Const SM_MOUSEPRESENT = 19
Private Const SM_SWAPBUTTON = 23
Private Const SM_CXDOUBLECLK = 36
Private Const SM_CYDOUBLECLK = 37
Private Const SM_CMOUSEBUTTONS = 43
Private Const SM_CXDRAG = 68
Private Const SM_CYDRAG = 69
Private Const SM_MOUSEWHEELPRESENT = 75
Private Declare Function GetSystemMetrics Lib "user32" _
  (ByVal nIndex As Long) As Long
```

This set of declarations declares the API function and provides the necessary constant values needed by the class. (All the constants beginning with "SM_" will be used by GetSystemMetrics.)

Using the SystemParametersInfo Function

Calling the SystemParametersInfo function is more complex than calling GetSystem-Metrics. Because SystemParametersInfo allows you to either set or retrieve information concerning your system's hardware and configuration, depending on the constant you send it, it must provide methods for both returning information and returning status (success or failure) information.

To make this possible, SystemParametersInfo requires four parameters:

- A constant representing the information to be set or retrieved, beginning with SPI_.

- A long integer, passed by value, sending information to SystemParameters-Info. Normally, this is where you place information to be used by System-ParametersInfo when it's setting values for you.

- A long integer, passed by reference. This long integer can be the address of a variable or data structure, and it's through this parameter (declared "As Any" in your VBA code) that SystemParametersInfo can send information back to your functions.

- A long integer, passed by value, which tells SystemParametersInfo how you want it to broadcast information about the changes you've asked it to make. You can have your change made only for this session, or, if you want to make the change persistent, you can tell SystemParametersInfo to write the change to the Registry. In addition, if you write the change to the Registry, you can also instruct SystemParametersInfo to inform all other running Windows applications that you've made the change.

Of course, you needn't be concerned with all this information if you're just going to use the classes as we've provided them. If you want to add to the classes or modify the existing functionality, though, you'll need to be aware of how SystemParametersInfo uses each of these parameters.

WARNING   In the sample classes, we opted for the "save and tell all" option when calling SystemParametersInfo; if you make any change, the code will write the change to the Registry and broadcast a message to all other running applications as well. If you want to change this behavior, change the value of the SPIF_TELLALL constant in each module. Set the constant to 0 to do nothing, or set it to be one or more of SPIF_UPDATEINIFILE and SPIF_SENDWININICHANGE, combined with the Or operator. The classes currently use the two constants combined.

For example, to get and set the number of screen lines to scroll when you scroll your mouse wheel (if you have a mouse wheel, of course), you can use SystemParametersInfo with its SPI_GETWHEELSCROLLLINES and SPI_SETWHEELSCROLLLINES constants. The WheelScrollLines property of the Mouse class (MOUSE.CLS) uses the Property Let and Get procedures, as shown in Listing 9.1.

In this example, the Property Let procedure is simple—it calls SystemParametersInfo, passing the SPI_SETWHEELSCROLLLINES constant, a value indicating the requested scroll lines, a 0 placeholder for the third parameter, and the SPIF_TELLALL constant indicating that the function call should save the information and update any running application. The Property Get procedure, however, is a bit more complex. In this case, you must first declare a variable to hold the returned value; call SystemParametersInfo, passing that variable as the third parameter; and return the filled-in value of the variable as the Property Get return value. (In each procedure, the mlngWindows and mlngNT module-level variables make sure that you don't attempt to run the procedure if you're on the wrong operating system. The ability to set and retrieve the mouse scroll lines is only available with

Windows 98 or Windows 2000, not Windows 95 or Windows NT, so you want to make sure to just back out of the procedure if the current operating system doesn't support the feature.)

Listing 9.1: Use SystemParametersInfo to Get and Set System Information

```
Public Property Get WheelScrollLines() As Long
    Dim lngValue As Long
    If mlngWINDOWS >= 410& Or mlngNT >= 4& Then
        Call SystemParametersInfo( _
          SPI_GETWHEELSCROLLLINES, 0, lngValue, 0)
        WheelScrollLines = lngValue
    End If
End Property

Public Property Let WheelScrollLines(Value As Long)
    ' Set to 0 to disable wheel scrolling.
    ' Set to -1 to cause a scroll to act
    ' like a click in the PageUp or PageDown regions of the
    ' scroll bar.
    If mlngWINDOWS >= 410& Or mlngNT >= 4& Then
        Call SystemParametersInfo( _
          SPI_SETWHEELSCROLLLINES, Value, 0, SPIF_TELLALL)
    End If
End Property
```

In some cases, the Property Let and Get pairings require one call to GetSystem-Metrics (to get the value) and one to SystemParametersInfo (to set the value). This is, of course, the sort of thing that makes the class module wrappers so convenient; you don't have to dig through the reference manuals to find that it requires two separate function calls to get your work done. For example, Windows allows you to control the width (and height) of the rectangle bordering the mouse position that determines whether the next click constitutes a double-click. To get this value, you call GetSystemMetrics. To set the value, however, you must call SystemParametersInfo. Listing 9.2 shows the code used by the DoubleClickX property of the Mouse class, which calls both functions.

Listing 9.2: Some Properties Require Both GetSystemMetrics and SystemParametersInfo

```
Public Property Get DoubleClickX() As Long
    ' Width, in pixels, of the rectangle enclosing the
    ' location of the first mouse click in a double-click sequence.
    ' Second click must occur within the boundaries
    ' of this rectangle.
    DoubleClickX = GetSystemMetrics(SM_CXDOUBLECLK)
End Property

Public Property Let DoubleClickX(Width As Long)
    Call SystemParametersInfo( _
      SPI_SETDOUBLECLKWIDTH, Width, 0, SPIF_TELLALL)
End Property
```

The third parameter in a call to SystemParametersInfo might also need to be a user-defined type. If it is, SystemParametersInfo will fill in the data type with the appropriate information on return. For example, the MinAnimation property of the ScreenInfo class (SCREENINFO.CLS) indicates whether Windows should display animation as it's minimizing windows. The code for the associated Property Get procedure is shown in Listing 9.3. This call to the SystemParametersInfo function requires you to send a variable of the ANIMATIONINFO data type, with its lngSize member filled in with the size of the structure. SystemParametersInfo either fills in the lngMinAnimate member of the structure with the current animation setting (in the Property Get procedure) or gets the value from this member and applies it (in the Property Let procedure). In either case, you need to use the Len function to find the length of the data structure and place that value in the lngSize member of the structure before calling SystemParametersInfo. The class modules in this chapter use this technique several times, calling SystemParametersInfo with various data types.

Listing 9.3: Use SystemParametersInfo with a User-Defined Type

```
Private Type ANIMATIONINFO
    cbSize As Long
    iMinAnimate As Long
End Type
```

```
Public Property Get MinAnimation() As Boolean
    ' Sets or returns the state of minimize animation.
    Dim ai As ANIMATIONINFO

    ai.cbSize = Len(ai)
    Call SystemParametersInfo( _
     SPI_GETANIMATION, ai.cbSize, ai, 0)
    MinAnimation = ai.iMinAnimate
End Property
```

Functions That Require Data Structures

Several API functions used in this chapter require you to send them a user-defined type, and they supply values to fill the elements of the structure. Depending on the circumstances, the wrapper class may call the function in either of two ways, in terms of information retrieval:

- It may call the function once, in the Initialize event of the class. If the information is relatively static, this makes sense. There's no point in calling the function each time you need to retrieve information from the function. (This is how the operating system version information is retrieved in all the classes in this chapter, except in the SystemInfo class, which provides individual properties to retrieve this information.)

- It may set up the function call in the Initialize event of the class but call the function each time you request information from the class. This technique is useful for situations in which the data changes rapidly; the MemoryStatus class uses this technique because memory information is so volatile.

All the API functions in this chapter that pass information in this manner provide information that's read-only. Therefore, there are no issues involved in saving information back to the API.

For example, the GetVersionEx API call requires you to supply it a data structure of type OSVERSIONINFO. (If you're running in Windows 2000, you can pass a data structure of type OSVERSIONINFOEX to get even more information. The SystemInfo class takes advantage of this new data structure. If you look carefully at the definitions of the two classes, you'll see that OSVERSIONINFOEX simply adds a few more items onto the same items already provided by the OSVERSION-INFO structure.) Listing 9.4 shows the necessary declarations, and the class Initialize event procedure, from the SystemInfo class (SYSTEMINFO.CLS). The event procedure first fills in the dwOSVersionInfoSize element of the structure with the length of the structure itself (many API calls require this step), and then it passes the structure to the GetVersionEx function. This function fills in the various members of the osvi variable, and other properties of the class use these members in order to supply their information. For example, the OSMajorVersion property, also shown in Listing 9.4, uses the dwMajorVersion member of the OSVERSION-INFO structure to do its work.

Listing 9.4: Use the GetVersionEx API Function (Code Gathered from the SystemInfo Class Module)

```
Private Type OSVERSIONINFOEX
    dwOSVersionInfoSize  As Long
    dwMajorVersion As Long
    dwMinorVersion As Long
    dwBuildNumber As Long
    dwPlatformId As Long
    szCSDVersion As String * 128
    wServicePackMajor As Integer
    wServicePackMinor As Integer
    wSuiteMask As Integer
    wProductType As Byte
    wReserved As Byte
End Type

Private Type OSVERSIONINFO
    dwOSVersionInfoSize As Long
    dwMajorVersion As Long
    dwMinorVersion As Long
    dwBuildNumber As Long
    dwPlatformId As Long
    szCSDVersion As String * 128
End Type

Private osvi As OSVERSIONINFOEX

Private Declare Function GetVersionEx Lib "kernel32" _
 Alias "GetVersionExA" _
 (lpVersionInformation As Any) As Long
```

```
Private Sub Class_Initialize()
    Dim osviTmp As OSVERSIONINFO

    ' Set the flag to true so that an error is raised
    ' if a non-applicable property is used for a particular
    ' operating system.
    RaiseErrors = True

    ' First try with OSVersionInfoEx
    osvi.dwOSVersionInfoSize = Len(osvi)
    mblnVersionInfoEx = CBool(GetVersionEx(osvi))
    If Not mblnVersionInfoEx Then
        ' If it failed, then you aren't running Win2000
        ' so try with OSVersionInfo.
        ' Changing the Size member tells the OS
        ' which UDT you want the info for.
        osvi.dwOSVersionInfoSize = Len(osviTmp)
        Call GetVersionEx(osvi)
    End If
    ' Get the other information as well
    Call GetSystemInfo(si)
End Sub

Public Property Get OSMajorVersion() As Long
    ' Retrieve the major version number of the operating system.
    ' For example, for Windows NT version 3.51, the major version
    ' number is 3; and for Windows NT version 4.0, the major version
    ' number is 4.
    OSMajorVersion = osvi.dwMajorVersion
End Property
```

Because the information retrieved by the GetVersionEx API function isn't likely to change as your application runs, there's no reason to call the function more than once during the lifetime of your class. The properties of the MemoryStatus class, however, return data that changes constantly. Therefore, it makes sense to call the GlobalMemoryStatus (or GlobalMemoryStatusEx, under Windows 2000) API function each time you access any property of the MemoryStatus class. This ensures that the property values are always up to date. The code in Listing 9.5 has been excerpted from the MemoryStatus class (MEMORYSTATUS.CLS). This listing shows the type and API declarations, as well as the Initialize event procedure of the class and one of the property procedures. The Initialize event procedure of the class fills in the dwLength member of the structure, and this information never changes. The TotalPhysical property then calls the GlobalMemoryStatus API function, passing in the structure, and returns the dwTotalPhys (ullTotalPhys under Windows 2000) member of the structure as its return value.

TIP   Although it's unusual, the code in Listing 9.5 uses the Currency data type to hold very long integers (that is, 64-bit values). Code here and throughout this chapter will use this technique. Because VBA provides no support for 64-bit integers, you must "fake it" using a Currency value. More on this later in the chapter.

Listing 9.5: Excerpts from the MemoryStatus Class Module

```
Private Type MEMORYSTATUS
    dwLength As Long
    dwMemoryLoad As Long
    dwTotalPhys As Long
    dwAvailPhys As Long
    dwTotalPageFile As Long
    dwAvailPageFile As Long
    dwTotalVirtual As Long
    dwAvailVirtual As Long
End Type
Private ms As MEMORYSTATUS

Private Type MEMORYSTATUSEX
    dwLength As Long
    dwMemoryLoad As Long
    ullTotalPhys As Currency
    ullAvailPhys As Currency
    ullTotalPageFile As Currency
    ullAvailPageFile As Currency
    ullTotalVirtual As Currency
    ullAvailVirtual As Currency
    ullAvailExtendedVirtual As Currency
End Type
Private msEx As MEMORYSTATUSEX

Private Declare Sub GlobalMemoryStatus _
 Lib "kernel32" _
 (lpBuffer As MEMORYSTATUS)
```

```vb
Private Declare Sub GlobalMemoryStatusEx _
 Lib "kernel32" _
 (lpBuffer As MEMORYSTATUSEX)

Private Sub Class_Initialize()
    Const VER_PLATFORM_WIN32_NT = 2

    ' Set the flag to true so that an error is raised
    ' if a non-applicable property is used for a particular
    ' operating system
    RaiseErrors = True

    ' First, confirm whether the OS is Win2000.
    osvi.dwOSVersionInfoSize = Len(osvi)
    If CBool(GetVersionEx(osvi)) Then
        With osvi
            mblnIsWin2000 = _
            (.dwPlatformId = VER_PLATFORM_WIN32_NT _
             And .dwMajorVersion = 5)
        End With
    End If

    ' ms and msEx are declared at the module level.
    If mblnIsWin2000 Then
        ' On Win2000, the recommended
        ' extended version of the function
        ' will be called.
        msEx.dwLength = Len(msEx)
    Else
        ' Other platforms use the original version.
        ms.dwLength = Len(ms)
    End If
End Sub

Public Property Get TotalPhysical() As Long
    ' Indicates the total number of bytes of physical memory.
    If mblnIsWin2000 Then
        Call GlobalMemoryStatusEx(msEx)
        TotalPhysical = CurrencyToLong(msEx.ullTotalPhys)
    Else
        Call GlobalMemoryStatus(ms)
        TotalPhysical = ms.dwTotalPhys
    End If
End Property
```

The remainder of the chapter provides details on each of the nine system information classes we've created. In each case, you'll find a table listing all the properties and methods of the class. If creating the class provided an unusual challenge (aside from the issues already discussed in the chapter), the sections will also include a description of the coding techniques used by the specific class.

TIP   To make it easier for you to experiment with the various classes presented in this chapter, we've created public automatically instantiated variables, one per class, in SysInfoTest.bas. Although we don't recommend defining variables this way in real applications, in this test case, you can simply open the Immediate window and start using one of the variables declared in this module. When you first use the variable, VBA will instantiate the associated object for you.

Computer and Operating System Information

The first class in this chapter provides information on and, in a few cases, allows you to set information about, your computer and the operating system. As you will see, all the classes in this chapter contain code to retrieve the operating system version, code that really belongs in the SystemInfo class (and it does). But in order to allow for portability and reduce class dependencies, only relevant sections of code from SystemInfo class were copied.

Of course, most of the properties of the SystemInfo class (SYSTEMINFO.CLS) must be read-only. Only the Beep, ComputerName, RaiseErrors, ScreenSaverActive, and ScreenSaverTimeout properties allow you to specify a value; the rest simply return information about your environment. Table 9.2 lists all the properties of the SystemInfo class.

TIP   Run the TestSystemInfo procedure, in the SysInfoTest module, to see almost all the properties of the SystemInfo object.

NOTE   Not all of these properties are available on every operating system. For the most detailed information, look at the source code available in the SystemInfo class.

TABLE 9.2: Properties of the SystemInfo Class

Property	Data Type	Description
ActiveProcessorMask	Long	Specifies a mask representing the set of processors configured into the system
AllocationGranularity	Long	Specifies the granularity with which virtual memory is allocated
Beep	Boolean	(Read/write) Turns the system warning beep on or off
BootMethod	Long	Retrieves the boot method. Possible values: 0 (normal boot), 1 (fail-safe boot), 2 (fail-safe boot with network)
ComputerName	String	(Read/write) Sets or retrieves the name of the computer
IsDBCS	Boolean	Returns True if the operating system is working with DBCS characters
IsIMMEnabled	Boolean	Returns True if the operating system is ready to use a Unicode-based Input Method Manager/Input Method Editor (IME) on a Unicode application
IsRemoteSession	Boolean	Returns True if the calling application is associated with a Terminal Services client session
IsSuiteInstalled	Boolean	Returns True if a specific product suite (BackOffice components, Windows 2000 Datacenter or Advanced Servers, Small Business Server, or Terminal Services) is available on the system
IsWin2000	Boolean	Returns True if the operating system is Windows 2000
IsWin95	Boolean	Returns True if the operating system is Windows 95
IsWin98	Boolean	Returns True if the operating system is Windows 98
IsWinNT	Boolean	Returns True if the operating system is Windows NT
MaxAppAddress	Long	Pointer to the highest memory address accessible to applications and Dynamic Link Libraries (DLLs)
MidEastEnabled	Boolean	Returns True if the system is enabled for Hebrew/Arabic languages
MinAppAddress	Long	Pointer to the lowest memory address accessible to applications and DLLs
NetworkPresent	Boolean	Returns True if a network is present

TABLE 9.2:   Properties of the SystemInfo Class *(continued)*

Property	Data Type	Description
NumberOfProcessors	Long	Specifies the number of processors in the system
OSBuild	Long	Retrieves the build number of the operating system
OSExtraInfo	String	Retrieves extra operating system information, like "Service Pack 3"
OSMajorVersion	Long	Retrieves the major version number of the operating system. For example, for Windows NT version 3.51, the major version number is 3; for Windows NT version 4.0, the major version number is 4.
OSMinorVersion	Long	Retrieves the minor version number of the operating system. For example, for Windows NT version 3.51, the minor version number is 51; for Windows NT version 4.0, the minor version number is 0.
OSVersion	String	Retrieves a string containing most of the relevant operating system version information. For example, for a machine with Windows 2000 Professional installed, the string returned can be "Microsoft Windows 2000 Professional version 5.0 (Build 2128)."
PageSize	Long	Specifies the page size and the granularity of page protection and commitment
ProcessorArchitecture	Integer	Specifies the system's processor architecture
ProcessorLevel	Integer	Windows 95: not used. Windows NT: specifies the system's architecture-dependent processor level
ProcessorRevision	Integer	Windows 95: not used. Windows NT: specifies an architecture-dependent processor revision
ProcessorType	Long	Windows 95: specifies the type of processor in the system. WindowsNT: uses ProcessorArchitecture, ProcessorLevel, and ProcessorRevision values
ProductType	String	Returns additional information about the operating system. For example, for Windows 2000 Professional, the ProductType is "Professional," and for Windows 2000 Server, the ProductType is "Server."
RaiseErrors	Boolean	(Read/write) Indicates whether the class should raise a runtime error if you attempt to call a property that is not valid for the current operating system. The default value is True.

TABLE 9.2: Properties of the SystemInfo Class *(continued)*

Property	Data Type	Description
ScreenSaverActive	Boolean	(Read/write) Sets or retrieves the state of the screen saver
ScreenSaverRunning	Boolean	Returns True if a screen saver is currently active on the desktop
ScreenSaverTimeout	Long	(Read/write) Sets or retrieves the screen saver timeout value in seconds
Secure	Boolean	Returns True if security is present
ServicePackMajorVersion	Integer	Returns the major version number of the latest Service Pack installed on the system
ServicePackMinorVersion	Integer	Returns the minor version number of the latest Service Pack installed on the system
ShowSounds	Boolean	Returns True if the user requires an application to present information visually in situations where it would otherwise present the information only in audible form
SlowMachine	Boolean	Returns True if the computer has a low-end processor (definition of low-end is somewhat unclear)
SpecialFolderLocation	String	Location of one of the many special Windows folders. See Table 9.7 for more information.
SystemDirectory	String	Retrieves the system directory. The value does not end with a trailing backslash (\).
TempPath	String	Retrieves the temporary path. The GetTempPath function gets the temporary file path from one of the following locations: the path specified by the TMP environment variable; the path specified by the TEMP environment variable, if TMP is not defined; the current directory, if both TMP and TEMP are not defined. Path always ends with a backslash (\).
UserName	String	Retrieves the name of the logged-in user
WIN32_IE	Long	Returns a specific long value that's dependent on the installed version of Internet Explorer. Possible values: 3 (IE 3.0); 4 (IE 4.0, 4.01, 4.01 Service Pack 1, 4.02 Service Pack 2); 5 (Internet Explorer 5)

TABLE 9.2:   Properties of the SystemInfo Class *(continued)*

Property	Data Type	Description
WIN32_WINDOWS	Long	Return value indicates whether Windows 98 or Windows 95 is installed. Possible values: 410 (Windows 98); 4 (Windows 95)
WIN32_WINNT	Long	Return value indicates whether Windows NT or Windows 2000 is installed. Possible values: 4 (Windows NT); 5 (Windows 2000)
WindowsDirectory	String	Retrieves the Windows directory. The value does not end with a trailing backslash (\).
WindowsExtension	Boolean	(Win95 only) Indicates whether the Windows extension, Windows Plus!, is installed
WINVER	Long	Returns the major build of the operating system. Possible values: 4 (Windows 95 or Windows NT); 5 (Windows 2000 or Windows 98)

The properties of the SystemInfo class can be broken down into five basic categories, as shown in Table 9.3. The next section of this chapter provides more information on these categories

TABLE 9.3:   Categories of SystemInfo Class Properties

Category	Properties
Computer/User	ComputerName, UserName
Paths	SpecialFolderLocation, SystemDirectory, TempPath, WindowsDirectory
Processor Info	ActiveProcessorMask, AllocationGranularity, MaxAppAddress, MinAppAddress, NumberOfProcessors, PageSize, ProcessorArchitecture, ProcessorLevel, ProcessorRevision, ProcessorType
Version	IsWin2000, IsWin95, IsWin98, IsWinNT, OSBuild, OSExtraInfo, OSMajorVersion, OSMinorVersion, OSVersion, ProductType, ServicePackMajorVersion, ServicePackMinorVersion, WIN32_IE, WIN32_WINDOWS, WIN32_WINNT, WINVER
Miscellaneous	Beep, BootMethod, IsDBCS, IsIMMEnabled, IsRemoteSession, IsSuiteInstalled, MidEastEnabled, NetworkPresent, RaiseErrors, ScreenSaverActive, ScreenSaverRunning, ScreenSaverTimeout, Secure, SlowMachine, ShowSounds, WindowsExtension

Using the SystemInfo Class

This section describes each of the categories of properties in the SystemInfo class, explaining both how to use them and how they were implemented.

Computer and User Information

The two properties ComputerName and UserName provide information about the network name for the computer and the logged-in user's name. Both properties return strings, and the ComputerName property also allows you to set the name of the computer. For example, you might write code like this to use the properties:

```
Dim si As SystemInfo
Set si = New SystemInfo
Dim strOut As String
strOut = si.UserName & " is logged into " & si.ComputerName
MsgBox strOut
si.ComputerName = "CompuLand"
```

NOTE   As you'll see mentioned later, changing the ComputerName property modifies only the setting in the Registry, until you reboot. At that point, Windows loads the value from the Registry and makes it the current computer name.

Under Windows 9x, retrieving and setting these properties is simple. The Windows API provides the GetComputerName and GetUserName functions. In both cases, you pass in a buffer to contain the name and a long integer variable containing the length of the buffer. Windows fills in the buffer and places the length of the string it returned into the long integer variable. If the function returns a nonzero value, the code can use the Left function to retrieve as many characters from the buffer as Windows said it filled in.

Under Windows 2000, there are several different types of Computer and User names, all of which are listed in Tables 9.4 and 9.5. The ComputerName and UserName properties accept optional arguments and then call GetComputerNameEx (or SetComputerNameEx) and GetUserNameEx API functions respectively, which allow you to refer to one of the listed name types. (These extended user and computer names are available only if you're logged into a Windows 2000 server from a Windows 2000 workstation.)

WARNING   The UserName property will raise errors if you pass it an invalid name format because it doesn't check the server type before making the request for the name. If you don't want to see those errors, make sure you set the RaiseErrors property of the SystemInfo class to be False before using the property.

TIP   Try out the TestNames procedure in the SysInfoTest module to try out the various computer and username options. Note that most will return no value, unless you're attached to a Windows 2000 server.

TABLE 9.4:   Available Computer Name Formats for Windows 2000

Name Format	Description
ComputerNameNetBIOS	Represents the NetBIOS name of the local computer or the cluster associated with the local computer. This name type is read-only and cannot be changed by assigning a new value to ComputerName. (Doesn't require Windows 2000 server.)
ComputerNameDnsHostname	Represents the DNS name of the local computer or the cluster associated with the local computer. This name type is read-only and cannot be changed by assigning a new value to ComputerName.
ComputerNameDnsDomain	Represents the name of the DNS domain assigned to the local computer or the cluster associated with the local computer. This name type is read-only and cannot be changed by assigning a new value to ComputerName.
ComputerNameDnsFullyQualified	Represents the fully qualified DNS name that uniquely identifies the local computer or the cluster associated with the local computer. This name is a combination of the DNS host name and the DNS domain name, using the form HostName.DomainName (for example, compuland.mydomain.com). This name type is read-only and cannot be changed by assigning a new value to ComputerName.
ComputerNamePhysicalNetbios	(Default) Represents the NetBIOS name of the local computer. On a cluster, this is the NetBIOS name of the local node on the cluster. The returned name is the same as the return value of GetComputerName on Windows 9x.

TABLE 9.4: Available Computer Name Formats for Windows 2000 *(continued)*

Name Format	Description
ComputerNamePhysicalDnsHostname	Represents the DNS host name of the local computer. On a cluster, this is the DNS host name of the local node on the cluster.
ComputerNamePhysicalDnsDomain	Represents the name of the DNS domain assigned to the local computer. On a cluster, this is the DNS domain of the local node on the cluster.
ComputerNamePhysicalDnsFullyQualified	Represents the fully qualified DNS name that uniquely identifies the computer. On a cluster, this is the fully qualified DNS name of the local node on the cluster. The fully qualified DNS name is a combination of the DNS host name and the DNS domain name, using the form HostName.DomainName (for example, compuland.mydomain.com). This name type is read-only and cannot be changed by assigning a new value to ComputerName.

TABLE 9.5: Available Username Formats for Windows 2000

Name Format	Description
NameUnknown	(Default) Represents an Unknown name type. The returned name is the same as the return value of GetUserName on Windows 9x. (Doesn't require Windows 2000 server.)
	Represents a fully qualified distinguished name (for example, CN=John Smith,OU=Users,DC=Engineering,DC=Microsoft,DC=Com)
NameSamCompatible	Represents the Windows NT 4 account name (for example, Engineering\JSmith). The domain-only version includes trailing backslashes (\\). (Doesn't require Windows 2000 server.)
NameDisplay	Returns a "friendly" display name (for example, John Smith)
NameUniqueId	Returns a GUID string that represents the name
NameCanonical	Returns a complete canonical name (for example, engineering.microsoft.com/software/someone). The domain-only version includes a trailing forward slash (/).
NameUserPrincipal	Represents the User principal name (for example, someone@engineering.microsoft.com)

TABLE 9.5:   Available Username Formats for Windows 2000 *(continued)*

Name Format	Description
NameCanonicalEx	Same as NameCanonical except that the right-most forward slash (/) is replaced with a newline character (vbCrLf), even in a domain-only case (for example, engineering.microsoft.com/software\nsomeone)
NameServicePrincipal	Represents the generalized service principal name (for example, www/www.microsoft.com@microsoft.com)

Listing 9.6 shows the code for retrieving the ComputerName and UserName properties.

Listing 9.6: Code for the ComputerName and UserName Properties

```
Public Property Get ComputerName( _
 Optional NameFormat As ComputerNameFormat = cnfComputerNameNetBIOS) _
As String

    Dim strBuffer As String
    Dim lngLen As Long

    If IsWin2000 Then
        If NameFormat <> cnfComputerNameNetBIOS Then
            ' If a particular NameFormat is requested and the
            ' OS is Windows 2000, then use the Extended
            ' version of the API function.

            ' To determine the required buffer size for the
            ' particular value of NameFormat, pass vbNullString
            ' for strBuffer. When the function returns, lngLen will
            ' contain the length of the required buffer.
            Call GetComputerNameEx(NameFormat, vbNullString, lngLen)
            strBuffer = String$(lngLen + 1, vbNullChar)
            If CBool(GetComputerNameEx( _
             NameFormat, strBuffer, lngLen)) Then
                ComputerName = Left$(strBuffer, lngLen)
            End If
        Else
            ' Specified NameFormat is cnfComputerNameNetBios
            ' in which case, use GetComputerName API
            strBuffer = String$(dhcMaxComputerName + 1, vbNullChar)
```

```
                        lngLen = Len(strBuffer)
                        If CBool(GetComputerName(strBuffer, lngLen)) Then
                            ' If successful, return the buffer
                            ComputerName = Left$(strBuffer, lngLen)
                        End If
                    End If
            Else
                ' The OS is not Win2000
                ' Only cnfComputerNameNetBios is valid for NameFormat
                If NameFormat = cnfComputerNameNetBIOS Then
                    strBuffer = String$(dhcMaxComputerName + 1, vbNullChar)
                    lngLen = Len(strBuffer)
                    If CBool(GetComputerName(strBuffer, lngLen)) Then
                        ' If successful, return the buffer
                        ComputerName = Left$(strBuffer, lngLen)
                    End If
                Else
                    If RaiseErrors Then
                        Call HandleErrors(ERR_INVALID_OS)
                    End If
                End If
            End If
        End If
End Property


Public Property Get UserName( _
 Optional ExtendedFormat As ExtendedNameFormat = enfNameUnknown) _
 As String

    Dim lngLen As Long
    Dim strBuffer As String
    Dim lngRet As Long

    Const dhcMaxUserName = 255

    ' Initialize the buffer strings
    strBuffer = String$(dhcMaxUserName, vbNullChar)
    lngLen = dhcMaxUserName
    If IsWin2000 Then
        If ExtendedFormat <> enfNameUnknown Then
            ' If a particular ExtendedFormat is requested and the
```

```
                ' OS is Windows 2000, then use the Extended version
                ' of the API function.
                lngRet = GetUserNameEx(ExtendedFormat, strBuffer, lngLen)
                ' Even if lngRet and Err.LastDLLError indicate that
                ' the call to GetUserNameEx was successful,
                ' strBuffer and lngLen may not get modified, in which case
                ' strBuffer will still contain only vbNullChars. To make
                ' sure that a valid string was returned in strBuffer,
                ' check lngRet and the length of strBuffer
                ' after trimming to the first instance of vbNullChar
                If lngRet And Len(dhTrimNull(strBuffer)) > 0 Then
                    ' If successful, return the username
                    UserName = Left$(strBuffer, lngLen - 1)
                Else
                    If RaiseErrors Then
                        With Err
                            .Raise .LastDllError, _
                                "SystemInfo.UserName", APIErr(.LastDllError)
                        End With
                    End If
                End If
            Else
                ' Specified ExtendedFormat was enfNameUnknown
                ' use GetUserName instead
                If CBool(GetUserName(strBuffer, lngLen)) Then
                    UserName = Left$(strBuffer, lngLen - 1)
                End If
            End If
        Else
            ' OS is not Win2000
            ' In this case, only enfNameUnknown is valid
            If ExtendedFormat = enfNameUnknown Then
                ' use GetUserName API function
                If CBool(GetUserName(strBuffer, lngLen)) Then
                    UserName = Left$(strBuffer, lngLen - 1)
                End If
            Else
                If RaiseErrors Then
                    Call HandleErrors(ERR_INVALID_OS)
                End If
            End If
        End If
    End If
End Property
```

The code to set the computer name, although quite simple for Windows 9*x* and NT, requires special considerations for Windows 2000. Only certain NameFormats are allowed, and even those allowed enforce restrictions on the length of the new name. For example, in the case of ComputerNamePhysicalDnsHostname, if the new name is longer than the maximum allowed length of 15 characters, the API function will truncate the name. Rather than let this happen unexpectedly, the ComputerName property will raise a runtime error if you attempt to pass it a name longer than 15 characters.

```
Public Property Let ComputerName( _
  Optional NameFormat As ComputerNameFormat = cnfComputerNameNetBIOS, _
  Name As String)

    If NameFormat <> cnfComputerNameNetBIOS And IsWin2000 Then
        Select Case NameFormat
            Case cnfComputerNamePhysicalNetbios
                If Len(Name) > dhcMaxComputerName Then
                    With Err
                        .Raise ERR_INVALID_NAME, _
                        "SystemInfo.ComputerNameEx", _
                        "Name cannot exceed " & _
                        dhcMaxComputerName & " characters."
                    End With
                End If
            Case cnfComputerNamePhysicalDnsHostname
                If Len(Name) > dhcMaxComputerName Then
                    Call HandleErrors(ERR_NAME_TOO_LONG, _
                    "NetBIOS name is longer than " & _
                    dhcMaxComputerName & " characters.")
                End If
            Case cnfComputerNamePhysicalDnsDomain
                ' It's here just so that we can escape the Else clause.
            Case Else
                ' For Public Property Let, only the above three
                ' values are acceptable.
                Err.Raise 5
        End Select
        Call SetComputerNameEx(NameFormat, Name)
    Else
        ' Either the OS is not Win2000 or NameFormat
        ' is 0 or cnfComputerNameNetBIOS, so use the
        ' normal API functions
```

```
        If NameFormat = cnfComputerNameNetBIOS Then
            Call SetComputerName(Name)
        Else
            If RaiseErrors Then
                Call HandleErrors(ERR_INVALID_OS)
            End If
        End If
    End If
End Property
```

TIP   The SetComputerName API call only writes the new computer name to the Registry. It doesn't (and it really can't) change the name of the computer as it's currently used on the network. The next time you restart the computer, it will use the new name.

Path Information

The SpecialFolderLocation, SystemDirectory, TempPath, and WindowsDirectory properties retrieve information about where you can expect to find files on your computer. In each case, Windows provides a single function to call in order to retrieve the information, and in each case the code is almost identical. For example, Listing 9.7 includes the code for the WindowsDirectory property. You should be familiar with this code if you've ever done any work with the Windows API that involves strings. In the WindowsDirectory property procedure, the code first creates a buffer to hold the output string and makes sure it's large enough for the largest expected result, using the String function. Then it calls the GetWindowsDirectory API function, passing the buffer and the length of the buffer. GetWindowsDirectory attempts to place the path into the buffer and returns the length of the string it placed into the buffer. If the buffer wasn't large enough, the function returns the length it would need to place into the buffer. If the function returns a value larger than the length passed into it, the property procedure resizes the buffer and tries again. This time, the string is guaranteed to fit.

Listing 9.7: Code for the WindowsDirectory Property

```
Public Property Get WindowsDirectory() As String
    ' Retrieve the Windows directory.
    Dim strBuffer As String
    Dim lngLen As Long
```

```
        strBuffer = Space(dhcMaxPath)
        lngLen = dhcMaxPath
        lngLen = GetWindowsDirectory(strBuffer, lngLen)
        ' If the path is longer than dhcMaxPath, then
        ' lngLen contains the correct length. Resize the
        ' buffer and try again.
        If lngLen > dhcMaxPath Then
            strBuffer = Space(lngLen)
            lngLen = GetWindowsDirectory(strBuffer, lngLen)
        End If
        WindowsDirectory = Left$(strBuffer, lngLen)
    End Property
```

NOTE   The functions used in the SystemDirectory, TempPath, and WindowsDirectory properties provide a perfect example of the non-uniformity of Windows API functions. For example, GetWindowsDirectory and GetSystemDirectory accept first a string and then its length. GetTempPath takes its parameters in the opposite order. In addition, GetTempPath returns a path that always ends with a trailing backslash, yet both the others return paths without the trailing backslash.

The SpecialFolderLocation property returns the path to any one of several special folders on a user's machine. There are a number of commonly used folders that have specific purposes under Windows, each of which is marked as special. These folders include standard virtual folders, such as Network Neighborhood and My Documents, along with standard file system folders, for example, System and Program Files. For such folders, Windows provides a standard, reliable way of retrieving the names and locations (which can vary on a per machine basis) by specifying one of the several defined CSIDL values.

Each special folder has a unique identification value (called a CSIDL value) assigned to it. For example, the Program Files file system folder has a CSIDL of CSIDL_PROGRAM_FILES, and the Network Neighborhood virtual folder has a CSIDL of CSIDL_NETWORK. The SpecialFolderLocation property accepts a predefined constant value and, provided that the requested folder is valid under the current operating system, attempts to return the location of the associated special folder.

Most of the shell features are encapsulated in three core DLLs: Comctl32.dll, Shell32.dll, and Shlwapi.dll. Because each version of Internet Explorer and the operating system updates these dlls, some of these CSIDLs may not be available on your particular system. Table 9.6 lists the different DLL versions and how they were distributed, and Table 9.7 lists currently available CSIDLs. If a particular CSIDL value is affected by one of these versions, it's noted in Table 9.7.

TIP

The SHGetSpecialFolderLocation API used in the SpecialFolderLocation property, although fully functional in Windows 2000, has been superseded by the ShGetFolderLocation API function, introduced in Windows 2000. If you wish to use the newer ShGetFolderLocation API in earlier systems, you can include a redistributable DLL, ShFolder.dll, with your applications. However, because distributing controls and DLLs with a VBA application may not be completely seamless, we have opted to use the older SHGetSpecialFolderLocation API function in the SystemInfo class—that way, you needn't distribute the ShFolder.dll with your applications. If you are interested in using this newer API function, your best bet is to search the Microsoft Knowledge Base for the details.

TABLE 9.6: Version and Distribution Methods for Comctl32.dll, Shell32.dll, and Shlwapi.dll

Version	DLL	Distribution Platform
4.00	All	Windows 95/Windows NT 4
4.70	All	Internet Explorer 3.x
4.71	All	Internet Explorer 4 (see Note 1)
4.72	All	Internet Explorer 4.01 and Windows 98 (see Note 1)
5.00	Shlwapi.dll	Internet Explorer 5 (see Note 2)
5.00	Shell32.dll	Windows 2000 (see Note 2)
5.80	Comctl32.dll	Internet Explorer 5 (see Note 2)
5.81	Comctl32.dll	Windows 2000 (see Note 2)

Note 1: All systems with Internet Explorer 4 or 4.01 will have the associated version of Comctl32.dll and Shlwapi.dll (4.71 or 4.72, respectively). However, for systems prior to Windows 98, Internet Explorer 4 and 4.01 can be installed with or without the integrated shell. If they are installed with the integrated shell, the associated version of Shell32.dll will be installed. If they are installed without the integrated shell, Shell32.dll is not updated. In other words, the presence of version 4.71 or 4.72 of Comctl32.dll or Shlwapi.dll on a system does not guarantee that Shell32.dll has the same version number. All Windows 98 systems have version 4.72 of Shell32.dll.

Note 2: Version 5.80 of Comctl32.dll and version 5 of Shlwapi.dll are distributed with Internet Explorer 5. They will be found on all systems on which Internet Explorer 5 is installed, except Windows 2000. Internet Explorer 5 does not update the shell, so version 5 of Shell32.dll will not be found on Windows NT, Windows 95, or Windows 98 systems. Version 5 of Shell32.dll will be distributed with Windows 2000, along with version 5 of Shlwapi.dll and version 5.81 of Comctl32.dll.

TABLE 9.7: CSIDL Values for the SpecialFolderLocation Property (siCSIDL_VALUES Enumeration Data Type)

CSIDL Value	Version	Description
CSIDL_FLAG_CREATE	5	If a special folder does not exist, this CSIDL can be combined with one of the other CSIDLs (using the Or operator or a "+" sign) to force the folder to be created.
CSIDL_ADMINTOOLS	5	File system directory that is used to store administrative tools for an individual user. The Microsoft Management Console will save customized consoles to this directory and will roam with the user.
CSIDL_ALTSTARTUP		File system directory that corresponds to the user's nonlocalized Startup program group
CSIDL_APPDATA	4.71	File system directory that serves as a common repository for application-specific data. A typical path is C:\Documents and Settings\username\Application Data. This CSIDL is supported by the redistributable ShFolder.dll for systems that do not have the Internet Explorer 4 integrated shell installed.
CSIDL_BITBUCKET		Virtual folder containing the objects in the user's Recycle Bin
CSIDL_COMMON_ADMINTOOLS	5	File system directory containing administrative tools for all users of the computer
CSIDL_COMMON_ALTSTARTUP		File system directory that corresponds to the nonlocalized Startup program group for all users. Valid only for Windows NT systems
CSIDL_COMMON_APPDATA	5	Application data for all users. A typical path is C:\Documents and Settings\All Users\Application Data.
CSIDL_COMMON_DESKTOPDIRECTORY		File system directory that contains files and folders that appear on the desktop for all users. A typical path is C:\Documents and Settings\All Users\Desktop. Valid only for Windows NT systems

TABLE 9.7: CSIDL Values for the SpecialFolderLocation Property (siCSIDL_VALUES Enumeration Data Type) *(continued)*

CSIDL Value	Version	Description
CSIDL_COMMON_DOCUMENTS		File system directory that contains documents that are common to all users. A typical path is C:\Documents and Settings\All Users\Documents. Valid for Windows NT systems and Windows 95 and Windows 98 systems with Shfolder.dll installed
CSIDL_COMMON_FAVORITES		File system directory that serves as a common repository for all users' favorite items. Valid only for Windows NT systems
CSIDL_COMMON_PROGRAMS		File system directory that contains the directories for the common program groups that appear on the Start menu for all users. A typical path is C:\Documents and Settings\All Users\Start Menu\Programs. Valid only for Windows NT systems
CSIDL_COMMON_STARTMENU		File system directory that contains the programs and folders that appear on the Start menu for all users. A typical path is C:\Documents and Settings\All Users\Start Menu. Valid only for Windows NT systems
CSIDL_COMMON_STARTUP		File system directory that contains the programs that appear in the Startup folder for all users. A typical path is C:\Documents and Settings\All Users\Start Menu\Programs\Startup. Valid only for Windows NT systems
CSIDL_COMMON_TEMPLATES		File system directory that contains the templates that are available to all users. A typical path is C:\Documents and Settings\All Users\Templates. Valid only for Windows NT systems
CSIDL_CONTROLS		Virtual folder containing icons for the Control Panel applications
CSIDL_COOKIES		File system directory that serves as a common repository for Internet cookies. A typical path is C:\Documents and Settings\username\Cookies.
CSIDL_DESKTOP		Windows Desktop–virtual folder that is the root of the namespace

TABLE 9.7: CSIDL Values for the SpecialFolderLocation Property (siCSIDL_VALUES Enumeration Data Type) *(continued)*

CSIDL Value	Version	Description
CSIDL_DESKTOPDIRECTORY		File system directory used to physically store file objects on the desktop (not to be confused with the desktop folder itself). A typical path is C:\Documents and Settings\username\Desktop.
CSIDL_DRIVES		My Computer–virtual folder containing everything on the local computer: storage devices, printers, and Control Panel. The folder may also contain mapped network drives.
CSIDL_FAVORITES		File system directory that serves as a common repository for the user's favorite items. A typical path is C:\Documents and Settings\username\Favorites.
CSIDL_FONTS		Virtual folder containing fonts. A typical path is C:\WINNT\Fonts.
CSIDL_HISTORY		File system directory that serves as a common repository for Internet history items.
CSIDL_INTERNET		Virtual folder representing the Internet
CSIDL_INTERNET_CACHE		File system directory that serves as a common repository for temporary Internet files. A typical path is C:\Documents and Settings\username\Temporary Internet Files.
CSIDL_LOCAL_APPDATA	5	File system directory that serves as a data repository for local (non-roaming) applications. A typical path is C:\Documents and Settings\username\Local Settings\Application Data.
CSIDL_MYPICTURES	5	My Pictures folder. A typical path is C:\Documents and Settings\username\My Documents\My Pictures.
CSIDL_NETHOOD		A file system folder containing the link objects that may exist in the My Network Places virtual folder. It is not the same as CSIDL_NETWORK, which represents the network namespace root. A typical path is C:\Documents and Settings\username\NetHood.

TABLE 9.7: CSIDL Values for the SpecialFolderLocation Property (siCSIDL_VALUES Enumeration Data Type) *(continued)*

CSIDL Value	Version	Description
CSIDL_NETWORK		Network Neighborhood–virtual folder representing the root of the network namespace hierarchy.
CSIDL_PERSONAL		File system directory that serves as a common repository for documents. A typical path is C:\Documents and Settings\username\My Documents.
CSIDL_PRINTERS		Virtual folder containing installed printers
CSIDL_PRINTHOOD		File system directory that contains the link objects that may exist in the Printers virtual folder. A typical path is C:\Documents and Settings\username\PrintHood.
CSIDL_PROFILE	5	User's profile folder
CSIDL_PROGRAM_FILES	5	Program Files folder. A typical path is C:\Program Files.
CSIDL_PROGRAM_FILES_COMMON	5	A folder for components that are shared across applications. A typical path is C:\Program Files\Common. Valid only for Windows NT and Windows 2000 systems.
CSIDL_PROGRAMS		File system directory that contains the user's program groups (which are also file system directories). A typical path is C:\Documents and Settings\username\Start Menu\Programs.
CSIDL_RECENT		File system directory that contains the user's most recently used documents. A typical path is C:\Documents and Settings\username\Recent.
CSIDL_SENDTO		File system directory that contains Send To menu items. A typical path is C:\Documents and Settings\username\SendTo.
CSIDL_STARTMENU		File system directory containing Start menu items. A typical path is C:\Documents and Settings\username\Start Menu.
CSIDL_STARTUP		File system directory that corresponds to the user's Startup program group. The system starts these programs whenever any user logs onto Windows NT or starts Windows 95. A typical path is C:\Documents and Settings\username\Start Menu\Programs\Startup.

T A B L E 9 . 7 : CSIDL Values for the SpecialFolderLocation Property (siCSIDL_VALUES Enumeration Data Type) *(continued)*

CSIDL Value	Version	Description
CSIDL_SYSTEM	5	System folder. A typical path is \WINNT\SYSTEM32.
CSIDL_TEMPLATES		File system directory that serves as a common repository for document templates.
CSIDL_WINDOWS		Windows directory or SYSROOT. This corresponds to the %windir% or %SYSTEMROOT% environment variables. A typical path is C:\WINNT.

Processor Information

To retrieve processor information, the SystemInfo class uses the GetSystemInfo API function. This function fills a SYSTEM_INFO data structure with data. (See the class module for the gory details.) The Initialize event procedure of the System-Info class calls the API function, and the various properties retrieve information from the elements of the SYSTEM_INFO structure.

Although the processor information returned by the GetSystemInfo API function isn't necessary for every application, it can be useful. The next few sections provide the details necessary to interpret the information provided by these properties.

NumberOfProcessors

Specifies the number of processors in the system.

ActiveProcessorMask

Specifies a mask value representing the processors in the system. The bit or bits set in the mask indicate the active processor (bit 0 is processor 0; bit 31 is processor 31). This value will be 1 for most computers.

PageSize

Specifies the page size and the granularity of page protection and commitment. This isn't generally of much interest to VBA programmers.

AllocationGranularity

Specifies the granularity with which virtual memory is allocated. This value was hard-coded as 64K in the past; because the Windows environment expands to different hardware platforms, other values may be necessary. Again, this value isn't of much interest to VBA programmers.

MinimumApplicationAddress, MaximumApplicationAddress

Pointers to the lowest and highest memory addresses accessible to applications and Dynamic Link Libraries. Not generally needed for VBA programmers unless they're making serious use of the Windows API functions that care about these addresses.

ProcessorType

Not relevant to Windows NT, which uses the ProcessorArchitecture, Processor-Level, and ProcessorRevision properties to provide information about the processor. This property provides the only means in Windows 95 to gather such information. The value will be one of the items in the following list:

Value	Processor
386	Intel 386
486	Intel 486
586	Intel Pentium
4000	MIPS R4000 (NT only)
21064	Alpha 21064 (NT only)

ProcessorArchitecture

Specifies the system's processor architecture. For Windows 95, this value will always be 0 (Intel). Otherwise, the value can be any from the following list (from the ProcessorType enum in the SystemInfo class):

Constant	Value	Processor
PROCESSOR_ARCHITECTURE_INTEL	0	Intel
PROCESSOR_ARCHITECTURE_MIPS	1	MIPS
PROCESSOR_ARCHITECTURE_ALPHA	2	Alpha
PROCESSOR_ARCHITECTURE_PPC	3	PPC
PROCESSOR_ARCHITECTURE_UNKNOWN	-1	Unknown

ProcessorLevel

Not used in Windows 9*x*, but in Windows NT/2000 it returns the system's architecture-dependent processor level. The values can be any of the items in the first column of the following list. Use the ProcessorArchitecture value in the second column to determine the actual processor level.

Value	Processor Architecture	Description
3	0	Intel 80386
4	0	Intel 80486
5	0	Intel Pentium
6	0	Intel Pentium Pro
4	1	MIPS R4000
21064	2	Alpha 21064
21066	2	Alpha 21066
21164	2	Alpha 21164
1	3	PPC 601
3	3	PPC 603
4	3	PPC 604
6	3	PPC 603+
9	3	PPC 604+
20	3	PPC 620

ProcessorRevision

Not used in Windows 95, but in Windows NT this property specifies an architecture-dependent processor revision.

Version Information

The properties in this area mostly use the GetVersionEx API function to fill in a structure with information about the operating system. In the Initialize event procedure for the SystemInfo class, the code calls GetVersionEx, passing it OSVERSION-INFO structure for Windows 9*x* and Windows NT, or OSVERSIONINFOEX structure for Windows 2000. All the various properties need do is retrieve information from a module-level variable.

If you have ever looked at the C/Visual C++ header files that ship with Microsoft Visual Studio or Platform SDK, you might have noticed syntax similar to the lines of code in Listing 9.8.

Listing 9.8: Code from WinUser.h C++ Header File

```
#if(WINVER >= 0x0400)
#define SPI_GETSERIALKEYS          62
#define SPI_SETSERIALKEYS          63
#endif /* WINVER >= 0x0400 */
#define SPI_GETSOUNDSENTRY         64
#define SPI_SETSOUNDSENTRY         65
#if(_WIN32_WINNT >= 0x0400)
#define SPI_GETSNAPTODEFBUTTON     95
#define SPI_SETSNAPTODEFBUTTON     96
#endif /* _WIN32_WINNT >= 0x0400 */
#if (_WIN32_WINNT >= 0x0400) || (_WIN32_WINDOWS > 0x0400)
#define SPI_GETMENUSHOWDELAY       106
#define SPI_SETMENUSHOWDELAY       107
#endif
```

The #if and #endif are preprocessor directives that, when used together, control compilation of portions of source code. If the expression after #if has a nonzero value, the line group immediately following the #if directive is retained and used during the generation of the executable file. Visual C++ programmers use this technique to reuse the same code base for multiple platforms and options. VBA also allows you to specify conditional compilation in similar type by using the #Const and #If-#Else-#End If constructs.

Instead of using conditional compilation, most classes in this chapter perform runtime checks of the operating system version and raise an error (unless you specify otherwise by setting the RaiseErrors property to be False) to alert the developer that the specified option is not valid for the current operating system, as shown in Listing 9.9.

Listing 9.9: Performing Runtime Version Checks and Handling Errors

```
' code removed...
If mlngWINVER >= 5& Then
    IsSystemResumeAuto = CBool(IsSystemResumeAutomatic)
Else
    Call HandleErrors(ERR_INVALID_OS)
End If
' code removed...

Private Sub HandleErrors( _
 lngErrCode As Long, _
 Optional strErrMsg As String)
    ' Centralized error handler to raise
    ' the errors to the client
    With Err
        If RaiseErrors Then
            If Len(strErrMsg) > 0 Then
                .Raise .Number, "PowerStatus", .Description, _
                 .HelpFile, .HelpContext
            Else
                .Raise lngErrCode, "SystemInfo", ERR_STRING
            End If
        End If
    End With
End Sub
```

The local variables mlngWINVER, mblnIsWin95, mblnIsWin2000, and so on, used in other classes, are quite similar to their corresponding public properties in the SystemInfo class. For example, the WINVER property of the SystemInfo class is defined in Listing 9.10.

NOTE   We could have set up all these classes so that they required you to include both the SystemInfo class and the class you were interested in so you could use the classes in your own projects. Instead, we made sure that each class is independent. That's why you'll find some redundant code if you look at the classes as a whole. All the version-checking code in the classes besides SystemInfo is quite similar to the version-checking code you'll find in the SystemInfo class.

Listing 9.10: WINVER Property Definition from SystemInfo Class

```
Public Property Get WINVER() As Long
    ' Equivalent to SDK's WINVER environment variable

    If IsWin95 Or IsWinNT Then
        WINVER = 4&
    End If
    If IsWin98 Or IsWin2000 Then
        WINVER = 5&
    End If
End Property
```

The corresponding mlngWINVER local variable in the ScreenInfo class gets its value from code that's run in the Initialize event of the class, as shown in Listing 9.11.

Listing 9.11: Retrieving Version Information in the Initialize Event of the ScreenInfo Class

```
Private Sub Class_Initialize()
    Dim blnIsWinNT As Boolean
    Dim blnIsWin95 As Boolean
    Dim blnIsWin98 As Boolean

    Const VER_PLATFORM_WIN32_WINDOWS = 1
    Const VER_PLATFORM_WIN32_NT = 2

    ' Set the flag to true so that an error is raised
    ' if a non-applicable property is used for a particular
    ' operating system
    RaiseErrors = True

    ' First find out the version of the OS
    osvi.dwOSVersionInfoSize = Len(osvi)
    If CBool(GetVersionEx(osvi)) Then
        With osvi
            mblnIsWin2000 = _
              (.dwPlatformId = VER_PLATFORM_WIN32_NT And _
              .dwMajorVersion = 5)
            blnIsWin98 = (.dwMajorVersion > 4 And _
```

```
            (.dwPlatformId = VER_PLATFORM_WIN32_WINDOWS And _
            .dwMinorVersion > 0))

        blnIsWinNT = _
            (.dwPlatformId = VER_PLATFORM_WIN32_NT And _
            .dwMajorVersion <= 4)
        blnIsWin95 = _
            (.dwPlatformId = VER_PLATFORM_WIN32_WINDOWS And _
            .dwMinorVersion = 0)

        If blnIsWin95 Or blnIsWinNT Then
            mlngWINVER = 4&
        ElseIf blnIsWin98 Or mblnIsWin2000 Then
            mlngWINVER = 5&
        End If
    End With
End If

End Sub
```

Handling Internet Explorer

The only version property in the SystemInfo class that does not get its value from the OSVERSIONINFO structure is the WIN32_IE property, which returns a value based on the version of Internet Explorer's ShDocVW.dll file installed on the system. As you may have noticed, each new version of Internet Explorer also updates several core operating system files in an effort to introduce more features. For example, some features that were introduced in Windows 98 may also be present under Windows 95 if you've installed Internet Explorer 5. Table 9.8 lists all the released versions of Internet Explorer (at the time this book was written) and the corresponding return value of the WIN32_IE property.

TABLE 9.8: Microsoft Internet Explorer Released Versions

Version	Product	WIN32_IE
4.70.1155	Internet Explorer 3	3
4.70.1158	Internet Explorer 3 (OSR2)	3
4.70.1215	Internet Explorer 3.01	3

TABLE 9.8: Microsoft Internet Explorer Released Versions

Version	Product	WIN32_IE
4.70.1300	Internet Explorer 3.02	3
4.71.1008.3	Internet Explorer 4 PP2	4
4.71.1712.5	Internet Explorer 4	4
4.72.2106.7	Internet Explorer 4.01	4
4.72.3110.3	Internet Explorer 4.01 Service Pack 1	4
4.72.3612.1707	Internet Explorer 4.01 SP2	4
5.00.0518.5	Internet Explorer 5 Developer Preview (Beta 1)	5
5.00.0910.1308	Internet Explorer 5 Beta (Beta 2)	5
5.00.2014.213	Internet Explorer 5	5

This version information is derived from the ShDocVW.dll file, which is installed by Internet Explorer. Because the version information is stored in the file itself, the SystemInfo class uses the GetFileVersionInfo and VerQueryValue API functions, which retrieve information about disk files. If you are curious about the code, you can take a look at the GetFileVersion procedure in the SystemInfo class.

Windows Accessibility

The Win32 API includes a number of features that make it easier for persons with disabilities to use their computers. These features are extensions to the operating system, and they affect the behavior of the system, no matter which application is currently running.

To make it easy for you to work with these settings from within your applications, we've created a single class module, Accessibility (ACCESSIBILITY.CLS), that provides six groups of properties representing the six areas of functionality. Table 9.9 describes the six areas of functionality, with pointers to Tables 9.10 through 9.16, which describe each of the properties in greater detail and provide references to the figures displaying the appropriate dialog boxes. In addition, because almost all these properties are available through the Windows Control Panel, Figures 9.1 through 9.11 show how users can set the same properties directly. The figures are presented in the order in which you'll come across them as you work through the accessibility dialogs. Each figure contains labels pointing to controls on the dialog box. The text for each label indicates either the corresponding property in the Accessibility class or the figure that corresponds to the dialog box you'll see if you click the button.

NOTE   In Figure 9.11, the prefix "xx" acts as a placeholder for any one of "sk," "mk," and so on, prefixes for the various groups of properties.

NOTE   When writing this book, we were using a beta version of Windows 2000 and were unable to get the Control Panel applet concerning the high contrast settings to work at all. Therefore, we are unable to provide the appropriate figure here. You may find, in your operating system, that this feature is working. Or it may be pulled completely. We have no way of knowing. We've provided the code and its description in this chapter's samples, hoping that the feature will survive last-minute cuts in the product.

T A B L E 9 . 9 :   Win32 Accessibility Features

Feature	Description
AccessTimeout	Enables a user to specify a timeout interval after which system-wide accessibility features are automatically turned off. The AccessTimeout feature is intended for computers that are shared by several users with different preferences. Each individual can use hot keys or the Control Panel to enable preferred features. After a user leaves, the enabled features will be automatically disabled by the timeout. The accessibility features affected by the timeout are FilterKeys, MouseKeys, StickyKeys, and ToggleKeys. AccessTimeout properties in the Accessibility class are described in Table 9.10.
FilterKeys	Enables control of keyboard properties, such as the amount of time before a keystroke is accepted as input and the amount of time before a keystroke begins to repeat. FilterKeys properties in the Accessibility class are described in Table 9.11.
MouseKeys	Enables the user to control the mouse pointer using the numeric keypad. MouseKeys properties in the Accessibility class are described in Table 9.13.
StickyKeys	Enables the user to type key combinations, such as Ctrl+Alt+Del, in sequence rather than at the same time. StickyKeys properties in the Accessibility class are described in Table 9.14.

TABLE 9.9:   Win32 Accessibility Features *(continued)*

Feature	Description
SoundSentry	Displays a visual signal when a sound is generated by a Windows-based application or an MS-DOS application running in a window. SoundSentry properties in the Accessibility class are described in Table 9.15.
ToggleKeys	Provides sound feedback when the user turns on or off the CapsLock, ScrollLock, or NumLock key. ToggleKeys properties in the Accessibility class are described in Table 9.16.

TABLE 9.10:   AccessTimeOut Properties Provided by the Accessibility Class

Property	Description	Figure
atActive	If True, a timeout has been set. Unless set, the Timeout value will have no effect.	9.11
atAvailable	If True, you can set a timeout period (read-only).	N/A
atFeedback	If True, a sound effect is played when the timeout period elapses.	9.11
atTimeOutMilliseconds	The number of milliseconds of idle time before Accessibility turns off. Only 5, 10, 15, 20, 25, and 30 minutes (each value multiplied by 60,000 to convert to milliseconds) are allowed.	9.11

TABLE 9.11:   FilterKeys Properties Provided by the Accessibility Class

Property	Description	Figure
fkActive	If True, the FilterKeys features are on.	9.1
fkAvailable	If True, the FilterKeys features are available (read-only).	N/A
fkBounceMSec	Specifies the amount of time, in milliseconds, that must elapse after a key is released before the computer will accept a subsequent press of the same key. If you set fkBounceMSec, you must set fkDelayMSec to 0, or you can't set the value. They can both be 0, but they can't both be nonzero. Valid values are 500, 700, 1000, 1500, and 2000.	9.4
fkClickOn	If True, the computer makes a click sound when a key is pressed or accepted.	9.3

TABLE 9.11: FilterKeys Properties Provided by the Accessibility Class *(continued)*

Property	Description	Figure
fkDelayMSec	Specifies the length of time, in milliseconds, the user must hold down a key before it begins to repeat. If you set fkDelayMSec, you must set fkBounceMSec to 0, or you can't set the value. They can both be 0, but they can't both be nonzero. Valid values are 300, 700, 1000, 1500, and 2000.	9.5
fkHotkeyActive	If True, the user can turn the FilterKeys feature on and off by holding down the Shift key for eight seconds.	9.3
fkHotKeyConfirm	(Win95, Win98, Windows 2000 only) If True, a confirmation dialog box appears when the FilterKeys features are activated with the hot key.	9.11
fkHotKeySound	If True, the computer plays a sound when the user turns the FilterKeys feature on or off with the hot key.	9.11
fkIndicator	(Win95, Win98, Windows 2000 only) If True, visual indicator is displayed when the FilterKeys features are on.	9.3
fkRepeatMSec	Specifies the length of time, in milliseconds, between repetitions of the keystroke. Valid values are 300, 500, 700, 1000, 1500, and 2000.	9.5
fkWaitMSec	Specifies the length of time, in milliseconds, the user must hold down a key before it is accepted by the computer. The only acceptable values are 0, 300, 500, 700, 1000, 1400, and 2000. All others will be rounded to the next larger value within the range. (Values larger than 2000 are cut back to 1000, the default.)	9.5

TABLE 9.12: HighContrast Properties Provided by the Accessibility Class (No Figure Available)

Property	Description	Figure
hcAvailable	If True, the High Contrast feature is available.	N/A
hcConfirmHotKey	A confirmation dialog appears when the high contrast feature is activated by using the hot key.	N/A
hcHighContrastOn	If True, the high contrast feature is on.	N/A
hcHotKeyActive	If True, the user can turn the high contrast feature on and off by simultaneously pressing the left ALT, left SHIFT, and PRINT SCREEN keys.	N/A

TABLE 9.12: HighContrast Properties Provided by the Accessibility Class (No Figure Available) *(continued)*

Property	Description	Figure
hcHotKeyAvailable	(Read Only) If True, the hot key associated with the high contrast feature can be enabled.	N/A
hcHotKeySound	If True, a siren is played when the user turns the high contrast feature on or off by using the hot key.	N/A

TABLE 9.13: MouseKeys Properties Provided by the Accessibility Class

Property	Description	Figure
mkActive	If True, the MouseKeys feature is active.	9.9
mkAvailable	If True, the MouseKeys feature is available (read-only).	N/A
mkConfirmHotKey	(Windows 95/98, Windows 2000) If True, a confirmation dialog box appears when the MouseKeys feature is activated by using the hot key.	9.11
mkCtrlSpeed	Specifies the multiplier to apply to the mouse cursor speed when the user holds down the Ctrl key while using the arrow keys to move the cursor. Documented by Microsoft as not working in NT, but it appears to work fine in NT 4.	9.10
mkHotKeyActive	Sets or retrieves whether the user can turn the MouseKeys feature on and off using the hot key: Alt (left-hand key) + Shift (left-hand key) + NumLock	9.10
mkHotKeySound	If True, the system plays a sound when the user turns the MouseKeys feature on or off with the hot key.	9.11
mkIndicator	(Windows 95/98, Windows 2000) If True, a visual indicator is displayed when the MouseKeys feature is on.	9.10
mkLeftButtonDown	(Windows 98, Windows 2000) The left button is in the down state.	N/A
mkLeftButtonSel	(Windows 98, Windows 2000) The user has selected the left button for mouse-button actions.	N/A
mkMaxSpeed	Specifies the maximum speed the mouse cursor attains when an arrow key is held down	9.10

TABLE 9.13: MouseKeys Properties Provided by the Accessibility Class

Property	Description	Figure
mkModifiers	(Windows 95/98, Windows 2000) The CTRL key increases cursor speed by the value specified by the iCtrlSpeed member, and the SHIFT key causes the cursor to delay briefly after moving a single pixel, allowing fine positioning of the cursor.	9.10
mkMouseKeysOn	If True, the MouseKeys feature is on.	N/A
mkMouseMode	(Windows 98, Windows 2000) If True, the system is processing numeric keypad input as mouse commands.	9.10
mkReplaceNumbers	(Windows 95/98, Windows 2000) If True, the numeric keypad moves the mouse when the NUM LOCK key is on.	9.10
mkRightButtonDown	(Windows 98, Windows 2000) The left button is in the down state.	N/A
mkRightButtonSel	(Windows 98, Windows 2000) If True, the user has selected the right button for mouse-button actions.	N/A
mkTimeToMaxSpeed	Specifies the length of time, in milliseconds, it takes for the mouse cursor to reach maximum speed when an arrow key is held down. Must be a value between 1000 and 5000, in milliseconds. Acceptable values are in 500-millisecond intervals (5000, 4500, etc.). Others in the range are rounded off. Values outside the range cause the call to SystemParameters Info to fail.	9.10

TABLE 9.14: StickyKeys Properties Supplied by the Accessibility Class

Property	Description	Figure
skActive	If True, the StickyKeys feature is active.	9.1
skAudibleFeedback	If True, the system plays a sound when the user sets keys using the StickyKeys feature.	9.2
skAvailable	If True, the StickyKeys feature is available (read-only).	N/A
skConfirmHotKey	(Windows 95/98, Windows 2000) If True, a confirmation dialog appears when the StickyKeys feature is activated by using the hot key.	9.2
skHotKeyActive	If True, the user can turn the StickyKeys feature on and off by pressing the Shift key five times.	9.2

TABLE 9.14: StickyKeys Properties Supplied by the Accessibility Class *(continued)*

Property	Description	Figure
skHotKeySound	If True, the system plays a sound when the user toggles the StickyKeys feature with the hot key.	9.11
skIndicator	(Windows 95/98, Windows 2000) If True, a visual indicator is displayed when the StickyKeys feature is on.	9.2
skLeftAltLatched	(Windows 98, Windows 2000) (read-only) True if the left ALT key is latched.	N/A
skLeftAltLocked	(Windows 98, Windows 2000) (read-only) True if the left ALT key is locked.	N/A
skLeftCtlLatched	(Windows 98, Windows 2000) (read-only) True if the left CTL key is latched.	N/A
skLeftCtlLocked	(Windows 98, Windows 2000) (read-only) True if the left CTL key is locked.	N/A
skLeftShiftLatched	(Windows 98, Windows 2000) (read-only) True if the left SHIFT key is latched.	N/A
skLeftShiftLocked	(Windows 98, Windows 2000) (read-only) True if the left SHIFT key is locked.	N/A
skLeftWinLatched	(Windows 98, Windows 2000) True if the left WIN key is latched.	N/A
skLeftWinLocked	(Windows 98, Windows 2000) True if the left WIN key is locked.	N/A
skRightAltLatched	(Windows 98, Windows 2000) (read-only) True if the right ALT key is latched.	N/A
skRightAltLocked	(Windows 98, Windows 2000) (read-only) True if the right ALT key is locked.	N/A
skRightCtlLatched	(Windows 98, Windows 2000) (read-only) True if the right CTL key is latched.	N/A
skRightCtlLocked	(Windows 98, Windows 2000) (read-only) True if the right CTL key is locked.	N/A
skRightShiftLatched	(Windows 98, Windows 2000) (read-only) True if the right SHIFT key is latched.	N/A
skRightShiftLocked	(Windows 98, Windows 2000) (read-only) True if the right SHIFT key is locked.	N/A

TABLE 9.14: StickyKeys Properties Supplied by the Accessibility Class *(continued)*

Property	Description	Figure
skRightWinLatched	(Windows 98, Windows 2000) True if the right WIN key is latched.	N/A
skRightWinLocked	(Windows 98, Windows 2000) True if the right WIN key is locked.	N/A
skTriState	If True, pressing a modifier key twice in a row locks down the key until the user presses it a third time.	9.2
skTwoKeysOff	If True, releasing a modifier key that has been pressed in combination with any other key turns off the StickyKeys feature.	9.2

TABLE 9.15: SoundSentry Properties Supplied by the Accessibility Class

Property	Description	Figure
ssActive	If True, the SoundSentry feature is active.	9.7
ssAvailable	If True, the SoundSentry feature is available (read-only).	N/A
ssFSGraphicEffect	(Windows 95, Windows 98) Specifies the visual signal to present when a graphics-mode application generates a sound while running in a full-screen virtual machine. This member can be one of the following values: 3 (no visual signal); 0 (flash the entire display).	N/A
ssFSGraphicEffectColor	(Windows 95, Windows 98) Specifies the RGB value of the color to be used when displaying the visual signal shown when a full-screen, graphics-mode application generates a sound.	N/A
ssFSGraphicEffectMSec	(Windows 95, Windows 98) Specifies the duration, in milliseconds, of the visual signal that is displayed when a full-screen, graphics-mode application generates a sound.	N/A
ssFSTextEffect	(Windows 95, Windows 98) If True, a visual signal appears when a text-mode application generates a sound while running in a full-screen virtual machine. Can be one of the following values: 0 (no visual indication is used), 1 (flash characters in the corner of the screen), 2 (flash the screen border [overscan area]), 3 (flash the entire display).	9.8

TABLE 9.15:   SoundSentry Properties Supplied by the Accessibility Class *(continued)*

Property	Description	Figure
ssFSTextEffectColorBits	(Windows 95, Windows 98) Specifies the RGB value of the color to be used when displaying the visual signal shown when a full-screen, text-mode application generates a sound.	N/A
ssFSTextEffectMSec	(Windows 95, Windows 98) Specifies the duration, in milliseconds, of the visual signal that is displayed when a full-screen, text-mode application generates a sound.	N/A
ssWindowsEffect	If True, visual signal appears when a graphics-mode application generates a sound while running in a full-screen virtual machine. Can be one of the following values: 0 (no visual indication is used), 1 (flash characters in the corner of the screen), 2 (Flash the screen border [overscan area]), 3 (flash the entire display).	9.8
ssWindowsEffectMSec	(Windows 95, Windows 98) Specifies the duration, in milliseconds, of the visual signal that is displayed when a Win32-based application (or an application running in a window) generates a sound.	N/A

TABLE 9.16:   ToggleKeys Properties Supplied by the Accessibility Class

Property	Description	Figure
tkActive	If True, the ToggleKeys feature is active.	9.1
tkAvailable	If True, the ToggleKeys feature is available (read-only).	N/A
tkHotKeyActive	If True, the user can turn the ToggleKeys feature on and off by holding the NumLock key for 5 seconds.	9.6
tkHotKeyConfirm	(Windows 95/98, Windows 2000) If True, a confirmation dialog appears when the ToggleKeys feature is activated with the hot key.	9.11
tkHotKeySound	If True, the system plays a sound when the user toggles the ToggleKeys feature with the hot key.	9.11

FIGURE 9.1

Accessibility Properties
(Keyboard) dialog box

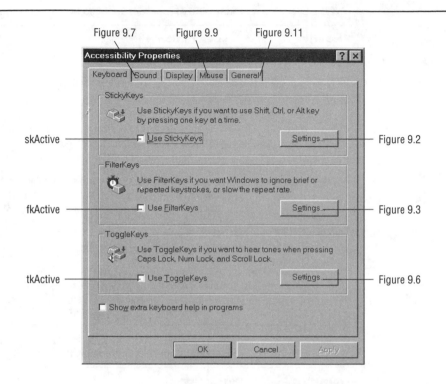

FIGURE 9.2

Settings for the StickyKeys
dialog box

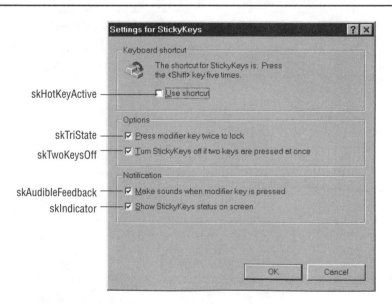

FIGURE 9.3
Settings for the FilterKeys
dialog box

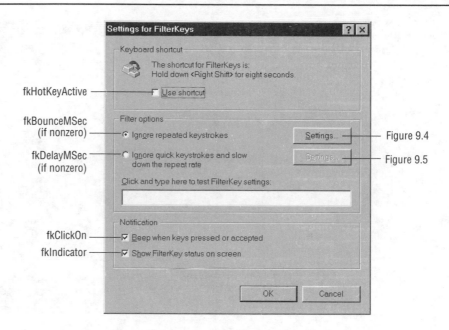

fkHotKeyActive

fkBounceMSec
(if nonzero)

fkDelayMSec
(if nonzero)

fkClickOn

fkIndicator

Figure 9.4

Figure 9.5

FIGURE 9.4
Advanced settings for the
FilterKeys (Bounce) dialog
box

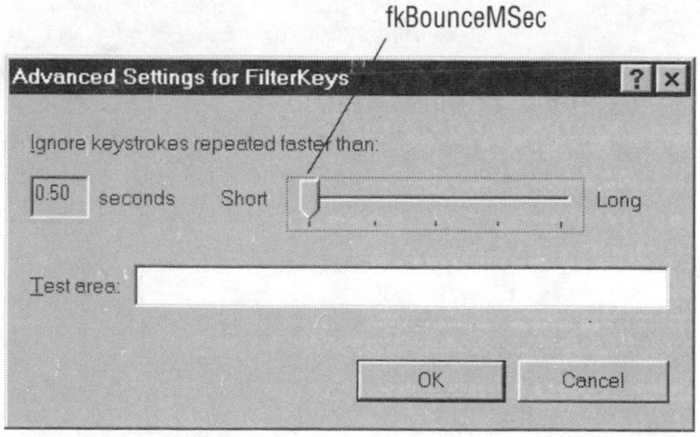

FIGURE 9.5
Advanced settings for the
FilterKeys (Delay)
dialog box

fkDelayMSec = 0,
fkRepeatMSec = 0

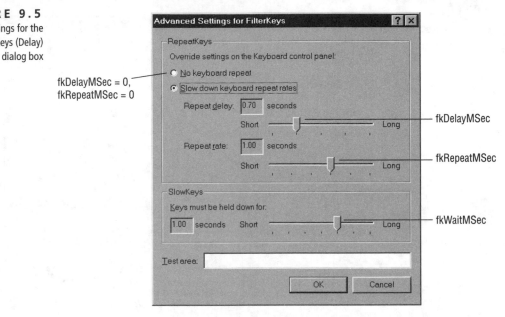

FIGURE 9.6
Settings for the ToggleKeys
dialog box

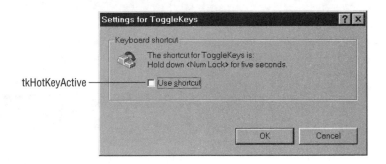

FIGURE 9.7
Accessibility Properties
(Sound) dialog box

ssActive

shActive

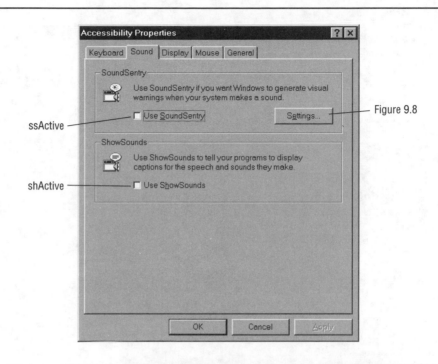

Figure 9.8

FIGURE 9.8
Settings for the
SoundSentry dialog box

ssWindowsEffect

ssFSTextEffect

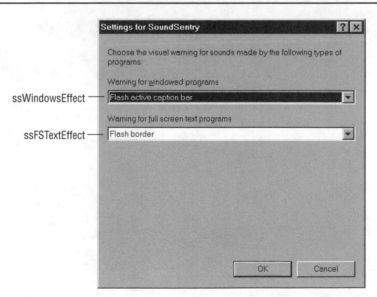

FIGURE 9.9
Accessibility Properties
(Mouse) dialog box

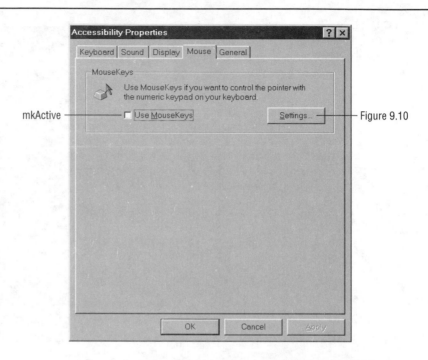

mkActive

Figure 9.10

FIGURE 9.10
Settings for the MouseKeys
dialog box

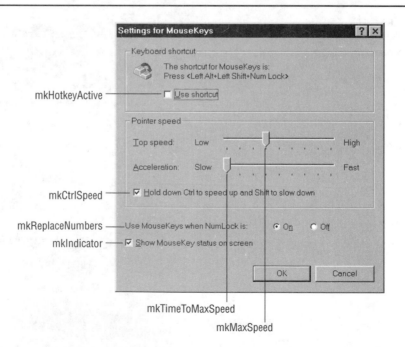

mkHotkeyActive

mkCtrlSpeed

mkReplaceNumbers

mkIndicator

mkTimeToMaxSpeed

mkMaxSpeed

FIGURE 9.11
Accessibility Properties
(General) dialog box

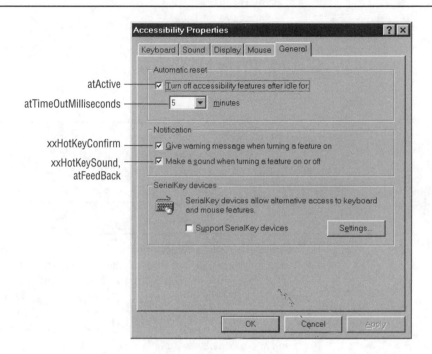

atActive
atTimeOutMilliseconds

xxHotKeyConfirm
xxHotKeySound,
atFeedBack

Using the Accessibility Class

As with any other class module, you'll need to create a new instance of the Accessibility class before you can use its properties. To do so, you create a variable that will refer to the new instance and work with that variable directly, like this:

```
Dim oAccess As Accessibility
' and then, later in your code:
Set oAccess = New Accessibility
```

Once you've created the object, use it as you would any other object, setting and retrieving its properties. For example, the following fragment enables the Sticky-Keys functionality, enables the hot key, and turns on the sound effect when users use the feature:

```
Dim oAccess As Accessibility
Set oAccess = New Accessibility
With oAccess
    ' No point working with this feature if it's not
    ' available on this computer.
```

```
        If .skAvailable Then
            .skActive = True
            .skHotKeyActive = True
            .skAudibleFeedback = True
        End If
    End With
```

WARNING   Some of the Accessibility class properties are interrelated, so read the descriptions carefully. For example, you cannot set both the fkBounceMSec and fkDelayMSec properties to nonzero values. If you try to set them both, Windows disregards your changes.

TIP   If you receive error 91, "Object variable or With block variable not set," it's almost guaranteed that you've declared an object variable but haven't instantiated it yet. You must use the New keyword to create an object; otherwise, you're just creating a variable that can refer to the object. Make sure you either use New when you declare the object or use the Set keyword to point the variable you created to a new instance of the object. (See Chapter 5 for more information on creating and using object variables.)

TIP   To try out all the properties of the Accessibility class, run the TestAccessibility procedure in the SysInfoTest module.

Creating the Accessibility Class

Each area in the Accessibility class (AccessTimeOut, FilterKeys, and so on) uses a particular user-defined type to retrieve and set its information. To retrieve the information, you call SystemParametersInfo with a flag indicating you want to retrieve the information and a data structure in which to place the information. To send the information back to Windows, you repeat the operation, using a flag indicating you want to send information back.

Each group of properties has its own module-level variable and its own procedure (named xxReset) that retrieves a data structure full of information. For example, Listing 9.12 shows the fkReset subroutine, which fills in the module-level fk variable with all the current FilterKeys settings.

Listing 9.12: Use fkReset to Retrieve Current FilterKeys Settings

```
Private Sub fkReset()
    ' Retrieve current values.
    fk.lngSize = Len(fk)
    Call SystemParametersInfo(SPI_GETFILTERKEYS, _
        fk.lngSize, fk, 0)
End Sub
```

The Accessibility class uses a similar technique to save changed values back to Windows, the xxApply set of procedures. Each function in this series returns a Boolean value indicating the success or failure of the procedure. Although the properties in Accessibility do not use the return value, you could easily modify the class so that it handles errors when you set the various parameters. Listing 9.13 shows the fkApply function, similar to the functions used by all the Accessibility class groups.

Listing 9.13: Use fkApply to Set the New FilterKeys Settings

```
Private Function fkApply() As Boolean
    fkApply = CBool(SystemParametersInfo(SPI_SETFILTERKEYS, _
        fk.lngSize, fk, SPIF_TELLALL))
End Function
```

What's in those user-defined structures? In general, you'll find two kinds of information there: quantitative values (such as the number of milliseconds to wait before repeating a key) and long integer flag values, containing a series of bits indicating Boolean values. In addition, each structure begins with a long integer containing the size of the structure. For example, the simplest structure, ACCESS-TIMEOUT, looks like this:

```
Private Type ACCESSTIMEOUT
    lngSize As Long
    lngFlags As Long
    lngTimeOutSecs As Long
End Type
```

In this case, code must supply the lngSize value before calling SystemParameters-Info so the function knows how many bytes it has to work with. The lngTimeOut-Secs member indicates how many milliseconds Windows waits before turning off Accessibility functions. (See the atTimeOutMillisecs Let and Get Property procedures in ACCESSIBILITY.CLS.) The lngFlags member groups a number of Boolean values (up to 32) into the single long integer value. In the case of the ACCESSTIME-OUT structure, there are only three possible values: ATF_AVAILABLE, ATF_TIMEOUTON, and ATF_ONOFFFEEDBACK, all defined in ACCESSIBILITY .CLS. Other structures use a different set of flags, and it's up to the programmer to know which flag coincides with which property of the feature. (This is why the class module makes this so much easier than working with SystemParametersInfo directly—you don't need to dig into each flag individually.)

To work with these Boolean flags, the Accessibility class includes two private procedures, IsBitSet and SetBit (shown in Listing 9.14), that handle the bits for you. To check whether a particular bit flag is set, property procedures can call IsBitSet, providing the flag value and particular bit to check. For example, the following procedure checks whether the FilterKeys click is enabled:

```
Public Property Get fkClickOn() As Boolean
    Call fkReset
    fkClickOn = IsBitSet(fk.lngFlags, FKF_CLICKON)
End Property
```

To use this property, you might include code like this in your own application:

```
Dim oAccess As Accessibility
Set oAccess = New Accessibility
If oAccess.fkClickOn Then
    ' You know the click is on.
End If
```

To set or clear a particular feature, property procedures can call SetBit, indicating the current flag's value, the particular feature to work with, and the new value. For example, the following procedure controls whether the FilterKeys click is enabled:

```
Public Property Let fkClickOn(Value As Boolean)
    Call SetBit(fk.lngFlags, FKF_CLICKON, Value)
    Call fkApply
End Property
```

To set this property, you might use code like this:

```
Dim oAccess As Accessibility
Set oAccess = New Accessibility
' Force the sound to be on when FilterKeys is active.
oAccess.fkClickOn = True
```

Listing 9.14: Retrieve, Set, and Clear Bits Using These Procedures

```
Private Function IsBitSet(lngFlags As Long, lngValue As Long) _
As Boolean
    ' Use logical AND to see if a particular bit within
    ' a long integer is set.
    IsBitSet = CBool((lngFlags And lngValue) = lngValue)
End Function

Private Sub SetBit(lngFlags As Long, lngValue As Long, _
fSet As Boolean)
    ' Use logical OR to set a particular bit.
    ' Use logical AND NOT to turn off a particular bit.
    If fSet Then
        lngFlags = lngFlags Or lngValue
    Else
        lngFlags = lngFlags And Not lngValue
    End If
End Sub
```

WARNING   As you can see from Tables 9.10 through 9.16, which list information about the various properties, some of the numeric properties (especially those related to FilterKeys) allow only specific numeric values. These values aren't documented, nor is the behavior when you supply a value that's out of range. Test your application carefully if you attempt to set these values, and make sure you understand the ramifications of changing these numeric values. For example, setting the fkDelayMSec property to 15 may seem like a good idea, but when you next retrieve the setting, the value will certainly not be the value you think you set—Windows will have set it to 0 instead.

Keyboard Information

The Keyboard class (KEYBOARD.CLS) allows you to set and retrieve information about the keyboard hardware. Obviously, many of the properties are read-only, but several allow you to control the settings used by the keyboard. Table 9.17 lists and describes all the properties of the Keyboard class. Figure 9.12 shows the properties supplied by the Keyboard class that have equivalents in the Windows user interface.

TABLE 9.17:   Properties Supplied by the Keyboard Class

Property	Read/Write?	Description
CapsLock	Yes	Returns or sets the CapsLock toggle
CaretBlinkTime	Yes	Sets or retrieves the number of milliseconds between blinks of the caret. Allowable values: 200 to 1200 (in multiples of 100)
CaretOn	No	Shows or hides the caret. Most apps control the caret themselves, and this call will have little or no effect except in limited circumstances.
Delay	Yes	Sets the keyboard repeat-delay setting. Only values 0 through 3 are acceptable.
FunctionKeys	No	Determines the number of function keys on the keyboard. The return value can be any of the values in Table 9.18.
KeyboardType	No	Determines the type of keyboard on the system. The return value can be any of the values in Table 9.19.
NumLock	Yes	Returns or sets the NumLock toggle
ScrollLock	Yes	Returns or sets the ScrollLock toggle
Speed	Yes	Sets the keyboard repeat-speed setting. Only values 0 through 31 are acceptable.

Using the Keyboard Class

The following brief sections demonstrate how to use each of the Keyboard class properties. In general, to use the Keyboard class, create a new instance of the class, and then set or retrieve its available properties. For example, to work with the current keyboard delay setting, you might use code like this:

```
Dim kb As Keyboard
Set kb = New Keyboard
If kb.Delay < 3 Then
    kb.Delay = kb.Delay + 1
End If
Set kb = Nothing
```

FIGURE 9.12
Control Panel interface for
properties of a Keyboard
object

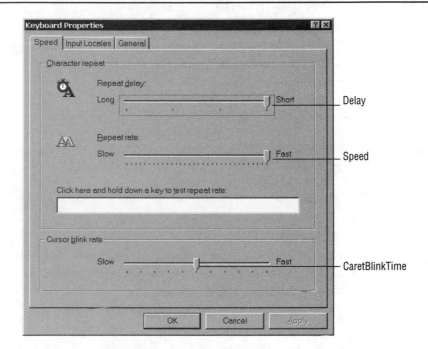

CapsLock, NumLock, and ScrollLock

Use the CapsLock property to set or retrieve the state of the CapsLock keyboard
toggle. It accepts and returns a Boolean parameter, so you might use code like this
to retrieve the current state of the toggle, set the CapsLock toggle on, do some
work, and then reset the toggle to its original state:

```
Dim blnOldState As Boolean
Dim kb As Keyboard
Set kb = New Keyboard
blnOldState = kb.CapsLock
kb.CapsLock = True
' Do work with CapsLock on.
kb.Capslock = blnOldState
```

Use the NumLock and ScrollLock properties just as you do the CapsLock
property.

CaretBlinkTime

The CaretBlinkTime property allows you to control the number of milliseconds between the "blinks" of the text input caret. To make the caret blink more slowly, you could use code like this:

```
Dim kb As Keyboard
Set kb = New Keyboard
' Slow down the caret blink rate one "notch"
If kb.CaretBlinkTime < 1200 Then
    kb.CaretBlinkTime = kb.CaretBlinkTime + 100
End If
Set kb = Nothing
```

CaretOn

Use the CaretOn property to show or hide the text-input caret. Most applications control this setting themselves, so you can't count on a global effect when you change this property, nor would you want to, for the most part. To retrieve the current state of the caret and hide it, you might use code like this:

```
Dim kb As Keyboard
Set kb = New Keyboard
' Hide the text caret.
kb.CaretOn = False
Set kb = Nothing
```

> **TIP**
>
> The effect of hiding the caret is cumulative. If your application hides the caret five times in a row, it must also unhide the caret five times before the caret reappears. Of course, because most VBA host applications control the caret themselves, you won't get much use from this property. Test carefully when using CaretOn; it may work for you, but it may not.

Delay

Use the Delay property to control the amount of time the keyboard waits, while you're pressing a particular key, before starting the autorepeat action. (See the section "Speed," coming up in a moment, for information on controlling the speed at which the key autorepeats.) You can set this property to any value between 0 and 3, inclusive. The following code sets the keyboard delay to its smallest possible value:

```
Dim kb As Keyboard
Set kb = New Keyboard
kb.Delay = 0
Set kb = Nothing
```

FunctionKeys

The FunctionKeys property simply returns the number of function keys on the installed keyboard. It returns one of the (admittedly ambiguous, but we didn't define these) values in Table 9.18:

```
Dim kb As Keyboard
Set kb = New Keyboard
Select Case kb.FunctionKeys
    Case 1,3,5
        ' Only 10 function keys. You need more for your
        ' application.
        MsgBox "You don't have enough function keys!"
End Select
Set kb = Nothing
```

TABLE 9.18:   Possible Values for the FunctionKeys Property

Return Value	Number of Function Keys
1	10
2	12 (sometimes 18)
3	10
4	12
5	10
6	24
7	Hardware-dependent and specified by the OEM

KeyboardType

The KeyboardType property returns the specific type of keyboard that's currently installed, as one of the values listed in Table 9.19. If your application requires a 101- or 102-key keyboard, you might include code like this:

```
Dim kb As Keyboard
Set kb = New Keyboard
If kb.KeyBoardType <> 4 Then
    MsgBox "This application works only with the new keyboard."
End If
```

TABLE 9.19: Possible Values for the KeyboardType Property

Return Value	Keyboard Type
1	IBM PC/XT or compatible (83-key) keyboard
2	Olivetti "ICO" (102-key) keyboard
3	IBM PC/AT (84-key) or similar keyboard
4	IBM enhanced (101- or 102-key) keyboard
5	Nokia 1050 and similar keyboards
6	Nokia 9140 and similar keyboards
7	Japanese keyboard

Speed

Use the Speed property to set the rate at which characters repeat while you're holding down a key. (See the section "Delay" above for information on controlling the waiting period before the repeat.) Windows allows values between 0 and 31 for this property:

```
Dim kb As Keyboard
Set kb = New Keyboard
' Set the fastest repeat rate.
kb.Speed = 31
Set kb = Nothing
```

Creating the Keyboard Class

Except for the key-state toggling properties (CapsLock, NumLock, and ScrollLock), creating the Keyboard class was simple. Each other property corresponds either to a single function call or to the conglomerate SystemParametersInfo function. For example, to retrieve the keyboard type, the class calls the GetKeyboardType API function. To modify the caret blink rate, the code calls the GetCaretBlinkTime and SetCaretBlinkTime API functions.

The CapsLock, NumLock, and ScrollLock properties each use the same Windows API function, GetKeyState, to check the state of the specific key. To use the function, you must pass it a specific *virtual key code*. Windows assigns every physical key a mapping so that Windows can run on machines with keyboards that differ slightly from the standard PC keyboard; these mappings are called virtual key codes. Windows supports a maximum of 256 such mappings. Windows uses the value 20 for the CapsLock key, 144 for the NumLock key, and 145 for the ScrollLock key. VBA provides constants representing these (and most other) virtual key codes: vbKeyCapital for the CapsLock key, vbKeyNumLock for the NumLock key, and vbKeyScrollLock for the ScrollLock key. (Actually, not all VBA hosts define the vbKeyScrollLock constant, so we've included a declaration for this value in KEYBOARD.CLS.) Therefore, the following fragment will return the current state of the CapsLock key:

```
lngState = GetKeyState(vbKeyCapital)
```

GetKeyState returns an integer containing 1 in its lowest bit if the key is toggled on or 0 in the lowest bit if the key is toggled off. (GetKeyState returns the highest bit set if the key is currently being held down, but the key being held down adds no information as to whether the key is currently toggled on or off.) The property procedures then convert these values to True or False, looking at just the lowest bit by using the logical And operator:

```
Public Property Get Capslock() As Boolean
    ' Return or set the Capslock toggle.
    Capslock = CBool(GetKeyState(vbKeyCapital) And 1)
End Property
```

Setting the CapsLock, NumLock, and ScrollLock states on the keyboard requires different techniques, depending on the operating system. Windows 95 and 98 require one technique, and Windows NT and 2000 require another.

For Windows 95 and 98, the CapsLock, NumLock, and ScrollLock Property Let procedures each call the same subroutine, SetKeyState, to do their work. SetKeyState uses the API functions GetKeyboardState and SetKeyboardState; each of these functions uses a 256-byte buffer in which to retrieve or set the full set of 256 key settings. Each virtual key code maps to one element in this array of values. Once you've used GetKeyboardState to retrieve the bufferful of settings, you can modify the specific key setting you care about and then store the settings back using SetKeyboardState. (To toggle the key on, you need to set the lowest-order bit in the byte. To toggle it off, you must clear that same bit. The SetKeyState procedure uses the Or and And Not operators to set that bit correctly.) This will change just the keys you've modified. This method allows you to change the state of the CapsLock, NumLock, or ScrollLock key. Listing 9.15 shows the SetKeyState procedure.

Listing 9.15: The SetKeyState Procedure Allows You to Alter the State of a Particular Key

```
Private Sub SetKeyState(intKey As Integer, fTurnOn As Boolean)
    ' Retrieve the keyboard state, set the particular
    ' key in which you're interested, and then set
    ' the entire keyboard state back the way it
    ' was, with the one key altered.
    Dim abytBuffer(0 To 255) As Byte
    GetKeyboardState abytBuffer(0)
    If fTurnOn Then
        abytBuffer(intKey) = abytBuffer(intKey) Or 1
    Else
        abytBuffer(intKey) = abytBuffer(intKey) And Not 1
    End If
    SetKeyboardState abytBuffer(0)
End Sub
```

NOTE   The only parameter the GetKeyboardState and SetKeyboardState API functions expect to receive is the address of a 256-byte memory block. In VBA, you emulate this block using a 256-element byte array. To pass an array to an API call, you normally pass the first element of the array. Because VBA stores arrays contiguously in memory, the API function can take the address of the first element of the array and find the rest of the elements. Procedures such as SetKeyState depend on this behavior when passing an array to an API call that doesn't understand anything about VBA arrays.

When called from Windows NT or Windows 2000, the property procedures must emulate keystrokes—that is, they must convince Windows that the user pressed the appropriate key. To do that, the procedures call the keybd_event API function twice (once to press the key, again to release the key), passing in the key to be pressed and information on whether to press or release the key. For example, the full Numlock Property Let procedure looks like this:

```
Public Property Let Numlock(Value As Boolean)
    ' Return or set the Numlock toggle.

    If mblnIsWinNT Then
        ' Under NT/2000, you must send keystrokes
        ' through the keyboard buffer to toggle
        ' NumLock.

        ' Simulate Key Press
        keybd_event vbKeyNumlock, 0, _
         KEYEVENTF_EXTENDEDKEY, 0
        ' Simulate Key Release
        keybd_event vbKeyNumlock, 0, _
         KEYEVENTF_EXTENDEDKEY Or KEYEVENTF_KEYUP, 0
    Else
        ' Under Win95/98, simply set the value in the keyboard.
        Call SetKeyState(vbKeyNumlock, Value)
    End If
End Property
```

Memory Status

The MemoryStatus class (MEMORYSTATUS.CLS) is simple, with just a few properties, most of them read-only (except RaiseErrors, of course). The properties, listed in Table 9.20, allow you to peek at the current memory situation in the computer that's running your application.

TABLE 9.20: Properties for the MemoryStatus Class

Property	Description
AvailableExtendedVirtual	Indicates the number of bytes of unreserved and uncommitted memory in the VLM portion of the virtual address space (Windows 2000 only)
AvailablePageFile	Indicates the number of bytes available in the paging file
AvailablePhysical	Indicates the number of bytes of physical memory available
AvailableVirtual	Indicates the number of bytes of unreserved and uncommitted memory in the user mode portion of the virtual address space of the calling process
MemoryLoad	Number between 0–100 that gives a general idea of current memory utilization, in which 0 indicates no memory use and 100 indicates full memory use
RaiseErrors	(Read/write) Indicates whether the class should raise a runtime error if you attempt to call a property that is not valid for the current operating system. The default value is True.
TotalPhysical	Indicates the total number of bytes of physical memory
TotalPageFile	Indicates the total number of bytes that can be stored in the paging file, not the size of the paging file on disk
TotalVirtual	Indicates the total number of bytes that can be described in the user mode portion of the virtual address space of the calling process

NOTE There are no properties in the MemoryStatus class dealing with available resources, as there might have been in a class written for a 16-bit operating system. The Win32 API does not contain any tools to retrieve information about available resources because this isn't supposed to be an issue in 32-bit Windows. (Anyone who's used Windows 9x extensively knows this isn't the case, but under Windows NT/2000, you certainly won't be worrying about resource usage.)

Using the MemoryStatus Class

To use the MemoryStatus class, first declare a new instance of the class, and then retrieve any of its properties. For example, the most interesting property of the MemoryStatus class is the MemoryLoad property, which tells you the approximate current memory utilization. To retrieve the value of this property, you write code like this:

```
Dim oms As MemoryStatus
Set oms = New MemoryStatus
Debug.Print "The current memory load is: " & oms.MemoryLoad
Set oms = Nothing
```

Use the same technique with any or all of the MemoryStatus class properties.

TIP   Try out the TestMemoryStatus procedure in the SysInfoTest module to see all the properties' values on your machine.

Creating the MemoryStatus Class

The MemoryStatus class is one of the classes that's centered on a single user-defined data structure, the MEMORYSTATUS structure.

```
Private Type MEMORYSTATUS
    dwLength As Long
    dwMemoryLoad As Long
    dwTotalPhys As Long
    dwAvailPhys As Long
    dwTotalPageFile As Long
    dwAvailPageFile As Long
    dwTotalVirtual As Long
    dwAvailVirtual As Long
End Type
```

To gather information about the current memory situation, call the GlobalMemory-Status API function, passing a MEMORYSTATUS variable.

NOTE   On computers with more than four gigabytes of memory (not that many computers contain that kind of memory), the MEMORYSTATUS structure can return incorrect information—it will report the real amount of memory MOD 4 (that is, if you have six gigabytes of memory, you'll only see two). Windows 2000 introduces an extended version of this structure (MemoryStatusEx) and a related extended API function (GlobalMemoryStatusEx). The code in the MemoryStatus class uses the new function if it determines that the code is running on a Windows 2000 installation.

The extended structure, MEMORYSTATUSEX, introduces one additional member, containing information about the available extended virtual memory, along with the data type changes to all other members that contain information about actual memory size:

```
Private Type MEMORYSTATUSEX
    dwLength As Long
    dwMemoryLoad As Long
    ullTotalPhys As Currency
    ullAvailPhys As Currency
    ullTotalPageFile As Currency
    ullAvailPageFile As Currency
    ullTotalVirtual As Currency
    ullAvailVirtual As Currency
    ullAvailExtendedVirtual As Currency
End Type
```

You may find this definition strange: Why are we defining the data type of these variables as Currency when we will be passing this structure to the Windows API? They certainly aren't maintaining currency values!

As it turns out, the VBA Currency data type is a 64-bit integer, which is what this API function expects to find in the MEMORYSTATUSEX data structure. In VBA, the Currency data type is the only native 64-bit numeric data type. (Internally, the Currency data type contains a 64-bit integer; when you display or work with a Currency value, VBA divides the internal representation by 10,000 to come up with the value you see in your code.) To get the real value from the Currency variable, you need to multiply whatever value the variable holds by 10,000.

Because all the properties of the MemoryStatus class need to call either Global-MemoryStatus or GlobalMemoryStatusEx with the appropriate data structure, the Initialize event procedure fills in the size of the structures after determining the operating system version, so that the properties don't all need to take this extra step:

```
Private Sub Class_Initialize()
    Const VER_PLATFORM_WIN32_NT = 2

    ' Set the flag to true so that an error is raised
    ' if a non-applicable property is used for a particular
    ' operating system
    RaiseErrors = True

    ' First, confirm whether the OS is Win2000.
    osvi.dwOSVersionInfoSize = Len(osvi)
```

```
        If CBool(GetVersionEx(osvi)) Then
            With osvi
                mblnIsWin2000 = _
                (.dwPlatformId = VER_PLATFORM_WIN32_NT _
                 And .dwMajorVersion = 5)
            End With
        End If


        ' ms and msEx are declared at the module level.
        If mblnIsWin2000 Then
            ' On Win2000, the recommended
            ' extended version of the function
            ' will be called.
            msEx.dwLength = Len(msEx)
        Else
            ' Other platforms use the original version.
            ms.dwLength = Len(ms)
        End If
    End Sub
```

Once that task has been taken care of, retrieving any property requires only that the class call the GlobalMemoryStatus function to refresh the data structure's values. For example, the TotalPageFile property looks like this:

```
Property Get TotalPageFile() As Long
    ' Indicates the total number of bytes that can be stored
    ' in the paging file, not the size of the paging file on disk.
    If mblnIsWin2000 Then
        Call GlobalMemoryStatusEx(msEx)
        TotalPageFile = CurrencyToLong(msEx.ullTotalPageFile)
    Else
        Call GlobalMemoryStatus(ms)
        TotalPageFile = ms.dwTotalPageFile
    End If
End Property


Private Function CurrencyToLong(curValue As Currency) As Long
    ' Converts a 64-bit Currency value to a Long value
    '
    CurrencyToLong = curValue * 10000
End Function
```

All the Property Get procedures in the MemoryStatus class work exactly the same way.

Mouse Information

The Mouse class (MOUSE.CLS) contains information pertinent to (what else?) the mouse and its activities on the screen. Table 9.21 lists all the properties of the class, along with their data types and descriptions.

TABLE 9.21:   Properties of the Mouse Class

Property	Read/ Write?	Data Type	Description
ActiveWindowTracking	Yes	Boolean	Enables or disables active window tracking (The window is automatically activated when the mouse is on it. This, however, does not bring the window to the foreground or on top of other windows.) (Windows 2000 only)
ActiveWindowTrackingTimeOut	Yes	Long	Retrieves or sets the active window tracking delay, in milliseconds (Windows 2000 only)
Buttons	No	Long	Retrieves the number of mouse buttons
CaretWidth	Yes	Long	Sets or retrieves the caret width in edit controls (Windows 2000 only)
CursorOn	Write-only	Boolean	Shows or hides the mouse cursor
CursorShadow	Yes	Boolean	Sets or removes the shadow around the mouse cursor (Windows 2000 only)
CursorX	No	Long	Retrieves the width, in pixels, of a cursor
CursorY	No	Long	Retrieves the height, in pixels, of a cursor
DoubleClickTime	No (write-only)	Long	Number of milliseconds between clicks, indicating to Windows that you've double-clicked. Normal value is around 450–500. To read double-click time, look in HKEY_CURRENT_USER\Control Panel\Mouse\DoubleClickSpeed.

TABLE 9.21: Properties of the Mouse Class *(continued)*

Property	Read/ Write?	Data Type	Description
DoubleClickX	Yes	Long	Width, in pixels, around the location of the first click in a double-click sequence. Second click must occur within the boundaries of this rectangle.
DoubleClickY	Yes	Long	Height, in pixels, around the location of the first click in a double-click sequence. Second click must occur within the boundaries of this rectangle.
DragX	Yes	Long	Width, in pixels, of a rectangle centered on a drag point to allow for limited movement of the mouse before the drag begins.
DragY	Yes	Long	Height, in pixels, of a rectangle centered on a drag point to allow for limited movement of the mouse before the drag begins.
HoverDelay	Yes	Long	Retrieves or sets the time, in milliseconds, for which the mouse pointer has to stay in the hover rectangle for a Hover event to occur. Available under Windows 98, Windows NT, and Windows 2000
HoverX	Yes	Long	Retrieves or sets the width, in pixels, of the rectangle within which the mouse pointer has to stay for a Hover event to occur. Available under Windows 98, Windows NT, and Windows 2000
HoverY	Yes	Long	Retrieves or sets the height, in pixels, of the rectangle within which the mouse pointer has to stay for a Hover event to occur. Available under Windows 98, Windows NT, and Windows 2000
MenuDelay	Yes	Long	Sets or retrieves the time, in milliseconds, that the system waits before displaying a shortcut menu when the mouse cursor is over a submenu item.

TABLE 9.21: Properties of the Mouse Class *(continued)*

Property	Read/Write?	Data Type	Description
MouseButtonSwap	Yes	Boolean	Sets or retrieves the swapped mouse button state. (Button1 is on the right.)
MousePresent	No	Boolean	Returns True if a mouse is installed
MouseSpeed, MouseThreshold1, MouseThreshold2	Yes	Long	MouseSpeed, combined with MouseThreshold1 and MouseThreshold2, creates the real mouse speed.
MouseTrails	Yes	Long	(Windows 95 and Windows 98 only) Controls mouse trails. If the value is greater than 1, MouseTrails is on, and the higher the value, the more trails you get.
SnapToDefault	Yes	Boolean	Determines whether the snap-to-default-button feature is enabled. If enabled, the mouse cursor automatically moves to the default button, such as "OK" or "Apply," of a dialog box. Available under Windows 98, Windows NT, and Windows 2000
TrackedWindowToTop	Yes	Boolean	If True, then the windows activated through active window tracking will be brought to the top.
WheelPresent	No	Boolean	Returns True if a wheel with a mouse is present. Available under Windows 98, Windows NT, and Windows 2000
WheelScrollLines	Yes	Boolean	Determines the number of lines scrolled with each movement of the mouse wheel. Available under Windows 98, Windows NT, and Windows 2000

NOTE   Even though the wheeled mouse functions properly in Windows 95, there's no support in that older operating system for determining whether the wheeled mouse is present or for controlling the number of lines to scroll when you move the wheel. Therefore, the WheelPresent and WheelScrollLines properties work properly only with Windows NT 4.*x*, Windows 98, and Windows 2000. On the other hand, Windows NT and Windows 2000 just don't support the MouseTrails property, which Windows 95 and Windows 98 do support.

Using the Mouse Class

The mouse class consists of three types of properties:

Read-only properties   The Buttons property returns the number of buttons on the mouse, and the WheelPresent property returns whether the mouse includes a middle wheel. To use these (and other read-only) properties, simply retrieve the return value. For example, to use the MousePresent property, you might write code like this:

```
Dim oMouse As Mouse
Set oMouse = New Mouse
If Not oMouse.MousePresent Then
    MsgBox "You must have a mouse to use this application."
End If
```

Write-only properties   Actually, there's but one of these misbegotten, poorly conceived properties: the DoubleClickTime property. To retrieve this value, you'll need to inspect the HKEY_CURRENT_USER\Control Panel\Mouse\DoubleClickSpeed Registry entry. We could have added the appropriate code to this class, but to do so would have involved borrowing code from Chapter 10. If you need to both set and retrieve this value, you may want to import the necessary classes from that chapter and retrieve the Registry setting in a Property Get procedure. In addition, the CursorOn property only allows you to set its value. That is, you can tell Windows to show the mouse cursor or to hide it. But there's no corresponding property to determine if the cursor is visible or not. When you tell Windows to display the cursor, it increments an internal counter. As long as that counter's value is greater than or equal to 0, the cursor is visible. When you tell Windows to hide the cursor, it decrements the value. When it becomes –1, Windows hides the cursor until you increment the counter (by calling the ShowCursor API function with a True value) so that it's greater than or equal to 0 again.

Read/write properties   Properties such as MouseButtonSwap and SnapToDefault are read/write properties that accept and return Boolean values. Others, such as MouseSpeed, DragX, and MouseTrails, all accept and return long integers. In all these cases, you use the properties the same way you use properties of any object. For example, to cause the mouse to swap its buttons (the right-hand button becomes the main button, popular among left-handed users), use code like this:

```
Dim oMouse As Mouse
Set oMouse = New Mouse
oMouse.MouseButtonSwap = True
```

The MouseSpeed and Related Properties

The only group of properties that requires any special explanation is the set of three properties: MouseSpeed, MouseThreshold1, and MouseThreshold2. These three work together to control how quickly the mouse cursor moves across the screen as you move the mouse physically. The MouseSpeed parameter can take on values between 0 and 2, representing the speed of the mouse cursor relative to the distance you've moved the mouse. The MouseThreshold (1 and 2) properties can take on values between 0 and 12. The following paragraphs explain how these three properties are related.

As you may have noticed, the more quickly you move the mouse, the farther the mouse cursor moves on the screen. This means you don't have to lift the mouse and reposition it as often as you might otherwise have to. Windows uses three values to calculate the distance it will move the mouse cursor every time you move the mouse, based on two tests.

At measured time intervals, as you move the mouse, Windows polls the position of the mouse and the speed at which you're moving it. If, during one interval, the distance along either the x or y axis is greater than the first mouse threshold value (MouseThreshold1) and the mouse speed (MouseSpeed) is not 0, Windows doubles the distance. If the distance along either the x or y axis is greater than the second mouse threshold value and the mouse speed is 2, the operating system doubles the distance that resulted from applying the first threshold test. It is thus possible for the operating system to multiply relatively specified mouse motion along the x or y axis by up to four times.

If you use the Mouse Control Panel applet, you'll see only a single linear slider control to manage the mouse speed. Windows takes the seven possible settings on the slider and converts them into preset values for the three properties. Table 9.22 lists these preset triplets of values, starting with the slowest and ending with the fastest setting. Figure 9.13 shows the Mouse Control Panel applet, with the first, middle, and last MouseSpeed triplets pointed out.

TABLE 9.22: Preset Values for the Three Mouse Parameters

Speed	Threshold1	Threshold2
0	0	0
1	10	0
1	7	0

TABLE 9.22: Preset Values for the Three Mouse Parameters *(continued)*

Speed	Threshold1	Threshold2
1	4	0
2	4	12
2	4	9
2	4	6

FIGURE 9.13
Mouse Control Panel applet, showing MouseSpeed triplets

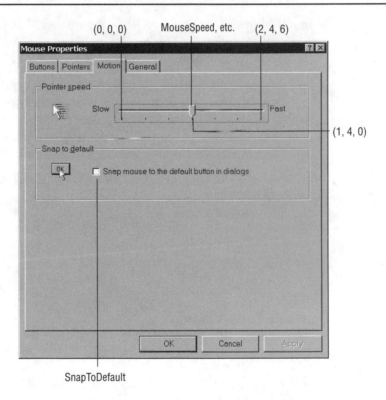

Therefore, the MouseSpeed parameter controls the general speed of the mouse. As you move the mouse, if the MouseSpeed parameter is greater than 0 and the mouse is moved more physical units than the value specified in Threshold1, Windows doubles the distance, and the cursor moves farther. If the MouseSpeed is 2 and the distance moved was also greater than the value in the MouseThreshold2 parameter, Windows again doubles the distance. You can see that it makes no sense to have both the MouseSpeed parameter set to 1 and the Threshold2 parameter set to anything except 0—Windows will never even look at the Threshold2 value in that case.

If you intend to set these values, here are some general rules to help you:

- If the MouseSpeed parameter is set to 0, Windows never looks at the Threshold values, and they should both be set to 0.

- If the MouseSpeed parameter is set to 1, Windows never looks at the Threshold2 parameter, and it should be set to 0.

- If MouseSpeed is set to 1, then the smaller Threshold1 is, the faster the mouse will move. This is why the Threshold1 values in Table 9.22 decrease from top to bottom while MouseSpeed stays at 1.

- If MouseSpeed is set to 2, then the value of MouseThreshold2 becomes significant, but it should never be less than the MouseThreshold1 value. MouseThreshold2 is used only if the mouse has moved farther than the value in MouseThreshold1, so having a value that's smaller than the MouseThreshold1 value won't add any speed.

Therefore, if your MouseSpeed, MouseThreshold1, and MouseThreshold2 values are (0, 0, 0), there's no acceleration as you move the mouse. As long as the first value is 0, Windows never even looks at the next two.

If the values are (1, 10, 0), and

- You move the mouse 8 units, the cursor moves 8 units

- You move the mouse 11 units, you've crossed the threshold, and Windows doubles the cursor movement to 22 units

If the values are (2, 4, 6), and

- You move the mouse 3 units, the cursor moves 3 units

- You move the mouse 5 units, you've crossed the first threshold, and Windows doubles the movement to 10 units for the cursor

- You move the mouse 7 units, you've crossed both thresholds, so Windows doubles the distance twice, moving the cursor 28 units.

As you can see, it's important to understand the relationship between the movement of the mouse and the MouseSpeed, MouseThreshold1, and MouseThreshold2 parameters in controlling the speed and acceleration of the mouse cursor.

Non-Client Metrics

Non-client metrics are the settings for the width, height, and fonts of items on a window's border. Setting the properties of a NonClientMetrics object (NONCLIENTMETRICS.CLS) affects the entire Windows display and allows you to control display attributes such as the size of the buttons on a window's caption bar and the font used by the MsgBox function.

The properties supplied by the NonClientMetrics class break down into two categories: simple properties and font properties. The simple properties, described in Table 9.23, allow you to control the size of various border settings, such as the buttons that appear on windows' caption bars. The font properties, listed in Table 9.24, allow you to change various font settings for the five Font objects. Finally, each of these Font objects supports the properties shown in Table 9.25.

T A B L E   9 . 2 3 :   Simple Properties Supplied by the NonClientMetrics Class

Property	Description
BorderWidth	Sets or retrieves the standard window-sizing border width
ScrollWidth	Sets or retrieves the width of buttons on scrollbars (or height, for horizontal scrollbars). Also returns the width of vertical scrollbars. Changing this value affects the dimensions of the scrollbars as well.
ScrollHeight	Sets or retrieves the height of buttons on scrollbars (or width, for horizontal scrollbars). Also returns the height of horizontal scrollbars
CaptionWidth	Sets or retrieves the width of caption bar buttons
CaptionHeight	Sets or retrieves the height of caption bar buttons
SmallCaptionButtonWidth	Sets or retrieves the width of small caption bar buttons
SmallCaptionButtonHeight	Sets or retrieves the height of small caption bar buttons
MenuWidth	Sets or retrieves the width of menu bar buttons
MenuHeight	Sets or retrieves the height of menu bar buttons

TABLE 9.23: Simple Properties Supplied by the NonClientMetrics Class *(continued)*

Property	Description
Caption	Retrieves the height, in pixels, of a normal caption bar
SmallCaption	Retrieves the height, in pixels, of a small caption bar
FixedBorderX	Retrieves the width, in pixels, of the frame around the perimeter of a window that has a caption but is not sizable
FixedBorderY	Retrieves the height, in pixels, of the frame around the perimeter of a window that has a caption but is not sizable

TABLE 9.24: Font Object Properties Supplied by the NonClientMetrics Class

Property	Description
CaptionFont	Retrieves the caption bar Font object
SmallCaptionFont	Retrieves the small caption bar Font object
MenuFont	Retrieves the menu Font object
StatusFont	Retrieves the status bar Font object
MessageFont	Retrieves the message box Font object

TABLE 9.25: Properties Supplied by the Font Class

Property	Type	Value
Size	Long	Point size for the font. Normally 8–127, but depends on the FaceName
Weight	Long	Integer between 100–900, where 100 is very light and 900 is very heavy. Normal is 400 and bold is 700.
Italic	Boolean	True or False
StrikeOut	Boolean	True or False
Underline	Boolean	True or False
FaceName	String	String containing font face name

Using the NonClientMetrics Class

Using the simple properties in the NonClientMetrics class is just like using properties in any other class. First, you create a new instance of the object, and then you set and retrieve its properties. For example, to add five pixels to the width of the scrollbars, you could use code like this:

```
Dim ncm As NonClientMetrics
Set ncm = New NonClientMetrics
ncm.ScrollWidth = ncm.ScrollWidth + 5
Set ncm = Nothing
```

To test out most of the simple properties, the code in Listing 9.16 (from the SysInfoText module) exercises most of the simple NonClientMetrics properties. Figure 9.14 shows a simple window before the code is called, and Figure 9.15 shows the same window after the code has done its work. As you can see, the NonClientMetrics class provides properties to control most of the visual aspects of the window border.

FIGURE 9.14
A simple window before FixNCM is called

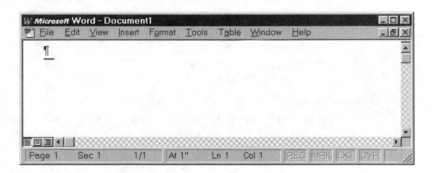

FIGURE 9.15
The same window after FixNCM is called

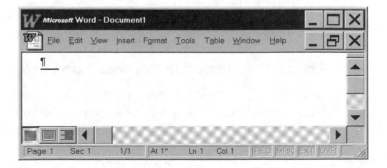

Listing 9.16: Modify Most of the Simple NonClientMetrics Properties

```
Sub FixNCM(Optional Bigger As Boolean = True)
    Dim ncm As NonClientMetrics
    Dim dblFactor As Double

    Set ncm = New NonClientMetrics
    If Bigger Then
        dblFactor = 2
    Else
        dblFactor = 0.5
    End If
    ncm.BorderWidth = ncm.BorderWidth * dblFactor
    ncm.CaptionHeight = ncm.CaptionHeight * dblFactor
    ncm.CaptionWidth = ncm.CaptionWidth * dblFactor
    ncm.MenuButtonHeight = ncm.MenuButtonHeight * dblFactor
    ncm.MenuButtonWidth = ncm.MenuButtonWidth * dblFactor
    ncm.ScrollHeight = ncm.ScrollHeight * dblFactor
    ncm.ScrollWidth = ncm.ScrollWidth * dblFactor
    Set ncm = Nothing
End Sub
```

> **TIP**
>
> Setting all these properties is a slow process. If you intend to change multiple NonClientMetrics properties often, consider removing the calls to SaveSettings in each property's code and explicitly calling the SaveSettings method yourself once you've made all the changes. That way, Windows won't attempt to change all the settings individually, and your code will run faster. To make these properties work like all simple properties, we wrote the code so that each Property Let procedure saves its changes. You're welcome to change this behavior if you like.

Using the NonClientMetrics Font Properties

In addition to its simple properties, the NonClientMetrics class provides five font properties. Each of these properties is a reference to a separate object, a Font object (FONT.CLS). Each Font object provides a set of properties describing a font used by a NonClientMetrics object, such as the font of the caption bar or the font used by the menus. In addition, the NonClientMetrics object maintains the font used by the form popped up by the MsgBox function. That's right: From your own applications, you can control the font used by the standard MsgBox function.

To use the font properties, treat them as objects contained within the NonClientMetrics object. For example, to retrieve the name of the font used by the MsgBox form, you could write code like this:

```
Dim ncm As NonClientMetrics
Set ncm = New NonClientMetrics
Debug.Print ncm.MessageFont.FaceName
Set ncm = Nothing
```

The real difference between using the simple properties and using the Font object properties is that changes to the fonts aren't saved until you explicitly call the SaveSettings method of the NonClientMetrics object. That is, once you've made all the font changes you need to make, you must use code like this:

```
Call ncm.SaveSettings
```

to cause the object to save all the new settings. You needn't call this method at all if you're only retrieving values or if you're working only with the simple properties. If you want to modify font values, however, your changes won't take effect until you call this method.

If you want to work extensively with the Font object, you could use the With statement, treating it like the real object it is. For example, the code in Listing 9.17 (from the SysInfoTest module) retrieves the current MsgBox font settings, modifies them, pops up a test message box, and then resets the values.

Listing 9.17: Sample Procedure That Modifies the MessageFont Object

```
Sub FixMsgBox()
    Dim ncm As NonClientMetrics
    Dim strOldFont As String
    Dim sglOldSize As Single

    Set ncm = New NonClientMetrics
    With ncm
        With .MessageFont
            strOldFont = .FaceName
            sglOldSize = .Size
            .FaceName = "Verdana"
            .Size = 24
```

```
            End With
            Call .SaveSettings
            MsgBox "This is a test"
            With .MessageFont
                .FaceName = strOldFont
                .Size = sglOldSize
            End With
            Call .SaveSettings
            MsgBox "This is a test"
        End With
    End Sub
```

As another example, the code in the following fragment sets the standard menu font to be two point sizes larger than it was originally and causes the font to be italic:

```
Dim ncm As NonClientMetrics
Set ncm = New NonClientMetrics
With ncm.MenuFont
    .Size = .Size + 2
    .Italic = True
End With
Call ncm.SaveSettings
```

NOTE   Some programs, including all of Microsoft's Office suite, eschew standard menus, instead using menus of their own creation. Changes you make to standard Windows menus using the classes provided here will have no effect in these applications.

Creating the NonClientMetrics Class

Although its read-only properties (Caption, SmallCaption, FixedBorderX, and FixedBorderY) rely on the GetSystemMetrics function to retrieve their values, like several other classes in this chapter, the NonClientMetrics class is centered around a single data structure, the typNonClientMetrics structure:

```
Private Type typNonClientMetrics
    cbSize As Long
    lngBorderWidth As Long
    lngScrollWidth As Long
```

```
        lngScrollHeight As Long
        lngCaptionWidth As Long
        lngCaptionHeight As Long
        lfCaptionFont As LogFont
        lngSMCaptionWidth As Long
        lngSMCaptionHeight As Long
        lfSMCaptionFont As LogFont
        lngMenuWidth As Long
        lngMenuHeight As Long
        lfMenuFont As LogFont
        lfStatusFont As LogFont
        lfMessageFont As LogFont
    End Type
```

In the Initialize event procedure for the class, the code calls the SystemParametersInfo function, passing a typNonClientMetrics structure to be filled in. From then on, all the properties use the settings in this structure for retrieving and setting properties.

The problem, as you can see, is that several members of this structure aren't simple variables; each is itself another data structure, the LogFont structure:

```
Const LF_FACESIZE = 32
Private Type LogFont
    lfHeight As Long
    lfWidth As Long
    lfEscapement As Long
    lfOrientation As Long
    lfWeight As Long
    lfItalic As Byte
    lfUnderline As Byte
    lfStrikeOut As Byte
    lfCharSet As Byte
    lfOutPrecision As Byte
    lfClipPrecision As Byte
    lfQuality As Byte
    lfPitchAndFamily As Byte
    lfFaceName(0 To LF_FACESIZE - 1) As Byte
End Type
```

Clearly, there is more information here than is necessary for the fonts used by the NonClientMetrics object. The question, then, was how to expose all the information you need in order to use the object but not end up with an overload of similar, but differently named, properties.

The answer, in this case, was to create a simple Font class with the properties shown earlier in Table 9.25. This way, the NonClientMetrics class can create five instances of the class to maintain the font information it needs for each of its five font properties, and you can access those properties using objects within your NonClient-Metrics object. In addition, the Font class can expose just the properties that make sense for this situation, not every portion of the LogFont data structure.

To use the Font class, the NonClientMetrics class needs to take three distinct steps:

1. **Declare the Font objects**. In the declarations section of the module, the code includes the following declarations:

```
Private oCaptionFont As Font
Private oSMCaptionFont As Font
Private oMenuFont As Font
Private oStatusFont As Font
Private oMessageFont As Font
```

2. **Copy the data into the Font objects**. In the Initialize event procedure, the class needs to copy the data from each LogFont structure to each separate Font object. The NonClientMetrics class contains a private procedure, SetFontInfo, which copies all the necessary data:

```
Private Sub Class_Initialize()
    Dim lngLen As Long

    lngLen = Len(ncm)
    ncm.cbSize = lngLen
    Call SystemParametersInfo(SPI_GETNONCLIENTMETRICS, _
     lngLen, ncm, 0)

    Set oCaptionFont = New Font
    Set oSMCaptionFont = New Font
    Set oMenuFont = New Font
    Set oStatusFont = New Font
    Set oMessageFont = New Font

    Call SetFontInfo(ncm.lfCaptionFont, oCaptionFont)
    Call SetFontInfo(ncm.lfMenuFont, oMenuFont)
    Call SetFontInfo(ncm.lfMessageFont, oMessageFont)
    Call SetFontInfo(ncm.lfSMCaptionFont, oSMCaptionFont)
    Call SetFontInfo(ncm.lfStatusFont, oStatusFont)
End Sub
```

3. **Copy the data back from the Font objects**. In the SaveSettings method of the class, the code must perform the reverse of the set of steps in the Initialize event procedure. Here, it must retrieve all the font information from the various Font objects, filling in the appropriate LogFont structures in the typNonClientMetrics structure. It uses the private GetFontInfo procedure to move the data back from the Font objects. Finally, it calls the SystemParametersInfo function to send the information back to Windows:

```
Public Sub SaveSettings()
    ' Save all changed settings.
    Dim lngLen As Long
    lngLen = Len(ncm)
    ncm.cbSize = lngLen
    ' Need to copy all the font values back into the
    ' LogFont structures.
    Call GetFontInfo(ncm.lfCaptionFont, oCaptionFont)
    Call GetFontInfo(ncm.lfMenuFont, oMenuFont)
    Call GetFontInfo(ncm.lfMessageFont, oMessageFont)
    Call GetFontInfo(ncm.lfSMCaptionFont, oSMCaptionFont)
    Call GetFontInfo(ncm.lfStatusFont, oStatusFont)
    ' Now save all the settings back to Windows.
    Call SystemParametersInfo(SPI_SETNONCLIENTMETRICS, _
        lngLen, ncm, SPIF_TELLALL)
End Sub
```

The SetFontInfo and GetFontInfo procedures are both simple, moving data from one data structure into an equivalent object and back. There are two interesting challenges along the way, however:

- Working with the array of bytes that contains the face name in the LogFont structure

- Converting the font size to and from the familiar point size, since that's not the way the LogFont structure stores it

The next two sections deal with these issues.

Working with the Face Name

In order to support international versions, VBA stores all its strings internally using the Unicode character mapping. In Unicode, each visible character takes up two bytes of internal storage. Because Windows 95 and Windows 98 do not support Unicode and support only the ANSI character mapping (with one byte for each character), VBA must convert strings it sends to and from the Windows API into ANSI. This happens regardless of which operating system the application is running under, although Windows NT and Windows 2000 do completely support Unicode.

The problem in working with the font name in the NonClientMetrics class is that the LogFont structure retrieves the font name (also referred to as its *face name*) into an ANSI string, which you must convert to Unicode before manipulating the font name within VBA. Luckily, VBA provides the StrConv function, which allows you to convert strings to and from Unicode. The NonClientMetrics class uses this function to perform the conversion. (See Chapter 1 for more information on working with strings and byte arrays.)

The font name member of the LogFont structure is declared like this:

```
lfFaceName(0 To LF_FACESIZE - 1) As Byte
```

where FACESIZE is a constant with a value of 32. Why isn't lfFaceName simply declared as a 32-byte string? The problem is that if you tell VBA that a variable contains a string, it assumes that that string is stored in Unicode and processes it as though it contained two bytes per character. Declaring the value as an array of bytes keeps VBA from mangling the string. Figure 9.16 shows the Immediate window displaying both the raw ANSI and converted Unicode versions of the value in the lfFaceName field of a LogFont structure.

FIGURE 9.16

ANSI and Unicode representations of the ANSI FaceName element

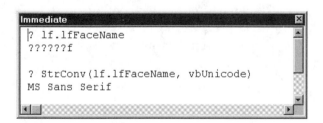

The problem, then, is getting the array of bytes in and out of a Unicode string. Getting it into a string is simple: Because the StrConv function can take a byte array as its input, you can use it to move the byte array, converted to Unicode, directly into a string. The SetFontInfo procedure in the NonClientMetrics class does just this:

```
With oFont
    ' Code removed...
    .FaceName = dhTrimNull(StrConv(lf.lfFaceName, vbUnicode))
End With
```

One final issue in this conversion is the removal of extra "junk" after the name of the font. The dhTrimNull function (borrowed from Chapter 1 of this book) looks for the first null character (vbNullChar) in a string and truncates the string at that point. Because the Windows API returns strings with an embedded Null indicating the end of the string, dhTrimNull is a useful tool whenever you're moving strings from a Windows API function call into VBA.

The tricky issue is getting the string back into the byte array in the LogFont structure in order to send the information back to Windows. Although you can assign a variant directly into a dynamic byte array, you cannot do the same with a fixed-size array, which is exactly what LogFont contains. Therefore, to get the text back into that array, the SetFaceName procedure in NonClientMetrics must traverse the input string, byte by byte, once it's converted the string back to ANSI.

Listing 9.18 shows the entire SetFaceName procedure. This procedure starts out by converting the Unicode string containing the new face name back into ANSI, using the StrConv function. StrConv places its return value into a dynamic byte array. (The byte array makes it fast and simple to traverse the string one byte at a time later on.)

```
abytTemp = StrConv(strValue, vbFromUnicode)
```

Then the code places the length of the string into the intLen variable. Because the array filled in by the StrConv function is zero-based, the number of items in the array is 1 greater than its UBound:

```
intLen = UBound(abytTemp) + 1
```

The LogFont fixed-sized array can hold only LF_FACESIZE – 1 characters, so the code next checks to make sure it's not going to try to write more characters than that to the structure:

```
If intLen > LF_FACESIZE - 1 Then
    intLen = LF_FACESIZE - 1
End If
```

Finally, it's time to write the bytes into the structure, using a simple loop:

```
For intI = 0 To intLen - 1
    lf.lfFaceName(intI) = abytTemp(intI)
Next intI
```

As the final step, the code inserts a null value (0) into the final position in the string. The Windows API expects to find this value as the string delimiter, and bypassing this step can cause trouble for your API calls. (Normally, when you pass a string to the API, you needn't worry about this—it's only because we've copied the string in, one byte at a time, that it's an issue at all.)

Listing 9.18: Moving a Unicode String Back into an ANSI Byte Array Takes a Few Steps.

```
Private Sub SetFaceName(lf As LogFont, strValue As String)
    ' Given a string, get it back into the ANSI byte array
    ' contained within a LOGFONT structure.
    Dim intLen As String
    Dim intI As Integer
    Dim varName As Variant
    Dim abytTemp() As Byte
    abytTemp = StrConv(strValue, vbFromUnicode)
    intLen = UBound(abytTemp) + 1
    ' Make sure the string isn't too long.
    If intLen > LF_FACESIZE - 1 Then
        intLen = LF_FACESIZE - 1
    End If
    For intI = 0 To intLen - 1
        lf.lfFaceName(intI) = abytTemp(intI)
    Next intI
    lf.lfFaceName(intI) = 0
End Sub
```

Although it's a bit more work to get the Unicode string back into the ANSI buffer than it was to get the ANSI buffer into a Unicode string, once you've got the code worked out, you needn't worry about it in the future. The NonClientMetrics class uses this code whenever you work with any of the Font objects, and should you need to use this functionality in any of your own classes (Windows uses the LogFont structure in many situations), you can lift the code from this class.

Working with Point Sizes

The LogFont structure maintains information about the font's height and width in pixels rather than its point size. It's the font's point size that you see when you choose a font in any Windows application, however. Therefore, to make the Font object's Size property work as you'd expect, the NonClientMetrics class must convert the font height into a standard point size.

When Windows provides the font width and height in the LogFont structure, it fills in 0 for the lfWidth member and a negative value for the lfHeight member. The negative value indicates internally that Windows should provide the closest match for the character height requested. The code in NonClientMetrics must, therefore, convert to and from that negative value in the lfHeight member of the LogFont structure.

When converting from the LogFont structure into points, the formula to use is

```
points = -Int(lngHeight * 72 / lngLogPixelsY)
```

where lngLogPixelsY is the number of pixels per logical inch on the screen. Because there are 72 points per logical inch, this calculation converts from pixels (the value in the LogFont structure) to points.

Where does the value for lngLogPixelsY come from? Windows itself provides this information, using the GetDeviceCaps API function. If you're interested, check out the code in the CalcSize procedure in the NonClientMetrics class. This value returns, for the specific screen driver, the number of screen pixels there are per logical inch of screen real estate. (The driver itself converts from logical inches to real inches, but that isn't part of this story.)

Converting back from points to pixels when saving a new font size is no more difficult. The formula for this conversion is

```
pixels = -Int(lngHeight * lngLogPixelsY / 72)
```

The CalcSize procedure in NonClientMetrics takes care of both translations for you. It's called whenever you move font information to or from a LogFont structure.

Power Status

To help applications take advantage of the power management features of portable (or desktop) computers that support these features, Windows 95, Windows 98, and Windows 2000 supply two API functions, GetSystemPowerStatus and SetSystemPowerState, that provide information about, and control over, the status of your computer's power. The PowerStatus class (POWERSTATUS.CLS) provides properties and methods you can use to investigate the computer's use of power and even to suspend the computer if it supports that functionality.

| **NOTE** | Unfortunately, power management features don't work in standard Windows NT 4 (and many unhappy Windows NT 4 users will attest to this). None of the features in the PowerStatus class will work under the current version of Windows NT unless you have installed software from other vendors that adds this functionality. Set the RaiseErrors property of the PowerStatus object to False if you don't want the properties to raise an error but to simply fail silently. |

Table 9.26 lists all the properties of the PowerStatus class. They're all read-only, as you'd expect. Many of the properties return numeric values grouped as enumerations. (See Table 9.28 for a list of the enumerated values.)

TABLE 9.26:   PowerStatus Class Properties

Property	Data Type	Description
ACLineStatus	pwrACLineStatus	AC power status. One of the following: 0 (offline, using batteries), 1 (online, plugged in), 2 (backup power), 255 (unknown)
BatteryCharging	Boolean	True or False
BatteryLifePercent	Byte	Percentage of battery charge remaining from 0–100; 255 if unknown
BatteryLifeTime	Long	Number of seconds of battery life remaining; –1 if unknown
BatteryFullLifeTime	Long	Number of seconds of battery life available when the battery is at full charge; –1 if unknown. This estimate is based on the BatteryLifeTime and BatteryLifePercent fields.
BatteryState	pwrBatteryFlag	Battery charge status. Any combination of one or more of the following: 1 (high), 2 (low), 4 (critical), 128 (no system battery), 255 (unknown)
DrivePowerState	Boolean	Returns True if the drive is fully turned on
IsSystemResumeAuto	Boolean	Returns True if the system was restored to the working state automatically and the user is not active

In addition to the properties defined in Table 9.26, the PowerStatus class includes a few methods as defined in Table 9.27.

TABLE 9.27: PowerStatus Class Methods

Method	Description
CancelWakeupRequest	Cancels a wake-up request issued by a previous call to RequestWakeUp. Returns False if the device does not support wake-up, the system is entering the sleeping state, or wake-up could not be enabled. The wake-up functionality may not be turned off immediately.
RequestWakeup	Issues a wake-up request to the specified device. Returns False if the device does not support wake-up, the system is entering the sleeping state, or wake-up could not be enabled.
RemainAwake	Enables the calling applications to inform the system that it is in use, thereby preventing the system from entering the sleeping power state while the application is running. Pass in a value from the pwrExecutionState enumeration.
Suspend	Attempts to use the computer's built-in power management to suspend the computer (not all computers support this functionality). If power has been suspended and subsequently restored, the return value is nonzero.
WakeUpLatency	Specifies roughly how quickly the computer should enter the working state. (Pass in a value from the pwrLatencyTime enumeration.)

Table 9.28 defines all the enumeration data types the PowerStatus class uses.

TABLE 9.28: PowerStatus Class Enumeration Data Types

Enumeration	Constant	Description
pwrACLineStatus	AC_LINE_OFFLINE	Offline mode, connected
	AC_LINE_ONLINE	Online mode, disconnected
	AC_LINE_BACKUP_POWER	Using Backup power
	AC_LINE_UNKNOWN	Unknown line status
pwrBatteryFlag	BATTERY_FLAG_HIGH	Battery charge status is High.
	BATTERY_FLAG_LOW	Battery charge status is Low.
	BATTERY_FLAG_CRITICAL	Battery charge status is Critical.
	BATTERY_FLAG_CHARGING	Battery is currently charging.
	BATTERY_FLAG_NO_BATTERY	No system battery
	BATTERY_FLAG_UNKNOWN	Unknown battery status

TABLE 9.28: PowerStatus Class Enumeration Data Types *(continued)*

Enumeration	Constant	Description
pwrExecutionState	ES_SYSTEM_REQUIRED	Informs the system that the application is performing some operation that is not normally detected as activity by the system
	ES_DISPLAY_REQUIRED	Informs the system that the application is performing some operation that is not normally detected as display activity by the system
	ES_USER_PRESENT	Indicates that a user is present, in which case the system will use the power management policies set up by the user. Otherwise, the system will return to the sleeping state as soon as possible.
	ES_CONTINUOUS	Tells the system to use the state being set until the next call that uses ES_CONTINUOUS with one of the other state flags cleared
pwrLatencyTime	LT_DONT_CARE	Any latency (default).
	LT_LOWEST_LATENCY	Advanced Power Management is suspended, and it takes the least amount of time (when compared to working state) for the computer to wake up.

Using the PowerStatus Class

The PowerStatus class consists of a few read-only properties, so it's simple to use. The following short sections demonstrate using each of the properties.

NOTE None of the following fragments will function correctly under standard Windows NT 4.*x* because it doesn't support power management functionality. However, if you're using a specialized version of Windows NT, modified by your computer manufacturer, these functions may work.

The ACLineStatus Property

The ACLineStatus property indicates whether the power connection is online or offline. The property returns one of the flags pwrACLineOffline, pwrACLine-Online, pwrACLineBackupPower, or pwrACLineUnknown. For example, you could write code like the following to display the AC power status:

```
Dim ps As PowerStatus
Set ps = New PowerStatus
Dim strOut As String
Select Case ps.ACLineStatus
    Case AC_LINE_OFFLINE
        strOut = "Batteries"
    Case AC_LINE_ONLINE
        strOut = "Plugged in"
    Case AC_LINE_BACKUP_POWER
        strOut = "Using backup power"
    Case AC_LINE_UNKNOWN
        strOut = "Unknown"
End Select
```

The BatteryState Property

The BatteryState property returns information about the charge state of the computer's battery. It returns one of the flags BATTERY_FLAG_HIGH, BATTERY_FLAG_LOW, BATTERY_FLAG_CRITICAL, BATTERY_FLAG_NO_BATTERY, or BATTERY_FLAG_UNKNOWN, all of which are contained within the pwrBatteryFlag enumeration data type. You could write code like this to display the battery-charging status:

```
Dim ps As PowerStatus
Set ps = New PowerStatus
Dim strOut As String
Select Case ps.BatteryState
    Case BATTERY_FLAG_HIGH
        strOut = "Full charge"
    Case BATTERY_FLAG_LOW
        strOut = "Low charge"
    Case BATTERY_FLAG_CRITICAL
        strOut = "Critical"
```

```
        Case BATTERY_FLAG_NO_BATTERY
            strOut = "No battery"
        Case BATTERY_FLAG_UNKNOWN
            strOut = "Unknown"
    End Select
```

The BatteryCharging Property

The BatteryCharging property simply returns a Boolean True or False, indicating the current charging state of the battery. If the state is unknown, the property returns False.

The BatteryLifePercent, BatteryLifeTime, and BatteryFullLifetime Properties

These three properties work together to provide information about how long the battery will provide power. The BatteryLifeTime property returns the number of remaining seconds the battery has, and the BatteryFullLifeTime property returns the total number of seconds the battery should last if fully charged. The Battery-LifePercent property returns the percentage of lifetime remaining, as an integer between 0 and 100. Both the BatteryLifeTime and BatteryFullLifeTime properties return the prwBatteryLifeUnknown constant if their status is unknown. The BatteryLifePercent property returns the pwrBatteryPercentageUnknown constant if its value is unknown.

The DrivePowerState Property

The DrivePowerState property allows you to find out whether the specific drive is fully spun up or not. The return value is True if the drive is fully on or False if the drive is in sleep mode. Ideally, if the hard drive is powered down, you should defer accessing it.

The IsSystemResumeAuto Property

This property will return True if the system was restored to the working state automatically and the user is not active at call time.

The Suspend Method

Call the Suspend method of the PowerStatus class to suspend the computer, if it supports the functionality. The method returns 0 if it fails, so you can check the return value to see whether the computer was actually suspended.

The RemainAwake Method

The RemainAwake method lets the operating system know that the system is being currently used, in which case the system will be prevented from entering sleep mode. There are four different types of working states that you can pass to this method, each described in Table 9.28.

The WakeUpLatency Method

This method tells the operating system how quickly the computer should recover from sleep mode. There are five possible sleep states, out of which only two can be used from code, as listed in Table 9.28. The LT_LOWEST_LATENCY constant is the only valid latency value you can pass to this function (the other choice, LT_DONT_CARE, being the default). As the constant's name indicates, this is the quickest amount of time in which the system can recover from a sleep state; in other words, it's the lowest possible latency period.

TIP   To see some of the PowerStatus methods and properties in action, try out the TestPowerStatus procedure in the SysInfoTest module. This procedure attempts to suspend your computer, so make sure you save all your work before trying it (you never know how stable Suspend really is, right?).

Screen and Window Information

Windows provides a great deal of information about the screen and the objects displayed on the screen, such as icons and windows. The NonClientMetrics class includes information about the window borders, but the ScreenInfo class contains properties and methods that work with the screen and icons.

Although the ScreenInfo class (SCREENINFO.CLS) exposes a large number of properties, they're all quite simple. Each read-only property (see Table 9.29) provides a single piece of information about the screen, such as the width or height of the screen or the minimum height or width of a window. Table 9.30 includes a list of read/write properties supplied by the ScreenInfo object, including the data type to specify for each property. Many of these properties allow you to enable or disable new interface features introduced in Windows 98 and Windows 2000, such as the Menu Fade effect and Hot Tracking. The ScreenInfo class, like other classes in this chapter, tracks applicable properties internally by retrieving operating system versions, so include error handling code in your procedures, and double-check these tables to find out if the property that interests you is valid for your operating system. (Make sure you set the RaiseErrors property of the ScreenInfo object to be False, if you don't want to trap errors because of incorrect operating system calls.) Table 9.29 lists the read-only ScreenInfo class properties. Table 9.30 lists the read/write properties, and Table 9.31 lists the methods of the class.

TABLE 9.29: ScreenInfo Class Read-Only Properties

Property	Description
Border3DX	Width, in pixels, of a Window border
Border3DY	Height, in pixels, of a Window border
CaptionBarButtonX	Width, in pixels, of a button in a window's caption or title bar
CaptionBarButtonY	Height, in pixels, of a button in a window's caption or title bar
CaptionButtonX	Width, in pixels, of small caption buttons
CaptionButtonY	Height, in pixels, of small caption buttons
CaptionHeight	Height, in pixels, of a normal caption bar
FixedBorderX	Width, in pixels, of the frame around the perimeter of a window that has a caption but is not sizable
FixedBorderY	Height, in pixels, of the frame around the perimeter of a window that has a caption but is not sizable
FullScreenX	Width of the inside area of a full-screen window. Use GetWorkArea to get the portion of the screen not obscured by docked trays.
FullScreenY	Height of the inside area of a full-screen window. Use GetWorkArea to get the portion of the screen not obscured by docked trays.
HorizontalScrollX	Width, in pixels, of the arrow bitmap on a horizontal scroll bar
HorizontalScrollY	Height, in pixels, of a horizontal scroll bar

TABLE 9.29: ScreenInfo Class Read-Only Properties *(continued)*

Property	Description
IconSizeX	Default width, in pixels, for an icon
IconSizeY	Default height, in pixels, for an icon
IconSpacingX	Width, in pixels, of grid cells for items in Large Icon view
IconSpacingY	Height, in pixels, of grid cells for items in Large Icon view
KanjiWindow	For DBCS versions of Windows, height in pixels of the Kanji window
MaximizedX	Width, in pixels, of a maximized top-level window
MaximizedY	Height, in pixels, of a maximized top-level window
MaxTrackX	Default maximum width, in pixels, of a window that has a caption and sizing borders
MaxTrackY	Default maximum height, in pixels, of a window that has a caption and sizing borders
MenuBarButtonsX	Width, in pixels, of menu bar buttons, such as the child window Close button
MenuBarButtonsY	Height, in pixels, of menu bar buttons, such as the child window Close button
MenuCheckX	Width, in pixels, of the default menu check-mark bitmap
MenuCheckY	Height, in pixels, of the default menu check-mark bitmap
MenuHeight	Height, in pixels, of a normal single-line menu
MinimizedX	Width, in pixels, of a normal minimized window
MinimizedY	Height, in pixels, of a normal minimized window
MinimumX	Minimum width, in pixels, of a window
MinimumY	Minimum height, in pixels, of a window
MinSpacingX	Width, in pixels, of a grid cell for minimized windows
MinSpacingY	Height, in pixels, of a grid cell for minimized windows
MinTrackX	Minimum tracking width, in pixels, of a window
MinTrackY	Minimum tracking height, in pixels, of a window
MonitorCount	Number of display monitors on the desktop under Windows 98 and Windows 2000

TABLE 9.29: ScreenInfo Class Read-Only Properties *(continued)*

Property	Description
PenWindows	True if Microsoft Windows for Pen computing extensions are installed
SameDisplayFormat	True if all the display monitors have the same color format under Windows 2000 and Windows 98. Note that two displays can have the same bit depth but different color formats. For example, the red, green, and blue pixels can be encoded with different numbers of bits, or those bits can be located in different places in a pixel's color value.
ScreenX	Width of the screen, in pixels
ScreenY	Height of the screen, in pixels
SizingBorderX	Width of the horizontal border, in pixels, around the perimeter of a window that can be resized
SizingBorderY	Height of the vertical border, in pixels, around the perimeter of a window that can be resized
SmallCaption	Height, in pixels, of a small caption bar
SmallIconX	Recommended width for a small icon
SmallIconY	Recommended height for a small icon
ThumbX	Width, in pixels, of the thumb box in a horizontal scroll bar
ThumbY	Height, in pixels, of the thumb box in a vertical scroll bar
VerticalScrollX	Width, in pixels, of a vertical scroll bar
VerticalScrollY	Height, in pixels, of the arrow bitmap on a vertical scroll bar
VirtualScreenHeight	Height, in pixels, of the virtual screen under Windows 98 and Windows 2000. The virtual screen is the bounding rectangle of all display monitors.
VirtualScreenWidth	Width, in pixels, of the virtual screen under Windows 98 and Windows 2000
VirtualScreenX	Coordinates for the left side of the virtual screen under Windows 98 and Windows 2000
VirtualScreenY	Coordinates for the top of the virtual screen under Windows 98 and Windows 2000
WindowBorderX	Width, in pixels, of a window border
WindowBorderY	Height, in pixels, of a window border

TABLE 9.30: ScreenInfo Class Read/Write Properties

Property	Data Type	Description
BorderMultiplier	Long	The multiplier factor that determines the width of a window's sizing border
ComboBoxAnimation	Boolean	Sets/returns True if the slide-open effect for combo boxes is enabled
DesktopWallpaper	String	Returns the path of the desktop wallpaper on Windows 2000 (does not work with JPG/GIF files); sets the wallpaper for all other operating systems. Supply a string containing a filename, or "(None)" to display no wallpaper. To get the wallpaper value, look in the Registry's HKEY_CURRENT_USER\Control Panel\Desktop\WallPaper key.
DragFullWindows	Boolean	Determines whether dragging of full windows is enabled. If True, Windows displays the entire window contents as you move the window. If False, it displays only a border.
FontSmoothing	Boolean	Indicates whether the font-smoothing feature is enabled
ForegroundFlashCount	Long	Sets or returns the number of times Windows will flash the taskbar button when rejecting a foreground switch request under Windows 2000 and Windows 98
ForegroundLockTimeOut	Long	Sets or returns the amount of time following user input, in milliseconds, during which the system will not allow applications to force themselves into the foreground under Windows 2000 and Windows 98
GradientCaptions	Boolean	Enables or disables the gradient effect for window title bars under Windows 2000 and Windows 98
GridGranularity	Long	Granularity value of the desktop sizing grid. This granularity establishes how much control you have over the size of windows; the larger this setting, the fewer options you have.
HotTracking	Boolean	Enables or disables hot tracking of user-interface elements, such as menu names on menu bars, under Windows 2000 and Windows 98. Hot tracking means that when the cursor moves over an item, it is highlighted but not selected.

TABLE 9.30:   ScreenInfo Class Read/Write Properties *(continued)*

Property	Data Type	Description
IconFontName	String	Font name for icons
IconFontSize	Long	Icon font size
IconHorizontalSpacing	Long	Width of an icon cell
IconTitleWrap	Boolean	Turns icon-title wrapping on or off
IconVerticalSpacing	Long	Height of an icon cell
ListboxSmoothScrolling	Boolean	Enables or disables smooth-scrolling effect for list boxes under Windows 98 and Windows 2000
MenuAnimation	Boolean	Enables or disables menu animation under Windows 98 and Windows 2000
MenuFade	Boolean	Enables or disables menu fade animation under Windows 2000
MenuKeysAlwaysUnderlined	Boolean	Enables or disables the underlining of menu access keys under Windows 98 and Windows 2000
MenuDropAlignment	Boolean	Alignment of pop-up menus. Specify True for right alignment and False for left alignment (the normal state).
MinAnimation	Boolean	Determines the state of minimize animation. If False, Windows doesn't display animation as you minimize a window. Setting this property to False makes Windows appear to run faster.
SelectionFade	Boolean	Enables or disables the selection fade effect under Windows 2000. The selection fade effect causes the menu item selected by the user to remain on the screen briefly while fading out after the menu is dismissed.
TooltipAnimation	Boolean	Enables or disables ToolTip animation under Windows 2000
TooltipFade	Boolean	Sets or returns ToolTip animation under Windows 2000 that is being currently used. True specifies fade effect; False specifies a slide effect.
UIEffects	Boolean	Enables or disables all UI effects en masse under Windows 2000.

TABLE 9.31: ScreenInfo Class Methods

Method	Description
GetWorkarea	Gets the size of the work area. The work area is the portion of the screen not obscured by the taskbar.
SetDeskPattern	Sets the current desktop pattern by causing Windows to read the Pattern setting from the WIN.INI file. To get a desktop pattern, look in HKCU\Control Panel\Desktop\Pattern.
SetWorkArea	Sets the size of the work area. The work area is the portion of the screen not obscured by the taskbar.

Using the ScreenInfo Class

The ScreenInfo class exposes many properties, all useful in particular circumstances, but all very specific. If you're not using a Japanese version of Windows, for example, you'll never have a need for the KanjiWindow property. On the other hand, you may often need the ScreenX and ScreenY properties. We can't begin to suggest reasons you'd need all these properties; we've simply provided them here, as properties of a ScreenInfo object, because Windows makes them available. Experiment with the read/write properties to see their effect on your environment before unleashing them in your applications.

As with other objects, working with these properties requires only creating an instance of the ScreenInfo object:

```
Dim oScreen As ScreenInfo
Set oScreen = New ScreenInfo
oScreen.MinAnimation = False
oScreen.IconFontName = "Tahoma"
If oScreen.ScreenX > 1024 Then
    MsgBox "You have a very large amount of screen real estate!"
End If
```

Working with the methods of the ScreenInfo object requires a bit more information. The GetWorkArea and SetWorkArea methods allow you to control the area that Windows thinks is available for maximized windows. You can retrieve the coordinates of this region, and you can modify them as well.

To retrieve the coordinates of the work area, you must pass four long integer variables to the GetWorkArea method. It fills in the value of the four long integers for you. To set the new work area, call SetWorkArea, passing one or more of the four coordinates. If you omit a coordinate when you call SetWorkArea, the code will use the current setting for that coordinate. This way, you can modify one or more of the coordinates without having to pass them all in. Once you've called the following code fragment, maximizing a window will leave empty space at the bottom because you've changed what Windows thinks is its work area for maximized windows:

```
Dim lngLeft As Long
Dim lngTop As Long
Dim lngRight As Long
Dim lngBottom As Long
Dim oScreen As ScreenInfo
Set oScreen = New ScreenInfo
' Get the current work area:
Call oScreen.GetWorkArea(lngLeft, lngTop, lngRight, lngBottom)
' Move the bottom up by 10%:
lngBottom = Int(.90 * lngBottom)
Call oScreen.SetWorkArea(Bottom:=lngBottom)
```

Creating the ScreenInfo Class

Like several other classes, most of the properties in the ScreenInfo class get their values from either the GetSystemMetrics or the SystemParametersInfo function. The only properties that required any extra code were the IconFontName and IconFontSize properties. Because both of these properties get their values from a LogFont structure, the ScreenInfo class faces the same obstacles that the NonClientMetrics class faced. The problems were solved with similar code. (See the "Working with the Face Name" and "Working with Point Sizes" sections earlier in this chapter for more information.)

TIP   To try out the properties of the ScreenInfo class, run the TestScreen procedure in the SysInfoTest module.

System Colors

Windows provides a set of system colors, which it uses when displaying any window. Any application can override the system colors, of course, but the colors are there for Windows', and your, use. Table 9.32 lists the properties of the System-Colors class (SYSTEMCOLORS.CLS), all read/write, that you can use to retrieve and set the Windows system colors.

TABLE 9.32: Properties of the SystemColors Class

Property	Description
ActiveBorder	Border of active window system color
ActiveCaption	Caption of active window system color. Specifies the left-side color in the color gradient of an active window's title bar under Windows 98 and Windows 2000
ActiveGradientColor	Right-side color in the color gradient of an active window's title bar under Windows 2000 and Windows 98
AppWorkspace	Background of MDI desktop system color
Background	Windows desktop system color
ButtonFace	Button system color
ButtonHighlight	3-D highlight of button system color
ButtonShadow	3-D shading of button system color
ButtonText	Button text system color
CaptionText	Text in window caption system color
DarkShadow3D	3-D dark shadow system color
GrayText	Gray text system color
Highlight	Selected item background system color
HighlightText	Selected item text system color
HotTrackItem	Color for a hot-tracked item under Windows 2000 and Windows 98
InactiveBorder	Border of inactive window system color
InactiveCaption	Caption of inactive window system color
InactiveCaptionText	Text of inactive window system color

TABLE 9.32:   Properties of the SystemColors Class *(continued)*

Property	Description
InactiveGradientColor	Right-side color in the color gradient of an inactive window's title bar under Windows 2000 and Windows 98
Light3D	Light color for 3-D shaded objects
Menu	Menu system color
MenuText	Menu text system color
ScrollBar	Scrollbar system color
TooltipBackground	Tooltip background system color
TooltipText	Tooltip text system color
Window	Window background system color
WindowFrame	Window frame system color
WindowText	Window text system color

Using the SystemColors Class

To use the SystemColors class, just as with the other classes in this chapter, first create a new instance of the class, and then work with its properties. For example, to change the background color of buttons, you could use code like this:

```
Dim sc As SystemColors
Set sc = New SystemColors
Dim lngColor As Long
lngColor = sc.ButtonFace
' Set the button background to be red.
sc.ButtonFace = 255
' Later, put the color back:
sc.ButtonFace = lngColor
```

By the way, should you try this experiment, you may be surprised; changing the ButtonFace property also changes the color of many other objects in Windows, including scrollbars and menu bars. Unfortunately, there's no support in the API for controlling the Windows color scheme, so you'll need to work with each color separately. It's also unfortunate that we could find no documentation on the interrelations between various screen artifacts and the system colors—you'll find that changing one of the properties of the SystemColors object may, in fact, change the color of a seemingly unrelated object. Experiment carefully when using these properties in applications.

Using System Colors in Your User Interface

If you intend to assign the system color values to elements of your application's user interface, don't assign the value you retrieved from properties of the System-Colors object. Although you can do this if you like, it will defeat your purpose. If a user changes the system colors, you want your interface to automatically alter itself to match the new colors. If you hard-code a value you retrieve at design time, your interface cannot magically alter itself.

If, instead, you choose a value from Table 9.33, your user interface will always match the settings chosen in the Windows color scheme. Use the values in the first column in your VBA code and the values in the second column in property sheets.

TABLE 9.33: System Color Constants for Use in the User Interface

VBA Constant	Value for Property Sheet	Description
vbScrollBars	&H80000000	Scrollbar color
vbDesktop	&H80000001	Desktop color
vbActiveTitleBar	&H80000002	Color of the title bar for the active window
vbInactiveTitleBar	&H80000003	Color of the title bar for the inactive window
vbMenuBar	&H80000004	Menu background color
vbWindowBackground	&H80000005	Window background color
vbWindowFrame	&H80000006	Window frame color
vbMenuText	&H80000007	Color of text on menus
vbWindowText	&H80000008	Color of text in windows
vbTitleBarText	&H80000009	Color of text in caption, size box, and scroll arrow
vbActiveBorder	&H8000000A	Border color of active window
vbInactiveBorder	&H8000000B	Border color of inactive window
vbApplicationWorkspace	&H8000000C	Background color of multiple document interface (MDI) applications

TABLE 9.33:   System Color Constants for Use in the User Interface *(continued)*

VBA Constant	Value for Property Sheet	Description
vbHighlight	&H8000000D	Background color of items selected in a control
vbHighlightText	&H8000000E	Text color of items selected in a control
vbButtonFace	&H8000000F	Color of shading on the face of command buttons
vbButtonShadow	&H80000010	Color of shading on the edge of command buttons
vbGrayText	&H80000011	Grayed (disabled) text
vbButtonText	&H80000012	Text color on push buttons
vbInactiveCaptionText	&H80000013	Color of text in an inactive caption
vb3DHighlight	&H80000014	Highlight color for 3-D display elements
vb3DDKShadow	&H80000015	Darkest shadow color for 3-D display elements
vb3DLight	&H80000016	Second-lightest 3-D color after vb3DHighlight
vbInfoText	&H80000017	Color of text in ToolTips
vbInfoBackground	&H80000018	Background color of ToolTips

Creating the SystemColors Class

The SystemColors class was one of the simplest in this chapter to create. It relies on only two API functions: GetSysColor and SetSysColors. GetSysColor retrieves a single system color, given a constant representing the item to be retrieved. For example, the following excerpt from the SystemColors class retrieves the background color for ToolTips:

```
Public Property Get TooltipBackground() As Long
    ' ToolTip background color system color.
    TooltipBackground = GetSysColor(COLOR_INFOBK)
End Property
```

Setting a system color requires a tiny bit more effort because the SetSysColors function is capable of setting multiple colors at once. The code in Listing 9.13 sets the background color for ToolTips, using the SystemColors' SetColor procedure.

This procedure calls the SetSysColors API procedure, which allows you to send as many colors as you like. SetColor is sending only a single color, but it could work with a group of colors at a time. In this case, it passes 1 as the first parameter, indicating that it's supplying only a single color. The second parameter indicates which color it's sending (COLOR_INFOBK, a predefined constant, indicates that this color is the background for ToolTips), and the third supplies the new color.

Listing 9.13: Setting a System Color Calls the SetColor Procedure

```
Public Property Let TooltipBackground(Value As Long)
    ' ToolTip background color system color.
    Call SetColor(COLOR_INFOBK, Value)
End Property
Private Sub SetColor(lngID As Long, lngValue As Long)
    Call SetSysColors(1, lngID, lngValue)
End Sub
```

TIP   You may find that you'd rather have the SystemColors class allow you to set a number of new colors before sending the information to Windows. This will make the update faster because Windows won't try to repaint the screen after each color change. To do this, you'll need to create an array of colors, one for each constant in the SystemColors class module. Then, in each Property Let, modify the value in the appropriate row of the array rather than calling SetColor. Finally, you'll need to add a new method of the class that you'll call when you're ready to update all the colors. This method will call SetSysColors, passing the number of items in the array (29, if you use the colors in the class module), an array containing the numbers 0 through 28, and an array containing all the new colors. That will cause Windows to set all 29 colors at once. One more tip: Make sure you initialize the color array with all the current colors in the Initialize event of the class. Otherwise, when you set the new colors, all the colors you haven't modified will contain 0 (black) and your Windows environment will become very difficult to use. The sample project includes a class that works this way—the SystemColorsFast class.

Summary

This chapter has presented, through a series of nine class modules, a demonstration of some of the system and device information that's available as part of the Windows API. By exposing the various bits of information as properties of the classes and grouping the wildly jumbled API calls into logical units, we've attempted to make this large body of information more useful to you as a solution developer.

On the other hand, this chapter just barely skimmed the surface of the system information available from the Win32 API. Although the chapter may seem fairly exhaustive, this is not the case. There are many more corners of the API to be poked at. For example, the GetDeviceCaps and DeviceCapabilities functions offer a treasure trove of information about devices such as the installed video and printer drivers. The properties discussed in this chapter should go a long way toward getting you the information you need for your solutions. In addition, should you need to add more information gathered from the API, the class modules provided in this chapter should be a good start for your own coding.

In particular, this chapter provided class modules dealing with the following areas of the Win32 API:

- Accessibility features
- Keyboard
- Memory status
- Mouse
- Non-client metrics
- Power status
- Screen and window information
- System colors
- Operating system and computer information

Other chapters in this book discuss additional issues that are pertinent to the discussion in this chapter. For example, for information on working with disks and files and gathering information about these objects, see Chapter 12. For information on working with the System Registry, see Chapter 10.

Managing Windows Registry Data

■ Understanding the Windows Registry

■ Exploring the Registry API

■ Writing functions to read and write Registry entries

■ Wrapping Registry functions in class modules

The Registry is at the heart of 32-bit Windows. It is a hierarchical database that contains configuration information for Windows applications, as well as for Windows itself. Windows 9*x* and Windows NT simply cannot function without the information stored in their Registries. Being able to view and edit information contained in the Registry is an essential ability for serious developers.

This chapter looks at how the Registry works and how you can interact with it. We begin with an explanation of its structure and how to use the graphical Registry Editor application to view and change information stored there. We then examine the Registry API, a subset of the Windows API that includes functions for manipulating Registry information. Finally, you'll see how to encapsulate these functions in VBA class modules, making adding Registry support to your applications as simple as including a few module files. Table 10.1 lists the sample files included on the CD-ROM.

TABLE 10.1: Sample Files

Filename	Description
REGISTRY.XLS	Excel file with class modules and a test procedure
REGISTRY.MDB	Access 2000 database with class modules and a test procedure
REGISTRY.VBP	Visual Basic project containing sample code
REGTEST.BAS	Text file with sample functions
SAMPREG.BAS	Sample Registry procedures from examples in this chapter
SIMPREG.BAS	Simple registry wrapper functions
KEY.CLS	Example class module as text
KEYS.CLS	Example class module as text
VALUE.CLS	Example class module as text
VALUES.CLS	Example class module as text
MAIN.FRM	Start-up form for the Visual Basic project
WIN32REG.CLS	Example class module as text

Registry Structure

If you're a longtime Windows developer and/or user, it should come as no shock that the Registry evolved as a way to organize application information that was once stored in a multitude of INI files. While INI files offered many advantages (for example, as text files, you could edit them using a simple tool like Notepad), as more Windows applications were developed, it became hard to keep track of all the associated configuration information. Furthermore, it was difficult to store some types of information, such as binary data, in text files.

Microsoft created the Registry as a hierarchically structured database and created a special API to deal with it. Initially (in Windows 3.*x*) it was used to store information related to OLE. In Windows NT, and then Windows 95, it was expanded to store other configuration information, and application developers were encouraged to move away from INI files and keep their program information in the Registry.

Today, information in the Registry is actually stored in two separate files (USER .DAT and SYSTEM.DAT in the Windows directory). Additionally, part of the Registry is not stored at all but instead is generated based on a computer's hardware configuration. However, applications that use the information need not be aware of this since they all interact with the Registry using a standard set of API functions.

The two primary items of interest in the Registry are keys and values. You use *keys*, sometimes referred to as *folders*, to organize Registry information in a hierarchical structure, much the way directories organize files in the file system. Like a directory, a key can have multiple subkeys, which themselves can have subkeys, and so forth. On the other hand, *values* are the actual data stored within each key. In our file system analogy, values represent individual files. However, unlike a directory, a key can have a value directly associated with it (called its *default* value), as well as other values that it contains. This structure is illustrated graphically in Figure 10.1, which shows the Windows Registry Editor application. You can launch this application by running REGEDIT.EXE.

As you can see in Figure 10.1, at the Registry's root are keys that contain distinct categories of information. In Registry nomenclature, these are referred to as *hives*. Of particular interest are HKEY_CURRENT_USER, which contains settings and preferences for the current user, and HKEY_LOCAL_MACHINE, which contains configuration information that applies to the computer itself. HKEY_ CLASSES_ ROOT exists for backward compatibility with the Windows 3.1 Registry and 16-bit Registry functions, and contains information on installed software and file associations. HKEY_USERS contains configuration options for all users who have accounts on the computer. In fact, HKEY_CURRENT_USER is a virtual hive and is actually a subkey of HKEY_USERS.

FIGURE 10.1
REGEDIT, the Windows
Registry editor

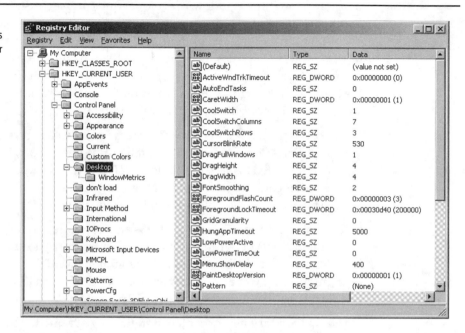

FIGURE 10.1
REGEDIT, the Windows
Registry editor

Figure 10.1 shows the HKEY_CURRENT_USER hive expanded to reveal its subkeys. In the right-hand pane, you can see the values associated with the Desktop key. Each value has a unique name, except for the default value (shown at the top of the value list), which has no name. The icon to the left of each value indicates its data type. The Windows 3.1 Registry supported only string values. The Win32 registry supports a variety of data types, each of which is described in Table 10.2. (The Constant column lists VBA constants that we've defined in the sample code.) However, the most common data types are String and DWORD (Long Integer).

TABLE 10.2: Data Types Supported by Windows 95 and Windows NT Registries

Data Type	Constant	Value	Description
String	dhcRegSz	1	A variable length, null-terminated text string.
DWORD	dhcRegDword	4	A 32-bit long integer.
Binary	dhcRegBinary	3	Binary data. Microsoft recommends limiting each value to 1MB or less.

TABLE 10.2: Data Types Supported by Windows 95 and Windows NT Registries *(continued)*

Data Type	Constant	Value	Description
Multiple strings	dhcRegMultiSz	7	An array of strings terminated by two null characters.
Unexpanded	dhcRegExpandSz	2	A null-terminated string that contains unexpanded references to environment variables, for example, "%PATH%".
Little-endian DWORD	dhcRegDwordLitt leEndian	4	A 32-bit number in little-endian format (same as dhcRegDword). In little-endian format, the most significant byte of a word is the high-order byte. This is the most common format for computers running Windows NT and Windows 95.
Big-endian DWORD	dhcRegDwordBi gEndian	5	A 32-bit number in big-endian format. In big-endian format, the most significant byte of a word is the low-order byte.
Symbolic link	dhcRegLink	6	A Unicode symbolic link.
Resource list	dhcResourceList	8	A device driver resource list
None	dhcRegNone	0	No defined type.

Referring to Registry Keys and Values

Since this chapter discusses individual Registry keys and values, it makes sense to present a format for describing them. In this book (and in most other sources of documentation on the Registry), individual keys are described by their relationship to one of the root hives, using syntax reminiscent of that used by the file system. Specifically, the backslash (\) denotes the key-subkey relationship. Therefore, you would express the Desktop key shown in Figure 10.1 as HKEY_CURRENT_USER\Control Panel\Desktop. Similarly, you would express the Wallpaper value as HKEY_CURRENT_USER\Control Panel\Desktop\Wallpaper. Since it may not be immediately clear from a given example whether the right-most string represents a key or a value, we have tried to make our examples as clear as possible.

VBA Registry Functions

If your needs are simple, VBA provides several built-in functions you can use to read and write Registry values. Microsoft made these functions available as part of VBA so application developers would have an easy way to store configuration options without having to resort to the Windows API. The major drawback of these functions, though, is that they let you work only with keys and values below a given key, namely, HKEY_CURRENT_USER\Software\Microsoft\VB and VBA Program Settings. If you need more flexibility or want to read values from another part of the Registry, you'll need the API functions discussed in the section "Working with Registry Values" later in this chapter. Table 10.3 lists the four VBA Registry functions.

T A B L E 1 0 . 3 :   VBA Functions for Manipulating the Windows Registry

Function	Arguments	Description
GetSetting	App, subkey, value[, default]	Retrieves a single value from a given Registry key.
GetAllSettings	App, subkey	Retrieves all the values for a given key as an array.
SaveSetting	App, subkey, value,	Saves or creates a Registry value for a given key setting.
DeleteSetting	app, subkey[, value]	Deletes a Registry key or a value from a given key.

Each of the Registry functions accepts an argument (app) corresponding to an application name. In the Registry itself, this name refers to a subkey immediately beneath HKEY_CURRENT_USER\Software\VB and VBA Program Settings. The idea is that developers will group all the configuration settings for a single application under one subkey. The second argument (subkey) is the name of another subkey beneath the application key. The screen in Figure 10.2 shows REGEDIT open to a subkey called MyCoolApp\Windows. In this example, you would pass "MyCoolApp" as the first argument to the functions and "Windows" as the second.

The other arguments vary depending on the function being called. For those that call for a value argument, you pass the name of one of the values beneath the specified subkey. In our example, there is one value, "Main". GetSetting lets you pass a default value as an optional fourth argument. If the value name passed as the third argument is not found, GetSetting returns the default. Finally, SaveSetting requires you to pass the setting you want to save as its fourth argument.

FIGURE 10.2
The Registry Editor displays
a VB program setting.

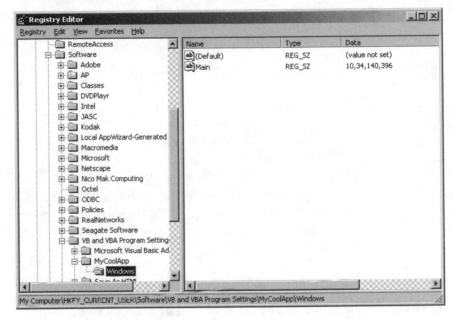

To see how these functions work, open the Immediate window, type the following code snippet, and press Enter:

```
SaveSetting "MyCoolApp", "Windows", "Main", "10,34,140,396"
```

This makes an entry like the one shown in Figure 10.2. To retrieve the value, just enter

```
?GetSetting("MyCoolApp", "Windows", "Main")
```

VBA should respond by printing the string "10,34,140,396" to the Immediate window.

You can delete either the Main value or the entire Windows subkey easily by calling DeleteSetting. Using GetAllSettings is a bit trickier, however, because it returns an array of values as a Variant. To demonstrate this function, first add another string value or two to the Windows subkey, by using either SaveSetting or REGEDIT. Then create the procedure shown in Listing 10.1. The GetAllSettings function supports only string values. (Not surprisingly, this is the only type supported by SaveSetting.)

WARNING   If you create values of another type using REGEDIT and subsequently try to read them using GetAllSettings, VBA raises Error 5, "Invalid procedure call or argument."

Listing 10.1: Print All the Values for a Given Subkey

```
Sub dhPrintValues(strApp As String, strKey As String)
  Dim varValues As Variant
  Dim cValue As Long

  varValues = GetAllSettings(strApp, strKey)
  For cValue = LBound(varValues, 1) To UBound(varValues, 1)
    Debug.Print varValues(cValue, 0), varValues(cValue, 1)
  Next
End Sub
```

PrintValues works by declaring a Variant variable to hold the results of GetAll-Settings. A counter variable, cValues, is used to iterate through all the values contained in the results. Run PrintValues from the Immediate window to see it in action.

Windows Registry Functions

The Windows API implements 25 functions for manipulating the Registry. Of those, only a handful are used very often, and these are geared primarily toward creating, opening, and deleting keys and setting and deleting values. Table 10.4 lists the functions we'll be using in our examples. You'll find all the functions in ADVAPI32.DLL. The examples in the section are contained in the basRegistryTest module in REGISTRY.XLS.

TABLE 10.4: Windows Registry Functions Used in the Examples

Function	Description
RegCloseKey	Closes an open key.
RegCreateKeyEx	Creates a new key or opens an existing key.
RegDeleteKey	Deletes an existing key along with its values and, under Windows 9x, all its subkeys. Under Windows NT or Windows 2000, you must manually delete the subkeys.
RegDeleteValue	Deletes a value from a key.
RegEnumKeyEx	Lists all the subkeys for a given key.
RegEnumValue	Lists all the values for a given key.

TABLE 10.4: Windows Registry Functions Used in the Examples *(continued)*

Function	Description
RegOpenKeyEx	Opens a key for reading and/or writing values.
RegSetValueEx	Sets the contents of a given value.
RegQueryValueEx	Reads the contents of a given value.

Like other elements of Windows, Registry keys are managed using handles, unique 32-bit integers. Before you manipulate a key or its values, you must open it, using RegCreateKeyEx or RegOpenKeyEx. You pass a pointer to a long integer that these functions fill in with the key's handle. You can then use the handle as an input to other Registry functions. Top-level keys have fixed handle values that you can use to open subordinate keys using RegOpenKeyEx. All Registry functions will return either a 0, representing successful completion, or an error code.

Opening, Closing, and Creating Keys

The most basic task in working with the Registry is examining keys and subkeys. This section explains how to use the functions to open and close existing keys, as well as how to create new keys.

The RegOpenKeyEx Function

The declaration for the RegOpenKeyEx function is

```
Declare Function RegOpenKeyEx _
  Lib "advapi32.dll" Alias "RegOpenKeyExA" _
  (ByVal hKey As Long, ByVal lpSubKey As String, _
  ByVal ulOptions As Long, ByVal samDesired As Long, _
  phkResult As Long) As Long
```

The function's first argument is a handle to an existing key. This can be either one of the predefined values representing a root hive or the handle of a key you've previously opened yourself. The second argument is the name of the subkey you wish to open. To specify an immediate subkey, just pass the subkey's name. You can also open a subkey several levels below the current key by passing the relative path of the subkey using the syntax described earlier in this chapter. For example, to open the HKEY_CURRENT_USER\Control Panel\Desktop key, you would supply the predefined handle for HKEY_CURRENT_USER and the string "Control Panel\Desktop" as the second argument to RegOpenKeyEx.

RegOpenKeyEx's third and fourth arguments control how the function treats the key you're trying to open. The ulOptions argument is currently being reserved for future use and must be 0. On the other hand, the samDesired argument defines your desired security access and is a bit-masked value consisting of a number of constants. The constants are listed in Table 10.5; spend a moment reviewing them. Many of the other Registry functions have a security argument. By passing one of these values, you are, in effect, telling the Registry what you intend to do with the key once you've opened it.

TABLE 10.5: Security Bit Masks for Registry Functions

Constant	Value (Hex)	Value (Decimal)	Description
dhcReadControl	&H20000	131072	Bit mask for read permission
dhcKeyCreateLink	&H20	32	Permission to create a symbolic link
dhcKeyCreateSubKey	&H4	4	Permission to create subkeys
dhcKeyEnumerate	&H8	8	Permission to enumerate subkeys
dhcKeyExecute	&H20019	131097	Permission for read access (same as dhcKeyRead)
dhcKeyNotify	&H10	16	Permission for change notification
dhcKeyQueryValue	&H1	1	Permission to read subkey data
dhcKeySetValue	&H2	2	Permission to write subkey data
dhcKeyRead	&H20019	131097	Combination of dhcReadControl, dhcKeyQueryValue, dhcKey-EnumerateSubKeys, and dhcKeyNotify
dhcKeyWrite	&H20006	131078	Combination of dhcReadControl, dhcKeySetValue, and dhcKeyCreateSubKey
dhcKeyAllAccess	&H2003F	131135	Combination of dhcReadControl, dhcKeyQueryValue, dhcKey-EnumerateSubKeys, dhcKeyNotify, dhcKeyCreateSubKey, dhcKeyCreateLink, and dhcKeySetValue

Finally, the phkResult argument is a pointer to a long integer that RegOpenKeyEx will fill in with a handle to the opened key. You should declare a Long variable and pass it to RegOpenKeyEx. If the function returns a 0 (for success), the hKey variable will hold a valid subkey handle and can be used with other functions. Listing 10.2, shown a little later in this chapter, illustrates how to open the HKEY_CURRENT_USER\Control Panel\Desktop key.

The RegCloseKey Function

After opening a key using RegOpenKeyEx or RegCreateKeyEx (explained in the next section), you must close it using RegCloseKey. Leaving a key open consumes memory, and you may, under rare conditions, corrupt your Registry. RegCloseKey accepts a single argument, the handle to an open key, and returns 0 if the key was successfully closed.

The RegCreateKeyEx Function

As its name implies, RegCreateKeyEx creates a new Registry key. However, not so obvious is that you can also use it to open an existing key. If you specify an existing key, RegCreateKeyEx opens it; otherwise, the function creates it. This behavior differs from that of RegOpenKeyEx, which returns an error code if the key does not exist.

RegCreateKeyEx is similar to RegOpenKeyEx, but it takes a few extra arguments. Its declaration is shown here:

```
Private Declare Function RegCreateKeyEx _
  Lib "advapi32.dll" Alias "RegCreateKeyExA" _
  (ByVal hKey As Long, ByVal lpSubKey As String, _
  ByVal ulReserved As Long, ByVal lpClass As String, _
  ByVal dwOptions As Long, ByVal samDesired As Long, _
  lpSecurityAttributes As Any, phkResult As Long, _
  lpdwDisposition As Long) As Long
```

You should recognize the hKey, lpSubkey, samDesired, and phkResult arguments—they're the same as those in RegOpenKeyEx. ulReserved is an unused argument and must be 0. The lpClass argument lets you specify a class descriptor for the key. This information is available to the RegEnumKeyEx function, which is explained in the section "The RegEnumKeyEx Function" later in this chapter.

The dwOptions argument controls what type of key is created. The most common settings for this argument are 0 (dhcRegOptionNonVolatile) and 1 (dhcRegOptionVolatile). Setting this argument to 1 creates a volatile Registry key. Volatile keys are not saved when you shut down your computer and are useful for storing temporary options that are valid only for the current session.

The lpSecurityAttributes argument is a pointer to a SECURITY_ATTRIBUTES structure. This structure defines the Windows NT security attributes you want placed on the new key. Windows 9x does not support operating system security attributes, so this argument is ignored. You'll notice that we've used the Any data type in the declaration. Under Windows NT or Windows 2000, if you pass a null pointer (represented by the value 0&), NT applies the default security attributes. That's what we've done in our examples.

TIP   If you plan to run these examples under Windows NT or Windows 2000 and don't want the default security attributes applied to the new key, pass a pointer to a SECURITY_ATTRIBUTES structure with valid values. You'll find this structure declared in the sample code module.

Finally, the lpdwDisposition argument is a pointer to a Long Integer variable that you pass to the function. When the function returns, the variable will be set either to 1, meaning the key did not previously exist and was created; or to 2, meaning the key was already there and was just opened.

Listing 10.2 shows the dhCreateNewKey procedure, which demonstrates how to create a new Registry key beneath the Desktop key, shown in Figure 10.1. After opening the Desktop key using RegOpenKeyEx, the procedure calls RegCreateKeyEx, passing the Desktop key's handle (hKeyDesktop) and the name of a new key (New Key).

Listing 10.2: Open the Desktop Key and Create a New Subkey

```
Sub dhCreateNewKey()
  Dim hKeyDesktop As Long
  Dim hKeyNew As Long
  Dim lngResult As Long
  Dim lngDisposition As Long

  ' Open the KHEY_CURRENT_USER\Control Panel\Desktop key
  lngResult = RegOpenKeyEx(dhcHKeyCurrentUser, _
   "Control Panel\Desktop", 0&, dhcKeyAllAccess, hKeyDesktop)
```

```
        ' Make sure the call succeeded
    If lngResult = dhcSuccess Then

        ' Create the new subkey
        lngDisposition = 0&
        lngResult = RegCreateKeyEx(hKeyDesktop, _
         "New Key", 0&, "", dhcRegOptionNonVolatile, _
         dhcKeyAllAccess, 0&, hKeyNew, lngDisposition)

        ' If successful, we're done--close the key
        If lngResult = dhcSuccess Then
            lngResult = RegCloseKey(hKeyNew)
        End If

        ' Close the Desktop key
        lngResult = RegCloseKey(hKeyDesktop)
    End If

End Sub
```

Working with Registry Values

Registry values have come along way since the days of Windows 3.1. In the Windows 3.1 Registry, you were limited to a single value per key, and that value had to contain string data. Now you can have an unlimited number of values in each key, and you choose from a wide variety of data types. The following sections discuss how to read, create, and write Registry values.

The RegQueryValueEx Function

Unlike keys, values do not use handles, and you don't need to open them before you can use them. Once you have a key handle, you can read, write, create, or delete any value it contains. RegQueryValueEx is the Registry function used to read an existing value's data. Its declaration is shown here:

```
Private Declare Function RegQueryValueEx _
  Lib "advapi32.dll" Alias "RegQueryValueExA" _
  (ByVal hKey As Long, ByVal lpValueName As String, _
  ByVal dwReserved As Long, lpType As Long, _
  lpData As Any, lpcbData As Long) As Long
```

You'll notice that the function's first argument is a key handle. You pass the handle of a valid, open key. The second argument is the name of the value you want to query. The third argument is another reserved argument and must be 0.

TIP   If you want to access data stored in the default value for a key (all values migrated from the Windows 3.1 Registry will be stored this way), pass an empty string as the name of the value.

The last three arguments retrieve the actual data stored in the value. Since the Registry can store various types of data, you must tell RegQueryValueEx the data type being read, using the lpType argument. You should pass one of the constants listed in Table 10.2 earlier in this chapter.

Finally, lpData and lpcbData specify a buffer you must create to hold the Registry data. lpData is defined as type Any in the function declaration. Depending on the type of data being read, you must pass a String or Long variable, or an array of Bytes (for binary data). Additionally, you must pass the size of the buffer in the lpcbData argument.

WARNING   Always use caution when passing an argument to an API function declared as Any. If you pass a data type that the API function does not expect, or fail to pass the correct size, the result is almost always an Invalid Page Fault (IPF). Remember to save your work before calling any API functions, especially those that use the Any data type.

Listing 10.3 shows a simple example of reading the Wallpaper value of the Desktop key. Wallpaper is a string that specifies the current desktop wallpaper bitmap. Pay special attention to the code that allocates the string buffer. The Space function creates a string buffer 255 bytes in size, and the cb variable is set to this length. After the procedure calls RegQueryValueEx, cb will contain the number of bytes written to the buffer.

Note also the ByVal keyword used in the call to RegQueryValueEx. This is necessary to coerce the VBA String variable into the null-terminated string expected by the API function. Normally, ByVal appears in the declaration of an API function, but we've left it out because we're using the Any data type. If you leave out ByVal in the function call, you will generate an IPF.

⤷ Listing 10.3: Read the Current Windows Wallpaper Setting

```
Sub dhReadWallpaper()
  Dim hKeyDesktop As Long
  Dim lngResult As Long
  Dim strBuffer As String
  Dim cb As Long

  ' Open the KHEY_CURRENT_USER\Control Panel\Desktop key
  lngResult = RegOpenKeyEx(dhcHKeyCurrentUser, _
   "Control Panel\Desktop", 0&, dhcKeyAllAccess, hKeyDesktop)

  ' Make sure the call succeeded
  If lngResult = dhcSuccess Then

    ' Create the buffer
    strBuffer = Space(255)
    cb = Len(strBuffer)

    ' Read the wallpaper value
    lngResult = RegQueryValueEx(hKeyDesktop, "Wallpaper", _
     0&, dhcRegSz, ByVal strBuffer, cb)

    ' Check return value
    If lngResult = dhcSuccess Then

      ' Display the current value
      MsgBox Left(strBuffer, cb), vbInformation, _
        "Current Wallpaper"
    End If

    ' Close the Desktop key
    lngResult = RegCloseKey(hKeyDesktop)
  End If
End Sub
```

Our dhReadWallpaper procedure is coded to deal with string data. For examples of how to handle other data types, see the section "The Value Property" later in this chapter.

The RegSetValueEx Function

You write a value to the Registry in much the same manner as you read a value. In fact, the declaration for RegSetValueEx is nearly identical to RegQueryValueEx:

```
Private Declare Function RegSetValueEx _
  Lib "advapi32.dll" Alias "RegSetValueExA" _
  (ByVal hKey As Long, ByVal lpValueName As String, _
  ByVal dwReserved As Long, ByVal dwType As Long, _
  lpData As Any, ByVal cbData As Long) As Long
```

The only difference, besides the function name, is that instead of passing an empty buffer to the function, you pass data in the lpData argument. You can see this in the dhWriteWallpaper procedure shown in Listing 10.4. It accepts the path to a file as its sole argument and writes this string to the Wallpaper value in the Desktop key.

Listing 10.4: Use the dhWriteWallpaper Procedure to Change the Wallpaper Registry Setting

```
Sub dhWriteWallpaper(strFile As String)
  Dim hKeyDesktop As Long
  Dim lngResult As Long

  ' Open the KHEY_CURRENT_USER\Control Panel\Desktop key
  lngResult = RegOpenKeyEx(dhcHKeyCurrentUser, _
   "Control Panel\Desktop", 0&, dhcKeyAllAccess, hKeyDesktop)

  ' Make sure the call succeeded
  If lngResult = dhcSuccess Then

    ' Save the wallpaper value
    lngResult = RegSetValueEx(hKeyDesktop, "Wallpaper", _
     0&, dhcRegSz, ByVal strFile, Len(strFile))

    ' Check return value
    If lngResult = dhcSuccess Then

      ' Display the success message
      MsgBox "Wallpaper changed to " & strFile, _
        vbInformation, "Wallpaper Changed"
    Else
      ' Display failure message
```

```
        MsgBox "Could not saved wallpaper.", _
          vbExclamation, "Wallpaper Not Changed"
      End If

      ' Close the Desktop key
      lngResult = RegCloseKey(hKeyDesktop)
    End If
End Sub
```

NOTE   Changing the Wallpaper Registry setting does not actually change the Windows wallpaper until you restart your computer. That's because Windows does not monitor this value for changes.

Changes made to the Registry are asynchronous. That is, calling RegSetValueEx does not write the change immediately. Instead, the setting is cached and written later. This is similar to so-called "lazy writes" implemented by the file system. If you are concerned about the delay, you can call the RegFlushKey function, which flushes the Registry cache immediately. Its very simple declaration is shown here:

```
Declare Function RegFlushKey Lib "advapi32.dll" _
(ByVal hKey As Long) As Long
```

Enumerating Keys and Values

The functions described thus far in this chapter are great as long as you know what keys and values you want to manipulate. But what if you don't? What if you want to create an application that lists subkeys or values for an arbitrary Registry key? Fortunately, there are Registry functions that let you do this, as discussed in the next two sections.

The RegEnumKeyEx Function

RegEnumKeyEx (and its counterpart, RegEnumValuesEx) enumerates the subkeys (and values) of a given key. RegEnumKeyEx's declaration is shown here:

```
Declare Function RegEnumKeyEx _
  Lib "advapi32.dll" Alias "RegEnumKeyExA" _
  (ByVal hKey As Long, ByVal dwIndex As Long, _
  ByVal lpName As String, lpcbName As Long, _
  lpReserved As Long, ByVal lpClass As String, _
  lpcbClass As Long, lpftLastWriteTime As Any) As Long
```

You pass RegEnumKeyEx a key handle and the numeric index of the subkey you want information on. Index values run from 0 to one less than the number of subkeys. You also pass buffers to hold the subkey's name and class, as well as a pointer to a FILETIME structure to hold the date and time when the key was last updated. If the specified subkey exists, RegEnumKeyEx populates the buffers and returns a 0, indicating success. If the dwIndex argument lies outside the valid range for existing subkeys, RegEnumKeyEx returns a nonzero result.

Using this information and a simple Do loop, you can write code to list all the subkeys of any existing Registry key. That's what we've done with the dhListSubkeys procedure shown in Listing 10.5.

Listing 10.5: Use RegEnumKeysEx to List a Key's Subkeys

```
Sub dhListSubkeys(hKeyRoot As Long, strSubkey As String)
    Dim hSubkey As Long
    Dim cEnum As Long
    Dim hKey As Long
    Dim lngResult As Long
    Dim strNameBuff As String
    Dim cbNameBuff As Long
    Dim strClassBuff As String
    Dim cbClassBuff As Long
    Dim typFileTime As FILETIME

    ' Open the key passed in
    lngResult = RegOpenKeyEx(hKeyRoot, strSubkey, _
     0&, dhcKeyAllAccess, hSubkey)

    ' Make sure the call succeeded
    If lngResult = dhcSuccess Then

        ' Loop through all subkeys
        Do
          ' Set up buffers
          strNameBuff = Space$(255)
          cbNameBuff = Len(strNameBuff)
          strClassBuff = Space$(255)
          cbClassBuff = Len(strClassBuff)

          ' Call RegEnumKeyEx
```

```
    lngResult = RegEnumKeyEx(hSubkey, cEnum, _
     strNameBuff, cbNameBuff, 0&, _
     strClassBuff, cbClassBuff, typFileTime)

    ' If successful, print subkey name
    If lngResult = dhcSuccess Then
       Debug.Print Left(strNameBuff, cbNameBuff)
    End If

    ' Increment subkey index
    cEnum = cEnum + 1
  Loop Until lngResult <> 0

    ' Close the subkey
    lngResult = RegCloseKey(hSubkey)
  End If
End Sub
```

The RegEnumValue Function

RegEnumValue works in a similar fashion. As you can see from the following declaration, it, too, accepts a key handle and an index number as its first two arguments:

```
Declare Function RegEnumValue _
  Lib "advapi32.dll" Alias "RegEnumValueA" _
  (ByVal hKey As Long, ByVal dwIndex As Long, _
  ByVal lpValueName As String, lpcbValueName As Long, _
  lpReserved As Long, lpType As Long, _
  lpData As Any, lpcbData As Any) As Long
```

In addition, you pass a buffer to hold the value's name. What's interesting about RegEnumValue is that you can also pass a data buffer. This allows you to determine the value's name and the data it contains at the same time. The only drawback is that the method to retrieve a value's data differs depending on its type. To account for any type that may be present, you must pass a pointer to a Byte array as the lpData argument and then interpret the array's contents after the call to RegEnumValue returns.

NOTE   RegEnumValue does not return the default value for a key. It is assumed that this value (which has an empty string for a name) always exists.

---

dhListValues, shown in Listing 10.6, enumerates the values associated with a given key. The screen in Figure 10.3 illustrates how to call the procedure from the Immediate window, as well as a possible result. The numbers shown indicate the data type stored in the value.

NOTE	You can see a list of subkeys by calling the dhListSubkeys procedure with the same set of arguments.

FIGURE 10.3
What happens when you call dhListValues from the Immediate window

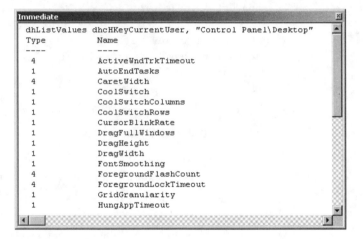

Listing 10.6: Enumerating Registry Key Values

```
Sub dhListValues(hKeyRoot As Long, strSubkey As String)
    Dim hSubkey As Long
    Dim cEnum As Long
    Dim lngResult As Long
    Dim strNameBuff As String
    Dim cbNameBuff As Long
    Dim lngType As Long
    Dim abytData(1 To 2048) As Byte
    Dim cbData As Long

     Open the key passed in
    lngResult = RegOpenKeyEx(hKeyRoot, strSubkey, _
     0&, dhcKeyAllAccess, hSubkey)

    ' Make sure the call succeeded
    If lngResult = dhcSuccess Then
```

```
        ' Print header
        Debug.Print "Type", "Name"
        Debug.Print "----", "----"
        ' Loop through all values
        Do
            ' Set up buffers
            strNameBuff = Space$(255)
            cbNameBuff = Len(strNameBuff)
            Erase abytData
            cbData = UBound(abytData)

            ' Call RegEnumValue
            lngResult = RegEnumValue(hSubkey, cEnum, _
             strNameBuff, cbNameBuff, 0&, _
             lngType, abytData(1), cbData)

            ' Print value name to Immediate window
            If lngResult = dhcSuccess Then
                Debug.Print lngType, Left(strNameBuff, _
                cbNameBuff)

            End If

            ' Increment value index
            cEnum = cEnum + 1
        Loop Until lngResult <> 0

        ' Close the key
        lngResult = RegCloseKey(hSubkey)
    End If
End Sub
```

An Object Model for the Registry

While Registry functions are interesting and useful in their own right, if you are planning on doing any serious Registry manipulation, a function call-based interface can get very cumbersome. The answer (which you should already know if you've read the preceding chapters) is to create an object-based interface using VBA class modules. Fortunately for you, we've already done most of the work.

The remainder of this chapter explains how our Registry object model is constructed, how it works, and how you can use it in your applications.

Not Another Object Model!

As you've no doubt noticed, we're quite fond of promoting the benefits of a well-designed object model implemented using VBA class modules. We also know that sometimes all you need is just a small fraction of the functionality they provide. That's why we've implemented the Registry object model to be modular. In total, there are five class modules that implement the full-featured object model. But it takes just one, WIN32REG.CLS, to get basic read/write functionality.

If all you need to do is read and write Registry values, just import the class module and look for the conditional compilation statement near the end of the declarations section. By changing the following expression:

```
#If True Then
```

to

```
#If False Then
```

you don't need to include any other class modules in your project. Just instantiate the Win32Registry class and call its ReadValue and WriteValue methods.

An Overview

The object model for our Registry components is extremely simple. It consists of only three base classes: Win32Registry, Key, and Value. Two collection classes supplement these classes. The reason it's so simple is because of the hierarchical nature of the Registry. Since a key can contain a number of values, as well as other keys, we can reuse each class over and over. The diagram in Figure 10.4 illustrates the object model for keys and values.

To implement this model using VBA, we need four class modules to represent the objects and collections and a fifth class module to give us a root for the Registry. Table 10.6 lists the class names and their properties and methods. The table also lists the CLS files that define the classes, which we've provided on the CD-ROM.

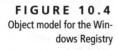

FIGURE 10.4
Object model for the Windows Registry

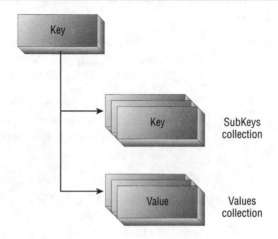

TABLE 10.6: Registry Classes, Properties, and Methods

Class	Filename	Properties	Methods
Win32Registry	WIN32REG.CLS	KeyUser KeyMachine KeyUsers KeyClasses	ReadValue WriteValue
Key	KEY.CLS	Name Handle Parent FullPath Values Subkeys	OpenKey OpenSubKey SubKeyExists DeleteSubkeys
Keys	KEYS.CLS	Count Parent	Add Item Remove Refresh
Value	VALUE.CLS	Name DataType Value Parent FullPath	*None*
Values	VALUES.CLS	Count Parent	Add Item Remove Refresh

Some of the properties and methods shown in the table are worth describing in more detail:

- The root class, Win32Registry, has properties that provide instant pointers to the four most commonly used Registry hives: HKEY_CURRENT_USER, HKEY_LOCAL_MACHINE, HKEY_USERS, and HKEY_CLASSES_ROOT.

- Key objects have a Handle property that is set to the handle returned by the Registry functions when the key is opened. Since all Registry functions depend on handles to keys, creating a Handle property for the Key object makes a lot of sense.

- Key objects have an OpenSubKey method that returns a reference to a descendant key. Unlike the SubKeys collection, which contains one key for each subkey exactly one level below the current key, OpenSubKey lets you open a subkey that is several levels deep by using a qualified relative path (for example, Control Panel\Desktop\WindowMetrics).

- The Keys and Values collection classes both have a Refresh method. Refresh resets each class' internal Collection object and repopulates it with Key and Value objects representing the subkeys and values of the current key. OpenSubKey calls the Refresh methods of each class. You can also call this yourself to update the collections with the most recent contents.

- All objects have a Parent property. In each case, this refers to a Key object that represents a given object's parent key.

Implementing the Classes

This section highlights certain interesting characteristics and procedures of the sample code in our class modules.

NOTE   Registry constants are implemented as enumerated types declared in the Win32-Registry class.

ReadValue and WriteValue Methods

Because sometimes all you want to do is read or write a particular subkey's value, we've implemented two methods that do this directly: ReadValue and WriteValue. Both take four arguments, the first of which is a constant representing the hive key you want to work with. The next two arguments are the names of a subkey and value, respectively. The fourth argument differs, depending on which method you call. ReadValue accepts an optional long integer that it will fill in with the data type of the value read. WriteValue accepts the actual data you want written, as a variant.

The following code snippet shows how you might use these methods to write a new value to the Registry and then read it back again:

```
Dim objReg As Win32Registry

Set objReg = New Win32Registry
objReg.WriteValue HKeyCurrentUser, "Control Panel", "Custom", 1024
Debug.Print objReg.ReadValue(HKeyCurrentUser, "Control Panel", _
    "Custom")
```

NOTE   The subkey name should always be in the form of a relative path to the hive key with no leading or trailing backslashes.

The Add Methods

The Add method defined in the Keys class module (shown in Listing 10.7) accepts a key name and calls the RegCreateKeyEx Registry function. RegCreateKeyEx will either create a new, or open an existing, subkey of a given key, specified by a key handle. We get the handle from the parent key's Handle property. If the function executes successfully, the Add method creates a new Key instance, sets its property values (including Parent), and adds it to the Private mcolKeys collection.

⤵ Listing 10.7: Add Method of the Keys Class

```
Public Function Add(ByVal Name As String) As Key
    Dim objKey As New Key
    Dim lngRet As Long
    Dim lngDisp As Long
    Dim hKey As Long

    ' Call RegCreateKey--for existing keys this will
    ' open them; for nonexistent keys this will
    ' create them
```

```
lngRet = RegCreateKeyEx(hKey:=mobjParent.Handle,
 lpSubKey:=Name, ulReserved:=0&, _
 lpClass:="", dwOptions:=RegOptionNonVolatile, _
 samDesired:=KeyAllAccess, _
 lpSecurityAttributes:=ByVal 0&, phkResult:=hKey, _
 lpdwDisposition:=lngDisp)

' If successful, add key to the collection and
' set the return value to point to it
If lngRet = Success Then
  objKey.Name = Name
  objKey.Handle = hKey

  ' Add item for default value
  objKey.Values.Add "", RegSz

  Set objKey.Parent = mobjParent
  mcolKeys.Add objKey, objKey.Name
  Set Add = objKey
End If
End Function
```

NOTE   You must manually add a member to the Values collection for the key's default value because it always exists and does not show up when you use the Refresh method (and because RegEnumValue doesn't return a value representing the key's default value).

The Add method of the Values class (Listing 10.8) works similarly, except that it does not call a Registry function. Instead, it just adds a new Value object to the mcolValues collection of the class. Note that it accepts an optional argument that can contain the new Value object's value. If you supply this argument, the Add method sets the Value property after creating a new object instance. Using optional arguments allows for greater coding flexibility. You can either set all the property values as part of the Add method or set them individually after adding the object to the collection. In both cases, the Add method returns a pointer to the newly added object. This makes it very easy to set additional property values by capturing the pointer in an object variable. An alternative to passing arguments and returning an object reference is to pass an entire object to the Add method. See the sidebar "Passing Objects to the Add Method" for more details on this approach.

Listing 10.8: Add Method of the Values Class

```
Public Function Add(ByVal Name As String, _
  ByVal DataType As Variant, _
  Optional ByVal Value As Variant) As Value

    ' Create new Value instance
    Dim objValue As New Value

    ' Set the new Value's Parent property
    ' to point to the collection's Parent
    Set objValue.Parent = mobjParent

    ' Set the requisite property values
    objValue.Name = Name
    objValue.DataType = DataType

    ' If optional argument was supplied,
    ' set the Value property value
    If Not IsMissing(Value) Then
        objValue.Value = Value
    End If

    ' Add new instance to the collection,
    ' using its Name as the unique key
    mcolValues.Add objValue, objValue.Name

    ' Set the return value to reference the
    ' new object
    Set Add = objValue
End Function
```

The Value Property

Our Value class implements a Value property that represents the contents of an individual Registry value. There are two interesting characteristics of this property. First, since the contents of a Registry value can be different data types, we must treat this property as a variant. In our object model, it will be one of three types: String, Long Integer, or an array of Bytes (for binary values). Second, we never cache the value in our class. That is, when the Value property is used by

Passing Objects to the Add Method

An alternative to the approach used for the Add methods in our example is to pass an object reference to the Add method instead of simple values. You should consider this method if you would otherwise have to pass a large number of parameters or if your object model does not support the idea of independent objects. For instance, the Jet DAO model allows you to create new tables in an Access database using TableDef and Field objects. (Jet is the database engine that manages Microsoft Access databases.) For instance, to create a new field in a table, you first create a new instance of a Field object. You then set a variety of property values and add it to the table's Fields collection using the Append method. For example:

```
Dim tdf As TableDef
Dim fld As Field
' Get a pointer to a TableDef
Set tdf = db.TableDefs("SomeTable")
' Create the new Field object by calling CreateField
Set fld = tdf.CreateField("NewField")
' Set some property values
fld.Type = dbText
fld.Size = 20
' Append it to the existing Fields collection
tdf.Fields.Append fld
```

Append is Jet's equivalent to the Add method. Again, note that it is an object reference, not a scalar value, that is passed to the method. This makes sense because a Field object isn't useful until several property values have been set and it has been added to the existing fields.

On the other hand, the approach we used is similar to the way Excel's object model works. For example, to add a new Worksheet object to the workbook, you call the Worksheets collection's Add method. You can call it without arguments to add a default worksheet to the workbook or specify optional arguments to dictate position or sheet type. Add also returns a reference to the newly added Worksheet object that you can capture in an object variable (to facilitate setting additional property values) or ignore.

another procedure, we read from or write to the Registry directly. Therefore, any changes to a Value object's Value property are immediately saved to the Registry.

Listing 10.9 shows the Property Get procedure for the Value property. We use a Select Case statement to determine the type of data contained in the Registry value and then call RegQueryValueEx to retrieve it. The function call differs (specifically, the lpData argument) depending on the type of data being requested.

Listing 10.9: Implement the Value Property of the Value Class

```vb
Property Get Value() As Variant
    Dim strBuffer As String
    Dim lngBuffer As Long
    Dim lngRet As Long
    Dim abytData() As Byte
    Dim cb As Long

    ' To return a value we need to figure out
    ' what datatype the value is and then call
    ' RegQueryValueEx using an appropriate lpData
    ' argument
    Select Case mlngDataType

        ' String
        Case RegSz

            ' Create a string buffer and set the
            ' size variable to pass
            strBuffer = Space(RegMaxDataSize)
            cb = Len(strBuffer)

            ' Call RegQueryValueEx passing
            ' address of string buffer
            lngRet = RegQueryValueEx( _
             mobjParent.Handle, mstrName, 0&, _
             mlngDataType, ByVal strBuffer, cb)

            ' If successful, return portion of
            ' buffer filled in by the function
            If lngRet = Success Then
                Value = Left(strBuffer, cb - 1)
            End If

        ' Long Integer
        Case RegDWord
```

```
                ' Set size argument to size of Long
                cb = Len(lngBuffer)

                ' Call RegQueryValueEx passing
                ' address to Long Integer variable
                lngRet = RegQueryValueEx( _
                 mobjParent.Handle, mstrName, 0&, _
                 mlngDataType, lngBuffer, cb)

                ' If successful, return value
                If lngRet = Success Then
                   Value = lngBuffer
                End If

          ' Binary
          Case RegBinary

                ' Create an array of bytes
                ReDim abytData(1 To RegMaxDataSize)
                cb = UBound(abytData)

                ' Call RegQueryValueEx passing
                ' address of first array element
                lngRet = RegQueryValueEx( _
                 mobjParent.Handle, mstrName, 0&, _
                 mlngDataType, abytData(1), cb)

                ' If successful, resize array and
                ' return a pointer to it
                If lngRet = Success And cb > 0 Then
                   ReDim Preserve abytData(1 To cb)
                   Value = abytData
                End If
          End Select
    End Property
```

Determining the Full Path of Keys and Values

Occasionally, you'll want to know what the full path of a particular Registry key or value is. The Name property will give you the name or relative path, but what about the full path, starting at the root? As it turns out, this is easy to compute, given the Parent properties of the class. By using the Parent property to work backward up the Registry hierarchy, you can build a full path by looking at the Name properties of all the interceding objects.

Listing 10.10 shows the FullPath property of the Key class. (The Value class uses almost identical code.) Notice that we first set a pointer to the key's immediate parent and then use a Do loop to build the path string. Each time through the loop, we reset the `objParent` pointer to the current object's parent. Eventually, we reach the top of the hierarchy, and `objParent` becomes Nothing. This causes our loop to terminate, at which point we append the original key's name and return the result.

Listing 10.10: Use the Parents of a Key to Generate Its Full Path

```
Property Get FullPath() As String
  Dim objParent As Key
  Dim strTemp As String

  ' Set starting point
  Set objParent = mobjParent

  ' Loop until objParent is Nothing (at the root)
  Do Until objParent Is Nothing
    strTemp = objParent.Name & "\" & strTemp
    Set objParent = objParent.Parent
  Loop

  ' Add this key's name
  strTemp = strTemp & mstrName

  ' Set return value
  FullPath = strTemp
End Property
```

Removing Registry Keys

The Remove method of the Keys class is worth mentioning because it uses recursive method calls to delete all the subkeys beneath the key being removed. This is necessary under Windows NT or Windows 2000 because the RegDeleteKey function will fail if the key being deleted has subkeys. (It works perfectly well under Windows 9x, however.) Listing 10.11 shows the code for the Remove method.

⟳ Listing 10.11: Remove Method of the Keys Class

```
Public Sub Remove(ByVal ID As Variant)
  Dim lngRet As Long
  Dim objSubKey As Key
  Dim lngSubKeys As Long
  Dim cSubKeys As Long

  ' This code removes all of the current key's
  ' subkeys by calling the Remove method recursively
  ' First refresh the subkeys
  mcolKeys(ID).SubKeys.Refresh

  ' Get a count (because the property will change)
  lngSubKeys = mcolKeys(ID).SubKeys.Count

  ' Loop through all the subkeys
  For cSubKeys = lngSubKeys To 1 Step -1
    ' Call Remove recursively
    mcolKeys(ID).SubKeys.Remove cSubKeys
  Next

  ' Call RegDeleteKey to delete the subkey
  lngRet = RegDeleteKey(mobjParent.Handle, _
   mcolKeys(ID).Name)
  ' If successful then remove it from the collection
  If lngRet = Success Then
    mcolKeys.Remove ID
  End If

End Sub
```

Note that the method first calls the Refresh method of the key's SubKeys collection. This is necessary to ensure that we get all the subkeys. The method then stores a count of the subkeys and loops backward from the total number to 1. You must loop backward because the number of items in the collection changes inside the loop.

TIP   You'll probably want to be able to check whether you were, in fact, running under Windows NT, since deleting a large number of subkeys can be time consuming. Chapter 9 describes code that will tell you the current operating system. It should be a simple matter to integrate it into this Keys class module.

Using the Registry Objects

Now that we've explained the highlights of our Registry classes, this section shows you how to use them. All the code in this section can be found in the TestRegClasses procedure that we've included in a global module in REGISTRY.XLS (and independently as TESTREG.BAS). To really see what's going on, place a breakpoint on the first line of code in the procedure and step through the code as it executes.

Opening a Subkey

To use the Registry classes, you must first instantiate it. This automatically opens the four common hive keys and provides you with pointers to them. It's then easy to open a subkey by calling the OpenSubkey method of whichever hive you're interested in. OpenSubKey accepts a relative path to the subkey (without leading or trailing backslashes) and returns a Key object reference if the call is successful. Listing 10.12 shows an example that opens the HKEY_CURRENT_USER\Control Panel\Desktop key. Note the use of the Key's FullPath property to print the full path of the newly opened key.

Listing 10.12: Open HKEY_CURRENT_USER\Control Panel\Desktop

```
Dim objRegistry As Win32Registry
Dim objKey As Key
' Open the registry
Set objRegistry = New Win32Registry

' Open the Control Panel\Desktop subkey
Set objKey = objRegistry.KeyUser.OpenSubKey( _
  "Control Panel\Desktop")

' Print the key's full path
Debug.Print "Opened: " & objKey.FullPath
```

Listing Subkeys and Values

OpenSubKey also calls the Refresh methods of the key's SubKeys and Values collections. You can then manipulate any of these using the appropriate collection reference. For example, Listing 10.13 shows how you would print the names and handles of any subordinate keys, and the names and contents of any values.

Listing 10.13: List a Key's Subkeys and Values

```
Dim objSubKey As Key
Dim objValue As Value
Dim cObject As Long

' List any subkeys
Debug.Print "Subkeys:"
For cObject = 1 To objKey.SubKeys.Count
  Set objSubKey = objKey.SubKeys.Item(cObject)
  Debug.Print objSubKey.Name, objSubKey.Handle
Next
' List any values
Debug.Print "Values:"
For cObject = 1 To objKey.Values.Count
  Set objValue = objKey.Values.Item(cObject)
  Debug.Print objValue.Name, objValue.Value
Next
```

Creating New Keys and Values

To create new subkeys and values, just add new objects to the SubKeys and Values collections. Listing 10.14 demonstrates how to add a new subkey called "CustomOptions". We first use the SubKeyExists method to determine whether the key already exists. If it does, we use the Remove method of the SubKeys collection to delete it.

Listing 10.14: Add a New Subkey and Values

```
' Check to see whether it exists, and if so, delete it
If objKey.SubKeyExists("CustomOptions") Then
  objKey.SubKeys.Remove "CustomOptions"
End If

' Add a new subkey beneath ...\Desktop
Set objNewKey = objKey.SubKeys.Add("CustomOptions")
Debug.Print "Added: " & objNewKey.FullPath

' Set the default value
objNewKey.Values.Item("").Value = "Default"
```

```
' Add a string value
Set objNewValue = objNewKey.Values. _
 Add("SomeString", rc.RegSz)
objNewValue.Value = "This is great fun!"
Debug.Print "Added: " & objNewValue.FullPath

' Add a DWORD (long) value
Set objNewValue = objNewKey.Values. _
 Add("SomeDWORD", rc.RegDWord)
objNewValue.Value = 1024
Debug.Print "Added: " & objNewValue.FullPath

' Add a binary value
Set objNewValue = objNewKey.Values. _
 Add("SomeBinary", rc.RegBinary)
objNewValue.Value = Array(0, 1, 2, 4, 8, 16, 32, 64, 128)
Debug.Print "Added: " & objNewValue.FullPath
```

After the procedure adds the new subkey, it adds some new values to it. It starts with the default value, which was added to the Values collection when the subkey was created. It then creates a new string, DWORD, and binary values. Note that the binary value is created using an array of integers between 0 and 255. The screen in Figure 10.5 shows the new subkey and values displayed in REGEDIT.

FIGURE 10.5
Viewing the newly added information

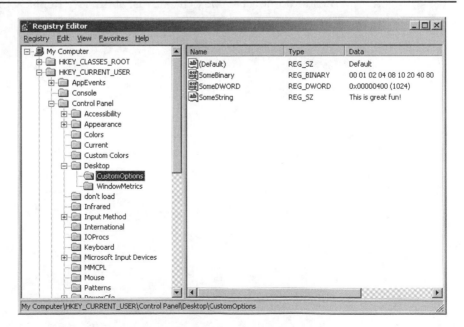

Summary

If you're a serious developer, you'll have to delve into the Registry sooner or later. Although you can use the Windows Registry Editor application, it is not practical to force your users to do this. In this chapter, we've looked at two ways to programmatically manipulate the contents of the Registry, including built-in VBA functions, as well as a number of API functions. Specifically, we discussed the following topics:

- Understanding the structure of the Windows Registry
- Using the VBA functions GetSetting, GetAllSettings, DeleteSetting, and SaveSetting
- Manipulating keys using the API functions RegOpenKeyEx, RegCreateKeyEx, and RegCloseKey
- Manipulating values using the API functions RegQueryValueEx and RegSetValueEx
- Enumerating keys and values using the API functions RegEnumKeyEx and RegEnumValue
- Building an object model for the Registry using VBA class modules

You should now be able to tackle just about any Registry problem.

chapter 11

The Windows Networking API

- Using common network dialogs

- Connecting to and disconnecting from shared network resources

- Retrieving network information

- Enumerating network resources

- Using the LAN Manager API

VBA does not directly expose many of the networking capabilities of Windows 95 and 98 or Windows NT and Windows 2000. Although it does allow you to make use of objects, such as mapped drives and network paths, once they exist, the ability to find, connect to, disconnect from, or enumerate these objects is not available in VBA. However, all of these actions are available through the Windows API. In this chapter, we cover many of the most useful functions in the WNet and LAN Manager APIs to help you make your applications more "network aware."

NOTE Why cover both WNet and LAN Manager API calls? In general, the WNet API calls are simpler to use and solve most of your networking needs. The LAN Manager API functions are more general purpose, require a bit more work to use, and can be a bit intimidating, with over 100 different functions to choose from. In this chapter, we provide an overview of both sets of networking API functions, with the emphasis on WNet functions—the ones most people need. In addition, several of the LAN Manager API functions are not available from Windows 95/98, but only from Windows NT/2000, so their use is limited by that distinction, as well. We include samples of functions that are supported under Windows 95 and 98, and ones that are not.

NOTE In this chapter (and throughout the book) we'll use Windows 95/98 to refer to behaviors that apply to both Windows 95 and Windows 98. We'll use Windows NT/2000 to refer to both Windows NT 4 and higher, and Windows 2000. Where behaviors are specific to Windows NT 3.51, we'll mention that version separately.

Table 11.1 lists the sample files you'll find on the CD-ROM.

T A B L E   1 1 . 1 :   Sample Files

Filename	Description
NETWORK.XLS	Excel 2000 file with sample functions
NETWORK.MDB	Access 2000 database with sample functions
NETWORK.BAS	Text file with sample functions
NETRESOURCEINFO.CLS	A helper class used by some of the functions in NETWORK.BAS

TABLE 11.1: Sample Files

Filename	Description
TESTPROCEDURES.BAS	Test procedures
NETWORK.VBP	VB project file with sample functions
MAIN.FRM	Start-up form for the VB project

WARNING   Many of the API calls in this chapter count on NetBIOS for their functionality. In all versions of Windows before Windows 2000, you could be guaranteed that the user had NetBIOS installed. In Windows 2000, although it's not the default configuration, it's possible that users can opt not to install NetBIOS. In that case, many of the functions in this chapter will fail. If you're using code from this chapter in your own applications, you'll need to make it clear to users, as part of your installation instructions, that they must have NetBIOS installed.

Basic Network Functionality

This section examines the basic network functions you might want to use in your applications, such as:

- Connecting to network resources with standard dialogs
- Disconnecting from network resources with standard dialogs
- Connecting to network resources via code
- Disconnecting from network resources via code
- Retrieving information about network resources

Using Common Network Dialogs

The easiest way, and the one users will find most familiar, to add network awareness to your applications is to use the dialogs the operating system provides that allow you to connect to and disconnect from network resources.

Connecting to a Network Resource with a Dialog

Figure 11.1 shows an example of the Windows NT 4 Network Connection dialog. However, be aware that network connection dialog boxes vary between operating systems. Although Windows NT 3.51 and 4 use similar dialog boxes, the dialog box Windows 95/98 uses is very different. It requires you to type in a UNC path, and it provides an MRU (Most Recently Used) list of connections made previously, but there are none of the browse capabilities you find in Windows NT. The corresponding dialog box in Windows 2000 makes things even easier for you— you can browse, or not, to find the path you need. The more limited Windows 95/98 dialog is shown in Figure 11.2.

FIGURE 11.1

Connecting to network resources with the Windows NT 4 Map Network Drive connection dialog

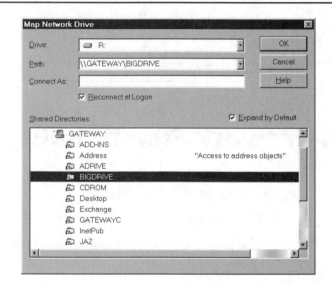

FIGURE 11.2

Connecting to network resources with the Windows 95/98 Map Network Drive connection dialog

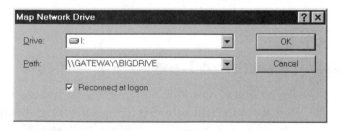

You'll use the following declaration to invoke the dialog:

```
Private Declare Function WNetConnectionDialog Lib "mpr.dll" _
    (ByVal hwnd As Long, ByVal dwType As Long) As Long
```

The only information you need to pass to the dialog is the window handle that will be the parent of the dialog (or specify 0 to use the Windows screen as the parent, effectively specifying no parent window) and the type of resources to display. Constants representing the common values used by the dialog are shown in Table 11.2.

TABLE 11.2: Commonly Used Constants for the Network Dialogs

Constant	Value	Meaning
dhcNoError	0&	Function call was successful.
dhcDlgCancelled	−1&	User cancelled the dialog.
dhcErrorExtendedError	1208&	An extended error occurred.
dhcErrorInvalidPassword	86&	Given password is invalid.
dhcErrorNoNetwork	1222&	No network was detected.
dhcErrorNotEnoughMemory	8&	There is not enough memory to display the dialog.
dhcResourceTypeDisk	1&	Use a resource of "disk" type.
dhcResourceTypePrint	2&	Use a resource of "print" type.

TIP   In general, we've found it easier not to call the networking API functions directly, because it's important to make sure all the parameters are set up properly. We've provided wrapper functions for each API function to ensure that each function is called correctly. Most of the API calls return an error code that tells you whether the call succeeded; in some cases, the wrapper functions will do the same, and in other cases, they will use the return value internally.

Listing 11.1 demonstrates a function you can use to call the WNetConnection-Dialog API.

Listing 11.1: Wrapper Function to Call the Network Connection Dialog

```
Public Function dhConnectDlg( _
Optional ByVal hWnd As Long = 0) As dhcNetworkErrors
    ' Display the dialog to connect to network resources
    Dim lngReturn As dhcNetworkErrors
```

```
        Dim lngExtendedError As Long

        ' Call the net connection dialog
        lngReturn = WNetConnectionDialog(hWnd, dhcResourceTypeDisk)

        ' If the call failed, get error information
        If lngReturn <> dhcNoError Then
            lngExtendedError = dhGetLastNetworkError(True)
            ' If there was an extended error,
            ' return it instead of the standard error
            If lngExtendedError = dhcNoError Then
                dhConnectDlg = lngReturn
            Else
                dhConnectDlg = lngExtendedError
            End If
        End If
    End Function
```

Under Windows NT/2000, you can pass only the dhcResourceTypeDisk flag to WNetConnectionDialog, but under Windows 95/98, you can pass the dhcResourceTypePrint flag as well, which allows you to connect to network printers.

Retrieving Extended Network Error Information

One interesting thing to note about the code in Listing 11.1 is the extra work dhConnectDlg does to decide which error code to return:

```
If lngExtendedError = dhcNoError Then
    dhConnectDlg = lngReturn
Else
    dhConnectDlg = lngExtendedError
End If
```

The main reason for this extra work is historical: The WNetConnectionDialog function, which has been around for quite some time, returns the same basic error values that its 16-bit version did: 0 for success, –1 for cancellation, and a few specific error values. Rather than change the return values for this function, which would break compatibility with converted applications, Microsoft chose to use the extended error capability provided by the WNetGetLastError function in order to return detailed information. Other network API functions use it as well, but the WNetDisconnectDialog function uses it extensively because it doesn't return much error information on its own.

The dhConnectDlg function, as well as several other functions in this chapter, calls the dhGetLastNetworkError function to retrieve extended error information. Many of the WNet API functions may return dhcErrorExtendedError, which requires you to call the WNetGetLastError API immediately to retrieve more detailed error information. We've provided dhGetLastNetworkError as a wrapper around the WNetGetLastError API function; this wrapper returns the extended error number and, optionally, if more information is available, displays a message box providing that information. The code for dhGetLastNetworkError is shown in Listing 11.2.

Listing 11.2: Get Information about the Last Network Error That Occurred

```
Public Function dhGetLastNetworkError( _
 Optional fDisplayError As Boolean = False) As dhcNetworkErrors
    ' Get error information from the last network operation

    Dim lngReturn As dhcNetworkErrors
    Dim lngError As Long
    Dim strError As String
    Dim lngErrorLen As Long
    Dim strProvider As String
    Dim lngProviderLen As Long

    ' Set up buffers for the error info (they should be
    ' at least 256 characters but it does not hurt to
    ' make them longer).
    strError = String$(256, vbNullChar)
    strProvider = String$(256, vbNullChar)
    lngErrorLen = Len(strError)
    lngProviderLen = Len(strProvider)

    ' Try to get the last error
    lngReturn = WNetGetLastError(lngError, strError, _
     lngErrorLen, strProvider, lngProviderLen)

    If lngReturn = dhcNoError Then
        dhGetLastNetworkError = lngError
        ' If there was extended error info and the calling
        ' procedure wanted it to be displayed here,
        ' then display it.
```

```
        If fDisplayError And (lngError <> dhcNoError) Then
            strError = dhTrimNull(strError)
            strProvider = dhTrimNull(strProvider)
            MsgBox "Error " & lngError & ": " & strError, _
             vbInformation, strProvider
        End If
    End If
End Function
```

WARNING   The most important thing to note about the WNetGetLastError API call is that it returns only the *most recent* error value. You must call dhGetLastNetworkError immediately after you call a function that might have returned an error. If the user performs any network operation, either manually or through some other application, before you call the dhGetLastNetworkError function, the information about your program's error will be lost.

Disconnecting from a Network Resource with a Dialog

As part of your application, you may need to provide a method for users to break a network connection. This functionality is provided by the WNetDisconnectDialog API function, and its declaration is almost identical to that for WNetConnectionDialog:

```
Private Declare Function WNetDisconnectDialog Lib "mpr.dll" _
  (ByVal hwnd As Long, ByVal dwType As Long) As Long
```

This function brings up the dialog shown in Figure 11.3. To call it, you can use the wrapper function dhDisconnectDlg, shown in Listing 11.3.

FIGURE 11.3
Disconnecting from network resources with the Windows NT Disconnect Network Drive dialog box

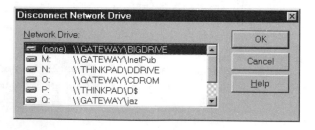

Listing 11.3: Disconnecting from Network Resources

```
Public Function dhDisconnectDlg(Optional ByVal hWnd As Long = 0) _
 As dhcNetworkErrors
    ' Display the dialog to disconnect from network resources

    Dim lngReturn As dhcNetworkErrors
    Dim lngExtendedError As Long

    ' Call the net disconnect dialog
    lngReturn = WNetDisconnectDialog(hWnd, dhcResourceTypeDisk)

    ' If the call failed, get error information
    If lngReturn <> dhcNoError Then
        lngExtendedError = dhGetLastNetworkError(True)
        ' If there was an extended error, return it instead
        ' of the standard error
        If lngExtendedError = dhcNoError Then
            dhDisconnectDlg = lngReturn
        Else
            dhDisconnectDlg = lngExtendedError
        End If
    End If
End Function
```

As with dhConnectDlg, the return value will usually be either dhcNoError, if the dialog disconnected something, or dhcDialogCancelled, if the user cancelled the dialog. It may also be one of the values listed earlier in Table 11.2.

Other Dialogs You Can Use

In addition to the dialogs displayed by the dhConnectDlg and dhDisconnectDlg functions, you can use the standard Windows File Open dialog, discussed in Chapter 12, which contains a convenient Network button that allows the user to connect to a network resource. This dialog is also familiar to most users and is easy to add to your application. When you wish to connect to a network resource, you often also want to select a file once you're connected, so this may be the easiest way to add network awareness to your application.

There are several advantages to using the dialogs the operating system provides:

- They are easy to call and integrate into your applications.

- Their look and feel will be familiar to the user.

- All the work of doing the actual network connections and disconnects is handled by the dialogs themselves.

Of course, there are also some disadvantages:

- When the function call succeeds, you have no easy way of knowing what resources the user connected to.

- There is no way to customize the interface of the dialogs to help them fit into your applications.

- You cannot control the way a connection is made. (For example, you cannot specify whether this connection should persist if the user reboots the machine.)

Because of these problems, many applications that need to add networking capabilities also need to do the work themselves rather than let these dialogs do the work for them. The following section provides information on bypassing the standard dialog boxes.

Handling Network Resources Yourself

Sometimes, you'll want your application to handle all the details of connecting to and disconnecting from network resources. This section covers many of these basic functions.

Connecting to a Network Resource

There are two Win32 API functions that let you connect to a network resource: WNetAddConnection and WNetAddConnection2. The first API call maintains compatibility with the older 16-bit API and is simpler to call, but it isn't as flexible and doesn't return as much information as the newer version. We present both functions here, but you'll normally want to use WNetAddConnection2 in your applications.

The declarations and types for these functions are shown here:

```
Public Type NETRESOURCE
    dwScope As dhcResourceScope
    dwType As dhcResourceType
    dwDisplayType As dhcResourceDisplayType
    dwUsage As dhcResourceUsage
```

```
        ' Pointers to strings
        lpLocalName As Long
        lpRemoteName As Long
        lpComment As Long
        lpProvider As Long

        ' Buffer that contains string data
        abyt(dhcMaxPath * 4) As Byte

        ' Actual location of the final strings
        strLocalName As String
        strRemoteName As String
        strComment As String
        strProvider As String
End Type

Private Declare Function WNetAddConnection Lib "mpr.dll" Alias _
    "WNetAddConnectionA" (ByVal strNetPath As String, _
    ByVal strPassword As String, ByVal strLocalName As String) _
    As Long

Private Declare Function WNetAddConnection2 Lib "mpr.dll" Alias _
    "WNetAddConnection2A" (lpNetResource As NETRESOURCE, _
    ByVal strPassword As String, ByVal strUserName As String, _
    ByVal lngFlags As Long) As Long
```

To call WNetAddConnection, you need only pass in the following parameters:

- Path to which you wish to connect

- Password (if there is one) or a zero-length string

- Local name to which you wish to map this new resource

You can use the dhAddConnection1 function, shown in Listing 11.4, to call WNet-AddConnection.

Listing 11.4: Connect Resources with WNetAddConnection

```
Function dhAddConnection1( _
    strNetPath As String, strPwd As String, _
    strLocalName As String) As dhcNetworkErrors
        ' Adds a network connection
```

```
        dhAddConnection1 = WNetAddConnection(strNetPath, _
            strPwd, strLocalName)
    End Function
```

You can call dhAddConnection1 as follows:

```
lngReturn = dhAddConnection1("\\middlemarch\setup", _
    "password","J:")
```

This connects the local J drive to the specified network share using a password of "password". If you are using an NT domain security model for your network, the function will create a connection with the permissions of the currently logged-in user.

Table 11.3 lists the various constants returned from, and sent to, both the WNetAddConnection and WNetAddConnection2 functions.

TABLE 11.3:   Commonly Used Constants for WNetAddConnection and WNetAddConnection2

Constant	Value	Meaning
dhcNoError	0&	Function call was successful.
dhcErrorAccessDenied	5&	Insufficient permissions to the specified resource.
dhcErrorAlreadyAssigned	85&	Given local name is already assigned to another resource.
dhcErrorBadDevType	66&	Device type and resource type do not match.
dhcErrorBadDevice	1200&	Device is invalid.
dhcErrorBadNetName	67&	Remote resource is invalid or cannot be found.
dhcErrorBadProfile	1206&	User profile is in an incorrect format.
dhcErrorCannotOpenProfile	1205&	User profile cannot be accessed to update persistent information.
dhcErrorDeviceAlreadyRemembered	1202&	An entry for the specified local name is already in the user profile.
dhcErrorExtendedError	1208&	An extended error has occurred.
dhcErrorInvalidPassword	86&	Given password is invalid.
dhcErrorNoNetOrBadPath	1203&	Specified remote resource could not be found or the name is invalid.
dhcErrorNoNetwork	1222&	No network was detected.

TABLE 11.3: Commonly Used Constants for WNetAddConnection and WNetAddConnection2 *(continued)*

Constant	Value	Meaning
dhcResourceTypeAny	0&	Use a resource of any type.
dhcResourceTypeDisk	1&	Use a resource of "disk" type.
dhcResourceTypePrint	2&	Use a resource of "print" type.
dhcMaxPath	260	Maximum number of characters allowed in a path for the remote name.
dhcConnectUpdateProfile	1&	Update the user profile to retain this connection after the user reboots.
dhcConnectDontUpdateProfile	0&	Don't update the user profile.

In many cases, WNetAddConnection is simply not flexible enough. You may need to connect with the username and password of another user (perhaps one with different permissions). You may want to control whether this connection will be persistent if the user reboots the machine, or you may want to specify the network provider when there are multiple networks. If you require these options, you need to use WNetAddConnection2, and you can do so using the dhAddConnection2 wrapper, shown in Listing 11.5.

Listing 11.5: Connect Resources with WNetAddConnection2

```
Public Function dhAddConnection2( _
 strNetPath As String, strLocalName As String, _
 strUserName As String, strPwd As String, _
 Optional lngConnectType As _
  dhcConnectType = dhcConnectUpdateProfile, _
 Optional fIsDiskResource As Boolean = True) As dhcNetworkErrors
    ' Adds a network connection

    Dim usrNetResource As NETRESOURCE

    With usrNetResource
        If fIsDiskResource Then
            .dwType = dhcResourceTypeDisk
        Else
            .dwType = dhcResourceTypePrint
```

```
        End If
        ' Convert the text into ANSI format.
        .strLocalName = StrConv(strLocalName, vbFromUnicode)
        .strRemoteName = StrConv(strNetPath, vbFromUnicode)

        ' Get the pointers to the text strings.
        ' Pass a null pointer (0&) for the
        ' provider.
        .lpLocalName = StrPtr(.strLocalName)
        .lpRemoteName = StrPtr(.strRemoteName)
        .lpProvider = 0&
    End With
    dhAddConnection2 = WNetAddConnection2(usrNetResource, _
      strPwd, strUserName, CLng(lngConnectType))
End Function
```

The function takes the following parameters:

Parameter	Description
strNetPath	UNC path to which to connect.
strLocalName	Local name for the resource (such as K:).
strUserName	User whose permissions should be used for logging in.
strPwd	Password for the user given by strUserName.
lngConnectType	Indicates whether to retain this connection after the user reboots. (Optional; default is dhcConnectUpdateProfile.)
fIsDiskResource	Indicates whether this is a disk resource. True indicates a disk resource; False indicates a print resource. (Optional; default is True.)

The function fills in the members of the NETRESOURCE structure and then calls WNetAddConnection2 for you. Here is an example of calling dhAddConnection2:

```
lngReturn = dhAddConnection2( _
  "\\middlemarch\setup", "K:", "Sam", "", False)
```

This call will connect the K drive to the specified resource with the permissions of the user named Sam (who has no password). When the user reboots, this connection will not be reestablished.

ANSI and Unicode, Again

Sprinkled throughout this book, you'll find references to ANSI and Unicode character sets, and converting between the two. The WNet and LAN Manager API functions really bring this all to the forefront. That is, you can't really work with this set of API functions without running head-on into ANSI versus Unicode issues.

First of all, VBA uses Unicode internally for all its strings. If you are calling an API function that requires ANSI strings, you'll need to convert the strings into ANSI before calling the function. If your API call passes parameters "As String", this isn't an issue—this conversion happens for you. On the other hand, if you're passing strings as part of a user-defined type, VBA doesn't do the conversion for you, and you'll need to call the StrConv function, using the vbFromUnicode option. (Listing 11.5 shows this type of code.)

Because of this ANSI/Unicode duality, VBA attempts to help out when you're calling API functions. That is, VBA assumes that all API function calls require ANSI strings, so any parameter you send will always be converted to ANSI on the way out, and then converted back to Unicode on the return. This works great for API functions that pass strings to functions that expect to receive ANSI strings. What about functions that expect to receive Unicode strings? Later in the chapter, when we're working with LAN Manager API functions, you'll need to pass Unicode strings to the functions. Therefore, you cannot use "As String" to define the parameters in the declaration. Instead, you must use "As Long" and pass the address of the string. By tricking VBA this way, you can pass the address of the string, no conversion takes place, and the API call gets the correct value. You can accomplish this goal using the undocumented StrPtr function—this function takes in a string as a parameter, and returns the address the string occupies in memory. You'll see this technique used all over this chapter.

Disconnecting from a Network Resource

Just as there are two ways to add a network resource, there are two API functions for disconnecting them: WNetCancelConnection and WNetCancelConnection2. The only added feature of the second function is that you can choose whether to update the user's profile with the information that you have disconnected the resource. (If you do not update the user's profile, the resource will be back the next time the user logs in.) The declarations for these functions are shown here:

```
Private Declare Function WNetCancelConnection Lib _
 "mpr.dll" Alias "WNetCancelConnectionA" _
(ByVal lpszName As String, ByVal fForce As Long) As Long

Private Declare Function WNetCancelConnection2 Lib _
 "mpr.dll" Alias "WNetCancelConnection2A" _
(ByVal lpName As String, ByVal dwFlags As Long, _
 ByVal fForce As Long) As Long
```

The common constants that can be used with these functions are shown in Table 11.4.

T A B L E   1 1 . 4 :   Commonly Used Constants for WNetCancelConnection and WNetCancelConnection2

Constant	Value	Meaning
dhcNoError	0&	Function call was successful.
dhcErrorBadProfile	1206&	User profile is in an incorrect format.
dhcErrorCannotOpenProfile	1205&	User profile cannot be accessed to update persistent information.
dhcErrorDeviceInUse	2404&	Device is currently in use and the Force parameter was not set to True.
dhcErrorExtendedError	1208&	An extended error has occurred.
dhcErrorNotConnected	2205&	Given resource is not currently connected.
dhcErrorOpenFiles	2401&	Device is currently in use and files on it are open, and the Force parameter was not set to True.
dhcConnectUpdateProfile	1&	Update the user profile to reflect that this resource was disconnected.
dhcConnectDontUpdateProfile	0&	Don't update the user profile.

To call WNetCancelConnection, you can use the dhCancelConnection1 wrapper function, shown in Listing 11.6. Pass this function the name of the resource to disconnect from and an optional Boolean value (its default is False), indicating whether you want to force the disconnect even if files are open or devices are in use.

Listing 11.6: Disconnect from Resources with WNetCancelConnection

```
Public Function dhCancelConnection1(strLocalName As String, _
Optional fForceDisconnect As Boolean = False) as Long
    ' Cancels a network connection
    dhCancelConnection1 = WNetCancelConnection( _
    strLocalName, Abs(fForceDisconnect))
End Function
```

TIP	The dhCancelConnection1 function uses the Abs (absolute value) function when passing the Boolean parameter fForceDisconnect. Many API calls specify that they accept a Boolean parameter, but C++ defines True as 1, while VBA defines True as −1. In most cases, the API calls check for any value that's not False (that is, anything except 0), so this difference isn't relevant. However, there are exceptions, for example, when a DLL is checking specifically for a True (1) value, in which case, passing a VBA Boolean True (−1) will fail. By the way, this isn't an issue when a DLL passes a value back to your program: If you define a variable as a Boolean and a DLL passes a 1 into that variable, VBA correctly treats the value as True.

Calling WNetCancelConnection2 using the dhCancelConnection2 function (shown in Listing 11.7) is similar. This function adds one more flag, in which you can specify whether you'd like the user's profile to be updated.

Listing 11.7: Disconnect from Resources with WNetCancelConnection2

```
Public Function dhCancelConnection2(strLocalName As String, _
Optional fForceDisconnect As Boolean = False, _
Optional lngConnectType As _
 dhcConnectType = dhcConnectUpdateProfile) As dhcNetworkErrors
    ' Cancels a network connection
    Dim lngFlags As Long

    lngFlags = lngConnectType
    dhCancelConnection2 = _
     WNetCancelConnection2(strLocalName, _
        lngFlags, Abs(fForceDisconnect))
End Function
```

Your users will most likely be somewhat frustrated and confused if you disconnect network resources that they're currently using. Because of this, you should *always* call dhCancelConnection1 and dhCancelConnection2 with the fForceDisconnect parameter set to False. If the return value is dhcErrorOpenFiles or dhcErrorDeviceInUse, you can warn the user that there are open files and that there is a risk of losing unsaved data in these files. If the user confirms wanting to disconnect the connection, you can try to cancel it again, this time setting fForceDisconnect to True.

Retrieving Information about Network Resources

As part of your networked application, you may need to know the UNC path of a specific mapped network drive or the name of the currently logged-in user, or perhaps you need to get (or even change) the name of the computer. This section discusses these topics.

Chapter 9 included methods similar to the dhGetUserName, dhGetComputerName, and dhSetComputerName functions. Because you're likely to use these functions when working with other networking functionality, it seemed worthwhile to repeat their use, in slightly different format, in this chapter.

Getting a UNC Path from a Mapped Network Drive

Imagine this common scenario: In the current session, your application's user has modified a file on a mapped network drive. The next time the user logs in, the drive mapping has changed, and your application can no longer find the same file. How do you work around this problem? Rather than store information about the mapped drive, you convert the drive mapping into a UNC path (including the server and drive name), using the WNetGetConnection API call. This function takes a local path as its input parameter, and it attempts to return a UNC path. (Of course, it may fail because there may not be a corresponding remote path if you've specified an incorrect local path.)

The declaration for WNetGetConnection looks like this:

```
Private Declare Function WNetGetConnection Lib "mpr.dll" _
  Alias "WNetGetConnectionA" (ByVal strLocalName As String, _
  ByVal strRemoteName As String, lngRemoteNameLen As Long) As Long
```

This function accepts the local name, a buffer to contain the UNC path, and the length of the buffer. On return, it will have filled in the buffer with the UNC path (if it succeeded). The return value will be dhcNoError on success, or one of the standard error codes on failure. The most common constants associated with this function are listed in Table 11.5.

TABLE 11.5: Commonly Used Constants for WNetGetConnection

Constant	Value	Meaning
dhcNoError	0&	Function call was successful.
dhcErrorBadDevice	1200&	Local name is invalid.
dhcErrorNotConnected	2205&	Given resource is not currently connected.
dhcErrorMoreData	234&	Buffer is too small. (The buffer length parameter will contain the length that is needed when the function returns this error.)
dhcErrorExtendedError	1208&	An extended error has occurred.
dhcErrorConnectionUnavailable	1201&	Device is not currently connected, but it is a persistent connection.
dhcErrorNoNetwork	1222&	No network is present.
dhcErrorNoNetOrBadPath	1203&	Specified remote resource could not be found or the name is invalid.

To call WNetGetConnection, you can use the dhGetRemoteName wrapper function, which takes the local name and returns the UNC path (or a zero-length string if it fails). The code for this function is shown in Listing 11.8.

Listing 11.8: Get a UNC Path from a Mapped Network Drive

```
Public Function dhGetRemoteName(strLocalName As String) As String
    ' Given a mapped network resource, returns the UNC path

    Dim lngRemoteNameLen As Long
    Dim strRemoteName As String
    Dim lngReturn As dhcNetworkErrors
```

```
Do
    ' Set up the buffer
    strRemoteName = String$(lngRemoteNameLen, vbNullChar)

    lngReturn = WNetGetConnection( _
     strLocalName, strRemoteName, lngRemoteNameLen)

    ' Continue looping until the call succeeds or the error is
    ' anything besides "there's more data"
Loop Until lngReturn <> dhcErrorMoreData

If lngReturn = dhcNoError Then
    dhGetRemoteName = dhTrimNull(strRemoteName)
End If
End Function
```

The Do…Loop structure in dhGetRemoteName uses an interesting, and somewhat common, technique to fill the output buffer. Initially, the value of lngRemote-
NameLen is 0, and the first pass through the loop sets strRemoteName to contain
0 characters, using the String function:

```
Do
    ' Set up the buffer
    strRemoteName = String$(lngRemoteNameLen, vbNullChar)
    ' Code removed here...
Loop
```

When you call WNetGetConnection with a buffer that's too small for its returned
data, the function fills its lngRemoteNameLen parameter with the length of the
buffer it needs and returns dhcErrorMoreData:

```
Do
    ' Code removed here...
    lngReturn = WNetGetConnection( _
     strLocalName, strRemoteName, lngRemoteNameLen)
    ' Continue looping until the call succeeds or the error is
    ' anything besides "there's more data"
Loop Until lngReturn <> dhcErrorMoreData
```

The second time through the loop, the code sets strRemoteName to contain enough
space for the return value, so WNetGetConnection will correctly fill the buffer and
return a value other than dhcErrorMoreData.

The following code fragment provides an example of using dhGetRemoteName to replace a mapped network drive with a UNC path when one exists:

```
' Convert from "T:\SAMPLE.TXT" to
' \\GATEWAY\JAZ\SAMPLE.TXT", assuming that
' T:\ is mapped to \\GATEWAY\JAZ.
If Mid$(strFilePath, 2, 1) = ":" Then
    strRemote = dhGetRemoteName(Left$(strFilePath, 2))
    If Len(strRemote) > 0 Then
        strFilePath = strRemote & Mid$(strFilePath, 3)
    End If
End If
```

NOTE   Rather than use WNetGetConnection, as dhGetRemoteName does, you can use another API function Windows provides that will do the work of putting the path together for you; it even splits up the server and share portions of the UNC path (the connection information) automatically from the rest of the path. This API function, WNetGetUniversalName, is covered in the section "Retrieving Universal Name Information" later in this chapter.

Retrieving the Name of the Currently Logged-In User

You may have applications in which you wish to integrate network security by changing the application's interface or actions based on the currently logged-in user. Whether you're doing this to add security, maintain user preferences and settings, or track usage, knowing who is using the application can be valuable. You can retrieve this information using the WNetGetUser API call, declared like this:

```
Private Declare Function WNetGetUser Lib "mpr" Alias _
  "WNetGetUserA" (ByVal strName As String, _
  ByVal strUserName As String, lngLength As Long) As Long
```

This function actually has two uses, depending on what you pass into the first parameter. If you pass an empty string in the strName parameter, the strUserName buffer will contain the name of the currently logged-in user. If you specify a resource, such as a mapped drive, the buffer will contain the username (or Windows NT domain and username) that was specified when the connection was created. This function can be called both ways with the dhGetUserName function, which takes an optional parameter that is passed in as the strName parameter to WNetGetUser. Listing 11.9 contains the code for dhGetUserName, which is similar to the code in the dhGetRemoteName function. Table 11.6 lists the constants that WnetGetUser most commonly returns.

Listing 11.9: Use WNetGetUser to Identify the Currently Logged-In User

```
Public Function dhGetUserName( _
 Optional strLocalName As String = vbNullString) As String
    ' Retrieve the current network user name

    Dim lngUserNameLen As Long
    Dim strUserName As String
    Dim lngReturn As dhcNetworkErrors

    Do
        ' Set up the buffer
        strUserName = String$(lngUserNameLen, vbNullChar)

        lngReturn = WNetGetUser( _
         strLocalName, strUserName, lngUserNameLen)

        ' Continue looping until the call succeeds or the error is not
    Loop Until lngReturn <> dhcErrorMoreData

    If lngReturn = dhcNoError Then
        dhGetUserName = dhTrimNull(strUserName)
    End If
End Function
```

TABLE 11.6: Commonly Used Constants for WNetGetUser

Constant	Value	Meaning
dhcNoError	0&	Function call was successful.
dhcErrorNotConnected	2205&	Given resource is not currently connected.
dhcErrorMoreData	234&	Buffer is too small. (The buffer length parameter will contain the length that is needed when the function returns this error.)
dhcErrorExtendedError	1208&	An extended error has occurred.
dhcErrorNoNetwork	1222&	No network is present.
dhcErrorNoNetOrBadPath	1203&	Specified remote resource could not be found or the name is invalid.

Getting (and Setting) the Computer Name

In an application that is network aware, you might want to be able to obtain the name of the workstation on which the application is running. The Registry contains this information, and the value is initialized when you log in to Windows. Although you could simply read this information from the Registry, when you change this value (through the Network Properties dialog or the Windows API, or by using REGEDIT.EXE), the computer's "knowledge" of its name does not change until the computer is rebooted. Therefore, the value in the Registry may not be the actual name of the computer.

The Win32 API provides two functions—GetComputerName and SetComputer-Name—to get and retrieve the information. Their declarations are shown here:

```
Private Declare Function GetComputerName Lib "kernel32" _
  Alias "GetComputerNameA" (ByVal strBuffer As String, _
  lngSize As Long) As Long

Private Declare Function SetComputerName Lib "kernel32" _
  Alias "SetComputerNameA" (ByVal strComputerName As String) _
  As Long
```

GetComputerName takes a buffer and the buffer's size as parameters; it fills in the buffer with the computer name and returns a nonzero value when successful. Set-ComputerName takes the new computer name and sets it. (The name will not actually change until you reboot the machine.) You can call the API functions with the dhGetComputerName and dhSetComputerName wrappers, shown in Listing 11.10.

Listing 11.10: Get and Set the Computer Name

```
Public Function dhGetComputerName() As String
    ' Return the workstation's computer name

    Dim lngReturn As Long
    Dim lngBufferSize As Long
    Dim strBuffer As String

    ' Make the buffer big enough for the name plus a vbNullChar
    lngBufferSize = dhcMaxComputernameLength + 1
    strBuffer = String$(lngBufferSize, vbNullChar)

    lngReturn = GetComputerName(strBuffer, lngBufferSize)
```

```
          ' lngReturn will be True on success
          If CBool(lngReturn) Then
              dhGetComputerName = Left(strBuffer, lngBufferSize)
          End If
      End Function

      Public Function dhSetComputerName(strComputerName) As Boolean
          ' Sets the workstation's computer name

          Dim lngReturn As Long

          lngReturn = SetComputerName(strComputerName)

          ' lngReturn will be non-zero on success
          dhSetComputerName = CBool(lngReturn)
      End Function
```

TIP   We've used the simplest code possible in this chapter. For more advanced versions of these functions using the GetComputerNameEx and SetComputerNameEx API functions, see the SystemInfo class in Chapter 9.

Advanced Networking Functionality

The basic network functions discussed in the first part of this chapter can handle most of your networking requirements. However, sometimes you need more than just the basics. This section covers some of the advanced networking features you can add to your VBA applications, such as:

- Retrieving more information about remote resources than WNetGetConnection can provide

- Enumerating connected network resources

- Enumerating available network shares

- Enumerating computers on the network

- Using the LAN Manager API

Retrieving Universal Name Information

The WNetGetUniversalName function can return either a UNC version of a particular remote path (for example, \\GATEWAY\JAZ\Updates when you pass it T:\Updates, when drive T is mapped to \\GATEWAY\JAZ), or a structure filled with information about the mapping, including the various portions of the string \\GATEWAY\JAZ\Updates, to keep you from having to parse the string yourself. However, calling the function presents some interesting challenges that are also applicable to other API function calls. This section discusses using the WNetGetUniversalName function and some of the difficulties involved in calling it from VBA. This discussion also serves as an introduction to the next section, "Enumerating Network Resources," which addresses the issues involved in performing network enumerations, where many of the same problems arise. Luckily, all of these problems can be solved, and the functions can be called successfully from VBA.

Introduction to the Buffer Problem

In theory, all the WNet functions should be as easy to call as the ones you have seen so far. However, in practice, Microsoft has made calling some of the WNet functions from VBA more difficult. The problem is that some of these functions use data structures containing addresses to strings, not the strings themselves, making it tricky to send and retrieve information from these API calls. For example, here is the declaration for the WNetGetUniversalName API:

```
Private Declare Function WNetGetUniversalName Lib "mpr" _
    Alias "WNetGetUniversalNameA" (ByVal strLocalPath As String, _
    ByVal lngInfoLevel As Long, lpBuffer As Any, _
    lngBufferSize As Long) As Long
```

At first glance, the lpBuffer and lngBufferSize parameters look the same as they did in other functions, such as WNetGetUser. However, this time, the buffer will contain a variable of one of the following user-defined types. However, these aren't the actual data types you'll find in the code—we'll discuss those in the next section. These represent the data types you might create if you were to begin doing the work here on your own:

```
Public Type UNIVERSAL_NAME_INFO
    lpUniversalName As String
End Type
```

```
Public Type REMOTE_NAME_INFO
    lpUniversalName As String
    lpConnectionName As String
    lpRemainingPath As String
End Type
```

The problem here is that the API function call allocates space for the strings used by these data structures in the buffer *immediately following the structure in memory.* But the strings inside these user-defined types aren't strings at all: Instead, they're actually pointers to buffers containing the text the function has retrieved.

It all boils down to this: If you call the function properly, you know that all the information is inside the buffer. However, without being able to decipher where the pointers in the REMOTE_NAME_INFO structure are pointing, you have no clean way to extract the information. You cannot even parse the three strings manually, because you can't assume their order within the buffer.

How to Solve the Buffer Problem

You can use a few tricks to solve the buffer problem. The first trick is to use the following two user-defined types instead of the ones given previously:

```
Public Type UNIVERSAL_NAME_INFO
    ' pointer to the string
    lpUniversalName As Long

    ' Add an extra buffer to the end which
    ' will be used to store the string
    abyt(dhcMaxPath) As Byte

    ' the actual location of the final string
    strUniversalName As String
End Type

Public Type REMOTE_NAME_INFO
    ' Pointers to strings
    lpUniversalName As Long
    lpConnectionName As Long
    lpRemainingPath As Long

    ' Add an extra buffer to the end which
    ' will be used to store the strings
    abyt(dhcMaxPath * 3) As Byte
```

```
                ' the actual location of the final strings
                strUniversalName As String
                strConnectionName As String
                strRemainingPath As String
        End Type
```

With those structures defined, you can "lie" about the buffer size so that the API function only sees the amount of memory that you've specified. That is, specify a size for the API function so that you don't include those last few strings (which are really there for your convenience, and the function has no need to know they're there), taking advantage of the fact that the API will not touch memory beyond what you tell it is valid. The heart of the function you use to work with Wnet-GetUniversalName might look like this code from dhGetRemoteInfo:

```
Dim lngReturn As dhcNetworkErrors
Dim lngBufferSize As Long

' Don't include the last three string pointers in the buffer size
' Each pointer takes up four bytes.
lngBufferSize = Len(usrRemoteNameInfo) - 12
lngReturn = WNetGetUniversalName( _
 strLocalPath, dhcRemoteNameInfoLevel, _
 usrRemoteNameInfo, lngBufferSize)
```

Notice that the code subtracts 12 from what it tells the API to use for the buffer size (that is, it removes the size of three long integers, which matches the three long pointers to strings in the structure).

Once you have made this call, you will have three empty strings and three pointers to ANSI strings (because you've called the ANSI version of the function, WnetOpenEnumA), as well as a byte array that happens to contain the data to be placed into those strings. So how do you turn these pointers into real strings that VBA can use? The dhStrFromAnsiPtr function does the work for you—it uses the lstrlen API function to find out how long the string is (lstrlen takes a pointer to a null-terminated string and tells you how many characters it contains), and the lstrcpyn API function to move the specified number of characters:

```
Private Declare Function lstrlen Lib "kernel32" _
 Alias "lstrlenA" (ByVal lpString As Long) As Long

Private Function dhStrFromANSIPtr(lngPtr As Long) As String
        ' Takes a long pointer to an ANSI string and returns
        ' the actual string
```

```
        Dim strTemp As String
        Dim lngLen As Long

        lngLen = lstrlen(lngPtr)
        strTemp = String$(lngLen, vbNullChar)
        If lstrcpyn(StrPtr(strTemp), lngPtr, lngLen + 1) <> 0 Then
            dhStrFromANSIPtr = dhTrimNull(StrConv(strTemp, vbUnicode))
        End If
End Function
```

The Unicode version of this function, which we'll use later when discussing several of the LAN Manager API functions under Windows NT/2000, is shown here. You will notice that the ANSI and Unicode versions are quite similar.

```
Private Declare Function lstrlenW Lib "kernel32" _
  (ByVal lpString As Long) As Long

Private Function dhStrFromPtr(lngPtr As Long) As String
    ' Takes a long pointer to a Unicode string and returns
    ' the actual string

    Dim strTemp As String
    Dim lngLen As Long

    lngLen = lstrlenW(lngPtr)
    strTemp = String$(lngLen, vbNullChar)
    If lstrcpynW(StrPtr(strTemp), lngPtr, lngLen + 1) <> 0 Then
        dhStrFromPtr = dhTrimNull(strTemp)
    End If
End Function
```

Using VarPtr, ObjPtr, and StrPtr

VBA 5 and 6 both contain three useful undocumented functions: VarPtr, StrPtr, and ObjPtr. VarPtr returns the address of the variable passed to it (otherwise referred to as a pointer to the variable). StrPtr returns a pointer to a string variable, and ObjPtr returns a pointer to an object variable. There are many situations, especially in API calls, in which these functions can be useful.

However, be careful! Because these functions are undocumented, they are not supported parts of the VBA function library. As such, they may not exist in future versions of VBA. Particularly looking toward the future with COM+ and moveable memory, these functions may have problems in future versions. However, given the huge dependency that VB, Access, and other Office wizards have on these methods (not to mention code written by users and developers!), if they do take them away, Microsoft will have to provide some other way to accomplish the same tasks.

Listing 11.11 shows two functions using the WNetGetUniversalName API function. The first function, dhGetRemoteInfo, allows you to pass in a local path and an empty REMOTE_NAME_INFO structure to retrieve information about the path. The function fills in the REMOTE_NAME_INFO structure with parsed information about the local path you supplied. The second, dhGetUniversalInfo, is a simpler function that takes a local path and an empty UNIVERSAL_NAME_INFO structure, and returns only the universal name associated with the path.

Listing 11.11: Calling WNetGetUniversalName in Two Ways

```
Public Function dhGetRemoteInfo(strLocalPath As String, _
  usrRemoteNameInfo As REMOTE_NAME_INFO) As dhcNetworkErrors

    Dim lngReturn As dhcNetworkErrors
    Dim lngBufferSize As Long

    ' Don't include the last three string pointers in the buffer size.
    lngBufferSize = Len(usrRemoteNameInfo) - 12
    lngReturn = WNetGetUniversalName(strLocalPath, _
      dhcRemoteNameInfoLevel, usrRemoteNameInfo, lngBufferSize)

    If lngReturn = dhcNoError Then
        ' If the call succeeded, fill the strings in the
        ' REMOTE_NAME_INFO structure.
        With usrRemoteNameInfo
            .strUniversalName = dhStrFromAnsiPtr(.lpUniversalName)
            .strConnectionName = dhStrFromAnsiPtr(.lpConnectionName)
            .strRemainingPath = dhStrFromAnsiPtr(.lpRemainingPath)
        End With
    End If
```

```
        dhGetRemoteInfo = lngReturn
End Function

Public Function dhGetUniversalInfo(strLocalPath As String, _
 usrUniversalNameInfo As UNIVERSAL_NAME_INFO) As dhcNetworkErrors

    Dim lngReturn As dhcNetworkErrors
    Dim lngBufferSize As Long

    ' Don't include the last string pointer in the buffer size.
    lngBufferSize = Len(usrUniversalNameInfo) - 4
    lngReturn = WNetGetUniversalName(strLocalPath, _
     dhcUniversalNameInfoLevel, usrUniversalNameInfo, lngBufferSize)

    If lngReturn = dhcNoError Then
        ' If the call succeeded, fill the string in the
        ' UNIVERSAL_NAME_INFO structure.
        With usrUniversalNameInfo
            .strUniversalName = dhStrFromAnsiPtr(.lpUniversalName)
        End With
    End If

    dhGetUniversalInfo = lngReturn
End Function
```

NOTE   The information provided in this section concerning the dhStrFromAnsiPtr function will also be important in the discussion of network enumerations in the next section of this chapter. The functions used in the next section use buffers in exactly the same way that WNetGetUniversalName does.

For example, to call these two functions, you might write code like this (from the TestProcedures module):

```
Sub TestUniversal(strPath As String)
    Dim uni As UNIVERSAL_NAME_INFO
    Dim rni As REMOTE_NAME_INFO

    If dhGetUniversalInfo(strPath, uni) = dhcNoError Then
        Debug.Print "Universal Name : " & uni.strUniversalName
    End If
```

```
      If dhGetRemoteInfo(strPath, rni) = dhcNoError Then
          Debug.Print "Connection Path: " & rni.strConnectionName
          Debug.Print "Remaining Path : " & rni.strRemainingPath
          Debug.Print "Universal Name : " & rni.strUniversalName
      End If
  End Sub
```

For a path like T:\Updates, where you've mapped drive T to \\GATEWAY\JAZ, the results should look like this:

```
Universal Name : \\GATEWAY\jaz\Updates
Connection Path: \\GATEWAY\jaz
Remaining Path : \Updates
Universal Name : \\GATEWAY\jaz\Updates
```

You can see that both functions return the UNC name, and the dhGetRemoteInfo function can save you from having to parse the full UNC path name yourself.

Enumerating Network Resources

The discussions earlier in this chapter on connecting to, disconnecting from, and getting information about network resources assumed that either you or your users know what devices are available. Other than dhConnectDlg, we have presented no interface that gives you a choice of available network devices. What if you want to provide your own interface, allowing users to select network devices? You'll need to use some sort of enumeration technique, asking the Windows API to provide you with a list of available devices.

Enumerating network devices is a three-step process:

1. Retrieve an enumeration handle, given the starting point for your enumeration.

2. Given the enumeration handle, work through all the contained resources, performing whatever action you need with each resource. Usually, you'll just want to retrieve each device's name to place into a list of your own.

3. Close the enumeration handle once you're done with it.

The Windows API provides three functions that handle the three steps of network enumerations: WNetOpenEnum, WNetEnumResource, and WNetCloseEnum. You'll need to call all three in order to retrieve a list of devices. Think of an enumeration handle as a conduit through which the API returns information about devices. Before you can retrieve a list of devices, you must retrieve an enumeration handle from Windows. To do that, you call WNetOpenEnum, passing several flags about the type of resources you wish to enumerate, and it supplies an enumeration handle. You'll use this handle to retrieve your list of devices, and you enumerate the resources using the WNetEnumResource function. You call this function repeatedly—it fills in a NETRESOURCE structure containing information about each resource—until it's run out of available network resources to enumerate. When you're finished enumerating devices, you use the WNetCloseEnum function to release the enumeration handle.

The next few sections look at using the WNetOpenEnum, WNetEnumResource, and WNetCloseEnum functions to retrieve lists of available network resources.

Getting a Network Enumeration Handle

Retrieving the enumeration handle is the most critical part of the process of enumerating network resources because it's your only chance to indicate to Windows exactly what resources you're looking for. Because you can enumerate everything from connections that are currently on your machine to network shares on someone else's machine (and everything in between), the way you handle the call to WNetOpenEnum controls exactly what you get back from Windows. When you call WNetOpenEnum, you pass three pieces of information:

- Scope of the enumeration

- Types of resources for the enumeration

- Resource usage for the enumeration

The possible value for each parameter is shown in Tables 11.7, 11.8, and 11.9.

T A B L E   1 1 . 7 :   Enumeration Scope Constants

Constant	Value	Meaning
dhcResourceConnected	&H1	All currently connected resources
dhcResourceGlobalNet	&H2	All resources on the network
dhcResourceRemembered	&H3	All remembered (persistent) resources
dhcResourceRecent	&H4	All recently added resources
dhcRecourceContext	&H3	All resources in the current domain

TABLE 11.8: Enumeration Type Constants

Constant	Value	Meaning
dhcResourceTypeAny	&H0	All resource types
dhcResourceTypeDisk	&H1	All disk resources
dhcResourceTypePrint	&H2	All printer resources

TABLE 11.9: Enumeration Usage Constants

Constant	Value	Meaning
dhcResourceUsageAll	&H13	All resources
dhcResourceUsageConnectable	&H1	All connectable resources
dhcResourceUsageContainer	&H2	All container resources
dhcResourceUsageAttached	&H10	All validated resources

The scope of an enumeration tells Windows where to look for resources. Choose a value from Table 11.7 to specify the necessary scope. If you specify any value besides dhResourceGlobalNet, the enumeration will work only through the devices on a single machine. (In addition, the Usage flag will be ignored because it applies only when you're dealing with the global network-wide scope.)

The enumeration type constants are straightforward: They let you choose whether you want to look at disks or printers. In addition, if the server on which you're performing an enumeration supports sharing other resources, such as COM ports, they will show up only when you specify the dhcResourceTypeAny constant. If the operating system cannot distinguish among different resource types, it may return all resource types and ignore the enumeration type flag.

You use the enumeration usage flag when choosing the dhcResourceGlobalNet scope. The concept is a little confusing, but it boils down to this: Some resources (such as network shares) can be connected to, and some resources, instead, contain other resources. By specifying the correct flag from Table 11.9, you indicate which type of global resource you'd like to enumerate. Think of it this way: If a resource is a container, you can use it with a new call to WNetOpenEnum in order to see what resources are inside the container. If the resource is connectable, you can pass the remote name string right to WNetAddConnection2 (or the wrapper function, dhAddConnection2) and connect to the resource. Finally, adding the dhcResourceUsageAttached to any enumeration causes the call to fail if the user is not authenticated, even if the network allows browsing without authentication.

TIP   The following discussion of working with enumeration handles contains a great deal of detail concerning the use of the low-level enumeration functions. The "Putting It All Together" section later in this chapter provides some wrapper functions to make it simpler to enumerate resources without dealing directly with enumeration handles. You'll find it simpler to use the wrapper functions, and you'll most likely use these functions instead of the WNetEnum functions. It's important to understand the lower-level details first, especially if you need to perform network enumerations other than the four samples provided.

Here is the declaration for the WnetOpenEnum function:

```
Private Declare Function WNetOpenEnum Lib "mpr" Alias _
  "WNetOpenEnumA" (ByVal lngScope As Long, _
  ByVal lngType As Long, ByVal lngUsage As Long, _
  lpNetResource As Any, lngEnum As Long) As Long
```

The lpNetResource parameter can be either a variable of the NETRESOURCE type or a null value. The NETRESOURCE type was discussed in the section "Connecting to a Network Resource" earlier in this chapter. Its definition is as follows:

```
Private Type NETRESOURCE
    dwScope As Long
    dwType As Long
    dwDisplayType As Long
    dwUsage As Long
    lpLocalName As String
    lpRemoteName As String
    lpComment As String
    lpProvider As String
End Type
```

Or, use the modified version, as we used earlier in other types that contain the space for the buffer and the strings that we'll use to hold the actual values later:

```
Public Type NETRESOURCE
    dwScope As dhcResourceScope
    dwType As dhcResourceType
    dwDisplayType As dhcResourceDisplayType
    dwUsage As dhcResourceUsage
```

```
    ' Pointers to strings
    lpLocalName As Long
    lpRemoteName As Long
    lpComment As Long
    lpProvider As Long

    ' Add an extra buffer to the end which
    ' will be used to store the strings
    abyt(dhcMaxPath * 4) As Byte

    ' the actual location of the final strings
    strLocalName As String
    strRemoteName As String
    strComment As String
    strProvider As String
End Type
```

This structure contains information on the scope, type, and usage of the network resource, as well as the display type, dwDisplayType. Possible values for this member are listed in Table 11.10.

T A B L E 1 1 . 1 0 : NetResource Display Type Constants

Constant	Value	Meaning
dhcResourceDisplayTypeGeneric	&H0	Display type does not matter.
dhcResourceDisplayTypeDomain	&H1	Object should be displayed as a domain.
dhcResourceDisplayTypeServer	&H2	Object should be displayed as a server.
dhcResourceDisplayTypeShare	&H3	Object should be displayed as a network share.

If you pass a null value for the lpNetResource parameter (remembering that since all the lp* parameters are Long integers, "null" in this case means 0), the enumeration will start at the root of the network. If you supply a NETRESOURCE structure, you can enumerate resources within a specific network resource, such as a particular drive. That is, you can also call WNetOpenEnum with a NETRESOURCE structure filled in, as long as the dwUsage member is set to dhcResourceUsageContainer. (You can't enumerate the resources inside a resource that doesn't contain other resources; for example, a printer.)

There are two ways to use WNetOpenEnum:

- You can call WNetOpenEnum twice, passing a null value rather than a NETRESOURCE structure the first time. Once you've got a list of all the available resources, you can use any specific resource and call WNetOpenEnum again, using the information about the particular resource.

- You can call WNetOpenEnum once if you already know the name of the resource you want to enumerate. If you can fill in the NETRESOURCE structure yourself, you don't need to call WNetOpenEnum twice.

To separate the two uses of WNetOpenEnum, we have provided two wrappers, dhGetTopLevelEnumHandle and dhGetNetResourceEnumHandle. The first function allows you to get the enumeration handle for the entire network, and the second allows you to get the handle for a specific container device. Both functions are shown in Listing 11.12.

> **WARNING** If you only use a single type of network, you never need to fill in the Provider parameter. (Or, if you prefer, you can fill it in with "Microsoft Windows Network.") However, if you use Novell Netware or any other network type, in addition to the Microsoft Windows network provider, you will want to include the appropriate network provider string for that network. Otherwise, you may not get the results you are expecting. Later in the chapter, one of the enumeration samples shows how to enumerate available network providers. By combining this function with others, you can potentially handle the situation of multiple network providers generically.

> **NOTE** Remember, WNetOpenEnum retrieves an enumeration handle that you'll be able to use if you want to enumerate resources (that is, retrieve information about all the specified network resources). However, to do that, you'll need to use the WNetEnumResource API call discussed in the section "Enumerating Resources" later in this chapter. The examples in this section merely retrieve the handle for you so you can later enumerate the specified set of resources.

Listing 11.12: Retrieve Enumeration Handles with WNetOpenEnum

```
Public Function dhGetTopLevelEnumHandle( _
  rsScope As dhcResourceScope, rtType As dhcResourceType, _
  rtUsage As dhcResourceUsage) As dhcNetworkErrors
    ' Opens a top-level network resource enumeration handle
```

```
        Dim lngReturn As dhcNetworkErrors
        Dim hEnum As Long

        ' Since this is a top level item, pass in the
        ' fourth parameter as the value 0.
        lngReturn = WNetOpenEnum(rsScope, rtType, rtUsage, _
         ByVal 0&, hEnum)

        If lngReturn = dhcNoError Then
            dhGetTopLevelEnumHandle = hEnum
        End If

End Function

Public Function dhGetNetResourceEnumHandle( _
 rsScope As dhcResourceScope, rtType As dhcResourceType, _
 rtUsage As dhcResourceUsage, _
 usrNetResource As NETRESOURCE) As dhcNetworkErrors
        ' Opens a resource enumeration handle for a given net resource.

        Dim lngReturn As dhcNetworkErrors
        Dim hEnum As Long

        lngReturn = WNetOpenEnum(rsScope, rtType, _
         rtUsage, usrNetResource, hEnum)

        If lngReturn = dhcNoError Then
            dhGetNetResourceEnumHandle = hEnum
        End If

End Function
```

Let's take a look at some examples to make this process a little clearer.

The easiest example is a simple call to dhGetTopLevelEnumHandle to find out all the currently connected network drives. (Note that under Windows NT/2000, some drives will be connected but may not have drive letters associated with them.) The call to open the network enumeration handle would look like this:

```
hEnum = dhGetTopLevelEnumHandle(dhcResourceConnected, _
 dhcResourceTypeDisk, dhcResourceUsageAll)
```

Or, you might want to get a top-level handle to the entire network. (In the Windows NT Network Connection dialog, this is the Microsoft Windows Network node that appears above the domains.)

```
hEnum = dhGetTopLevelEnumHandle(dhcResourceGlobalNet, _
    dhcResourceTypeAny, dhcResourceUsageAll)
```

After calling dhGetTopLevelEnumHandle, you'll be able to call WNetEnum-Resource to investigate all the resources on the network. For any resource that's a container, such as a domain or server, you'll be able to call dhGetNetResource-EnumHandle and enumerate the resources that that item contains. The Windows NT Network Connection dialog does something like this to fill the tree-view—like display in the bottom half of its window, as shown earlier in Figure 11.1.

For example, if you need to look at the network disk shares on another machine and you know its name, you can use code like the following to open the enumeration handle:

```
Dim usrNetResource As NETRESOURCE
Dim hEnum as Long
Dim strServerANSI As String

With usrNetResource
    .dwDisplayType = dhcResourceDisplayTypeServer
    .dwScope = dhcResourceGlobalNet
    .dwUsage = dhcResourceUsageContainer
    .dwType = dhcResourceTypeDisk

    strServerANSI = StrConv("\\YourServer", vbFromUnicode)
    .lpRemoteName = StrPtr(strServerANSI)
End With
hEnum = dhGetNetResourceEnumHandle(dhcResourceGlobalNet, _
    dhcResourceTypeDisk, dhcResourceUsageConnectable, usrNetResource)
```

You can then use this handle to obtain all the available network shares on the server whose name you've supplied. As another example, if you wanted to get the names of all computers in a particular domain, you could use code like this:

```
Dim usrNetResource As NETRESOURCE
Dim hEnum as Long
Dim strDomainANSI As string
```

```
With usrNetResource
    .dwDisplayType = dhcResourceDisplayTypeDomain
    .dwScope = dhcResourceGlobalNet
    .dwUsage = dhcResourceUsageContainer
    .dwType = dhcResourceTypeDisk
    strDomainANSI = StrConv("\\YourDomain", vbFromUnicode)
    .lpRemoteName = StrPtr(strDomainANSI)
End With
hEnum = dhGetNetResourceEnumHandle(dhcResourceGlobalNet, _
  dhcResourceTypeDisk, dhcResourceUsageContainer, usrNetResource)
```

This handle allows you to enumerate all the machines in the network specified by your domain name. Code presented in the section "Enumerating Resources" a little later in this chapter shows you how to use the enumeration handles you've opened. (There will also be several examples of the sample code for the chapter.)

Closing an Enumeration Handle

You should always close anything you open (a prime rule for getting along in life, as well as in programming), and network enumeration handles are no exception. You use the WNetCloseEnum API function to do this, and its declaration looks like this:

```
Private Declare Function WNetCloseEnum Lib "mpr.dll" _
  (ByVal hEnum As Long) As Long
```

For the sake of consistency, we've provided a wrapper for this call, although calling this function directly is simple enough. The function, dhCloseEnum, is shown in Listing 11.13.

Listing 11.13: Use dhCloseEnum to Close Enumeration Handles

```
Public Function dhCloseEnum(hEnum As Long) As dhcNetworkErrors
    ' Closes a resource enumeration handle

    dhCloseEnum = WNetCloseEnum(hEnum)
End Function
```

It's a good idea to have your code close a handle as soon as you're done with it. In theory, even if you don't close the handles, they will be closed when you shut down the host application you opened them from (Word, Excel, Access, and so on), but an explicit close is cleaner and frees up the resources right away.

Enumerating Resources

It's finally time to start using the previously discussed enumeration handles to obtain information. This section discusses the use of WnetEnumResource, the API function that actually performs the real work. This function is the workhorse that takes the enumeration handle from WNetOpenEnum and uses it to retrieve information about each available network resource.

The declaration of WNetEnumResource is as follows:

```
Private Declare Function WNetEnumResource Lib "mpr.dll" _
  Alias "WNetEnumResourceA" (ByVal hEnum As Long, _
  lngCount As Long, lpBuffer As Any, lngBufferSize As Long) _
  As Long
```

The hEnum parameter is a handle obtained by WNetOpenEnum. (You can use either of the two wrapper functions, dhGetNetResourceEnumHandle or dhGetTopLevelEnumHandle, to obtain the handle.) The lngCount parameter specifies the number of items you wish to receive. We've seen some unpredictable results trying to obtain more than one at a time, so the wrapper function we provide, dhEnumNext, requests only one at a time. As it turns out, there is no substantial performance hit for multiple calls to WnetEnumResource. Although calls to WNetOpenEnum can take a little while, calls to WNetEnumResource do their work quickly.

The heart of the dhEnumNext function will look similar to some of the other calls that you've seen already. Although you've seen the NETRESOURCE structure used previously, this is the first time we've used it for retrieving data. In this case, the code must set the buffer length to be the size of the structure, taking away the size of the four string pointers (16 bytes) at the end:

```
Dim lngReturn As dhcNetworkErrors
Dim lngBufferLength As Long

' Don't include the last four string pointers in the buffer size
lngBufferLength = Len(usrNetResource) - 16
lngReturn = WNetEnumResource(hEnum, 1, _
  usrNetResource, lngBufferLength)
```

The second half of the dhEnumNext function contains the logic that takes the elements out of the byte array and puts them into a NETRESOURCE type. Before you do this, take another look at the NETRESOURCE definition:

```
Public Type NETRESOURCE
    dwScope As dhcResourceScope
    dwType As dhcResourceType
```

```
                    dwDisplayType As dhcResourceDisplayType
                    dwUsage As dhcResourceUsage

                    ' Pointers to strings
                    lpLocalName As Long
                    lpRemoteName As Long
                    lpComment As Long
                    lpProvider As Long

                    ' Add an extra buffer to the end which
                    ' will be used to store the strings
                    abyt(dhcMaxPath * 4) As Byte

                    ' the actual location of the final strings
                    strLocalName As String
                    strRemoteName As String
                    strComment As String
                    strProvider As String
                End Type
```

As shown earlier with the REMOTE_NAME_INFO structure, any code that uses the NETRESOURCE structure for retrieving information must copy data from the string pointers into the associated string members manually. For example, if you are enumerating connected network resources (drive mappings to UNC paths), the code will look like the following:

```
If lngReturn = dhcNoError Then
    With usrNetResource
        .strLocalName = dhStrFromAnsiPtr(.lpLocalName)
        .strRemoteName = dhStrFromAnsiPtr(.lpRemoteName)
        .strComment = dhStrFromAnsiPtr(.lpComment)
        .strProvider = dhStrFromAnsiPtr(.lpProvider)
    End With
End If
```

Listing 11.14 contains the complete code for the dhEnumNext function.

Listing 11.14: Enumeration with dhEnumNext

```
Public Function dhEnumNext(hEnum As Long, _
  usrNetResource As NETRESOURCE) As dhcNetworkErrors
        ' Enumerate the next resource in hEnum and put the info
        ' in usrNetResource
```

```
Dim lngReturn As dhcNetworkErrors
Dim lngBufferLength As Long

' Don't include the last four string pointers in the buffer size
lngBufferLength = Len(usrNetResource) - 16
lngReturn = WNetEnumResource(hEnum, 1, _
 usrNetResource, lngBufferLength)

If lngReturn = dhcNoError Then
    ' If the call succeeded, there are several pointers to data.
    ' Use the pointers to get the actual strings
        With usrNetResource
            .strLocalName = dhStrFromANSIPtr(.lpLocalName)
            .strRemoteName = dhStrFromANSIPtr(.lpRemoteName)
            .strComment = dhStrFromANSIPtr(.lpComment)
            .strProvider = dhStrFromANSIPtr(.lpProvider)
        End With
End If

    dhEnumNext = lngReturn
End Function
```

In some applications, you may need to enumerate network resources one by one until you find the one you're searching for, or perhaps you'll have some other reason to enumerate network resources individually. However, in most cases, you'll need to specify the type of resources you want and then have a function return an array of NETRESOURCE structures that meet your criteria. We present a wrapper function that does this in the next section.

Putting It All Together

The wrapper function, dhGetNetResourceInfo, does all the work of calling the enumeration functions for you. This function takes the following parameters:

Parameter	Description
rsScope	One of the values in Table 11.7.
rtType	One of the values in Table 11.8.
rtUsage	One of the values in Table 11.9.

fSpecifyStart	A Boolean value that tells the function whether the next parameter (usrNetResourceStart) is going to be passed; it should be False if you want to use the network root to start your enumeration, and True if you wish to pass in usrNetResourceStart as the root of the enumeration.
usrNetResourceStart	A NETRESOURCE type specifying the beginning of the enumeration if you want to start anywhere but at the network root. This must be passed in even if fSpecifyStart is False, but, in that case, its members can be empty because it will not be used.

The dhGetNetResourceInfo function returns a VBA Collection object, filled with the resources that match your request. You must use code like this to work with the return value:

```
Dim col As Collection
Set col = dhGetNetResourceInfo(...parameters go here...)
```

Each item in the output collection is an object based on the NetResourceInfo class. Therefore, you can use code like this to enumerate the results:

```
Dim nri As NetResourceInfo

If Not (col Is Nothing) Then
    For Each nri In col
        ' Do something with nri; perhaps print the RemoteName
        ' or some other property value.
    Next nri
End If
```

Listing 11.15 contains the entire dhGetNetResource function. Notice how it allows you to pass in the values you need to as the string values in our custom NET-RESOURCE type, and it changes them to the pointers that the API call needs with the StrPtr function.

Listing 11.15: Doing It All with dhGetNetResourceInfo

```
Public Function dhGetNetResourceInfo(rsScope As dhcResourceScope, _
rtType As dhcResourceType, rtUsage As dhcResourceUsage, _
fSpecifyStart As Boolean, usrNetResourceStart As NETRESOURCE) _
As Collection
    ' Retrieve all the net resources specified by the parameters

    Dim lngReturn As dhcNetworkErrors
    Dim hEnum As Long
    Dim nri As NetResourceInfo
    Dim usrNetResource As NETRESOURCE
    Dim colNetResource As Collection

    On Error GoTo HandleErrors

    ' If fSpecifyStart is selected use the usrNetResourceStart
    ' info as the root for the enumeration. Otherwise, assume
    ' the top level.
    If fSpecifyStart Then
        With usrNetResourceStart
            ' In case strings were specified, set them
            ' into the pointers now
            If Len(.strComment) > 0 Then
                .lpComment = StrPtr(.strComment)
            End If
            If Len(.strLocalName) > 0 Then
                .lpLocalName = StrPtr(.strLocalName)
            End If
            If Len(.strProvider) > 0 Then
                .lpProvider = StrPtr(.strProvider)
            End If
            If Len(.strRemoteName) > 0 Then
                .lpRemoteName = StrPtr(.strRemoteName)
            End If
        End With
        hEnum = dhGetNetResourceEnumHandle( _
          rsScope, rtType, rtUsage, usrNetResourceStart)
    Else
        hEnum = dhGetTopLevelEnumHandle(rsScope, rtType, rtUsage)
    End If
```

```
        If hEnum <> 0 Then
            ' init the collection
            Set colNetResource = New Collection

            Do While lngReturn = dhcNoError

                lngReturn = dhEnumNext(hEnum, usrNetResource)
                ' lngReturn will be dhcErrorNoMoreItems when we are done.
                If lngReturn <> dhcErrorNoMoreItems Then
                    Set nri = New NetResourceInfo

                    With usrNetResource
                        nri.Comment = .strComment
                        nri.LocalName = .strLocalName
                        nri.Provider = .strProvider
                        nri.RemoteName = .strRemoteName
                    End With

                    colNetResource.Add nri
                End If
            Loop

            lngReturn = dhCloseEnum(hEnum)
        End If
        ' If there was an error, colNetResource
        ' (and the return value) will be Nothing.

ExitHere:
    Set dhGetNetResourceInfo = colNetResource
    Exit Function

HandleErrors:
    ' Raise the error back out.
    Err.Raise Err.Number, Err.Source, Err.Description
End Function
```

The four examples shown in Listing 11.16 (from the TestProcedures module) all call the dhGetNetResourceInfo function. One example obtains all the computers in a given domain (dhEnumPCsInDomain). The second one obtains all the network shares available on a given computer (dhEnumSharesOnPC). The third one obtains all the mapped network resources on the current machine (dhEnumConnectedResourcesOnLocalPC). The final enumeration sample, which was already mentioned earlier in connection with handling multiple networks, obtains the names of all the network providers that are available (dhEnumAvailableNetworks). The difference in each case is the specific parameters passed in, and possibly the values placed in the usrNetResourceStart parameter (depending on the function you've called).

NOTE   In each sample function, the dhGetNetResourceInfo function returns a collection object as its return value. (The return value will be Nothing if the enumeration didn't find any matching resources.) This function fills in the collection, and, on return from the function call, the collection contains one object for each network resource the function found that matches the criteria you specified when you called the function. The sample functions enumerate through the collection with a For...Each construct, displaying text in the Immediate window. But, obviously, you would do something more useful with the enumerated values in your own application.

Listing 11.16: Sample Functions That Call dhGetNetResourceInfo

```
Public Sub dhEnumPCsInDomain(strDomainName As String)

    ' Retrieve all the servers in the given domain

    Dim col As Collection
    Dim nri As NetResourceInfo
    Dim usrNetResourceStart As NETRESOURCE
    Dim strDomainNameANSI As String

    strDomainNameANSI = StrConv(strDomainName, vbFromUnicode)

    With usrNetResourceStart
        .dwScope = dhcResourceGlobalNet
        .strRemoteName = strDomainNameANSI
    End With

    Set col = dhGetNetResourceInfo(dhcResourceGlobalNet, _
      dhcResourceTypeDisk, dhcResourceUsageContainer, _
      True, usrNetResourceStart)
```

```vb
        If Not (col Is Nothing) Then
            For Each nri In col
                Debug.Print nri.RemoteName
            Next nri
        End If

End Sub

Public Sub dhEnumSharesOnPC(ByVal strMachineName As String)

    Dim col As Collection
    Dim nri As NetResourceInfo
    Dim usrNetResourceStart As NETRESOURCE
    Dim strMachineNameANSI As String

    If Left$(strMachineName, 2) <> "\\" Then
        strMachineName = "\\" & strMachineName
    End If
    strMachineNameANSI = StrConv(strMachineName, vbFromUnicode)

    With usrNetResourceStart
        .dwScope = dhcResourceGlobalNet
        .strRemoteName = strMachineNameANSI
    End With

    Set col = dhGetNetResourceInfo( _
     dhcResourceGlobalNet, dhcResourceTypeDisk, _
     dhcResourceUsageConnectable, True, _
     usrNetResourceStart)

    If Not (col Is Nothing) Then
        For Each nri In col
            Debug.Print nri.RemoteName
        Next nri
    End If

End Sub

Public Sub dhEnumConnectedResourcesOnLocalPC()
    ' Retrieve all the connections on the current machine
```

```
        Dim col As Collection
        Dim nri As NetResourceInfo
        Dim usrNetResourceStart As NETRESOURCE

        Set col = dhGetNetResourceInfo(dhcResourceConnected, _
         dhcResourceTypeDisk, 0, False, usrNetResourceStart)
        If Not (col Is Nothing) Then
            For Each nri In col
                Debug.Print nri.LocalName; _
                  " is connected to "; nri.RemoteName
            Next nri
        End If
End Sub

Public Sub dhEnumAvailableNetworks()

    ' Retrieve all the network types available (usually this will just
    ' be the 'Microsoft Windows Network' but can also be Novell or
      other
    ' types when they are available.

    Dim col As Collection
    Dim nri As NetResourceInfo
    Dim usrNetResourceStart As NETRESOURCE

    Set col = dhGetNetResourceInfo(dhcResourceGlobalNet, _
     dhcResourceTypeDisk, dhcResourceUsageConnectable, _
     False, usrNetResourceStart)
    If Not (col Is Nothing) Then
        For Each nri In col
            Debug.Print nri.RemoteName
        Next nri
    End If
  End Sub
```

As you can see, WNetEnumResource is extremely powerful: It can perform many different operations and return a great deal of information. Unfortunately, this quick look just scratches the surface of what this function can do, but it should be enough to get you going.

The LAN Manager API

The functions we've discussed so far provide a rich set of features that can make your applications network aware, and they are available on any Windows 95/98 or Windows NT/2000 machine. However, as solid as the WNet API is, some necessary functionality is missing. To get the rest of the functionality you need, you must use the LAN Manager API, available only on Windows NT/2000 (with the exception of 20 or so functions, which are available in some format in Windows 95/98). The full API consists of over 120 functions (as compared to the 14 in the WNet API). They used to be rather underdocumented and widely unsupported, but in the more recent version of the Win32 Platform SDK, Microsoft has backed down from calling it unsupported and has promoted many of these functions to being the "blessed" way of doing things. This section will cover how to perform the following actions:

- Sharing resources (adding network shares)

- Deleting network shares

- Changing a user's network password

- Retrieving the name of the primary domain controller (PDC) of the domain

- Getting the time of day from another machine

There are four interesting items to note about the LAN Manager functions:

- Some of these functions work only under Windows NT/2000; those functions are not available to Windows 95 users. Out of 120 available functions, those supported on Windows 95/98 are (there may be others we've missed)

    - NetAccessAdd

    - NetAccessCheck

    - NetAccessDel

    - NetAccessEnum

    - NetAccessGetInfo

    - NetAccessGetUserPerms

    - NetAccessSetInfo

- NetConnectionEnum

- NetFileClose2

- NetFileEnum

- NetSecurityGetInfo

- NetServerGetInfo

- NetSessionDel

- NetSessionEnum

- NetSessionGetInfo

- NetShareAdd

- NetShareDel

- NetShareEnum

- NetShareGetInfo

- NetShareSetInfo

- All the strings you pass to LAN Manager API functions must be Unicode, rather than ANSI, strings when you are calling them from Windows NT/ 2000. This is in contrast to most Win32 APIs, which are implemented in both ANSI and Unicode versions on Windows NT/2000. The examples shown here force the use of Unicode by using the StrPtr function to use the actual Unicode string stored in VBA.

TIP
Because the LAN Manager APIs require that you call a different API function depending on whether you are running on Windows 95/98 or Windows NT/2000, the wrappers we've provided determine which operating system is running and will work on all platforms, making the correct API call. Rather than using the calls to GetVersionEx, covered in Chapter 9 (which provides more information than you need here), the functions in this chapter call the simpler GetVersion function to determine the current operating system. For details, see the sample code and its IsWinNT() function, which will return True on Windows NT/2000 machines.

- The API functions have a consistent naming style that makes it easy to tell what they do. Each function starts with a *Net* prefix, followed by a noun that describes what object is being manipulated and a verb indicating what the function does to that object. For example, if you wanted to add a user, you would use the NetUserAdd function.

- These API functions have much in common. Learning one LAN Manager API and how to call it is the key to calling dozens of others just like it.

WARNING   Of course, not all the news is good news. Many of the LAN Manager functions are not easily accessible to VBA programmers because they return pointers to pointers to memory addresses. VBA has no supported mechanism for dereferencing these pointers. However, this limitation can be worked around using API functions like lstrcpy, lstrcpyn, and RtlMoveMemory. Although we are not specifically focusing on covering those functions here, the dhStrFromAnsiPtr and dhStrFromPtr functions discussed earlier show examples of dereferencing pointers with the lstrcpyn/lstrcpynW functions. Also, the dhGetTimeFromServer function (covered later in this section) provides an example that uses RtlMoveMemory.

Adding a Network Share

The WNet functions allow you to enumerate network shares but supply no way to create a new one. The LAN Manager API provides the NetShareAdd function, which does allow you to create a new share. For Windows NT/2000, use this declaration:

```
Private Declare Function NetShareAdd Lib "NETAPI32.DLL" _
  (ByVal strServername As String, ByVal lnglevel As Long, _
  strbuf As SHARE_INFO_2, lngParamErr As Long) As Long
```

For Windows 95/98, use this one:

```
Private Declare Function NetShareAdd9x Lib "srvapi.dll" _
  Alias "NetShareAdd" (ByVal pszServer As String, _
  ByVal lngLevel As Integer, strBuf As SHARE_INFO_50, _
  ByVal cbBuffer As Integer) As Long
```

The following list describes the parameters for NetShareAdd (the NetShareAdd9x function uses similar parameters):

Parameter	Description
strServerName	Machine name on which to add the share.
lngLevel	Specifies what level of share information will be in the strBuf parameter. In theory, you can pass either a SHARE_INFO_2 or SHARE_INFO_50 data structure, and this parameter indicates which you've sent. Supply either the dhcShareInfo2 or dhcShareInfo50 constants here. The Windows NT/2000 example shown here passes a SHARE_INFO_2 data structure, so you should pass dhcShareInfo2 constant in this parameter. The Windows 95/98 example passes a SHARE_INFO_50 structure, so there you should pass dhcShareInfo50 for this parameter.
strBuf	A buffer declared to be of type SHARE_INFO_2 or SHARE_INFO_50 (the Windows NT/2000 example uses SHARE_INFO_2, and the Windows 95/98 example uses SHARE_INFO_50), to be filled in by the function call. Choose which structure you use based on the information you want returned. The lngLevel parameter's value must indicate which structure you're sending.
lngParamErr	Indicates which parameter, if any, was invalid on return from the function call. (If only all API calls were this helpful!) (Windows NT/2000 only)
cbBuffer	The size of the buffer passed to the function (Windows 95/98 only).

WARNING To use NetShareAdd, the currently logged-in user must have permission to add the share. Otherwise, an error will occur. Unless you're a member of the Administrators or Account Operators local group or you have Communication, Print, or Server operator group membership, you won't be able to successfully execute NetShare-Add. Even with these rights, the Print operator can add only printer queues, and the Communication operator can add only communication-device queues.

The SHARE_INFO_2 structure contains the parameters described in the following list:

Parameter	Meaning
shi2_netname	Name for the new share.
shi2_type	Resource type, selected from the values in Table 11.11.
shi2_remark	A comment that will appear in Windows Explorer and in the network connection dialog under Windows NT.
shi2_permissions	Flag specifying permissions. (This parameter is ignored unless share-level security is set up on the machine.) See Table 11.12 for allowable values.
shi2_max_uses	Maximum number of concurrent users allowed. (−1 means no limit.)
shi2_current_uses	Current number of users (ignored when adding a new share).
shi2_path	Local path of the shared resource on the machine.
shi2_passwd	Password for the share. (Like shi2_permissions, this parameter is ignored unless share-level security is set up on the machine.)

The SHARE_INFO_50 structure contains the following members:

Parameter	Meaning
shi50_netname	Name for the new share.
shi50_type	Resource type, selected from the values in Table 11.11.
shi50_remark	A comment that will appear in Windows Explorer and in the network connection dialog under Windows NT.
shi50_flags	Flag specifying permissions. (This parameter is ignored unless share-level security is set up on the machine.) Possible values are listed in Table 11.13.

Parameter	Meaning
shi50_path	Local path of the shared resource on the machine.
shi50_rw_password	Read-write password for the share. (Like shi50_flags, this parameter is ignored unless share-level security is set up on the machine.)
shi50_ro_password	Read-only password for the share. (Like shi50_flags, this parameter is ignored unless share-level security is set up on the machine.)

The network share types are defined in Table 11.11. The permissions flags for Windows NT/2000 are defined in Table 11.12. Table 11.13 shows allowable values for Windows 95/98.

TABLE 11.11: Network Share Types (Used for the shi2_type Parameter)

Constant	Value	Meaning
dhcLanManStypeDisktree	&H0	Disk resource
dhcLanManStypePrintq	&H1	Printer resource
dhcLanManStypeDevice	&H2	Device resource (such as a COM port)
dhcLanManStypeIpc	&H3	IPC resource

TABLE 11.12: Permissions Flags (Used for the shi2_ permissions Parameter)

Constant	Value	Meaning
dhcLanManAccessNone	&H0	No access allowed
dhcLanManAccessRead	&H1	Permission to read from the resource
dhcLanManAccessWrite	&H2	Permission to write to the resource
dhcLanManAccessCreate	&H4	Permission to create an instance of the resource
dhcLanManAccessExec	&H8	Permission to execute the resource
dhcLanManAccessDelete	&H10	Permission to delete the resource
dhcLanManAccessAtrib	&H20	Permission to modify attributes
dhcLanManAccessPerm	&H40	Permission to modify permissions
dhcLanManAccessAll	&HFF	A bitmask that includes all the previous flags

TABLE 11.13: Windows 95/98 Flags (Used for the shi50_flags Parameter)

Constant	Value	Meaning
dhcLanManWin9xReadOnly	&H1	Read-only share.
dhcLanManWin9xFull	&H2	Full Access allowed.
dhcLanManWin9xAccessMask	&H3	Specifies both of the above permissions, who knows why they did this?
dhcLanManWin9xPersist	&H100	Share is reconnected on a system reboot (if not specified, the share will be removed on reboot).
dhcLanManWin9xSystem	&H200	The share will not normally be visible (similar to the functionality Windows NT/2000 provide when you name the share with a $ suffix).
dhcLanManStypeIpc	&H3	IPC resource.

To make all this simpler, we've provided a wrapper function, dhAddNetwork-Share, as shown in Listing 11.17. This wrapper function determines the operating system, fills in the appropriate data structures, and calls the correct API function. Note that several of the parameters are optional and some are ignored, depending on your platform. Table 11.14 describes each of the parameters for dhAddNet-workShare.

TABLE 11.14: Parameters for dhAddNetworkShare

Parameter	Optional?	Default Value	Description
strServer	No		Machine name on which to add the share. You can pass vbNullString to use the current machine.
strShareName	No		Name for the new share.
strPath	No		Local path of the shared resource on the machine.
strRemarks	Yes	" "	Comment for this share (appears in Windows Explorer)
fIsDiskResource	Yes	True	If True, share is for a drive. If False, share is for a printer.
lngMaxUsers	Yes	−1	Maximum number of concurrent users allowed (−1 means no limit).

TABLE 11.14: Parameters for dhAddNetworkShare *(continued)*

Parameter	Optional?	Default Value	Description
lngPermissions	Yes	dhcLanManAccess All on NT/2000, dhcLanManWin9x AccessMask on 95/98	Flag specifying permissions. (ignored unless share-level security is set up on the machine) See Tables 11.12 and 11.13 for allowable values.
strRwPassword	Yes	" "	Password for the share. (Like shi2_permissions, this parameter is ignored unless share-level security is set up on the machine.)
strRoPassword	Yes	" "	Read-only password for the share (ignored on NT/2000).

Listing 11.17: Add a Network Share

```
Public Function dhAddNetworkShare( _
  ByVal strServer As String, _
  strShareName As String, _
  strPath As String, _
  Optional strRemarks As String, _
  Optional fIsDiskResource As Boolean = True, _
  Optional lngMaxUsers As Long = -1, _
  Optional ByVal lngPermissions As Long = -1, _
  Optional strRwPassword As String = "", _
  Optional strRoPassword As String = "") As Long

    ' Adds a network share

    Dim si2 As SHARE_INFO_2
    Dim si50 As SHARE_INFO_50
    Dim lngParamError As Long

    If IsWinNT() Then
        If lngPermissions = -1 Then
            lngPermissions = dhcLanManAccessAll
        End If

        ' Place all strings in the structure as needed
```

```
        With si2
            .shi2_netname = StrPtr(strShareName)
            If fIsDiskResource Then
                .shi2_type = dhcLanManStypeDisktree
            Else
                .shi2_type = dhcLanManStypePrintq
            End If
            .shi2_remark = StrPtr(strRemarks)
            .shi2_permissions = lngPermissions
            .shi2_max_uses = lngMaxUsers
            .shi2_path = StrPtr(strPath)
            .shi2_passwd = StrPtr(strRwPassword)
        End With

        dhAddNetworkShare = _
         NetShareAdd(StrPtr(strServer), _
         dhcShareInfo2, si2, lngParamError)
    Else
        If lngPermissions = -1 Then
            lngPermissions = dhcLanManWin9xAccessMask
        End If

        ' Place all strings in the structure as needed
        With si50
            .shi50_netname = strShareName & vbNullChar
            If fIsDiskResource Then
                .shi50_type = dhcLanManStypeDisktree
            Else
                .shi50_type = dhcLanManStypePrintq
            End If
            .shi50_remark = strRemarks & vbNullChar
            .shi50_path = strPath & vbNullChar
            .shi50_ro_password = strRwPassword & vbNullChar
            .shi50_rw_password = strRoPassword & vbNullChar
        End With

        dhAddNetworkShare = NetShareAdd9x( _
         strServer, dhcShareInfo50, si50, LenB(si50))
    End If
End Function
```

Calling this function is also straightforward. For example, to add a share named ROOT, which points to the C drive on a machine named Hopper, you simply call

```
lngReturn = dhAddNetworkShare("\\Hopper","ROOT","c:\")
```

TIP
> The strPath parameter must be a complete, valid path. Don't fall into the same trap we did when testing this function: If you pass "C:" without the backslash, you'll receive Error 123, "File, path, or drive name is incorrect," for your efforts.

Deleting a Network Share

Deleting a network share requires less work and less explanation than adding a share. The NetShareDel API function is defined as follows for Windows NT/2000:

```
Private Declare Function NetShareDel Lib "NETAPI32.DLL" _
  (ByVal lpServername As Long, ByVal lpNetName As Long, _
  ByVal lngReserved As Long) As Long
```

For Windows 95/98, it is:

```
Private Declare Function NetShareDel9x Lib "srvapi.dll" _
  Alias "NetShareDel" (ByVal StrServer As String, _
  ByVal strNetName As String, _
  ByVal lngReserved As Long) As Long
```

NetShareDel accepts the server name and the name of the share to delete. (The lngReserved parameter is undocumented, and you should pass 0 in this parameter.) Listing 11.18 provides a wrapper function, dhDeleteNetworkShare, for NetShareDel. (The wrapper function calls the appropriate version of NetShareDel for the platform you are on).

WARNING
> Unless you're a member of the Administrators or Account Operators local group or you have Communication, Print, or Server operator group membership, you won't be able to successfully execute NetShareDel. Even with these rights, the Print operator can delete only printer queues, and the Communication operator can delete only communication-device queues.

Listing 11.18: Delete a Network Share

```
Public Function dhDeleteNetworkShare( _
 ByVal strServer As String, ByVal strShareName As String) As Long
    ' Deletes a network share

    If IsWinNT() Then
        dhDeleteNetworkShare = NetShareDel( _
         StrPtr(strServer), StrPtr(strShareName), 0&)
    Else
        dhDeleteNetworkShare = NetShareDel9x( _
         strServer, strShareName, 0&)
    End If
End Function
```

WARNING   If you are calling dhAddNetworkShare or dhDeleteNetworkShare on a Windows 95/98 machine, use caution! The NetShareAdd API in srvapi.dll is one of the most unforgiving of any that we have ever seen. In particular, you will see the vbNull-Chars that are concatenated to the end of the strings in the SHARE_INFO_50 structure. NetShareDel is case sensitive even when you are trying to delete share names, but only on Windows 95 and 98.

Changing a User's Password

It's simple to change a user's password using the LAN Manager's NetUserChange-Password API function (which is unfortunately *only* available on Windows NT and Windows 2000.) This function (and the wrapper we've written around it) takes four parameters, as shown here:

Parameter	Description
DomainName	Remote server or domain (If you don't pass a value for this parameter to the wrapper function, code in the function will convert the parameter value into vbNullString, so that the API function will use the current logon domain of the caller.)

Parameter	Description
UserName	Name of the user whose password is to be changed (If you don't specify this value, the wrapper function retrieves the currently logged-in username.)
OldPassword	Old password of the user
NewPassword	New password of the user

The declaration for NetUserChangePassword is shown here:

```
Private Declare Function NetUserChangePassword Lib "NETAPI32.DLL" _
(ByVal DomainName As Long, ByVal UserName As Long, _
ByVal OldPassword As Long, ByVal NewPassword As Long) As Long
```

As with the other LAN Manager APIs running on Windows NT/2000, the strings must be Unicode. The wrapper function, dhChangeUserPassword, uses the StrPtr function to accomplish this, passing the address of the strings directly to the API function. (See the sidebar "ANSI and Unicode, Again" earlier in the chapter for more information.) Listing 11.19 shows the wrapper function.

NOTE   This function takes advantage of the fact that passing the special value vbNullString to StrPtr returns 0. The NetUserChangePassword API function is written so that if you pass Null (0&) for the domain or the username, the function uses the current domain and/or currently logged-in user. Our wrapper handles this for you: If you don't pass in a value for the domain name or the username, the procedure uses the default value for the parameter—vbNullString. Therefore, when the wrapper calls the API function, the value for the strDomain and/or the strUser parameter will be vbNullString if you haven't supplied a value, and the return value from StrPtr will be 0, indicating that you want the API function to calculate the current domain and/or current user.

Listing 11.19: Change a User's Network Password (Windows NT/2000 Only)

```
Public Function dhChangeUserPassword( _
  ByVal strOldPwd As String, ByVal strNewPwd As String, _
  Optional strUser As String = vbNullString, _
  Optional strDomain As String = vbNullString) As Long
    ' Change a user's password
```

```
        dhChangeUserPassword = NetUserChangePassword( _
          StrPtr(strDomain), StrPtr(strUser), _
          StrPtr(strOldPwd), StrPtr(strNewPwd))
    End Function
```

For example, to change your own password from *oldpassword* to *newpassword*, you could make a call like this:

```
If dhChangeUserPassword( _
  "oldpassword", "newpassword") = dhcNoError Then
    ' You successfully changed the password
End If
```

The following is a list of the errors most likely to occur when calling dhChangeUserPassword:

Error	Description
dhcErrorInvalidPassword	Old password is not correct.
dhcErrorAccessDenied	User does not have access to the requested information.
dhcErrorInvalidComputer	Computer name is invalid.
dhcErrorNotPrimary	Operation is allowed only on the primary domain controller of the domain.
dhcErrorUserNotFound	Username could not be found.
dhcErrorPasswordTooShort	Password is shorter than required by the domain's password policies.

Retrieving the Name of the Primary Domain Controller (PDC) of the Domain

It's relatively easy to determine the name of the PDC using another LAN Manager function, but this function is also only supported on Windows NT/2000. The declarations for NetGetDCName and the NetApiBufferFree function required to free the buffer NetGetDCName creates on Windows NT/2000 are

```
Private Declare Function NetGetDCName Lib "NETAPI32.DLL" _
  (ByVal servername As Long, ByVal domainname As Long, _
  bufptr As Long) As Long

Private Declare Function NetApiBufferFree Lib "NETAPI32.DLL" _
  (ByVal bufptr As Long) As Long
```

WARNING   Many LAN Manager functions create an internal buffer for you, allocating a block of memory to contain some piece of information. It's up to you to make sure you deallocate that memory once you're done with it, using the NetApiBufferFree function. If you forget to call this function, you will cause your application to have a memory leak, and the memory won't be released back to Windows. For more details on whether individual LAN Manager functions have this requirement, see MSDN. This is not true of any of the LAN Manager functions on Windows 95/98, where the client is responsible for both creating and freeing the buffer.

TIP   In theory, you can find the PDC from Windows 95/98 in the same roundabout way that the Windows Explorer does when you click the Up One Level toolbar button (which means calling WNetGetResourceParent, followed by NetServerGetInfo). But even this method is explicitly called "inappropriate" in MSDN, so we do not document it here.

Just as with NetUserChangePassword, either parameter to NetGetDCName can be a null pointer. (When you don't specify the server name, the function assumes you want to use the current machine. When you don't specify the domain name, the function uses the domain to which the machine is logged in.) Listing 11.20 contains the wrapper function, dhGetPDC, that calls NetGetDCName.

Listing 11.20: Retrieving a PDC (Windows NT/2000 Only)

```
Public Function dhGetPDC( _
 Optional ByVal strServer As String = vbNullString, _
 Optional ByVal strDomainName As String = vbNullString) _
 As String
    ' Gets the name of the primary domain controller

    Dim lngBufptr As Long

    If NetGetDCName( _
     StrPtr(strServer), StrPtr(strDomainName), _
     lngBufptr) = dhcNoError Then
        dhGetPDC = dhStrFromPtr(lngBufptr)
        Call NetApiBufferFree(lngBufptr)
    End If
End Function
```

Common errors for the return of NetGetDCName are listed here:

Error	Description
dhcErrorDCNotFound	Could not find the name of the primary domain controller.
dbcErrorInvalidName	Could not find the specified name (can refer to either of the parameters).

As an interesting side note, we found that dhcErrorDCNotFound was almost always the guaranteed return value any time you log on to your machine with cached information, even if you do it on a remote machine and connect to the network later via RAS. The function seems to have no such problems when you log on to the network directly.

TIP
If your call to NetGetDCName fails, perhaps it's because you're logged in with cached domain information. (You get the error dhcErrorDCNotFound.) You may want to call the NetGetAnyDCName API function instead. This function (declared in the sample code but not used here) will get the name of any domain controller, not just the primary domain controller. You call it in the same way that you call NetGetDCName, but it returns any available domain controller. (If you need to know more information about the domain controller you have, you'll need to also call NetGetServerInfo.)

TIP
Although NetGetDCName isn't explicitly listed as obsolete under Windows 2000, MSDN recommends using the DsGetDcName function instead. DsGetDcName has more options pertaining to the type of domain controller you can get, but it's slightly more complicated to call, as well.

Getting the Time of Day from Another Server

Developers often need to be able to synchronize the times of two computers. That is, you may need to set the time of a workstation to be the same as the time on a network server. The LAN Manager function, NetRemoteTOD, handles this for you. Unfortunately, this function is again only supported on Windows NT/2000. In order to do its work, NetRemoteTOD requires you to copy memory from one place to another, so you'll also need the RtlMoveMemory API function. The declarations are as follows:

```
Private Declare Function NetRemoteTOD Lib "NETAPI32.DLL" _
 (ByVal server As Long, bufptr As Long) As Long

Private Declare Sub RtlMoveMemory Lib "kernel32" _
 (pDest As Any, pSrc As Any, ByVal ByteLen As Long)
```

Listing 11.21 shows the simple wrapper we've created around this function.

Listing 11.21: Retrieve the Date and Time from a Server (Windows NT/2000 Only)

```
Public Function dhGetTimeFromServer( _
 Optional ByVal strServer As String = vbNullString) As Date
     ' Gets the time of day from the specified server
     '
     Dim tdi As TIME_OF_DAY_INFO
     Dim lngBufptr As Long

     If NetRemoteTOD(StrPtr(strServer), lngBufptr) = 0 Then
         Call RtlMoveMemory(tdi, ByVal lngBufptr, Len(tdi))

         ' Convert to a real date/time, allowing for the
         ' time zone shift
         dhGetTimeFromServer = _
          DateSerial(tdi.t_year, tdi.t_month, tdi.t_day) + _
          TimeSerial(tdi.t_hours, tdi.t_mins, tdi.t_secs) - _
          (tdi.t_timezone / 60 / 24)

         Call NetApiBufferFree(lngBufptr)
     End If
 End Function
```

The NetRemoteTOD function expects to receive a Unicode string (hence the call to StrPtr) containing the name of the machine from which you want to retrieve the date/time, and it creates an internal buffer to contain the time info. The lngBufPtr parameter comes back to you, filled in with the address of the structure in memory. The wrapper function calls the RtlMoveMemory function, which copies the data from that buffer into the locally declared TIME_OF_DAY_INFO structure.

The TIME_OF_DAY_INFO structure has an interesting definition, as shown here:

```
Public Type TIME_OF_DAY_INFO
    t_elapsedt As Long
    t_msecs As Long
    t_hours As Long
    t_mins As Long
    t_secs As Long
    t_hunds As Long
    t_timezone As Long
    t_tinterval As Long
    t_day As Long
    t_month As Long
    t_year As Long
    t_weekday As Long
End Type
```

This structure includes a value representing the number of seconds since January 1, 1970 (t_elapsedt), in case you're interested in that particular value. It also includes all of the date/time information in separate members, for the rest of us. It does also include the important offset for the time zone (as compared to the current machine settings) since both sets of time information are provided in GMT (Greenwich Mean Time). We chose to use the actual values for the date, subtracting the value found in the t_timezone member to correct for the time zone difference.

Finally, the wrapper function calls the NetApiBufferFree function, to release the memory used by the internal TIME_OF_DAY_INFO structure. If you forget to call this function, that structure (containing 12 long integers) would remain allocated. It's really best that your applications deallocate memory they've used!

To set your computer to have the same time as a server named HOMER, you might write code like this:

```
Dim dtmValue As Date
dtmValue = dhGetTimeFromServer("\\HOMER")
Date = DateValue(dtmValue)
Time = TimeValue(dtmValue)
```

On Functions Not Covered

This section has just scratched the surface of the LAN Manager API. You'll find many useful functions among the large set of LAN Manager API calls (as well as some that have become obsolete or have been superseded). These functions cover all aspects of networking, including:

- Organizational unit information
- Domain "join" information
- Domain information
- Remote file information
- Handling local and global groups
- Sending messages
- Managing replicator import and export
- Scheduling services
- Managing servers and sessions
- Handling transports
- Managing users and workstations

Although some of these functions cannot easily be called from VBA because of the way they pass parameters, there are still many LAN Manager functions you can use (and, hopefully, some of the pointer tricks you've seen in this chapter will make it possible for you to call most of the functions you need). The examples we've provided in this chapter will help get you started.

As has been noted previously, Microsoft has backed down from the old position of stating that much of the LAN Manager API is unsupported, and they have provided good documentation for most of LAN Manager functions in the Win32 Platform SDK. Microsoft has also expanded the support for the API on Windows 2000, for example, adding functions to help you join and unjoin domains (NetJoinDomain/NetUnjoinDomain), getting information on how a machine is joined if it is (NetGetJoinInformation), on many NetDfs* functions for handling DFS (distributed file system) shares, and more.

TIP	Where do you find more information about the LAN Manager API? The answer is (as always) MSDN—the Microsoft Developer Network CD-ROM. If you're interested in this information, there's no excuse for not purchasing this incredibly useful compendium of information. Of course, you can find much of this information on Microsoft's Web site, as well, but it's not nearly as convenient as it is on the CD-ROM. Have we said this often enough? The MSDN CD-ROM is one of the most worthwhile purchases you can make if you want to use the Windows API as part of your application development. For people who are not sure if they want to join the MSDN subscription, you can easily look up information by going to the MSDN Web site at http://msdn.microsoft.com/.

Summary

Making applications network aware can be one of the most challenging aspects of programming in VBA, both because using the network APIs in VBA is not well documented, and because many of them were not written with VBA developers in mind. In this chapter, we covered most of the basic networking functions you may want to add to your application, as well as several advanced networking functions. In addition, we provided some special tricks to help you work around APIs that are not "VBA friendly." Specifically, we covered these topics:

- Using common network dialogs
  - The network connection dialog
  - The network disconnect dialog
- Making network connections manually
  - Creating network connections
  - Deleting network connections
- Retrieving basic network resource information
  - Getting a UNC path from a mapped network resource
  - Retrieving the name of the currently logged-in user
  - Getting (and setting) the workstation name
  - Getting advanced network information

- Enumerating network resources

    - Opening, using, and closing enumeration handles

    - Enumerating available network shares on a machine

    - Enumerating mapped network resources on the current machine

    - Enumerating the computers in a domain

- Calling the LAN Manager API

    - Adding network shares on a machine

    - Deleting network shares

    - Changing a user's network password

    - Retrieving the name of the primary domain controller

    - Getting the time of day from another server

For more extensive looks at string handling, see Chapter 1. For more information on using the system Registry, see Chapter 10. For more coverage of using the Windows API in general, see Appendix B, which is located on the companion CD-ROM that accompanies this book.

chapter 12

Working with Disks and Files

- Using built-in VBA disk and file functions

- Understanding the power of Windows API for managing files

- Using Windows Common Dialogs in your applications

Sooner or later, as you write VBA programs you'll have to interact with disks and files. Your interaction might be to perform simple tasks, such as copying or deleting files, or more complex ones, like opening and parsing a text file. This chapter explores the many things you can do with disks and files. It begins with a discussion of the built-in VBA disk and file functions. While adequate for performing most tasks, they do not provide all the functionality many developers desire. The second part of this chapter examines the numerous Windows API functions at your disposal for doing things the built-in functions aren't capable of.

NOTE   You'll find more information on working with disks and files using the Windows Scripting Runtime in Chapter 14.

Table 12.1 lists the sample files located on the CD-ROM for this chapter.

TABLE 12.1:   Sample Files

Filename	Description
DISKFILE.XLS	Microsoft Excel workbook containing the sample code
DISKFILE.MDB	Access 2000 database containing the sample code
DISKFILE.VBP	Visual Basic project containing the sample code
MAIN.FRM	Startup form for Visual Basic project
COMMDLG.BAS	Sample code for common dialog functions
DATETIME.BAS	Sample code for file date and time functions
DISKINFO.BAS	Sample code for disk information functions
HANDLES.BAS	Sample code for file handle examples
FILEIO.BAS	Sample code for VBA file I/O functions
FINDFUNC.BAS	Sample code for Windows API file-listing functions
MISCFILE.BAS	Miscellaneous Windows API functions
NOTIFY.BAS	Sample code for directory change notification functions
PATHFUN.BAS	Sample code for path parsing examples
FSEARCH.BAS	Sample code for file search functions
STRINGS.BAS	String manipulation code from Chapter 1

TABLE 12.1:   Sample Files *(continued)*

Filename	Description
TEMPFILE.BAS	Sample code for temporary file examples
VBAFILE.BAS	Sample code for built-in VBA file function examples
COMMDLG.CLS	Common dialog class
TESTCDLG.BAS	Sample code testing common dialog class
CALLBAK.CLS	Example callback object class
ICALLBAK.CLS	Callback interface class

The Built-In VBA Disk and File Functions

VBA offers several built-in functions designed to manipulate disks and files. In general, they are oriented toward tasks that are both common and simple. We take a look at them in this section for the sake of completeness. They are, for the most part, very old functions inherited from previous versions of BASIC. If you've used BASIC for any length of time, you've probably used them before, possibly dozens of times. If you're new to VBA and need more detail on these functions, you may want to reexamine the VBA documentation or another introductory text. All the code for this section is contained in the basVBABuiltIn module of the sample Excel workbook and the VBAFILE.BAS file.

The Dir Function Explained

While it's not the most powerful built-in VBA file function, the Dir function is probably one of the most commonly used. Its primary purpose is to return the names of files in a given directory. Dir accepts a file specification and returns a filename matching the specification. There are four ways you can call the Dir function:

1. If you pass a complete filename (with no wildcard characters), Dir returns the name of the file if it exists at the specified location. If the file doesn't exist, Dir returns an empty string.

2. If you pass a file specification (one that includes wildcard characters), Dir returns the first filename that matches the specification.

3. If you pass a directory name, Dir finds the first file in that directory.

4. If you don't pass anything, Dir returns the next matching filename. You can continue to call Dir in this manner until it returns an empty string indicating no further matches.

Furthermore, the following rules apply when you call Dir:

- You must pass a path the first time you call Dir or after Dir returns an empty string; otherwise, an error occurs.

- You can pass a complete path, relative path, or UNC path.

- If you don't specify a path, Dir searches the current drive and directory.

- Each time you call Dir with a new path, it abandons the prior directory search.

The procedure shown in Listing 12.1 shows a number of examples of calling the Dir function.

Listing 12.1: Various Ways to Call the Dir Function

```
Sub dhTestDir()
  Dim strFile As String

  ' Prints "WIN.INI" if the file exists
  Debug.Print Dir("C:\WINDOWS\WIN.INI")

  ' Prints the first file that starts with "W"
  Debug.Print Dir("C:\WINDOWS\W*")

  ' Prints the next file that starts with "W"
  Debug.Print Dir

  ' Prints all the files in the current directory
  strFile = Dir("*")
  Do Until strFile = ""
    Debug.Print strFile
    strFile = Dir
  Loop
End Sub
```

TIP   You can use relative paths, including the single-dot (.) and double-dot (..) symbols, which represent the current and parent directories, respectively, in all VBA file functions. For example, the command Dir("..*.*") returns the first file in the directory immediately above the current one.

Checking for a File's Existence

One common need in an application is to determine whether a particular file exists. You might need to do this before calling another VBA function, such as Kill (which deletes a file). Checking for a file's existence is easy using the Dir function. Listing 12.2 shows the dhFileExists function. You pass it a complete path to a file (with no wildcards); it returns True if the file exists and False if it doesn't.

Listing 12.2: A Simple Function to Check for a File's Existence

```
Function dhFileExists(strFile As String) As Boolean
  ' Call Dir with the passed file name--
  ' if the file exists Dir will return
  ' back the file name and the length
  ' of the string will be > 0
  On Error Resume Next
  dhFileExists = (Len(Dir(strFile)) > 0)
End Function
```

Using File Attributes

Files maintained in FAT or NTFS file systems have attributes that indicate whether they are read-only, hidden, to be archived, or part of the operating system. Under normal circumstances, the Dir function returns the names of all files that do not have the hidden or system attributes set, but you can instruct Dir to look for these files. You can also search for directories, as well as retrieve a disk's volume label. To accomplish all this, you pass a bit mask of values as the optional second argument. You can pass any combination of the following values:

Value	Constant	Description
0	vbNormal	Default file attributes
1	vbReadOnly	Finds read-only files
2	vbHidden	Finds hidden files
4	vbSystem	Finds system files
8	vbVolume	Returns disk volume label
16	vbDirectory	Finds directories

For example, to include hidden and system files in the list that Dir generates, you could use a statement like this:

```
strFile = Dir("C:\", vbHidden + vbSystem)
```

NOTE   Passing an attribute as the second argument does not limit the output only to files with that attribute set. It only adds them to the list of normal files returned by the Dir function.

GetAttr and SetAttr

You can also retrieve and set the attributes for a given file. VBA provides two functions for this purpose, GetAttr and SetAttr. GetAttr accepts a filename and returns a long integer containing a bit mask of the file's attributes. In addition to the ones listed above, you can check for the archive attribute (vbArchive, value 32). Similarly, SetAttr accepts a filename and a bit mask of attributes. Listing 12.3 shows the dhIsAttr function. It accepts a filename and a set of attributes and returns True if the file's attributes match those passed to the function.

Listing 12.3: Use the dhIsAttr Function to Check a File's Attributes.

```
Function dhIsAttr(strFile As String, lngAttr As Long) _
  As Boolean

    ' Check the attributes of the file against the
    ' specified attributes--return True if they match
    On Error Resume Next
    dhIsAttr = ((GetAttr(strFile) And lngAttr) = lngAttr)
End Function
```

You can call the function with any attribute or combination of attributes. For example,

```
' Is "C:\MSDOS.SYS" a system file?
Debug.Print dhIsAttr("C:\MSDOS.SYS", vbSystem)


' Is "C:\MSDOS.SYS" read-only AND a system file?
Debug.Print dhIsAttr("C:\MSDOS.SYS", vbSystem + vbReadOnly)
```

Another example of using GetAttr is shown in Listing 12.4. It shows three procedures that list all the files in the root directory, along with their file attributes. dhPrintAttr uses the Dir function to locate all the files and directories. (Note the bit mask passed as the second argument.) dhBuildAttrString and dhBuildAttr compare the attributes of each file against a given file attribute and construct a string based on the results. Figure 12.1 shows the output from running dhPrintAttr.

Listing 12.4: Two Procedures That Print Files and Attributes

```
Sub dhPrintAttr()
   Dim strFile As String
   Dim lngAttr As Long
   Dim strAttr As String

   ' Use the root directory of the current drive
   Const dhcDir = "\"

   ' Look for all types of files
   strFile = Dir(dhcDir, _
    vbHidden + vbSystem + vbDirectory)

   ' Loop until no more files are found
   Do Until strFile = ""

      ' Use GetAttr to get the file's attributes
      lngAttr = GetAttr(dhcDir & strFile)

      ' Print the file with its attributes
      Debug.Print strFile, dhBuildAttrString(lngAttr)

      ' Get the next file and reset the attribute string
      strFile = Dir
      strAttr = ""
   Loop
End Sub

Function dhBuildAttrString(lngAttr As Long) As String
   Dim strAttr As String

   ' Build up an attribute string
```

```
        dhBuildAttr strAttr, lngAttr, vbReadOnly, "R"
        dhBuildAttr strAttr, lngAttr, vbHidden, "H"
        dhBuildAttr strAttr, lngAttr, vbSystem, "S"
        dhBuildAttr strAttr, lngAttr, vbArchive, "A"
        dhBuildAttr strAttr, lngAttr, vbDirectory, "D"


    ' Return attribute string
    dhBuildAttrString = strAttr
End Function

Sub dhBuildAttr(strAttr As String, lngAttr As Long, _
  lngMask As Long, strSymbol As String)

    ' Compare the passed attributes with the
    ' mask--if it matches append the passed
    ' symbol to the string
    If (lngAttr And lngMask) = lngMask Then
        strAttr = strAttr & strSymbol
    Else
        strAttr = strAttr & " "
    End If
End Sub
```

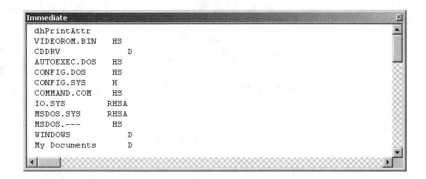

FIGURE 12.1
A list of files and their attributes

Listing Directory Names

File attributes are critical to locating specific file types, especially directories. (To the file system, directories are just like files but with a special attribute set.) Listing 12.5 shows a procedure that lists all the subdirectories beneath a given directory. Note that after using the Dir function to build the list, the procedure uses dhIsAttr to find the directories among the names returned.

Listing 12.5: A Procedure That Prints Subdirectory Names

```
Sub dhListSubDirs(strPath As String)
  Dim strFile As String

  ' Make sure strPath is a directory
  If Right(strPath, 1) <> "\" Then
    strPath = strPath & "\"
  End If

  If dhIsAttr(strPath, vbDirectory) Then

    ' Find all the files, including directories
    strFile = Dir(strPath, vbDirectory)
    Do Until strFile = ""

      ' If the file is a directory, print it
      If dhIsAttr(strPath & strFile, vbDirectory) Then

        ' Ignore "." and ".."
        If strFile <> "." And _
          strFile <> ".." Then

          Debug.Print strFile
        End If
      End If

      ' Get the next file
      strFile = Dir
    Loop
  End If
End Sub
```

Those Pesky Dir Dots

You'll notice that the code in Listing 12.5 includes an If…Then statement to weed out two values returned by Dir: "." and "..". These values represent the current directory and parent directory, respectively. Dir will return them whenever you scan for directory names in any directory beneath the root. As far as the operating system is concerned, they're perfectly valid directory names. Under most circumstances, though, you won't want to include them in the directory listing.

Doing the Disk File Shuffle

Probably the most common tasks related to files involve copying, moving, renaming, and deleting them. VBA has several functions, all of which are quite straightforward, designed to accomplish these tasks:

Function	Description
FileCopy	Copies a file
Name	Moves or renames a file
Kill	Deletes a file

Listing 12.6 shows a small procedure that demonstrates their syntax. It copies the WIN.INI file from the Windows directory to the root directory, renames it WIN.TMP, and then deletes it. What could be simpler?

⟳ Listing 12.6: Copy, Rename, and Delete Files.

```
Sub dhCopyRenameDelete()
  ' Copy WIN.INI to root directory
  FileCopy "C:\WINDOWS\WIN.INI", "C:\WIN.INI"

  ' Rename to WIN.TMP
  Name "C:\WIN.INI" As "C:\WIN.TMP"

  ' Delete the renamed file
  Kill "C:\WIN.TMP"
End Sub
```

While these functions are mostly unremarkable (except perhaps for Name's odd syntax), there are a few things you should know about them:

- FileCopy *will* overwrite the destination file if it exists.

- Name will *not* overwrite an existing file.

- You can copy and rename in one step by specifying a different destination name.

- You can move files using the Name function by specifying a different destination name.

Some File Information: FileLen and FileDateTime

Two other VBA file functions are worth mentioning: FileLen and FileDateTime. FileLen returns the size of a file in bytes, given its name. FileDateTime returns the date and time a given file was last modified. Listing 12.7 shows a very simple procedure that demonstrates their syntax. The sections "A Hardcore Replacement for Dir" and "Getting File Information Quickly" later in this chapter discuss looking to the Windows API to find out even more information about files.

Listing 12.7: Print a File's Size and Date of Last Modification.

```
Sub dhMoreFileInfo()
  ' How big is WIN.INI?
  Debug.Print FileLen("C:\WINDOWS\WIN.INI") & " bytes"

  ' When was it last modified?
  Debug.Print FileDateTime("C:\WINDOWS\WIN.INI")
End Sub
```

Directory Management

VBA features a number of functions for manipulating directories. Like the file management functions, they are all straightforward. Using these functions, you can set and retrieve the current directory, set the current drive, and create and remove directories.

Current Confusion

What can make using these functions a bit confusing is the concept of the current drive and directory. Each process (application) in Windows can set a *current directory.* Any operations on files that are not fully qualified affect the current directory. For example, if you were to issue the command

```
Debug.Print Dir("*.*")
```

the result would be the first file in the current directory. We recommend avoiding the current directory altogether and using fully qualified path names (complete with drive and directory), but sometimes it's convenient to use the current directory. So how do you find out what the current directory is? Use the CurDir function. For example,

```
Debug.Print CurDir
```

VBA includes the drive as well as the directory in the output. To change the current directory, use the ChDir function:

```
ChDir "C:\WINDOWS"
```

There is also a ChDrive function to change the current drive. This is where things get confusing. Shouldn't you be able to change the current drive using the ChDir command? The answer is no. The reason is that VBA tracks these elements separately. While you can include another drive letter in the ChDir statement, that drive does not become "active" until you use ChDrive. You can see this by running the code shown in Listing 12.8. (Just make sure you use drives and directories appropriate for your computer.)

Listing 12.8: Demonstrating the Confusion of ChDir and ChDrive

```
Sub dhTestCurrent()
    ' Print the first file in the current directory
    Debug.Print Dir("*.*"), "in " & CurDir

    ' Try to change to the D drive using ChDir
    ChDir "D:\SOMEDIR"

    ' Print the first file again--it's still on C!
    Debug.Print Dir("*.*"), "in " & CurDir

    ' Now use ChDrive to switch drives
    ChDrive "D"

    ' Print the first file again--this time it's D!
    Debug.Print Dir("*.*"), "in " & CurDir
End Sub
```

The procedure begins by printing the first filename in the current directory, which we assume is on the C drive, along with the directory name. It then tries to change to the D drive using just ChDir. While this appears to execute just fine, when the first filename is printed again, it's the same as before. Since you can't change drives using ChDir, the current directory remains the same. The procedure then uses ChDrive to change the current drive. When the filename is printed a third time, it's the first file in D:\SOMEDIR. This demonstrates that although you can use ChDir with a different drive *and* directory, VBA does not recognize the new current directory until you use ChDrive.

Creating and Deleting Directories and Directory Trees

You add and remove directories using the MkDir and RmDir functions. Both accept a directory path as arguments. You can include a fully qualified path, including a drive letter, or a partial one. If you omit a drive letter, MkDir and RmDir assume the current drive and resolve all relative paths based on the current directory. In other words, they work just like their namesake MS-DOS commands.

The only other item worth noting is that, like the MS-DOS command, RmDir will fail if you attempt to remove a directory containing files or subdirectories. You must use the Kill statement to delete any files that exist. Since subdirectories can be nested several levels deep, removing a high-level directory is problematic. The solution requires recursively looking for subdirectories and deleting any files they contain. This is not easy, however, because each recursive call to Dir resets any pending results from the previous call.

One possible solution is shown in Listing 12.9. The function, appropriately named dhDelTree after the utility that appeared in MS-DOS 5, accepts a directory and methodically deletes every nested file and subdirectory. It works by first storing the name of the current directory in a variable. It then changes to the target directory and deletes any existing files. Next, it searches for subdirectories and, upon finding one, calls itself recursively. When the recursive call returns, the function restarts its subdirectory search until no more subdirectories exist. Finally, it removes the target directory and resets the current directory to its original value.

Listing 12.9: A Function to Delete an Entire Directory Tree

```
Function dhDelTree(ByVal Directory As String, _
 Optional RemoveRoot As Boolean = True, _
 Optional ByVal Level As Integer = 1) As Boolean

    On Error GoTo HandleErrors

    Dim strFilename As String
    Dim strDirectory As String

    strDirectory = dhFixPath(Directory)

    ' Check to make sure the directory actually exists.
    ' If not, we don't have to do a thing.
```

```
If Len(Dir(strDirectory, vbDirectory)) = 0 Then
    GoTo ExitHere
End If

If dhFixPath(CurDir) = strDirectory Then
    MsgBox "Unable to delete the current directory. " & _
     "Move to a different directory, and try again."
    GoTo ExitHere
End If

' Delete all the files in the current directory
strFilename = Dir(strDirectory & "*.*")
Do Until strFilename = ""
    Kill strDirectory & strFilename
    strFilename = Dir
Loop

' Now build a list of subdirectories
Do
    strFilename = Dir(strDirectory & "*.*", vbDirectory)

    ' Skip "." and ".."
    Do While strFilename = "." Or strFilename = ".."
        strFilename = Dir
    Loop

    ' If there are no more files, exit the loop.
    ' Otherwise call dhDelTree again to wipe
    ' out the subdirectory.
    If strFilename = "" Then
        Exit Do
    Else
        ' Call dhDelTree recursively. Pass True for RemoveRoot,
        ' because you'll always want to remove subfolders.
        ' Indicate the level by passing Level + 1.
        If Not dhDelTree(strDirectory & strFilename, True, _
         Level + 1) Then
            GoTo ExitHere
        End If
    End If
Loop
```

```
' Finally, remove the target directory
' The following expression returns True unless
' the first factor is True and the
' second factor is False -- that is,
' it always removes the folder unless
' you're at level 1 (the root level) and you've
' been told not to remove the root.
If Level = 1 Imp RemoveRoot Then
    RmDir strDirectory
End If

dhDelTree = True

ExitHere:
    Exit Function

HandleErrors:
    Select Case Err.Number
        Case 75 ' Path or file access
            ' If a file or folder can't be deleted,
            ' just keep going.
            Resume Next
        Case Else
            dhDelTree = False
            MsgBox Err.Description, vbExclamation, _
              "Error " & Err.Number & " in dhDelTree"
            Resume ExitHere
    End Select
End Function
```

NOTE　　The dhFixPath function used in this procedure simply ensures that the path passed in has a trailing backslash.

You may notice that this solution is not tremendously efficient, due to the fact that it needs to change directories and restart subdirectory searches each time it's executed (which for large trees is many times). We offer a more elegant solution to a related problem, *copying* an entire subdirectory tree, in our file system object model, described in Appendix D, "An Object Model for Folders and Files" (which is included on the CD-ROM that accompanies this book).

WARNING   Be extremely careful when calling the dhDelTree function. The results of executing a statement like dhDelTree("C:\") could be highly counterproductive.

File I/O If You Must

BASIC, the language VBA is based on, is, in personal computing terms, very old. It evolved during a time when there were no high-level, object-oriented database tools. As such, it includes a number of functions that perform low-level file input/ output (I/O). While there are usually better ways to manipulate the contents of files, sometimes you have to roll up your sleeves and dig into the bits and bytes. This section briefly covers VBA's file I/O functions. Since they are unchanged from earlier versions of BASIC, we leave the advanced discussion of their usage to the numerous existing books on the subject. All the code for this section is contained in the basFileIO module of the sample Excel workbook and the FILEIO.BAS file.

NOTE   Thanks to COM and work by the scripting team at Microsoft, you have a much more attractive option for working with file I/O. Chapter 14 discusses the objects available through the Windows Scripting Runtime. If you have simple I/O needs you should probably take a look at Chapter 14.

Getting a Handle on Files

Before you can begin manipulating files and their contents, you need to understand the role of *file handles* (sometimes called *file numbers* in VBA documentation). Like other handles in Windows, file handles are simply numbers that uniquely identify open files to the operating system. The first step in opening a file using VBA is getting an unused file handle. You do this using the FreeFile function. For example,

```
Dim hFile As Long

' Get the next free file handle
hFile = FreeFile
```

If successful, FreeFile returns a nonzero value that you can use in the Open statement described in the next section. A file's handle is the key to using all the other VBA file I/O functions.

VBA's method of assigning file handles is different from that used by the Windows API. Windows API functions return file handles as part of opening or creating new files. The section "Getting a (Windows) Handle on Files" later in this chapter discusses this subject in depth.

Other books on BASIC file functions and even the VBA documentation often ignore the FreeFile function and use hard-coded file handles (for example "#1"). While this is perfectly legal syntax, we recommend you use variables and the FreeFile function to assign file handles, especially if you open more than one file at once. Hard-coded file handles can lead to confusion and unwanted results if you inadvertently write data to the wrong file.

Using the Open Function

You use the VBA Open function to open all disk files for reading, writing, or both. It can be a confusing function because of its odd syntax and many permutations. The general form of the Open function is shown here. (Square brackets indicate optional components.)

```
Open pathname For mode [Access access] [lock] _
    As [#]filenumber [Len=reclength]
```

Table 12.2 lists each of the elements of the function and describes what each is used for. As you can see, there are quite a few possible permutations!

T A B L E 1 2 . 2 : Elements of the Open Function

Element	Description
pathname	Path to the file to open
mode	File open mode. Must be one of Append, Binary, Input, Output, or Random
access	Access mode. Must be one of Read (default), Write, or Read Write
lock	Share mode. Must be one of Shared (default), Lock Read, Lock Write, or Lock Read Write

TABLE 12.2: Elements of the Open Function *(continued)*

Element	Description
filenumber	File handle. Can be a hard-coded number or a variable containing the handle obtained from FreeFile
reclength	Record length (for Random mode) or number of bytes buffered (for append, input, and output modes)

The options for mode, access, and lock are probably the most confusing. The next three sections explain each of them.

File Mode

The mode in which you open a file determines how Windows treats the opened file and what you can do with it. Unless you're constructing a random-access database application in VBA, you'll likely open a file in one of the sequential access modes: Append, Input, or Output. These are the preferred modes for working with text files. Files opened in Input mode are restricted to read-only access. Files opened in Output or Append mode can be read from or written to. The difference between the two is that Output always creates a new file, deleting an existing one with the same name, while Append adds text to the end of a file.

If you need to read and write data to a file on a byte-by-byte basis (such as when working with image files), open the file in binary mode. Random mode, on the other hand, is normally used for files that use a fixed record length, such as a dBase file. Operations on files opened in random mode operate on units that correspond to the size of the record specified by the *reclength* element of the Open function.

File Access

Somewhat related to the file open mode is the file access mode. You choose from three options: Read, Write, and Read Write. The meaning of each should be obvious. If you don't have appropriate access rights to open a file with the specified options, perhaps because of network or operating system security settings, an error occurs.

Locking

In multiuser scenarios, it is a good idea to select one of the locking options. The default is Shared. This lets other users read from and write to the file while you have it open. If this is not appropriate for your situation, you can select one of the other options. Lock Read prevents other users from reading the file but still allows them to write to it. Lock Write allows others to read the contents of the file but not to modify them. Lock Read Write is the most restrictive. It prevents other users from reading or writing.

NOTE   While we don't cover it in this chapter, you can lock parts of a file once you've opened it. Search VBA online help for more information on the Lock statement.

A Simple Example

Now let's look at a simple example of using the Open statement. The procedure shown in Listing 12.10 opens a file in sequential access mode. Note from the statement options that the procedure will only be able to read from the file. Note also that if you want to test this procedure, you should make sure the file specified in the Open statement exists.

Listing 12.10: Open a File for Sequential Read Access.

```
Sub dhTestOpen()
  Dim hFile As Long

  ' Get a new file handle
  hFile = FreeFile

  ' Open a file for sequential access
  Open "C:\TESTPROC.BAS" For Input Access Read _
   Shared As hFile

  ' Do something here...

  ' Close the file
  Close hFile
End Sub
```

Don't Forget to Close!

You'll notice that just before terminating, the procedure in Listing 12.10 calls the VBA Close statement, passing the file handle. The Close statement closes an open disk file. Closing a file after you're done using it is important. If you fail to close a file, you risk locking others out of it (if opened in non-shared mode) or losing data (if you shut down Windows).

You can close multiple files simultaneously by passing more than one file handle, separated by commas, to the Close statement. While we recommend using the Close statement to close each open file individually as soon as you're finished with it, you can also use the Reset statement to close all disk files opened by your application.

Manipulating File Position

Under most circumstances, you don't want to blindly read and write data to disk files. You normally need to know things like how big a file is, where the next read or write operation will take place, and when you've reached the end of the file. VBA offers several functio74ns to help you do this, described in the following sections.

LOF and EOF

No, we're not talking about two of the dwarfs from *The Hobbit*. LOF and EOF are two functions that tell you the size of a file and when you're at the end of a file, respectively. Each accepts a file handle as an argument. LOF simply returns the size of the open file in bytes.

EOF returns a Boolean value indicating whether the *current byte position* is at the end of the file. The current byte position is maintained internally by VBA. When you first open a file, VBA sets this value to 0. As you use file I/O functions, VBA changes this value. For example, after reading two bytes from a file opened in Binary mode, the current byte position is set to 2. The next read operation will occur at the next, or third, byte. When you have read the entire contents of a file, the current byte position is set to the final byte number, and EOF returns True. Any attempt to read more data will result in an error.

NOTE   For files opened in output mode, EOF always returns True.

Loc and Seek

If you need to know what the current byte position is, call the Loc function. Loc accepts a file handle as an argument and returns the current byte position. The number returned, however, varies depending on the mode the file was opened in. For files opened in binary mode, Loc returns the actual byte position. For files opened in random mode, Loc returns the record number instead of the byte number. For files opened in sequential mode (input, output, or append), however, the number returned by Loc is the current byte position divided by 128. (No, we don't know why.)

If you need to know the actual byte position of sequentially accessed files, use the Seek function instead. Seek works just like Loc for binary and random files but returns a true byte position for sequential files.

VBA also has a Seek statement that you can use to set the current byte or record position for files opened in binary or random mode. (As the term *sequential* implies, you can't change the current byte position for sequential files.)

Statements for Reading and Writing

Just as there are many permutations of the Open statement, there are numerous VBA statements for reading from and writing to disk files. Which one you use depends on which file open mode you used and how you want to format the incoming or outgoing data. Table 12.3 summarizes the different statements.

TABLE 12.3: VBA Statements for File I/O

Open Mode	Read Statement(s)	Write Statement(s)
Sequential (Input, Output, or Append)	Input, Line Input #, Input #	Print #, Write #
Random	Get	Put
Binary	Input, Get	Put

Sequential Access

Files opened in input, output, or append mode can be manipulated by any of five functions. For reading data you can use Input, Line Input #, or Input #. Writing to sequential files is accomplished with the Print # or Write # functions.

Input Input is the simplest function for reading data and is useful for dealing with text files that don't contain line breaks and files containing binary data. Listing 12.11 shows a procedure that accepts a filename and prints the contents of the file to the Immediate window. You'll notice that it uses the EOF function to determine when it's reached the end of the file.

Listing 12.11: Print the Contents of a File, Byte by Byte.

```
Sub dhPrintBytes(strFile As String)
  Dim hFile As Long

  ' Get a new file handle
  hFile = FreeFile

  ' Open the file for sequential access
  Open strFile For Input Access Read Shared As hFile

  ' Print the file contents
  Do Until EOF(hFile)
    Debug.Print Input(1, hFile);
  Loop

  ' Close the file
  Close hFile
End Sub
```

This procedure is not very efficient, however, because it makes two function calls (to EOF and Input) for each byte in a file. When using the Input function, it's best to fetch the data in chunks. Listing 12.12 shows an updated version of the procedure that does this. In addition to the filename, it accepts a chunk size and retrieves data in blocks rather than one byte at a time.

Listing 12.12: Print the Contents of a File, Using Chunks.

```
Sub dhPrintChunks(strFile As String, intSize As Integer)
  Dim hFile As Long
  Dim lngSize As Long
  Dim intChunk As Integer

  ' Get a new file handle
  hFile = FreeFile
```

```
' Open the file for sequential access
Open strFile For Input Access Read Shared As hFile

' Get the file size
lngSize = LOF(hFile)

' Print the file contents, first in chunks
For intChunk = 1 To lngSize \ intSize
  Debug.Print Input(intSize, hFile);
Next

' Then the remainder
If (lngSize Mod intSize) > 0 Then
  Debug.Print Input((lngSize Mod intSize), hFile)
End If

' Close the file
Close hFile
End Sub
```

You'll notice that the procedure uses a For…Next loop to read in each block of data. The number of iterations is computed by dividing the chunk size into the file size, using integer division. A final Input statement is used to read any remaining data, which will be left over if the file size is not equally divisible by the chunk size.

Of course, these methods of retrieving data evolved under early versions of BASIC that could not cope with large amounts of data. String variables were limited to 32K, for instance. With the 32-bit versions of VBA, however, String variables can now hold over two *billion* characters, so you could use a statement like this to read a file's entire contents at once:

```
Debug.Print Input(LOF(hFile), hFile)
```

Line Input #   For text files that contain line breaks (for example, configuration files like AUTOEXEC.BAT and WIN.INI), use the Line Input # statement instead. This statement accepts a file handle and a variable and reads the next line from the file into the variable. (It strips the trailing carriage return and line-feed characters.) Listing 12.13 shows a procedure that accepts a filename, opens that file for read-only access, and prints each line to the Immediate window. Using Line Input #, you don't have to worry about byte position or buffer size.

Listing 12.13: Print Text Files with Line Breaks Using Line Input #.

```
Sub dhPrintLines(strFile As String)
    Dim hFile As Long
    Dim strLine As String

    ' Get a new file handle
    hFile = FreeFile

    ' Open the file for sequential access
    Open strFile For Input Access Read Shared As hFile

    ' Print the file contents
    Do Until EOF(hFile)
        Line Input #hFile, strLine
        Debug.Print strLine
    Loop

    ' Close the file
    Close hFile
End Sub
```

Input #   Input #, the final sequential read statement, accepts a file handle and a series of variables (separated by commas) and loads file data into those variables. Input # is most useful for comma-delimited data since it treats each data element separately, loading it into a separate variable. It also automatically removes quotes around text values and converts date strings to VBA dates.

Write #   The counterpart of Input # is Write #. It accepts a file handle and a comma-delimited list of values and writes each value to the file. Additionally, the statement delimits the output with commas and encloses text in quotes and dates in number signs (#). This makes it ideal for reading using Input #. Listing 12.14 shows a procedure that demonstrates both statements.

Listing 12.14: Using Write # and Input #

```
Sub dhWriteAndInput(strFile As String)
    Dim hFile As Long
    ReDim varData(1 To 5) As Variant
    Dim i As Integer
```

```
' Open a file for output, write to it, and close it
hFile = FreeFile
Open strFile For Output Access Write As hFile
Write #hFile, "Some Text", "A Date:", Date, "A Number:", 100
Close hFile

' Now open it back up for reading
hFile = FreeFile
Open strFile For Input Access Read As hFile
Input #hFile, varData(1), varData(2), varData(3), _
  varData(4), varData(5)
Close hFile

' Print the data
For i = 1 To 5
  Debug.Print varData(i)
Next
End Sub
```

This procedure begins by opening a file for output and writing several values to it. If you stepped through the code, stopping just after the first Close statement, and opened the file, you would see that the contents look like this:

```
"Some Text","A Date:",#1997-01-21#,"A Number:",100
```

The procedure then opens the file again for read access; uses Input # to read the data into five Variant variables, stored as an array; and prints them to the Immediate window.

NOTE   When using Input #, the number of variables must match the number of data elements in the file.

Print #   Finally, there's the Print # statement. You may recognize the statement from the Print method of the Debug object. In fact, the two statements work in much the same manner. Print # writes a series of values to a file open in output or append mode. Unlike Write #, however, Print # does not format the data with quotes or number signs. Furthermore, Print # separates each value with tabs, not commas. If you were to substitute Print # for Write # in the previous example, the output file would look like this:

```
Some Text    A Date:  1/21/97  A Number:    100
```

Since there are no commas, you could not use Input # to read the file. You would need to use Input or Line Input instead.

The Print # statement is normally used with just one piece of data, commonly a line of text. Listing 12.15 contains a simple procedure to add line numbers to a text file. It opens one file in input mode and another, new file in output mode. It then loops through the input file, reads each line, and writes the line number and original text to the output file using Print #.

Listing 12.15: Use Print # to Add Line Numbers to a Text File.

```
Sub dhAddLineNumbers(strFileIn As String, strFileOut As String)
    Dim hFileIn As Long
    Dim hFileOut As Long
    Dim strInput As String
    Dim i As Integer

    ' Open first file for input
    hFileIn = FreeFile
    Open strFileIn For Input Access Read As hFileIn

    ' Open the second file for output
    hFileOut = FreeFile
    Open strFileOut For Output Access Write As hFileOut

    ' Read each line from the input file, add a line
    ' number and write it to the output file
    Do Until EOF(hFileIn)
        i = i + 1
        Line Input #hFileIn, strInput
        Print #hFileOut, i & ":", strInput
    Loop

    ' Close the files
    Close hFileIn
    Close hFileOut
End Sub
```

WARNING	When opening two or more files simultaneously, always call FreeFile for the second file handle after opening the first file. Otherwise, both file handles will be the same (since you haven't used the first handle, it's still free), and an error will occur when you try to open the second file.

Random Access

Although not often used in today's world of Automation-enabled database technologies like ADO, VBA's random-access file functions can still be used to produce database-like behavior with very little overhead. The functions work by manipulating "records" in the form of user-defined data types. When you open a file for random access, you pass the size of the record to the Open statement. All subsequent read and write operations then move data to and from variables of a given user-defined type in memory. Furthermore, these functions, Get and Put, transparently handle the task of overwriting existing records in the middle of a file.

To illustrate this functionality, assume the following user-defined data type:

```
Type dhEmployee
    ID As Integer
    FirstName As String * 10
    LastName As String * 10
    Department As Integer
    HireDate As Date
    Salary As Currency
End Type
```

This represents a fictitious employee record. Note the fixed-length String variables. You must use fixed-length strings to prevent the record-oriented nature of this process from breaking down. This is because you must tell VBA what the record size is when you open it. Errors will occur if the record is of variable size.

Listing 12.16 shows two functions designed to read and write data in this format to and from a file. Each function uses the same Open statement:

```
Open strFile For Random Access Read Write _
    As hFile Len = Len(empIn)
```

Note that the file is opened in random mode and that the record length (determined by applying the Len function to the record variable) is passed to the Open statement.

Listing 12.16: Read and Write to a Random-Access File

```
Function dhReadEmp(strFile As String, _
 emp As dhEmployee) As Boolean

  Dim hFile As Long
  Dim empIn As dhEmployee

   ' Open file for random access
   hFile = FreeFile
   Open strFile For Random Access Read Write _
    As hFile Len = Len(empIn)

   ' Try to find the employee in existing records
   Do Until EOF(hFile)

     ' Read in the record
     Get hFile, , empIn

     ' Check IDs
     If empIn.ID = emp.ID Then
       emp = empIn
       dhReadEmp = True
       Exit Do
     End If
   Loop

   Close hFile
End Function

Function dhSaveEmp(strFile As String, _
 empToSave As dhEmployee) As Boolean

  Dim hFile As Long
  Dim empIn As dhEmployee
  Dim lngRec As Long

   ' Open the file for random access
   hFile = FreeFile
   Open strFile For Random Access Read Write _
    As hFile Len = Len(empIn)
```

```
        ' Try to find the employee in existing records
        Do Until EOF(hFile)
          lngRec = lngRec + 1

          ' Read in the record
          Get hFile, lngRec, empIn

          ' Check IDs
          If empIn.ID = empToSave.ID Then

            ' Write the new data and get out
            Put hFile, lngRec, empToSave
            GoTo ExitHere
          End If
        Loop

          ' Record doesn't exist so write at end
          Put hFile, , empToSave

    ExitHere:
      dhSaveEmp = True
      Close hFile
    End Function
```

Each function loops through the contents of the file, loading existing data into a record variable, empIn. In the case of dhReadEmp, the function is not concerned with the record number per se. If the record is found, the function returns it to the calling procedure. dhSaveEmp, on the other hand, uses a variable to track the record number (lngRec). If an existing record is found, the procedure replaces it with the new record simply by specifying the record number in the Put statement. That's one reason this mode of data access is so powerful. You can read or write to *any* record in the file based on its number!

NOTE A procedure that demonstrates this functionality, dhTestRandom, is included in the sample code but not printed here.

Of course, it would be difficult to convince anyone that what we've just described constitutes a database. After all, to find a given record, our procedures loop through every record in the file! But by using complex data structures such as linked lists and embedded pointers, you could create a sophisticated database system using these functions. Why you would want to, given the availability of component-based technologies, is another question.

The Windows API: Where the Real Power Is

As good as the built-in VBA functions are, they don't do everything you might need to do in an application. For instance, what if you need to find out how much disk space is free or change the volume label of a disk? You'll need to use the Windows API to accomplish these tasks. This section examines a few of the many API functions that relate to disks and files.

Comparing API Functions with VBA Functions

Before looking at specific functions, let's compare the VBA functions we've already discussed with their Windows API equivalents. You'll see many similarities. After all, when you call a VBA function, VBA is making the associated API calls on your behalf.

Table 12.4 lists the VBA disk and file functions, along with their comparable Windows API counterparts. Where the functionality provided by the Windows API functions differs from the VBA functions, it is noted in the right-hand column. Because the Windows API is a more complex interface than VBA, if there is no appreciable benefit to using an API function, we don't cover it in this chapter.

TABLE 12.4: Comparing VBA and Windows API Disk and File Functions

VBA Function(s)	Comparable API Function(s)	How API Functions Differ
ChDir, ChDrive	SetCurrentDirectory	No added functionality
CurDir	GetCurrentDirectory	No added functionality
Dir	FindFirstFile, FindFirstFileEx, FindNextFile, FindClose	Requires more function calls but yields more information about each file
FileCopy	CopyFile, CopyFileEx	Allows you to prevent overwriting an existing file. CopyFileEx provides progress notification through a callback mechanism.

TABLE 12.4: Comparing VBA and Windows API Disk and File Functions *(continued)*

VBA Function(s)	Comparable API Function(s)	How API Functions Differ
FileDateTime	GetFileTime	Much more complex but gives you access to all three file times (creation, access, and last-written)
FileLen	GetFileSize, GetFileSizeEx	Works with really huge files (greater than 2GB)
GetAttr	GetFileAttributes, GetFileAttributesEx	No added functionality
Kill	DeleteFile	No added functionality
MkDir, RmDir	CreateDirectory, CreateDirectoryEx, RemoveDirectory	Support for NT security attributes
Name	MoveFile, MoveFileEx	Provides options on how to move the file (e.g., on reboot)
SetAttr	SetFileAttributes	No added functionality
Open, Input, Print, Write, Close	CreateFile, ReadFile, ReadFileEx, WriteFile, WriteFileEx, CloseHandle	This is like comparing apples and oranges. You must use the CreateFile API function to obtain file handles, but in general, using the VBA functions for file I/O is simpler.

In addition to the API calls that duplicate built-in functionality, there is a whole host of others that offer capabilities not found in VBA. Table 12.5 lists the ones mentioned in this chapter. There are certainly others, but most are too esoteric or too complex to warrant coverage here.

TABLE 12.5: Windows API Functions with No VBA Equivalent

Function(s)	Description
CompareFileTime	Compares the file time of two files
FindFirstChangeNotification, FindNextChangeNotification, FindCloseChangeNotification	Instruct Windows to notify your application when a file or directory changes
GetBinaryType	Determines whether a file is an executable and if it is, the type
GetDiskFreeSpace	Retrieves information about a disk drive, including available disk space

TABLE 12.5: Windows API Functions with No VBA Equivalent *(continued)*

Function(s)	Description
GetDriveType	Determines what type a drive is (fixed, removable, network, CD-ROM, or RAM disk)
GetFileInformationByHandle	Retrieves detailed file information in a single function call
GetFullPathName	Retrieves the full path name for a file, given a partial path
GetLogicalDrives, GetLogicalDriveStrings	Retrieve the logical drives for the computer either as a bit mask or as a null-delimited string
GetShortPathName	Retrieves the short (8.3) filename associated with a given long filename
GetTempFileName	Computes a temporary filename based on a directory name, prefix characters, and, optionally, a unique integer
GetTempPath	Retrieves the directory designated to hold temporary files
GetVolumeInformation	Retrieves information about the file system and specified volume
SearchPath	Searches for a file, given a search path or the default system paths
SetFileTime	Changes the times associated with a given file
SetVolumeLabel	Sets the volume label for a drive

NOTE   Some of the information in this section is available through the Windows Scripting Runtime, explained in Chapter 14. We've presented it here because sometimes it's desirable to call the Windows API directly, and it provides insight into what the runtime itself is doing.

Getting Disk Information

VBA has a number of functions that deal with files but very few that deal with disks. For example, there is no way to determine the disk space available on a given drive or the number and type of drives installed in your computer.

Fortunately, the Windows API comes to the rescue with a myriad of functions to accomplish these tasks as well as many others. All the code for this section is contained in the basDiskInfo module of the sample Excel workbook and the DISKINFO.BAS file.

How Many Drives Do You Have?

To find out how many drives you have, the best place to start is with two functions that determine the number of drives installed in your computer, including both physical drives and network connections. The two functions are GetLogicalDrives and GetLogicalDriveStrings. Which one you use will depend on what type of data you're dealing with.

GetLogicalDrives is a simple function call that returns drive information packed into a single long integer. Each bit represents a drive letter (the first bit for drive A, the second for drive B, and so on), with 1 indicating that the drive is installed. The declaration for GetLogicalDrives is

```
Declare Function GetLogicalDrives Lib "kernel32" () As Long
```

It's pretty simple. What little complexity there is comes in deciphering the bits. Listing 12.17 shows a procedure, dhGetDrivesByNum, that takes the result of calling GetLogicalDrives and performs a bit-wise comparison on the first 26 bits. If it finds a drive, the procedure adds the drive number to a VBA collection passed as an argument.

TIP   VBA Collection objects are extremely useful in situations like this. In fact, it's a good idea to consider a collection wherever you're thinking of using an array.

Listing 12.17: Fetch Logical Drives by Number.

```
Function dhGetDrivesByNum(colDrives As Collection) _
    As Integer

    Dim lngDrives As Long
    Dim intDrive As Integer

    ' Reset the collection
    Set colDrives = New Collection
```

```
' Get the logical drives
lngDrives = GetLogicalDrives()

' Do a bitwise compare on the first 26 bits
For intDrive = 0 To 25
  If (lngDrives And (2 ^ intDrive)) <> 0 Then
    colDrives.Add intDrive, Chr(65 + intDrive)
  End If
Next

' Return the number of drives found
dhGetDrivesByNum = colDrives.Count

End Function
```

Using GetLogicalDriveStrings presents a different type of complexity, although not daunting by any stretch of the imagination. GetLogicalDriveStrings returns drive letters in a single string buffer. Each drive letter is separated by a null character (ASCII code 0), with the entire string terminated by two Nulls. (This is often referred to as a *double null-terminated* string.) Listing 12.18 shows the counterpart to dhGetDrivesByNum, a procedure called dhGetDrivesByString. After allocating a buffer and calling GetLogicalDriveStrings, dhGetDrivesByString parses the buffer, looking for null characters. Like dhGetDrivesByNum, it also adds these drive letters to a VBA collection passed to the function.

⟳ Listing 12.18: Fetch Logical Drives, This Time by Letter.

```
Function dhGetDrivesByString(colDrives As Collection) _
 As Integer

    Dim strBuffer As String
    Dim lngBytes As Long
    Dim intPos As Integer
    Dim varArray As Variant
    Dim strDrive As String

    ' Reset the collection
    Set colDrives = New Collection

    ' Set up a buffer
    strBuffer = Space(255)
```

```
' Get the logical drive string
lngBytes = GetLogicalDriveStrings( _
 Len(strBuffer), strBuffer)

' Parse the drive string by looking
' for the null delimiter and add each to
' the collection
varArray = Split(strBuffer, Chr$(0))
Do
    strDrive = varArray(intPos)
    colDrives.Add strDrive, strDrive
    intPos = intPos + 1
Loop Until Len(varArray(intPos)) = 0

' Return the number of drives found
dhGetDrivesByString = colDrives.Count
End Function
```

TIP

Note the use of the new VBA 6 function Split, which converts a string into an array based on a given delimiter. In the last edition of this book we had to resort to a manual search for the null character. Using Split is much, much simpler (not to mention faster). You should keep this in mind when reviewing your own code from older versions of VBA.

Listing 12.19 shows a sample procedure that tests each method. You can run this code from the Immediate window. Figure 12.2 shows the results.

Listing 12.19: Test the Methods for Retrieving Logical Drives.

```
Sub dhPrintDrives()
    Dim colDrives As New Collection
    Dim varDrive As Variant

    ' First by number
    Debug.Print "Drives found: " & _
     dhGetDrivesByNum(colDrives)
    For Each varDrive In colDrives
      Debug.Print varDrive,
    Next

    Debug.Print
```

```
' Then by letter
Debug.Print "Drives found: " & _
  dhGetDrivesByString(colDrives)
For Each varDrive In colDrives
  Debug.Print varDrive,
Next
End Sub
```

FIGURE 12.2

Logical drive information

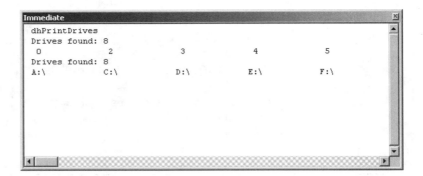

What Kind of Drives Are They?

Once you've determined which drives are on your system, you can call another Windows API function, GetDriveType, to find out what kind of drive each one is. GetDriveType's declaration is as follows:

```
Declare Function GetDriveType Lib "kernel32" _
  Alias "GetDriveTypeA" (ByVal nDrive As String) As Long
```

GetDriveType accepts a string representing the root directory of a drive (including the colon and backslash and like those produced by dhGetDrivesByString) and returns a code indicating what type of drive it is. It can be any one of the values listed in Table 12.6.

T A B L E 12.6:   Drive Type Constants for GetDriveType

Value	Constant	Description
0	DRIVE_UNKNOWN	Drive does not exist or type cannot be determined
1	DRIVE_NOROOT	String passed was not the root directory
2	DRIVE_REMOVABLE	Removable media

TABLE 12.6: Drive Type Constants for GetDriveType *(continued)*

Value	Constant	Description
3	DRIVE_FIXED	Fixed disk
4	DRIVE_REMOTE	Network drive
5	DRIVE_CDROM	CD-ROM
6	DRIVE_RAMDISK	RAM disk

TIP

If you pass the vbNullString constant as the drive letter, GetDriveType returns information on the current drive.

To demonstrate the GetDriveType API function, we created a sample procedure called dhPrintDriveTypes (shown in Listing 12.20) that prints the type of each installed drive to the Immediate window. Note that it uses dhGetDrivesByString to generate the list of drives. Figure 12.3 illustrates sample output.

Listing 12.20: Print the Type of Each Installed Drive.

```
Sub dhPrintDriveTypes()
    Dim colDrives As New Collection
    Dim varDrive As Variant
    Dim lngType As Long

    ' Get drive letters
    If dhGetDrivesByString(colDrives) > 0 Then
        For Each varDrive In colDrives
            ' Print drive letter
            Debug.Print varDrive,

            ' Print drive type
            lngType = GetDriveType(CStr(varDrive))
            Select Case lngType
                Case DRIVE_UNKNOWN
                    Debug.Print "Unknown"
                Case DRIVE_NOROOT
                    Debug.Print "Unknown"
                Case DRIVE_REMOVABLE
                    Debug.Print "Removable Media"
```

```
        Case DRIVE_FIXED
           Debug.Print "Fixed Disk"
        Case DRIVE_REMOTE
           Debug.Print "Network Drive"
        Case DRIVE_CDROM
           Debug.Print "CD-ROM"
        Case DRIVE_RAMDISK
           Debug.Print "RAM Disk"
        End Select
      Next
    End If
  End Sub
```

FIGURE 12.3

Printing drive types

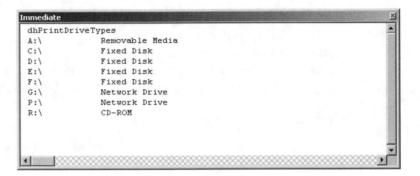

> **NOTE**   Strings passed to GetDriveType must represent the root directory; otherwise, the function will be unable to determine the drive type.

How Much Space Is Left?

Perhaps the most common question VBA developers want to ask concerning disk drives is, "How much disk space is available?" Answering this question was extremely difficult under 16-bit versions of BASIC because it involved making DOS interrupt calls—not an easy task from VBA. The Win32 API, however, added a simple function to retrieve this information, GetDiskFreeSpace. Of course, there was one problem with GetDiskFreeSpace. When it was written (way, way back in the early 90s), hard disk capacity was relatively limited compared to today and the function only worked with drives up to 2 gigabytes in size. Today it's not uncommon for new PCs to come with hard drives in excess of 30 gigabytes.

That's why Windows 95 OSR2, Windows 98, and Windows NT/2000/XP all support an improved function, GetDiskFreeSpaceEx. GetDiskFreeSpaceEx uses 64-bit integers to represent space and therefore supports drives up to 2^{63} bytes in size. (It's 2^{63} and not 2^{64} because one bit is used to indicate sign.)

One question you might ask is, "How do I call GetDiskFreeSpaceEx if it uses 64-bit integers and VBA only supports 32-bit integers?" The answer is actually quite simple. The VBA Currency data type is, in actuality, a 64-bit integer that's scaled by a factor of 10,000 to represent decimal values. As such, it's perfectly compatible with GetDiskFreeSpaceEx. The declaration for GetDiskFreeSpaceEx, therefore, is

```
Public Declare Function GetDiskFreeSpaceEx _
  Lib "kernel32" Alias "GetDiskFreeSpaceExA" _
  (ByVal lpRootPathName As String, _
  curFreeBytesAvailableToCaller As Currency, _
  curTotalNumberOfBytes As Currency, _
  curTotalNumberOfFreeBytes As Currency) As Boolean
```

As you can see from the declaration, you pass the root drive letter (e.g., "C:\"), as well as three Currency variables. After the function completes, the three variables indicate free disk space available to the function caller (i.e., the current user), total disk space, and overall free space. Note that the free disk space available to the current user may be different from overall free space on the drive if you're using space allocation policies (very common on network file shares).

TIP　　You can also pass UNC names (e.g., "\\MYSERVER\MYSHARE") to GetDiskFreeSpaceEx.

TIP　　If you pass the vbNullString constant as the drive letter, both GetDiskFreeSpace and GetFreeDiskSpaceEx return information on the current drive.

We've boiled GetDiskFreeSpaceEx down to three useful functions, dhFreeDiskSpaceEx, dhMyFreeDiskSpaceEx, and dhTotalDiskSpaceEx. To save paper, only dhTotalDiskSpaceEx is shown in Listing 12.21. The others are nearly identical, the only difference being they utilize other parameters to the API call. Listing 12.21

also shows a test procedure, dhPrintDiskSpaceEx, which demonstrates how to call the two functions. Figure 12.4 shows sample output.

FIGURE 12.4
Printing disk space for installed drives

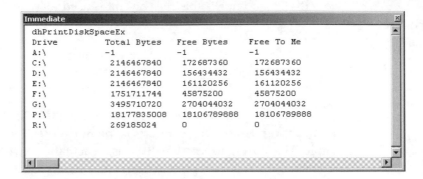

```
Immediate
dhPrintDiskSpaceEx
Drive          Total Bytes     Free Bytes      Free To Me
A:\            -1              -1              -1
C:\            2146467840      172687360       172687360
D:\            2146467840      156434432       156434432
E:\            2146467840      161120256       161120256
F:\            1751711744      45875200        45875200
G:\            3495710720      2704044032      2704044032
P:\            18177835008     18106789888     18106789888
R:\            269185024       0               0
```

TIP   As an optimization, you could create a single procedure that computes all three types of information using arguments passed by reference and a single call to GetFreeDiskSpaceEx. We created three separate functions so each could report the results as a single return value.

NOTE   If the GetDiskFreeSpaceEx function fails (returns False), then dhFreeDiskSpaceEx, dhMyFreeDiskSpaceEx, and dhTotalDiskSpaceEx return –1.

Listing 12.21: Functions for Determining Total Disk Space

```
Function dhTotalDiskSpaceEx(Optional strDrive As _
 String = vbNullString) As Currency

    Dim curTotal As Currency
    Dim curFree As Currency
    Dim curFreeToMe As Currency

    ' Call GetDiskFreeSpaceEx
    If GetDiskFreeSpaceEx(strDrive, _
     curFreeToMe, curTotal, curFree) Then
```

```
            ' If successful compute total disk space
            dhTotalDiskSpaceEx = curTotal * 10000
        Else
            dhTotalDiskSpaceEx = -1
        End If
    End Function

Sub dhPrintDiskSpaceEx()

    Dim colDrives As New Collection
    Dim varDrive As Variant

    ' Get drive letters
    If dhGetDrivesByString(colDrives) > 0 Then

        ' Print header
        Debug.Print "Drive", "Total Bytes", _
         "Free Bytes", "Free To Me"

        ' Print drive space for all drives
        For Each varDrive In colDrives

            Debug.Print varDrive, _
             dhTotalDiskSpaceEx(CStr(varDrive)), _
             dhFreeDiskSpaceEx(CStr(varDrive)), _
             dhMyFreeDiskSpaceEx(CStr(varDrive))

        Next
    End If
End Sub
```

TIP   For completeness we've included the old (and now obsolete) functions in the sample code. You should, however, use the new functions explained here in any new code you write. If you used the prior edition of this book we also recommend you search for the outdated functions (dhFreeDiskSpace and dhTotalDiskSpace) and replace them with the new ones.

What about Drive Labels?

The last disk-related API functions covered in this chapter concern a disk's volume label. You know that 11-character string you can set when you format a disk? Using the VBA Dir function, you can retrieve a disk's volume label, but you can't set it. With the Windows API functions GetVolumeInformation and SetVolumeLabel, you can do that and more.

In addition to the volume label, GetVolumeInformation returns information on the volume's serial number, the maximum filename length, and the name of the installed file system. The declaration for GetVolumeInformation is

```
Declare Function GetVolumeInformation Lib "kernel32" _
  Alias "GetVolumeInformationA" _
  (ByVal lpRootPathName As String, _
  ByVal lpVolumeNameBuffer As String, _
  ByVal nVolumeNameSize As Long, _
  lpVolumeSerialNumber As Long, _
  lpMaximumComponentLength As Long, _
  lpFileSystemFlags As Long, _
  ByVal lpFileSystemNameBuffer As String, _
  ByVal nFileSystemNameSize As Long) As Long
```

We created a procedure that accepts a drive's root directory (make sure to include the colon and backslash) and prints information about the volume to the Immediate window. Since the function call is straightforward, and to save space, we decided not to include the code listing here. You can find the procedure, called dhPrintVolInfo, in the basDiskInfo module in the sample Excel workbook or DISKFILE.BAS.

GetVolumeInformation's counterpart, SetVolumeLabel, is a simple function with a single purpose: to set the volume label of a disk drive. Its declaration is

```
Declare Function SetVolumeLabel Lib "kernel32" _
  Alias "SetVolumeLabelA" (ByVal lpRootPathName As String, _
  ByVal lpVolumeName As String) As Long
```

As with SetVolumeLabel's cousins, you pass a string containing the root directory of a drive as the first argument. The second argument is the string containing the new volume label. If you wish, you can remove the volume label completely. Due to a bug in Windows 95, however, there are two ways to do this. Under Windows 98 and Windows NT/2000/XP, the function works as designed. You pass a null pointer (vbNullString) to the function to delete the volume label. Under Windows 95, this doesn't work. Instead you must pass an empty string (""). If SetVolumeLabel is successful in changing the volume label, it returns True; otherwise it returns False.

Fun with Paths

One of the most common (and most tedious) tasks a VBA programmer must perform is manipulating file paths. Whether you're deriving the full path from a partial path, parsing paths, or determining the short form of a path, you'll undoubtedly devote more than a few moments to dealing with these issues during your programming career. All the code for this section is contained in the basPathFun module of the sample Excel workbook and the PATHFUN.BAS file.

Parsing Paths

Often you'll need to break a complete file path into its components. Typically, this means separating the filename from the path. You may also want to treat the file extension as a separate component. At the extreme end, breaking a path into individual directories is sometimes desirable. We've written two VBA functions to aid you in this process.

> **NOTE**   These and other functions in this chapter use string functions introduced in Chapter 1. For more information on how they work, see that chapter.

The first VBA function, shown in Listing 12.22, is dhParsePath, which takes a complete file path and separates it into path and filename components. Note that it accepts variables for the resulting components by reference and modifies them. An optional argument, varExt, represents a variable for the file extension. If this is passed to dhParsePath, the function strips the file extension from the name and places it in the variable. If this argument isn't passed, dhParsePath includes the extension with the filename. You can test this function by calling the dhTestParse-Path procedure, which is explained in the section "A Path-Parsing Example" a little later in this chapter.

Listing 12.22: A Function That Breaks Apart File Paths

```
Sub dhParsePath(ByVal strFullPath As String, _
  ByRef strPath As String, ByRef strFile As String, _
  Optional ByRef varExt As Variant, _
  Optional strPathSep = "\")

    Dim lngPos As Long
    Dim lngPos2 As Long
```

```
            ' If varExt was passed, get the file extension
         If Not IsMissing(varExt) Then
             ' Find the last "."
             lngPos = InStrRev(strFullPath, ".")
             ' If this is a web address find the last "/"
             If strPathSep = "/" Then
                 lngPos2 = InStrRev(strFullPath, strPathSep)
             End If
             ' If there's a "." after the last "/" assume it's
             ' the file extension
             If lngPos > 0 And lngPos > lngPos2 Then
                 varExt = Mid(strFullPath, lngPos + 1)
             Else
                 varExt = ""
             End If
         Else
             varExt = ""
         End If

             ' Now get the file name, removing the extension
             ' if necessary
         lngPos = InStrRev(strFullPath, strPathSep)
         If lngPos > 0 Then
             strFile = Mid(strFullPath, lngPos + 1, _
              Len(strFullPath) - lngPos - Len(varExt))
             If Len(varExt) Then
                 strFile = Left(strFile, Len(strFile) - 1)
             End If
             strPath = Left(strFullPath, lngPos - 1)
         End If
     End Sub
```

A more complex function is shown in Listing 12.23. The dhGetPathParts function breaks a complete path into numerous components, based on each subdirectory in the path. You call it by passing a path and a VBA Collection object. The function places the components, which include the drive letter, each subdirectory, and the filename, into the collection. We use this function in other procedures in the sample code contained on the CD-ROM.

NOTE	Note that for UNC paths the function treats "\\" as the drive letter and for Web addresses the function treats the protocol (e.g., "http:", "file:", etc.) as the drive letter.

Listing 12.23: Decompose a Path into Atomic Components.

```
Function dhGetPathParts(strPath As String, _
  colParts As Collection, _
  Optional strPathSep = "\") As Long

    Dim varParts As Variant
    Dim lngPos As Long

    Set colParts = New Collection

    ' For UNC paths treat "\\" as the drive letter
    If InStr(strPath, "\\") = 1 Then
        colParts.Add "\\"
        lngPos = 2
    End If

    ' Strip off web protcols
    lngPos = InStr(strPath, "//")
    If lngPos > 0 Then
        colParts.Add Left(strPath, lngPos - 1)
        lngPos = 2
    End If

    ' Split the path on the backslash
    varParts = Split(strPath, strPathSep)
    For lngPos = lngPos To UBound(varParts)
        colParts.Add varParts(lngPos)
    Next

    ' Return the number of parts
    dhGetPathParts = colParts.Count
End Function
```

Retrieving Complete and Short Path Names

The Windows API also offers several functions that deal with paths. Some, like GetTempPath, are discussed in other sections of this chapter because they relate to other topics. Two that can't be categorized with other functions are GetFullPath-Name and GetShortPathName. They are declared as

```
Declare Function GetFullPathName Lib "kernel32" _
  Alias "GetFullPathNameA" _
  (ByVal lpFileName As String, ByVal nBufferLength As Long, _
  ByVal lpBuffer As String, ByVal lpFilePart As String) As Long

Declare Function GetShortPathName Lib "kernel32" _
  Alias "GetShortPathNameA" _
  (ByVal lpszLongPath As String, _
  ByVal lpszShortPath As String, _
  ByVal cchBuffer As Long) As Long
```

The sole purpose of GetFullPathName is to create a fully qualified path from a given partial path and filename, based on the current directory. This means that if you simply pass a filename, GetFullPathName will append the path of the current directory to it. If you pass a relative path, such as "..\..\SOMEFILE.TXT", GetFull-PathName will resolve the relative path to the current directory and return the result. We've written a VBA wrapper for the GetFullPath function called dhFull-Path, shown in Listing 12.24.

Listing 12.24: The dhFullPath Function Resolves Relative Paths and Filenames.

```
Function dhFullPath(strPath As String) As String
  Dim strBuffer As String
  Dim strFilePart As String
  Dim lngBytes As Long

  ' Set up the buffer
  strBuffer = Space(MAX_PATH)

  ' Call GetFullPathName
  lngBytes = GetFullPathName(strPath, Len(strBuffer), _
   strBuffer, strFilePart)

  ' If successful, parse the buffer
```

```
    If lngBytes > 0 Then
        dhFullPath = Left(strBuffer, lngBytes)
    End If
End Function
```

To test this function, try running the following code from the Immediate window:

```
?dhFullPath(Dir("*.*"))
```

The Dir statement returns the first file in the current directory. dhFullPath then computes the complete path. Be careful when using this function, however, since GetFullPathName doesn't verify that the resulting filename is valid or that the file actually exists. For instance, the following statement retrieves the first file in the directory above the current one and appends it to the current directory name:

```
?dhFullPath(Dir("..\*.*"))
```

Even though the file exists, the path is invalid.

GetShortPathName is useful if you need to work with filenames in their old 8.3 form. For example, perhaps your application needs to exchange files with another system that doesn't support long filenames (such as Windows 3.x). GetShortPathName accepts a long filename and returns its associated short name. Again, we've provided a simple wrapper function you can call, dhShortPath, shown in Listing 12.25.

Listing 12.25: dhShortPath Returns a File's 8.3 Filename.

```
Function dhShortPath(strPath As String) As String
    Dim strBuffer As String
    Dim lngBytes As Long

    ' Set up a buffer
    strBuffer = Space(MAX_PATH)

    ' Call GetShortPathName
    lngBytes = GetShortPathName(strPath, strBuffer, _
    Len(strBuffer))

    ' If succcessful parse the buffer
    If lngBytes > 0 Then
        dhShortPath = Left(strBuffer, lngBytes)
    End If
End Function
```

A Path-Parsing Example

Listing 12.26 shows a procedure that demonstrates the functions we've just discussed. It begins by retrieving the first file in the current directory. It then calls the other functions to compute the full path, the short path, and the path parts. Some sample output is shown in Figure 12.5.

Listing 12.26: A Procedure to Demonstrate Path Parsing

```
Sub dhTestParsePath()
  Dim strCurrFile As String
  Dim strFullPath As String
  Dim strShortPath As String
  Dim strPath As String
  Dim strFile As String
  Dim varExt As Variant
  Dim lngParts As Long
  Dim colParts As New Collection
  Dim varPart As Variant

  ' Get first file from current directory
  strCurrFile = Dir("*.*")

  ' Get the full path name
  strFullPath = dhFullPath(strCurrFile)

  ' Get the short path name
  strShortPath = dhShortPath(strFullPath)

  ' Parse the path into its parts
  Call dhParsePath(strFullPath, strPath, strFile, varExt)

  ' Decompose the entire path
  lngParts = dhGetPathParts(strFullPath, colParts)

  ' Print the information
  Debug.Print "File:", strCurrFile
  Debug.Print "Full path:", strFullPath
  Debug.Print "Short path:", strShortPath
  Debug.Print "Path:", strPath
  Debug.Print "Filename:", strFile
```

```
        Debug.Print "Extension:", varExt
        Debug.Print "Path parts:", lngParts
        lngParts = 2
        For Each varPart In colParts
          Debug.Print Space(lngParts) & varPart
          lngParts = lngParts + 2
        Next
    End Sub
```

FIGURE 12.5

Result of parsing a file path

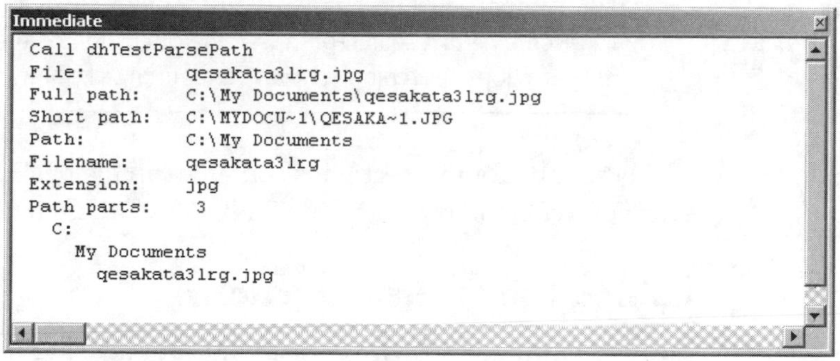

```
Immediate                                                    [x]
Call dhTestParsePath                                         [▲]
File:         qesakata3lrg.jpg
Full path:    C:\My Documents\qesakata3lrg.jpg
Short path:   C:\MYDOCU~1\QESAKA~1.JPG
Path:         C:\My Documents
Filename:     qesakata3lrg
Extension:    jpg
Path parts:   3
  C:
    My Documents
      qesakata3lrg.jpg
                                                             [▼]
[◄] [░░░░░░░░░░░░░░░░░░░░░░░░░░░░]                          [►]
```

A Replacement for Dir

If the VBA Dir function does not offer all the power you need, consider using the underlying Windows API functions that Dir is based on: FindFirstFile, FindNextFile, and FindClose. Individually, these three functions emulate the functionality of various forms of the VBA Dir function. FindFirstFile initiates a directory search and returns the first matching filename, just as Dir does when you pass a file specification. FindNextFile locates the next matching file, and FindClose terminates a search. Calling Dir again with a new file specification performs this last step implicitly.

These functions go even further than Dir, however. In addition to matching filenames, these functions return additional information, such as creation date, size, and short (8.3) filename. Declarations for the functions are shown here:

```
' Functions for searching for files in a given directory
Declare Function FindFirstFile Lib "kernel32" _
 Alias "FindFirstFileA" (ByVal lpFileName As String, _
 lpFindFileData As WIN32_FIND_DATA) As Long
```

```
Declare Function FindNextFile Lib "kernel32" _
  Alias "FindNextFileA" (ByVal hFindFile As Long, _
  lpFindFileData As WIN32_FIND_DATA) As Long

Declare Function FindClose Lib "kernel32" _
  (ByVal hFindFile As Long) As Long
```

> **NOTE**   These functions don't actually "find" files in the sense that they search your hard disk. For that you'll have to write custom VBA code. If you simply need to find a file given a certain search path, see the discussion of the SearchPath API function in the section "Searching for Files" later in this chapter.

All the code for this section is contained in the basFindFunctions module of the sample Excel workbook and the FINDFUNC.BAS file.

Calling the "Find" Functions

You call FindFirstFile with a file specification, using the same rules as when passing a file specification to Dir: You can pass a complete or partial path, including wildcards or UNC server names. You also pass a pointer to a WIN32_FIND_DATA structure. FindFirstFile fills in the members of this structure with information on the matching file. The definition of the structure is as follows:

```
Type WIN32_FIND_DATA
    lngFileAttributes As Long        ' File attributes
    ftCreationTime As FILETIME       ' Creation time
    ftLastAccessTime As FILETIME     ' Last access time
    ftLastWriteTime As FILETIME      ' Last modified time
    lngFileSizeHigh As Long          ' Size (high word)
    lngFileSizeLow As Long           ' Size (low word)
    lngReserved0 As Long             ' reserved
    lngReserved1 As Long             ' reserved
    strFileName As String * MAX_PATH ' File name
    strAlternate As String * 14      ' 8.3 name
End Type
```

> **NOTE**   MAX_PATH is defined as 260, the maximum path size for Windows.

As you can see from the type definition, you can gather quite a bit of information from a single function call. (For more information on the FILETIME structure, see the section "Windows API Dates and Times" later in this chapter.)

If FindFirstFile locates a file matching the passed specification, it fills in the WIN32_FIND_DATA structure and returns a handle to the find operation. You use this handle in subsequent calls to FindNextFile. When you no longer want to continue searching, call FindClose, passing the handle of the find operation you want to abandon.

If FindFirstFile fails, it returns –1. You can then inspect the LastDLLError property of VBA's Err object for the error code returned by the DLL function. FindNextFile simply returns True if the next find operation was successful and False if it wasn't.

With this information in hand, you can build a simple function that lists the files in a given directory. Listing 12.27 shows the dhFindFiles procedure, which does just that. It begins by calling FindFirstFile with a path passed as an argument. If this is successful, the procedure then calls FindNextFile inside a Do...Loop, continuing until FindNextFile returns False.

Listing 12.27: List Files in a Given Directory Using API Functions.

```
Sub dhFindFiles(strPath As String)
  Dim fd As WIN32_FIND_DATA
  Dim hFind As Long

  ' Find the first file
  hFind = FindFirstFile(strPath, fd)

  ' If successful...
  If hFind > 0 Then
    Do
      ' Print file information
      With fd
        Debug.Print dhTrimNull(.strFileName), _
          .lngFileSizeLow & " bytes", _
          dhBuildAttrString(.lngFileAttributes)
      End With
```

```
          ' Find the next file and continue as long
          ' as there are files to be found
          Loop While CBool(FindNextFile(hFind, fd))

          ' Terminate the find operation
          Call FindClose(hFind)
      End If
  End Sub
```

Since the filename members in WIN32_FIND_DATA are fixed-length strings, the procedure must parse the results, looking for a terminating null character.

To test this procedure, try calling it from the Immediate window. Figure 12.6 shows what the output might look like.

FIGURE 12.6

File information produced
by calling dhFindFiles

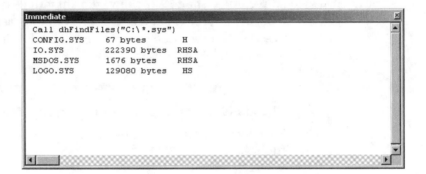

```
Immediate                                                    ×
  Call dhFindFiles("C:\*.sys")
  CONFIG.SYS     67 bytes        H
  IO.SYS         222390 bytes    RHSA
  MSDOS.SYS      1676 bytes      RHSA
  LOGO.SYS       129080 bytes    HS
```

A New and Improved Dir

Having all this extra information at your disposal creates some interesting possibilities. We've used these API functions to create a replacement for the VBA Dir function. Why have we done this? One drawback to the VBA Dir function is that, while it lets you include files with certain attributes in the search, it does not allow you to limit the search based on a set of attributes. Our replacement, dhDir, does.

Listing 12.28 shows the dhDir function, along with a helper function, dhFind-ByAttr. We've structured dhDir so you can call it just as you would the VBA Dir function. Specifically, you call it with a path name to begin a search and then call it with no arguments to continue retrieving matching filenames. Unlike Dir, however, our function executes an exclusive search when you provide an attribute value. You can override this behavior, and thus revert to the same functionality Dir provides, by passing False as the optional third argument.

NOTE   If you attempt to call either Dir or dhDir for the first time and don't pass any arguments, they both produce runtime error 5, "Invalid procedure call or argument."

Listing 12.28: Our Replacement for the VBA Dir Function

```
Function dhDir(Optional ByVal strPath As String = "", _
Optional lngAttributes As VbFileAttribute= vbNormal, _
Optional fExclusive As Boolean = True) As String

    Dim fd As WIN32_FIND_DATA
    Static hFind As Long
    Static lngAttr As Long
    Static fEx As Boolean
    Dim strOut As String

    ' If no path was passed, try to find the next file
    If strPath = "" Then
        If hFind > 0 Then
            If CBool(FindNextFile(hFind, fd)) Then
                strOut = dhFindByAttr(hFind, fd, lngAttr, fEx)
            End If
        Else
            Err.Raise 5 ' Invalid procedure call or argument
        End If

    ' Otherwise, start a new search
    Else
        ' Store the attributes and exclusive settings
        lngAttr = lngAttributes
        fEx = fExclusive

        ' If the path ends in a backslash, assume
        ' all files and append "*.*"
        If Right(strPath, 1) = "\" Then
            strPath = strPath & "*.*"
        End If

        ' Find the first file
        hFind = FindFirstFile(strPath, fd)
```

```
                If hFind > 0 Then
                    strOut = dhFindByAttr(hFind, fd, lngAttr, fEx)
                End If
            End If

            ' If the search failed, close the Find handle.
            If Len(strOut) = 0 Then
                If hFind > 0 Then
                    Call FindClose(hFind)
                End If
            End If
            dhDir = strOut
        End Function

        Function dhFindByAttr(hFind As Long, _
         fd As WIN32_FIND_DATA, lngAttr As VbFileAttribute, _
         fExclusive As Boolean) As String

            Dim fOk As Boolean

            ' Continue looking for files until one
            ' matches the given attributes exactly
            ' (if fExclusive is True) or just contains
            ' them (if fExclusive is False)
            Do
                If fExclusive Then
                    fOk = (fd.lngFileAttributes = lngAttr)
                Else
                    fOk = ((fd.lngFileAttributes And lngAttr)) = lngAttr
                End If

                If fOk Then
                    dhFindByAttr = dhTrimNull(fd.strFilename)
                    Exit Do
                End If
            Loop While FindNextFile(hFind, fd)
        End Function
```

TIP   Note our use of the VbFileAttribute data type in the function declarations. When you declare arguments using an enumerated type, VBA displays a list of constants as you type the parameter.

Our function works by first calling FindFirstFile to begin a new search (but only if you pass a file specification in the first argument). The dhFindByAttr function checks the file's attributes against the requested set and, if no match is found, uses FindNextFile to return the next filename. This continues until a match is found or no more files matching the original specification exist. Static variables in dhDir are used to store parameter values between function calls.

Figure 12.7 shows an example of calling dhDir to search for all files in the root directory that have the system and hidden attributes set. The first call to dhDir establishes the search parameters. Subsequent calls return other files with these exact three attributes.

FIGURE 12.7

Calling dhDir to perform an
exclusive directory search

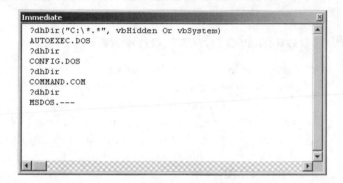

```
Immediate
?dhDir("C:\*.*", vbHidden Or vbSystem)
AUTOEXEC.DOS
?dhDir
CONFIG.DOS
?dhDir
COMMAND.COM
?dhDir
MSDOS.---
```

Figure 12.8 shows a similar directory search, but this time the search is not exclusive. It returns all files that have the three attributes set, regardless of whether they have any others set. As a result, the DBLSPACE.BIN file, which has all three attributes plus the archive attribute, is included in this search.

FIGURE 12.8

Calling dhDir to perform an
inclusive directory search

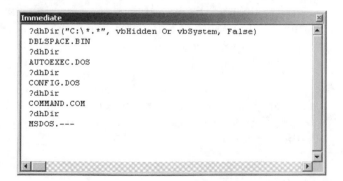

```
Immediate
?dhDir("C:\*.*", vbHidden Or vbSystem, False)
DBLSPACE.BIN
?dhDir
AUTOEXEC.DOS
?dhDir
CONFIG.DOS
?dhDir
COMMAND.COM
?dhDir
MSDOS.---
```

Exploiting the True Power of FindFirstFile

At this point you might be wondering why we went to all this trouble for what you might describe as a minimum gain in functionality over Dir. First of all, dhDir does serve a purpose. How often have you wanted to retrieve a list of *only* hidden files without having to weed out normal files? Second, the true power of these functions lies in the additional information you get as part of the function call.

NOTE　　　For another example of using these functions, see Appendix D (located on the CD-ROM that accompanies this book), where we describe an object model for folders and files constructed using VBA class modules.

Windows Notification Functions

Have you ever needed to know when the contents of a file or directory have changed? For example, suppose you're writing a "drop-box" application that monitors a network directory for incoming files. Wouldn't it be nice if Windows could tell your application when a file arrives? Well, it can, if you use the file notification functions discussed in this section. All the code for this section is contained in the basNotification module of the sample Excel workbook and the NOTIFY.BAS file.

How Change Notifications Work

The functions FindFirstChangeNotification, FindNextChangeNotification, and FindCloseChangeNotification are similar to the Find functions just described, except that instead of returning results right away, they establish *change handles* that you pass to the operating system. Each change handle denotes a particular state change, such as a directory being renamed. When the event occurs, Windows notifies your application. You can then continue monitoring the directory or cancel the change handle.

You may have noticed this effect when using Windows Explorer. If you leave a directory window open and use another application to copy a file to that directory, Explorer shows the new file immediately; you don't have to manually refresh the window contents.

You can choose to monitor one or more conditions using a bit mask of values from Table 12.7.

TABLE 12.7: Values for Monitoring Conditions

Constant	Description
FILE_NOTIFY_CHANGE_FILE_NAME	File creations, deletions, and name changes
FILE_NOTIFY_CHANGE_DIR_NAME	Directory creations, deletions, and name changes
FILE_NOTIFY_CHANGE_ATTRIBUTES	File or directory attribute changes
FILE_NOTIFY_CHANGE_SIZE	File size changes
FILE_NOTIFY_CHANGE_LAST_WRITE	Changes to a file's last write time
FILE_NOTIFY_CHANGE_SECURITY	File security descriptor changes (Windows NT only)

Setting Up a Change Notification

You establish a change notification using the FindFirstChangeNotification function. Its declaration is as follows:

```
Declare Function FindFirstChangeNotification Lib "kernel32" _
  Alias "FindFirstChangeNotificationA" _
  (ByVal lpPathName As String, ByVal bWatchSubtree As Long, _
  ByVal dwNotifyFilter As Long) As Long
```

The lpPathName argument is the name of a directory you want to monitor. If you want to monitor subdirectories as well, pass 1 as the second argument. The third argument is a combination of values from Table 12.7.

If successful, FindFirstChangeNotification returns a change handle. (If it fails, it returns –1.) You pass this change handle to another Windows API function, WaitForSingleObject:

```
Declare Function WaitForSingleObject Lib "kernel32" _
  (ByVal hHandle As Long, ByVal dwMilliseconds As Long) _
  As Long
```

WaitForSingleObject is a generic function designed to work with a number of Windows notification handles. When you call the function, it does not return until one of the following two things happens:

- The event associated with the change handle occurs.

- The number of milliseconds passed as the second argument elapses.

TIP   If you want to wait indefinitely, you can pass &HFFFF as the second argument. We don't recommend doing this, however, because your program may appear to hang if the event never happens.

This brings up the downside of using these functions: your VBA procedure waits until the event occurs, effectively halting your application. Therefore, these functions are of limited use in single-threaded environments like the current version of VBA (although if VBA ever becomes multithreaded, these functions will be extremely useful). Nonetheless, in some circumstances, like the drop-box scenario mentioned at the beginning of this section, you may not mind this behavior.

What to Do When a Notification Occurs

When WaitForSingleObject returns, the result indicates whether the event has occurred (WAIT_OBJECT_0) or the timeout period has elapsed (WAIT_TIMEOUT). Based on this value, you can take appropriate action. In our drop-box scenario, for example, a return value of WAIT_OBJECT_0 would be your cue to scan the directory for the new file and begin the file-manipulation process.

Then, if you want to continue waiting for another change, call FindNextChangeNotification, passing the change handle obtained earlier from FindFirstChangeNotification. FindNextChangeNotification returns True if Windows is ready to resume monitoring the directory for changes. Then you call WaitForSingleObject again, and the process repeats itself. When you no longer want to monitor changes, call FindCloseChangeNotification.

Using Change Notifications

For the reasons described earlier in this discussion, these functions are difficult to demonstrate using VBA. Nonetheless, we've put together a little "game" that demonstrates how to use the functions. You can think of it as a computerized version of the arcade game featuring little gophers that pop up from random holes. The object of that game is to whack each gopher with a rubber mallet before it disappears back into its den. Listing 12.29 shows the heart of our gopher-whacking game, the dhFunWithNotify procedure.

Listing 12.29: Test Notification Functions and Have Fun Too.

```
Sub dhFunWithNotify(strPath As String, ByVal lngTimeout As Long)
    Dim colPaths As New Collection
    Dim strFile As String
    Dim hChange As Long
    Dim lngStatus As Long
    Dim lngFlags As Long
    Dim fKeepGoing As Boolean
    Dim lngScore As Long
    Dim lngTotalScore As Long

    Const dhcBaseScore = 100000

    ' Build a list of subdirectories beneath strPath
    Debug.Print "Building directory list..."
    If dhGetSubdirectories(strPath, colPaths) = 0 Then
      Debug.Print "Could not build subdirectory list!"
      Exit Sub
    End If

    ' Set up flags
    lngFlags = FILE_NOTIFY_CHANGE_FILE_NAME

    ' Create the first file
    Debug.Print "Here we go!!!"
    strFile = dhCreateTempFile(dhGetRandomFile(colPaths), _
     "~DH")
    If strFile = "" Then
      Debug.Print "Error creating first file!"
      Exit Sub
    End If

    ' Create first change notification
    hChange = FindFirstChangeNotification(strPath, _
     1, lngFlags)

    ' Make sure it was successful
    If hChange > 0 Then
```

```
' Loop until timeout has occurred,
' the notification function fails,
' or our timeout reaches zero
Do

  ' Print the relative file name
  Debug.Print "You have " & lngTimeout / 1000 & _
   " seconds to delete:"
  Debug.Print "..\" & mid(strFile, Len(strPath) + 2)

  ' Wait for the change to happen
  lngStatus = WaitForSingleObject(hChange, _
   lngTimeout)

  ' What happened?
  Select Case lngStatus
    Case WAIT_OBJECT_0
      ' A change happened! Check to see if
      ' the right file was deleted
      If Dir(strFile) = "" Then

        ' File is gone! Compute score
        lngScore = CLng((dhcBaseScore * _
         colPaths.Count) / lngTimeout)
        lngTotalScore = lngTotalScore + _
         lngScore
        Debug.Print "Good job! Score " & _
         lngScore & " points"

        ' Create next temp file
        strFile = dhCreateTempFile( _
         dhGetRandomFile(colPaths), "~DH")
        fKeepGoing = CBool(Len(strFile))

        ' If successful...
        If fKeepGoing Then

          ' Call FindNextChangeNotification
          ' once to clear change handle
          Call FindNextChangeNotification( _
           hChange)
```

```
                   ' Call it again to establish the
                   ' next change event
                   fKeepGoing = CBool( _
                   FindNextChangeNotification( _
                   hChange))

                   ' Reduce timeout and wait again
                   lngTimeout = lngTimeout - 500

                Else
                   Debug.Print "Error creating file!"
                End If
             Else
                ' The file's still there!
                Debug.Print _
                  "Oh, no! You got the wrong file!"
                fKeepGoing = False
             End If
          Case WAIT_TIMEOUT
             ' The wait timed out!
             Debug.Print "Time's up! Timeout = " & _
              lngTimeout & " ms"
             fKeepGoing = False

          Case WAIT_FAILED
             ' This is bad, the wait didn't work
             Debug.Print "Wait failed!"
             fKeepGoing = False
       End Select

    Loop While fKeepGoing And (lngTimeout > 0)

    ' Close the change notification
    Call FindCloseChangeNotification(hChange)

    ' Print exit message
    Debug.Print "Total score: " & lngTotalScore
    Debug.Print "Thanks for playing"
  End If
End Sub
```

You start the game by calling dhFunWithNotify, passing a directory name and a timeout value in milliseconds. dhFunWithNotify then builds a list of all the subdirectories beneath the given directory and creates a zero-byte file in one of them. The object of the game is to find the file using Windows Explorer and delete it before time runs out. If you're successful, dhFunWithNotify creates a new file for you to find. To make things a bit more challenging, dhFunWithNotify also reduces the timeout value by 500 milliseconds (one half second) each time you successfully find the file! Your score is based on the number of subdirectories and how fast you can delete the file. See how long you can continue finding and deleting files before the timeout elapses. The more subdirectories you specify, the more challenging the game becomes.

TIP   To get the best results, position the VBA Immediate window so you can see it while working in Explorer.

While the example is whimsical, it does point out how you can use the notification functions. The procedure calls FindFirstChangeNotification to establish the initial change handle, passing the original directory name. Note that it also passes 1 as the second argument. Passing the number 1 forces the function to include subdirectories in the change notification. The other item worth noting is that Find-NextChangeNotification is called twice. This is necessary because the process requesting the change notification is also causing a change event (in this case, each time a new file is created). Calling FindNextChangeNotification the first time clears the notification for the newly created file. Calling it a second time sets up a new notification.

You can find the helper functions dhFunWithNotify uses here in the basNotification module of the sample Excel workbook or the NOTIFY.BAS file.

TIP   If you find yourself playing this wonderfully exciting game as often as we do, you'll accumulate a number of zero-byte files on your hard disk. To get rid of them, use the Windows Find dialog to search for all files that begin with "~DH".

Monitoring Multiple Changes

You can also monitor more than one change event simultaneously—for example, to monitor changes to two completely separate directory trees. To do this, you create an *array* of change handles, calling FindFirstNotificationHandle once for each condition. You then call another API function, WaitForMultipleObjects, passing the first element of the array and the total number of handles in the array. You can also specify whether WaitForMultipleObjects should wait for *all* the events to happen or any *one* of them. In the latter case, when an event occurs, the return value from WaitForMultipleObjects will be WAIT_OBJECT_0 plus a number indicating which event it was. If you wish, you can then call FindNextNotificationHandle just as in our example.

NOTE   We included the declaration for WaitForMultipleObjects in the sample code but did not create an example of how to use it. You should, however, be able to deduce this from the function declaration.

Searching for Files

Another common task many applications must perform is searching for a particular file. Simple searches in a known directory can be accomplished easily using Dir or dhDir. Sometimes, however, you don't know where to look for a file. You can write custom VBA procedures that utilize API functions to help you find files, and they can be simple or complex, depending on your needs. All the code for this section is contained in the basSearch module of the sample Excel workbook and the FSEARCH.BAS file.

Using the SearchPath API Function

The Windows API offers a simple solution in the form of the SearchPath function. SearchPath is designed to search for files in a series of directories. The declaration for SearchPath is shown here:

```
Declare Function SearchPath Lib "kernel32" _
  Alias "SearchPathA" (ByVal lpPath As String, _
  ByVal lpFileName As String, ByVal lpExtension As String, _
  ByVal nBufferLength As Long, ByVal lpBuffer As String, _
  ByVal lpFilePart As String) As Long
```

Which directories SearchPath looks in is controlled by the first argument, lpPath. If you pass a null pointer (using the vbNullString constant), SearchPath looks in the following directories, in order:

1. The directory from which your application loaded

2. The application's current directory

3. Under Windows 95/98, the Windows system directory. Under Windows NT/2000/XP, the 32-bit Windows system directory

4. Under Windows NT/2000/XP only, the 16-bit Windows system directory

5. The Windows directory

6. The directories listed in the PATH environment variable

You can override this behavior by passing a value in the lpPath argument. The value takes the form of a DOS PATH statement, with individual directories separated by semicolons. For example,

```
C:\MYDATA;C:\MYAPPS;D:\SOME OTHER FILES;C:\BACKUPS
```

You pass the filename you're looking for in the lpFileName argument. If the filename doesn't contain a file extension, you can pass one in the lpExtension argument, and SearchPath will append it to the results for you. Listing 12.30 shows the dhSearch function. We wrapped the SearchPath function inside this function so you could call it easily. Just pass a filename and, optionally, a search path, and the function will return the full path to the file, if found. Figure 12.9 shows an example of calling the function.

Listing 12.30: dhSearch Looks for Files in Particular Directories.

```
Function dhSearch(strFile As String, _
  Optional strPath As String = vbNullString) As String

    Dim strBuffer As String
    Dim lngBytes As Long
    Dim strFilePart As String

    ' Create a buffer
    strBuffer = Space(MAX_PATH)

    ' Call search path
```

```
    lngBytes = SearchPath(strPath, strFile, vbNullString, _
     Len(strBuffer), strBuffer, strFilePart)
    ' If successful, parse out the file name
    If lngBytes > 0 Then
        dhSearch = Left(strBuffer, lngBytes)
    End If
End Function
```

FIGURE 12.9
Calling the dhSearch function

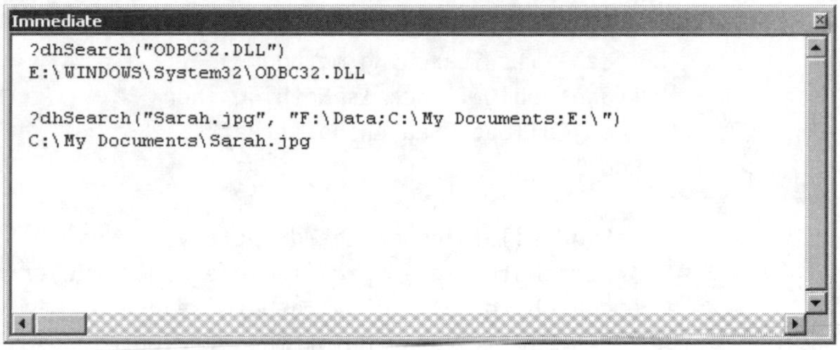

```
Immediate                                                          ⊠
?dhSearch("ODBC32.DLL")
E:\WINDOWS\System32\ODBC32.DLL

?dhSearch("Sarah.jpg", "F:\Data;C:\My Documents;E:\")
C:\My Documents\Sarah.jpg
```

Recursive Searches with VBA

SearchPath is a convenient and powerful function, but what if you need to search your entire hard disk? Unfortunately, there is no API function that will do that (we dearly wish there were), but you can write your own VBA function to do it. The key is to create a function that can be called recursively.

The dhFindAllFiles Function

We've created such a function for you, dhFindAllFiles, as shown in Listing 12.31. It may seem complex, but that's mostly because we added a few bells and whistles that aren't completely necessary but that make it much more fun.

↻ **Listing 12.31: Use the dhFindAllFiles Function to Search Your Entire Hard Disk.**

```
Function dhFindAllFiles(strSpec As String, _
 ByVal strPath As String, colFound As Collection, _
 Optional lngAttr As Long = -1, _
 Optional fRecursive As Boolean = True, _
 Optional objCallback As IFileFindCallback) As Long
```

```
Dim strFile As String
Dim colSubDir As New Collection
Dim varDir As Variant

' Make sure strPath ends in a backslash
If Right(strPath, 1) <> "\" Then
  strPath = strPath & "\"
End If

' If the callback object was supplied
' call its Searching method
If Not objCallback Is Nothing Then
  objCallback.Searching strPath
End If

' Find all files in the directory--if no
' attributes were specified use a non-exclusive
' search for all files, otherwise use a
' restrictive search for the attributes
If lngAttr = -1 Then
  strFile = dhDir(strPath & strSpec, , False)
Else
  strFile = dhDir(strPath & strSpec, lngAttr, True)
End If

Do Until strFile = ""

  ' Add file to collection if attributes match
  ' (special case directories "." and ".."
  If (strFile <> ".") And (strFile <> "..") Then
    colFound.Add strPath & strFile
  End If

  ' If the callback object was supplied
  ' call its Found method
  If Not objCallback Is Nothing Then
    objCallback.Found strPath, strFile
  End If

  ' Get the next file
  strFile = dhDir
Loop

' If the recursive flag is set build a list
```

```
                    ' of all the subdirectories
                If fRecursive Then

                    strFile = dhDir(strPath, vbDirectory, False)
                    Do Until strFile = ""
                        ' Ignore "." and ".."
                       If strFile <> "." And strFile <> ".." Then

                            ' Add each to the directory collection
                            colSubDir.Add strPath & strFile
                       End If
                       strFile = dhDir
                    Loop

                    ' Now recurse through each subdirectory
                    For Each varDir In colSubDir
                        dhFindAllFiles strSpec, varDir, colFound, _
                          lngAttr, fRecursive, objCallback
                    Next
                End If

                    ' Return the number of found files
                    dhFindAllFiles = colFound.Count
            End Function
```

Basically, the function works like this:

1. Given a file specification (such as *.TXT) and a starting directory, it scans the directory for all files matching the specification.

2. It adds each filename it finds to a VBA Collection object supplied by the calling procedure.

3. After finding all the files in the directory, it scans the directory a second time, looking for subdirectories.

4. It adds each subdirectory to an internal Collection object.

5. It iterates through each subdirectory in the Collection object and calls itself recursively, passing the subdirectory as a new starting point.

dhFindAllFiles passes the same collection of found files down the call chain into deeper and deeper subdirectory levels. When all the subdirectories have been scanned, the collection contains a complete list of files matching the original specification.

Testing dhFindAllFiles

To demonstrate this function, we've provided a procedure called dhPrintFound-Files, shown in Listing 12.32. dhPrintFoundFiles accepts a file specification and path and passes them directly to dhFindAllFiles. It also performs the other required task: it declares a new VBA Collection object and passes it to dhFindAllFiles along with the other information. Figure 12.10 shows you how to call dhPrintFoundFiles and what the output might look like.

Listing 12.32: This Procedure Tests dhFindAllFiles.

```
Sub dhPrintFoundFiles(strPath As String, strSpec As String)

    Dim colFound As New Collection
    Dim lngFound As Long
    Dim varFound As Variant

    ' Test the file find logic
    Debug.Print "Starting search..."

    ' Call dhFindAllFiles
    lngFound = dhFindAllFiles(strSpec, strPath, colFound)

    ' Print the results
    Debug.Print "Done. Found: " & lngFound

    ' With the collection of file names
    ' you can do something with them
    Debug.Print
    Debug.Print "What we found:"
    Debug.Print "=============="

    For Each varFound In colFound
        Debug.Print varFound
    Next
End Sub
```

Once you have the collection of found files, you can use them to drive another process. We simply print them to the Immediate window using a For Each loop, but you could use them in other file operations (copying, deleting, and so on).

FIGURE 12.10

Performing a file search
using dhPrintFoundFiles

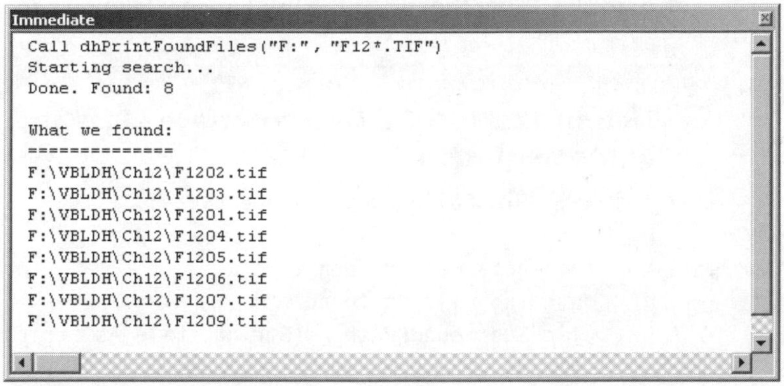

```
Immediate                                                              ⊠
Call dhPrintFoundFiles("F:", "F12*.TIF")                              ▲
Starting search...
Done. Found: 8

What we found:
==============
F:\VBLDH\Ch12\F1202.tif
F:\VBLDH\Ch12\F1203.tif
F:\VBLDH\Ch12\F1201.tif
F:\VBLDH\Ch12\F1204.tif
F:\VBLDH\Ch12\F1205.tif
F:\VBLDH\Ch12\F1206.tif
F:\VBLDH\Ch12\F1207.tif
F:\VBLDH\Ch12\F1209.tif                                              ▼
◄                                                                    ►
```

Embellishments to dhFindAllFiles

We dressed up the basic functionality in dhFindAllFiles in three ways. First, we added an optional argument to limit the search to files with a given set of attributes. By default, this argument, lngAttr, is set to −1. This instructs the dhDir functions to find all files matching the specification. You can override this by passing your own set of attributes. In this case, dhDir performs a restrictive search, finding only those files that have the given attributes.

Second, we provided an option (fRecursive) to control the recursive function calls. Setting this option to False forces dhFindAllFiles to search only the original starting directory.

The third embellishment we added is a provision for a callback object (objCallback). A *callback object* is a pointer to a VBA class that implements a set of required methods, Searching and Found. As each new subdirectory is searched, dhFindAllFiles calls the Searching method, passing the subdirectory name. Furthermore, when dhFindAllFiles finds a file, it calls the Found method, passing the path and filename. Since the search process may take a long time (especially if you're searching your whole hard disk), you may want to provide your users with feedback on the progress. If you've ever used the Windows Find dialog, you know it displays, in the status bar, the directory currently being searched. It also adds each file to a list as it is found. You can implement similar functionality using a callback object of your own.

To enforce the required interface we've created an interface class, IFileFindCallback, that declares the two methods. We've also written a very simple class called

FileFindCallback that implements the interface. Listing 12.33 shows both class modules. Note the use of the Implements keyword in the second class module.

Listing 12.33: A Callback Interface Class and a Simple Implementation

```
' IFileFindCallback interface class:

' This gets called each time a
' matching file is found
Public Sub Found(Path As String, File As String)

End Sub

' This gets called each time a new
' directory is searched
Public Sub Searching(Path As String)

End Sub

' FileFindCallback implementation:

Implements IFileFindCallback

Private Sub IFileFindCallback_Found(Path As String, File As String)
    Debug.Print "Found: " & Path & File
End Sub

Private Sub IFileFindCallback_Searching(Path As String)
    Debug.Print "Searching: " & Path
    Debug.Print "--------------------------------------"
End Sub
```

NOTE   For more information on interface classes and the Implements keyword see the section "Interface Classes and the Implements Keyword" in Chapter 6, "Advanced Class Module Techniques."

Listing 12.34 shows a modified version of the dhPrintFoundFiles procedure called dhPrintFoundFilesWithFeedback. It declares a new instance of the FileFind-Callback class and passes it to dhFindAllFiles. As each matching filename is found, it is printed to the Immediate window. Try this out yourself by calling dhPrintFoundFilesWithFeedback from the Immediate window.

Listing 12.34: dhPrintFoundFilesWithFeedback Uses a Callback Object.

```
Sub dhPrintFoundFilesWithFeedback(strPath As String, _
   strSpec As String)

   Dim colFound As Collection
   Dim lngFound As Long
   Dim objCallback As FindFileCallback

   Set colFound = New Collection
   Set objCallback = New FindFileCallback

   ' Test the file find logic
   Debug.Print "Starting search..."

   ' Call dhFindAllFiles, passing a callback
   ' object--the callback object will print
   ' the file names to the Immediate window
   ' as they are found
   lngFound = dhFindAllFiles(strSpec, strPath, _
   colFound, , , objCallback)

   ' Print the results
   Debug.Print "Done. Found: " & lngFound
End Sub
```

These embellishments are just the beginning. The Windows Find dialog, for instance, lets you customize the search by specifying file sizes, dates, and even the text the files contain. If you feel like a challenge, you can extend the dhFindAll-Files function using the other file functions mentioned in this chapter.

Procuring Temporary Filenames

Many applications use temporary files to store intermediate results while processing data. All the major Microsoft applications use them for various reasons. If your application needs to use temporary files, there are two API functions you should use to choose a filename and path. GetTempPath returns the directory designated to hold temporary files. The directory returned will be one of those listed below, evaluated in the order listed:

1. The directory specified by the TMP environmental variable

2. The directory specified by the TEMP environmental variable

3. The current directory (Windows 95/98) or the Windows directory (Windows NT/2000/XP) if neither TMP nor TEMP is defined

GetTempFileName creates a temporary filename, given a path, a prefix string, and, optionally, a unique integer. If you pass a nonzero value as the integer, GetTempFileName converts it to hexadecimal and concatenates it with the path and prefix. In this case, the function does not test to see whether the file already exists. If you pass a 0, GetTempFileName chooses a number based on the system clock. It continues to choose numbers until it can construct a filename that does not already exist.

All the code for this section is contained in the basTempFiles module of the sample Excel workbook and the TEMPFILE.BAS file.

The declaration for each function is shown here:

```
Declare Function GetTempPath Lib "kernel32" _
  Alias "GetTempPathA" (ByVal nBufferLength As Long, _
  ByVal lpBuffer As String) As Long

Declare Function GetTempFileName Lib "kernel32" _
  Alias "GetTempFileNameA" (ByVal lpszPath As String, _
  ByVal lpPrefixString As String, ByVal wUnique As Long, _
  ByVal lpTempFileName As String) As Long
```

Using these two functions together, you can create a single VBA function that returns a unique temporary filename. We've done this for you in the form of the dhTempFileName function shown in Listing 12.35. Note that the function accepts an optional argument for the file prefix. If you omit this argument, the string "~DH" is used.

Listing 12.35: dhTempFileName Computes a Unique Temporary Filename.

```
Function dhTempFileName( _
 Optional strPrefix As String = "~DH") As String

  Dim strPath As String
  Dim strBuffer As String
  Dim lngBytes As Long

  ' Set up a buffer
  strBuffer = Space(MAX_PATH)

  ' Call GetTempPath
  lngBytes = GetTempPath(Len(strBuffer), strBuffer)

  ' If successful extract the path
  If lngBytes > 0 Then
    strPath = Left(strBuffer, lngBytes)

    ' Reset the buffer and call GetTempFileName
    strBuffer = Space(MAX_PATH)
    lngBytes = GetTempFileName(strPath, _
     strPrefix, 0, strBuffer)

    ' If successful extract the file name
    If lngBytes > 0 Then
      dhTempFileName = Left(strBuffer, lngBytes)
    End If
  End If
End Function
```

Note that GetTempFileName actually creates the temporary file. If you don't use the file, be sure to delete it using the VBA Kill function.

Getting a (Windows) Handle on Files

The discussion of the VBA file I/O functions earlier in this chapter introduced the concept of file handles. To work with a file using some of the Windows API functions, you must also get a handle to it. These handles are not equivalent, however.

You cannot use a file handle derived from the VBA FreeFile function with Windows API functions.

All the code for this section is contained in the basFileHandles module of the sample Excel workbook and the HANDLES.BAS file.

Using the CreateFile Function

You obtain file handles by calling the CreateFile function. CreateFile has a myriad of uses in addition to opening and creating files. We could spend an entire chapter, and then some, fully explaining all the things you can use CreateFile for. For our purposes, however, we'll stick to opening a file for read-only access.

CreateFile is declared as follows:

```
Declare Function CreateFile Lib "kernel32" _
  Alias "CreateFileA" _
  (ByVal lpFileName As String, _
  ByVal dwDesiredAccess As Long, _
  ByVal dwShareMode As Long, _
  lpSecurityAttributes As Any, _
  ByVal dwCreationDisposition As Long, _
  ByVal dwFlagsAndAttributes As Long, _
  ByVal hTemplateFile As Long) As Long
```

NOTE   The lpSecurityAttributes parameter, declared As Any in our example, is normally a pointer to a SECURITY_ATTRIBUTES structure. These structures are used to set and retrieve Windows NT security descriptor information. Operating system security is a complex topic in its own right and beyond the scope of this book. In all our examples, we pass null pointers to functions that accept security attributes.

Table 12.8 lists the many arguments to CreateFile, along with the allowable constants, where applicable. The meanings of the constants should be self-explanatory. For more information on CreateFile and its arguments, consult the Windows Platform SDK documentation available online at http://msdn.microsoft.com/library/.

If you look carefully at the arguments and constants shown in Table 12.8, you should see a similarity between them and the options for the VBA Open statement. This is no coincidence; the capabilities are comparable.

TABLE 12.8:   Arguments to CreateFile

Argument	Description	Allowable Values
lpFileName	Path to the file or directory	Any valid, fully qualified file path to open
dwDesiredAccess	Desired file access (bit mask)	GENERIC_READ, GENERIC_WRITE
dwShareMode	File-sharing mode (bit mask)	FILE_SHARE_READ, FILE_SHARE_WRITE
lpSecurityAttributes	Windows NT security information	Pointer to SECURITY_ATTRIBUTES structure
dwCreationDisposition	Defines what action to take if file does (or does not) exist	CREATE_NEW, CREATE_ALWAYS, OPEN_EXISTING, OPEN_ALWAYS, TRUNCATE_EXISTING
dwFlagsAndAttributes	File attributes (bit mask)	FILE_ATTRIBUTE_ARCHIVE, FILE_ATTRIBUTE_COMPRESSED, FILE_ATTRIBUTE_NORMAL, FILE_ATTRIBUTE_HIDDEN, FILE_ATTRIBUTE_READONLY, FILE_ATTRIBUTE_SYSTEM, FILE_FLAG_WRITE_THROUGH, FILE_FLAG_OVERLAPPED, FILE_FLAG_NO_BUFFERING, FILE_FLAG_RANDOM_ACCESS, FILE_FLAG_SEQUENTIAL_SCAN, FILE_FLAG_DELETE_ON_CLOSE, FILE_FLAG_BACKUP_SEMANTICS, FILE_FLAG_POSIX_SEMANTICS
hTemplateFile	Defines the file to use as a template for attributes	File handle. Invalid under Windows 95 and ignored in our examples

A Quick and Dirty Wrapper

Since most of our examples involve opening a file for simple read-only access, we wrote a wrapper function for CreateFile called dhQuickOpenFile. Shown in Listing 12.36, it accepts a filename and an optional access mode (GENERIC_ READ is the default) and returns the result of calling CreateFile. If CreateFile is successful in opening the file, the result is a handle to the open file. If an error occurs, CreateFile returns –1. Any procedure calling dhQuickOpenFile should check for this value.

TIP Many Windows API functions, including CreateFile, return error codes via the GetLastError API function. You can use the LastDLLError property of VBA's Err object to determine this error code after a failed API call.

Listing 12.36: dhQuickOpenFile, a Wrapper Function for CreateFile

```
Function dhQuickOpenFile(strFile As String, _
 Optional lngMode As Long = GENERIC_READ) As Long

    ' Call CreateFile to open the file in
    ' read-only, shared mode unless the user
    ' has passed a different access method--
    ' return the resulting file handle
    dhQuickOpenFile = CreateFile(strFile, lngMode, _
     FILE_SHARE_READ Or FILE_SHARE_WRITE, _
     ByVal 0&, OPEN_EXISTING, _
     FILE_ATTRIBUTE_NORMAL Or _
     FILE_FLAG_RANDOM_ACCESS, 0&)

End Function
```

A Simple Example

To demonstrate dhQuickOpenFile (and thus CreateFile), the procedure in Listing 12.37 opens a given file and prints the file's size (using the GetFileSizeEx API function) to the Immediate window.

Listing 12.37: Print a File's Size the API Way.

```
Sub dhPrintSizeAPI(strFile As String)

    Dim hFile As Long
    Dim curSize As Currency

    ' Open the file and get the handle
    hFile = dhQuickOpenFile(strFile)
```

```
    ' If successful, print the size--
    ' if not, print the DLL error code
    If hFile > 0 Then

        ' Get the file size
        Call GetFileSizeEx(hFile, curSize)

        ' Print the results
        Debug.Print curSize * 10000 & " bytes"

        ' Close the file
        Call CloseHandle(hFile)
    Else
        Debug.Print "Error calling CreateFile: " & _
          Err.LastDllError
    End If
End Sub
```

You'll notice that, just like our VBA function examples, the procedure closes the file after it's finished using it. In this case, it calls the CloseHandle API function. (CloseHandle is a function used to close various Kernel object handles.)

A Word on File Sizes

As hard disks and files have continued to grow the operating system, developers at Microsoft have had to keep inventing ways to measure their sizes. The primary problem was that long (32-bit) integers can only hold values up to about 2 billion, far less than today's massive hard drive capacities. The now-obsolete GetFileSize API function provided a workaround by returning a large file's size in two 32-bit chunks, one as the return value of the function and one through a passed-in parameter. This worked but was less than convenient for VBA developers. With Windows NT, Windows 2000, and Windows XP, Microsoft provided GetFileSizeEx, which returns a file's size through a single 64-bit integer parameter. We've included a declaration for GetFileSizeEx (along with GetFileSize) in basFileHandles in case you're developing for Windows NT/2000/XP. The declaration is shown below:

```
Private Declare Function GetFileSizeEx Lib "kernel32" _
  (ByVal fhile As Long, curFileSize As Currency) As Long
```

To use the function, declare and pass a Currency variable as the second argument (just like with GetDiskFreeSpaceEx described earlier in the chapter). If the call succeeds, GetFile-SizeEx will return a non-zero value. If it fails it will return 0.

Getting File Information Quickly

Now that you understand what Windows file handles are and how to get them, you're ready for a little gem of an API function called GetFileInformationByHandle. In a single function call, you can retrieve almost everything you ever wanted to know about a file. The information returned is similar to what you get using the Find functions described earlier in this chapter, but you use an open file handle instead of performing a directory scan.

GetFileInformationByHandle uses a user-defined data type to hold the information. The declaration for this type, BY_HANDLE_FILE_INFORMATION, is as follows:

```
Type BY_HANDLE_FILE_INFORMATION
    lngFileAttributes As Long          ' File attributes
    ftCreationTime As FILETIME         ' Creation time
    ftLastAccessTime As FILETIME       ' Last access time
    ftLastWriteTime As FILETIME        ' Last write time
    lngVolumeSerialNumber As Long      ' Serial number
    lngFileSizeHigh As Long            ' File size high-order word
    lngFileSizeLow As Long             ' File size low-order word
    lngNumberOfLinks As Long           ' Links to file (1 for FAT)
    lngFileIndexHigh As Long           ' Unique ID high-order word
    lngFileIndexLow As Long            ' Unique ID low-order word
End Type
```

GetFileInformationByHandle accepts a file handle and pointer to an instance of this structure and returns True or False, indicating success or failure. For an explanation of the FILETIME members, see the next section.

Windows API Dates and Times

Before going any further in discussing Windows API file and disk functions, we need to spend some time discussing date and time issues because a number of tasks (like setting the creation date of a file) require expressing time values in a way the Windows API understands. Specifically, the API uses two time formats, system time and file time, neither of which is directly compatible with VBA. These formats are discussed in the following sections.

All the code for this discussion is contained in the basDatesAndTimes module of the sample Excel workbook and the DATETIME.BAS file.

System Time

System time is the format used internally by Windows. Functions that deal in system time express it using a user-defined data type called, appropriately, SYSTEM-TIME. The data type is structured as follows:

```
Type SYSTEMTIME
    intYear As Integer
    intMonth As Integer
    intDayOfWeek As Integer
    intDay As Integer
    intHour As Integer
    intMinute As Integer
    intSecond As Integer
    intMilliseconds As Integer
End Type
```

As you can see, each date and time element is represented by a separate integer value. Using this format, you can represent any date from January 1, 32768 B.C. to December 31, 32767. This date range is wide enough for most applications, except perhaps archeological or paleontological programs.

We've provided two procedures for converting between VBA and system time values. Listing 12.38 shows these functions, dhSysTimeToVBATime and dhVBA-TimeToSysTime.

Listing 12.38: Convert between VBA and System Time Formats.

```
Function dhSysTimeToVBATime(stSysTime As SYSTEMTIME) As Date
    ' Construct a VBA date/time value using the
    ' DateSerial and TimeSerial functions
    With stSysTime
        dhSysTimeToVBATime = _
            DateSerial(.intYear, .intMonth, .intDay) + _
            TimeSerial(.intHour, .intMinute, .intSecond)
    End With
End Function

Sub dhVBATimeToSysTime(datTime As Date, stSysTime As SYSTEMTIME)
    ' Fill in the structure with date and time parts
    With stSysTime
        .intMonth = Month(datTime)
        .intDay = Day(datTime)
        .intYear = Year(datTime)
```

```
      .intHour = Hour(datTime)
      .intMinute = Minute(datTime)
      .intSecond = Second(datTime)
   End With
End Sub
```

When working with system time data, keep in mind that Windows tracks time internally using *coordinated universal time* (*UTC*). Coordinated universal time is loosely defined as the current time of day in Greenwich, England, and is sometimes called Greenwich Mean Time (GMT). You can retrieve the current system time by calling the GetSystemTime API function. Most functions that utilize the SYSTEMTIME data type assume the time being passed is in UTC format.

Local time is the current time of day where you are, that is, in the time zone specified on your system. If you want to know the current local time, call the GetLocalTime API function. While there is no direct way to convert between the two time scales, you can retrieve time zone information by calling the GetTimeZoneInformation function. The information returned (via another user-defined type called TIME_ZONE_INFORMATION) contains, among other things, the time zone *bias*—the difference between local time and coordinated universal time.

File Time

The other type of time format you'll come across in disk and file functions, *file time*, is used to set and retrieve the three time values associated with files and directories. 32-bit Windows operating systems track the time a file was created, the time it was last accessed, and the time it was last modified.

Like system times, file times use a user-defined type. Called FILETIME, it's structured as follows:

```
Type FILETIME
   lngLowDateTime As Long
   lngHighDateTime As Long
End Type
```

The contents of a FILETIME structure are not quite as obvious as those of SYSTEMTIME. The two long integers that make up FILETIME represent a 64-bit number containing (and we're not making this up) the number of 100-nanosecond intervals since January 1, 1601!

Fortunately, you rarely have to work with FILETIME data in its raw format. The Windows API contains functions that convert from file time to system time and back. Using these functions, we were able to create the VBA time conversion functions shown in Listing 12.39.

Listing 12.39: Functions for Converting between File Time and VBA Time

```
Function dhFileTimeToVBATime(ftFileTime As FILETIME, _
 Optional fLocal As Boolean = True) As Date

  Dim stSystem As SYSTEMTIME
  Dim ftLocalFileTime As FILETIME

  ' If the user wants local time, convert the file
  ' time to local file time
  If fLocal Then
    Call FileTimeToLocalFileTime(ftFileTime, ftLocalFileTime)
    ftFileTime = ftLocalFileTime
  End If

  ' Convert the file time to system time then
  ' call our own function to convert to VBA time
  If CBool(FileTimeToSystemTime(ftFileTime, stSystem)) Then
    dhFileTimeToVBATime = dhSysTimeToVBATime(stSystem)
  End If
End Function

Sub dhVBATimeToFileTime(datTime As Date, ftTime As FILETIME, _
 Optional fLocal As Boolean = True)

  Dim stSystem As SYSTEMTIME
  Dim ftSystem As FILETIME

  ' Call our function to convert the VBA time to
  ' system time
  Call dhVBATimeToSysTime(datTime, stSystem)

  ' Convert the system time to file time
  If CBool(SystemTimeToFileTime(stSystem, ftTime)) Then

    ' If the VBA time was local time, convert the
    ' local file time to system file time
    If fLocal Then
      Call LocalFileTimeToFileTime(ftTime, ftSystem)
      ftTime = ftSystem
    End If
  End If
End Sub
```

Note that each function accepts a flag value, fLocal, as an optional argument. If this is set to True (the default), the VBA time value is treated as local time. If fLocal is False, it's treated as system, or UTC, time.

Working with File Times

With the discussion of time formats out of the way, let's take a look at API functions that deal in file dates and times. A common requirement for some applications is to be able to set the creation time of a file. You may have noticed that when you install an application from a company like Microsoft, all the files have the same creation date and time. As mentioned earlier in this discussion, the file system actually tracks three time values for each file. Using Windows API functions, you can set and retrieve all of them. This section shows you how this is done and how to compare the times of two files quickly and easily.

Getting and Setting File Times

The functions that enable you to get and set file times are GetFileTime and SetFileTime. The declarations for these functions are as follows (note that each accepts a file handle as the first argument):

```
Declare Function GetFileTime Lib "kernel32" _
  (ByVal hFile As Long, lpCreationTime As FILETIME, _
  lpLastAccessTime As FILETIME, _
  lpLastWriteTime As FILETIME) As Long

Declare Function SetFileTime Lib "kernel32" _
  (ByVal hFile As Long, lpCreationTime As FILETIME, _
  lpLastAccessTime As FILETIME, _
  lpLastWriteTime As FILETIME) As Long
```

Since the FILETIME format can be tricky to work with, we've come up with several wrapper functions you can use to set or retrieve file times. These functions open the file (using dhQuickOpenFile) and handle the conversion between time formats. Listing 12.40 shows the first two, dhGetFileTimes and dhSetFileTimes. Each uses a custom structure, dhtypFileTimes, not shown in Listing 12.40. We created this structure, which groups three VBA Date variables, to make it convenient to work with all three file time values at once.

⟩ Listing 12.40: Two Functions for Retrieving or Setting All Three File Times

```
Function dhGetFileTimes(strFile As String, _
 dftTimes As dhtypFileTimes) As Boolean

    Dim ftCreate As FILETIME
    Dim ftAccess As FILETIME
    Dim ftWrite As FILETIME
    Dim hFile As Long
    Dim lngRet As Long

    ' Open the file
    hFile = dhQuickOpenFile(strFile)
    If hFile > 0 Then

        ' Call GetFileTime to fetch time information
        ' into the local FILETIME structures
        If CBool(GetFileTime(hFile, ftCreate, _
         ftAccess, ftWrite)) Then

            ' If successful, convert the values to
            ' VBA Date format and return them in
            ' the passed dhtypFileTimes structure
            With dftTimes
                .datCreated = dhFileTimeToVBATime(ftCreate)
                .datAccessed = dhFileTimeToVBATime(ftAccess)
                .datModified = dhFileTimeToVBATime(ftWrite)
            End With

            ' Return success
            dhGetFileTimes = True
        End If

        ' Close the file
        Call CloseHandle(hFile)
    End If
End Function

Function dhSetFileTimes(strFile As String, _
 dftTimes As dhtypFileTimes) As Boolean
```

```
Dim ftCreated As FILETIME
Dim ftAccessed As FILETIME
Dim ftModified As FILETIME
Dim hFile As Long

' Open the file for write access
hFile = dhQuickOpenFile(strFile, GENERIC_WRITE)

' If successful then...
If hFile > 0 Then

    ' Convert the passed time to a FILETIME
    With dftTimes
        Call dhVBATimeToFileTime(.datCreated, ftCreated)
        Call dhVBATimeToFileTime(.datAccessed, ftAccessed)
        Call dhVBATimeToFileTime(.datModified, ftModified)
    End With

    ' Set the times
    If CBool(SetFileTime(hFile, ftCreated, _
     ftAccessed, ftModified)) Then

        ' Return success
        dhSetFileTimes = True
    End If

    ' Close the file
    Call CloseHandle(hFile)
End If
End Function
```

As an example, suppose you wanted to set the creation, last access, and last write times of a file to midnight, January 1, 1997. You could use code like this:

```
Dim dft As dhtypFileTimes

With dft
    .datCreated = #1/1/97 12:00:00 AM#
    .datAccessed = #1/1/97 12:00:00 AM#
    .datModified = #1/1/97 12:00:00 AM#
End With

Call dhSetFileTimes("C:\SOMEFILE.EXE", dft)
```

If you use dhSetFileTimes to change a file time value, be sure not to leave any of the structure elements blank. Doing so will set the file time to 0 or, expressed as a VBA date, Saturday, December 30, 1899!

Both functions require you to declare a dhtypFileTimes variable and pass it as the second argument. If you want to retrieve or modify only a single file time, you can use two other VBA functions we've provided, dhGetFileTimesEx and dhSetFileTimesEx. Instead of a user-defined data type, these functions accept an integer specifying which time or times you're interested in. In the case of dhGetFileTimesEx, this is a single number indicating *one* of the time values. dhSetFileTimesEx, on the other hand, accepts a bit mask of numbers and changes *one or more* time values to the supplied time. Both functions have reasonable defaults for these arguments, so you don't have to supply a value if you don't want to. The following code illustrates how you might call these functions:

```
' Get the last modified time for WIN.INI
Debug.Print dhGetFileTimesEx("C:\WINDOWS\WIN.INI")

' Get the last accessed time for WIN.INI
Debug.Print dhGetFileTimesEx("C:\WINDOWS\WIN.INI", _
 dhcFileTimeAccessed)

' Set the last modified and last accessed time for WIN.INI
' to right now
Debug.Print dhSetFileTimesEx("C:\WINDOWS\WIN.INI", Now)

' Set the created time for WIN.INI to yesterday
Debug.Print dhSetFileTimesEx("C:\WINDOWS\WIN.INI", Now - 1, _
 dhcFileTimeCreated)
```

Since dhGetFileTimesEx and dhSetFileTimesEx are basically modified versions of dhGetFileTimes and dhSetFileTimes, we haven't included their code here. You can find it, along with the constant definitions, in the sample files for this chapter.

Comparing File Times

In addition to simply retrieving the time values associated with a file, you'll sometimes need to compare them against those of another file. You might do this, for example, to determine whether a file on a desktop computer and another on a laptop are the same. While you could retrieve the times for both files using the functions described above, there is also a simple Windows API call you can use, CompareFileTime:

```
Declare Function CompareFileTime Lib "kernel32" _
  (lpFileTime1 As FILETIME, lpFileTime2 As FILETIME) As Long
```

CompareFileTime accepts pointers to two FILETIME structures and returns a result indicating the difference, if any, between them. It returns –1 if the first file time is less than the second, 1 if it's greater, and 0 if the two are equal. Listing 12.41 shows a function that uses CompareFileTime to compute the difference between the time values for two files. To use it, pass the path to both files, along with the time you want to check. Note that it returns the same values as CompareFileTime except in the event of an error (perhaps due to an invalid filename), in which case it returns –2.

Listing 12.41: Use the Windows API to Compare File Times.

```
Function dhCompareFileTime(strFile1 As String, _
  strFile2 As String, Optional intTime As _
  Integer = dhcFileTimeModified) As Long

  Dim ftCreate1 As FILETIME
  Dim ftAccess1 As FILETIME
  Dim ftWrite1 As FILETIME
  Dim hFile1 As Long
  Dim ftCreate2 As FILETIME
  Dim ftAccess2 As FILETIME
  Dim ftWrite2 As FILETIME
  Dim hFile2 As Long

  ' Set a return value in case things go wrong
  dhCompareFileTime = -2

  ' Open the first file
  hFile1 = dhQuickOpenFile(strFile1)
  If hFile1 > 0 Then

    ' Open the second file
    hFile2 = dhQuickOpenFile(strFile2)
    If hFile2 > 0 Then
```

```
            ' Get the file times
          If CBool(GetFileTime(hFile1, ftCreate1, _
            ftAccess1, ftWrite1)) Then
            If CBool(GetFileTime(hFile2, ftCreate2, _
              ftAccess2, ftWrite2)) Then

                ' Call CompareFileTime for the
                ' requested time and return the result
                Select Case intTime
                  Case dhcFileTimeCreated
                    dhCompareFileTime = _
                      CompareFileTime(ftCreate1, _
                      ftCreate2)
                  Case dhcFileTimeAccessed
                    dhCompareFileTime = _
                      CompareFileTime(ftAccess1, _
                      ftAccess2)
                  Case dhcFileTimeModified
                    dhCompareFileTime = _
                      CompareFileTime(ftWrite1, ftWrite2)
                End Select
            End If
          End If

            ' Close the second file
            Call CloseHandle(hFile2)
          End If

            ' Close the first file
            Call CloseHandle(hFile1)
        End If
End Function
```

| NOTE | For more information on comparing and manipulating dates and times using VBA, see Chapter 3. |

Using the Windows Common File Dialogs

The bulk of this chapter has discussed manipulating files once you know which ones you want to manipulate. Sometimes you'll need to ask the user to select a file. To standardize specific often-needed dialogs, including those for file selection, Windows provides a group of common dialogs all applications can use. If you want to allow your users to select a filename for opening or saving, Windows has a common dialog box to handle the selection. VBA provides no built-in mechanism for you to get to any of the common dialogs, but the Windows API makes it possible to use any of them.

Using these API functions is somewhat daunting, however, so we've wrapped up much of the code in a simpler-to-use class module, CommonDlg, and have provided several examples of using this class. The following sections discuss how you can use the CommonDlg class, making it easy for you to take advantage of these common dialogs in your own applications.

Using the CommonDlg Class

The CommonDlg class contains code that allows you to easily display the File Save, File Open, Font, and Color common dialogs. The class takes care of all the communication between VBA and the Windows API. It takes advantage of a number of user-defined types, enums, and API calls and provides a large number of methods and properties. In particular, the four methods you'll need to use in order to display the common dialogs are as follows:

Method	Action
ShowColor	Displays the Color chooser common dialog
ShowFont	Displays the Font chooser common dialog
ShowOpen	Displays the File Open common dialog
ShowSave	Displays the File Save common dialog

To use the dialogs in the simplest case, you can instantiate a new CommonDlg object and then call one of these methods. That is, the simplest usage for displaying the Font common dialog might look like this:

```
Dim cdl As CommonDlg
Set cdl = New CommonDlg
cdl.ShowOpen
Debug.Print cdl.FileName
```

NOTE   The color and font dialogs fall outside the scope of the chapter but are included in the class for completeness. More information on how they work can be found in Chapter 17 of *Access 2000 Developer's Handbook, Volume I: Desktop Edition* from Sybex.

How About the CommonDialog ActiveX Control?

If you have the Windows Common Dialog ActiveX control available, you're welcome to use that in place of the CommonDlg class we've provided here. We've encountered several issues using that control, however, including the following:

- The control must be placed on a form. If you want to use the common dialogs from multiple locations in your application, you'll either need to place the control on every form where you might need it or make sure that the form hosting the control is always open. Using the class module has no similar requirements.

- The control does not allow you to specify a callback function. It's in this callback function (that is, a function you supply that's called by the common dialog while it's displayed on screen) that you can position the dialog box where you want it, change the captions of controls on the dialog (in the case of the File Open/Save dialog boxes), or react to other actions taken on the dialog box. Our class can take advantage of this callback mechanism and includes an example callback function that centers the dialog box on the screen.

- The control does not allow you to specify the owner of the dialog box. Without this capability, it's difficult to manage what happens when you use the Alt+Tab keystroke to move to a different application while the dialog box is displayed. The CommonDlg class provides an hWndOwner property, which allows you to specify which window "owns" the dialog box.

- The control doesn't include source code. If you want to add features or modify the behavior of existing features, you're out of luck. Using the CommonDlg class, you have full control over the source code.

Common Steps

No matter which of the common dialogs you want to use, the steps are similar:

1. Make sure your project contains the CommonDlg class. (If you want to use a callback function described later, you might also want to import basCommonDlg and basCommon. These modules make it possible to use the sample callback functions.)

2. Create a variable of type CommonDlg to refer to the CommonDlg object in memory, like this:

```
Dim cdl As CommonDlg
```

3. Instantiate the variable:

```
Set cdl = New CommonDlg
```

4. Set properties of the CommonDlg object. You needn't set any properties at all, but you'll normally set the appropriate flags property (OpenFlags, ColorFlags, FontFlags), indicating specific preferences you have about the behavior of the dialog box. Use the Or operator to combine various settings. You might see code like this:

```
cdl.InitDir = "C:\"
cdl.OpenFlags = cdlOFNAllowMultiSelect Or _
  cdlOFNNoChangeDir
```

5. Call the appropriate method of the object (ShowOpen, ShowSave, ShowColor, or ShowFont) to display the selected dialog box. This will halt your code until the user has dismissed the dialog box. Your code might look like this:

```
cdl.ShowOpen
```

6. Once the user has dismissed the dialog box, retrieve the appropriate information from the CommonDlg object. For example, to retrieve the selected filename, you might write code like this:

```
Me.txtFileName = cdl.FileName
```

7. When you're done, destroy the CommonDlg object:

```
Set cdl = Nothing
```

TIP Generally, you'll also want to add a bit of code to determine whether the user clicked the Cancel button. To do this, you must set the CancelError property of the CommonDlg object to True. You must then add error handling to trap for the error raised by the object. This happens when the user cancels the dialog box by clicking the Cancel button. See the section "Checking for Cancellation" later in the chapter for more information on using this technique.

All that's left to take care of is the details. Describing those details is the job of the following sections, which show how to use File Open and File Save dialog boxes. Make sure you take the time to investigate all the options to see how the dialog boxes work.

Compatibility of Existing Code

To make it easier for you to migrate code that you may have already written using the CommonDialog ActiveX control, we decided to make the CommonDlg class compatible with the Common Dialog ActiveX control. That is, if you have code written using the ActiveX control, you should be able to remove the control from your project and use the CommonDlg class instead. Although we've added new options and properties, existing code that uses the ShowOpen, ShowSave, ShowColor, or ShowFont methods of the ActiveX control should work with this class as well.

Setting Options

Besides the basic properties of the CommonDlg class that you'll see described in the next few sections, the Windows common dialogs allow you to specify detailed properties all rolled into a single value. Internally, the CommonDlg class sends a user-defined type full of information to the Windows API, and one of the elements of that structure is named Flags. This long integer consists of 32 possible bits of information. By turning on various bits within the 32 available bits, you indicate to Windows exactly how you want the common dialog to behave.

We've mirrored that same behavior in the Flags property of the CommonDlg object. Each different type of dialog box interprets the bits in the Flags property differently, and we've provided groups of constants as enums to make your choice of bits easier. In the CommonDlg class module, you'll find the dhFileOpenConstants enumerated type for both the File Open and File Save dialogs. Internally, the CommonDlg class copies these individual values into the general Flags property for you.

Because the various flags properties can consist of combinations of zero or more of these constants, you'll need to combine them together to specify multiple values. To do this, you can either use the "+" or Or operator. Mathematically, these accomplish the same goal. We use Or in our code because that makes it clearer that we're combining bits together to create a long integer value. If you're more comfortable using "+", however, your code will still work fine. Figure 12.11 shows how you might select from available lists of constants to supply the value for the OpenFlags property.

FIGURE 12.11
Use IntelliSense to choose from lists of possible flag values combined with Or.

Using a Callback Function

The ability to have your own code executing while the Windows common dialog is onscreen is a powerful feature, and it's available to you using the CommonDlg class. We've supplied a simple callback function (it centers the dialog box on the screen after the dialog has been initialized), but this technique is powerful—and potentially dangerous—once you've studied the API documentation.

> **NOTE** For more information on using callback functions with Windows API procedures, see Appendix B (located on the CD-ROM accompanying this book).

In order to use a callback procedure with the Windows common dialogs, you must work through four issues:

- How do you indicate to the CommonDlg class that it should call your callback function?

- How do you declare the callback function so that the Windows common dialog can send information to it correctly?

- How do you supply the address of the procedure as a property of the CommonDlg class?

- What do you do from within the callback function?

The first question is the simplest: set the appropriate flag property to include the flag that enables a hook (that is, a callback) procedure. These flag values all include the text "EnableHook." If you don't set this flag, Windows will never call your procedure.

How do you specify the parameters for the callback function? When you create the procedure called by the common dialog, it's imperative that you get the data types, return type, and parameter-passing information correct. Because Windows calls your procedure directly, with no intervention from Visual Basic, any mistakes in the declaration of the procedure will generally cause your application to crash. For the common dialogs, your callback function must be declared like this:

```
Public Function SampleCallback( _
 ByVal hWnd As Long, ByVal uiMsg As Long, _
 ByVal wParam As Long, ByVal lParam As Long) As Long
```

The exact name of the procedure is inconsequential, as are the names of the parameters, but the data types, the parameter passing (that is, the use of ByVal), and the return type must match this example. If you use our sample callback functions, you won't have any trouble.

How do you tell Windows about this procedure? The CallBack property of the CommonDlg object requires you to send it the address of a VBA procedure. To do that, you use the AddressOf modifier (previously available only in Visual Basic, now available in all VBA hosts), which converts a procedure name into its address in memory. For this mechanism to work, this procedure must be a public procedure in a standard module—it can't be Private, and it can't be within a class module. (For more information on using the AddressOf modifier, see Appendix B, which is located on the CD-ROM accompanying this book.) One small problem: AddressOf only works within a procedure call. You can't write code like this:

```
cdl.CallBack = AddressOf SampleCallBack
```

because VBA won't compile this code. You need to supply the address of a procedure in the Callback property, however. To get around this problem, we've supplied the dhFnPtrToLong function in basTestCommonDlg, which takes one Long parameter and simply returns that value:

```
Public Function dhFnPtrToLong(lngAddress As Long) As Long
    dhFnPtrToLong = lngAddress
End Function
```

How is this useful? Although it looks like dhFnPtrToLong isn't really doing anything, it allows you to call it using the AddressOf modifier, and it returns the address you've sent it. With a procedure like this, you can now write:

```
cdl.CallBack = dhFnPtrToLong(AddressOf SampleCallBack)
```

and get the address you need in the CallBack property of the class. If you look at the samples that use the CommonDlg class, you'll see that they all use code similar to this in order to set the CallBack property.

What can you do within the callback procedure? From within the function itself, you react to messages sent to the callback function from Windows. These messages indicate the current state of the dialog box and allow you to make decisions about what to do. (You can think of messages in Windows as constants—they're actually long integers—that Windows uses to communicate to application windows.) Windows passes to your procedure a message value and the window handle for the open dialog box. Although, with enough research into the Windows API documentation, you can perform major tricks with the common dialogs, our example simply waits to receive the WM_INITDIALOG message (indicating that the dialog box has finished its initialization process) and then centers the dialog box on the screen. Listing 12.42 shows the callback function for the File Open and File Save dialogs. (You'll find both this and the CenterWindow procedure in the basCommonDlg module.)

TIP   For more information on using callback functions with common dialogs, you'll need to consult a good Windows API reference. If you have a subscription to the Microsoft Developer Network (MSDN), that's a good place to start. Go online at `http://msdn.microsoft.com`.

Listing 12.42: A Sample Callback Function for Use with Windows Common Dialogs

```
Public Function GFNCallback(ByVal hWnd As Long, ByVal uiMsg As Long, _
    ByVal wParam As Long, ByVal lParam As Long) As Long

    Dim hWndParent As Long

    Select Case uiMsg
        Case WM_INITDIALOG
```

```
                ' In this case, hWnd is the handle
                ' of the child dialog box. You need to
                ' call GetParent to get the handle of the main
                ' dialog box. Go figure.
                hWndParent = GetParent(hWnd)
                If hWndParent <> 0 Then

                    ' On initialization, center the dialog.
                    Call CenterWindow(hWndParent)
                End If

            #If False Then
                ' Now THIS is cool. You can send a message
                ' to the File Open/Save dialog box, and either change
                ' text or hide a control. Check out the
                ' CDM_* messages, and the fos* enum in the
                ' CommonDlg class for all the options.
                Call SendMessageText(hWndParent, CDM_SETCONTROLTEXT, _
                    fosOKButton, "&Select")
                Call SendMessageLong(hWndParent, CDM_HIDECONTROL, _
                    fosFilterListLabel, 0)
            #End If

                ' You could get many other messages here, as well.
                ' All the normal window messages get
                ' filtered through here, and you can
                ' react to any that you like.
        End Select
        ' Tell the original code to handle the message, too.
        ' Otherwise, things get pretty ugly.
        ' To do that, return 0.
        GFNCallback = 0
    End Function
```

Using the Windows File Open/Save Common Dialogs

The Windows File Open and File Save dialogs make it easy for you to allow users to select a file for opening or saving. The programmatic interface to these common dialogs requires you to send Windows some information, and then Windows will do its job, pop up the dialog, and return information to you.

No matter what options you choose and what file you select, the dialog box does no more than return to your application the choices made while the dialog box was visible. It does not open or save a file—it merely allows you to make choices. What you do with the information gathered by the dialog box is up to you.

In order to use the File Open or File Save common dialogs, you may want to set properties of the CommonDlg object that pertain to these dialogs. Table 12.9 lists the properties that apply to the dialogs.

NOTE   In Windows 98, Windows 2000, and Windows XP you can modify the size and position of the File Open and File Save dialog boxes and Windows will "remember" those settings for subsequent uses of the dialog box. See the notes in Table 12.10 on specific flags that alter this behavior. We've also noticed that if any VBA error occurs (if the user presses Cancel on the dialog box, for example, and you've got the CancelError property set to True), Windows seems to "forget" the size and location.

TABLE 12.9:   Properties of the CommonDlg Class That Pertain to the File Open and Save Dialogs

Property Name	Data Type	Description
CallBack	Long	Address of a procedure to be called while the dialog is displayed. This procedure can position the dialog box or take other actions, depending on the particular dialog box.
CancelError	Boolean	If True, pressing the Cancel button on the common dialog triggers a runtime error in the class. Check for the cdlCancel error if you've set this property to True.
DefaultExt	String	If you don't supply an extension, the dialog appends this to your filename. See also the cdlOFNExtensionDifferent value in Table 17.2.
DialogTitle	String	Text that appears in the dialog caption.
FileExtOffset	Long	After returning from the call to ShowOpen or ShowSave, contains the offset, in characters, to the file extension. This makes it easy to parse the filename.
FileList	String()	If you've specified the cdlOFNAllowMultiSelect flag setting, the user may have selected multiple files. After dismissing the dialog box, this array of strings will contain one element for each selected file. FileList(0) always contains the folder in which the user selected files, and FileList(1) through FileList(n) (where n is the total number of selected files) contain the names of the selected files. If the user only selected a single file, FileList(0) contains the folder, and FileList(1) contains the single filename.

TABLE 12.9: Properties of the CommonDlg Class That Pertain to the File Open and Save Dialogs *(continued)*

Property Name	Data Type	Description
FileName	String	The full name (including path) of the selected file. If you specify this value before calling ShowOpen or ShowSave, the dialog will display this filename as the default file to be selected.
FileNameBufferSize	Long	When you call the Open or Save dialog boxes, the CommonDlg class must allocate space for the returned filename(s). The default size allocated is 20,000 bytes. If you think you may need more space, you can specify your own size. Unless you know users are going to be choosing lots of files at once, the default should be sufficient.
FileOffset	Long	After returning from the call to ShowOpen or ShowSave, contains the offset, in characters, to the name of the file (that is, the offset of the beginning of the filename portion of the full path).
FileTitle	String	After returning from the call to ShowOpen or ShowSave, contains the filename and extension (no path information) of the selected file. If you've selected multiple files, this property will contain no text.

Filter	String	List of pairs of filter values, separated with "|". For example, you can use a string like the following:
		`"Text Files (*.txt)|`
		`*.txt|`
		`Database Files (*.mdb,*.mda,.mde)|`
		`*.mdb;*.mda;*.mde|`
		`All Files (*.*)|`
		`*.*"`
		The first half of each pair contains the text the user sees in the Files of Type combo box, and the second half of each pair indicates to Windows the file specification it should look for. (For multiple wildcards in the second half of a pair, use a semicolon to separate the items.) Supplying no filter is the same as requesting all files.

FilterIndex	Integer	One-based index of the filter item that you want to be selected when the dialog box opens (the default value is 1). After the dialog has been dismissed, contains the index of the currently selected filter.
Flags	Long	Zero or more values from Table 12.10, combined with the Or operator, indicating how you want the dialog box to be initialized and how it should behave. You can set the value of this or the OpenFlags property, but using the OpenFlags property supplies a drop-down list of values based on dhFileOpenConstants enumerated type. We suggest you use the OpenFlags property instead of this property, which is provided for compatibility with the CommonDialog ActiveX control.

TABLE 12.9: Properties of the CommonDlg Class That Pertain to the File Open and Save Dialogs *(continued)*

Property Name	Data Type	Description
hWndOwner	Long	Windows handle for the parent of the dialog. Normally, supply a form's hWnd property. If you're not using a form, supply Application.hWndAccessApp for this property.
InitDir	String	The folder in which you want the dialog to first show files. If you don't specify this property, the dialog box will start in the current folder. Once you make a selection, Windows makes the selected file's folder the new current folder, unless you also specify the cdlOFNNoChangeDir flag.
OpenFlags	dhFileOpen Constants	Zero or more values from Table 12.10, combined with the Or operator, indicating how you want the dialog box to be initialized and how it should behave. You can set the value of this or the Flags property, but using the OpenFlags property supplies a drop-down list of values based on adcFileOpenConstants enumeration. We suggest you use the OpenFlags property instead of the Flags property, which is provided for compatibility with the CommonDialog ActiveX control.
OpenFlagsEx	dhFileOpen ConstantsEx	Additional flags available only under Windows 2000/XP

TABLE 12.10: Possible Values for the Flags or OpenFlags Properties

Constant Name	Description
cdlOFNAllowMultiselect	Specifies that the File Name list box allows multiple selections. If you include this flag, use the FileList property to investigate the array of selected filenames (see Table 12.9).
cdlOFNCreatePrompt	If the user selects a file that doesn't exist, this flag causes the dialog box to prompt for permission to create the file. It doesn't actually create the file, however. If the user chooses to create the file, the dialog box closes and the FileName property contains the name of the selected file. Without this flag set, specifying a nonexistent file requires no intervention from the user. If you use this flag with the cdlOFNAllowMultiselect flag, only one nonexistent file is allowed.
cdlOFNEnableHook	If you include this flag, Windows will call the function specified in the CallBack property as it processes the dialog box. In Windows 98, Windows 2000, or Windows XP, setting this property causes the dialog box to not be sizable, unless you also set the cldOFNEnableSizing flag.

*Will require extra Windows API coding to fully support, so we recommend that you know what you're doing when using these flags.

TABLE 12.10:   Possible Values for the Flags or OpenFlags Properties *(continued)*

Constant Name	Description
cdEnableSizing	(Windows 98/2000/XP only) The ability to resize the dialog box is the default behavior, and Windows remembers the last position/size of the dialog box between uses. Generally, you won't need this flag, but if you also specify the cdlOFNEnableHook flag, Windows thinks you're providing your own form template for the dialog and disables sizing. Using this class, you cannot supply your own template, so if you specify the cdlOFNEnableHook flag, you'll also want to include this flag. This flag is ignored (and you cannot resize the dialog box) under Windows 95 and Windows NT.
cdlOFNExplorer	Causes the dialog box to use the newer "explorer-style" interface. The CommonDlg class always adds this flag to the value you specify for the Flags or OpenFlags property. If you want to alter this behavior, you'll need to modify the code in the CommonDlg class.

cdlOFNExtensionDifferent	On return from the dialog box, indicates that the user chose a file with an extension different from that in the DefaultExt property. If you haven't specified a value for DefaultExt, this flag will never be set. Use the And operator, like this, to check for this flag:
	`If cdl.OpenFlags And _`
	`  cdlOFNExtensionDifferent <> 0 Then`
	`    ' You know that you selected a`
	`    ' file whose extension is different`
	`    ' than that specified in the`
	`    ' DefaultExt property.`
	`End If`

cdlOFNFileMustExist	Specifies that the user can only enter names of existing files in the File Name entry field. If the user enters an invalid name, the dialog box displays a warning in a message box. If you specify this flag, the common dialog works as if you'd also specified the cdlOFNPathMustExist flag.
cdlOFNHelpButton	Displays a Help button on the dialog box. Although it's possible to react to the user clicking this button, it requires subclassing a form and reacting to Windows registered messages to make it work. Doing this is beyond the scope of this book, and this constant is only supplied for compatibility with the ActiveX control.*
cdlOFNHideReadOnly	If selected, this flag hides the Read Only check box on the dialog box.
cdlOFNLongNames	For old-style dialog boxes (see cdlOFNExplorer), causes the dialog to use long filenames. Has no effect in the CommonDlg class and is included for compatibility only.

*Will require extra Windows API coding to fully support, so we recommend that you know what you're doing when using these flags.

TABLE 12.10: Possible Values for the Flags or OpenFlags Properties *(continued)*

Constant Name	Description
cdlOFNNoChangeDir	If specified, Windows restores the directory to its original value if the user changed the directory while searching for a file.
cdlOFNNoDereferenceLinks	Causes the dialog box to return the path and filename of the selected shortcut (.LNK) file. If not specified, the dialog box returns the path and filename of the file referenced by the selected shortcut.
cdlOFNNoLongNames	If you're using the old-style dialog box, causes the dialog to display all filenames using 8.3 format. Has no effect in the CommonDlg class and is included for compatibility only.
cdlOFNNoNetworkButton	If you're using the old-style dialog box (see the cdlOFNExplorer flag), setting this flag removes the Network button from the dialog box. Has no effect in the CommonDlg class and is included for compatibility only.
cdlOFNNoReadOnlyReturn	On return from the dialog box, if this flag is set, the returned file does not have the Read Only check box checked and is not in a write-protected folder. Use the And operator (see the example shown in the cdlOFNExtensionDifferent flag) to find out if this flag has been set.
cdlOFNNoValidate	Specifies that the dialog box allows invalid characters in the filename. Generally, it's not a good idea to use this flag setting.*
cdlOFNOverwritePrompt	Causes the Save As dialog box to generate a message box if the selected file already exists. The developer can decide whether to allow the selection of this file.
cdlOFNPathMustExist	Specifies that the user can only select valid paths and filenames. If selected, this flag causes the dialog box to display a message box if the entered filename and path are invalid.
cdlOFNReadOnly	Causes the Read Only check box to be checked when the dialog box opens. After the dialog box has been dismissed, indicates whether the check box was checked at the time the user closed the dialog box. Use the And operator (see the example shown in the cdlOFNExtensionDifferent flag) to find out if this flag has been set.
cdlOFNShareAware	Specifies that if the user specifies a file that's in use, the error is ignored and the dialog box returns the selected name anyway.*

*Will require extra Windows API coding to fully support, so we recommend that you know what you're doing when using these flags.

You needn't set any of the CommonDlg properties if you're happy with the default behavior. When you're ready to select a file for opening or saving, call the appropriate method of the CommonDlg object (either ShowOpen or ShowSave).

That is, if you simply write code like this, you'll see the name of the file you select from the dialog box:

```
Dim cdl As CommonDlg
Set cdl = New CommonDlg
cdl.ShowOpen
MsgBox cdl.FileName
```

On the other hand, if you want to control which files are offered to the user, which folder the dialog starts in, whether the Read Only check box is displayed, or any other specific attributes of the dialog box, you'll want to investigate the many properties and flags shown in Tables 12.9 and 12.10. To demonstrate the use of many of the properties of the CommonDlg class, Listing 12.43 shows a test procedure from basTestCommonDlg.

Listing 12.43: Testing the CommDlg class

```
Sub dhTestFileOpen()

    Dim cdl As CommonDlg
    Set cdl = New CommonDlg

    cdl.hWndOwner = GetActiveWindow()
    cdl.CancelError = True

    On Error GoTo HandleErrors

    ' Set three pairs of values for the Filter.
    cdl.Filter = _
     "Text files (*.txt)|" & _
     "*.txt|" & _
     "Database files (*.mdb, *.mde, *.mda)|" & _
     "*.mdb;*.mde;*.mda|" & _
     "All files (*.*)|" & _
     "*.*"

    ' Select filter 2 (Database files) when
    ' the dialog opens.
    cdl.FilterIndex = 2

    ' Indicate that you want to use a callback function,
    ' change back to the original directory when
    ' you're done, and require that the selected
```

```
          ' file actually exists.
          cdl.OpenFlags = cdlOFNEnableHook Or _
           cdlOFNNoChangeDir Or cdlOFNFileMustExist

          ' Select the callback function.
          cdl.CallBack = dhFnPtrToLong(AddressOf GFNCallback)

          ' Set up miscellaneous properties.
          cdl.InitDir = "C:\"
          cdl.FileName = "autoexec.bat"
          cdl.DefaultExt = "bat"

          ' Open the file open dialog box,
          ' and wait for it to be dismissed.
          cdl.ShowOpen

          ' Retrieve the selected file name
          Debug.Print cdl.FileName

          ' Check the OpenFlags (or Flags) property to
          ' see if the selected extension is different than
          ' the default extension.
          If (cdl.OpenFlags And _
           cdlOFNExtensionDifferent) <> 0 Then
              MsgBox "You chose a different extension!"
          End If

      ExitHere:
          Set cdl = Nothing
          Exit Sub

      HandleErrors:
          Select Case Err.Number
              Case cdlCancel
                  ' Cancelled!
                  Resume ExitHere
              Case Else
                  MsgBox "Error: " & Err.Description & _
                   "(" & Err.Number & ")"
          End Select
          Resume ExitHere
      End Sub
```

This procedure takes the following actions:

- Declares and instantiates the CommonDlg object:

```
Dim cdl As CommonDlg
Set cdl = New CommonDlg
```

- Sets the owner of the dialog to be the current form:

```
cdl.hwndOwner = GetActiveWindow()
```

NOTE   So that this example would work from whatever client you happen to run it in, we've used the GetActiveWindow API function. In practice you'll want to assign the hWnd of one of your application's windows. For example, you could use the hWnd property of a VB form.

- Sets up the filter text, and selects a particular filter to be displayed when the dialog appears:

```
' Set three pairs of values for the Filter.
cdl.Filter = _
 "Text files (*.txt)|" & _
 "*.txt|" & _
 "Database files (*.mdb, *.mde, *.mda)|" & _
 "*.mdb;*.mde;*.mda|" & _
 "All files (*.*)|" & _
 "*.*"

' Select filter 2 (Database files) when
' the dialog opens.
cdl.FilterIndex = 2
```

- Sets the OpenFlags property, indicating how you want the dialog box to behave:

```
cdl.OpenFlags = cdlOFNEnableHook Or _
  cdlOFNNoChangeDir Or cdlOFNFileMustExist
```

- Sets up the callback function, pointing to our sample callback function (stored in basCommonDlg). This callback function must be a public function in a standard module and must meet the requirements described in the previous section, "Using a Callback Function." Note that you must call the dhFnPtr-ToLong function in order to store the address of the procedure into a variable:

```
cdl.CallBack = dhFnPtrToLong(AddressOf GFNCallback)
```

- Sets up other miscellaneous properties:

```
cdl.InitDir = "C:\"
cdl.FileName = "autoexec.bat"
cdl.DefaultExt = "bat"
```

- Calls the ShowOpen method of the object. This causes your code to halt, waiting for the dialog box to be dismissed:

```
cdl.ShowOpen
```

- After the dialog has been dismissed, retrieves the selected filename:

```
txtFileOpen = cdl.FileName
```

- Checks to see if the selected file had a different extension from that provided in the DefaultExt property. If so, handles that situation:

```
If (cdl.OpenFlags And _
  cdlOFNExtensionDifferent) <> 0 Then
    MsgBox "You chose a different extension!"
End If
```

You can see the entire procedure by looking at the sample code.

To use this functionality in your own applications, make sure you've imported the CommonDlg class module. If you want to use callbacks, you'll also want to import basTestCommonDlg.

NOTE   For information on using the CancelError property to trap when a user cancels the dialog box, see the upcoming section, "Checking for Cancellation."

The only real difference between the File Open and File Save dialog boxes is the interpretation of some of the flag values shown in Table 12.10. Otherwise, the usage and behavior of the common dialog is the same whether you use the Show-Open or ShowSave methods. In either case, use the OpenFlags property to specify the flags you'd like to apply.

TIP   If you'd rather have this all wrapped up for you, check out the dhFileDialog procedure in basCommonDialog. This procedure allows you to pass in parameters indicating the behavior you'd like, and the procedure does all the work of instantiating the object for you. It then returns the filename that was selected.

Changes for Windows 2000 and Windows XP

Common dialog functionality remained relatively unchanged from Windows 95 to Windows NT 4 and Windows 98. Beginning with Windows 2000 and continuing with Windows XP, Microsoft modified the File Open and File Save dialogs to look and work more like those in Office 2000 (and now Office XP). That is, they now have the familiar Outlook-like *places bar* on the left-hand side (see Figure 12.12).

FIGURE 12.12
New Windows 2000/XP
common-file open dialog

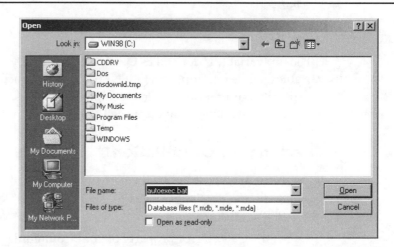

Unfortunately, to make sure you enable the new functionality you must use an extended version of the OPENFILENAME structure that includes four more member variables. If you try to use the older version of this user-defined type *and* you specify a callback function, you'll get the old-style dialog like the one shown in Figure 12.13.

FIGURE 12.13
Old-style open file
dialog that appears if
you don't use the right
OPENFILENAME structure

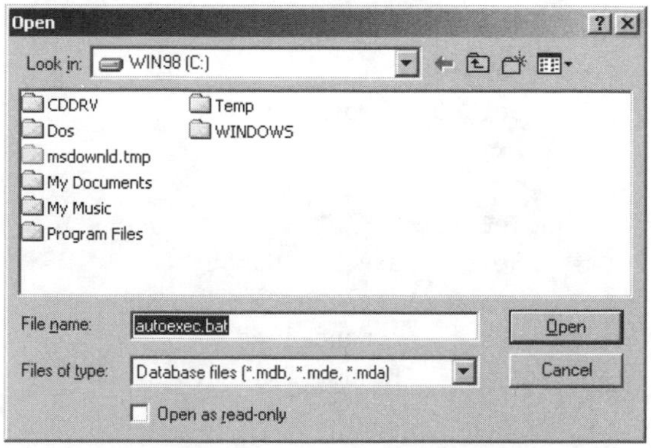

The CommonDlg class accounts for this automatically by checking for the Windows version in the Class_Initialize procedure. If you're running Windows 2000 or Windows XP it sets a flag that's used later on in the SetOpenProperties procedure:

```
' If we're not running Windows 2000/XP set structure
' size equal to the older UDT
If mblnIsWin2000 Then
    .lStructSize = Len(ofn)
Else
    .lStructSize = Len(ofnTmp)
End If
```

The ofn variable is defined as OPENFILENAMEEX, which includes the extra variables, while ofnTmp is an OPENFILENAME structure. By setting the lStructSize member appropriately, GetOpenFileName works correctly. For more information on system information as well as this technique, see Chapter 9.

Checking for Cancellation

If you want to know whether the user pressed the Cancel button (as opposed to clicking OK with no file selected), you'll need to add code to handle this. Specifically, follow these steps:

1. Set the CancelError property of your CommonDlg object to True.

2. Add an error handler to your procedure, and specifically check for the error cdlCancel (32755). This is the error the CommonDlg class will raise if the user clicks the Cancel button (or presses Escape) while the dialog is displayed.

In your error handler, you may decide to do something if the user pressed Cancel. Most of the time, however, you'll simply go on with your application without taking any action. For example, the following code, excerpted from the dhTestFileOpen procedure, reacts to the user pressing Cancel by doing nothing at all:

```
ExitHere:
    Set cdl = Nothing
    Exit Sub

HandleErrors:
    Select Case Err.Number
        Case cdlCancel
            ' Cancelled!
            Resume ExitHere
```

```
        Case Else
            MsgBox "Error: " & Err.Description & _
            "(" & Err.Number & ")"
    End Select
    Resume ExitHere
End Sub
```

WARNING   Make sure you check the VBA Error Trapping property (the General tab on the Tools ➤ Options dialog) when running in a VBA host. If it's set to Break in Class Module, none of these classes will work correctly. If this setting is checked, that means that even if you have error handling in a class module, the code will drop into break mode if a runtime error occurs. Although this setting may make sense when you're working in Visual Basic, which creates standalone executables, it never makes sense when you distribute VBA applications. You must make sure to set this option to Break on Unhandled Errors, or you won't be able to make use of the CancelError property of this class. To try this out, open a module, make sure the setting is set to Break in Class Module, and then try the code in dhTestFileOpen, pressing the Cancel button. Although you wouldn't expect it, you'll hit a breakpoint in the error handler. Not cool. If you use error handling, make sure you verify this option setting for each and every project you distribute.

Modifying the Look of the File Open or Save Common Dialog Box

Although it's not simple, you can modify the text displayed in any command button or label on the common dialog boxes, and you can control the visibility of any item on the form, as well. To accomplish these goals, you'll need to modify code in the callback function used by the dialog. To modify the dialog box's layout, you must use the Windows API Send Message function to send the dialog box messages indicating that you want to change its appearance. Windows provides a long integer that uniquely identifies each of the controls on the form, and you can find an enumeration of those values in the dhFileOpenSaveControls enum in the CommonDlg class. To change the text of a control, call the SendMessageText variation on the SendMessage API (see the code in basCommonDlg), specifying the window handle for the dialog box, the CDM_SETCONTROLTEXT message, the identifier of the control you want to change, and the new text. The following example shows how you might do this:

```
Call SendMessageText(hWndParent, CDM_SETCONTROLTEXT, _
    fosOKButton, "&Select")
```

> To change the visibility of a control on the dialog box, call the SendMessageLong variation on the SendMessage API, passing the window handle, the CDM_HIDECONTROL message, the identifier of the control, and 0, like this:
>
> ```
> Call SendMessageLong(hWndParent, CDM_HIDECONTROL, _
>     fosFilterListLabel, 0)
> ```
>
> (Note that there's no message available to redisplay a hidden control.) Remove the conditional compilation statements in the GFNCallBack procedure (in basTestCommonDlg) to see this code working. When you make this change and run the dhTestFileOpen procedure, you'll see that the label for the Open button is now Select, and the "Files of Type" label is invisible.

Summary

This chapter has presented a lot of information regarding disk and file manipulation using VBA. Specifically, we covered the following topics:

- How to use VBA file and directory information functions such as Dir, GetAttr, FileLen, and FileDateTime

- How to copy, move, create, and delete files and directories

- How to create and modify files using VBA file I/O functions

- How to search for files on your hard disk

- How to manipulate path names and temporary files

- Using Windows API functions to retrieve file and disk information such as the volume label, disk types, and free space

- How to set and retrieve file dates and times

- How to force Windows to inform you when the contents of a directory have changed

- Using a VBA class module–based system for easing file and directory management

In addition to supplying you with "out of the box" functions you can use in your applications, we've tried to help you understand how you can utilize both VBA and Windows API functions to get the most out of the file system.

chapter 16

Adding Multimedia to Your Applications

- Understanding Windows multimedia services

- Playing WAV files

- Controlling your CD player

- Exploring digital video with AVI files

To help round out this book on Visual Basic language development, we decided to include a chapter on multimedia. Why, you might ask? After all, it's such an immense subject that entire books have been written about it. We couldn't possibly explain everything you need to know to write complete multimedia titles. Fortunately, that's not what we wanted to do. Our intent was to provide you with a few simple tricks you can use to enhance your application. Even the most serious developers have, from time to time, wanted to play sound files or video clips in their applications. In this chapter, you'll learn a few easy techniques to make this happen. The chapter begins with a discussion of the multimedia capabilities of Windows. Then we'll take a look at individual topics that range from playing sound files to running video clips in a window. By the end of this chapter, you should have a basic understanding of how Windows handles multimedia, as well as a grab bag of useful VBA functions to add to your applications.

Table 13.1 lists the sample files included on the CD-ROM for this chapter.

T A B L E 1 3 . 1 : Sample Files

Filename	Description
MMEDIA.XLS	Excel file with sample functions
MMEDIA.MDB	Access 2000 database with sample functions
MMEDIA.VBP	Visual Basic project containing the sample code
MAIN.FRM	Start-up form for the Visual Basic project
FRMVIDEO.FRM	VBA user form for AVI example
FRMVIDEO.FRX	Binary components of the VBA user form
CLASSEX.BAS	Code for class modules
CSTRING.BAS	Code for MCI command string example
MCIBASE.BAS	MCI function, type, and constant declarations
REGISTRY.BAS	Registry functions
SIMPLE.BAS	Simple multimedia examples
CDPLAY.CLS	CDPlayer class module
VIDPLAY.CLS	VideoPlayer class module
WAVEPLAY.CLS	WavePlayer class module

TABLE 13.1: Sample Files *(continued)*

Filename	Description
GO.WAV	Sample WAV file
NORTH.WAV	Sample WAV file
EAST.WAV	Sample WAV file
SOUTH.WAV	Sample WAV file
WEST.WAV	Sample WAV file
WAVE.DLL	Resource-only DLL containing embedded WAV files
WAVE.RC	Resource script for WAVE.DLL
WAVE.RES	Compiled resource file
WAVE.MAK	Make file for WAVE.DLL

NOTE   To test the sample code in this chapter, you will need a multimedia-capable computer, including a CD player and a sound card.

An Introduction to Windows Multimedia

Before exploring the various techniques for manipulating multimedia elements, let's take a look at the foundation on which they are based: the Windows multimedia subsystems. While the examples in this chapter are just the tip of the iceberg as far as multimedia is concerned, this section gives you an overview of the many multimedia capabilities Windows offers.

Multimedia Services and MCI

Microsoft first introduced real multimedia support as an add-on to Windows 3.*x*, called the Multimedia Extensions. These were additional DLLs that implemented functions for playing digital sound and video, as well as MIDI (Musical Instrument Digital Interface) files. With the advent of Windows 95, Microsoft integrated these functions directly into the operating system. Even though they still exist as separate DLLs apart from the traditional Windows API triad of User, Kernel, and

GDI, you can now be assured that the functions are available on any machine running Windows 95, Windows 98, Windows NT 4, or Windows 2000. (However, this does not mean that you can count on the presence of multimedia hardware necessary to make them work!)

The multimedia support in the current versions of Windows has matured into a robust environment with support for numerous and varied hardware devices, such as digital audio and laser disc players, audio compact discs, overlay video (a.k.a. TV-in-a-window), and animation. Much of this is coordinated through the Media Control Interface (MCI). MCI defines a function interface to control different multimedia devices. Even though the features of the devices themselves vary greatly, they all share a more or less common set of abilities. For example, all must open some sort of multimedia data (referred to as a *media object* in this chapter), be it a sound file or an audio compact disc track. All have the ability to play the data, as well as manipulate the current position (rewind, fast forward, and so on). This section reviews the capabilities of several multimedia devices. Later sections in this chapter demonstrate how to control them using MCI commands.

NOTE   MCI is considered a *high-level* multimedia interface because the devices themselves handle most of the work of manipulating media objects. Windows also has a host of *low-level* multimedia functions that give you a fine degree of control over multimedia data. Since it's unlikely that you'll choose Visual Basic to build an application such as, say, a speech recognition system, we decided to stick with the high-level functions in this chapter.

Waveform Audio

Waveform audio is the correct term for the ever-popular WAV file format so familiar to Windows users. You create waveform audio using a sound card capable of taking analog input from a microphone and converting it to a digital signal. Waveform audio is the most common way of providing sound effects for applications because of its ability to duplicate sounds exactly, with a high degree of clarity. You can affect the level of quality by controlling the following input parameters:

Sample rate   The number of digital "snapshots" taken each second (often denoted by the term *hertz,* abbreviated Hz). The more samples you take, the better the quality. You can choose one of three distinct values: 11025 Hz (radio or voice quality), 22050 Hz (medium quality), or 44100 Hz (CD quality).

Bits per sample   Determines how accurate each sample is. The more data per sample you store, the better the quality. You can store either 8 or 16 bits per sample.

Channels   Refers to whether you record in stereophonic (2 channels) or monophonic (1 channel).

The downside to waveform audio is the amount of storage space required for sound data. For example, 60 seconds of CD-quality, 16-bit stereo sound requires 10,584,000 bytes of storage! (That's 60 x 44100 x (16 / 8) x 2.) Fortunately, you rarely need this level of clarity. Due to the mediocre quality of many sound cards, plus the inefficiency of the human ear, 11025 Hz, 8-bit monophonic sounds are usually adequate for sound effects and voice prompts.

Compact Disc Audio

If you really need CD-quality audio, you should use CD audio tracks. MCI offers simple functions for playing CD audio, and the storage requirements are zero because the media are on a compact disc. However, the one problem with CD audio is the difficulty of producing it. Unless you purchase the right to use existing content, you'll have to create your own. This is a time-consuming process requiring considerable artistic talent.

MIDI Audio

MIDI audio offers a compromise between waveform audio and CD audio. MIDI (which stands for Musical Instrument Digital Interface) is the format understood by electronic synthesizers. Most sound cards include an FM synthesizer chip capable of producing music from MIDI commands. Unlike waveform audio, which stores an exact replica of recorded sound, MIDI audio is stored as "songs" made up of information regarding musical instruments, notes, pitch, duration, and so on. For this reason, the storage requirements are quite low. For example, Windows 98 and Windows 2000 ship with a MIDI-encoded file named CANYON .MID. Despite the fact that the song is over two minutes long, the song file is only about 21K in size.

However, there are three drawbacks to MIDI files. First, since the songs don't store actual sounds but instead define musical instruments, it's up to the sound card to supply the actual sound, so the output will vary from one sound card to the next. The second problem is that unless you have a specially designed sound card, the CPU must process the musical information, adding to the overall system load. Third, sound cards that use FM synthesizers to produce the output can only *approximate* the true sound of an instrument by modulating the frequency of a carrier wave. Newer sound cards that store digital samples of actual instruments (so-called *wave table* sound cards) reproduce the intended music much more accurately, but they are still more expensive and less prevalent than FM synthesizer-based cards. For these reasons, MIDI songs are normally used as background music for games where instrumental fidelity is not essential.

Digital Video

One of the best features of Windows is its ability to process digital video. You probably know this feature better as AVI files. Microsoft shipped software called Video for Windows that allowed you to view AVI files under Windows 3.*x*. In fact, Video for Windows defined the AVI file format, which is the most popular format around today. Starting with Windows 95 and NT 4, digital video became an integral part of the multimedia subsystem.

NOTE   Other digital video formats include Apple QuickTime, MPEG, and DVI (Digital Video Interactive).

Digital video files are created using special hardware that converts the analog signal from a television tuner or VCR into digital images. The quality of the image can vary greatly depending on the size of the image, the speed of playback (measured in frames per second), and the compression algorithms used. For example, compression is used so that not every pixel an image comprises needs to be updated if it doesn't change from frame to frame. A variety of compression algorithms offer different levels of speed and size reduction.

In addition to using analog-to-digital converter hardware, you can create AVI files with software products such as Lotus ScreenCam. These products produce computer-generated frames based on screen captures or other means and are particularly useful for creating demos or instructional videos for software programs.

Like digital audio, digital video suffers the problem of media size. Even a short video clip recorded at small frame size can take up 500K or more of disk space. To further complicate matters, to view an AVI file, you must have the same *codec* (*co*mpression/*dec*ompression software) used to create the file on your computer. While most computers have numerous codecs installed, which allow them to play back most videos, there is a chance for incompatibility. You can see which ones you have using the Control Panel Multimedia applet under Windows 95, Windows 98, or Windows NT 4; or under Windows 2000 by using the Computer Management applet, shown in Figure 13.1.

FIGURE 13.1
Viewing audio and video codecs in the Windows 2000 Computer Management applet

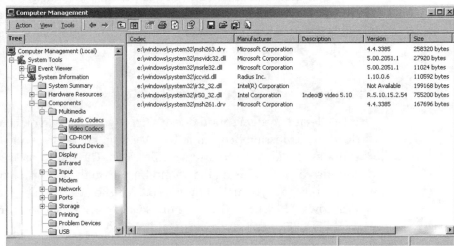

NOTE

You can also access codec information through the Control Panel under Windows 2000, but it's not easy. First open the Sound and Multimedia applet and click the Hardware tab in the dialog. Locate the Video Codecs entry in the list of devices and double-click it. This opens the Device Property dialog. From here, click the Properties tab. At this point, you can double-click *again* to get more information on a particular codec, but what's the point? Just use the new Windows 2000 Computer Management applet, which lists all the information in one place. (If the Start Menu icon of the applet is not listed after you install Windows 2000, you can display it via the Start Menu Properties dialog.)

One-Step Multimedia

Unless you're writing a complete multimedia title, your multimedia needs are probably quite simple. For example, you may just want to generate a simple sound or play a certain WAV file. This section explains how to do this using single VBA statements.

Beeping Away

If all you want to do is generate a simple, obvious noise, nothing beats the VBA Beep statement. This single statement generates a sound regardless of the presence of multimedia hardware. If no hardware is installed, the result is just a "beep" from the computer's speaker. On the other hand, if a sound card is installed, VBA plays the default system sound. (For more information on system sounds, see the section "Playing System Event Sounds" later in this chapter.)

MessageBeep: One Step Better

If the default system sound doesn't tickle your fancy, you can resort to the Windows API MessageBeep function. MessageBeep plays one of five predefined sounds associated with a Message Box icon. These sounds are based on the system sounds you define using the Sounds applet in the Control Panel. You can use the same constants you use with the VBA MsgBox function or those defined by the Windows API. Table 13.2 lists both sets of constants. (You can also pass the value &HFFFFFFFF to produce the default sound.)

TABLE 13.2: VBA and Windows API Constants for Producing System Sounds

Value	VBA Constant	Windows API Constant
0	none	MB_OK
16	vbCritical	MB_ICONHAND or MB_ICONSTOP
32	vbQuestion	MB_ICONQUESTION
48	vbExclamation	MB_ICONEXCLAMATION
64	vbInformation	MB_ICONASTERISK or MB_ICONINFORMATION

MessageBeep is a simple function that accepts one of the constants listed in Table 13.2 and produces that sound. If no sound card is installed, the function simply produces a beep from the computer speaker.

If your development tool doesn't already play a system sound when it displays a message box, you can use the MessageBeep and MsgBox functions together to do this. The dhMsgBeep function, shown in Listing 13.1, provides an example.

Listing 13.1: Make a Message Box Make Noise

```
Function dhMsgBeep(strMsg As String, _
  Optional lngType As Long = 0, _
  Optional strCaption As String = "") As Long

  Dim lngSound As Long

  ' Get sound type
  lngSound = lngType And &HF0

  ' Play sound
  Call MessageBeep(lngSound)

  ' Show message box
  If strCaption = "" Then
    dhMsgBeep = MsgBox(strMsg, lngType)
  Else
    dhMsgBeep = MsgBox(strMsg, lngType, strCaption)
  End If
End Function
```

Playing Waveform Audio with PlaySound

For the ultimate in one-step multimedia, you can use the PlaySound API function. This simple function lets you play any arbitrary waveform audio file, including system sounds and waveform data contained in executable files. The declaration of the PlaySound function is as follows:

```
Declare Function PlaySound Lib "winmm.dll" _
  Alias "PlaySoundA" (ByVal lpszSoundName As String, _
  ByVal hMod As Long, ByVal uFlags As Long) As Long
```

As you can see, PlaySound accepts only three arguments: the name of a sound, the handle to a loaded module (more on that in a moment), and a set of flags. The function is nonetheless highly versatile. Table 13.3 lists the flags you can pass to the function.

TABLE 13.3: PlaySound Flag Constants

PlaySound Flag	Description
SND_SYNC	Plays the sound synchronously (the default).
SND_ASYNC	Plays the sound asynchronously.
SND_NODEFAULT	If the specified sound is invalid, PlaySound does not play the default sound.
SND_LOOP	Loops the sound until the next call to PlaySound.
SND_NOSTOP	Does not stop the sound currently playing.
SND_NOWAIT	Doesn't wait if the sound driver is busy.
SND_MEMORY	The lpszSoundName argument is a pointer to a sound in memory.
SND_ALIAS	Sound is a system sound name.
SND_ALIAS_ID	Sound is a system sound identifier.
SND_FILENAME	Sound is a filename.
SND_RESOURCE	Sound is a resource name.

Regardless of the other flags you choose to pass to the function, you should pass one of the following: SND_FILENAME, SND_ALIAS, or SND_MEMORY. These flags tell PlaySound how to interpret the lpszSoundName argument—as a filename, as a system event name, or as a memory address. The following sections discuss each of these methods.

> **NOTE** If you don't pass one of these flags, PlaySound tries to determine the meaning of the lpszSoundName argument on its own. However, it's usually better to do this yourself.

> **NOTE** The hMod argument is used only to play embedded resources with the SND_MEMORY flag; otherwise, it must be set to 0.

Playing WAV Files

The most obvious use for PlaySound is to play arbitrary WAV files. You pass the path to the wave file and a set of flags. The most common flags, along with SND_FILENAME, are SND_SYNC and SND_ASYNC. Passing the SND_SYNC flag forces PlaySound to play the entire file before returning control to your application. Conversely, the SND_ASYNC flag tells PlaySound to cue the sound, begin playback, and return immediately. For example, suppose you wanted to play a WAV file containing instructions on how to use your application while a user was using it. You could use a statement like this:

```
Call PlaySound("C:\MYAPP\SOUNDS\HOWTO.WAV", 0&, _
  SND_ANSYC Or SND_FILENAME)
```

This would play the sound asynchronously, allowing the user to interact with your application while the sound was playing.

> **NOTE**
> If you don't specify a path, PlaySound will look for the file using the same search rules followed by the SearchPath function described in Chapter 12.

If PlaySound cannot play the requested sound, perhaps because the filename you passed does not exist, it plays the default Windows sound (the familiar electronic "ding"). If you don't want to hear this sound, pass the SND_NODEFAULT flag. The function's return value will tell you whether the sound was played successfully, as the following code illustrates:

```
If Not CBool(PlaySound("MYSOUND.WAV", 0&, SND_NODEFAULT)) Then
  ' Something went wrong!
End If
```

> **NOTE**
> If you don't include the SND_NODEFAULT flag and PlaySound can't play the requested sound, it plays the default sound *and* returns a value of 1, indicating success!

If you want to repeat a sound continuously, pass the SND_LOOP flag. PlaySound will continue to call the sound over and over until you call the function again. You can call it with another sound or an empty string to stop the current sound from looping. For instance, suppose you wanted to create the illusion of a barking dog for a theft-deterrent system. You might use code like this:

```
' Make the dog bark
Call PlaySound("BARK.WAV", 0&, SND_FILENAME Or SND_LOOP)

' Okay, that's enough!
Call PlaySound("", 0&, SND_NODEFAULT)
```

Playing System Event Sounds

The PlaySound function also provides an easy way to play Windows system event sounds. The discussion of the MessageBeep function earlier in this chapter explained a few of the system sounds. Other system sounds include system start and stop, window minimize and maximize, and the infamous critical stop. (That's the event associated with an IPF.) You can change the sounds associated with various events using the Sounds applet in the Control Panel, which is shown in Figure 13.2.

FIGURE 13.2
You can change system sounds using the Sounds applet in the Control Panel

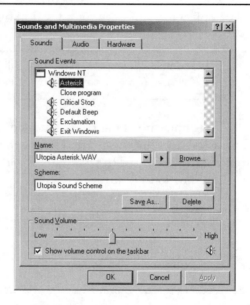

Playing Stock System Sounds

To play a system sound using PlaySound, you must specify its name along with the SND_ALIAS flag. For example:

```
Call PlaySound("AppGPFault", 0&, SND_ALIAS Or SND_NODEFAULT)
```

Table 13.4 lists the system sounds recognized by the PlaySound function, as well as the descriptions shown in the Sounds applet. Note that the two are different. The system sound names are fixed and are mapped to the descriptive text shown in the Sounds applet through the use of registry settings. You can find the mappings in the HKEY_CURRENT_USER\AppEvents\EventLabels key.

TABLE 13.4:   System Sounds You Can Play Using PlaySound

System Sound Name	Default Description in Control Panel
.Default	Default sound
AppGPFault	Program error
Close	Close program
EmptyRecycleBin	Empty Recycle Bin
MailBeep	New mail notification
Maximize	Maximize
MenuCommand	Menu command
MenuPopup	Menu popup
Minimize	Minimize
Open	Open program
RestoreDown	Restore down
RestoreUp	Restore up
SystemAsterisk	Asterisk
SystemExclamation	Exclamation
SystemExit	Exit Windows
SystemHand	Critical Stop
SystemQuestion	Question
SystemStart	Start Windows

Playing Application Event Sounds

In addition to the system sounds listed in Table 13.4, other applications may add event sounds that can also be customized using the Sounds applet. Unfortunately, you can't play these sounds directly using PlaySound and the SND_ALIAS flag. To play application-specific sounds, you must first look in the Registry to locate the sound entry, read the name of the WAV file, and then call PlaySound.

All event sounds, including the system sounds, are stored in the HKEY_CURRENT_USER\AppEvents\Schemes\Apps key. Windows system sounds are stored in a subkey called .Default (note the leading period). Other applications may add additional subkeys with their own event sounds. Beneath every subkey there are other subkeys for each event, and beneath those are subkeys representing the default sound associated with the event, the sound that is currently assigned, and the sounds associated with any sound schemes you may have installed. Figure 13.3 shows the Registry Editor open to a portion of this wild Registry branch.

FIGURE 13.3
Registry entries for
event sounds

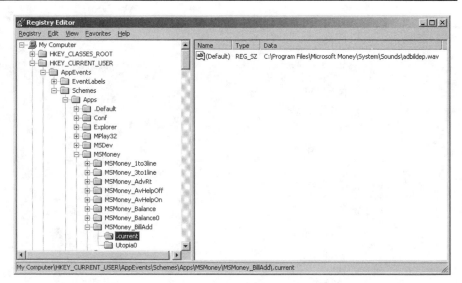

To make retrieving the name of the sound file associated with an application event easier, we created a function called dhGetEventSound. This function uses the Registry functions explained in Chapter 10 to retrieve the sound associated with any event, be it system or application specific. Listing 13.2 shows the dhGetEventSound function.

NOTE For those of you keeping score at home, the dhGetEventSound function was adapted from the dhReadWallpaper procedure described in the section "Working with Registry Values" in Chapter 10.

Listing 13.2: Retrieve Any Event Sound from the Registry

```
Function dhGetEventSound( _
 Optional strApp As String = ".Default", _
 Optional strEvent As String = ".Default", _
 Optional strScheme As String = ".Current") As String

   Dim hKeySound As Long
   Dim strKeySound As String
   Dim lngResult As Long
   Dim strBuffer As String
   Dim cb As Long

   ' Build the key name
   strKeySound = "AppEvents\Schemes\Apps\" & _
    strApp & "\" & strEvent & "\" & strScheme

   ' Open the sound key
   lngResult = RegOpenKeyEx(dhcHKeyCurrentUser, _
    strKeySound, 0&, dhcKeyAllAccess, hKeySound)

   ' Make sure the call succeeded
   If lngResult = dhcSuccess Then

      ' Create the buffer
      strBuffer = Space(255)
      cb = Len(strBuffer)

      ' Read the default value
      lngResult = RegQueryValueEx(hKeySound, "", _
       0&, dhcRegSz, ByVal strBuffer, cb)

      ' Check return value
      If lngResult = dhcSuccess Then

         ' Return the value
         dhGetEventSound = Left(strBuffer, cb)
      End If

      ' Close the sound key
      lngResult = RegCloseKey(hKeySound)
   End If
End Function
```

As you can see from the function declaration, dhGetEventSound accepts three optional arguments representing the application name, event name, and sound scheme. We've supplied default values that, if you call the function with no arguments, cause dhGetEventSound to return the default system sound. You can override these defaults with settings of your own. For example, the following code plays the WAV file associated with starting Microsoft Money 2000. (Naturally, you must have installed Money for this to work since its installation program copies the WAV files to your system and sets up the right Registry entries.)

```
Dim strFile As String

' Get the name of the WAV file
strFile = dhGetEventSound("MSMoney", "MSMoney_Intro")

' Play the WAV file if successful
If strFile <> "" Then
  Call PlaySound(strFile, 0&, SND_FILENAME Or SND_NODEFAULT)
End If
```

TIP   Unless you want to play a sound associated with a sound scheme other than the current one, leave the third argument to dhGetEventSound blank.

Playing Embedded Sounds

The last use for PlaySound is to play sounds that are embedded within an EXE or DLL file. Executable files (we'll consider DLLs executable files for the purpose of this discussion) usually contain numerous embedded objects known generically as *resources*. Common resources include icons, bitmaps, menus, string tables, and dialog box definitions. Application developers embed resources because doing so reduces the number of additional files that must be distributed with the application. Furthermore, it's difficult, although by no means impossible, to extract embedded resources from an executable. Therefore, embedding a resource is a convenient way to protect intellectual property.

Creating Embedded WAV Files

If you plan on using numerous WAV files in your application, you may want to consider embedding them in a DLL, even though it may not contain any program code. Developers commonly create *resource-only* DLLs for this purpose. Creating a resource-only DLL requires only two steps:

1. Compile individual WAV files (or other resources) into a resource file using a *resource compiler* such as RC.EXE, which ships with Microsoft Visual C++.

2. Link the resource file into a DLL using a linker such as LINK.EXE, which also comes with Microsoft Visual C++.

Accomplishing the first step requires that you create a resource script. A *resource script* tells the resource compiler what files to include and how to identify them in the resource file. Listing 13.3 shows the contents of WAVE.RC, a sample resource script we've provided for this chapter.

Listing 13.3: A Sample Resource Script

```
//////////////////////////////////////////////////////////
//
// Resource script for creating embedded WAV files
//
// Make sure each WAVE resource is assigned a unique number!
//
//////////////////////////////////////////////////////////

101 WAVE DISCARDABLE "GO.WAV"

201 WAVE DISCARDABLE "NORTH.WAV"
202 WAVE DISCARDABLE "EAST.WAV"
203 WAVE DISCARDABLE "SOUTH.WAV"
204 WAVE DISCARDABLE "WEST.WAV"

// End RC file
```

Each line in the script file (except those beginning with //, which are comments) identifies a resource. For each line you must include

- A unique number or name (without quotes) identifying the resource

- The type of resource (WAVE, in this case)

- The keyword DISCARDABLE (which tells Windows it can dynamically load and unload the resource)

- The path to the resource

NOTE   If the files are not located in the same directory as the RC file, you need to include the path. Furthermore, since RC.EXE conforms to the same rules as a C compiler, you must double all path separators (for example, C:\\WAVE\\GO.WAV).

You compile the resource script into a resource file by running RC.EXE from the command line. For example,

```
RC WAVE.RC
```

results in a resource file with the same name as the resource script and an .RES file extension.

At this point you need to link the resource file into a DLL. Since this is a resource-only DLL, which requires no other object files, you can use a command line like the following (assuming you're using Microsoft's LINK.EXE linker):

```
LINK /out:WAVE.DLL /dll /machine:i386 /noentry wave.res
```

Each part of the command line has a specific meaning:

- /out:*outputfile* defines the output file.

- /dll informs LINK.EXE to produce a DLL.

- /machine:*machinetype* defines the binary executable format.

- /noentry informs LINK.EXE that there is no entry point (that is, this is a resource-only DLL).

- The remaining entries are the input files separated by spaces.

TIP   You can also use a make file instead of specifying all the options on the command line. Use the syntax LINK @*makefile*, where *makefile* is the name of the make file. We've included a make file, WAVE.MAK, with the sample code.

Playing an Embedded WAV File

Once you've compiled a series of WAV files into a DLL, you can use PlaySound to play one. However, it's not quite that simple because you have to load the resource into memory first. That involves loading the DLL, finding the resource, loading the resource, and calling PlaySound with the SND_MEMORY flag. Don't despair, though; we've created a wrapper function, dhPlayResource, that takes care of all these tasks for you. It's shown in Listing 13.4.

TIP

If you're using Visual Basic as your development tool, you can use VB's LoadResource function to obtain a memory pointer to the resource in place of the library- and resource-loading code in Listing 13.4.

Listing 13.4: The dhPlayResource Function Plays an Embedded WAV File

```vb
Function dhPlayResource(strLibrary As String, _
 varResource As Variant, Optional lngFlags As Long = 0) _
 As Boolean

  Dim hMod As Long
  Dim hRes As Long
  Dim lngRes As Long
  Dim fOk As Boolean

  ' Load the library as a data file
  hMod = LoadLibraryEx(strLibrary, 0&, _
  LOAD_LIBRARY_AS_DATAFILE)
  If hMod <> 0 Then

    ' If the resource is a number add the "#",
    ' otherwise just use it
    If IsNumeric(varResource) Then
      varResource = "#" & varResource
    End If

    ' Find the WAVE resource in the library
    lngRes = FindResource(hMod, CStr(varResource), "WAVE")
    If lngRes <> 0 Then
      ' Load the resource
      hRes = LoadResource(hMod, lngRes)
      If hRes <> 0 Then
        ' Lock the resource and play it
        If CBool(LockResource(hRes)) Then
          dhPlayResource = CBool(PlayResSound( _
            hRes, 0&, SND_MEMORY Or lngFlags))
        End If
```

```
        ' Free the resource
        Call FreeResource(hRes)
      End If
    End If

    ' Free the library
    Call FreeLibrary(hMod)
  End If
End Function
```

Since a discussion of loading resources from an executable file goes beyond the scope of this book, you'll have to deduce how the function works on your own. (However, do notice that the call to PlaySound includes the SND_MEMORY flag.) You can try out the function by calling it with WAVE.DLL, the sample DLL provided with this chapter. It contains the five WAV files referenced in the WAVE.RC file. To play these sounds and hear one of the author's lovely voices, try executing the following code:

```
?dhPlayResource("WAVE.DLL", 101), dhPlayResource("WAVE.DLL", 201)
```

If the sounds don't play for you, it may be because the current directory is not set to the one containing the DLL. In this case, edit the filename to include the path where the DLL is located.

NOTE   Because you must supply a pointer to the resource in memory as a Long integer, we created a second declaration for PlaySound, called PlayResSound, which defines the first argument as Long.

TIP   If you're using Visual Basic *and* you have compiled WAVE resources into your executable file, you can use a much more convenient form of PlaySound. Simply pass the instance handle of your VB application as the second argument in addition to the resource name and the SND_RESOURCE flag—for example: PlaySound("WAVENAME", App.hInstance, SND_RESOURCE).

WARNING   Whatever you do, don't call the dhPlayResource function with the SND_ ASYNC flag! This will cause the library to be unloaded before the sound is finished playing, resulting in a very nasty IPF.

Understanding the Media Control Interface

The Media Control Interface component of Windows' multimedia services is an extremely powerful mechanism for controlling multimedia devices. Using just a few (three!) functions, it can play audio CDs, record digital audio, control VCRs. (You get the idea.) Furthermore, it offers two ways of controlling devices: a command string-based approach and a command message-based approach. This section looks at MCI in detail, including both interfaces.

Due to space limitations, we couldn't provide a complete listing of MCI commands and their options. If the examples in this book aren't enough for you to accomplish your tasks, consult additional resources, such as the Microsoft Developer Network (MSDN) library CD-ROM. You can also find MSDN online at `http://msdn.microsoft.com/`.

Working with MCI Devices

MCI was designed from the start to support a number of different multimedia devices. Each device is assigned a unique device type that can be expressed as a text description or a number. You use these designations in MCI functions. Table 13.5 provides a summary of the device types, along with their identifiers.

TABLE 13.5: Multimedia Device Types and MCI Designations

Device	Device Type Constant	Device Type String
Compact disc audio	MCI_DEVTYPE_CD_AUDIO	cdaudio
Digital video in a window	MCI_DEVTYPE_DIGITAL_VIDEO	digitalvideo or avivideo
Digital-audio tape player	MCI_DEVTYPE_DAT	dat
Image scanner	MCI_DEVTYPE_SCANNER	scanner
MIDI sequencer	MCI_DEVTYPE_SEQUENCER	sequencer
Other MCI devices	MCI_DEVTYPE_OTHER	other
Overlay video (analog)	MCI_DEVTYPE_OVERLAY	overlay or avivideo
Video-cassette recorder	MCI_DEVTYPE_VCR	vcr or player
Videodisc player	MCI_DEVTYPE_VIDEODISC	videodisc
Waveform audio	MCI_DEVTYPE_WAVEFORM_AUDIO	waveaudio

Simple versus Complex Device Types

As far as MCI is concerned, there are two broad classes of multimedia devices: simple and complex. *Simple devices* are those that are more or less inseparable from the media they handle. For example, audio CD players are simple devices because they can handle only one media object at a time (the compact disc), and the media is either available for playing or it isn't. On the other hand, *complex devices* can create, save, load, and unload media objects dynamically. Windows' waveform audio driver is an example of a complex device. You can use it to create and save new WAV files or to load and play existing ones.

Determining Which Devices Are Installed

Device information is stored in the system Registry in the HKEY_LOCAL_ MACHINE\System\CurrentControlSet\Control\MediaResources\mci key. Figure 13.4 shows REGEDIT open to this branch. You can use the Registry functions explained in Chapter 10 to retrieve this information.

FIGURE 13.4

Viewing installed MCI devices in the Registry

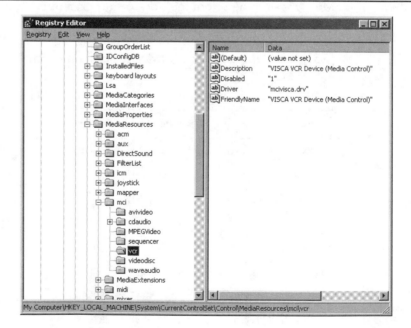

Note the Disabled value for the Registry key shown in Figure 13.4. While there may be a number of MCI devices listed, those that aren't actually installed in the computer will have a Disabled setting of 1.

Working with Devices

Regardless of which type of device you decide to use, working with devices follows the same overall pattern. You begin by *opening* the device. This tells MCI what device you intend to use and prepares it for subsequent commands. If the device is available (which may not be the case—a device could be in use by another process), MCI assigns the device a unique *device ID* that your application uses to control the device.

Once you've opened a device, you use it by sending various commands, using one of the two supported interfaces. The following sections describe the interfaces in detail.

Finally, when you're finished using a device, you *close* it. Closing a device releases any memory allocated by MCI for the session. It also makes the device available for other applications or processes. This is important for media types such as compact disc audio because they cannot be shared among multiple applications.

MCI Commands

Whether you decide to use the command string interface or the command message interface, you control devices using a fixed set of commands. These commands are represented by both strings and numeric constants for use with the different interfaces. While all devices must support a core set of commands, some commands apply only to certain device types. MCI categorizes commands in one of four ways: system, required, basic, and extended. The next few sections explain each category and summarize the commands that make it up. Later sections give examples of using these commands to play CD audio, waveform audio, and digital video devices.

System Commands

System commands, of which there are only two, are handled directly by MCI rather than by individual devices. The MCI_BREAK command (also represented by the command string "break") sets a *break key* for an MCI device. You press the break key to interrupt device actions, such as playing and recording. The MCI_SYSINFO command (command string "sysinfo") requests information about MCI devices.

Required Commands

All MCI devices must support a set of *required commands.* These commands, along with a standard set of options, represent the common capabilities of all MCI devices. Table 13.6 summarizes the MCI required commands. (This and other tables in this section list the command message constant, as well as the command string and description.)

T A B L E 1 3 . 6 : MCI Required Commands

Command Message Constant	Command String	Description
MCI_GETDEVCAPS	capability	Obtains device capabilities (for example, whether the device can record media objects).
MCI_CLOSE	close	Closes the device.
MCI_INFO	info	Obtains textual device information.
MCI_OPEN	open	Opens the device and, optionally, a media object.
MCI_STATUS	status	Obtains status information (for example, whether the device is currently playing.)

Basic Commands

As you can see from Table 13.6, required commands supply only the minimum functionality needed to initialize, query, and close a device. To control a device for a useful purpose, you must call one of the *basic commands* shown in Table 13.7. Most, but not all, devices implement these commands. If you need to know whether a device supports a particular command before calling it, you can use the MCI_ GETDEVCAPS command listed in Table 13.6. Most of the examples later in this chapter focus on these commands.

T A B L E 1 3 . 7 : MCI Basic Commands

Command Message Constant	Command String	Description
MCI_LOAD	load	Loads a media object from a file.
MCI_PAUSE	pause	Pauses playback or recording.
MCI_PLAY	play	Starts playback.

TABLE 13.7: MCI Basic Commands *(continued)*

Command Message Constant	Command String	Description
MCI_RECORD	record	Starts recording.
MCI_RESUME	resume	Resumes paused playback or recording.
MCI_SAVE	save	Saves media object to disk.
MCI_SEEK	seek	Positions current playback or recording position.
MCI_SET	set	Sets various operating parameters.
MCI_STATUS	status	Obtains status information. (Note that this is also a required command.)
MCI_STOP	stop	Stops playback.

Extended Commands

A few devices, such as digital video and videodisc players, support *extended commands*. These tend to be the most complex of the lot, designed to enable features specific to a particular device. Table 13.8 summarizes these commands, along with the devices they apply to.

TABLE 13.8: MCI Extended Commands

Command Message	Command String	Description	Applies to
MCI_CONFIGURE	configure	Displays a configuration dialog.	digitalvideo
MCI_CUE	cue	Cues a file for playback.	digitalvideo, waveaudio
MCI_DELETE	delete	Deletes a portion of a media object.	waveaudio
MCI_ESCAPE	escape	Sends escape codes to a device.	videodisc
MCI_FREEZE	freeze	Freezes video signal acquisition.	overlay
MCI_PUT	put	Defines source, destination, and frame windows.	digitalvideo, overlay
MCI_REALIZE	realize	Realizes a device's palette into a device context.	digitalvideo
MCI_SETAUDIO	setaudio	Sets audio parameters.	digitalvideo

T A B L E   1 3 . 8 :   MCI Extended Commands *(continued)*

Command Message	Command String	Description	Applies to
MCI_SETVIDEO	setvideo	Sets video parameters.	digitalvideo
MCI_SIGNAL	signal	Identifies a specific position within a signal.	digitalvideo
MCI_SPIN	spin	Starts or stops disc spinning.	videodisc
MCI_STEP	step	Steps through playback frame by frame.	digitalvideo, videodisc
MCI_UNFREEZE	unfreeze	Enables video signal acquisition.	overlay
MCI_UPDATE	update	Repaints the current frame.	digitalvideo
MCI_WHERE	where	Defines source, destination, or frame areas.	digitalvideo, overlay
MCI_WINDOW	window	Controls the display window.	digitalvideo, overlay

The MCI Command String Interface

The MCI command string interface was designed to allow control of multimedia devices using simple string-based commands. Originally aimed at programming languages that could not easily handle complex data structures, it has been mostly supplanted by the more powerful and flexible command message interface described in the next section. Nonetheless, we cover this interface here both for completeness and because, for simple tasks, it's easier to implement than command messages.

The mciSendString Function

All the command string capabilities are accessed with a single function, mciSend-String. Its declaration is as follows:

```
Declare Function mciSendString _
  Lib "winmm.dll" Alias "mciSendStringA" _
  (ByVal lpstrCommand As String, _
  ByVal lpstrReturnString As String, _
  ByVal uReturnLength As Long, _
  ByVal hwndCallback As Long) As Long
```

As you can see, mciSendString accepts four arguments that dictate the command carried out by the device. It returns 0 on success and a nonzero error code on failure. The error codes are the same as those used by the command message interface. (For more information, see the section "MCI Errors" later in this chapter.)

Of the four arguments, you'll be primarily interested in only the first two. These two arguments allow you to send commands and receive results from MCI. The third argument, uReturnLength, is merely an indicator of the size of the data returned. The final argument, hwndCallback, is the handle of the window that you want to receive status messages from MCI. Using this argument requires hacking a window's message loop—a topic well beyond the scope of this book.

Constructing Command Strings

You instruct MCI to take action by passing a command string in the lpstrCommand argument. Constructing command strings is probably the second most tedious part of working with the command string interface. (Parsing return information is the first!) The more complex the action you want to take, the more tedious it is. Command strings use a standard verb-object-modifier syntax:

command mediatype | filename | alias [options]

All command strings begin with a predefined MCI command. The command is followed by the media type descriptor string, a registered multimedia filename, or an *alias* (which is just a unique string). Specifying an alias when you open a device makes it easier to refer back to the device in subsequent commands. Following the device or alias are any options a particular command requires.

Listing 13.5 shows a simple procedure that plays a MIDI file. You can see that command strings are constructed by concatenating the filename to MCI commands and that an alias is used to refer back to the open device.

NOTE   For all our examples involving MCI, you should step through the code one line at a time. Otherwise, the device will be closed before you have a chance to see or hear the results.

⟶ **Listing 13.5: Play a MIDI File Using the MCI Command String Interface**

```
Sub dhPlayMIDIFile(strFile As String)
  Dim strCommand As String
  Dim strRet As String
  Dim lngBytes As Long
  Dim lngRet As Long

  ' Open the file (must have a .MID or .RMI extension)
  strCommand = "open " & strFile & " alias seq"
  strRet = Space(255)
  lngRet = mciSendString(strCommand, strRet, lngBytes, 0&)

  ' If successful, start playback
  If lngRet = 0 Then
    strCommand = "play seq"
    strRet = Space(255)
    lngRet = mciSendString(strCommand, strRet, lngBytes, 0&)
  End If

  ' Close the device
  strCommand = "close seq"
  strRet = Space(255)
  lngRet = mciSendString(strCommand, strRet, lngBytes, 0&)
End Sub
```

NOTE   If the filename passed in an MCI command string contains spaces, you must enclose the filename in double quotation marks.

In this example, no information is returned by MCI, so allocating space for a buffer in the strRet variable is unnecessary. For those commands that do return information (such as the "where" command), you should allocate the buffer prior to calling mciSendString and inspect its contents afterward. This section has considered the command string interface as a simple method of playing multimedia elements. For information on retrieving information using the command message interface, see the section "MCI Information Functions" later in this chapter.

The MCI Command Message Interface

The MCI command message interface is a simple but powerful mechanism for controlling multimedia devices. Like the command string interface, its purpose is to allow you to send commands to devices. However, rather than using text strings, the command message interface uses integer commands and structures to specify options.

The mciSendCommand Function

You use the command message interface by calling the mciSendCommand function, which is declared as follows:

```
Declare Function mciSendCommand _
  Lib "winmm.dll" Alias "mciSendCommandA" _
  (ByVal wDeviceID As Long, ByVal uMessage As Long, _
  ByVal dwParam1 As Long, dwParam2 As Any) As Long
```

You pass four pieces of information in the function's arguments:

- The device ID of an open device. This can be 0 for devices not yet opened or MCI_ALL_DEVICE_ID to send a message to all open devices.

- The message expressed as a numeric constant.

- A bitmask of flags associated with the message.

- A pointer to a structure containing details concerning the message.

Like its counterpart mciSendString, mciSendCommand returns 0 on success or an MCI error code on failure. The beauty of mciSendCommand is that it works with a variety of devices through its ability to accept different data types as the fourth argument.

General Message Flags

The third argument to mciSendCommand is a combination of flags that fine-tune the behavior of the command. Most of the flag values are associated with certain commands and the data structures they use. (See the next section, "Message Information Structures.") However, there are two flags you can use with all commands: MCI_WAIT and MCI_NOTIFY.

The MCI_WAIT flag instructs MCI to wait until the command has been carried out. Depending on the device, this may take a considerable amount of time. For example, audio CD devices must spin up in response to an MCI_OPEN command.

Loading a large WAV file into a waveform audio device can also be time consuming. Omitting this flag causes the mciSendCommand function to return immediately, but use this option with care—if you attempt to carry out a second, dependent action before the first action completes (playing a WAV file before it's finished loading, for instance), the command may fail.

TIP If you choose not to use the MCI_WAIT flag, you can determine the status of a device by issuing the MCI_STATUS command. (See the section "MCI Information Functions" a little later in this chapter for more information.)

The MCI_NOTIFY flag instructs MCI to notify your application when the command completes. Specifically, it sends an MM_MCINOTIFY message to a window that you designate. If you are using a development tool capable of intercepting window messages, you can use this flag to detect, for instance, when MCI has finished loading a file.

Message Information Structures

MCI defines numerous data types that you use in conjunction with different commands. We've included the declarations for these types (along with the API functions and constants) in the basMCIBase module. Since there are so many, the ones used in this chapter are explained in the sections describing our sample code.

In general, each command message has an associated structure. For example, the MCI_OPEN command uses the MCI_OPEN_PARMS structure:

```
Type MCI_OPEN_PARMS
    lngCallback As Long
    lngDeviceID As Long
    strDeviceType As String
    strElementName As String
    strAlias As String
End Type
```

NOTE Every structure designed to work with MCI commands has a lngCallback member. You use this to specify the handle of a window that will receive an MM_MCINOTIFY message when the command finishes. Of course, this feature is useful only if you're using a development tool that can hook into a window's message queue or if you have an ActiveX control that can do so.

The MCI message interface does not require you to use every member variable of a structure. Instead, you fill in the values you need and pass a bitmask of flags to mciSendCommand that indicate which elements are used. For example, if you were opening a waveform audio device and set the strElementName member to the name of a WAV file, you would also need to pass the MCI_OPEN_ELEMENT flag as part of the call to mciSendCommand. If you pass a flag but don't fill in the member variable with a valid value, an error occurs.

Additionally, some devices may use more complex structures for certain commands. For example, overlay video devices use the MCI_OVLY_OPEN_PARMS structure with the MCI_OPEN command instead of MCI_OPEN_PARMS. These structures let you supply additional information that is unique to the device.

MCI Errors

If an error occurs during a call to mciSendCommand, the result is a nonzero error code. MCI has conveniently provided a function called mciGetErrorString that returns a description for a given error code. You should always check the result of calling mciSendCommand and, if it's greater than 0, call mciGetErrorString to retrieve the text. We've written a wrapper function called dhMCIError to enable you to do this. Listing 13.6 shows the function, along with the declaration for mciGetErrorString.

Listing 13.6: A Function for Retrieving MCI Error Descriptions

```
Declare Function mciGetErrorString _
 Lib "winmm.dll" Alias "mciGetErrorStringA" _
 (ByVal dwError As Long, ByVal lpstrBuffer As String, _
 ByVal uLength As Long) As Long

Function dhMCIError(ByVal lngErr As Long, _
 Optional varTag As Variant) As String

  Dim strBuffer As String
  Dim lngPos As Long
  Dim lngRet As Long

  If lngErr <> 0 Then
    ' Set up a buffer
    strBuffer = Space(1024)
```

```
      Call mciGetErrorString(lngErr, strBuffer, _
       Len(strBuffer))

      ' Trim string
      lngPos = InStr(strBuffer, vbNullChar)
      If lngPos > 0 Then
        strBuffer = Left(strBuffer, lngPos - 1)

        ' Get tag?
        lngPos = InStr(strBuffer, " ")
        If Not IsMissing(varTag) And lngPos > 0 Then
          varTag = Left(strBuffer, lngPos - 1)
        End If

        ' Return result
        dhMCIError = Mid(strBuffer, lngPos + 1)
      End If
    End If
  End Function
```

You can pass an optional Variant argument to the function. All MCI error messages begin with the string "MMSYSTEM*xxx* ", where *xxx* is the error code. dhMCIError normally strips this encoded error string from the text it returns. However, if you supply a variable as the varTag argument, dhMCIError places the prefix text in it.

MCI Time Formats

MCI expresses time intervals for devices using a number of different formats. Retrieving the current position and controlling playback depend on your understanding of these formats. Table 13.9 lists the numeric constant and description of each format.

TABLE 13.9: MCI Time Formats

Time Format Constant	Description
MCI_FORMAT_BYTES	Bytes (in pulse code modulated [PCM] format files)
MCI_FORMAT_MILLISECONDS	Milliseconds
MCI_FORMAT_MSF	Minute/second/frame

TABLE 13.9: MCI Time Formats *(continued)*

Time Format Constant	Description
MCI_FORMAT_SAMPLES	Samples
MCI_FORMAT_SMPTE_24	SMPTE, 24 frame
MCI_FORMAT_SMPTE_25	SMPTE, 25 frame
MCI_FORMAT_SMPTE_30	SMPTE, 30 frame
MCI_FORMAT_SMPTE_30DROP	SMPTE, 30 frame drop
MCI_FORMAT_TMSF	Track/minute/second/frame
MCI_SEQ_FORMAT_SONGPTR	MIDI song pointer

Not all time formats are appropriate for all device types. In general, you'll use TMSF format for compact disc audio, milliseconds, or samples for waveform audio; and the SMPTE (Society of Motion Picture and Television Engineers) formats for all video devices.

Regardless of the format, MCI stores time information in a Long integer. For TMSF, MSF, and SMPTE types, each byte represents a distinct unit of time. Table 13.10 lists these formats and the information packed into each byte.

TABLE 13.10: Data Storage for Different Time Formats

Byte Position	TMSF	MSF	SMPTE
High-order word/high-order byte	Frames	Unused	Frames
High-order word/low-order byte	Seconds	Frames	Seconds
Low-order word/high-order byte	Minutes	Seconds	Minutes
Low-order word/low-order byte	Tracks	Minutes	Hours

To make it easy to convert from MCI to VBA time formats, we created the function shown in Listing 13.7. You call it with the value and format of an MCI time interval. The result is a VBA Date variable. Listing 13.7 also shows the user-defined data types we created to make splitting a Long integer into its component bytes easier.

Listing 13.7: Convert between MCI and VBA Time Formats

```
Type dhDoubleWordByByte
  LowWordLowByte As Byte
  LowWordHighByte As Byte
  HighWordLowByte As Byte
  HighWordHighByte As Byte
End Type

Type dhDoubleWordLong
  DoubleWord As Long
End Type

Function dhMCITimeToVBATime(lngTime As Long, _
  lngTimeFormat As Long) As Date

  Dim dwb As dhDoubleWordByByte
  Dim dwl As dhDoubleWordLong
  Dim datResult As Date

  ' Break up long into four bytes using LSet
  dwl.DoubleWord = lngTime
  LSet dwb = dwl

  ' Use the busted-up bytes
  With dwb
    ' Which time format?
    Select Case lngTimeFormat
      ' frames (assume 30/sec)
      Case MCI_FORMAT_FRAMES
        datResult = TimeSerial(0, _
          0, lngTime / 30)
      ' minute/second/frame
      Case MCI_FORMAT_MSF
        datResult = TimeSerial(0, _
          .LowWordLowByte, _
          .LowWordHighByte)
      ' track/minute/second/frame
      Case MCI_FORMAT_TMSF
        datResult = TimeSerial(0, _
          .LowWordHighByte, _
          .HighWordLowByte)
```

```
' Society of Motion Picture Engineers
' (hour/minute/second/frame)
Case MCI_FORMAT_SMPTE_24, _
 MCI_FORMAT_SMPTE_25, _
 MCI_FORMAT_SMPTE_30, _
 MCI_FORMAT_SMPTE_30DROP, _
 MCI_FORMAT_HMS
   datResult = TimeSerial( _
    .LowWordLowByte, _
    .LowWordHighByte, _
    .HighWordLowByte)
  ' Milliseconds
  Case MCI_FORMAT_MILLISECONDS
    datResult = lngTime / 86400000
End Select
End With


' Set the return value
dhMCITimeToVBATime = datResult
End Function
```

MCI Information Functions

In addition to specific examples of controlling multimedia devices, there are two commands you can use to obtain information about a device. We've encapsulated these commands, MCI_STATUS and MCI_INFO, in two wrapper functions.

MCI_STATUS

You use the MCI_STATUS command to obtain status information regarding a device. For example, you can determine whether a CD audio device is ready to play. We've written a wrapper function for this command, dhMCIStatus, which is shown in Listing 13.8.

Listing 13.8: A Wrapper Function for the MCI_STATUS Command

```
Function dhMCIStatus(lngDevID As Long, lngItem As Long, _
 Optional lngAddlFlags As Long = 0, _
 Optional bytTrack As Byte = 0) As Long

 Dim mst As MCI_STATUS_PARMS
 Dim lngRet As Long
```

```
' Make sure device ID is valid
If lngDevID Then

  ' Set values of MCI_STATUS_ITEM structure
  With mst
    .lngItem = lngItem
    .lngTrack = bytTrack

    ' Call mciSendCommand
    lngRet = mciSendCommand(lngDevID, MCI_STATUS, _
    MCI_STATUS_ITEM Or lngAddlFlags, mst)

    ' If successful, return lngReturn
    ' member of MCI_STATUS_ITEM structure
    If lngRet = 0 Then
      dhMCIStatus = .lngReturn
    End If
  End With
End If
End Function
```

dhMCIStatus accepts a device ID and a status item number. A complete list of status items is shown in Table 13.11. You can also pass an optional bit mask of additional flags that dhMCIStatus merges with the required flag (MCI_STATUS_ITEM) before passing it to mciSendCommand. Finally, for status information that applies to a particular media track, you can pass the track number.

NOTE   For track-dependent information, you must pass the MCI_TRACK flag in the lngAddlFlags argument in addition to the track number.

TABLE 13.11: MCI_STATUS_ITEM Types

Status Item Constant	Description
MCI_STATUS_LENGTH	Length of a particular media object or track.
MCI_STATUS_POSITION	Current position (in the current time format).
MCI_STATUS_NUMBER_OF_TRACKS	Number of tracks for the current audio compact disc.
MCI_STATUS_MODE	Current device mode (stopped, playing, and so on).

TABLE 13.11: MCI_STATUS_ITEM Types *(continued)*

Status Item Constant	Description
MCI_STATUS_MEDIA_PRESENT	Returns 1 if CD audio media is present.
MCI_STATUS_TIME_FORMAT	Current time format.
MCI_STATUS_READY	Returns 1 if the device is ready to play or record.
MCI_STATUS_CURRENT_TRACK	The CD audio track currently playing.
MCI_WAVE_STATUS_BLOCKALIGN	Waveform audio block alignment.
MCI_WAVE_STATUS_FORMATTAG	Waveform audio format tag (for example, "PCM" for pulse code modulation).
MCI_WAVE_STATUS_CHANNELS	Waveform audio channels (1 = mono, 2 = stereo).
MCI_WAVE_STATUS_SAMPLESPERSEC	Waveform audio sample rate in Hertz (11,025; 22,050; or 44,100).
MCI_WAVE_STATUS_AVGBYTESPERSEC	Average storage size for 1 second of waveform audio.
MCI_WAVE_STATUS_BITSPERSAMPLE	Waveform audio bits per sample (8 or 16).
MCI_WAVE_STATUS_LEVEL	Waveform audio record level.
MCI_SEQ_STATUS_TEMPO	MIDI sequencer tempo.
MCI_SEQ_STATUS_PORT	MIDI sequencer port.
MCI_SEQ_STATUS_OFFSET	MIDI sequencer SMPTE offset.
MCI_SEQ_STATUS_DIVTYPE	MIDI sequencer file division type.

To determine whether a CD audio device is ready to play, you would use a statement like this:

```
fReady = CBool(dhMCIStatus(lngDeviceID, MCI_STATUS_READY))
```

You can use the MCI_STATUS command to return the current operating mode of a device. Calling dhMCIStatus with the MCI_STATUS_MODE constant results in one of the constant values listed in Table 13.12. For example, you can determine whether a device, such as a CD audio player, is currently playing by using code like this:

```
fIsPlaying = (dhMCIStatus(lngDeviceID, MCI_STATUS_MODE) = _
    MCI_MODE_PLAY)
```

TABLE 13.12:   Device Modes

Device Mode Constant	Description
MCI_MODE_NOT_READY	Device is not ready to play or record.
MCI_MODE_STOP	Device is currently stopped.
MCI_MODE_PLAY	Device is currently playing.
MCI_MODE_RECORD	Device is currently recording.
MCI_MODE_SEEK	Device is currently seeking (moving to new position).
MCI_MODE_PAUSE	Device is currently paused.
MCI_MODE_OPEN	Device door is open.

MCI_INFO

You use the MCI_INFO command to obtain textual information for a device. For example, you can determine the unique media ID assigned to audio compact discs. We've written a wrapper function for the MCI_INFO command called dhMCIInfo, shown in Listing 13.9.

Listing 13.9: A Wrapper Function for the MCI_INFO Command

```
Function dhMCIInfo(lngDevID As Long, lngInfo As Long) As String
   Dim min As MCI_INFO_PARMS
   Dim lngRet As Long

   If lngDevID Then
     With min
       ' Set up buffer
       .strReturn = Space(255)
       .lngRetSize = Len(.strReturn)
       lngRet = mciSendCommand(lngDevID, MCI_INFO, _
        lngInfo, min)

       ' If successful, return portion of
       ' strReturn buffer
       If lngRet = 0 Then
         dhMCIInfo = Left(.strReturn, _
          InStr(.strReturn, vbNullChar) - 1)
```

```
            End If
          End With
        End If
      End Function
```

You call dhMCIInfo with a device ID and one of the item constants listed in Table 13.13. Therefore, to return the media ID for a compact disc, you would use code like this:

```
strMediaID = dhMCIInfo(lngDeviceID, MCI_INFO_MEDIA_IDENTITY)
```

TABLE 13.13: MCI_INFO Types

Information Item Constant	Description
MCI_INFO_PRODUCT	Description of the device hardware
MCI_INFO_FILE	Media filename
MCI_INFO_MEDIA_UPC	Media UPC (Universal Product Code)
MCI_INFO_MEDIA_IDENTITY	Unique media identifier
MCI_INFO_NAME	Name of the current track or MIDI sequence
MCI_INFO_COPYRIGHT	Media copyright information

NOTE   Not all information items apply to all devices and media types. If you request an inappropriate item, the result is an empty string.

Putting MCI to Work

To demonstrate the power of the Media Control Interface, we've constructed several working examples that do such things as playing audio CDs and recording waveform audio. We've implemented all of these as class modules to make them easy to integrate into your applications. The next several sections use the samples to explain the basic elements of MCI's command message interface.

NOTE   If you want to use these classes in your applications, be sure to include basMCIBase, as well as the class module.

Playing Audio CDs

One of the simplest applications of MCI is playing audio compact discs. It's simple because all you really have to do is open the CD audio device and start playback. However, we've added a few additional features to our class module, such as the ability to retrieve track times and play individual tracks. You'll find all the sample code in the CDPlayer class module. Table 13.14 provides a complete listing of its properties and methods.

TABLE 13.14:   CDPlayer Class Properties and Methods

Member Type	Name	Description
Properties	Frame	Current track position in frames.
	IsReady	Returns True if the device is ready to play.
	IsPlaying	Returns True if the device is playing.
	MediaID	Compact disc media identifier.
	Minute	Current track position in minutes.
	Mode	Current device mode.
	Second	Current track position in seconds.
	Time	Current track position as a VBA Date value.
	Track	Current track.
	Tracks	Number of tracks.
	TrackTime	Track length for a given track.
Methods	Pause	Pauses playback.
	Play	Starts playback at current position or plays a given track.
	Position	Positions the device to a given track, minute, and second.
	StopPlaying	Stops playback.

Opening a Device

To open any device, you send the MCI_OPEN command, specifying the device type you want to open. This information is contained in an instance of the MCI_OPEN_PARMS data type:

```
Type MCI_OPEN_PARMS
    lngCallback As Long
    lngDeviceID As Long
    strDeviceType As String
    strElementName As String
    strAlias As String
End Type
```

At a minimum, you must specify the device type in the strDeviceType member. You can optionally supply the name of a media object (such as a WAV file for waveform audio devices) in the strElementName member. If you want to assign an alias to the open device, pass it in the strAlias member.

Since an audio compact disc device is a simple device, you needn't supply an element name. Our CDPlayer class opens the device in a procedure called OpenDevice. Listing 13.10 shows the portion of the procedure that calls mciSendCommand.

Listing 13.10: Open an Audio Compact Disc Device

```
Dim lngRet As Long
Dim mop As MCI_OPEN_PARMS

' If we're already open then close
If mlngDevID Then
  Call CloseDevice
End If

' Set device type
mop.strDeviceType = "cdaudio"

' Open the device
lngRet = mciSendCommand(0&, MCI_OPEN, MCI_OPEN_TYPE, mop)
If lngRet = 0 Then
  ' Store the device id
  mlngDevID = mop.lngDeviceID
```

```
Else
  Err.Raise lngRet, "CDPlayer::OpenDevice", _
    dhMCIError(lngRet)
End If
```

Note the device type, "cdaudio". This informs MCI of the device to open. The flag in the function call, MCI_OPEN_TYPE, instructs MCI to look at the strDevice-Type member of the MCI_OPEN_PARMS structure.

If the function call is successful, the procedure stores the contents of the lng-DeviceID member in a class-level variable, mlngDevID. We use this in subsequent calls to identify the device.

Getting Track Information

After opening the device, OpenDevice retrieves information on the number and length of tracks on the compact disc. Listing 13.11 shows the code that accomplishes this.

Listing 13.11: Retrieve Compact Disk Track Information

```
' Get number of tracks
lngRet = dhMCIStatus(mlngDevID, _
 MCI_STATUS_NUMBER_OF_TRACKS)
If lngRet > 0 Then

  ' Get track times (note: these
  ' will be in MSF time format)
  Set mcolTracks = New Collection
  For bytTrack = 1 To lngRet

    ' Get time for one track
    lngRet = dhMCIStatus(mlngDevID, _
     MCI_STATUS_LENGTH, MCI_TRACK, bytTrack)

    ' Add track time to collection
    mcolTracks.Add lngRet, "Track" & bytTrack
  Next
End If
```

The procedure uses the dhMCIStatus function (described in the section "MCI Information Functions" earlier in this chapter) to obtain the number of tracks. It then calls the function again, once for each track, to retrieve the length of each track in MSF time format. To make it easy to retrieve this information later, the procedure adds the data to a class-level Collection object, mcolTracks.

Setting the Time Format

Once the track information has been collected, the procedure sets the time format of the device to TMSF (tracks/minutes/seconds/frames). It does this so it will be easy to play an individual track. If the procedure didn't change the format, all commands to play a portion of the compact disc would have to be expressed in MSF format. A single function call using the MCI_SET command changes the time format:

```
msp.lngTimeFormat = MCI_FORMAT_TMSF
lngRet = mciSendCommand(mlngDevID, MCI_SET, _
  MCI_SET_TIME_FORMAT, msp)
```

Note that setting the lngTimeFormat member of an MCI_SET_PARMS structure specifies the new time format.

Starting Playback

The Play method is a good example of using the MCI_PLAY command. You can use MCI_PLAY to start playback at a particular point in a media object or at the current position. Listing 13.12 shows CDPlayer's Play method, as well as the MCI_PLAY_PARMS declaration.

> ### Listing 13.12: Play a CD Audio Track

```
Type MCI_PLAY_PARMS
  lngCallback As Long
  lngFrom As Long
  lngTo As Long
End Type

Public Sub Play(Optional Track As Byte = 0)
  Dim mpp As MCI_PLAY_PARMS
  Dim lngRet As Long

  If mlngDevID Then
```

```
      ' If no track was supplied play from
      ' the current position
      If Track = 0 Then
        lngRet = mciSendCommand(mlngDevID, _
         MCI_PLAY, 0&, 0&)

      ' Otherwise, set begin and end tracks
      ' and play just that track
      Else
        mpp.lngFrom = Track
        mpp.lngTo = Track + 1
        lngRet = mciSendCommand(mlngDevID, MCI_PLAY, _
         MCI_FROM Or MCI_TO, mpp)
      End If

      If lngRet <> 0 Then
        Err.Raise lngRet, "CDPlayer::Play", _
         dhMCIError(lngRet)
      End If
    End If
  End Sub
```

You'll notice that Play accepts an optional track number. If this is omitted, Play simply starts playback at the current position by calling the MCI_PLAY command with no additional flags and a null pointer in place of the MCI_PLAY_PARMS structure. On the other hand, if a track number is supplied, it sets the lngFrom and lngTo members of the structure and calls MCI_PLAY with the MCI_FROM and MCI_TO flags.

NOTE   Even though the lngFrom and lngTo members of the MCI_PLAY_PARMS structure should be expressed using the TMSF time format, that's not important in this case. Since, in TMFS format, the track number is stored in the low-order byte of the low-order word, you can just set the value of these members to the track number directly.

Changing Playback Position

On most devices, you can change the current playback or recording position by issuing the MCI_SEEK command. You use the MCI_SEEK_PARMS structure, setting its lngTo member variable to the new position expressed in the device's current time format. Listing 13.13 shows the Position method that accomplishes this task for the CDPlayer class, along with the definition of the MCI_SEEK_ PARMS structure.

Listing 13.13: Change the Playback Position with MCI_SEEK

```
Type MCI_SEEK_PARMS
  lngCallback As Long
  lngTo As Long
End Type

Public Sub Position( _
 Optional Track As Byte = 0, _
 Optional Minute As Byte = 0, _
 Optional Second As Byte = 0)

  Dim dwb As dhDoubleWordByByte
  Dim dwl As dhDoubleWordLong
  Dim msk As MCI_SEEK_PARMS
  Dim lngRet As Long
  Dim fWasPlaying As Boolean

  If mlngDevID Then
    ' If the disc is playing, pause it
    If IsPlaying Then
      Me.Pause
      fWasPlaying = True
    End If

    ' If no track was supplied then assume
    ' the current one
    If Track = 0 Then
      Track = Me.Track
    End If

    ' Construct position in TMSF format
    With dwb
      .LowWordLowByte = Track
      .LowWordHighByte = Minute
      .HighWordLowByte = Second
    End With
    LSet dwl = dwb
```

```
            ' Set time and call MCI_SEEK
            msk.lngTo = dwl.DoubleWord
            lngRet = mciSendCommand(mlngDevID, _
             MCI_SEEK, MCI_TO, msk)

            If lngRet = 0 Then
              ' If cd was playing when this was
              ' called, resume playing
              If fWasPlaying Then
                Me.Play
              End If
            Else
              Err.Raise lngRet, "CDPlayer::Position", _
               dhMCIError(lngRet)
            End If
          End If
        End Sub
```

The Position method accepts track, minute, and second values as optional arguments, assuming the current track if none was supplied. It creates a TMSF time value from these arguments using the user-defined data types explained in the section "MCI Time Formats" earlier in this chapter. After checking to see whether the disc is currently playing, and pausing it if it is, the Position method issues the MCI_SEEK command, passing the MCI_TO flag and a pointer to the MCI_SEEK_ PARMS structure. If the call to mciSendCommand was successful, the method restarts the CD if necessary by calling the Play method.

NOTE   The IsPlaying property referenced in Listing 13.13 is implemented using the dhMCIStatus function explained in the section "MCI Information Functions" earlier in this chapter.

Pausing and Stopping Playback

The last general topic in this section is pausing and stopping playback. While we use CD audio as an example, you can apply these techniques to most MCI devices. Listing 13.14 shows the Pause and StopPlaying methods. Note that all they do is issue the appropriate MCI command (MCI_PAUSE or MCI_STOP).

Listing 13.14: Pause and Stop Playback

```
Public Sub Pause()
  Dim lngRet As Long

  If mlngDevID Then
    ' Pause playback by issuing the MCI_PAUSE command
    lngRet = mciSendCommand(mlngDevID, MCI_PAUSE, 0&, 0&)
    If lngRet <> 0 Then
      Err.Raise lngRet, "CDPlayer::Pause", _
        dhMCIError(lngRet)
    End If
  End If
End Sub

Public Sub StopPlaying()
  Dim lngRet As Long

  If mlngDevID Then
    ' Stop playback by issuing the MCI_STOP command
    lngRet = mciSendCommand(mlngDevID, MCI_STOP, 0&, 0&)
    If lngRet <> 0 Then
      Err.Raise lngRet, "CDPlayer::StopPlaying", _
        dhMCIError(lngRet)
    End If
  End If
End Sub
```

An Example

We've created a simple procedure to show off our CDPlayer class. Shown in Listing 13.15, this procedure prints information about the currently loaded compact disc, starts playback, pauses playback, and moves to different tracks and locations.

Listing 13.15: Play Around with an Audio Compact Disc

```
Sub dhTestCD()
  Dim cd As CDPlayer
  Dim bytTrack As Byte
```

```
    ' Create a new instance
    Set cd = New CDPlayer
    With cd

        ' Make sure the device is ready
        If .IsReady Then

            ' Print CD and track information
            Debug.Print "Media ID: " & .MediaID
            Debug.Print .Tracks & " tracks"
            Debug.Print "=========="
            For bytTrack = 1 To .Tracks
                Debug.Print "Track " & bytTrack & ": " & _
                Format(.TrackTime(bytTrack), "nn:ss")
            Next

            ' Start playback
            .Play

            ' Print the current position
            Debug.Print .Track & " " & .Minute & _
            ":" & Format(.Second, "00")

            ' Move to second track
            .Position Track:=2

            ' Pause playback
            .Pause

            ' Skip ahead to the 1-minute mark
            .Position Minute:=1

            ' Restart playback
            .Play

            ' Stop playback
            .StopPlaying
        End If
    End With

    ' Terminate instance
    Set cd = Nothing
End Sub
```

Figure 13.5 shows the VBA Immediate window with the results of running dhTestCD with the *Austin Powers: The Spy Who Shagged Me* soundtrack compact disc.

FIGURE 13.5
Playing the *Austin Powers: The Spy Who Shagged Me* compact disc

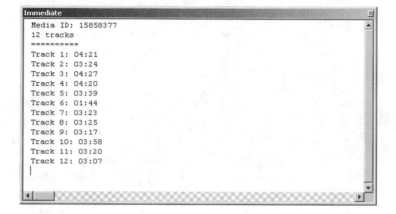

Recording and Playing Waveform Audio

Now let's take a look at another MCI device, waveform audio, better known as WAV files. Waveform audio devices can be used to record, store, and play digital audio sounds. We've created a class called WavePlayer that demonstrates these capabilities. Table 13.15 lists WavePlayer's properties and methods.

TABLE 13.15: WavePlayer Class Properties and Methods

Member Type	Name	Description
Properties	AvgBytesPerSecond	Average storage required for 1 second of audio.
	BitsPerSample	Number of bits to use for recording (8 or 16).
	Channels	Number of channels to use for recording (1 or 2).
	Filename	Name of the current WAV file.
	FormatTag	Format of recorded media (normally PCM).
	Length	Length of the sample in milliseconds.
	Position	Current playback or record position in number of milliseconds from start of sample.

T A B L E 1 3 . 1 5 :   WavePlayer Class Properties and Methods *(continued)*

Member Type	Name	Description
	SampleRate	Sample rate to use for recording (11,025; 22,050; or 44,100).
	Wait	Specifies whether sounds play synchronously or asynchronously.
Methods	Delete	Removes a portion of the current sample.
	OpenFile	Opens a WAV file.
	Play	Plays the current sample.
	Record	Records sound into the current sample.
	Reset	Clears the current sample from the device.
	Save	Saves the current sample using the current filename.
	SaveAs	Saves the current sample using a new filename.
	StopRecording	Stops asynchronous recording.

Loading Files with Complex Devices

Waveform audio is a *complex* MCI device, which means it operates on a data file instead of on a fixed media object like an audio CD. Before you can begin playback on a complex device, you must load or record a sample. You can load a file by specifying a filename when opening a device or by issuing the MCI_LOAD command after the device has been opened.

Waveform audio devices do not support loading a file dynamically. Instead, you must load the file at the same time you open the device. Listing 13.16 shows the Private OpenDevice procedure, as well as the Open method. Note that all the Open method does is call OpenDevice with a filename.

NOTE   We created a separate OpenDevice procedure so we could call it in the Class_Initialize event procedure. This procedure opens the device and prepares it for recording.

Listing 13.16: Open a Waveform Audio File

```
Public Sub OpenFile(WaveFile As String)
  Call OpenDevice(WaveFile)
End Sub

Private Sub OpenDevice(Optional strFile As String = "")
  Dim lngRet As Long
  Dim mwo As MCI_WAVE_OPEN_PARMS

  If mlngDevID Then

    ' Close the device
    Call CloseDevice
  End If

  ' Set member variables
  With mwo
    .strDeviceType = "waveaudio"
    .strElementName = strFile
    .lngBufferSeconds = 10
  End With

  ' Load the requested file
  lngRet = mciSendCommand(mlngDevID, MCI_OPEN, _
   MCI_OPEN_ELEMENT Or MCI_OPEN_TYPE, mwo)
  If lngRet = 0 Then
    mlngDevID = mwo.lngDeviceID
  Else
    Err.Raise lngRet, "WavePlayer::OpenDevice", _
      dhMCIError(lngRet)
  End If
End Sub
```

WavePlayer's OpenDevice procedure, shown in Listing 13.16, differs from the same procedure in the CDPlayer class in three significant ways:

- It uses an MCI_WAVE_OPEN_PARMS structure instead of the standard MCI_OPEN_PARMS. MCI_WAVE_OPEN_PARMS includes an additional member, lngBufferSeconds, which lets you specify the size of the buffer used by the device.

- It passes the name of the file to open in the strElementName member variable.

- It includes the MCI_OPEN_ELEMENT flag in the call to mciSendCommand.

Playing Waveform Audio

Like the CDPlayer class, the WavePlayer class features a Play method. However, playing waveform audio is unlike playing CD audio because waveform audio is not broken into tracks. Therefore, WavePlayer's Play method is designed to accept starting and stopping positions in milliseconds rather than as a track number. Listing 13.17 shows the code behind the Play method.

Listing 13.17: Play Waveform Audio

```
Public Sub Play(Optional StartTime As Long, _
  Optional StopTime As Long)

  Dim mpp As MCI_PLAY_PARMS
  Dim lngLength As Long
  Dim lngRet As Long

  If mlngDevID Then

    ' Validate inputs
    lngLength = Length()
    If StartTime < 0 Or StartTime > lngLength Then
      StartTime = 0
    End If
    If StopTime <= StartTime Or StopTime > lngLength Then
      StopTime = lngLength
    End If

    ' Play the wave file
    mpp.lngFrom = StartTime
    mpp.lngTo = StopTime
    lngRet = mciSendCommand(mlngDevID, MCI_PLAY, _
      MCI_FROM Or MCI_TO Or mlngWait, mpp)
    If lngRet <> 0 Then
      Err.Raise lngRet, "WavePlayer::Play", _
        dhMCIError(lngRet)
    End If
  End If
End Sub
```

The Play method validates the start and stop values against the length of the current audio sample. If neither argument is supplied, the method plays the entire sample.

Determining the total length of the sample is easy, as the code behind the Length property illustrates:

```
Property Get Length() As Long
    Length = dhMCIStatus(mlngDevID, MCI_STATUS_LENGTH)
End Property
```

NOTE   With waveform audio, time is measured in milliseconds, eliminating the need to convert to and from complex time forms, such as TMSF.

Recording Waveform Audio

Recording waveform audio is perhaps the most relevant use for the WavePlayer class (since you can play a WAV file simply by calling PlaySound). To record with an MCI device, you issue the MCI_RECORD command, passing a pointer to an instance of the MCI_RECORD_PARMS structure. MCI automatically allocates a buffer for the recorded sound based on settings in the MCI_RECORD_PARMS member variables. You can also start recording without specifying a time interval, and the waveform audio device will record until it receives an MCI_STOP command, or until you run out of virtual memory.

Listing 13.18 shows the Record method of the WavePlayer class. It accepts three optional arguments: Milliseconds, StartTime, and Overwrite. *Milliseconds* specifies the length of time for the recording. *StartTime* represents the point in the current waveform audio file to start recording. The *Overwrite argument* controls whether the newly recorded sound is inserted into the current file (the default) or replaces existing contents.

Listing 13.18: Record Waveform Audio

```
Type MCI_RECORD_PARMS
    lngCallback As Long
    lngFrom As Long
    lngTo As Long
End Type
```

```
Public Sub Record( _
 Optional Milliseconds As Integer = 0, _
 Optional StartTime As Long = -1, _
 Optional Overwrite As Boolean = False)

  Dim mrp As MCI_RECORD_PARMS
  Dim lngLength As Long
  Dim lngFlags As Long
  Dim lngRet As Long

  If mlngDevID And Milliseconds >= 0 Then

    ' If StartTime is -1, get current position
    lngLength = Length
    If StartTime < 0 Or StartTime > lngLength Then
      StartTime = Position
    End If

    ' Set flag values
    If Milliseconds > 0 Then
      lngFlags = MCI_FROM Or MCI_TO Or MCI_WAIT
    End If
    If Overwrite Then
      lngFlags = lngFlags Or MCI_RECORD_OVERWRITE
    Else
      lngFlags = lngFlags Or MCI_RECORD_INSERT
    End If

    ' Record for a given number of seconds
    With mrp
      .lngFrom = StartTime
      .lngTo = StartTime + Milliseconds
    End With
    lngRet = mciSendCommand(mlngDevID, MCI_RECORD, _
     lngFlags, mrp)
    If lngRet <> 0 Then
      Err.Raise lngRet, "WavePlayer::Record", _
      dhMCIError(lngRet)
    End If
  End If
End Sub
```

If no start time is specified (or if it exceeds the current size of the file), the start position is set to the current position. The current position is determined by calling dhMCIStatus with the MCI_STATUS_POSITION flag. Our class encapsulates this in the Position property.

The Record method determines the flags to send to mciSendCommand based on the arguments passed to the procedure. If you call Record with a positive value for Milliseconds, the method sets the MCI_FROM, MCI_TO and MCI_WAIT flags. If you call the method with no arguments (Milliseconds equals 0), no flags are set. This causes the waveform audio device to start recording and continue until you issue the MCI_STOP command. WavePlayer features a StopRecording method that does just this.

WARNING   If you issue the MCI_RECORD command with no time interval specified, make sure you don't include the MCI_WAIT flag in the function call. This will cause MCI to continue recording forever.

In either case, the Record method adds either the MCI_RECORD_INSERT or MCI_RECORD_OVERWRITE flag based on the value of the Overwrite argument. This flag controls whether the new sample is inserted into the current file at the specified position or replaces the contents at that position.

Starting and ending positions are determined by the StartTime and Milliseconds arguments. These values are written to the MCI_RECORD_PARMS structure before the call to mciSendCommand.

Setting Input Parameters

Waveform audio devices have a number of configurable parameters that control the quality of input and, subsequently, the quality of output. Our WavePlayer class lets you set and retrieve these values through a series of properties. Table 13.15, presented earlier in this section, listed these properties: AvgBytesPerSecond, BitsPerSample, Channels, and SampleRate. The higher the sample rate, channel, or bits-per-sample setting, the better the quality is. However, be aware that as the quality increases, so does the space required to store the sample.

Retrieving these values is accomplished simply by calling the dhMCIStatus function and passing the appropriate status item constant. (See Table 13.11 earlier in this chapter for a list of these constants.) On the other hand, setting the values requires issuing the MCI_SET command. Listing 13.19 shows the Private Change-Setting procedure, which is called by the Property Let procedures for the properties.

Listing 13.19: Change Waveform Audio Device Input Parameters

```
Private Sub ChangeSetting(lngSetting As Long, lngNewValue _
As Long)
 Dim mws As MCI_WAVE_SET_PARMS
 Dim lngRet As Long

  ' Make sure device ID is valid
  If mlngDevID Then

    ' Use the MCI_WAVE_SET_PARMS structure
    With mws

      ' Get the existing values
      .intFormatTag = Me.FormatTag
      .intBitsPerSample = Me.BitsPerSample
      .intChannels = Me.Channels
      .lngSamplesPerSec = Me.SampleRate

      ' Change the desired setting
      Select Case lngSetting
        Case MCI_WAVE_STATUS_FORMATTAG
          .intFormatTag = lngNewValue
        Case MCI_WAVE_STATUS_CHANNELS
          .intChannels = lngNewValue
        Case MCI_WAVE_STATUS_SAMPLESPERSEC
          .lngSamplesPerSec = lngNewValue
        Case MCI_WAVE_STATUS_BITSPERSAMPLE
          .intBitsPerSample = lngNewValue
      End Select

      ' Compute derived settings
      .lngAvgBytesPerSec = ((.intBitsPerSample / 8) * _
      .intChannels * .lngSamplesPerSec)
      .intBlockAlign = ((.intBitsPerSample / 8) * _
      .intChannels)
```

```
          ' Call mciSendCommand
          lngRet = mciSendCommand(mlngDevID, MCI_SET, _
           MCI_WAIT Or MCI_WAVE_SET_FORMATTAG Or _
           MCI_WAVE_SET_BITSPERSAMPLE Or _
           MCI_WAVE_SET_CHANNELS Or _
           MCI_WAVE_SET_SAMPLESPERSEC Or _
           MCI_WAVE_SET_AVGBYTESPERSEC Or _
           MCI_WAVE_SET_BLOCKALIGN, mws)

          If lngRet <> 0 Then
            Err.Raise lngRet, "WavePlayer::ChangeSetting", _
             dhMCIError(lngRet)
          End If
        End With
      End If
    End Sub
```

The procedure works by first retrieving the existing settings into a MCI_WAVE_SET_PARMS structure. It then changes one of those settings based on the value of the lngSetting argument. Two settings, average bytes per second and block alignment, are derived values, so the ChangeSetting procedure computes them based on the new settings. Finally, the procedure issues the MCI_SET command, passing a reference to the MCI_WAVE_SET_PARMS structure and a series of flags representing the various settings.

NOTE   While it would appear that you can change settings individually, Microsoft recommends changing all of them at once in the manner we've just described. Failing to do this could result in the waveform audio device falling back into its lowest-quality mode.

Removing Portions of a Waveform Audio File

Unlike most other types of devices, waveform audio devices are capable of deleting portions of the media object they work with. To accomplish this, you issue the MCI_DELETE command with beginning and ending time periods stored in an instance of the MCI_WAVE_DELETE_PARMS structure. Listing 13.20 shows the Delete method of our WavePlayer class. (We omitted the structure declaration because it's identical to the MCI_RECORD_PARMS structure.)

Listing 13.20: Delete a Portion of a Waveform Audio File

```
Public Sub Delete(StartTime As Long, _
Milliseconds As Long)

  Dim mdp As MCI_WAVE_DELETE_PARMS
  Dim lngLength As Long
  Dim lngRet As Long

  If mlngDevID Then

    ' Validate inputs
    lngLength = Length()
    If StartTime < 0 Or StartTime > lngLength Then
      StartTime = 0
    End If

    ' Delete the specified portion
    With mdp
      .lngFrom = StartTime
      .lngTo = StartTime + Milliseconds
      If .lngTo > lngLength Then
        .lngTo = lngLength
      End If
    End With
    lngRet = mciSendCommand(mlngDevID, MCI_DELETE, _
    MCI_FROM Or MCI_TO, mdp)
    If lngRet <> 0 Then
      Err.Raise lngRet, "WavePlayer::Delete", _
      dhMCIError(lngRet)
    End If
  End If
End Sub
```

After validating the inputs—the starting point and the length of the sample to delete—the Delete method issues the MCI_DELETE command. If it's successful, a portion of the current file will be completely removed.

Saving a Waveform Audio File

The final bit of waveform audio functionality to look at is saving a recorded or modified file to disk. You do this by issuing the MCI_SAVE command. As you can imagine, there is an associated MCI_SAVE_PARMS structure to go along with the command. We've implemented two methods to perform this task: SaveAs and Save. Listing 13.21 shows both methods, the Private procedure they call to get the job done, and the declaration of the MCI_SAVE_PARMS structure.

Listing 13.21: Save a Waveform Audio File to Disk

```
Type MCI_SAVE_PARMS
  lngCallback As Long
  lpFileName As String
End Type

Public Sub SaveAs(Filename As String)
  If Filename <> "" Then
    Call SaveFile(Filename)
  End If
End Sub

Public Sub Save()
  Dim strFile As String

  ' Use the current file name
  strFile = Me.Filename
  Call SaveAs(strFile)
End Sub

Private Sub SaveFile(strFile As String)
  Dim lngRet As Long
  Dim msp As MCI_SAVE_PARMS

  If mlngDevID Then

    ' Save the file
    msp.lpFileName = strFile
    lngRet = mciSendCommand(mlngDevID, MCI_SAVE, _
     MCI_SAVE_FILE Or MCI_WAIT, msp)
    If lngRet <> 0 Then
```

```
        Err.Raise lngRet, "WavePlayer::SaveFile",
          dhMCIError(lngRet)
      End If
    End If
  End Sub
```

After calling SaveAs for the first time, you can call Save to save the file with the same name. The Save method uses the dhMCIInfo function to obtain the name of the current waveform audio file. If you want to save the file with a different name, just call SaveAs again.

WARNING   When you save a file using the MCI_SAVE command, any existing file is overwritten without warning.

An Example

Our example to demonstrate the WavePlayer class is shown in Listing 13.22. After initializing the class and playing a saved WAV file, the procedure changes the input settings and records three seconds of sound. It then plays the sample back, removes the middle one second, plays it again, and saves it to disk.

Listing 13.22: Play and Record Waveform Audio

```
Sub dhTestWave()
  Dim wav As WavePlayer

  ' Create new instance
  Set wav = New WavePlayer
  With wav

    ' Open and play a saved WAV file
    .OpenFile "C:\Windows\Media\Chord.wav"
    .Play

    ' Reset the device and record for 3 seconds
    .Reset
    .SampleRate = 22050
    .BitsPerSample = 16
    .Record Milliseconds:=3000

    ' Play the recorded sound
    .Play
```

```
      ' Now remove the middle 1 second
      .Delete StartTime:=1000, Milliseconds:=1000

      ' Play it again and then save it
      .Play
      .SaveAs "C:\NEWWAVE.WAV"
   End With

      ' Terminate instance
   Set wav = Nothing
End Sub
```

Putting Digital Video in a Window

Digital video, better known as AVI files, is being used increasingly in multimedia training applications and even as a supplement to standard online help topics. This section shows you how to load an AVI file and play it in any arbitrary window on your desktop. As with the other examples, we created a class (Video-Player) to encapsulate the functionality. Table 13.16 lists VideoPlayer's properties and methods.

TABLE 13.16: VideoPlayer Class Properties and Methods

Member Type	Name	Description
Properties	Caption	Title of display window.
	Filename	Name of AVI file.
	hWnd	Window handle of display window.
	IsPlaying	True if a video clip is playing.
	Length	Length of the current clip in milliseconds.
	Stretch	True if image is to be stretched to fill the display window.
Methods	Center	Centers the image in the display window.
	OpenFile	Opens an AVI file.
	Play	Plays the current video clip.
	StopPlaying	Stops playing the current video clip.

NOTE To demonstrate this class, we've included a form (frmVideo) in the sample Excel workbook. If you don't have a copy of Excel, you'll need to create a new form in whatever development tool you use.

MCI Video Types

MCI defines two broad categories of video: digital and overlay. *Digital video* is recorded and saved in a file. *Overlay video* is based on a direct analog feed and is the basis for those "TV-in-a-window" applications you've no doubt seen advertised. Overlay video requires special hardware in order to operate. Digital video does not.

While MCI defines these two categories and supplies separate commands and structures to manipulate them, they share many characteristics. For example, each must be played in a window, and you can define which portion of that window is used. In describing the techniques required to play digital video, we've "borrowed" some functionality from MCI's overlay video features.

Basic AVI Functionality

There's not much to say about the basic functionality in the VideoPlayer class. You open and close it in much the same manner as you do the CDPlayer and WavePlayer classes. You use "avivideo" as the device type and, optionally, the path to an AVI file as the element name. The class implements a number of the same properties and methods as the CDPlayer and WavePlayer classes, such as IsPlaying, Play, and StopPlaying. In fact, the code used to implement these is almost identical. What makes this class unique is how it interacts visually with the system.

Putting Digital Video in a Window

Digital and overlay video must have a window in which to display themselves. You can either specify an existing window or let them create their own. If you choose not to specify a window, the result is the same as if you had simply run an AVI from Explorer. Under Windows 95, Windows 98, and Windows NT 4, the device creates a window using attributes defined in the Video section of the Multimedia Control Panel applet (shown in Figure 13.6) and in the Windows Media Player Options dialog (shown in Figure 13.7). In Windows 2000, you change video options only through the Media Player applet.

FIGURE 13.6
Multimedia video settings
in the Control Panel

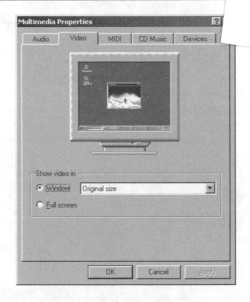

FIGURE 13.7
AVI settings in the Windows Media Player

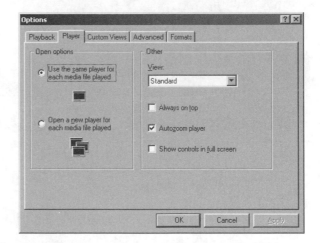

Under most circumstances, you'll want to control the playback, restricting it to a certain window and size. To do this, you must issue the MCI_WINDOW command after opening the device. Among other things, you pass the handle to the window in which you want playback to happen. We've implemented an hWnd property of the VideoPlayerclass that accomplishes this. Listing 13.23 shows the Property Let procedure.

Listing 13.23: Setting the hWnd Property Assigns a Window to the Device

```
Property Let hWnd(hWnd As Long)
    Dim mow As MCI_OVLY_WINDOW_PARMS
    Dim lngFlags As Long
    Dim lngRet As Long

    If mlngDevID Then
        ' Set default flags
        lngFlags = MCI_OVLY_WINDOW_HWND

        ' Set stretch flag
        If mfStretch Then
            lngFlags = lngFlags Or _
            MCI_OVLY_WINDOW_ENABLE_STRETCH
        Else
            lngFlags = lngFlags Or _
            MCI_OVLY_WINDOW_DISABLE_STRETCH
        End If

        ' Set the window handle and, optionally, the caption
        mow.hWnd = hWnd
        If Len(mstrCaption) Then
            mow.strText = mstrCaption
            lngFlags = lngFlags Or _
            MCI_OVLY_WINDOW_TEXT
        End If

        ' Issue the MCI_WINDOW command
        lngRet = mciSendCommand(mlngDevID, MCI_WINDOW, _
        lngFlags, mow)

        ' If successful, store the window handle
        If lngRet = 0 Then
            mHwnd = hWnd
        Else
            mHwnd = 0
            Err.Raise lngRet, "VideoPlayer::hWnd (Let)", _
            dhMCIError(lngRet)
        End If
    End If
End Property
```

The procedure uses an MCI_OVLY_WINDOW_PARMS structure to define the window attributes. The members of this structure let you supply a window handle, a caption, and a display mode (maximized, normal, and so on). Flags passed to the mciSendCommand function validate each of these members. In our example, we maintain a class-level variable, mstrCaption, for a window caption. If the variable is set (nonblank), the procedure adds the MCI_OVLY_WINDOW_TEXT flag to the current set of flags. MCI will, in turn, change the caption of the specified window.

We also maintain another class variable, mfStretch, which controls whether the video image will be stretched to fill the entire window. If this variable is set to True (via the Stretch property of the class), MCI will stretch the image to completely fill the window's client area. (A window's *client area* is the area inside a window, excluding the window's border and caption.) To further control the size and position, you can issue the MCI_PUT command, described in the next section.

Positioning Playback

If you need to further refine the position of a video clip within the window specified in the MCI_WINDOW command, you issue the MCI_PUT command. MCI_PUT, and its counterpart MCI_GET, set and retrieve window coordinates for both video source and output elements. To demonstrate how to use these commands, we've implemented a Center method that centers the output in the window when called after you assign a window handle to the video device. Listing 13.24 shows the Center method.

Listing 13.24: Center a Video Clip in a Window

```
Public Sub Center()
  Dim morSource As MCI_OVLY_RECT_PARMS
  Dim morDest As MCI_OVLY_RECT_PARMS
  Dim rc As RECT
  Dim lngRet As Long

  ' Make sure we've got something loaded and that
  ' the user has specified a window
  If mlngDevID And Len(Me.Filename) > 0 And _
    CBool(mHwnd) Then
```

```
' Issue the MCI_WHERE command to get the
' size of the current AVI file
lngRet = mciSendCommand(mlngDevID, MCI_WHERE, _
 MCI_OVLY_WHERE_SOURCE, morSource)
If lngRet = 0 Then

    ' Get the available client area
    If CBool(GetClientRect(mHwnd, rc)) Then

        ' Do the math to center the image
        With rc
          morDest.rc.Top = (.Bottom - .Top - _
           morSource.rc.Bottom) / 2
          morDest.rc.Left = (.Right - .Left - _
           morSource.rc.Right) / 2
        End With

        ' Issue the MCI_PUT command to place the
        ' output at the computed position in the
        ' destination window
        lngRet = mciSendCommand(mlngDevID, _
         MCI_PUT, MCI_OVLY_PUT_DESTINATION Or _
         MCI_OVLY_RECT, morDest)
        If lngRet <> 0 Then
          Err.Raise lngRet, "VideoPlayer::Center", _
            dhMCIError(lngRet)
        End If
    Else
        Err.Raise lngRet, "VideoPlayer::Center", _
          dhMCIError(lngRet)
    End If
Else
    Err.Raise lngRet, "VideoPlayer::Center", _
      dhMCIError(lngRet)
End If
  End If
End Sub
```

Both commands rely on two user-defined data types. The MCI_OVLY_RECT_ PARMS structure includes the standard callback member, as well as a pointer to the second data type, RECT. The RECT type is a standard Windows API type used to define the boundaries of a rectangle.

Centering a video clip in a window involves four steps:

1. Determining the size of the source video

2. Determining the size of the window's client area

3. Computing the correct position for the output based on the video and window sizes

4. Setting the destination area to reflect this position

The Center method accomplishes the first step by issuing the MCI_WHERE command. You can use this command to determine the size and position of both the current source video and the output region. The method passes the MCI_OVLY_WHERE_SOURCE flag, indicating that it wants to know the size of the source video. If the command is successful, the dimensions are stored in the RECT structure within the passed MCI_OVLY_RECT_PARMS variable. The Top and Left member variables will contain the *position* of the video's upper-left corner (initially, these are both 0), and the Bottom and Right members will contain the *height* and *width* of the image, respectively.

> **NOTE**   MCI uses the RECT structure differently from most other Windows API functions. Usually, API functions use the Bottom and Right members to represent the extent of a rectangle relative to the upper-left corner of the client area, not to its size.

Determining the size of the target window's client area is easy. The method calls the standard Windows API GetClientRect function to grab the dimensions and place them in the passed RECT structure.

Finally, after performing some simple arithmetic to determine the new position for the video, the Center method issues the MCI_PUT command, passing a pointer to the MCI_OVLY_RECT_PARMS structure containing the new dimensions and the MCI_OVLY_PUT_DESTINATION and MCI_OVLY_RECT flags.

An Example

Our example uses a form in Excel VBA (shown in Figure 13.8) to display an AVI file. (The one shown is from Microsoft Flight Simulator 2000.) However, you can use just about any window you can get a handle to. Listing 13.25 shows the code behind the form. You'll need to enter a valid path to an AVI file in the form's text box.

FIGURE 13.8

Displaying an AVI file in a window

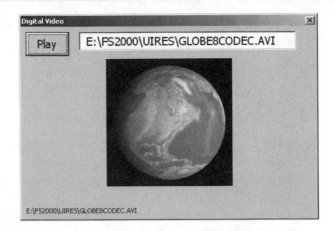

Listing 13.25: Code Required to Use the VideoPlayer Class

```
Option Explicit

' This is required to get a handle to the form
Private Declare Function GetActiveWindow _
 Lib "user32" () As Long

' Private instance of VideoPlayer class
Private vid As VideoPlayer

Private Sub cmdPlay_Click()
  ' Create a new instance
  Set vid = New VideoPlayer

  ' Open a file
  vid.OpenFile Me.txtAVI.Text

  ' Set the window and caption
  vid.Caption = "Window Caption"
  vid.hWnd = GetActiveWindow()

  ' Center the video in the window and play it
  vid.Center
  vid.Play
End Sub
```

```
Private Sub UserForm_QueryClose(Cancel As Integer, _
 CloseMode As Integer)

  ' If video is still playing, stop it
  If vid.IsPlaying Then
    vid.StopPlaying
  End If
End Sub

Private Sub UserForm_Terminate()
  ' Terminate the instance
  Set vid = Nothing
End Sub
```

You can see how the form uses the class to open an AVI file, center it on the screen, and play it. The only other item worth pointing out is the use of the GetActive-Window API function. This function is necessary because VBA forms do not expose their window handle directly. On the other hand, if you're using a tool like Visual Basic or Access, you can reference this value directly via a form's hWnd property.

Summary

In this chapter, we've presented a few simple techniques for integrating multimedia into your VBA applications. While we could not be as thorough as we would have liked due to space considerations, we've given you several tools that should add a little life to your programs. We examined the multimedia capabilities of Windows, and the Media Control Interface in particular, as a way of accomplishing the following tasks:

- Play audio compact disc tracks.
- Record and play waveform audio.
- Display digital video in a window.

We hope this chapter has also given you the insight to add other multimedia elements to your applications.

chapter 14

Using the Scripting Runtime Library Objects

- Use objects provided by SCRRUN.DLL, part of the Windows Script Host.

- Use the FileSystemObject, and its Drive, Folder, and File objects, to manage files, folders, and drives.

- Use the TextStream object to work with text files.

- Take advantage of the Dictionary object, a data structure similar to a collection but more powerful.

The sample files you'll find on the CD-ROM that accompanies this book are listed in Table 14.1.

TIP

The examples in this chapter are provided in a VB6 project, SCRIPTING.VBP. We've compiled the project into an executable, SCRIPTING.EXE, so you can simply run the program to test out the various methods and properties. If you have a copy of VB6, open the project to investigate its source code. If you don't, you can open the various BAS and FRM files with a text editor and view the sample code there or use the XLS or MDB projects containing the code (but not the forms). There's very little reusable code in this chapter—it's mostly demonstrations of the various objects, properties, and methods—so you needn't worry that you can't simply use the modules "as is." We've grouped any code you might want to use in your own projects into standard modules (which you can easily import into any VBA host) and have noted these situations throughout the chapter. In addition, if you attempt to run SCRIPTING.EXE and the application fails, run the SETUP.EXE program in the folder associated with this chapter to install the program, the VB runtime libraries, and the scripting DLL.

WARNING

If you have an out-of-date version of the Scripting Runtime Library, none of the code in this chapter will compile or execute. In that case, you'll need to go to `http://msdn.microsoft.com/scripting` and download the latest Microsoft Scripting (version 5.1 or higher).

T A B L E 1 4 . 1: Demonstration Files

Filename	Description
SCRIPTING.EXE	Demonstration program for this chapter
SCRIPTING.XLS	Demonstration Excel 2000 spreadsheet
SCRIPTING.MDB	Demonstration Access 2000 database
SCRIPTING.VBP	Project file for the VB6 project
DRIVES.FRM	Sample VB form
FILEFOLDERNAMES.FRM	Sample VB form
FILES.FRM	Sample VB form
FOLDER.FRM	Sample VB form

TABLE 14.1:   Demonstration Files *(continued)*

Filename	Description
SWITCHBOARD.FRM	Sample VB form
ATTRIBUTES.BAS	Sample module
DICTIONARY.BAS	Sample module
NAVIGATEFOLDERS.BAS	Sample module
TESTATTRIBUTES.BAS	Sample module
TESTPROCEDURES.BAS	Sample module
TRANSLATE.BAS	Sample module
COMMONDLG.CLS	Sample class module
SETUP.EXE (and associated files, SETUP.LST, SCRIPTING.CAB)	Setup program for VB compiled project (SCRIPTING.EXE), in case you don't own a copy of Visual Basic 6

Why Is This Chapter Different?

The world of ActiveX components is huge and constantly growing. It would be, as far as we can tell, impossible to write a book containing information on all the available objects, properties, and methods out there, even if we limited it to just a single developer's products, such as those from Microsoft. The problem is that every day there are many new libraries full of objects out there.

Because the playing field is huge, one option would have been for us to simply sidestep the issue and avoid discussion of the available components entirely. On the other hand, one ActiveX component that Microsoft provides is so universally available and so useful that we thought it important to treat it as if it was part of VBA. (And, therefore, this becomes the only chapter in the book where we've looked at a particular ActiveX component and described it in detail.) That is, the SCRRUN.DLL component of the Windows Script Host. This ActiveX component provides three areas of functionality that are useful, important, and somewhat difficult to re-create yourself. Boiled down to the bare minimum, SCRRUN.DLL provides objects that allow you to

- Work with the file system, retrieving information on and working with drives, folders, and files.

- Work with text files, both reading and writing to the files.

- Work with a data structure similar to a VBA Collection object but with more features.

TIP   This chapter introduces you to all the objects provided by SCRRUN.DLL and includes explanation of all the properties and methods of the objects. Along the way, you'll see how to use the objects and find some of the pitfalls to avoid. This DLL comes with VB6 and with Internet Explorer. Most likely, if you're using Microsoft products, it's already available on your machine. If not, you can always browse to `http://msdn.microsoft.com/scripting` and download the pieces you need. Your users can download it from here as well, or you can distribute the pieces you need along with your applications.

What Is the Windows Script Host?

The Windows Script Host is a tool provided by Microsoft that makes it possible for developers to create scripts (like batch files) that can run natively within the operating system. Using this tool, end users don't require a full development environment, or even the runtime libraries associated with VB, to run scripts. In order to make it possible for script developers to access drives, folders, and files; to work with text files; and to use in-memory data structures, Microsoft provided an ActiveX component, SCRRUN.DLL (generally called "Windows Scripting Runtime"). This chapter describes this component of the Windows Script Host in detail, so you can take advantage of it, too.

Referencing and Using SCRRUN.DLL

Before you can take advantage of the objects provided by SCRRUN.DLL, you'll need to set a reference to the component from within your development environment. In VB, use the Project ➤ Reference menu, and in other VBA hosts, use the Tools ➤ References menu item. Either way, scroll down through the list until you find the Microsoft Scripting Runtime entry, shown in Figure 14.1.

FIGURE 14.1

Use the Tools ➤ References (or Project ➤ References) menu item, and select Microsoft Scripting Runtime.

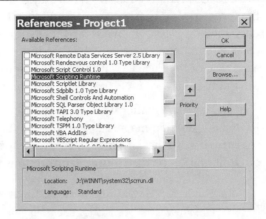

Once you've set a reference to this library of objects, you can use the objects as if they were built into your project. For the most part, you'll simply need to declare a variable and then instantiate it, like this:

```
Dim fso As Scripting.FileSystemObject
Set fso = New Scripting.FileSystemObject
```

TIP

For more information on using VBA to automate other applications, see Chapter 4. In this case, the application you're controlling has a project name of "Scripting" (just as Microsoft Excel's project name is "Excel," for example). In addition, pay careful attention to the use of the project name in front of each reference to any object from the Scripting library—this makes your code run slightly faster and makes the code more readable, as well. Again, see Chapter 4 for more information on this technique.

TIP

If, for some reason, you don't find Microsoft Scripting Runtime in your list of available references, and you're sure it should already be installed on your machine, you can always use the Browse button on the dialog box to allow you to go search for SCRRUN.DLL on your own. It should be in the System (Win9X) or System32 (Windows NT/2000) folder, underneath your installation of Windows.

If you want to distribute an application to other users, and you've taken advantage of the Scripting objects, you'll need to make sure your users also have a copy of SCRRUN.DLL on their own machines. To do that, you'll need to use some tool that creates a setup program of some sort. If you're using VB, you can use the Package and Deployment wizard that comes with that product. If you've purchased the Microsoft Office 2000 Developer product, you'll find that it also includes a version of the Package and Deployment wizard. Besides these two tools, there are many other products that help you create and install packaged applications.

In any case, no matter what tool you use, your users need to have a copy of SCR-RUN.DLL on their machines, and it needs to have been registered (in their system registry) before they attempt to run your application. See your host application's documentation on distributing applications to end users for more information.

> **WARNING** Microsoft was in the midst of releasing a new version of the Windows Script Host as we were writing this book, and we based this chapter on the latest version. Some features of the objects demonstrated in this chapter may not work with your version of SCRRUN.DLL. If you find this to be true, visit `http://msdn.microsoft.com/scripting` and download the latest version of the Scripting Runtime Library files.

The rest of the chapter is devoted to introducing, demonstrating, and explaining each of the objects provided by the SCRRUN.DLL library.

The FileSystemObject Object

Yes, the name seems redundant. And so it is. But the FileSystemObject (you'll understand what we mean if we leave off that extra "object," right?) allows you to access any other object in the file system, including drives, folders, and files. It has but a single property (Drives, a collection containing all the drives available in the file system), and plenty of methods for managing drives, folders, and files.

In order to take advantage of the FileSystemObject and all the other file system objects, you must first declare and create a new instance of the class, like this:

```
Dim fso As Scripting.FileSystemObject
Set fso = New Scripting.FileSystemObject
```

The FileSystemObject makes all the other file system objects available, and it's the only creatable object in the Scripting library.

> **NOTE**
>
> Actually, the FileSystemObject isn't the only creatable Scripting object. It is, however, the only creatable object that allows you to work with the file system. You can also instantiate a Dictionary object, described later in the chapter. In addition, if you're using the Scripting library associated with Windows Script Host 2, you can also instantiate an Encoder object, allowing you to encode scripting code. This isn't something you're likely to need in a VBA application, and we won't cover this object in this book.

Declaring and Instantiating in One Step

It's tempting to declare and instantiate the FileSystemObject in the same line of code (using the "As New" syntax), and you'll see this done often in other publications. As we've mentioned in other places throughout this book, there's generally nothing to be gained by collapsing the two lines down into one. That is, you'll see this line of code:

```
Dim fso As New Scripting.FileSystemObject
```

instead of the two-line version:

```
Dim fso As Scripting.FileSystemObject
Set fso = New Scripting.FileSystemObject
```

When you collapse these two lines together, you cause two problems:

- VBA can't tell when it should instantiate the object (it only instantiates the object when you first use it), so VBA must insert checks throughout your code to see if it's time to instantiate the object. This slows down your application's execution.

- If you collapse the two lines into one, you won't be able to compare your variable to Nothing—the moment you try, VBA will instantiate the object (because it thinks you now want to use the object, whether it had already been instantiated), in which case it won't be Nothing anymore. That is, code like this will always instantiate the object referred to by **fso**, even though it ought not, and the code inside the **If Then** statement will never run:

```
Dim fso As New Scripting.FileSystemObject
' Later in your code...
If fso Is Nothing Then
    ' Too late! This code will never run.
End If
```

We can only think of one good reason to use the combined declaration/instantiation: if you're writing code and want to test out methods and properties of an object in the Immediate window, it's useful to temporarily create an object in a standard module, like this:

```
Public fso As New Scripting.FileSystemObject
```

Then, at any time, you can open the Immediate window and work with methods and properties of **fso**. Other than this, we think you're better off using two lines of code for declaration and instantiation of any object.

Methods of the FileSystemObject

The FileSystemObject provides a number of methods that allow you to manage and manipulate files, folders, and drives. In addition, the object provides a few methods for creating and opening text files, using the TextStream object. Tables 14.2, 14.3, and 14.4 list and describe the methods of the FileSystemObject, and the subsequent sections dig into some of the methods in greater detail. (Examples in the tables assume you've already declared and instantiated a FileSystemObject named **fso**.)

NOTE   We won't discuss the TextStream object, nor the three methods of the FileSystemObject that manipulate text files, in this section. For more information, see the section titled "The TextStream Object" later in the chapter.

WARNING   Windows Script Host 2 added some new methods for the FileSystemObject. We've noted those by adding an asterisk to the method name. If you're using an earlier version of the Scripting library, these methods won't be available.

TABLE 14.2:   FileSystemObject Methods Allowing You to Manage File and Folder Names and Versions

Method	Return Type	Description
BuildPath	String	Given a filename and path name, concatenates the two pieces. Inserts a path separator character if necessary. (This method is simple: it does nothing more than relieve you of the burden of having to determine if a path name includes a trailing slash before you concatenate a filename onto the path.) This function doesn't ensure that either the path or the file actually exists: it simply performs a string manipulation on whatever strings you send it.

TABLE 14.2: FileSystemObject Methods Allowing You to Manage File and Folder Names and Versions *(continued)*

Method	Return Type	Description
GetAbsolutePathName	String	Given a relative path, returns a complete and unambiguous path based on the current selected Windows path.
GetBaseName	String	Returns the base name (the filename portion) of the last component of the passed-in path. This method doesn't ensure that the file exists—it simply performs a string manipulation, looking for "\" and "." characters.
GetDriveName	String	Returns the drive name portion of the passed-in path. This method doesn't ensure that the drive exists—it simply performs a string manipulation, looking for "\" characters. The method correctly handles drives in either C: or \\share\drive format.
GetExtensionName	String	Returns the extension name (after the final "." in the filename) of the last component of the passed-in path. This method doesn't ensure that the file exists—it simply performs a string manipulation, looking for "\" and "." characters.
GetFileName	String	Returns the filename portion (including the base name and extension) of the last component of the passed-in path. This method doesn't ensure that the file exists—it simply performs a string manipulation, looking for "\" and "." characters.
GetFileVersion*	String	Returns the internal file version (supplied by the original application developer), for executable, DLL, and driver files that support this feature. For other files, returns an empty string.
GetParentFolderName	String	Returns the drive and folder name portion of the passed-in path. This method doesn't ensure that the drive or folder exists—it simply performs a string manipulation, looking for "\" characters. The method correctly handles drives in either C: or \\share\drive format.
GetSpecialFolder	Folder	Returns the path to one of three special folders (the Windows, Windows System, or Temp folder). Pass in one of the following constants: WindowsFolder (0), SystemFolder (1), or TemporaryFolder (2), and the method returns the full path to the requested special folder.

TABLE 14.2: FileSystemObject Methods Allowing You to Manage File and Folder Names and Versions *(continued)*

Method	Return Type	Description
GetTempName	String	Returns a unique name, which you can use for creating a file or folder. The method does not actually create anything—it simply returns a name you can use for creating your own file or folder. Although the documentation doesn't state the scope of the unique name, our assumption is that it guarantees a unique name within the Windows temporary folder.

TABLE 14.3: FileSystemObject Methods Allowing You to Manipulate Files, Folders, and Drives

Method	Return Type	Description
CopyFile		Copy a file (or files) from one location to another.
CopyFolder		Copy a folder (or folders) from one location to another.
CreateFolder	Folder	Create a folder with the specified name, and return a reference to the newly created folder. If the entire path to the new folder doesn't exist, the method raises error 76 ("Path not found"). If the folder already exists, the method raises error 58 ("File already exists"). See "The Folder Object," later in the chapter, for information on working with Folder objects. For example, you might write code like this: `Set fld = fso.CreateFolder("C:\NewFolder")`

DeleteFile		Deletes one or more files, given a file specification. Optionally, forces the deletion of system and/or read-only files. Files deleted using this method are not placed into the Recycle Bin. For example:
		`fso.DeleteFile "C:\Autoexec.bak"`
		`fso.DeleteFile "C:\*.bat"`

DeleteFolder		Deletes one or more folders (even if the folder includes files—in that case, the files are deleted along with the folder). If you specify a wildcard, so that multiple folders are deleted, the method stops at the first error but makes no attempt to roll back deletions before the error. Folders and files deleted using this method are not placed into the Recycle Bin. For example: `fso.DeleteFolder "C:\NewFolder"`

T A B L E   1 4 . 3 : FileSystemObject Methods Allowing You to Manipulate Files, Folders, and Drives *(continued)*

Method	Return Type	Description

DriveExists	Boolean	Given a drive letter or complete file specification, determines if the drive exists. This method does not attempt to see if the drive is available or if media has been inserted. See the IsReady property of the Drive object for more information on checking the readiness of a drive. For example:
		`If fso.DriveExists("Q:") Then`
		`    ' You know drive Q exists.`
		`End If`

FileExists	Boolean	Determines if the specified file exists. Either include a full or relative path—otherwise, the method only looks in the current folder (and it's not always clear in Windows exactly what the current folder is). For example:
		`If fso.FileExists("C:\Autoexec.bat") Then`
		`    ' You know the file exists.`
		`End If`

FolderExists	Boolean	Determines if the specified folder exists. Either include a full or relative path—otherwise, the method only looks in the current folder. For example:
		`If fso.FolderExists("C:\Backup") Then`
		`    ' You know the folder exists.`
		`End If`

GetDrive	Drive	Given a drive letter (D), a drive specification (D:\), or a network share (\\share\path), return a Drive object referring to the selected drive. For example:
		`Dim drv As Scripting.Drive`
		`Set drv = fso.GetDrive("C")`

GetFile	File	Given a relative or absolute file path, return a File object corresponding to the selected item. For example:
		`Dim fil As Scripting.File`
		`Set fil = fso.GetFile("C:\Autoexec.bat")`

GetFolder	Folder	Given a relative or absolute folder path, return a Folder object corresponding to the selected item. For example:
		`Dim fld As Scripting.Folder`
		`Set fld = fso.GetFolder("C:\Backup")`

MoveFile		Move a file (or files) to new location.
MoveFolder		Move a folder (or folders) to a new location.

TABLE 14.4: FileSystemObject Methods Allowing You to Work with TextStream Objects

Method	Return Type	Description
CreateTextFile	TextStream	Given a filename, creates a new text file and returns a TextStream object so that you can manipulate the file programmatically.
GetStandardStream*	TextStream	In order to work with the standard I/O streams, this method allows you to open the StdIn, StdOut, or StdErr devices. If you need to create CGI applications for use on a Web site, or if you want to allow input or output from one of the standard operating system streams, you can finally do so from within VBA. Pass in one of the constants StdIn (0), StdOut (1), or StdErr (2), and the method returns a TextStream object with which you can either read or write. We've not had a compelling reason to need this feature and won't dwell on it here.
OpenTextFile	TextStream	Opens a specified file and returns a TextStream object that can be used to read from or append to the file

Testing the Simple FileSystemObject Methods

The sample form, frmFileFolderNames, shown in Figure 14.2, allows you to test out most of the methods described in Table 14.2. If you dig into the form's code, you'll find that the Load event procedure for the form instantiates a form-level FileSystemObject, and the form's Unload event procedure destroys it. (That way, none of the individual procedures needs to create an instance.) The code within the form's events uses simple methods of the FileSystemObject, like this fragment that fills in labels on the form with portions of a selected filename:

```
lblFilePart(1).Caption = fso.GetBaseName(strFile)
lblFilePart(2).Caption = fso.GetDriveName(strFile)
lblFilePart(3).Caption = fso.GetExtensionName(strFile)
lblFilePart(4).Caption = fso.GetParentFolderName(strFile)
```

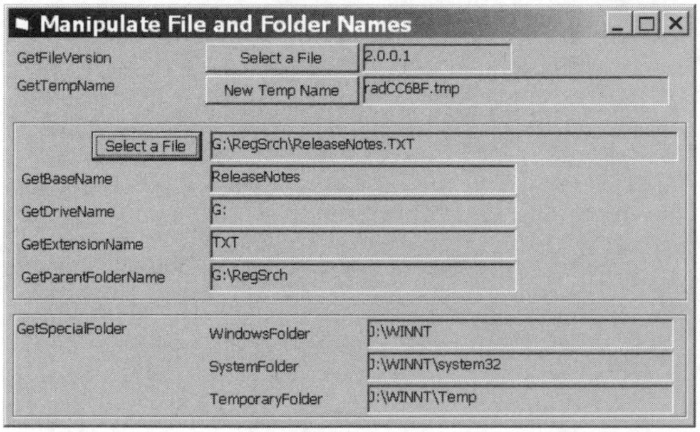

FIGURE 14.2
Use this sample form, frmFileFolderNames, to test out several of the FileSystemObject methods and properties.

Copying and Moving Files and Folders

The FileSystemObject's methods make it easy to copy and move files and folders. This power comes at a price: Copying and moving files and/or folders using the FileSystemObject can be treacherous because of the flexibility inherent in these methods. In each case, you specify a source and a destination. When copying files or folders (not when moving), you can also specify whether you want the copied files or folders to overwrite existing items.

> **NOTE**   Every example in this section assumes you've already declared and instantiated a FileSystemObject named **fso**.

For example, if you want to copy one file to a new location (the new location must be a valid, existing folder), you could write code like this:

```
fso.CopyFile "C:\autoexec.bat", _
  "D:\SaveFolder\"
```

Note the trailing backslash on the output folder name: if you don't specify the trailing backslash, the method assumes you're specifying a filename to copy the file to. If you already have a folder with the specified name, you'll get a runtime error. If you do want to copy the file to a folder and give it a new name, you can write code like this:

```
fso.CopyFile "C:\autoexec.bat", "D:\SaveFolder\save.bat"
```

To copy multiple files, you might write code like this:

```
fso.CopyFile "C:\*.bat", "D:\SaveFolder\"
```

Note that you cannot rename the files as you copy them. That is, this code will fail:

```
fso.CopyFile "C:\*.bat", "D:\SaveFolder\*.sav"
```

If you want to overwrite existing files without raising an error, pass True as the optional third parameter, like this:

```
fso.CopyFile "C:\*.bat", "D:\SaveFolder\", True
```

The CopyFolder method works the same way, except that this method copies a folder and all its contents to a new location. You can write code like this:

```
fso.CopyFolder "D:\SaveFolder", "D:\NewFolder"
```

and you'll find a new folder with all the contents of the original. As when copying files, you can specify the third optional parameter, telling the method to overwrite existing files without complaint.

WARNING   Don't attempt to copy a folder to a subfolder of itself. This is an illegal operation, no matter how you try it.

Moving files and folders works basically the same as copying, except you cannot overwrite existing files or folders as you move. In other words, there's no parameter that allows you to overwrite existing items, and attempting to do so will trigger a runtime error.

TIP   If you need to move files or folders, and you're not sure whether they already exist, you'll need to use error handling to your advantage. If the attempt to move fails, you can use the appropriate method to delete the file or folder, and use the Resume statement to attempt the move again.

The Drives Collection

The FileSystemObject provides a single property: the Drives collection. You can use this property to access the entire file system hierarchy associated with your computer. Once you've created an instance of the FileSystemObject, you can work your way down through the Drives collection to a particular drive. From there, you can use the RootFolder property to retrieve a reference to the Folder object corresponding to the root folder of the drive. Once there, you can use the SubFolders property to retrieve a Folders collection, representing all the folders on the drive. Given a Folders collection, you can work with individual Folder objects and the Files collection within them.

TIP   Generally, you won't iterate through Drive, Folder, and File objects to work with individual items. Instead, you'll use the GetDrive, GetFolder, and GetFile methods of the FileSystemObject, mentioned in earlier sections. If you need to iterate through and work with all the drives, folders, and files on your computer, however, you can easily use For Each...Next loops to visit each and every item in the file system. The following sections detail how you can loop through the various collections.

To retrieve a reference to a particular drive on your computer, you might write code like this:

```
Dim fso As Scripting.FileSystemObject
Dim drv As Scripting.Drive
Set fso = New Scripting.FileSystemObject
Set drv = fso.Drives("C")
```

This code declares and instantiates a new FileSystemObject and retrieves a reference to the C: drive. Once you have that reference, you can use the Drive object and all its properties, as described in the next section.

To demonstrate the use of the Drives collection and the Drive object (see the next section for details on the individual properties of the Drive object), check out the frmDrives demo form, shown in Figure 14.3. This form displays all the available drives in a list box. Once you select a particular drive, the form displays formatted information about that drive's properties in controls on the form.

To do its job, the sample form uses code like this in its Load event procedure, filling the list box with the list of available drives:

```
Private Sub Form_Load()
    Dim drv As Scripting.Drive

    On Error Resume Next

    Set fso = New Scripting.FileSystemObject

    For Each drv In fso.Drives
        lstDrives.AddItem drv.DriveLetter
    Next drv

    ' This will fail if the current
    ' drive is a UNC drive. That's why
    ' we added the "On Error Resume Next"
    ' in here.
    lstDrives.Text = Left$(CurDir, 1)
End Sub
```

FIGURE 14.3

The sample form frmDrives displays a list of all available drives, and information about each particular drive.

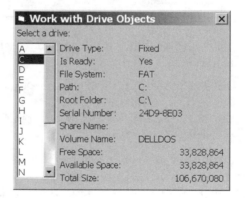

The Drive Object

The Drive object represents a particular drive within your computer's file system. You can either use the Drives property or the GetDrive method of the FileSystem object to retrieve a particular drive. That is, the following fragment demonstrates two methods for retrieving a reference to a particular drive:

```
Dim fso As Scripting.FileSystemObject
Dim drv As Scripting.Drive

Set fso = New Scripting.FileSystemObject
' Use this technique:
Set drv = fso.Drives("C")

' or this one. It doesn't matter:
Set drv = fso.GetDrive("C")
```

Table 14.5 lists all the properties of the Drive object. (The Drive object has no methods.)

TABLE 14.5:   Properties of the Drive Object

Property	Type	Description
AvailableSpace	Variant	Available space on the drive for the current user, taking into account disk quotas applied by the system administrator.
DriveLetter	String	The drive letter associated with the drive. If the drive is mapped from a network share, the ShareName property will indicate the original share's location.
DriveType	DriveTypeConst; one of CDROM (4), Fixed (2), RamDisk (5), Remote (3), Removable (1), Unknown (0)	Returns the type of the selected drive. Unfortunately, this property can gather no more information than the six available return values. If you're using a particular brand of removable drive, for example, there's no way to differentiate different manufacturer's drives, given this information.
FileSystem	String	Type of file system in use on the drive. Generally, this will be one of "FAT," "CDFS," or "NTFS."
FreeSpace	Variant	Available space on the selected drive, not taking into account quotas for the current user. That is, this value will return all available space, even if the current user cannot access all that space.
IsReady	Boolean	Returns True if the selected drive is ready. Only applicable for removable drives (see the DriveType property for more information), this property is True when the media is inserted and ready for access.

TABLE 14.5: Properties of the Drive Object *(continued)*

Property	Type	Description
Path	String	The path for the specified drive. Doesn't include a trailing backslash.
RootFolder	Folder	Folder object representing the root folder. Use the Files property to work with files in the root folder or the SubFolders property to work with folders under the root. See the section titled "The Folder Object" for more information.
SerialNumber	Long	Long integer (in base 10) containing the unique serial number for the drive. Normally, you see this value formatted in hex, and the sample form contains a function to perform this conversion for you.
ShareName	String	If the drive represents a mapped share, this property contains the name of the share. If the drive isn't mapped, ShareName returns an empty string ("").
TotalSize	Variant	Returns the total size for the drive, in bytes. Divide by 1024 to convert to Kb (kilobytes).
VolumeName	String	Set or get the volume name for the drive. This is the only read/write property of the Drive object. You can set this property's value to change the volume name of the drive.

NOTE   The Drive object returns Variant values for its drive size properties—AvailableSpace, FreeSpace, and TotalSize—rather than returning Long integers. The problem is that a single drive can be larger than 2 gigabytes (and that's the maximum size a Long can hold). Therefore, by using Variants, the return type can be a Long, Single, or Double, as required by the individual drive. We tested this object with drives up to 18 gigabytes, and it worked fine for all the drives we threw at it.

NOTE   The AvailableSpace and FreeSpace properties seem redundant, but they're not. In some environments, system administrators place disk quotas on individual users. The AvailableSpace property takes disk quotas into account, and the FreeSpace property simply returns the amount of free space on the drive.

Several of the Drive properties displayed on the form in Figure 14.3 require formatting. For example, if you want to display the drive type, you'll need a function like the following to convert from the DriveTypeConst value into a string:

```
Private Function DriveType( _
  lngType As Scripting.DriveTypeConst) As String
    Select Case lngType
        Case Fixed
            DriveType = "Fixed"
        Case Remote
            DriveType = "Remote"
        Case CDRom
            DriveType = "CDRom"
        Case Removable
            DriveType = "Removable"
        Case Unknown
            DriveType = "Unknown"
        Case RamDisk
            DriveType = "RamDisk"
    End Select
End Function
```

Generally, programs display a drive's SerialNumber property in Hex, formatted as XXXX-YYYY, where X and Y represent hexadecimal values. To take care of this conversion, the sample form includes the following function:

```
Private Function FormatHex(lngValue As Long) As String
    Dim strTemp As String
    ' This guarantees that the string has 8 characters,
    ' left-padded with 0's.
    strTemp = Right$(String(8, "0") & Hex(lngValue), 8)
    FormatHex = Format$(strTemp, "@@@@-@@@@")
End Function
```

The Folder Object

The Folder object represents a single folder within the file system, and the Folders object provides a collection of Folder objects. Each Folder object exposes the properties listed in Table 14.6. The sample VB form, frmFolder, shown in Figure 14.4, demonstrates each of these properties for a folder you select. (Select a file first and then click the link provided in the ParentFolder property to view the sample form.)

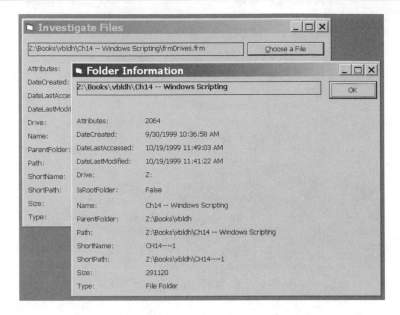

FIGURE 14.4
The sample form frmFiles allows you to select a file and then displays all the Folder object properties associated with the Parent-Folder property.

TABLE 14.6: Properties of the Folder Object

Property	Type	Description	Comments
Attributes (read/write)	FileAttribute	One or more of the values from Table 14.8, added together	Set this property to modify the attributes of a folder. Use a combination of the values in Table 14.8, adding the values together. Some combinations of values are invalid.
DateCreated	Date	Date the folder was created	Includes both the date and time
DateLastAccessed	Date	Date the folder was last accessed	Includes both the date and time
DateLastModified	Date	Date the folder was last modified	Includes both the date and time
Drive	Drive	Drive object representing the drive containing the folder	This property will return a UNC path, if the drive isn't local
Files	Files	Collection containing all the File objects in the folder	

TABLE 14.6: Properties of the Folder Object *(continued)*

Property	Type	Description	Comments
IsRootFolder	Boolean	Indicates whether the specified folder is the root folder of a drive	Returns True even for the root folder of UNC shares, even if the actual folder mapped isn't the root of a physical drive.
Name (read/write)	String	Name of the folder	You can set this property to effectively rename the Folder. Returns the name portion only, so a folder such as "C:\" will return an empty string for this property.
ParentFolder	Folder	Parent folder of the current folder	
Path	String	Full path name of the file	This property includes long filenames. The ShortPath property provides the 8.3 version of the path and filename.
ShortName	String	8.3 (8 character file name, 3 character extension) version of the filename	
ShortPath	String	8.3 version of the full path	
Size	Variant	Sum of the sizes of all the files in the folder and its subfolders	In order to accommodate drives larger than the value a Long can contain, this property returns a Variant. Divide this value by 1024 to calculate the Kb size. This property returns the same value as if you'd right-clicked the folder in Windows Explorer and selected Properties.
SubFolders	Folders	Collection containing all the folders within the selected folder, at the current level. This collection does not contain folders within the current level's folders.	Clearly, this data structure becomes recursive if a folder contains subfolders, each of which can contain subfolders.
Type	String	The file type association for the folder	Although this isn't documented, our testing found that local drives returned "Local Disk," and UNC paths on remote drives returned "File" as the value of this property.

Many of these properties are shared with the File object. See the section titled "The File Object" for examples of using some of the properties. Navigating through folders, however, is an issue specific to the Folders collection, Folder objects, and the ParentFolder and SubFolders properties. The following paragraphs describe using these objects and properties.

WARNING Although the Folders collection provided by the SubFolders property looks like a normal VBA collection (it provides only Count and Item methods, however, leaving out the Add and Remove methods), its Item method accepts only a string as its parameter. That is, if you want to reference a particular folder within the SubFolders collection, you cannot do it by position within the collection. You must specify a folder name as the key. If you want to iterate through all the items in the SubFolders collection, you may not use a For...Next loop: instead, you must use a For Each... Next loop.

Navigating through Folders

The two procedures in Listing 14.1 demonstrate how you might recursively iterate down through subfolders and how you might work your way back up the folder hierarchy to the root folder.

Listing 14.1: You Can Work Your Way Down through the Hierarchy of Subfolders, or Back Up to the Root Folder, as Shown in These Procedures from basNavigateFolders.

```
Public Sub IterateFolders( _
 fld As Scripting.Folder, _
 Optional Level As Integer = 0)

    ' Demo recursive procedure to iterate through
    ' folders, including subfolders.

    Dim fldSub As Scripting.Folder
    ' Print out the current folder, indented.
    Debug.Print Space(2 * Level); fld.Path

    ' Now loop through all the subfolders.
```

```
        For Each fldSub In fld.SubFolders
            Call IterateFolders(fldSub, Level + 1)
        Next fldSub
End Sub

Public Sub GetParentFolder(fld As Scripting.Folder)
    ' Demo procedure to work back through
    ' folders, up to the root.

    Do Until fld.IsRootFolder
        Debug.Print fld.Path
        Set fld = fld.ParentFolder
    Loop
    Debug.Print fld.Path
End Sub
```

The IterateFolders procedure first prints out the current folder's Path property, and then loops through all the folders in its SubFolders collection. For each sub-folder, the code calls the IterateFolders procedure recursively, effectively working its way through all the folders under the selected folder. To test this procedure, try this code from basNavigateFolders:

```
Public Sub TestIterateFolders()
    Dim fso As Scripting.FileSystemObject
    Set fso = New Scripting.FileSystemObject
    Call IterateFolders(fso.GetFolder("C:\"))
    Set fso = Nothing
End Sub
```

The GetParentFolder procedure is simpler: it uses the ParentFolder property of each folder, working its way uphill until the selected folder's IsRootFolder property returns True. The TestGetParent procedure, shown here, demonstrates the use of GetParentFolder:

```
Public Sub TestGetParent()
    Dim fso As Scripting.FileSystemObject
    Set fso = New Scripting.FileSystemObject
    ' Substitute your own folder for the hard-coded
    ' folder used in this example.
    Call GetParentFolder( _
     fso.GetFolder("C:\OPG\SAMPLES\CH02"))
    Set fso = Nothing
End Sub
```

The Files Collection

Once you've selected a particular folder, you can use the Files property of the Folder object to retrieve a collection of File objects. The next section describes the File object in detail, but the following code demonstrates how you might iterate through the Files collection to work with each File object in a folder:

```
Public Sub ListFiles()
    Dim fso As Scripting.FileSystemObject
    Dim fld As Scripting.Folder
    Dim fil As Scripting.File

    Set fso = New Scripting.FileSystemObject
    Set fld = fso.GetFolder("C:\")

    Debug.Print "There are " & fld.Files.Count & " files."

    ' This loop doesn't work, and it would
    ' be the slowest solution, even if it DID work.
    'Dim i As Integer
    'For i = 1 To fld.Files.Count
    '    Debug.Print fld.Files.Item(i).Name
    'Next i

    For Each fil In fld.Files
        Debug.Print fil.Name
    Next fil
End Sub
```

WARNING   Just as mentioned earlier with the SubFolders collection, the Files collection looks like a normal VBA collection but its Item method only accepts a string as its parameter. That is, if you want to reference a particular file within the Files collection, you cannot do it by position within the collection. You must specify a filename as the key. If you want to iterate through all the items in the Files collection, you may not use a For...Next loop: instead, you must use a For Each...Next loop.

The File Object

Each item in the Files collection is itself a File object, and each File object exposes the properties listed in Table 14.7. (Table 14.8 lists possible values for the Attributes property of a File object.) The sample VB form, frmFiles, shown in Figure 14.5, demonstrates each of these properties for a file that you select.

FIGURE 14.5
The sample form allows you to select a file and then displays all the File object properties associated with that file.

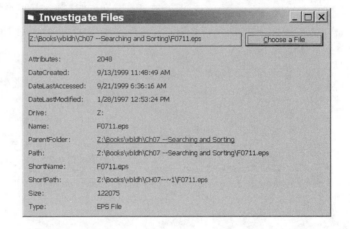

TABLE 14.7: File Object Properties. All Properties Are Read-Only Unless Otherwise Specified.

Property	Type	Description	Comments
Attributes (read/write)	FileAttribute	One or more of the values from Table 14.8, added together	Set this property to modify the attributes of a file. Use a combination of the values in Table 14.8, adding the values together. Some combinations of values are invalid.
DateCreated	Date	Date the file was created	Includes both the date and time
DateLastAccessed	Date	Date the file was last accessed	Includes both the date and time
DateLastModified	Date	Date the file was last modified	Includes both the date and time

T A B L E 1 4 . 7 : File Object Properties. All Properties Are Read-Only Unless Otherwise Specified. *(continued)*

Property	Type	Description	Comments
Drive	Drive	Drive object representing the drive containing the file	
Name (read/write)	String	Full name of the file, including the extension	You can set this property to effectively rename the file.
ParentFolder	Folder	Folder containing the file	
Path	String	Full path name of the file	This property includes long filenames. The ShortPath property provides the 8.3 version of the path and filename.
ShortName	String	8.3 (8 character filename, 3 character extension) version of the filename	
ShortPath	String	8.3 version of the full path	
Size	Variant	Actual size of the file, in bytes	In order to accommodate drives larger than the value a Long can contain, this property returns a Variant. Divide this value by 1024 to calculate the Kb size.
Type	String	The file type association for the file	

T A B L E 1 4 . 8 : FileAttribute Enumeration

Constant	Value	Description	Can Be Set
Normal	0	Normal file, with no attributes set	No (this is the absence of any other attribute)
ReadOnly	1	Read-only file	Yes
Hidden	2	Hidden file	Yes
System	4	System file	Yes
Volume	8	Disk volume label	No

TABLE 14.8: FileAttribute Enumeration *(continued)*

Constant	Value	Description	Can Be Set
Directory	16	Folder or directory	No
Archive	32	File has been changed since most recent backup	Yes
Alias	1024	File is link or shortcut	No
Compressed	2048	File is compressed	No

Most of the properties listed in Table 14.7 require no explanation. Some of the properties, however, are not so clear:

- The "Modifying Attributes" section below provides details on using the Attributes property.

- The Drive property returns a Drive object representing the drive containing the file. Because the Path property of the Drive object is the object's default member, if you type something like this (where fil is a File object referring to an existing file), you'll get the Path property without explicitly requesting it:

  ```
  Debug.Print fil.Drive
  ```

- You can change the name of a File object by modifying its Name property.

- The ParentFolder property returns a Folder object, and the default member of the Folder object is the Path property. Therefore, if you simply write code like the following, you'll get the Path property of the parent folder. If you need more information about the parent folder, you can use the other properties of the Folder object returned by the ParentFolder property:

  ```
  Debug.Print fil.ParentFolder
  ```

Methods of File Objects

The File object provides just four methods, shown in Table 14.9. The Copy, Delete, and Move methods are similar to the parallel methods of the FileSystemObject. Here, however, you needn't specify source filenames—that information comes from the File object you've already referenced. (Using the CopyFile method of the

FileSystemObject, however, you can copy multiple files at once, specifying a source using wildcards. Here, you can only copy a single file—the selected file.)

TABLE 14.9: Methods of the File Object

Method	Return Value	Description
Copy		Copy the selected file to a new location, optionally overwriting an existing output file.
Delete		Delete the selected file, optionally allowing you to delete system and read-only files. Files deleted this way are permanently deleted, not moved to the Recycle Bin.
Move		Move the selected file to a new location.
OpenAsTextStream	TextStream	Open the selected file as a TextStream object, allowing you to work with its contents. See "The TextStream Object," later in the chapter, for more information.

Copying a File

To call the Copy method, use syntax like this:

```
fil.Copy Destination[, OverWrite]
```

where:

- *Destination* is a string representing the location for the new file. Wildcard characters are not allowed.

- *Overwrite* is an optional Boolean (default is True), indicating whether you want to have the copy operation overwrite an existing file. If set to False, the Copy method raises an error if the file already exists. (You'll get error 58, "File already exists," if you set this parameter to False and the destination file already exists.)

For example, if `fil` is a Scripting.File object referring to an existing file, you might write code like this to copy the file to the root of your D: drive, raising an error if the output file already exists:

```
fil.Copy "D:\", False
```

TIP   Although VBA provides a FileCopy method, it doesn't work with open files, and it cannot be made to raise an error if the output file exists. In addition, you must specify the full output filename, rather than just the path, as you can with the Copy method of the Scripting.File object.

Deleting a File

To delete a file, use the Delete method of the Scripting.File object, like this:

```
fil.Delete [Force]
```

where:

- *Force* is an optional Boolean (default is False) indicating whether the method should delete read-only and system files without raising an error. (Normally, attempting to delete read-only files raises error 70, "Permission denied.")

For example, if `fil` is a Scripting.File object referring to an existing file, you might write code like this to delete the file, forcing a delete even if the file is read-only:

```
fil.Delete True
```

TIP   VBA includes the Kill statement, which allows you to delete some files. It doesn't, however, allow you to delete system or hidden files. (Perhaps that's a good thing?) If you want to delete multiple files using the Scripting objects, use the DeleteFile method of the FileSystemObject.

Moving a File

To call the Move method, use syntax like this:

```
fil.Move Destination
```

where:

- *Destination* is a string representing the location for the new file. Wildcard characters are not allowed.

For example, if `fil` is a Scripting.File object referring to an existing file, you might write code like this to move the file to the root of your D: drive:

```
fil.Move "D:\"
```

WARNING	Unlike the Copy method, the Move method does not provide any means for over-writing existing files. If a file with the same name already exists in the output location, the Move method will raise error 58, "File already exists." You'll need to add error handling to your code in order to handle this occurrence.

TIP	If you want to move multiple files using a wildcard specifier, see the MoveFile method of the FileSystemObject. If you want to move an entire folder, you can use the Move method of a Folder object. If you want to move multiple folders, use the MoveFolder method of the FileSystemObject.

Opening a TextStream Based on a File

If you want to open a File object as a text stream and work with its contents as text, you can use the OpenAsTextStream method of the File object. The syntax for the OpenAsTextStream method looks like this:

```
Set ts = fil.OpenAsTextStream [IOMode][, Format]
```

where:

- *ts* is previously declared as Scripting.TextStream.

- *IOMode* is optional and is one of the values ForReading, ForWriting, or ForAppending, indicating the mode to be used when opening the file. The default value is ForReading.

- *Format* is optional and is one of the values TristateUseDefault (use the system default file format), TriStateTrue (open the file as Unicode), or TriState-False (open the file as ASCII). The default is TristateFalse, indicating that the file will be opened as an ASCII file unless you specify otherwise.

This method provides the same functionality as the FileSystemObject's Open-TextFile method. You'll find that method described in the section titled "The Text-Stream Object" later in the chapter.

Retrieving a Specific File Object

You can use the Drives, SubFolders, and Files collections of the FileSystemObject to drill down to a particular file. On the other hand, if you need information on a particular file, given its name, you can also use the GetFile method of the FileSystemObject. For example, you're more likely to use the second code example, rather than the first (both are in basTestProcedures), to retrieve a reference to J:\WINNT\WIN.INI:

```
Sub GetAFile1()
    ' Get a reference to a file, the hard way.
    Dim fso As Scripting.FileSystemObject
    Dim drv As Scripting.Drive
    Dim fld As Scripting.Folder
    Dim fil As Scripting.File

    Set fso = New Scripting.FileSystemObject
    Set drv = fso.Drives("J:")
    Set fld = drv.RootFolder.SubFolders("WINNT")
    Set fil = fld.Files("WIN.INI")
    Debug.Print fil.Size
End Sub

Sub GetAFile2()
    ' Get a reference to a file, the easy way.
    Dim fso As Scripting.FileSystemObject
    Dim fil As Scripting.File

    Set fso = New Scripting.FileSystemObject
    Set fil = fso.GetFile("J:\WINNT\WIN.INI")
    Debug.Print fil.Size
End Sub
```

Modifying Attributes

The Attributes property of a File object allows you to modify its attributes within the file system. You modify a file's Attributes property using only four of the possible attributes: ReadOnly, Hidden, System, and Archive. In each case, you must modify a bitwise value, toggling bits as needed to set these values. In other words, you can't simply set the Attributes property to equal one of these values—doing so would modify existing attributes. Therefore, you must use the Or operator to add one or more attributes to a file's attribute settings, and the And Not operators to remove one or more attributes. You can use the And operator to check whether a particular attribute is set. The procedures in Listing 14.2, from basAttributes, allow you to check, set, or clear one or more attributes.

Listing 14.2: Use These Procedures to Check, Set, or Clear One or More File Attributes.

```
Public Function CheckAttributes( _
 lngValue As Scripting.FileAttribute, _
 lngAttribute As Scripting.FileAttribute) As Boolean

    ' Given a file attribute and one or more
    ' attributes to check, return True if all
    ' the requested attributes are set, and False
    ' otherwise.
    CheckAttributes = ((lngValue And lngAttribute) = lngAttribute)
End Function



Public Function SetAttributes( _
 lngValue As Scripting.FileAttribute, _
 lngAttribute As Scripting.FileAttribute) As Scripting.FileAttribute

    ' Given a file attribute and one or more
    ' attributes to set, return the modified
    ' file attribute.
    SetAttributes = lngValue Or lngAttribute
End Function

Public Function ClearAttributes( _
 lngValue As Scripting.FileAttribute, _
 lngAttribute As Scripting.FileAttribute) As Scripting.FileAttribute

    ' Given a file attribute and one or more
    ' attributes to clear, return the modified
    ' file attribute.
    ClearAttributes = lngValue And Not lngAttribute
End Function
```

The procedures in Listing 14.3, from basTestAttributes, demonstrate the use of the three attribute-handling functions. ClearAllAttributes clears all file attributes from the file whose name you supply. SetReadOnly sets the read-only attribute for the selected file, and CopyIfArchived copies the selected file to a new location if its archive attribute has been set.

Listing 14.3: Test Procedures for the Procedures in Listing 14.2

```
Public Sub ClearAllAttributes(strPath As String)
    ' Given a full file name, clear
    ' all the modifiable attributes:
    ' Archive, ReadOnly, System, and Hidden.

    Dim fso As Scripting.FileSystemObject
    Dim fil As Scripting.File

    Set fso = New Scripting.FileSystemObject
    Set fil = fso.GetFile(strPath)

    ' Clear all modifiable attributes.
    fil.Attributes = ClearAttributes(fil.Attributes, _
     Archive + System + Hidden + ReadOnly)

    Set fil = Nothing
    Set fso = Nothing
End Sub

Public Sub SetReadOnly(strPath As String)
    ' Given a full file name, set the
    ' ReadOnly attribute for the file.

    Dim fso As Scripting.FileSystemObject
    Dim fil As Scripting.File

    Set fso = New Scripting.FileSystemObject
    Set fil = fso.GetFile(strPath)

    ' Set read-only attribute.
    fil.Attributes = SetAttributes( _
     fil.Attributes, ReadOnly)

    Set fil = Nothing
    Set fso = Nothing
End Sub

Public Function CopyIfArchived( _
 strInPath As String, strOutPath As String) As Boolean
```

```
        ' If the selected file has its Archive bit set,
        ' copy it to the output path.

        ' Return True if the file was copied,
        ' False otherwise.

        Dim fso As Scripting.FileSystemObject
        Dim fil As Scripting.File

        ' Assume the file won't be copied.
        CopyIfArchived = False

        Set fso = New Scripting.FileSystemObject
        Set fil = fso.GetFile(strInPath)

        ' Set read-only attribute.
        If CheckAttributes(fil.Attributes, Archive) Then
            fso.CopyFile strInPath, strOutPath, True
            CopyIfArchived = True
        End If

        Set fil = Nothing
        Set fso = Nothing
    End Function
```

TIP   For more information on working with files and file attributes, see Chapter 12.

Bitwise Arithmetic

The Attributes property of a File object is a long integer but is actually a set of bits (0s and 1s), each representing one possible file attribute. The position of each bit within the integer indicates the meaning of the bit. For example, if a file's Attributes property is 2051, the bits that are set represent 2048 + 2 + 1, indicating a compressed, hidden, and read-only file.

Each of the constant values shown in Table 14.8 (except Normal) has one bit set, indicating the particular bit within the Attributes property representing that particular attribute. For example, because the bit farthest to the right in the Attributes property represents the read-only attribute of a file, the ReadOnly constant contains all 0s except for the right-most bit, which is set to 1.

To modify the Attributes property, you use either the And or the Or bitwise operator. The And operator takes any two values and returns 1 in any of the positions that was 1 in both values and returns 0 in any of the positions where either or both were 0. The Or operator sets any position to 1 if either of the corresponding positions is 1, and 0 otherwise.

Therefore, to force a specific bit to be on, you use the Or operator with a number that has all zeros except in the particular bit you care about, where you have a 1. (This works because any value Or'd with 0 isn't changed, but any value Or'd with 1 is set to 1.) The SetAttributes procedure in basAttributes demonstrates this behavior.

To force a bit to be off, you use the And operator with 1s in all the bits except the one you care about, where you have a 0. (This works because any value And'd with 1 isn't changed, but any value And'd with 0 is set to 0.) To control whether you're turning bits on or off, you can apply the Not logical operator to the constant representing the bit you're attempting to toggle, which flips all the bits of a value from 0 to 1 or from 1 to 0. The ClearAttributes procedure in basAttributes demonstrates this behavior.

Therefore, because the constant ReadOnly contains the correct bit settings to set the file attribute so that it's read-only, you could Or it with the value returned from the file's Attributes property to set the file to be read-only. To turn it off, you And it with Not ReadOnly. This leaves all the bits alone except the one controlling the ReadOnly attribute of the file, which is set to 0.

To determine if a particular bit is set, you can use the And operator. If the file's Attribute property And'd with an attribute to check returns a value that's the same as the attribute to be checked, you know that the particular bit you were interested in is, in fact, set on. The CheckAttribute procedure in basAttributes demonstrates this behavior.

The TextStream Object

If you have a need to work with text files, you'll appreciate the TextStream object. Yes, we've introduced other techniques for working with text files in other chapters (see Chapter 12, in particular), but all the built-in VBA techniques are painful, at best.

The TextStream object in SCRRUN.DLL allows you to read and write text in a text file. In addition, you can choose to work with text a line at a time or on a character-by-character basis. (A line consists of characters up to, but not including, a carriage return/linefeed pair of characters.)

You can open the text file for reading, for writing, or for appending (depending on options you choose when you open the file). You cannot mix these options: that is, once you've opened a file for writing, you cannot go back and read text without closing the file and re-opening it. If you've opened the file to append text to it, the same limitation applies: you'll need to close and re-open the file before you can read any text. Basically, you can never move backwards within a text file without closing and opening the file again. You can only read characters moving forward and can only write characters with a forward-moving file pointer.

Opening a TextStream

You can create a TextStream object in one of three ways:

- You can call the *CreateTextFile* method of either a FileSystemObject or of a Folder object. This method creates a new text file and returns a TextStream object so you can programmatically manipulate the new file. The syntax for this method is as follows:

```
Set TextStreamVariable = FSOOrFolder.CreateTextFile( _
    FileName[, OverWrite][, Unicode]
```

where:

  - *FileName* is a string containing the name of the new file, including its path.

  - *OverWrite* is an optional Boolean (default value True), indicating whether an existing file can be overwritten without raising an error. Currently, the documentation incorrectly states that the default is False. It is not—if you omit this parameter, files get overwritten.

  - *Unicode* is an optional Boolean, indicating whether the file should be created using the Unicode character set (True) or using the ASCII character set (False). The default is False.

- You can call the *OpenAsTextStream* method of a File object. In this case, the syntax is as follows:

```
Set TextStreamVariable = fil.OpenAsTextStream( _
    [IOMode][, Format])
```

where:

  - *IOMode* is an optional value that can be one of ForAppending, For-Reading, or ForWriting. This tells the File object how you want to use the TextStream object that it's creating. The default choice is For-Reading.

- *Format* is an optional value that indicates whether to use ASCII (TristateFalse), Unicode (TristateTrue), or the system default (TristateUseDefault). The default value is TristateFalse, meaning that you'll get an ASCII file.

- You can call the *OpenTextFile* method of the FileSystemObject to open an existing file as a TextStream object. The syntax is as follows:

```
Set TextStreamVariable = fso.OpenTextFile( _
FileName[, IOMode][, Create][, Format]
```

- *FileName* is a string containing the name of the new file, including its path.

- *IOMode* is an optional value that can be one of ForAppending, ForReading, or ForWriting. This tells the File object how you want to use the TextStream object that it's creating. The default choice is ForReading.

- *Create* is an optional Boolean value (default is False) indicating whether the method should create a new text file if one with the specified name doesn't already exist.

- *Format* is an optional value that indicates whether to use ASCII (TristateFalse), Unicode (TristateTrue), or the system default (TristateUseDefault). The default value is TristateFalse, meaning that you'll get an ASCII file.

You can use any of these methods to retrieve a TextStream object. The OpenText-File and OpenAsTextFile methods can open an existing text file, and the Create-TextFile and OpenTextFile methods can create a new text file. Which technique you use is up to you—choose the one that's most convenient, depending on the objects you currently have available.

Making the TextStream Object Work

Once you've opened a TextStream object, representing a text file on disk, you can use methods of the object to read, write, and move within the text file. Table 14.10 lists all the methods of the TextStream object.

TABLE 14.10: Methods of the TextStream Object

Method	Description
Close	Close an open TextStream object. Although VBA will do this for you when the variable referring to the text file goes out of scope, it's best to close the file explicitly—this forces any open buffers to be flushed and guarantees that any data written to the file is actually placed into the file on disk.
Read	Starting at the current location in the text file, read the specified number of characters, move the current position forward by the specified amount of characters, and return the characters read from the file.
ReadAll	Read the remaining contents of the text file, starting at the current position within the text file, and return the text. Moves the current position within the text file to the end of the file. For large files, consider reading one line at a time or, at least, smaller chunks than the entire file.
ReadLine	Starting at the current position, read the remainder of the current line, move the current position to the beginning of the next line, and return the characters read.
Skip	Move the file pointer ahead by the number of characters specified in the parameter to Skip. Skipped characters are discarded—that is, they don't show up in the output in any of the methods that read from the file.
SkipLine	Starting at the current file location, skip to the beginning of the next line, disregarding any characters skipped along the way, and the carriage return/line feed between the current position and the new line. After a call to this method, the file pointer will either be at the beginning of a new line or at the end of the file.
Write	Write the specified text to the end of the file. This method doesn't insert spaces or line breaks, so use the WriteLines method if you want to insert a line at a time.
WriteBlankLines	Write the specified number of carriage return/line feed pairs to the output file, effectively inserting a specified number of blank lines.
WriteLine	Write the text you specify, and a carriage return/line feed, to the output file. If you call this without specifying any text, it will be as if you'd called WriteBlankLines(1)— that is, the object will simply insert a single blank line into the file.

Some points to consider:

- All methods that read and write from or to the text file take into account the current position (sometimes called the *file pointer*) within the text file. That is, calling the ReadAll method starts at the current position within the text file and reads all the text from there. The ReadAll method does not go back to the beginning of the file if you've already moved the file pointer.

- If you attempt to read when the file pointer is at the end of the file, you'll get error 62 ("Past end of file"). You'll get this same error if you attempt to read from an empty file.

- If you're reading from a file and want to go back to the beginning, don't attempt to use the Skip method to move. You'll need to close and re-open the text file to move the pointer backwards.

- The Skip method only works when you're reading. That means you cannot move to an arbitrary location in a file and start writing there. You can only create a new file and write continuously or append to an existing file. (This is just a limitation with this implementation of the TextStream object.) If you attempt to use the Skip or SkipLine methods when your TextStream object is open for writing, you'll receive a runtime error.

Properties of the TextStream Object

In addition to the methods listed in Table 14.10, the TextStream object provides four simple properties, shown in Table 14.11. You're most likely to use the AtEnd-OfStream property, which returns True once you've reached the end of the input file), but the others can be useful as well. (All the properties shown in Table 14.11 are read-only.)

TABLE 14.11: Properties of the TextStream Object

Property	Return Value	Description
AtEndOfLine	Boolean	Returns True if the file pointer is just about to reach the end of a line. This property is only valid when reading from a text file.
AtEndOfStream	Boolean	Returns True when the file pointer is at the end of the text file. This property is only valid when reading from a text file.
Column	Long	Returns the current column within the current line of text. This property is available either when reading or writing. After you write a new line, the Column property returns 1.
Line	Long	Returns the line number containing the file pointer. When you first open a file for reading or for writing, the Line property returns 1.

Using the TextStream Object

As a simple example of using the TextStream object, we've provided the AddLine-Numbers procedure (from basTestProcedures), shown in Listing 14.4. This procedure allows you to specify input and output filenames and, optionally, a starting line number, the amount to increment for each line, and the fixed width (padded with 0s) for the line numbers. For example, calling the procedure as shown here will create a file named OUT.TXT containing the contents of TEMP.TXT with line numbers starting at 10, incrementing by 10s, and with a fixed width of 4 characters. Figure 14.6 shows a portion of both the input and output text files:

```
AddLineNumbers "C:\temp.txt", "C:\out.txt", 10, 10, 4
```

FIGURE 14.6

Before and after photos, using AddLineNumbers to modify the text file

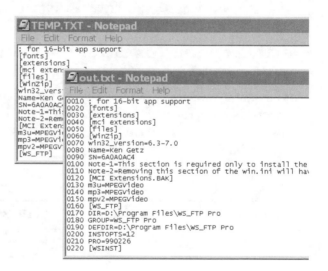

Listing 14.4: AddLineNumbers Demonstrates Reading and Writing Text Files Using the TextStream Object.

```
Public Sub AddLineNumbers( _
  strInFile As String, _
  strOutFile As String, _
  Optional Start As Long = 1, _
  Optional Increment As Long = 1, _
  Optional Width = 6)
```

```
Dim fso As Scripting.FileSystemObject
Dim tsIn As Scripting.TextStream
Dim tsOut As Scripting.TextStream
Dim lngCount As Long
Dim strLead As String
Dim strText As String
Dim strNumber As String

On Error GoTo HandleErrors

Set fso = New Scripting.FileSystemObject
Set tsIn = fso.OpenTextFile(strInFile)
' Accept all the defaults: Overwrite, use ASCII.
Set tsOut = fso.CreateTextFile(strOutFile)

' Create the leader text, by default: "000000"
If Width < 0 Then Width = 0
If Width > 10 Then Width = 10
strLead = String(Width, "0")
lngCount = Start

Do Until tsIn.AtEndOfStream
    strText = tsIn.ReadLine
    ' Add the line number to the piece of text.
    If Width = 0 Then
        strNumber = CStr(lngCount)
    Else
        strNumber = Right$(strLead & lngCount, Width)
    End If
    strText = strNumber & " " & strText
    tsOut.WriteLine strText
    lngCount = lngCount + Increment
Loop

ExitHere:
    On Error Resume Next
    tsIn.Close
    tsOut.Close
    Set tsIn = Nothing
    Set tsOut = Nothing
    Set fso = Nothing
    Exit Sub
```

```
HandleErrors:
    Select Case Err.Number
        ' Handle all errors the same.
        Case Else
            MsgBox "Error: " & Err.Description & _
            " (" & Err.Number & ")"
    End Select
    Resume ExitHere
End Sub
```

Working with the Dictionary Object

Although it seems like a poor fit for the rest of the objects in this chapter, the Windows Script Host also provides a useful in-memory data structure, the Dictionary object. Much like the VBA Collection object, the Dictionary object acts as an associative array. That is, you can add items to the dictionary, and for each item, assign a string (or any other data type) that uniquely identifies the item. In this section, you'll learn the properties and methods of the Dictionary object and why it's better than the built-in Collection object.

To create a Dictionary object, you can write code like this:

```
Dim dct As Scripting.Dictionary
Set dct = New Scripting.Dictionary
' Then, start adding items using the Item property
' or the Add method.
```

To get you started, Tables 14.12 and 14.13 list the properties and methods of the Dictionary object.

TABLE 14.12: Methods of the Dictionary Object

Method	Description

Add	Given a unique Key value and an item (both can be of any data type), add a new Key/Item pair to the dictionary. For example, you might write code like this:
	`dct.Add "Integer", 5`
	`dct.Add "Form", frmMain`
	In this example, the Key value was "Integer" or "Form," and the Item value was the value 5 or a reference to the opened form, frmMain. The first parameter (the Key value) must be unique within the dictionary.

TABLE 14.12: Methods of the Dictionary Object *(continued)*

Method	Description
Exists	Given a unique Key value, indicates whether a particular item exists within the dictionary. Just as when adding an item to the dictionary, the Key value can be of any data type. If the key exists, the Exists method returns True. Otherwise, it returns False. For example, the following expression returns True, given the items added in the example code for the Add method: `If dct.Exists("Form") Then`

Items	Zero-based array of all the items associated with the Dictionary object. You can write code like this to iterate through all the items:
	`For i = 0 To dct.Count - 1`
	`    Debug.Print dct.Items(i)`
	`Next i`

Keys	Zero-based array of all the keys associated with the Dictionary object. You can write code like this to iterate through all the keys:
	`For i = 0 To dct.Count - 1`
	`    Debug.Print dct.Keys(i)`
	`Next i`

Remove	Removes both a key and its item from the specified Dictionary object. If you attempt to remove a pair that doesn't exist, you'll get a runtime error. You must supply a Key value in order to remove a specific Key/Item pair from the dictionary. (Using a collection, you can specify an index to remove the item corresponding to that index from the collection—here, you cannot.) To remove the Key/Item pair associated with the Key value "Hello," you might write code like this: `dct.Remove "Hello"`
RemoveAll	Removes all Key/Item pairs from the dictionary: `dct.RemoveAll`

TABLE 14.13: Properties of the Dictionary Object

Property	Data Type	Description
CompareMode	CompareMethod	One of the constants BinaryCompare, DatabaseCompare, or TextCompare. In addition, you can specify a LocaleID value to specify comparisons for a specific locale. See Chapter 1, with information on the various string functions that compare two values. You can only set this property when there are no items in the dictionary.
Count	Long	Number of items in the dictionary.

TABLE 14.13: Properties of the Dictionary Object *(continued)*

Property	Data Type	Description
Item	Variant	Sets or returns an item for a specified Key value. If the key doesn't already exist in the dictionary, it gets created using the specified key and item. If you attempt to retrieve an item for a key that doesn't exist, a new key is created and its item is left empty. We suggest you use this technique (shown in the first bullet point in the upcoming section "Why Is a Dictionary Better Than a Collection?") rather than using the Add method, unless your goal is to raise an error when you attempt to add the same Key value more than once. You can use the Item property like this to return the value of an item: `varItem = dct.Item("Keyword")` To set the value of an item, you can use code like this: `dct.Item("Keyword") = "NewValue"` One interesting thing to note: the Key value of an item in a dictionary can be of any data type. It needn't be just a string. For example, you could add an item to a Dictionary object, using a form reference as the key: `dct.Item(frmMain) = Time` This code would add a new item to the dictionary, using the form named frmMain as the Key value, with an item containing the current time. Were you to call this code in the Load event procedure of every form, your dictionary would contain one item per form and the time each form was loaded.
Key	Variant	Can only be used to set the Key property for an existing key. That is, you can use the Key property to modify an existing element of the Dictionary, like this: `dct.Key("OldItem") = "NewItem"`

Taking the Dictionary for a Spin

Given that a dictionary looks and feels so much like a VBA Collection object, you may be tempted to use it as if it was a collection—you won't be making the best use of the object, and you'll likely be frustrated by the differences.

First and foremost, the Add method of a Collection object and the Add method of a Dictionary object look strikingly similar. For example, the following code (from the TestDictionary procedure, in basDictionary) adds items to a Dictionary object, dct:

```
Dim dct As Scripting.Dictionary
Set dct = New Scripting.Dictionary
```

```
dct.Add "Butter", "Dairy"
dct.Add "Carrots", "Vegetable"
dct.Add "Beets", "Vegetable"
dct.Add "Apple", "Fruit"
dct.Add "Milk", "Dairy"
dct.Add "Yogurt", "Dairy"
```

Given this code, the Dictionary object contains six Key/Item pairs, and the Key values are "Butter," "Carrots," "Beets," and so on (remember, the Key values must all be unique). The Item values are "Dairy," "Vegetable," and so on.

If you want to iterate through all the keys in the dictionary, you can use code like this:

```
Dim varItem As Variant
For Each varItem In dct.Keys
    Debug.Print varItem
Next varItem
```

TIP   The dictionary assumes you want to iterate through the Keys array, unless you specify otherwise. In other words, the previous loop would have worked without the explicit ".Keys" reference.

To iterate through all the items in a dictionary, you might write code like this:

```
For Each varItem In dct.Items
    Debug.Print varItem
Next varItem
```

You can also use a For...Next loop to iterate through the items or keys, like this:

```
Dim i As Long
For i = 0 To dct.Count - 1
    Debug.Print dct.Items(i)
Next i
```

TIP   Dictionary objects' Items and Keys arrays are 0-based.

You can modify a Key/Item pair's Key value, simply by setting the Key property to a new value, like this:

```
dct.Key("Yogurt") = "Frozen Yogurt"
```

You can, likewise, change the Item property of any Key/Item pair by simply changing the value, like this:

```
' The Item value was originally "Dairy".
' After this, it will be "Fruit".
dct.Item("Frozen Yogurt") = "Fruit"
```

To retrieve an Item value within the Dictionary object, you can either use the Item property, specifying the Key value; or you can use the Items array, specifying the location within the dictionary, like this:

```
Debug.Print dct.Item("Frozen Yogurt")
' You can also loop through the array, using
' a For Next loop.
Debug.Print dct.Items(5)
```

You can only retrieve a Key value using the Keys array, like this:

```
' You can also loop through the array, using
' a For Next loop.
Debug.Print dct.Keys(5)
```

A Simple Example

Back in Programmer School (we went there, a long time ago), we suffered through homework exercises where we were required to create a data structure to count the number of times each unique word appeared within a text file. Back in the dark ages, the best solution was to use a hash table (a somewhat complex data structure). Now, we've repeated the same experiment using a Dictionary object, and it's a lot simpler.

To test this technique, try out the CountWords procedure in basDictionary. You specify a text file, and this procedure fills a module-level Dictionary object with Key/Item pairs using the individual words as the Key values and the number of times the word has appeared as the Item value. Once this procedure has done its work, you can use the ListItems procedure to display all the words and counts. Figure 14.7 shows part of the output of running this procedure, in the Immediate window. Listing 14.5 shows the full code for both procedures.

FIGURE 14.7

Use the CountWords and ListItems procedures to test out a Dictionary object.

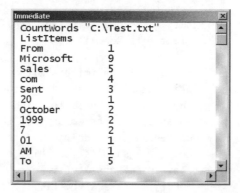

○ **Listing 14.5: The CountWords and ListItems Procedures Use a Dictionary Object to Maintain a Listing of Words and the Number of Times Each Occurs within a Text File.**

```
Private mdct As Scripting.Dictionary

Public Sub CountWords(strFileName As String)

    ' Given a text file name, add an item to
    ' mdct for each distinct word. Keep track
    ' of the number of times each word appears
    ' in the text file.

    Dim fso As Scripting.FileSystemObject
    Dim ts As Scripting.TextStream

    Dim strText As String
    Dim astrItems() As String
    Dim i As Long

    On Error GoTo HandleErrors

    Set fso = New Scripting.FileSystemObject
    Set mdct = New Scripting.Dictionary
```

```
    ' Open the text file, and read it all
    ' into a string.
    Set ts = fso.OpenTextFile(strFileName)
    strText = ts.ReadAll

    ' Replace all delimiters with spaces.
    ' Trim out all the extra white space, and
    ' then call the Split function to retrieve
    ' an array full of words from the file.
    ' dhTranslate and dhTrimAll are copied from the
    ' Chapter 1 samples for this book.
    strText = dhTranslate(strText, _
      " @()[]{},;:.-" & vbCrLf, " ")
    strText = dhTrimAll(strText)
    astrItems = Split(strText)

    mdct.CompareMode = TextCompare
    For i = LBound(astrItems) To UBound(astrItems)
        strText = astrItems(i)
        If mdct.Exists(strText) Then
            mdct.Item(strText) = mdct.Item(strText) + 1
        Else
            mdct.Item(strText) = 1
        End If
    Next i

ExitHere:
    ts.Close
    Set fso = Nothing
    Exit Sub

HandleErrors:
    Select Case Err.Number
        Case Else
            MsgBox "Error: " & Err.Desciption & _
              " (" & Err.Number & ")"
    End Select
End Sub
```

```
Public Sub ListItems()
    Dim i As Integer

    For i = 0 To mdct.Count - 1
        Debug.Print mdct.Keys(i), mdct.Items(i)
    Next i
End Sub
```

The sample code starts by instantiating both a FileSystemObject and the module-level dictionary:

```
Set fso = New Scripting.FileSystemObject
Set mdct = New Scripting.Dictionary
```

Next, the code opens the specified text file and reads its entire contents into a string variable:

```
' Open the text file, and read it all
' into a string.
Set ts = fso.OpenTextFile(strFileName)
strText = ts.ReadAll
```

The next chunk of code translates all text delimiters into a space character, trims off all excess white space, and then uses the built-in Split function to return an array full of all the words from the original text file.

```
' Replace all delimiters with spaces.
' Trim out all the extra white space, and
' then call the Split function to retrieve
' an array full of words from the file.
' dhTranslate and dhTrimAll are copied from the
' Chapter 1 samples for this book.
strText = dhTranslate(strText, _
  " @()[]{},;:.-" & vbCrLf, " ")
strText = dhTrimAll(strText)
astrItems = Split(strText)
```

TIP   See Chapter 1 for more information about the dhTranslate and dhTrimAll functions, provided in the sample code for that chapter.

It's important in this example that the Dictionary object disregard capitalization and treat uppercase, mixed-case, and lowercase versions of the same word as the same. Therefore, the next line of code sets the CompareMode property of the dictionary to treat all versions of a word the same:

```
mdct.CompareMode = TextCompare
```

Finally, the code that does all the work: The following fragment loops through all the items in the array returned by the Split function and, if the word already exists in the dictionary, increments its Item value. If the word doesn't exist, the code sets the Item value to be 1. Study this code fragment carefully—it points out how you can effectively use the Item property of a dictionary to add items to the data structure:

```
For i = LBound(astrItems) To UBound(astrItems)
    strText = astrItems(i)
    If mdct.Exists(strText) Then
        mdct.Item(strText) = mdct.Item(strText) + 1
    Else
        mdct.Item(strText) = 1
    End If
Next I
```

The ListItems procedure simply loops through all the items in the dictionary by position and prints out the Key and Item properties for each Key/Item pair:

```
For i = 0 To mdct.Count - 1
    Debug.Print mdct.Keys(i), mdct.Items(i)
Next i
```

Why Is a Dictionary Better Than a Collection?

The Dictionary object fixes several of the glaring errors in the design of the VBA Collection object—errors that continue even after several versions. Perhaps the VBA team doesn't see these issues as "errors," but they make the Collection object difficult, if not impossible, to use. In specific,

- You can add items to the dictionary using the Item property. That is, you can write code like this, to add a new word and initialize its count in a dictionary named dct:

  ```
  dct.Item("NewWord") = 1
  ```

- You can retrieve both keys and items, given a Dictionary object. That is, because of the Items and Keys properties, you can retrieve items from either array. In a collection, you can only retrieve the items, not the Key values. For example, you might write code like this to iterate through a Dictionary object, printing out the keys and values:

```
Dim i As Integer

For i = 0 To mdct.Count - 1
    Debug.Print dct.Keys(i), dct.Items(i)
Next I
```

- You can modify a key once it's been added to the dictionary. For example, imagine Excel's workbook, a collection of worksheet objects. Each worksheet must have a unique name within its collection (that is, the Name property acts as the Key value within its collection), yet you have always been able to change the Name property of a worksheet. Using a Collection object, the Key property of an object is write-only and write-once. If you need to change the Key value, you must delete the item from the collection and then re-add it with the new key. Using a dictionary, you can modify the Key property at any time (the value must continue to be unique within the Dictionary object, however). For example, to change the Key property from "lowercase" to "UPPERCASE," you might write code like this:

```
dct.Key("lowercase") = "UPPERCASE"
```

From then on, the item associated with the key "lowercase" would now be associated with the key "UPPERCASE" instead.

- You're not limited to using strings as the Key values for items in a dictionary. In a collection, each object can either have no Key value, or a unique string value. In a dictionary, each object must have a unique Key value associated with it, but that key can be of any data type.

- A Collection object provides no easy way to determine if a particular item has already been added to the collection. The Dictionary object provides the Exists method, which returns True if the specified Key value already exists within the dictionary.

- A collection provides no obvious way to remove all its items. The Dictionary class provides a RemoveAll method, effectively resetting the dictionary.

Summary

Although we could never attempt to cover all the available ActiveX components or even a small subset, we find the Scripting Runtime Library and its FileSystem-Object, TextStream, and Dictionary objects to be so useful and so easy to get that it made sense to spend a chapter digging into these objects. Just as with any other component, you'll need to worry about distributing the DLL and getting it registered on users' machines—don't underplay the importance of this step in your development efforts.

As you've seen, the Scripting Runtime Library provides a unique set of objects that allow you to

- Work with the hierarchy of drives, folders, and files in your computer's file system.

- Work with individual drives, folders, and files.

- Recursively drill into the file system, or work up from a specific folder back to the root folder.

- Open a text file, and read and write text in the file.

- Create a fast, simple-to-use in-memory data structure similar to, but more powerful than, the VBA Collection object.

Although we didn't cover it here, you may also find the other set of objects provided by the Windows Script Host to be useful. That is, take a look at the Windows Script Host Object Model (using the References dialog) for a whole group of more objects. To be honest, we didn't focus on this set of objects for two reasons:

- They're more limited than they need to be.

- We cover almost all of the functionality provided by those objects elsewhere in this book, with more flexibility available to you.

If nothing else, we hope that this chapter provided insight into the power of using external components in your VBA applications. If you have some extra hours, take the time to set a reference to other libraries you find available in the References dialog, look in the Object Browser to see what objects the library provides, and try working with the objects programmatically. It's a great way to while away the time on a long plane flight!

chapter 15

Writing Add-Ins for the Visual Basic IDE

- Understanding the VB and VBA IDE Automation interfaces

- Writing code that manipulates the user interface

- Modifying code programmatically

- Developing COM add-ins

Developers are unique among computer users in the fact that, when faced with a problem, they are more likely to invent their own solution than to look for an existing one. In particular, developers are fond of creating their own specialized tools that help them work with their purchased development tools. The Visual Basic Integrated Development Environment (IDE) affords programmers this ability by implementing both an Automation interface and an add-in architecture. Using the Automation interface, you can manage projects; manipulate components, such as modules and forms; and modify source code. This new feature opens the door for a whole new breed of utilities and add-ins. Furthermore, all of this is exposed with a consistent, COM-based add-in architecture now used by Microsoft Office 2000, Visual Basic, VBA, and the Microsoft Development Environment (the shell that hosts Visual C++).

In this chapter, we explain the basic concepts of Microsoft COM Add-in architecture and the add-in interfaces exposed by Visual Basic and VBA. (There are subtle differences.) We also discuss the IDE object model, focusing on the most useful classes, properties, and methods for managing your projects programmatically. We also introduce you to a custom object model, which we created to supplement the IDE's object model. We use this object model to add capabilities that are lacking in the IDE classes. If you've ever wanted to create tools to help you program, or if you just want to understand what's under the hood of the Visual Basic programming environment, this chapter is for you.

NOTE   To fully explore the add-in described in this chapter, you will need either a copy of Visual Basic 6 or a copy of Microsoft Office 2000 Developer, which includes the add-in designer necessary to compile the sample files. If you do not have either of these, we have included on the CD-ROM an Access 2000 database and an Excel workbook file containing material from the prior edition of this book that demonstrates VBA IDE Automation but cannot be used to create a true COM Add-in.

Table 15.1 lists the sample files for this chapter.

TABLE 15.1: Sample Files

Filename	Description
VBAIDE.XLS	Excel workbook containing sample code
VBAIDE.MDB	Access 2000 database containing sample code
IDEEX.BAS	IDE code examples

TABLE 15.1: Sample Files *(continued)*

Filename	Description
TESTPROC.BAS	Sample code module for testing the IDE object model
EVENTS.CLS	Class module for hooking VBA IDE command bar events
CBARNUMS.TXT	Command Bar button IDs for the VBA IDE
CODEEX.BAS	VBA code examples
CLASSEX.BAS	Custom object module examples
PROJECT.CLS	Sample Project class
MODULE.CLS	Sample Module class
MODULES.CLS	Sample Modules class
PROC.CLS	Sample Procedure class
PROCS.CLS	Sample Procedures class
VB IDE Addin.VBP	Project file for VB IDE add-in template
VBA IDE Addin.VBP	Project file for VBA IDE add-in template
VBIDET.DSR	VB IDE add-in designer template
VBAIDET.DSR	VBA IDE add-in designer template
IDEADDNT.FRM	VB form template with basic functionality
VBIDE.VBP	VB project for sample VB IDE COM Add-in
VBAIDE.VBP	VB project for sample VBA IDE COM Add-in
VBAIDE.VBA	VBA IDE COM Add-in project for VBA Add-in Designer
VBIDE.DSR	Add-in designer for sample VB IDE project
VBAIDE.DSR	Add-in designer for sample VBA IDE project
IDEADDIN.FRM	Sample add-in form
CODE.FRM	Sample add-in form
VBAIDE.DLL	Compiled VB IDE add-in
VBIDE.DLL	Compiled VBA IDE add-in

Working with the IDE Object Model

Before you can create a COM Add-in for either the VB or VBA IDE, you'll need to become familiar with the classes that make up their object models. Fortunately, they are very easy to experiment with, independent of an add-in, by using VBA in Microsoft Office. That's because the VBE object is exposed as part of an Office application's object model. This means you can write code in the VBA environment and run it from the Immediate window. The object model is relatively simple and easy to grasp. This section gives you an overview of the class structure, as well as examples of using it.

> **NOTE**   If you want to use the VBA or VBA IDE object models in your applications without using the COM add-in designer described later in this chapter, you'll need to add a reference to your project. To do so, open the References dialog box and select either "Microsoft Visual Basic for Applications 5.3 Extensibility" for VBA, or "Microsoft Visual Basic 6.0 Extensibility" for VB.

> **WARNING**   It's an unfortunate fact that the VB IDE and VBA IDE Automation interfaces differ ever so slightly. For example, project items in VB represent actual disk files, while in VBA, every project item is contained in a single file. As such, the properties and methods are not identical. In this chapter, we focus on the similarities, using the VBA IDE as an example and calling out the differences where applicable. If you're developing add-ins for Visual Basic as opposed to VBA, make sure you pay close attention to these differences and double-check the VB documentation.

The Class Hierarchies

The IDE class hierarchy features the VBE (Visual Basic Environment) class at its head. This is similar to the Application class used by many VBA host applications—it represents the top-level class of the hierarchy.

> **NOTE**   COM Add-ins receive a pointer to the VBE object passed in during the initialization stage.

Descending from the VBE class are a number of collections representing objects in the development environment: Addins, CodePanes, CommandBars, VBProjects, and Windows. Several properties of the VBE (ActiveCodePane, ActiveVBProject, and so on) return convenient references to other objects. Depending on what you're trying to do, you might find using these properties easier than using the related collections.

Table 15.2 shows a complete list of the classes implemented in the VB and VBA IDE type libraries. Note that some, like ContainedVBControls, are only supported in Visual Basic due its slightly different development capabilities.

TABLE 15.2: Classes in the IDE Type Library

Class	Description	VB IDE?	VBA IDE?
Addin	IDE COM Add-in	Yes	Yes
Addins	Addins collection	Yes	Yes
CodeModule	VB code module (normal or class)	Yes	Yes
CodePane	Code window	Yes	Yes
CodePanes	CodePanes collection	Yes	Yes
CommandBarEvents	Command bar control event interface	Yes	Yes
ContainedVBControls	Collection of controls contained within a control or form	Yes	No
Events	Global event interface	Yes	Yes
FileControlEvents	Project file event interface	Yes	No
IDTExtensibility	Obsolete add-in interface—add-in designers now implement IDTExtensibility2	Yes	No
LinkedWindows	Collection of dock-able windows	Yes	Yes
Member	Procedure within a code module	Yes	No
Members	Members collection	Yes	No
Property	VB component attribute	Yes	Yes
Properties	Properties collection	Yes	Yes
Reference	Project reference (e.g., type library)	Yes	Yes
References	References collection	Yes	Yes

TABLE 15.2: Classes in the IDE Type Library *(continued)*

Class	Description	VB IDE?	VBA IDE?
ReferencesEvents	References event interface	Yes	Yes
SelectedVBControls	Collection of selected controls within the UI	Yes	No
SelectedVBControlsEvents	SelectedVBControls event interface	Yes	No
VBComponent	Project component (e.g., module, form, etc.)	Yes	Yes
VBComponents	VBComponents collection	Yes	Yes
VBComponentsEvents	VBComponents event interface	Yes	No
VBControl	VB control (e.g., command button)	Yes	No
VBControls	VBControls collection	Yes	No
VBControlsEvents	VBControls event interface	Yes	No
VBE	Main IDE object	Yes	Yes
VBForm	VB form	Yes	No
VBNewProjects	A collection of new projects added to the environment after a given operation	Yes	No
VBProject	Root object for a VB or VBA project	Yes	Yes
VBProjects	VBProjects collection	Yes	Yes
VBProjectsEvents	VBProjects event interface	Yes	No
Window	VB IDE window (e.g., Code window, toolbox, etc.)	Yes	Yes
Windows	Windows collection	Yes	Yes

In this section, we show you a few ways to manipulate IDE objects by highlighting and describing each class. We also mention some of the more noteworthy properties and methods of the classes. While we focus on the VBA IDE object model, almost everything here also applies if you're writing add-ins for the VB IDE. However, this section is not meant to be a complete dissertation on the object model. For a complete list of the properties and methods of these classes, refer to the Object Browser and online help.

NOTE   You'll find the sample code for the first half of this section in the basIDEExamples module in VBAIDE.XLS. For the second half—the part that deals with modifying source code programmatically—you'll find the examples in the basCodeExamples module.

Working with Windows

The VBA IDE classes offer a surprising degree of control over the physical appearance of the IDE itself. You can write code to manipulate the main IDE window, as well as its children and command bars. Why is this surprising? Normally, when you consider what you'd like to do with the VBA object model, you think about modifying the objects and code that make up your project. (At least it's what we think about.) The IDE's user interface is immaterial. Nonetheless, it is a big part of the object model, so let's look at what you can do.

The Window Class

The Window class is a generic class that represents all windows in the IDE, including the IDE's main window. You access individual Window objects using the Windows collection of the VBE class (which contains references to the IDE's child windows) or its MainWindow property (which refers to the IDE's main window). The class features obvious properties, such as Top, Left, Height, Width, Visible, WindowState, and Caption, as well as SetFocus and Close methods. It also has a Type property that returns the type of a given window. Table 15.3 lists the possible values for the Type property. Finally, the Window class implements two properties, LinkedWindows and LinkedWindowFrame, which we explain in the next section.

TABLE 15.3:   Possible Values of the Type Property of the Window Class

Value	Constant	Window Type
0	vbext_wt_CodeWindow	Code window
1	vbext_wt_Designer	Object Designer window
2	vbext_wt_Browser	Object Browser
3	vbext_wt_Watch	Watch window

TABLE 15.3:   Possible Values of the Type Property of the Window Class *(continued)*

Value	Constant	Window Type
4	vbext_wt_Locals	Locals window
5	vbext_wt_Immediate	Immediate window
6	vbext_wt_ProjectWindow	Project Explorer
7	vbext_wt_PropertyWindow	Properties window
8	vbext_wt_Find	Find window
9	vbext_wt_FindReplace	Find-and-replace window
10	vbext_wt_Toolbox	VB Form toolbox (not applicable to VBA)
11	vbext_wt_LinkedWindowFrame	Frame for a linked (docked) window
12	vbext_wt_MainWindow	The IDE main window
13	vbext_wt_Preview	VB form layout Preview window (not applicable to VBA)
14	vbext_wt_ColorPalette	VB Color Palette window (not applicable to VBA)
15	vbext_wt_ToolWindow	VBA Form toolbox

Linked Windows

The VBA IDE features a number of windows (for example, the Project and Properties windows) that can be *docked* to the main IDE window. You dock a window by dragging it close to one of the main window's borders. When you release the mouse, the window "sticks" to the edge of the main window. Within the object model, these are known as *linked windows.* The Window class implements two properties that allow you to control the docking behavior. Both the LinkedWindowFrame and LinkedWindows properties return references to other Window objects.

If a given Window object is docked, its LinkedWindowFrame property will return a reference to the window it is docked to. In the current incarnation of the VBA IDE, this is always the IDE main window. (Presumably, Microsoft left the door open for future user interface designs in which a window might be docked to multiple objects.) If the window is not docked, LinkedWindowFrame returns Nothing.

LinkedWindows works in the opposite direction. It tells you which windows are docked to the current one via a collection of Window objects. Again, in the current version of the IDE, the only window that can have linked windows is the IDE main window.

WARNING   If you try to reference the LinkedWindows collection of a normal window (other than the IDE main window), VBA generates Error 91, "Object variable or With block variable not set."

As a collection, LinkedWindows has several properties and methods, including Count, Add, and Remove. Add and Remove both accept references to other windows and, when used, toggle the docked state of a given window. For example, the code shown in Listing 15.1 "undocks" all the docked windows in the IDE.

⟳ Listing 15.1: Undock Windows in the VBA IDE

```
Sub dhUndockAllWindows()
  Dim intWindow As Integer

  ' Use the LinkedWindows collection of the
  ' VBE object's MainWindow
  With Application.VBE.MainWindow.LinkedWindows

    ' Loop backward through each linked
    ' window, removing it from the collection
    For intWindow = .Count To 1 Step -1
      .Remove .Item(intWindow)
    Next
  End With
End Sub
```

Docking windows is a bit trickier because only certain types of windows (such as the Project, Properties, and Watch windows) can be docked Code windows, and other windows (like user forms) that appear in the main IDE workspace cannot be docked. Listing 15.2 shows a procedure that docks all dockable windows. Also, if you run the procedure, you'll notice that the configuration of the docked windows changes. (They dock in different places.) There does not appear to be any way to control where windows dock.

Listing 15.2: Dock Windows in the VBA IDE

```
Sub dhDockAllWindows()
  On Error GoTo HandleError

  Dim objWindow As VBIDE.Window

  Const conErrCantDock = &H80004005

  ' Use the VBE object
  With Application.VBE

    ' Loop through all its windows
    For Each objWindow In .Windows

      ' If the window is visible, dock it by
      ' adding it to the LinkedWindows collection
      If objWindow.Visible Then
        .MainWindow.LinkedWindows.Add objWindow
      End If
    Next
  End With

ExitHere:
  Exit Sub
HandleError:
  Select Case Err.Number
    ' Check for error when adding
    ' a window that can't be docked
    Case conErrCantDock
      Resume Next
    Case Else
      MsgBox Err.Description, vbExclamation, _
        "Error " & Err.Number
      Resume ExitHere
  End Select
End Sub
```

The dhDockAllWindows procedure, shown in Listing 15.2, works by looping through the Windows collection of the VBE object, attempting to add each window to the LinkedWindows collection. Note that before attempting this, the procedure checks the window's Visible property. This is necessary because when you launch the IDE, VBA opens all the environment windows (Locals, Immediate, and so on) and displays only those that were visible during the last editing session. If you attempt to add a hidden window to the LinkedWindows collection, VBA makes it visible. Normally, this is not a desirable side effect, and that's why the procedure first checks each window's Visible property.

Note also the error handling in the procedure. Since the For Each loop will iterate through *all* open windows and since some, like Code windows, can't be docked, the Add method may fail. The error handler traps this error and simply resumes executing at the next statement.

The CodePane Class

So far, we've discussed the general Window class. The CodePane class is a specific window type that corresponds to a Code window in the IDE. VBA maintains a separate CodePanes collection within the VBE object, in addition to the Windows collection. You also use the ActiveCodePane property. The most important property of a CodePane is CodeModule. It gives you access to your project's actual source code. We examine the CodeModule class in the section "Manipulating Code Modules" later in this chapter.

What can you do with a CodePane that you can't do with a normal window? Not much, as it turns out. You can determine how many lines of code are visible (using the CountOfVisibleLines property) and which line of code is at the top of the window (using TopLine). You can also retrieve and set the text selection using the GetSelection and SetSelection methods, respectively.

Listing 15.3 shows the dhCodePaneInfo procedure, which prints information about the active code pane to the Immediate window. To test the procedure, highlight some code in a Module window and then run the procedure from the Immediate window. Figure 15.1 shows an example of the output.

Listing 15.3: Print Details about a CodePane Object

```
Sub dhCodePaneInfo()
   On Error GoTo ExitHere

   Dim lngRowStart As Long
   Dim lngColStart As Long
   Dim lngRowEnd As Long
   Dim lngColEnd As Long
```

```
' Use the active code pane
With Application.VBE.ActiveCodePane
  ' Print window caption
  Debug.Print "Information on: " & .Window.Caption
  Debug.Print "==================================="

  ' Print visible lines and top line
  Debug.Print "Visible lines: " & .CountOfVisibleLines
  Debug.Print "Top line: " & .TopLine

  ' Print selection info
  Call .GetSelection(lngRowStart, lngColStart, _
    lngRowEnd, lngColEnd)

  Debug.Print "Selection:"
  Debug.Print " Start line:   " & lngRowStart
  Debug.Print " Start column: " & lngColStart
  Debug.Print " End line:     " & lngRowEnd
  Debug.Print " End column:   " & lngColEnd
End With
ExitHere:
End Sub
```

FIGURE 15.1

Printing information about the code selection to the Immediate window

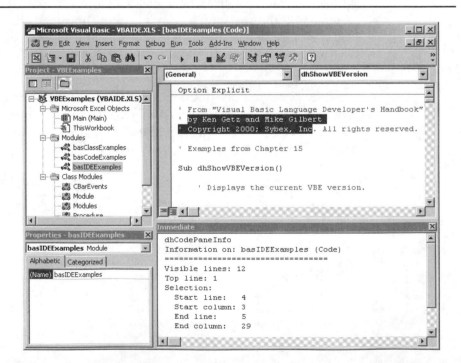

There are two items worth noting in this procedure:

- CodePane objects have a Window property that is a pointer to the associated window. You can use this property to access properties of the Window class described earlier in this chapter.

- The GetSelection method accepts four Long integer variables by reference and modifies them to represent the current selection. Make sure you declare these variables before calling the method.

What about Command Bars?

In the prior edition of this book, we spent several pages explaining how to manipulate command bars in the IDE. We've omitted that material from this version for two reasons: First, when we last wrote about the IDE, command bars were still relatively new, appearing for the first time in Office 97, and there weren't that many other sources of information. Second, before the advent of COM Add-in support in the IDE, the only way to manipulate command bars was by accessing them through the host application's object model, just as in the rest of the examples in this section.

Today there are abundant sources of information on programmatically controlling command bars, and it would be mostly redundant to cover the topic here. (For an extensive discussion of command bars, you can consult our *Access 2000 Developer's Handbook, Volume I: Desktop Edition*, also from Sybex.) Furthermore, it's likely you'll only want to manipulate command bars from within a COM Add-in. This is because pointers to Command Bar buttons (as well as their associated event hooks) are destroyed when the VBA run-time environment is reset—something that happens often in an Office application. That's why we cover command bars in the COM Add-ins section later in the chapter, and then, only briefly.

Working with VBA Projects

The remainder of this section discusses the most interesting aspect of programming the VBA IDE: working with VBA projects. This is where the fun starts, because it is this portion of the object model that deals with programmatic control of project components and source code.

The VBProject Class

The VBA IDE is a shared component, capable of hosting multiple projects at the same time. You would expect the object model to represent this. In fact, it does so by means of the VBProjects collection of the VBE object. Each VBProject object in the collection represents a loaded VBA project.

> **NOTE** When working with the VBA IDE object model, you cannot directly add or remove objects from the VBProjects collection. This must be done by the host application, but you can write code that instructs the host application to load a project. For example, you could write Microsoft Excel Automation code to open an XLS file containing VBA code. The VB IDE object model lets you create new projects, as well as open existing ones.

The VBProject class implements properties that map to those in the project options dialog (see Figure 15.2 for an example). For example, you can set and retrieve the Name, Description, HelpFile, and HelpContextID properties. Changing these through code changes the values in the options dialog and vice versa.

FIGURE 15.2

Project options you can set and retrieve using VBA code

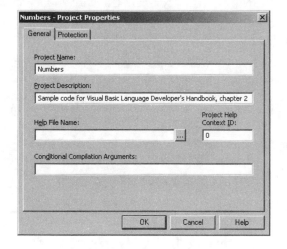

The class also implements several read-only properties that can give you additional information about the project. Specifically, the Mode property tells you whether the project is in Run, Break, or Design mode. These states are represented by the integer values 0, 1, and 2 and by the constants vbext_vm_Run, vbext_vm_Break, and vbext_vm_Design, respectively. Furthermore, the Protection property returns the value 1 (vbext_pp_locked) if the project is password protected and 0 (vbext_pp_none) if it is not. Finally, the Saved property tells you whether the project has changed since the last time it was saved. A True value indicates that no changes have been made, while False indicates that changes have been made but not yet saved.

Use the VBE object's ActiveVBProject property to return a reference to the project that is currently active in the VBA IDE.

The Reference Class

Part of a VBA project is the set of type library references for any Automation components it uses. Simple projects will have but a few references, such as those for VBA itself, Automation, and the host application. Complex projects—those that use additional Automation components or ActiveX controls—will have numerous references. You can manage references interactively using the References dialog shown in Figure 15.3. You can also manipulate them programmatically using the References collection of the VBProject class.

FIGURE 15.3
The References dialog showing type library references for a VBA project

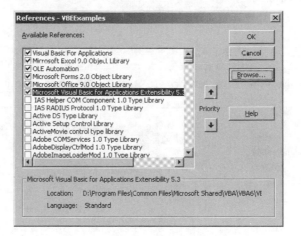

NOTE   If you're working through the examples in this chapter, your project will also have a reference to the VBA IDE extensibility type library.

As you might expect, the References collection contains one element for each reference in a particular project. The Reference class itself defines properties that describe the reference, such as Name, Major and Minor version numbers, Description, FullPath, Guid (for type library references), Type, Builtin, and IsBroken. The IsBroken property is of particular interest because when a reference is broken (because a type library or an application has been moved or deleted), the VBA project containing it won't compile. When you determine that a reference is broken, you can delete and re-create it using methods of the References collection.

WARNING   Be careful when manipulating VBA References using Microsoft Access 2000. Access implements its own References collection and Reference class that are slightly different from those implemented by VBA. This is a holdover from prior versions that did not have the full VBA IDE. You should disambiguate any object references in your code to use a specific class. For example, "Dim objRef As VBIDE.Reference" will force VBA to use its own Reference class, not Access'.

NOTE   Built-in references are required by the VBA project and will normally include references to VBA and the host application. You cannot remove a built-in reference from a project.

Listing 15.4 shows a procedure that prints information on the active project's references to the Immediate window. Figure 15.4 illustrates some sample output. Note the references to VBA and the host application (Microsoft Excel in this case).

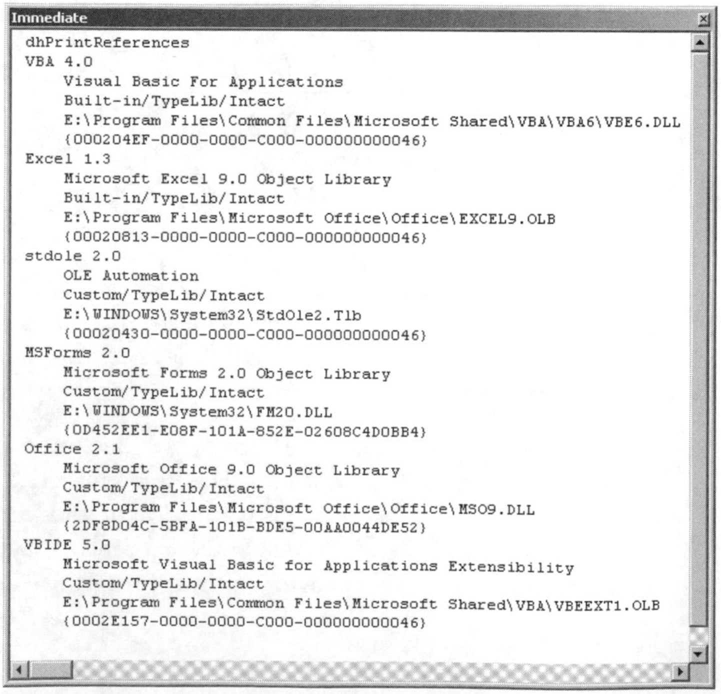

FIGURE 15.4

Reference information printed to the Immediate window

```
Immediate
dhPrintReferences
VBA 4.0
     Visual Basic For Applications
     Built-in/TypeLib/Intact
     E:\Program Files\Common Files\Microsoft Shared\VBA\VBA6\VBE6.DLL
     {000204EF-0000-0000-C000-000000000046}
Excel 1.3
     Microsoft Excel 9.0 Object Library
     Built-in/TypeLib/Intact
     E:\Program Files\Microsoft Office\Office\EXCEL9.OLB
     {00020813-0000-0000-C000-000000000046}
stdole 2.0
     OLE Automation
     Custom/TypeLib/Intact
     E:\WINDOWS\System32\StdOle2.Tlb
     {00020430-0000-0000-C000-000000000046}
MSForms 2.0
     Microsoft Forms 2.0 Object Library
     Custom/TypeLib/Intact
     E:\WINDOWS\System32\FM20.DLL
     {0D452EE1-E08F-101A-852E-02608C4D0BB4}
Office 2.1
     Microsoft Office 9.0 Object Library
     Custom/TypeLib/Intact
     E:\Program Files\Microsoft Office\Office\MSO9.DLL
     {2DF8D04C-5BFA-101B-BDE5-00AA0044DE52}
VBIDE 5.0
     Microsoft Visual Basic for Applications Extensibility
     Custom/TypeLib/Intact
     E:\Program Files\Common Files\Microsoft Shared\VBA\VBEEXT1.OLB
     {0002E157-0000-0000-C000-000000000046}
```

Listing 15.4: Print Reference Information to the Immediate Window

```
Sub dhPrintReferences()
  Dim ref As Reference

  ' Iterate the references of the active project
  For Each ref In Application.VBE. _
   ActiveVBProject.References

    ' Use each reference and print:
    ' Name and version
    '  Description
    '  Built-in or custom?
    '  Project or typelib?
    '  Broken or intact?
    '  Full path
    '  GUID
    With ref
      Debug.Print .Name & " " & .Major & "." & .Minor
      If Not .IsBroken Then
        Debug.Print "  " & .Description
      End If
      Debug.Print "  "; IIf(.BuiltIn, "Built-in/", _
        "Custom/");
      Debug.Print IIf(.Type = vbext_rk_Project, _
        "Project/", "TypeLib/");
      Debug.Print IIf(.IsBroken, "Broken!", "Intact")
      Debug.Print "  "; .FullPath
      Debug.Print "  "; IIf(.Type = _
        vbext_rk_TypeLib, .GUID, "")
    End With
  Next
End Sub
```

WARNING   You cannot access the Description property of a broken reference. Attempting to do so will result in a run-time error.

Removing References

If a reference is broken, you can rebuild it using methods of the References collection. You can't use Reference class properties because they are all read only and are set when the reference is added to the project. Therefore, you must first delete the invalid reference using the References collection's Remove method. Remove accepts a pointer to a Reference object as an argument. Listing 15.5 shows the dhRemoveAllBadRefs procedure, which removes all broken references from the active project.

Listing 15.5: Procedure for Removing All Broken References

```
Sub dhRemoveAllBadRefs()
  Dim ref As Reference

  ' Use the active project
  With Application.VBE.ActiveVBProject

    ' Iterate through the references
    For Each ref In .References

      ' If reference is broken, remove it
      If ref.IsBroken Then
        .References.Remove ref
      End If
    Next
  End With
End Sub
```

Adding References

Once you've removed the offending reference, you can then add it back to the project. You can add a reference using one of two methods of the References collection: AddFromFile or AddFromGuid. (Of course, this works the same way for new references, as well.) Use AddFromFile to create a reference to a DLL, an EXE, or another VBA project. For example, to add a reference to an Excel add-in, you might use code like this:

```
Application.VBE.ActiveVBProject.References.AddFromFile _
  "C:\Excel\Addins\MinMax.xla"
```

If the file does not exist and a path is specified, a run-time error occurs. If no path is specified, VBA searches for the file in the Windows and Windows\System directories, as well as in the current directory.

AddFromGuid adds a reference to a type library or other component based on its Globally Unique Identifier (GUID), which is stored in the Registry. You pass the GUID as a string, along with major and minor version numbers. VBA attempts to find the component in the Registry and, if successful, creates a reference to it in the project. For example, to add a reference to Microsoft Access 2000's type library, you would use a statement like this:

```
Application.VBE.ActiveVBProject.References.AddFromGuid _
  "{4AFFC9A0-5F99-101B-AF4E-00AA003F0F07}", 9, 0
```

If VBA can't find the reference, it raises a run-time error. If the exact version specified doesn't exist but a more recent version does, VBA adds a reference to the more recent version.

TIP   The easiest way to determine the GUID for a given type library is to add a reference to the type library to a project using the References dialog and then print the Guid property of the associated Reference object.

Modifying Project Components

Manipulating projects and references is fine, but what about the real meat of an application—the code-bearing components, such as modules, forms, and host-application objects? The VBComponent class represents all these objects. Each VBA project has a VBComponents collection that contains one object for each component.

VBA code modules (both class modules and regular code modules) are examples of VBComponent objects. The types of other components you can add to your project will depend on the host application. For instance, if you're using Microsoft Excel, your project will contain one Worksheet object for each worksheet in the workbook, as well as a reference to the workbook itself. A Microsoft Word VBA project would contain a reference to the associated document file. You can also add VBA user forms to projects based on Excel, Word, Outlook, FrontPage, and PowerPoint. (Visual Basic and Access have their own form design tools.)

The number of different object types that fall under the heading of VBComponents is quite large. However, as far as VBA is concerned, there are only five types of components: standard modules, class modules, user forms, ActiveX designers, and documents. The exact manifestation of the last category will depend on the host application. On the other hand, VB has a much richer set of components, including resource files, user controls, and ActiveX document objects.

Listing 15.6 shows dhDumpComps, a procedure that prints the components of a VBA project to the Immediate window. It accepts a pointer to a project as an argument and uses a For Each loop to iterate through each component. Figure 15.5 illustrates the output produced when calling the procedure from the Immediate window, passing a reference to the active project.

FIGURE 15.5
Sample output from the
dhDumpComps procedure

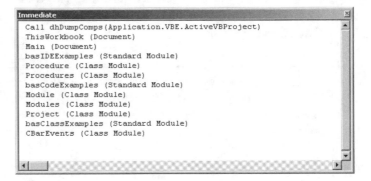

```
Call dhDumpComps(Application.VBE.ActiveVBProject)
ThisWorkbook (Document)
Main (Document)
basIDEExamples (Standard Module)
Procedure (Class Module)
Procedures (Class Module)
basCodeExamples (Standard Module)
Module (Class Module)
Modules (Class Module)
Project (Class Module)
basClassExamples (Standard Module)
CBarEvents (Class Module)
```

Listing 15.6: Procedure That Prints the Components of a VBA Project

```
Sub dhDumpComps(vbp As VBProject)
  Dim vbc As VBComponent

  ' Loop through each component in the project
  For Each vbc In vbp.VBComponents

    ' Print the component's name
    Debug.Print vbc.Name & " (";

    ' Print the component's type
    Select Case vbc.Type
```

```
        Case vbext_ct_StdModule
           Debug.Print "Standard Module";
        Case vbext_ct_ClassModule
           Debug.Print "Class Module";
        Case vbext_ct_MSForm
           Debug.Print "User Form";
        Case vbext_ct_Document
           Debug.Print "Document";
        Case 11 ' vbext_ct_ActiveXDesigner
           Debug.Print "ActiveX Designer";
        Case Else
           Debug.Print "Unknown"
      End Select
      Debug.Print ")"
   Next
End Sub
```

NOTE   There is no enumeration associated with an ActiveX designer declared in the VBA
IDE type library. However, the constant vbext_ct_ActiveXDesigner is defined in the
VB IDE type library as the value 11. Our procedure uses that value to indicate that
the component is a designer, such as the COM Add-in Designer or Data
Environment.

The VBComponent Class

From a programming perspective, the VBComponent class is simple. It features
Name and Type properties that correspond to a component's name and classifica-
tion (one of the five types mentioned in the "Modifying Project Components" section). Like the VBProject class that it's a part of, the VBComponent class has a
Saved property.

The VBComponent class also implements several methods. The Activate method
gives the component the input focus in the VBA IDE. The Export method accepts a
filename and exports the component's definition as text. You can use Export to
produce individual source files from a VBA project stored as part of a host application's document. For instance, to export the contents of a code module stored in
an Excel workbook, you might use code like this:

```
Application.VBE.ActiveVBProject.VBComponents("basMain") _
   .Export "C:\MAIN.BAS"
```

<table>
<tr><td>**NOTE**</td><td>While you can use the Export method of any VBComponent object, only the VBA-specific portions of the object will be exported. For instance, VBA exports an Excel worksheet object as a class module, including any code attached to the object's events. However, VBE does not include the Excel worksheet properties in the output file.</td></tr>
</table>

Creating New Components

Unlike most of the collections in the VBA IDE, you *can* add new members to the VBComponents collection, thus creating new components in your project. The Add method accepts an argument that defines the component type, but you cannot use this method to add an ActiveX designer. For that, you must use the AddCustom method. For example, to create a new code module in the active project, you could use code like this:

```
Set vbcNew = Application.VBE.ActiveVBProject. _
    VBComponents.Add(vbext_ct_StdModule)
```

Note that the Add method returns a pointer to the newly created component. In the preceding example, a VBComponent object variable, vbcNew, stores this pointer.

The AddCustom method, newly added to VBA 6, let's you add a custom component to your project. This is how you programmatically add ActiveX designers. You call AddCustom by passing the designer's GUID. Table 15.4 lists the GUIDs for designers that ship with Visual Basic 6 and Microsoft Office 2000 Developer.

TABLE 15.4:   ActiveX Designer GUIDs

Designer	GUID
Add-in	{AC0714F6-3D04-11D1-AE7D-00A0C90F26F4}
Data Environment	{C0E45035-5775-11D0-B388-00A0C9055D8E}
Data Report	{78E93846-85FD-11D0-8487-00A0C90DC8A9}
DHTML Page	{90290CCD-F27D-11D0-8031-00C04FB6C701}
Web Class	{17016CEE-E118-11D0-94B8-00A0C91110ED}

Keep in mind that with VBA you cannot add designers to standard VBA projects, you can only add them to stand-alone or add-in projects. As an example, assuming an add-in project is open in the environment, the following line of code would add a new data environment designer to it:

```
Application.VBE.VBProjects(2).VBComponents.AddCustom _
  "{C0E45035-5775-11D0-B388-00A0C9055D8E}"
```

You can also create new components by importing them from a text file. The VBComponents collection's Import method accepts a filename and returns a pointer to the new component, provided VBA was able to process the file contents successfully.

Finally, if you want to eliminate a component from your project, simply call the Remove method, passing a pointer to the VBComponent object.

Component Properties

What makes the VBComponent class truly useful is its collection of Property objects. Each Property object corresponds to a property of the particular component. These are the same properties that appear in the IDE's Properties window. You can iterate the collection to examine the name and value of each property. Listing 15.7 shows a procedure, dhDumpProps, that does just that. It accepts a pointer to a VBComponent object as an argument and uses a For Each loop to examine each of the component's properties. You can call the procedure from the Immediate window, as the following code illustrates:

```
Call dhDumpProps(Application.VBE. _
  ActiveVBProject.VBComponents(1))
```

Listing 15.7: Printing VBComponent Property Values

```
Sub dhDumpProps(vbc As VBComponent)
  On Error GoTo HandleError

  Dim prp As Property
  Dim var As Variant
  Dim fReadingValue As Boolean

  Const dhcPadding = 25

  ' Iterate the properties of the given
  ' component and print the names and values
  For Each prp In vbc.Properties

    ' Use each property
    With prp
```

```
' Print the property name, padded
' with spaces
If Len(.Name) >= dhcPadding Then
  Debug.Print .Name & " ";
Else
  Debug.Print .Name & _
    Space(dhcPadding - Len(.Name));
End If

' Set a flag indicating we're about
' to try to read the actual value
fReadingValue = True

' If this is an indexed property,
' print the number of indices
If .NumIndices > 0 Then
  Debug.Print "<indexed (" & _
    .NumIndices & ")>"

' If the value is an object, just print
' "<object>"
ElseIf IsObject(.Value) Then
  Debug.Print "<object (" & _
    TypeName(prp.Object) & ")>"

' If the value is an array, print
' each element
ElseIf IsArray(.Value) Then
  For Each var In .Value
    Debug.Print var,
  Next
  Debug.Print

' If the value is not an object
' or an array, just print it
Else
  Debug.Print prp.Value
End If

' Reset flag
fReadingValue = False
End With
```

```
NextProp:
  Next
ExitHere:
  Exit Sub
HandleError:
  ' If we were trying to read the value,
  ' print the error we got and move on
  If fReadingValue Then
    Debug.Print "<error " & Err.Number & _
      ": " & Err.Description & ">"
    Resume NextProp
  ' Otherwise, bail out
  Else
    MsgBox Err.Description, vbExclamation, _
      "Error " & Err.Number
    Resume ExitHere
  End If
End Sub
```

While the dhDumpProps procedure might seem needlessly complex, it actually is not. All the code is necessary due to the intricacy of a VBA Property object. To fully understand this, let's look at what the procedure does with each property.

After printing the property name, along with some padding to make the output look nice, dhDumpProps sets a Boolean flag variable that indicates it is about to try to read the property's value. The procedure does this so that if an error occurs, the error handler can skip to the next property rather than abort the entire procedure. For some reason, trying to read the value of certain properties results in run-time errors, despite efforts to trap for these cases.

TIP   Our procedure prints all the properties of a component, including hidden ones. Hidden properties often have an underscore as the first character of their name. To view hidden properties and methods in Object Browser, right-click anywhere in the Object Browser window and select Show Hidden Members from the context menu.

Indexed Properties

After determining that a property value can be read, a series of If and ElseIf statements try to determine what type of property the current Property object is and how best to deal with it. The first If statement checks the property's NumIndices property. Some component properties are indexed, which means that to read their values, you must supply up to four index values. An example of an indexed property is the Colors property of an Excel Workbook object. The Colors property is made up of 56 separate values representing the individual RGB color values used for the workbook's palette. You can write VBA code to set or retrieve any one of these values. To do so, you must use the Property object's IndexedValue property, passing a number from 1 to 56. For example:

```
Application.VBE.ActiveVBProject. _
  VBComponents("ThisWorkbook").Properties("Colors"). _
  IndexedValue(2) = RGB(255, 255, 0)
```

Since dhDumpProps is a generic procedure and doesn't know what type of component it is manipulating. When it come across an indexed property, it simply prints the string "<indexed>", along with the number of indices. If you were writing VBA code to manipulate a specific component type, you would certainly want to use the IndexedValue property with particular index values.

Object Properties

Next, the procedure uses the VBA IsObject function to determine whether the current Property object's Value property is itself an object. You will find that many component properties are objects with their own sets of properties and methods. Again, since dhDumpProps is a generic procedure, it simply prints the string "<object>" and the object type after the property name.

If you know the type of object being returned, you can manipulate the object's properties and methods. However, here's where things get a bit strange. The VBA documentation states that if a property value returns an object, you must use the Property object's Object property to access the returned object's properties and methods. For instance, to manipulate the font properties of a VBA user form, you should be able to use code like this:

```
Application.VBE.ActiveVBProject.VBComponents("UserForm1"). _
  Properties("Font").Object.Size = 10
```

However, in our testing, this did not work. VBA generated a compile-time error, "Method or data member not found" on the Size property.

What did work was using the Property object's Value property, although not as you'd expect. You might think you could use it in place of the Object property in the preceding statement. In reality, the Value property returned a collection containing the properties of the Font object. We were then able to use a statement like this one:

```
Application.VBE.ActiveVBProject.VBComponents("UserForm1"). _
  Properties("Font").Value.Item("Size") = 10
```

Note that the Item method is required when passing the property name (Size). While we can't explain why VBA behaves like this with object properties, it at least appears to be consistent.

We did find that the Object property worked when we assigned an object pointer to it. For instance, we were able to set the Picture property of a VBA user form using the following statement:

```
Set Application.VBE.ActiveVBProject. _
  VBComponents("UserForm1").Properties("Picure"). _
  Object = LoadPicture("C:\WINDOWS\WAVES.BMP")
```

LoadPicture loads an image file from disk and returns a pointer to it.

Scalar and Array Properties

If the Value property doesn't yield an object, it still might be an array, so the next ElseIf statement checks for this using the IsArray function. If IsArray returns True, the procedure uses another For Each loop to print each element of the array.

Finally, if none of the preceding conditions have been met, dhDumpProps assumes that Value is a scalar value and just prints it to the Immediate window. The last thing the procedure does is reset the flag variable.

Figure 15.6 shows some sample output from running the dhDumpProps procedure. The property values shown belong to an Excel Workbook object.

FIGURE 15.6
Property names and values
for a workbook

Component Designers

Components can also have designers. In the context of components, *designers* are supplemental windows that allow you to change the design of a component. The most common example of a designer is the VBA User Form Design window, but other examples may include things like the COM Add-in designer or the Data Environment designer. Designers allow you to easily change property values (in conjunction with the Properties window).

NOTE   VBA standard and class modules do not have designers.

The VBComponent class implements one method and two properties that allow you to interact with component designers. First, the DesignerWindow method returns a pointer to the component's Designer window. The object returned belongs to the VBA IDE Window class, so you can use all the properties and methods described earlier in this chapter. For example, to display the Designer window for a VBA user form, you could use a statement like this:

```
Application.VBE.ActiveVBProject. _
  VBComponents("UserForm1").DesignerWindow.Visible = True
```

You can tell whether a particular Designer window is open by inspecting the HasOpenDesigner property.

The Designer method of the VBComponent class gives you direct control over the designer itself. Depending on the component, this may give you additional design capabilities. For instance, a VBA user form designer provides access to a UserForm object from the MSForms type library. By using properties and methods of the UserForm class, you can change the appearance of the form, as well as its controls. The following statement prints the number of controls on a user form, named UserForm1, to the Immediate window:

```
Debug.Print Application.VBE.ActiveVBProject. _
  VBComponents("UserForm1").Designer.Controls.Count
```

TIP   Exploring the MSForms type library is beyond the scope of this book. However, you can check it out yourself by using Object Browser. A reference to the type library is added to all VBA projects hosted by Microsoft Excel, PowerPoint, Outlook, FrontPage, and Word.

Manipulating Code Modules

You'll find VBA code in two places within the IDE object model: as properties of both the CodePane and VBComponent classes. Each class has a CodeModule property that returns a pointer to the associated CodeModule object. The CodeModule class is perhaps the most complex of the VBA IDE classes. It is also the most fun and most rewarding to work with.

Counting Code Lines

The CodeModule class implements a number of properties that provide numerical counts of code lines. The CountOfLines and CountOfDeclarationLines properties return the total number of lines in the module and the number of lines in the declarations section, respectively. Obviously, the number of lines occupied by procedures is the difference between the two. Listing 15.8 shows a code fragment that illustrates how to use these properties.

Listing 15.8: Count Lines of Code in a Module

```
With Application.VBE.ActiveVBProject. _
  VBComponents("basCodeExamples").CodeModule

  Debug.Print "Total lines: " & .CountOfLines
  Debug.Print "Declarations: " & .CountOfDeclarationLines
  Debug.Print "Procedures: " & .CountOfLines - _
    .CountOfDeclarationLines
End With
```

CodeModule objects also have a ProcCountLines property that returns the number of lines in a given procedure. We'll discuss that in a moment, in the section "Working with Procedures."

Getting at the Code

To return the actual contents of a module, use the Lines property. Lines accepts two arguments: a starting line number and a line count. It returns the text specified by the two values. Listing 15.9 shows code that complements that shown in Listing 15.8. Instead of printing the number of lines to the Immediate window, the code in Listing 15.9 prints the actual text.

Listing 15.9: Print the Contents of a Module

```
With Application.VBE.ActiveVBProject. _
  VBComponents("basCodeExamples").CodeModule

  Debug.Print "All code:"
  Debug.Print .Lines(1, .CountOfLines)

  Debug.Print "Declarations:"
  Debug.Print .Lines(1, .CountOfDeclarationLines)

  Debug.Print "Procedures:"
  Debug.Print .Lines(.CountOfDeclarationLines + 1, _
    .CountOfLines - .CountOfDeclarationLines)
End With
```

Working with Procedures

Using the CodeModule class, you can work with VBA procedures programmatically. Unfortunately, the VBA IDE object module does not subdivide code modules into procedures. To work with procedures, you call methods of the CodeModule class, passing (among other things) the name of the procedure you want to work with. Of course, this assumes you *know* the name of the procedure! Fortunately, there is a way, albeit not simple, to determine the procedures contained within a code module: You use the ProcOfLine property to pass a line number. The result is the name of the procedure that contains that line of code. For example, to determine the name of the procedure that contains the tenth line of code in the basIDE-Examples module, you would use the following statement:

```
Debug.Print Application.VBE.ActiveVBProject. _
  VBComponents("basIDEExamples").CodeModule. _
  ProcOfLine(10, lngType)
```

If you executed this line of code in the sample project for this chapter, the result would be "dhShowVBEVersion". The second argument to ProcOfLine, lngType, is a Long integer that the ProcOfLine property will fill in with the type of procedure on the specified line. It will contain a value from 0 to 3, which represents standard procedures (Subs and Functions) and Property Let, Set, and Get statements, respectively.

Once you know the name and type of a procedure in a module, there are several other properties you can use. All of the following properties accept a procedure name and type as arguments:

ProcStartLine   Returns the line on which a procedure begins.

ProcBodyLine   Returns the line on which a procedure's code begins (the line containing the Sub, Function, or Property statement). This differs from ProcStartLine, which may include preceding comments or blank lines.

ProcCountLines   Returns the length of the procedure, in lines, including any preceding comments or blank lines.

Using these properties, you can quickly list all the procedures in a module. Listing 15.10 shows a procedure that does just this. dhListProcs accepts a CodeModule object as an argument and uses the CountOfLines property to loop through each line of code. For each line, the procedure employs the ProcOfLine property to determine whether the current line is contained within a procedure definition.

Listing 15.10: Procedure That Lists the Procedures in a Module

```
Sub dhListProcs(modAny As CodeModule)
    Dim cLines As Long
    Dim lngType As Long
    Dim strProc As String

    ' Use the passed CodeModule
    With modAny
        ' Loop through all the code lines,
        ' looking for a procedure
        For cLines = 1 To .CountOfLines

            ' Get the name of the procedure
            ' on the current line
            strProc = .ProcOfLine(cLines, lngType)

            ' If non-blank we've found a proc
            If strProc <> "" Then

                ' Print the line number, proc
                ' name, and type
                Debug.Print "Line " & cLines, _
                 strProc & "(" & lngType & ")"
```

```
                ' Skip the code lines by adding the
                ' number of lines in the proc (less one)
                ' to the current line number
                cLines = cLines + _
                  .ProcCountLines(strProc, lngType) - 1
            End If
        Next
    End With
End Sub
```

Most lines in a typical module will be part of some procedure, so it doesn't make sense to loop through every line. Instead, once dhListProcs has found the line at the start of a procedure, it skips the line following the end of the procedure. It does this by adding the number of lines in the procedure (obtained using the ProcCountLines property), minus 1, to the current line number. This results in a procedure that executes quite quickly, even on a large module. Figure 15.7 shows sample output obtained by running the procedure.

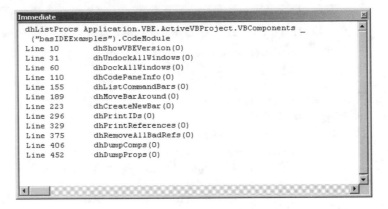

In the section "Putting It Together: An Alternative Object Model" later in this chapter, you'll see how to integrate this code into a class module that creates and maintains a collection of procedures.

NOTE   The VB IDE object model does give you a more direct way to access procedures via its Members collection. This collection contains objects that provide you with the starting line of each procedure within a module.

CodeModule Methods

As good as the VBA IDE object model is, it is not very granular when it comes to modifying code. We've already explained that there is no direct support for procedures. You perform code modifications indirectly, as well. Specifically, there are seven methods of the CodeModule class that you can use to modify code:

AddFromFile   Accepts a filename and adds the contents of the file to the module after the declarations section but before the first existing procedure.

AddFromString   Works like AddFromFile, but it accepts a text string as an argument rather than a filename.

CreateEventProc   Accepts object and event names, both as text, and creates a new event procedure in the module. It returns the number of the line on which the new event procedure starts.

DeleteLines   Accepts a starting line number and an optional number of lines. It deletes the specified number of lines of code (the default is 1) from the module, starting at the line passed as the first argument.

Find   Locates text within the module. It accepts a number of arguments that affect its search logic. (We explain Find in more detail in the section "Finding and Replacing Code" later in this chapter.)

InsertLines   Accepts a line number and a text string as arguments. It inserts the contents of the text string at the specified line.

ReplaceLine   Accepts a line number and a text string as arguments. It replaces the existing line at the specified location with the supplied text.

Adding and Removing Code

What could be easier than adding code to a module? The AddFromFile and AddFromString methods are fairly self-explanatory. AddFromFile inserts the contents of a text file containing VBA code into a module after the declarations section. AddFromString simply inserts whatever you pass as an argument. For example, the code in Listing 15.11 creates a new code module in the active project, inserts a global variable declaration, and then inserts the contents of a file. Figure 15.8 shows the new code module.

Listing 15.11: Create a New Module and Insert Some Code

```
Sub dhNewModule()
  ' Use the active project
  With Application.VBE.ActiveVBProject

    ' Create and use a new module
    With .VBComponents.Add(vbext_ct_StdModule)

      ' Change the module name
      .Name = "basTest"

      ' Use the code module
      With .CodeModule

        ' Add a variable declaration
        .AddFromString "Global gintText As Integer"

        ' Add the contents of a file
        .AddFromFile "C:\TESTPROC.BAS"
      End With
    End With
  End With
End Sub
```

FIGURE 15.8

A new module created using VBA code

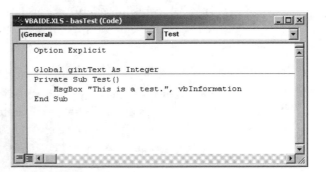

TIP

You don't have to add the Option Explicit directive to the new module if you've enabled the Require Variable Declaration option. If you're not sure if this option is enabled, you can use the Lines and CountOfDeclarationLines properties (or the Find method described in the section "Finding and Replacing Code") to search the declarations section.

Like AddFromString, the InsertLines method accepts a text string and inserts it into the module. However, it inserts the string at a location specified by its first argument. Suppose, for example, you wanted to insert a comment block at the beginning of a module. You couldn't use AddFromString, because that method inserts text at the *end* of the declarations section. By using InsertLines, on the other hand, you can put the text wherever you want. The following code illustrates this.

```
' Add a comment block
With Application.VBE.ActiveVBProject. _
 VBComponents("basTest").CodeModule

    .InsertLines 1, "'========================"
    .InsertLines 2, "' Created by me, " & Date
    .InsertLines 3, "'========================"
End With
```

NOTE

AddFromFile, AddFromString, and InsertLines each append a carriage return to any text inserted into a module. If you want to add additional carriage returns, you must embed them in the inserted text (using the vbCrLf constant, for example).

You can remove lines of code using the DeleteLines method. DeleteLines accepts a starting line and an optional line count. It removes one or more lines of code (one is the default) from the module, starting at the specified line. Therefore, to remove the comment block, you might use code like this:

```
' Remove comment block
Application.VBE.ActiveVBProject. _
 VBComponents("basTest").CodeModule. _
 DeleteLines 1, 3
```

WARNING   Use caution when calling the DeleteLines method. Make sure you know what you're deleting! You can inspect the text on the affected lines using the Lines property. You can also use the Find method (explained in the section "Finding and Replacing Code") to locate specific text before deleting it.

Event Procedures

Event procedures are special procedures that VBA calls in response to an event for a given object. The CodeModule class implements a special method for creating them: CreateEventProc. CreateEventProc accepts an object name and an event name as arguments and creates a new event procedure in a given module. It returns the line number on which the procedure definition begins. You can use this number to insert additional lines of code in the body of the procedure.

The code in Listing 15.12 creates an event procedure for the Initialize event of a new class module. It then inserts code (a comment and a MsgBox statement) after the procedure declaration. Note that it uses the line number returned by Create-EventProc as the starting line for the inserted code. Figure 15.9 illustrates the results of running the procedure.

NOTE   The object name for class modules will always be Class.

Listing 15.12: Create a New Event Procedure

```
Sub dhSampleEventProc()
    Dim lngStart As Long
    Dim strQuotes As String

    strQuotes = Chr(34)

    ' Create a new class module
    With Application.VBE.ActiveVBProject. _
     VBComponents.Add(vbext_ct_ClassModule).CodeModule

        ' Add a new event proc
        lngStart = .CreateEventProc("Initialize", "Class")
```

```
        ' Add some code
        .InsertLines lngStart + 1, "    ' This is a test"
        .InsertLines lngStart + 2, "    MsgBox " & _
         strQuotes & "Test" & strQuotes & ", " & _
         "vbInformation"
    End With
End Sub
```

FIGURE 15.9

A new class module with a
newly created Initialize
event procedure

One important consideration when using CreateEventProc is to make sure that the object in question exists and that it supports the specified event. If it does not exist or it does not support the event, VBA generates an "Event handler is invalid" error. However, you can create event procedures using the methods described earlier in this chapter for inserting code into a module. VBA does not verify the correctness of procedures created in this manner.

NOTE   You cannot create event procedures in standard modules. The only event procedures allowed for class modules are Initialize and Terminate.

Making full use of the CreateEventProc method goes beyond the scope of this book. It requires knowledge of the particular event-generating components in your project.

Finding and Replacing Code

The last way to modify a project's source code is by using the Find and Replace methods. Find is a powerful method that searches the code within a module, given a search string and a set of rules. It accepts five required and three optional arguments and returns a Boolean value indicating success or failure. These arguments are shown in Table 15.5.

TABLE 15.5: Arguments to the Find Method

Argument	Data Type	Required	Description (Default)
Target	String	Yes	The string you want to find.
StartLine	Long	Yes	The line on which to start searching.
StartColumn	Long	Yes	The column in which to start searching.
EndLine	Long	Yes	The line on which to stop searching.
EndColumn	Long	Yes	The column in which to stop searching.
WholeWord	Boolean	No	Specifies a whole word search. (False)
MatchCase	Boolean	No	Specifies a case-sensitive search. (False)
PatternSearch	Boolean	No	If True, allows the use of a wildcard. (False)

We can best describe how to use the Find method through an example. Listing 15.13 shows a procedure designed to search through a given module looking for the string "Copyright 2000". Once the string is found, the procedure replaces the line with one that reads "Copyright © 2000". (Listing 15.16 also illustrates the use of the Replace method.)

NOTE The Find method is case insensitive.

⟳ Listing 15.13: Example of Search-and-Replace

```
Sub dhFindAndReplace(modAny As CodeModule)
    Dim lngStartLine As Long
    Dim lngStartCol As Long
    Dim lngEndLine As Long
    Dim lngEndCol As Long
    Dim strLine As String

    Const dhcFind = "Copyright 2000"
    Const dhcReplace = "Copyright © 2000"
```

```
    ' Use the passed code module
    With modAny

        ' Set initial parameters
        lngStartLine = 1
        lngStartCol = 1
        lngEndLine = .CountOfLines
        lngEndCol = Len(.Lines(.CountOfLines, 1))

        ' Keep searching until no other
        ' occurrences are found
        Do While .Find(dhcFind, lngStartLine, _
         lngStartCol, lngEndLine, lngEndCol, True)

            ' Replace the line that contains
            ' the text with a new one
            strLine = .Lines(lngStartLine, 1)
            strLine = Left(strLine, lngStartCol - 1) & _
             dhcReplace & Mid(strLine, lngEndCol)
            .ReplaceLine lngStartLine, strLine

            ' Reset parameters
            lngStartLine = lngEndLine + 1
            lngStartCol = 1
            lngEndLine = .CountOfLines
            lngEndCol = Len(.Lines(.CountOfLines, 1))
        Loop
    End With
End Sub
```

The most interesting aspect of the procedure is how the Long integer variables are used. Before calling the Find method for the first time, the procedure initializes these variables to specify the entire contents of the code module. The starting line and column (lngStartLine and lngStartCol) are both set to 1. Ending line and column numbers are computed using properties of the CodeModule object. lngEndLine is set to the number of lines in the module, while lngEndCol is set to the length of the last line.

These values (along with the search string) are passed to the Find method inside a Do While loop. Since Find returns True only if a match was found, this ensures that it will be called repeatedly until it finds no other matches.

When the Find method is called and a match is found, the method sets the four long integers to values indicating where the search string was located. For example, if the second line in the module was

```
' Sample code copyright 2000 by Sybex
```

the lngStartLine, lngStartCol, lngEndLine, and lngEndCol would be set to 2, 15, 2, and 28, respectively. This would indicate that the search string started at line 2, column 15, and ended at line 2, column 28.

Our sample procedure uses this information, in conjunction with the Left and Mid functions, to substitute the new text for the old. Once it has constructed the new line of code, it calls the module's ReplaceLine method to replace the entire line with a new one. VBA limits you to replacing an entire line. You cannot replace individual characters directly.

Finally, after finding the text and making the substitution, it's important to reset the four numbers before calling Find again. Otherwise, the search area will be limited to the last known location of the search string! Our procedure resets the numbers at the bottom of the loop. Note that it sets the starting line number equal to the ending line number, plus one. That forces VBA to begin a subsequent search at the next line of code.

WARNING   Be very careful when modifying code in the currently executing module or a module containing procedures called by the current module. You might inadvertently alter compiled, running code, which may lead to unpredictable (and probably undesirable) results.

Putting It Together: An Alternative Object Model

So far, we've explained the individual classes, properties, and methods that make up the VBA IDE Automation interface. In this final section, we put it all together by building our own object model to represent VBA project components. The reason for doing this is to add functionality that the VBA IDE object model lacks. For instance, we've created a Procedure class that encapsulates individual procedures within a module. Creating our own object model also gives us additional flexibility in manipulating VBA projects and could be the basis for useful add-ins and utilities.

NOTE   You'll find all the nonclass module sample code for this section in the basClass-Examples module in VBAIDE.XLS.

Examining Our Object Model

We've created a very simple object model, consisting of three classes, two of which have associated collections. This required a total of five class modules to implement.

The Project Class

At the root of the hierarchy is the Project class. It has but one property, VBProject, in addition to its Modules collection. The VBProject property is a direct pointer to a normal VBProject object. We created this single property rather than replicating each of the properties of the VBProject class in our class. You can use the VBProject property to access any property of the VBProject object. Listing 15.14 shows a sample procedure that creates a new instance of our Project class, sets its VBProject property, and then reads the VBProject's Name property. If you want to use our object model, you'll need to instantiate the Project class in a similar manner.

NOTE   Because Modules is a class name defined by Microsoft Access, you cannot use it for a custom class module. You'll notice that we named the class VBModules in VBAIDE.MDB.

Listing 15.14: Instantiate and Use the Project Class

```
Sub dhUseProjectClass()
  Dim objProject As Project

  ' Instantiate the project
  Set objProject = New Project

  ' Set the new Project object's
  ' VBProject property to the active project
  Set objProject.VBProject = _
   Application.VBE.ActiveVBProject

  ' Print the VBProject's name
  Debug.Print objProject.VBProject.Name
End Sub
```

The Module Class

Our Module class is a thin layer over the VBA CodeModule class. The only real difference is that it appears as a child of the Project class. CodeModule objects are grandchildren of a VBProject. We're not interested in the project components, just their code, so we left them out.

Our class features Name and Kind properties, both of which are derived from the VBComponent object that contains the code module. You can access the Code-Module object directly through the Module property of our class in the same manner as the VBProject property of the Project class described in the previous section.

Finally, the Module class implements a Declarations property that lets you set or retrieve the contents of a module's declarations section. The property is initially set when the Module property is set. Listing 15.15 shows the Property Set statement.

Listing 15.15: Property Set Statement for the Module Property

```
Property Set Module(modModule As CodeModule)
  ' Make sure property hasn't been set
  If mmodModule Is Nothing Then

    ' Store the module pointer
    Set mmodModule = modModule

    ' Set the Module property of the
    ' Procedures collection
    Set mobjProcs.Module = modModule

    ' Read the declarations section
    mstrDeclarations = modModule. _
      Lines(1, modModule.CountOfDeclarationLines)
  End If
End Property
```

The Procedure Class

Going one step further than the VBA IDE object model, we've implemented a Procedure class that represents a procedure in a code module. This, combined with the Procedures collection class, lets us model a code module from a more detailed perspective. The class features Name and Kind properties, the latter based on the

VBA procedure types described in the section "Working with Procedures" earlier in this chapter.

Our class also has a Code property, which contains the body of the procedure, including the declaration and any preceding comments. The Lines property of the class dynamically computes the number of lines in the procedure, based on the code it currently contains.

The Collections

There are two collections represented in our object model: Modules and Procedures. We've implemented these as two class modules. In addition to the standard collection properties and methods (Count, Item, Add, and Remove), we've added a Refresh method. Refresh iterates through existing modules or procedures, adding them to the appropriate collection. Listing 15.16 shows the code from the Modules collection's Refresh method. Its implementation is straightforward. It uses a For Each loop to iterate through all the components in the project, checking their CodeModule property. If the method finds a valid CodeModule, it calls the Add method to add it to the collection.

Listing 15.16: The Modules Collection's Refresh Method

```
Public Sub Refresh()
  Dim vbc As VBComponent

  ' Clear out any existing objects
  Set mcolModules = New Collection

  ' Loop through each component in the
  ' project, adding its module (if it has one)
  For Each vbc In mvbpProject.VBComponents
    If Not vbc.CodeModule Is Nothing Then
      Call Add(vbc.Name, _
        vbc.Type, vbc.CodeModule)
    End If
  Next
End Sub
```

The reason the code in Listing 15.16 is so simple is that the VBA IDE object model features a collection of CodeModule objects (accessed indirectly through the VBComponents collection). Implementing a Refresh method for our Procedures collection (see Listing 15.17) is a bit more difficult. However, the code in Listing 15.17 should seem familiar; it's just an adaptation of the code we presented in the section "Working with Procedures" earlier in this chapter.

Listing 15.17: The Procedures Collection's Refresh Method

```
Public Sub Refresh()
   Dim cLines As Long
   Dim lngType As Long
   Dim strProc As String
   Dim objProc As Procedure

   ' Clear out any existing objects
   Set mcolProcs = New Collection

   ' Use the private code module
   With mobjModule
      ' Loop through all the lines
      For cLines = 1 To .CountOfLines

         ' If a procedure is on this line
         ' add it to the collection
         strProc = .ProcOfLine(cLines, lngType)
         If strProc <> "" Then

            ' Add a new Procedure object
            Set objProc = Add(strProc, lngType)

            ' Set its Code property
            objProc.Code = .Lines(cLines, _
             .ProcCountLines(strProc, lngType))

            ' Skip to the next line after
            ' this procedure
            cLines = cLines + _
             .ProcCountLines(strProc, lngType) - 1
         End If
      Next
   End With
End Sub
```

The only difference this time around is that instead of printing procedure names to the Immediate window, the Refresh method adds new Procedure objects to the collection.

If you look at the complete source code for our object model, you'll see that both collections implement properties that are pointers to VBA IDE objects. The Modules collection features a Project property that points to a VBProject object, while the Procedures collection features a Module property that points to an associated CodeModule object. We trigger the Refresh methods when these properties are set. For example, the code for the Modules collection's Project Property Set procedure is shown in Listing 15.18.

Listing 15.18: Setting the Project Property Triggers the Refresh Method

```
Property Set Project(vbpProject As VBProject)
  ' Make sure the property hasn't been set
  If mvbpProject Is Nothing Then
    ' Store the object pointer
    Set mvbpProject = vbpProject
    ' Call the Refresh method
    Refresh
  End If
End Property
```

All of this is triggered when the VBProject property of our Project class is set. Therefore, all you need to do to populate an instance of our object model is to instantiate a Project object and set its VBProject property. What could be easier?

Using Our Object Model

While we've constructed an object model for representing the code in a VBA project, we haven't done much with it. That's up to you. What kinds of things might you do with it? You could create a reporting tool that prints statistics on, and the contents of, a VBA project. Listing 15.19 shows a sample procedure that does this. After creating a new Project object, the procedure simply loops through each object in the hierarchy, printing selected information to the Immediate window. Figure 15.10 shows some sample output.

Listing 15.19: A Procedure That Prints Detailed Project Information

```
Sub dhPrintProjectInfo()
   Dim objProject As Project
   Dim cModule As Long
   Dim cProc As Long

   Set objProject = New Project

   ' Set the new Project object's
   ' VBProject property to the active project
   Set objProject.VBProject = _
    Application.VBE.ActiveVBProject

   ' Print project information
   With objProject.VBProject
     Debug.Print "Information for: " & .Name
     Debug.Print " Description: " & .Description
     Debug.Print " HelpFile: " & .HelpFile
     Debug.Print " HelpContext: " & .HelpContextID
     Debug.Print " Reference count: " & .References.Count
   End With

   ' Print module and procedure info
   With objProject.Modules
     Debug.Print " Module count: " & .Count

     ' Loop through each module
     For cModule = 1 To .Count

       ' Print module info
       With .Item(cModule)
         Debug.Print " Module: " & .Name
         Debug.Print " Type: " & .KindName

         ' Print procedure info
         With .Procedures
           Debug.Print " Procedures: " & .Count
```

```
                  ' Loop through each procedure
                  For cProc = 1 To .Count

                      ' Print procedure info
                      With .Item(cProc)
                        Debug.Print "   " & .Name & _
                          " (" & .KindName & ", " & _
                          .Lines & " lines)"
                      End With
                    Next
                  End With
                End With
              Next
            End With
        End Sub
```

FIGURE 15.10

Example of running the
dhPrintProjectInfo
procedure

```
Immediate                                                              ×
 dhPrintProjectInfo
 Information for: VBEExamples
  Description: Demonstrates how to use the VBA IDE Automation inter
  HelpFile:
  HelpContext: 0
  Reference count: 6
  Module count: 11
  Module: ThisWorkbook
   Type: Document
   Procedures: 0
  Module: Main
   Type: Document
   Procedures: 1
    shpStar_Click (Sub or Function, 3 lines)
  Module: basIDEExamples
   Type: Standard
   Procedures: 12
    dhShowVBEVersion (Sub or Function, 20 lines)
    dhUndockAllWindows (Sub or Function, 28 lines)
    dhDockAllWindows (Sub or Function, 49 lines)
    dhCodePaneInfo (Sub or Function, 44 lines)
    dhListCommandBars (Sub or Function, 33 lines)
    dhMoveBarAround (Sub or Function, 33 lines)
    dhCreateNewBar (Sub or Function, 72 lines)
    dhPrintIDs (Sub or Function, 32 lines)
    dhPrintReferences (Sub or Function, 45 lines)
    dhRemoveAllBadRefs (Sub or Function, 30 lines)
    dhDumpComps (Sub or Function, 45 lines)
    dhDumpProps (Sub or Function, 95 lines)
```

Coincidentally, this is more or less what we've decided to use as the example for
our COM Add-in. So, without further delay, let's explore that topic.

COM Add-Ins

Starting with Visual Basic 6 and Office 2000, Microsoft has taken a bold step toward unifying the programming experience for developers creating add-ins. Prior to these versions, if you wanted to write add-ins for multiple applications or development environments, you needed to cope not only with object model differences but also with differences in project, storage, and deployment models. However, this has all changed with the COM Add-in architecture in VB and VBA. Before we get to the individual extensibility models, we begin this section with a discussion of the COM Add-in architecture.

> **NOTE**   This section assumes some level of familiarity with COM and creating COM components. If you've never written a COM component with, say, Visual Basic, you may want to consult a resource like *Visual Basic Developer's Handbook* or *Visual Basic Developer's Guide to COM and COM+*, both from Sybex.

The primary benefit of the new COM Add-in architecture is that it's the same, regardless of application. Defined around a COM interface called IDTExtensibility2, the architecture defines how an add-in is registered with an application, how the add-in gets loaded, and what information is passed to the add-in regarding the application that it is running. What this means is that the add-in need only worry about the application's object model, not the idiosyncrasies of how it gets loaded, unloaded, and so on.

Since the new architecture is based on COM, you can use any COM-enabled tool, such as Microsoft Visual Basic, to create COM Add-ins. COM Add-ins are really nothing more than COM EXEs or DLLs that you can create with VB, C++, Delphi, or a host of other tools. You can also create add-ins in VBA using the COM Add-in Designer that comes with Microsoft Office 2000 Developer.

Using the COM Add-Ins Dialog

Both VB and VBA include a new dialog for managing add-ins. Figure 15.11 shows the dialog that you can access with the Add-ins ➢ Add-In Manager menu command.

FIGURE 15.11
The COM Add-ins dialog shows those add-ins registered with VB or VBA.

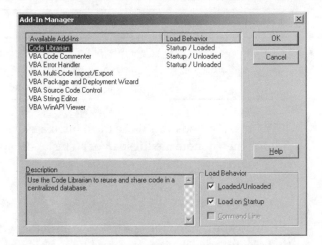

You can change the loaded or unloaded state of individual add-ins by selecting the add-in and checking or unchecking the appropriate check box. You can also change whether individual add-ins are loaded automatically when the development environment loads. Initial load behavior is covered later in this chapter.

Exploring IDTExtensibility2

The COM Add-in model is based on a COM interface called IDTExtensibility2. A *COM interface* is a defined set of properties and methods that a COM component must support. In this case, IDTExtensibility2 defines a set of methods that allow an application to load and unload add-ins and pass them useful information. Table 15.6 lists the methods that make up IDTExtensibilty2. When you create your own COM Add-ins, they must implement these methods.

TABLE 15.6: Methods Defined by IDTExtensibility2

Method	Description
OnAddinsUpdate	Called when an application's list of add-ins changes, for instance, if another add-in is loaded or unloaded
OnBeginShutdown	Called by the application prior to shutting down
OnConnection	Called when the add-in is loaded

TABLE 15.6: Methods Defined by IDTExtensibility2 *(continued)*

Method	Description
OnDisconnection	Called when the add-in is unloaded
OnStartupComplete	Called by the applications when it finishes its start-up routines (i.e., when the application is in a ready state)

The two methods you'll use most often are OnConnection and OnDisconnection, as they denote the lifespan of an instance of your add-in. The others also have interesting uses.

OnConnection

When an application loads a COM Add-in that you've created and installed, it first creates an instance of your add-in using the COM CoCreateInstance function call. Once it has a pointer to an instance of your add-in, it attempts to call the OnConnection method. OnConnection accepts a number of parameters, as you see from its prototype:

```
Private Sub AddinInstance_OnConnection( _
  ByVal Application As Object, _
  ByVal ConnectMode As AddInDesignerObjects.ext_ConnectMode, _
  ByVal AddInInst As Object, _
  custom() As Variant)

End Sub
```

The first argument, Application, is a pointer to the host application that's loading the add-in. In the case of VB or VBA, this will be a pointer to the VBE object described later in this chapter. Since IDTExtensibility2 can be used by any application, you can use the Application object to determine what application you're running in using the VBA TypeName function. OnConnection is also where you set up the mechanism for responding to events. (We'll explore this later in the section "Coding the Add-in.")

Additionally, OnConnection accepts a value indicating when the add-in was loaded. Table 15.7 lists the possible values for this argument.

TABLE 15.7: Startup Methods for a COM Add-In

Constant	Value	Description
ext_cm_AfterStartup	0	The add-in was loaded after the application was already running, either by selecting it in the COM Add-ins dialog or programmatically.
ext_cm_Startup	1	The add-in was loaded at application startup.
ext_cm_External	2	The add-in was loaded from an external source, such as from the VB Wizard Toolbar through Automation.
ext_cm_CommandLine	3	The add-in is an EXE loaded from the command line. This is only applicable to Visual Basic add-ins.

NOTE
The enumerated constants in Table 15.7 are defined by the COM Add-in Designer DLL that ships with Visual Basic and Microsoft Office 2000 Developer. We used the Designer to create our sample add-in. If you choose not to use the Designer or to create your add-in using other tools like C++ or Delphi, you'll need to either define these constants yourself or to use the numeric values in Table 15.7.

The AddInInst argument is a pointer to the instance of the add-in itself. It's useful for determining properties of the add-in at runtime.

Finally, the last argument, custom, is a Variant array that contains additional information that may be passed by the application. For example, Office 2000 applications pass one piece of information in the first array element indicating how the host application was started. Custom(1) will return 1 if the application was loaded normally (i.e., from the Start menu or by opening an Office document), 2 if the application was started by embedding one document inside another, and 3 if the application was started via Automation. You can use this to decide not to enable your add-in's functionality if, for instance, the host application was started by activating an embedded document.

OnDisconnection

OnDisconnection is the counterpart to OnConnection. It's called when an add-in is being unloaded from the host application. It's your chance to perform housekeeping tasks like deleting menu items or dropping database connections. OnDisconnection is similar to OnConnection in that your add-in will be passed information during the event. Take a look at the procedure definition:

```
Private Sub AddinInstance_OnDisconnection( _
  ByVal RemoveMode As AddInDesignerObjects.ext_DisconnectMode, _
  custom() As Variant)

End Sub
```

RemoveMode will be one of two values: ext_dm_HostShutdown (0) if the host application itself is shutting down, or ext_dm_UserClosed (1) if the user deselected the add-in using the COM Add-ins dialog. (RemoveMode will also be ext_dm_UserClosed if an application programmatically unloads the add-in.)

The custom argument contains the same information as the argument of the same name in OnConenction.

Other Add-in Methods

While you'll probably use OnConnection and OnDisconnection the most, you may occasionally write code for the other add-in methods. For instance, if your add-in depends on the host application being in a completely ready state, you delay taking any action until the OnStartupComplete method is called.

Likewise, if your add-in depends on other add-ins, you can write code in the OnAddInsUpdate method to check to see if the add-ins are still loaded. OnAddIns-Update is called whenever an application's list of loaded add-ins changes, either by the user selecting or deselecting them from the COM Add-ins dialog or through code. Both VB and VBA implement an AddIns collection that your add-in can query for the existence of other add-ins (and even load or unload them).

Building a COM Add-In for the VBA IDE

There's no better way to explore the ins and outs of COM Add-ins than by building a sample add-in. To demonstrate these techniques, we've created an add-in that provides information on projects loaded in the VBA IDE using our object model that was described earlier. In this section, we'll show how to create an add-in project and set up a reference to the IDE type library. Coding examples will come later, as we explore the IDE object model.

Using the COM Add-In Designer

The easiest way to create COM Add-ins is by using the COM Add-in designer that ships as part of Visual Basic 6 or Microsoft Office 2000 Developer. The Designer takes care of implementing the IDTExtensibility2 COM interface and includes a user interface for specifying options that enable the add-in to register itself with an application. If you don't use the Designer, you'll need to handle all these details yourself. Figure 15.12 shows the Designer window open in our add-in project.

FIGURE 15.12
COM Add-in Designer window showing options for the sample project

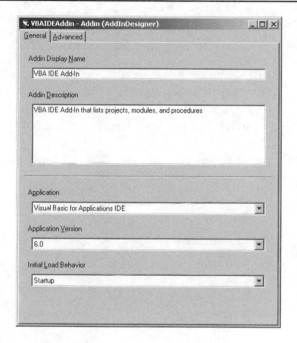

There are two ways to create a new add-in project, depending on whether you are using Visual Basic or VBA. In Visual Basic, you begin by selecting File ➢ New Project and choosing Add-in from the list of project types shown in Figure 15.13. Since VB creates new projects based on a list of templates, a new add-in project includes the add-in designer *plus* a default form and code module.

FIGURE 15.13
Creating a new add-in
project in Visual Basic

The template's sample code is optimized only for the VB IDE. We've included replacement project template files that enable you to create add-ins that work with the VB IDE or the VBA IDE. To use these, you must copy the files listed in Table 15.8 to the Templates\Projects subdirectory in the VB installation folder.

TABLE 15.8: Files That Compose Our Enhanced IDE Add-In Project Templates

File	Description
VB IDE Addin.VBP	Project file for VB IDE add-in
VBA IDE Addin.VBP	Project file for VBA IDE add-in
IDEADDNT.FRM	VB form with basic functionality
VBIDET.DSR	Add-in designer for VB IDE
VBAIDET.DSR	Add-in designer for VBA IDE

Once you've copied the files, two new entries will appear in the VB New Project dialog: VB IDE Add-in and VBA IDE Add-in (see Figure 15.14)

If you're using VBA and Office 2000 Developer, you create a new add-in project by selecting it from the New Project dialog, shown in Figure 15.15 (also accessible via the File ➤ New Project command). Unlike VB, the VBA add-in project does not include a form or any code. You'll have to write the code yourself. To make this easy, you can copy the VBA code (and only the VBA code) from the VBIDE.DSR or VBAIDE.DSR files into the designer's code module to create add-ins for VB or VBA, respectively.

FIGURE 15.14

Two new project templates
for IDE add-ins

FIGURE 15.15

Creating a new add-in
project in VBA

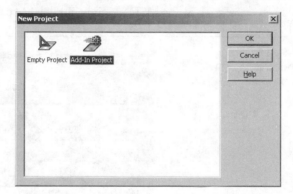

NOTE   The New Project command is only available in the VBA IDE if you've installed
Microsoft Office 2000 Developer.

Once you've created a new add-in project, you use the Designer's UI to set basic
options for the add-in. Table 15.9 lists each field and its purpose.

TABLE 15.9:   Settable Options in the COM Add-In Designer

Option	Description
Addin Display Name	Sets the display name as it will appear in the COM Add-ins dialog. Also sets the value of the COMAddIn object's Description property.
Addin Description	Sets the description as it will appear in the COM Add-ins dialog when a user selects the add-in from the list.

T A B L E 1 5 . 9 :   Settable Options in the COM Add-In Designer *(continued)*

Option	Description
Application	Defines the host application for this instance of the designer.
Application Version	Controls the version for which this add-in is intended.
Initial Load Behavior	Sets the initial load behavior of the add-in (see next).

The Advanced tab of the Designer lets you supply additional information that will be compiled into the add-in. Figure 15.16 shows the Advanced tab. Using this tab, you can specify a satellite DLL for your project. Satellite DLLs are used to provide localized resources separate from the add-in to aid developers who distribute solutions in multiple languages. For more information on satellite DLLs, consult a Visual Basic resource, such as the MSDN online library (`http://msdn.microsoft.com/`).

FIGURE 15.16

Advanced COM Add-in properties

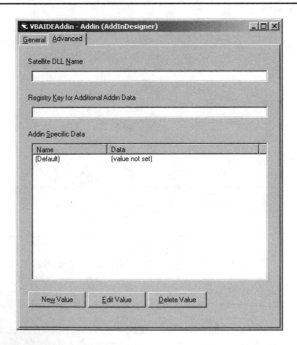

The Advanced tab also lets you specify additional Registry values under a key of your choosing that the add-in will create when it's registered with the operating system. You could use this, for instance, to set preference data into the Registry when the add-in is first installed. Simply set the Registry key you want to use to store the data (e.g., HKEY_CURRENT_USER\Software\VB & VBA Program Settings) and then use the command buttons to add, edit, or delete Registry values.

Specifying Add-In Load Behavior

Add-in load behavior is probably the most important setting on the Designer's dialog because it controls how and when your add-in gets loaded into the host application. There are four possible settings for this option: None, Startup, Load at Startup Only, and Load on Demand.

None

When you choose None as the load behavior, your add-in will not be loaded automatically by the host application. However, it will still show up in the COM Add-ins dialog so the user can load it. You can also load it programmatically by setting the add-in's Connect property to True using the object model.

Startup

Loading an add-in at startup will likely be the option you choose most often. When an add-in loads at startup, it appears as if it's part of the host application—a new feature—and the user never has to deal with the COM Add-ins dialog.

Command Line

This setting indicates that the add-in is an executable file and should be started from the command line. Command line startup is only valid for add-ins created with Visual Basic since the add-in designer that ships with Microsoft Office 2000 Developer can only create DLLs.

Command Line/Startup

This setting indicates that the add-in is an executable file and should be started when the environment loads but can *also* be launched from the command line.

Adding the Type Library Reference

After creating a new add-in project, you must set a reference to the IDE's type library to the add-in project. To do this, open the References dialog and make sure either "Microsoft Visual Basic 6.0 Extensibility" for the VB IDE or "Microsoft Visual Basic for Applications Extensibility 5.3" for VBA (see Figure 15.17) is selected.

FIGURE 15.17
Selecting the VBA IDE type library reference

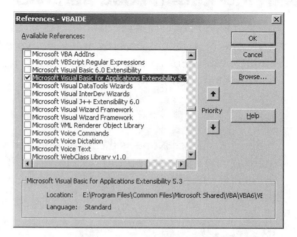

Many add-ins you'll create will want to add a custom menu command to the Add-ins or other menu. For this, you'll also need a reference in your project to the Microsoft Office 9.0 type library, which implements the command bars for the IDE.

TIP   If you use our enhanced VB add-in project templates, you don't need to do this since the correct references are already included.

Coding the Add-in

When you create a COM Add-in to work with the VB or VBA IDE, your add-in will receive a pointer to the IDE object (represented by the VBE class in Table 15.2) as part of the OnConnection event procedure. You must store this pointer in a module-level variable so you can access the IDE after the procedure terminates.

The most important coding task is writing code in the OnConnection event to somehow "hook" your add-in into the host application. This can be done through a custom menu command, a toolbar button, or through sinking to one of the IDE's events. Unfortunately, only Visual Basic's IDE offers any really useful events. Our sample add-in uses a Command Bar button to open the add-in's form but otherwise doesn't leverage any other events. Listing 15.20 shows the relatively small amount of code from our add-in designer.

Listing 15.20: Source Code from Our IDE Add-In Designer

```vb
Option Explicit

Public IDEInstance As VBIDE.VBE

Private mfrmAddin As frmAddIn
Private WithEvents mcbeAddin As VBIDE.CommandBarEvents
Private mcbbAddin As Office.CommandBarControl

Const conAddinMenuName = "IDE Add-in"

Private Sub AddinInstance_OnConnection( _
 ByVal Application As Object, _
 ByVal ConnectMode As ext_ConnectMode, _
 ByVal AddInInst As Object, _
 custom() As Variant)

    On Error GoTo HandleErrors

    Dim cbrAddins As Object
    Dim cbbNew As Office.CommandBarControl

    ' Store a pointer to the IDE
    Set IDEInstance = Application

    ' Create a new command bar button
    Set mcbbAddin = IDEInstance.CommandBars("Add-ins"). _
     Controls.Add(msoControlButton)
    mcbbAddin.Caption = conAddinMenuName

    ' Set its event hook
    Set mcbeAddin = IDEInstance.Events.CommandBarEvents(mcbbAddin)

    ' If launched from an external source (e.g. the
    ' wizard toolbar) show the form right away
    ' (VB IDE only)
    If ConnectMode = ext_cm_External Then
        Me.Show
    End If
```

```
ExitHere:
    Exit Sub
HandleErrors:
    Select Case Err.Number
        Case Else
            MsgBox Err.Description, vbExclamation, _
            "Error " & Err.Number & Err.Number & _
            " in Addin::OnConnection"
    End Select
    Resume ExitHere
End Sub

Private Sub AddinInstance_OnDisconnection( _
 ByVal RemoveMode As ext_DisconnectMode, _
 custom() As Variant)

    On Error Resume Next

    ' Delete the command bar button
    mcbbAddin.Delete

    ' Unload the form
    Unload mfrmAddin
End Sub

Public Sub Show()
    ' Load the form, give it a pointer to the IDE
    ' and show the form
    On Error GoTo HandleErrors

    Set mfrmAddin = New frmAddIn
    Set mfrmAddin.IDEInstance = Me.IDEInstance

    ' Refresh the lists of projects, etc.
    mfrmAddin.RefreshLists

    mfrmAddin.Show
ExitHere:
    Exit Sub
HandleErrors:
    Select Case Err.Number
        Case Else
```

```
                MsgBox Err.Description, vbExclamation, _
                   "Error " & Err.Number & " in Addin::Show"
        End Select
        Resume ExitHere
    End Sub

    Public Sub Hide()
        ' Unload the form
        On Error Resume Next
        Unload mfrmAddin
    End Sub

    Private Sub mcbeAddin_Click( _
     ByVal CommandBarControl As Object, _
     handled As Boolean, _
     CancelDefault As Boolean)

        ' Show the form
        Me.Show
    End Sub
```

Note the use of the WithEvents keyword in the declarations section to provide an event hook for the Command Bar button. After creating the new Command Bar button, the procedure references the IDE's Events collection to establish the hook for the new button.

The listing also shows the OnDisconnection event procedure, where the Command Bar button is removed, and the Show method, which handles the task of displaying the add-in's form.

Using Our Object Model

Our add-in uses the object model we described earlier in the chapter to provide a list of projects and their components. Figure 15.18 shows the add-in's form when it is open and displaying project information.

All of the project-specific code is contained in the form's module. Since the classes we created do most of the hard work, the form's code is relatively straightforward. For example, code behind the form's RefreshLists method simply uses the IDE's VBProjects collection to populate the form's Projects combo box. Listing 15.21 shows the code.

FIGURE 15.18

Displaying information on loaded projects

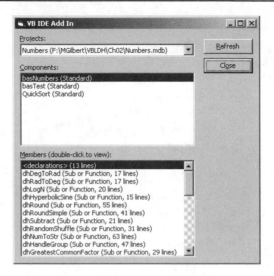

Listing 15.21: Building a List of Loaded Projects

```
Public Sub RefreshLists()
    Dim vbp As VBIDE.VBProject

    ' Clear the combo box and restock it with
    ' a list of loaded projects
    cboProjects.Clear
    For Each vbp In IDEInstance.VBProjects
        cboProjects.AddItem vbp.Name & " (" & _
        GetFileName(vbp) & ")"
    Next

    ' If there are projects, select the first one
    ' in the list (this will trigger the Click event)
    If cboProjects.ListCount > 0 Then
        cboProjects.ListIndex = 0
    End If
End Sub
```

The combo box's Click event is triggered when the procedure sets the control's ListIndex property. Code in the event procedure creates a new instance of our Project class, sets its VBProject property, and then uses its Modules collection to populate the Modules list box. Listing 15.22 shows the event procedure.

Listing 15.22: Populating the Modules List Using Our Object Model

```
Private Sub cboProjects_Click()
    Dim modAny As Module
    Dim strTemp As String

    ' Declare a new project as the current one
    ' and set it equal to the selected VB project
    Set mprjCurrent = New Project
    Set mprjCurrent.VBProject = IDEInstance. _
     VBProjects(cboProjects.ListIndex + 1)

    ' Clear the list box and restock it with a list
    ' of the modules in the project
    lstComponents.Clear
    For Each modAny In mprjCurrent.Modules
        lstComponents.AddItem modAny.Name & _
         " (" & modAny.KindName & ")"
    Next

    ' If there are modules, select the first one
    ' in the list (this will trigger the Click event)
    If lstComponents.ListCount > 0 Then
        lstComponents.ListIndex = 0
    End If
End Sub
```

Just as with the project list, setting the ListIndex property triggers an event procedure that fills the Procedures list box. Refer to the sample project for the complete code listing.

Debugging, Compiling, and Distributing

Once you've completed coding a COM Add-in, you must explicitly execute the add-in before you can debug it. In the case of the Office 2000 Developer COM

Add-in Designer, you do this by clicking the Run Project button on the toolbar (as opposed to the Run Sub/Userform button). With add-ins created using Visual Basic, you simply click the Run button. Other than that, debugging works just like it does with regular VBA projects. For instance, you can add a breakpoint in the OnConnection event to step through the start-up code.

After you've tested and debugged your add-in, it's time to compile it. To do so, select the File ➢ Make command from the Visual Basic Editor. This creates a COM DLL (although you can create a COM EXE if you're using Visual Basic) on your hard disk. It also creates the required Registry entries that associate the add-in with a host application on your development machine. You still need to cope with deploying the add-in to your users.

Once you've created the add-in, you can distribute it to others. Since it's a COM component, you'll need to register the component of each user's computer. For instance, if you want to do this manually to test your add-in on another developer's computer, you can use the REGSVR32 program. Just copy your add-in to a directory on the hard drive and run REGSVR32 from a DOS prompt as follows:

```
REGSVR32 <addinpath>\<addinfile>
```

REGSVR32 is normally installed in the Windows\System directory. If this directory is not in your PATH statement, you'll need to modify the command line. You can also unregister the add-in using the /u flag, like this:

```
REGSVR32 /u <addinpath>\<addinfile>
```

It's unlikely you'll want to install your add-in manually on every user's workstation. Instead, you'll want to use a setup program that will automatically install and register the add-in. The Package and Deployment Wizard that ships with both Visual Basic and Microsoft Office 2000 Developer creates setup programs that will do this.

COM Add-In Registry Entries

One thing that differentiates an Office COM Add-in from regular COM components is the set of Registry entries that associates it with a particular host application. We'll document these here, although if you use the COM Add-in Designer to create your add-ins, you probably won't need to worry about them unless you need to troubleshoot a misbehaving add-in.

The VB and VBA IDEs look in two different locations in the Registry to determine which add-ins they should load. Add-in information is stored under HKEY_CURRENT_USER\Software\Microsoft\Visual Basic\6.0\Addins for Visual Basic and HKEY_CURRENT_USER\Software\Microsoft\VBA\VBE\ 6.0\Addins. Note that all add-ins are associated with a given user.

When you register a COM Add-in, it creates a subkey that is its Prog ID. Figure 15.19 shows the Windows Registry Editor open to the add-ins key for Visual Basic. You can see the subkey for our sample add-in—its Prog ID is VBIDEAddin.Addin.

FIGURE 15.19
Registry entries for the
sample VB IDE add-in

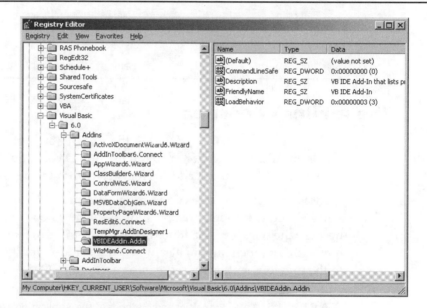

At load time, the IDE reads the subkeys looking for registered add-ins. It then looks at values for each key to determine whether to load the add-in. Table 15.10 lists the Registry values defined for COM Add-ins. LoadBehavior is the value that controls whether an application loads the add-in at startup or not.

TABLE 15.10: Registry Values for COM Add-Ins

Value Name	Data Type	Description
CommandLineSafe	DWORD	Determines whether the add-in can be launched from a command line.
Description	String	Description of the add-in that will appear in the COM Add-ins dialog.
FriendlyName	String	Name of the add-in that will appear in the list of add-ins in the COM Add-ins dialog.
LoadBehavior	DWORD	Load behavior of the add-in: 0 = none 3 = startup
SatelliteDLLName	String	Name of add-in's satellite DLL, if it has one.

The AddIns Collection

To help you manage COM Add-ins, the VB IDE (but not the VBA IDE) implements an AddIns collection. You can use this as you would any other collection to iterate through the list of add-ins registered with the development environment.

Table 15.11 lists the collection's properties and methods. You'll notice that while you can iterate through existing add-ins, there is no way to add new ones. That's because the only way to add new COM Add-ins is to make Registry entries. Normally, this happens automatically when the add-in itself is registered. Refer back to the previous section for more information on COM Add-in Registry entries.

TABLE 15.11: Properties and Methods of the Application's AddIns Collection

Property or Method	Description
VBE	Returns a pointer to the VBE object.
Count	Returns the number of add-ins in the collection.
Parent	Same as VBE.
Item	Returns a particular AddIn object.
Update	Updates the collection. This should be used after an add-in has been added or removed from the system while the development is running.

It's no surprise that the AddIns is a collection of AddIn objects. Table 15.12 lists the properties for the AddIn class.

TABLE 15.12: Properties of the COMAddIn Class

Property	Description
Collection	Returns a pointer to Addins collection.
Connect	True or False value indicating whether the add-in is loaded. You use this to load or unload individual add-ins.
Description	Description of the add-in as it appears in the Add-ins dialog.
Guid	Global unique identifier of the COM component that implements the add-in.
Object	Returns a pointer to the running instance of the add-in if it's loaded.
ProgId	Returns the ProgId for the add-in (for example, "MyAddin.Init").
VBE	Returns a pointer to the VBE object.

In addition to being able to see the description of each add-in, you can use the Connect property to load or unload individual add-ins. You might use this, say, to load a series of add-ins required by one of yours. Once loaded, you can use the Object property to return the running instance of each add-in. This lets your add-in communicate with other add-ins using any Public properties or methods they expose.

Summary

In this chapter, we've introduced you to the VB and VBA IDE object models and shown you how to use their classes, properties, and methods. By understanding the object model, you can create you own custom tools and utilities to help you write code and create applications. Most often, you'll want to implement these as COM Add-ins. This chapter also explained the COM Add-in architecture and showed you how to implement them. By now, you should be familiar with

- Adding a reference to the IDE type library
- Controlling the IDE user interface using the Window and CodePane classes

- Manipulating projects using the VBProject, Reference, VBComponent, and Property classes

- Modifying source code using the CodeModule class

- Creating COM Add-ins and the IDTExtensibility2 interface

- Using the COM Add-in designer

- Creating a simple COM Add-in

This chapter also provided a custom object model that enhances the IDE classes. You can use this model as the basis for your own utilities and add-ins.

The Reddick VBA Naming Conventions, Version 6

The purpose of the Reddick VBA (RVBA) Naming Conventions is to provide a guideline for naming objects in the Visual Basic for Applications (VBA) language. Having conventions is valuable in any programming project. When you use them, the name of the object conveys information about the meaning of the object. These conventions attempt to provide a way of standardizing that meaning across the body of VBA programmers.

VBA is implemented to interact with a host application—for example, Microsoft Access, Microsoft Visual Basic, AutoCAD, and Visio. The RVBA conventions cover all implementations of the VBA language, regardless of the host application. Some of the tags described in this appendix may not necessarily have an implementation within some of the particular host programs for VBA. The word *object,* in the context of this appendix, refers to simple variables and VBA objects, as well as to objects made available by the VBA host program.

While I am the editor of these conventions, they are the work of many people, including Charles Simonyi, who invented the Hungarian conventions on which these are based, and Stan Leszynski, who co-authored several versions of the conventions. Many others, too numerous to mention, have also contributed to the development and distribution of these conventions.

These conventions are intended as a guideline. If you disagree with a particular part of the conventions, simply replace that part with what you think works better. However, keep in mind that future generations of programmers may need to understand those changes, and place a comment in the header of a module indicating what changes have been made. The conventions are presented without rationalizations for how they were derived, although each of the ideas presented has a considerable history to it.

Changes to the Conventions

Some of the tags in the version of the conventions presented here have changed from previous versions. Consider all previous tags to be grandfathered into the conventions—you don't need to go back and make changes. For new development work, I leave it up to you to decide whether to use the older tags or the ones suggested here. In a few places in this appendix, older tags are shown in {braces}. As updates to this appendix are made, the current version can be found at `http://www.xoc.net`.

An Introduction to Hungarian

The RVBA conventions are based on the Hungarian conventions for constructing object names (they were named for the native country of the inventor, Charles Simonyi). The objective of Hungarian is to convey information about the object concisely and efficiently. Hungarian takes some getting used to, but once adopted, it quickly becomes second nature. The format of a Hungarian object name is

```
[prefixes]tag[BaseName[Suffixes]]
```

The square brackets indicate optional parts of the object name. These components have the following meanings:

Component	Meaning
Prefixes	Modify the tag to indicate additional information. Prefixes are all lowercase. They are usually picked from a standardized list of prefixes, given later in this appendix.
Tag	Short set of characters, usually mnemonic, that indicates the type of the object. The tag is all lowercase. It is usually selected from a standardized list of tags, given later in this appendix.
BaseName	One or more words that indicate what the object represents. The first letter of each word in the BaseName is capitalized.
Suffixes	Additional information about the meaning of the BaseName. The first letter of each word in the Suffix is capitalized. They are usually picked from a standardized list of suffixes, given later in this appendix.

Notice that the only required part of the object name is the tag. This may seem counterintuitive; you may feel that the BaseName is the most important part of the object name. However, consider a generic procedure that operates on any form. The fact that the routine operates on a form is the important thing, not what that form represents. Because the routine may operate on forms of many different types, you do not necessarily need a BaseName. However, if you have more than one object of a type referenced in the routine, you must have a BaseName on all but one of the object names to differentiate them. Also, unless the routine is generic, the BaseName conveys information about the variable. In most cases, a variable should include a BaseName.

Tags

You use tags to indicate the data type of an object, and you construct them using the techniques described in the following sections.

Variable Tags

Use the tags listed in Table A.1 for VBA data types. You can also use a specific tag instead of *obj* for any data type defined by the host application or one of its objects. (See the section "Host Application and Component Extensions to the Conventions" later in this appendix.)

TABLE A.1: Tables for VBA Variables

Tag	Object Type
bool {f, bln}	Boolean
byte {byt}	Byte
cur	Currency
date {dtm}	Date
dec	Decimal
dbl	Double
int	Integer
lng	Long
obj	Object
sng	Single
str	String
stf	String (fixed length)
var	Variant

Here are several examples:

```
lngCount
intValue
strInput
```

You should explicitly declare all variables, each on a line by itself. Do not use the old-type declaration characters, such as %, &, and $. They are extraneous if you use the naming conventions, and there is no character for some of the data types, such as Boolean. You should always explicitly declare all variables of type Variant using the *As Variant* clause, even though it is the default in VBA. For example:

```
Dim intTotal As Integer
Dim varField As Variant
Dim strName As String
```

Constructing Properties Names

Properties of a class present a particular problem: should they include the naming convention to indicate the type? To be consistent with the rest of these naming conventions, they should. However, it is permitted to have property names without the tags, especially if the class is to be made available to customers who may not be familiar with these naming conventions.

Collection Tags

You treat a collection object with a special tag. You construct the tag using the data type of the collection followed by the letter *s*. For example, if you had a collection of Longs, the tag would be lngs. If it were a collection of forms, the collection would be frms. Although, in theory, a collection can hold objects of different data types, in practice, each of the data types in the collection is the same. If you do want to use different data types in a collection, use the tag objs. For example:

```
intsEntries
frmsCustomerData
objsMisc
```

Constants

Constants always have a data type in VBA. Because VBA will choose this data type for you if you don't specify it, you should always specify the data type for a constant. Constants declared in the General Declarations section of a module should always have a scope keyword of Private or Public and be prefixed by the scope prefixes *m* or *g*, respectively. A constant is indicated by appending the letter *c* to the end of the data type for the constant. For example:

```
Const intcGray As Integer = 3
Private Const mdblcPi As Double = 3.14159265358979
```

Although this technique is the recommended method of naming constants, if you are more concerned about specifying that you are dealing with constants rather than their data type, you can alternatively use the generic tag *con* instead. For example:

```
Const conPi As Double = 3.14159265358979
```

Menu Items

The names of menu items should reflect their position in the menu hierarchy. All menu items should use the tag mnu, but the BaseName should indicate where in the hierarchy the menu item falls. Use *Sep* in the BaseName to indicate a menu separator bar, followed by an ordinal. For example:

```
mnuFile (on menu bar)
mnuFileNew (on File popup menu)
mnuFileNewForm (on File New flyout menu)
mnuFileNewReport (on File New flyout menu)
mnuFileSep1 (first separator bar on file popup menu)
mnuFileSaveAs (on File popup menu)
mnuFileSep2 (second separator bar on file popup menu)
mnuFileExit (on File popup menu)
mnuEdit (on menu bar)
```

Creating Data Types

VBA gives you three ways to create new data types: enumerated types, classes, and user-defined types. In each case, you will need to invent a new tag that represents the data type that you create.

Enumerated Types

Groups of constants of the *Long* data type should be made an enumerated type. Invent a tag for the type, append a *c*, then define the enumerated constants using that tag. Because the name used in the Enum line is seen in the object browser, you can add a BaseName to the tag to spell out the abbreviation indicated by the tag. For example:

```
Public Enum ervcErrorValue
    ervcInvalidType = 205
    ervcValueOutOfBounds
End Enum
```

The BaseName should be singular, so that the enumerated type should be ervcErrorValue, not ervcErrorValues. The tag that you invent for enumerated types can then be used for variables that can contain values of that type. For example:

```
Dim erv As ervcErrorValue
Private Sub Example(ByVal ervCur As ervcErrorValue)
```

While VBA only provides enumerated types of groups of the Long type, you can still create groups of constants of other types. Just create a set of constant definitions using an invented tag. For example:

```
Public Const estcError205 As String = "Invalid type"
Public Const estcError206 As String = "Value out of bounds"
```

Unfortunately, because this technique doesn't actually create a new type, you don't get the benefit of the VBA compiler performing type checking for you. You create variables that will hold constants using a similar syntax to variables meant to hold instances of enumerated types. For example:

```
Dim estError As String
```

Tags for Classes and User-Defined Types

A class defines a user-defined object. Because these invent a new data type, you will need to invent a new tag for the object. You can add a BaseName to the tag to spell out the abbreviation indicated by the tag. User-defined types are considered a simple class with only properties but in all other ways are used the same as class modules. For example:

```
gphGlyph
edtEdit
Public Type grbGrabber
```

You then define variables to refer to instances of the class using the same tag. For example:

```
Dim gphNext As New gphGlyph
Dim edtCurrent as edtEdit
Dim grbHandle as grbGrabber
```

Polymorphism

In VBA, you use the *Implements* statement to derive classes from a base class. The tag for the derived class should use the same tag as the base class. The derived classes, though, should use a different BaseName from the base class. For example:

```
anmAnimal (base class)
anmZebra (derived class of anmAnimal)
anmElephant (derived class of anmAnimal)
```

This logic of naming derived classes is used with forms, which are all derived from the predefined Form base class and use the frm tag. If a variable is defined to be of the type of the base class, then use the tag, as usual. For example:

```
Dim anmArbitrary As anmAnimal
Dim frmNew As Form
```

On the other hand, if you define a variable as an instance of a derived class, include the complete derived class name in the variable name. For example:

```
Dim anmZebraInstance As anmZebra
Dim anmElephantExample As anmElephant
Dim frmCustomerData As frmCustomer
```

Constructing Procedures

VBA procedures require you to name various items: procedure names, parameters, and labels. These objects are described in the following sections.

Constructing Procedure Names

VBA names event procedures, and you cannot change them. You should use the capitalization defined by the system. For user-defined procedure names, capitalize the first letter of each word in the name. For example:

```
cmdOK_Click
GetTitleBarString
PerformInitialization
```

Procedures should always have a scope keyword, Public or Private, when they are declared. For example:

```
Public Function GetTitleBarString() As String
Private Sub PerformInitialization
```

Naming Parameters

You should prefix all parameters in a procedure definition with ByVal or ByRef, even though ByRef is optional and redundant. Procedure parameters are named the same as simple variables of the same type, except that arguments passed by reference use the prefix *r*. For example:

```
Public Sub TestValue(ByVal intInput As Integer, _
  ByRef rlngOutput As Long)
Private Function GetReturnValue(ByVal strKey As String, _
  ByRef rgph As Glyph) As Boolean
```

Naming Labels

Labels are named using upper- and lowercase, capitalizing the first letter of each word. For example:

```
ErrorHandler:
ExitProcedure:
```

Prefixes

Prefixes modify an object tag to indicate more information about an object.

Arrays of Objects Prefix

Arrays of an object type use the prefix *a*. For example:

```
aintFontSizes
astrNames
```

Index Prefix

You indicate an index into an array by the prefix *i*, and, for consistency, the data type should always be a Long. You may also use the index prefix to index into other enumerated objects, such as a collection of user-defined classes. For example:

```
iaintFontSizes
iastrNames
igphsGlyphCollection
```

Prefixes for Scope and Lifetime

Three levels of scope exist for each variable in VBA: Public, Private, and Local. A variable also has a lifetime of the current procedure or the lifetime of the object in which it is defined. Use the prefixes in Table A.2 to indicate scope and lifetime.

TABLE A.2: Scope Prefixes

Prefix	Object Type
(none)	Local variable, procedure-level lifetime, declared with *Dim*
s	Local variable, object lifetime, declared with *Static*
m	Private (module) variable, object lifetime, declared with *Private*
g	Public (global) variable, object lifetime, declared with *Public*

You also use the *m* and *g* constants with other objects, such as constants, to indicate their scope. For example:

```
intLocalVariable
mintPrivateVariable
gintPublicVariable
mdblcPi
```

VBA allows several type declaration words for backward compatibility. The older keyword Global should always be replaced by Public, and the Dim keyword in the General Declarations section should be replaced by Private.

Other Prefixes

Table A.3 lists and describes some other prefixes:

TABLE A.3: Other Commonly Used Prefixes

Prefix	Object Type
c	Count of some object type
h	Handle to a Windows object
r	Parameter passed by reference

Here are some examples:

```
castrArray
hWndForm
```

Suffixes

Suffixes modify the base name of an object, indicating additional information about a variable. You'll likely create your own suffixes that are specific to your development work. Table A.4 lists some generic VBA suffixes.

TABLE A.4: Commonly Used Suffixes

Suffix	Object Type
Min	The absolute first element in an array or other kind of list
First	The first element to be used in an array or list during the current operation
Last	The last element to be used in an array or list during the current operation
Lim	The upper limit of elements to be used in an array or list. Lim is not a valid index. Generally, Lim equals Last + 1.
Max	The absolutely last element in an array or other kind of list
Cnt	Used with database elements to indicate that the item is a Counter. Counter fields are incremented by the system and are numbers of either type Long or type Replication Id.

Here are some examples:

```
iastrNamesMin
iastrNamesMax
iaintFontSizesFirst
igphsGlyphCollectionLast
lngCustomerIdCnt
varOrderIdCnt
```

Filenames

When naming items stored on the disk, no tag is needed because the extension already gives the object type. For example:

```
Test.Frm (frmTest form)
Globals.Bas (globals module)
Glyph.Cls (gphGlyph class module)
```

Host Application and Component Extensions to the Conventions

Each host application for VBA, as well as each component that can be installed, has a set of objects it can use. This section defines tags for the objects in the various host applications and components.

Access 2000, Version 9 Objects

Table A.5 lists Access object variable tags. Besides being used in code to refer to these object types, these same tags are used to name these kinds of objects in the form and report designers.

TABLE A.5: Access Object Variable Tags

Tag	Object Type
aob	AccessObject
aops	AccessObjectProperties
aop	AccessObjectProperty
app	Application
bfr	BoundObjectFrame
chk	CheckBox
cbo	ComboBox
cmd	CommandButton
ctl	Control
ctls	Controls

TABLE A.5: Access Object Variable Tags *(continued)*

Tag	Object Type
ocx	CustomControl
dap	DataAccessPage
dcm	DoCmd
frm	Form
fcd	FormatCondition
fcds	FormatConditions
frms	Forms
grl	GroupLevel
hyp	Hyperlink
img	Image
lbl	Label
lin	Line
lst	ListBox
bas	Module
ole	ObjectFrame
opt	OptionButton
fra	OptionGroup (frame)
brk	PageBreak
pal	PaletteButton
prps	Properties
shp	Rectangle
ref	Reference
refs	References
rpt	Report
rpts	Reports
scr	Screen

TABLE A.5: Access Object Variable Tags *(continued)*

Tag	Object Type
sec	Section
sfr	SubForm
srp	SubReport
tab	TabControl
txt	TextBox
tgl	ToggleButton

Some examples:

```
txtName
lblInput
```

For ActiveX custom controls, you can use the tag ocx as specified in Table A.5 or more specific object tags that are listed later in this appendix in Tables A.14 and A.15. For an ActiveX control that doesn't appear in the Tables A.14 or A.15, you can either use ocx or invent a new tag.

DAO 3.6 Objects

DAO is the programmatic interface to the Jet database engine shared by Access, Visual Basic, and Visual C++. The tags for DAO 3.6 objects are shown in Table A.6.

TABLE A.6: DAO Object Tags

Tag	Object Type
cnt	Container
cnts	Containers
db	Database
dbs	Databases
dbe	DBEngine
doc	Document
docs	Documents

T A B L E A . 6 : DAO Object Tags *(continued)*

Tag	Object Type
err	Error
errs	Errors
fld	Field
flds	Fields
grp	Group
grps	Groups
idx	Index
idxs	Indexes
prm	Parameter
prms	Parameters
pdbe	PrivDBEngine
prp	Property
prps	Properties
qry	QueryDef
qrys	QueryDefs
rst	Recordset
rsts	Recordsets
rel	Relation
rels	Relations
tbl	TableDef
tbls	TableDefs
usr	User
usrs	Users
wrk	Workspace
wrks	Workspaces

Here are some examples:

```
rstCustomers
idxPrimaryKey
```

Table A.7 lists the tags used to identify types of objects in a database.

TABLE A.7: Access Database Explorer Object Tags

Tag	Object Type
tbl	Table
qry	Query
frm	Form
rpt	Report
mcr	Macro
bas	Module
dap	DataAccessPage

If you wish, you can use more exact tags or suffixes to identify the purpose and type of a database object. If you use the suffix, use the tag given from Table A.7 to indicate the type. Use either the tag or the suffix found along with the more general tag, but not both. The tags and suffixes are shown in Table A.8.

TABLE A.8: Specfic Object Tags and Suffixes for Access Database Explorer Objects

Tag	Suffix	Object Type
tlkp	Lookup	Table (lookup)
qsel	(none)	Query (select)
qapp	Append	Query (append)
qxtb	XTab	Query (crosstab)
qddl	DDL	Query (DDL)
qdel	Delete	Query (delete)
qflt	Filter	Query (filter)
qlkp	Lookup	Query (lookup)

T A B L E A . 8 : Specfic Object Tags and Suffixes for Access Database
Explorer Objects *(continued)*

Tag	Suffix	Object Type
qmak	MakeTable	Query (make table)
qspt	PassThru	Query (SQL pass-through)
qtot	Totals	Query (totals)
quni	Union	Query (union)
qupd	Update	Query (update)
fdlg	Dlg	Form (dialog)
fmnu	Mnu	Form (menu)
fmsg	Msg	Form (message)
fsfr	SubForm	Form (subform)
rsrp	SubReport	Form (subreport)
mmnu	Mnu	Macro (menu)

Here are some examples:

```
tblValidNamesLookup
tlkpValidNames
fmsgError
mmnuFileMnu
```

When naming objects in a database, do not use spaces. Instead, capitalize the first letter of each word. For example, instead of Quarterly Sales Values Table, use tblQuarterlySalesValues.

There is strong debate over whether fields in a table should have tags. Whether you use them is up to you. However, if you do use them, use the tags from Table A.9.

T A B L E A . 9 : Field Tags (If You Decide to Use Them)

Tag	Object Type
lng	Autoincrementing (either sequential or random) Long (used with the suffix Cnt)
bin	Binary
byte	Byte

TABLE A.9: Field Tags (If You Decide to Use Them) *(continued)*

Tag	Object Type
cur	Currency
date	Date/time
dbl	Double
guid	Globally unique identified (GUID) used for replication AutoIncrement fields
int	Integer
lng	Long
mem	Memo
ole	OLE
sng	Single
str	Text
bool	Yes/No

Visual Basic 6 Objects

Table A.10 shows the tags for Visual Basic 6 objects.

TABLE A.10: Visual Basic 6 Object Tags

Tag	Object Type
app	App
chk	CheckBox
clp	Clipboard
cbo	ComboBox
cmd	CommandButton
ctl	Control
dat	Data
dir	DirListBox
drv	DriveListBox

TABLE A.10:   Visual Basic 6 Object Tags *(continued)*

Tag	Object Type
fil	FileListBox
frm	Form
fra	Frame
glb	Global
hsb	HScrollBar
img	Image
lbl	Label
lics	Licenses
lin	Line
lst	ListBox
mdi	MDIForm
mnu	Menu
ole	OLE
opt	OptionButton
pic	PictureBox
prt	Printer
prp	PropertyPage
scr	Screen
shp	Shape
txt	TextBox
tmr	Timer
uctl	UserControl
udoc	UserDocument
vsb	VscrollBar

Microsoft ActiveX Data Objects 2.1 Tags

Office 2000 provides version 2.1 of the ActiveX Data Objects library. Table A.11 lists the recommended tags for this version of ADO.

Avoiding Object Confusion

Many of the ADO, ADOX, and JRO tags overlap with existing DAO tags. Make sure you include the object library name in all references in your code, so there's never any possibility of confusion. For example, use

```
Dim rst As ADODB.Recordset
```

or

```
Dim cat As ADOX.Catalog
```

rather than using the object types without the library name. This will not only make your code more explicit and avoid confusion about the source of the object but will also make your code run a bit faster.

TABLE A.11: ADO 2.1 Object Tags

Tag	Object Type
cmd	Command
cnn {cnx}	Connection
err	Error
errs	Errors
fld	Field
flds	Fields
prm	Parameter
prms	Parameters
prps	Properties
prp	Property
rst	Recordset

Microsoft ADO Ext. 2.1 for DDL and Security (ADOX) Tags

In order to support DDL and security objects within Jet database, Microsoft provides ADOX, an additional ADO library of objects. Table A.12 lists tags for the ADOX objects.

T A B L E A . 1 2 : ADOX Object Tags

Tag	Object Type
cat	Catalog
clms	Column
clm	Columns
cmd	Command
grp	Group
grps	Groups
idx	Index
idxs	Indexes
key	Key
keys	Keys
prc	Procedure
prcs	Procedures
prps	Properties
prp	Property
tbl	Table
tbls	Tables
usr	User
usrs	Users
vw	View
vws	Views

Microsoft Jet and Replication Objects 2.1

In order to support Jet's replication features, ADO provides another library, JRO. Table A.13 lists suggested tags for the JRO objects.

TABLE A.13: JRO Object Tags

Tag	Object Type
flt	Filter
flts	Filters
jet	JetEngine
rpl	Replica

Microsoft SQL Server and Microsoft Data Engine (MSDE) Objects

Table A.14 lists tags for Microsoft SQL Server and the Microsoft Data Engine (a limited-connection version of SQL Server 7) objects.

TABLE A.14: SQL Server/MSDE Object Tags

Tag	Object Type
tbl	table
proc	stored procedure
trg	trigger
qry	view
dgm	database diagram
pk	primary key
fk	foreign key
idx	other (non-key) index
rul	check constraint
def	default

Microsoft Common Control Objects

Windows 95 and Windows NT have a set of common controls that are accessible from VBA. Table A.15 lists the tags for objects created using these controls.

TABLE A.15: Microsoft Common Control Object Tags

Tag	Object Type
ani	Animation
btn	Button (Toolbar)
bmn	ButtonMenu (Toolbar)
bmns	ButtonMenus (Toolbar)
bnd	Band (CoolBar)
bnds	Bands (CoolBar)
bnp	BandsPage (CoolBar)
btns	Buttons (Toolbar)
cbr	CoolBar
cbp	CoolBarPage (CoolBar)
hdr	ColumnHeader (ListView)
hdrs	ColumnHeaders (ListView)
cbi	ComboItem (ImageCombo)
cbis	ComboItems (ImageCombo)
ctls	Controls
dto	DataObject
dtf	DataObjectFiles
dtp	DTPicker
fsb	FlatScrollBar
imc	ImageCombo
iml	ImageList
lim	ListImage

TABLE A.15: Microsoft Common Control Object Tags *(continued)*

Tag	Object Type
lims	ListImages
lit	ListItem (ListView)
lits	ListItems (ListView)
lsi	ListSubItem (ListView)
lsis	ListSubItems (ListView)
lvw	ListView
mvw	MonthView
nod	Node (TreeView)
nods	Nodes (TreeView)
pnl	Panel (Status Bar)
pnls	Panels (Status Bar)
prb	ProgressBar
sld	Slider
sbr	StatusBar
tab	Tab (Tab Strip)
tabs	Tabs (Tab Strip)
tbs	TabStrip
tbr	Toolbar
tvw	TreeView
udn	UpDown

Other Custom Controls and Objects

Finally, Table A.16 lists the tags for other commonly used custom controls and objects.

TABLE A.16: Tags for Commonly Used Custom Controls

Tag	Object Type
cdl	CommonDialog (Common Dialog)
dbc	DBCombo (Data Bound Combo Box)
dbg	DBGrid (Data Bound Grid)
dls	DBList (Data Bound List Box)
gau	Gauge (Gauge)
gph	Graph (Graph)
grd	Grid (Grid)
msg	MAPIMessages (Messaging API Message Control)
ses	MAPISession (Messaging API Session Control)
msk	MaskEdBox (Masked Edit Textbox)
key	MhState (Key State)
mmc	MMControl (Multimedia Control)
com	MSComm (Communication Port)
out	Outline (Outline Control)
pcl	PictureClip (Picture Clip Control)
rtf	RichTextBox (Rich Textbox)
spn	SpinButton (Spin Button)

Summary

Using a naming convention requires a considerable initial effort on your part. The payoff comes when either you or another programmer has to revisit your code at a later time. Using the conventions given here will make your code more readable and maintainable.

Greg Reddick is the President of Xoc Software, a software development company developing programs in Visual Basic, Microsoft Access, and C/C++. He leads training seminars in Visual Basic for Application Developers Training Company and is a co-author of Microsoft Access 95 Developer's Handbook, *published by Sybex. He worked for four years on the Access development team at Microsoft. Greg can be reached at* grr@xoc.net *or at the Xoc Software Web site at* http://www.xoc.net.

INDEX

Note to the Reader: Throughout this index **boldfaced** page numbers indicate primary discussions of a topic. *Italicized* page numbers indicate illustrations.

D

F

H

I

J

K

L

M

N

S

T

W

X

Y

What's on the CD

This CD provides a wealth of information in a readily usable format to aid in your VBA development efforts. We've included every significant example presented in the text.

Here's just a sampling of what you'll find on the CD:

- Reusable functions that extend the power of VBA, along with a large number of cut-and-paste solutions to general-purpose problems—all the code from the book!

- In the README there is a link to Microsoft's download site from which you can obtain the latest version of the VBA SDK.

- WinZip, the premier Windows shareware program for zipping and unzipping files

- Adobe Acrobat 4.0 for viewing .pdf files, such as the appendices.

- Appendix B, a chapter borrowed from our "sister" book (*Access 2000 Developer's Handbook: Desktop Edition*), introducing the use of the Windows API in VBA applications

- Appendix C, which focuses on writing bulletproof, well-tuned VBA applications, including handling errors, creating event logs, and the creation of a procedure-tracking stack for your applications

- Appendix D, which contains a Folder and File object model—that is, a set of classes you can use for modeling the file system

For more information about the CD, including installation instructions, see the "About the CD" section in the Introduction of this book, and the README.HTML file in the root folder of the CD.

NOTE   If you use Windows Explorer to copy the book's sample files directly from the CD to your hard disk, the files will be marked as read-only. Either run the supplied Chapter.exe self-extracting zip file, or, after you've copied files manually, use Windows Explorer to clear the Read Only attribute of the file.